IDOL
WORSHIP

A Shameless Celebration
of Male Beauty in the Movies

By
MICHAEL FERGUSON

STARbooks Press
Sarasota, Fla.

For Dad and Mom,
who won't approve of the language, but fostered
my love of the movies and encouraged
my creative endeavors.

STARbooks Press
1370 Boulevard of the Arts
Sarasota, FL 34236-2902

Cover design by John Nail

Second Edition Published in the U.S. in May, 2004
First Edition Published in the U.S. in November, 2003
Library of Congress Card Catalogue No. Pending
ISBN No. 1-891855-48-4

Other Books by STARbooks Press

Matt Dillon, in his teen idol days, as *Tex* (1982). PHOTOFEST

CONTENTS

Gérard Philipe (right) bums a light in *Le Diable au corps* (1946). AUTHOR'S COLLECTION

Introduction

Brad Pitt with his shirt off. Jude Law climbing out of the bathtub. Jared Leto sniffing Robert Downey, Jr. Matt Dillon…just standing there.

It's time to indulge. *Idol Worship: A Shameless Celebration of Male Beauty in the Movies* is a guidebook to a century's worth of men who have quickened our hearts, put a sparkle in our eyes, and lulled us willingly into fantasy. All things considered, they may just be the very reason more than half of us go to the movies...period. Let's face it, there's not much more elemental than the sex drive; all the resplendent scenery, brilliant storytelling, and high-tech special effects in the world can't do for us what a gorgeous leading man can with just a glance. Here are the fellas—from Rudolph Valentino to Colin Farrell—whose beauty has made them the objects of intense fantasy and desire, as well as ridicule and scorn.

Not so very long ago, you didn't have to go to a drag show to discover which movie stars gay men were most often identified as idolizing. From Mae West, Bette Davis, and Joan Crawford to Marlene Dietrich, Judy Garland, and Barbra Streisand, the pantheon of players was so rigorously stereotyped that to be an urban gay was to be euphemistically encoded "a friend of Dorothy's," coined from Ms. Garland's role in *The Wizard of Oz* (1939).

It should come as no surprise, however, that gay men enjoy watching men in their movies, too. But there's a curious double standard. The grand dames of our cinema worship are expected to be no less than that. They're ballsy, tortured, emancipated, tragic, and exotic. They're beautiful on their own terms and definitely aren't up to playing the roles others want them or expect them to play. They can even get old on us. In fact, age, personal bouts with abusive men, liquor, drugs, and godawful movies make them even more glamorous.

1

The men, on the other hand, are strictly candy. We like them young. We like them cute. But we can never take them seriously. And they can't age. If and when they do, we replace them.

Well, revoke my membership card, because I love Dietrich and Davis, too, but it's the guys who keep me coming back to the movies…and I take them very seriously. I guess that's why I'm a homo.

Once upon a time, there were enough gay men who'd memorized entire Barbara Stanwyck movies that it was a foregone conclusion she'd never be forgotten. That no longer seems assured. And so, with a subculture on the verge of gleeful assimilation into a mass culture, and the resulting loss of our movie heroines in our collective cross-reference, I wish to do my part for the boys and keep the torches burning for the likes of Rudolph Valentino, John Ericson, Brandon de Wilde, Christopher Jones, and Matt Lattanzi.

Yep. Sometimes cute *is* enough. And while we're at it, let's hear it for that stunning young man who delivers a telegram halfway through the picture and can barely say his two lines!

It always floors me to hear a straight guy denying knowledge of whether another guy is good-looking or not. Men go out of their way to avoid admission, as if agreeing or simply having an opinion was akin to romantic culpability. Can a woman know that another woman is pretty? Sure. Can a woman say it, admit it, or even openly envy it? You bet. Men aren't allowed to and they'd rather not. "How would I know?" or "I'll take your word for it" are the most often heard responses to: "Man, is he good-lookin' or what?" They can mutter agreement in a playful or self-deprecating way, but never in the gushing, complimentary, or even jealous way that women are allowed.

Beauty is an asexual concept, though Western culture has prejudiced it as preferentially feminine. Women are beautiful, men are handsome is what I was taught. If a man is called beautiful, it's likely he's on the "feminine" side of good looks. Girly.

Gender-biased definitions of beauty as either masculine or feminine mean nothing to me. So whereas "pretty boy" is considered by most a derisive term, at the very least an emasculating one, to me, it's a term of endearment.

If I seem to be succumbing to the tyranny of youth and beauty that curses the gay social scene and places physical attributes above all else, then I may be guilty as charged, but to a decidedly lesser crime: a myth-shattering reality check that artlessly acknowledges movies are fantasy, movies are illusion, one of the few proper places we have to harmlessly indulge ourselves. Keep telling yourself that while you delve through this book and stare into the too-gorgeous faces of men of extraordinary talent (or lack thereof) who all arrive equal by virtue of their looks. The danger of beauty is not surrendering to it, but losing sight of what it is and what it is not.

The culture rebels against male beauty at the same time it slobbers over it, but the rebellion is a front. We love pretty. Pretty girls. And pretty boys. Unfortunately, we've also long suffered from a nasty bout of homophobic machismo and tend to subvert our jealous attraction to boys who are pretty through ridicule or "good-natured" ribbing. The best-looking guys are taunted for it. They're the ones singled out for verbal abuse and warned to stay out of jail where a pretty face like that can mean only one fate. The warning has merit, but it also speaks to the way in which to be a beauty, an object of desire, is to live with the threat of violence. If you've got something other people want but can't have, they'll figure out some way to make you pay for it.

There's a mysterious life-force that emanates from beauty. Not only are we attracted to it, but we get a buzz just being around it. If you're lucky enough to know a beauty, you know what I'm talking about. They somehow make you feel more alive. People look and stare and you get a vicarious high just because you're seen as an intimate. It approximates the rush of what we imagine to be celebrity. Ever wonder, though, what it must be like to be so attractive that you know people are always looking at you? (I have, especially whenever I get caught doing it.)

Conversely, some beautiful men are likely to suffer from an obnoxious degree of self-confidence, bloated ego, cocky attitude, and the expectation and unjustified reward of social privilege. We all remember the jock in high school who thought he was so good-looking—he was—but the biggest jerkoff in the class. Accordingly, he was handed awards, granted waivers on disciplinary actions, afforded opportunities for advancement ahead of others, and got himself crowned Prom King. The pathetic part was that you still wanted to sleep with him. Beauty could make you forgive an asshole in fantasy and yet despise him in reality.

Beautiful men are forced to prove themselves worthy of our ignoring their looks. If they happen to be great athletes, so much the better for both of us. We can say we admire their athleticism at the same time we secretly covet their beauty. If they're actors or models, though, we immediately suspect they're "himbos" or full of themselves...or gay. Admiring someone for such a superficial bundle of physical traits can't be allowed without finding some fault, subjecting them to some form of disempowerment or demonization. The cocky ones would say we're just jealous. We are, but only because we imagine what great things we could do with those powers. Just think how are lives would improve if we were both sexually desirable and allowed to keep our own brains.

"He's too pretty" is a criticism many young actors face when being considered and often not considered for roles outside their pretty boy niche: namely, the boring, underwritten, and underdeveloped leading man—the male ingenue. Many of them, notably Robert Taylor, Monty Clift, Paul Newman, and Brad Pitt, resented the accusation. What does "too pretty" mean? At its core, it suggests that the image has pre-conceived limitations about the kind of role a guy can acceptably play with a face like that. Typecasting in the truest sense of the word. No wonder pretty boys want to mess up their looks and play unattractive roles. All pretty actors want to be character actors. All character actors want to continue being character actors, but with leading man looks.

So where do you draw the line between who's pretty, who's beautiful, and who's handsome? When do you stop being pretty and start being handsome? Can't someone be all the above? Of course. And that's why Rock Hudson, a man surely on the handsome side of pretty, is in this book and Sean Connery, a man surely on the handsome side of handsome, is not. If that doesn't make sense to you, you're not alone. I have applied no strict rules to the selections other than my own sensibilities. Bruce Willis did not make the cut. Rob Lowe did.

A central problem with admitting that movie stars are also sex stars is that you're seen as reducing them to little more than objects—you are *objectifying* them, thereby making them less human. The criminal extrapolation of that argument is that, apparently, by responding to them sexually, you're this close to becoming a stalker. I love worst-case scenarios, because one can't help admitting they exist, but what have they got to do with you? Unless you're the worst case scenario.

Inescapably, though, movie stars are sex stars and always have been. What's more, the movie stars themselves know it, no matter how self-effacing, humble, and regular-Joe they appear to be. The reason they know it, even if they can't admit it outside a jokey attempt at self-denigration, is that they've all grown up lusting after movie stars themselves. In fact, they're lusting after co-stars, porn stars, would-be stars, and even has-been stars just like the rest of us.

Seeing movie stars as sex objects doesn't preclude also seeing them as human beings, because we ought to know what's fantasy and what's fiction. The very term "movie stars" is mythological, and we view these people in any number of different lights (as personalities, as performers, as talented or untalented, etc.), so taking time out to focus on the sexual aspects of their mythology ought to be just as viable.

The fascinating distinction is that unlike mythological heroes or literary monsters, the fantasy beings that constitute movie stars are also real. The flickering image corresponds with an actuality of flesh and blood. Their beauty is not a myth. But their existence in real life has the power to make us feel as though we're living in one.

So even while the movie sex scene is more often than not poorly filmed in terms of meeting our hopes and expectations to see juicy details instead of overlapping dissolves, cut-aways, and a disturbing lack of foreplay and exploration, the movies have romanticized sex for the good of all. They represent a controlled environment in which the best-looking faces with the best-looking bodies are suggestively given the best-looking angles and the best-looking partners with whom to have the best-looking sex without ever actually having it.

They are, in fact, so good-looking that when Brad Pitt tells an interviewer in all detumescent candor that movie sex scenes are difficult and that people don't realize that there's a make-up person there troweling putty on his butt to hide the occasional zit, even *that's* sexy. And if a visible pustule on Brad Pitt's backside was to escape the make-up people, the director, the cinematographer, the editor, and the studio pre-screenings, and end up the size of a prize-winning tomato on the multiplex big-screen, it would in no way impact his desirability, unless it was oozing.

Besides, it's satisfying to see beautiful people with everyday people characteristics. I refrain from calling them flaws, because they aren't, though I know people who say they find Brad so luscious because his beautiful face is "flawed" by that scar beneath his eye where a baseball once split him open. Flawed beauty is a misnomer when it comes to human beings. We may want to take a razor to bring symmetry and individuality to Ken Wahl's lycanthropic eyebrow, or pin back Matt Dillon's ears, but then they wouldn't be who they are. Cosmetic changes are part and parcel to the business, of course, and Wahl did eventually depilate, but does anyone really want to grind down Tom Cruise's nose or pancake away Harrison Ford's chin slash or sandblast Mark Wahlberg's third nipple?

When Keanu Reeves strips down and rolls around on the floor with his wife in *The Devil's Advocate* (1997), the fact that you can glimpse the black hairs between his buttcheeks is a plus, not a call for shears.

This book is dedicated to the proposition that being a sexy leading man, being a Hollywood hunk, or being a stunningly handsome movie star has as much to do with your professional training, years of study, or devotion to your craft as being queer has to do with a lifetime subscription to *The Advocate* and a condo in The Castro. We are not herewith assembled to pit the Actor's Studio emoting of Marlon Brando against the loincloth emoting of Christopher Atkins. This isn't a book about craft; it's a shameless celebration of sex appeal. For example, I'd like you to know that when it comes to surveying male beauty in the movies, a little film called *Calendar Girl* (1993) measurably adds to its appeal by having Jason Priestley noticeably bulging inside his pants, then later flopping into nanosecond view—because he simply cannot be contained at that natural length—when he jogs butt-nekkid toward the ocean. Jason hasn't made enough films to merit an official entry, mind you, but that shouldn't stop us from emblematically acknowledging his contribution.

You will note an unavoidable repetition of certain words in this text: beauty, beautiful, gorgeous, cute, handsome, lovely, hot, pretty, and stunning, among them. Such is the nature of this gushing beast.

While I'm gushing, I'd like to thank Robert J. Lentz, Michael Crouch, Robert and Gloria Carr, Alissa Wicklund, Rosalie Newman, Paul Engelman, Wenzel Roessler, Ted Satterthwaite, Jillene Schwindt, John Nail, Paul Marquis of STARbooks, Barb Davison, my sisters Denice and Kim, and my entire family for their enthusiastic support. I'd also like to thank the wealth of biographers, past interviewers, filmmakers, and photographers who laid the groundwork for this project.

The closet of my youth made me covet the men of the movies. For that, I can never fully express my gratitude, though this book is an attempt to do so.

Thanks to the following production companies and individuals representing the photos that appear in this volume: ABC Pictures Corporation, Alex Entertainment Inc., Alexander Korda Films, Alfa Cinematografica, Allied Artists Pictures, Altavista Films, Amblin Entertainment, Armada, Australian Film Commission, Bad Robot, Bel Ami Photo & Video Inc., BHE Films, Cannon Group, Castlezone, Channel Four Films, Cinecom Pictures, Cloud Nine Films Ltd., Columbia Pictures Corporation, Concord Productions Inc, Coronado Productions, Dino de Laurentiis Cinematografica, DisCina, Euro International Film, FilmDallas Pictures, First National Pictures Inc., Fox 2000 Pictures, Goldcrest Films Ltd., Goldwyn Pictures Corporation, Hanna Productions, Hart-Sharp Entertainment, Hemdale Film Corporation, David Hlynsky, Hollywood Pictures, Howard Hughes Productions, Interwest, Island, Jalem Productions, Kings Road Entertainment, Kingsgate Films, Lions Gate Films Inc., Liveplanet, London Film Productions, Malpaso Productions, Mansfield Productions, Merchant-Ivory Productions, Metro Pictures Corporation, Metro-Goldwyn-Mayer Pictures, Millennium Films, Miramax Films, Monogram Pictures Corporation, Morgan Creek Productions, New Line Cinema, New Regency Pictures, Panoramic Productions, Paramount Pictures, Paris Film, Paritalia, Pathé Entertainment, Brad Posey – Club 1821, Produzioni Europee Associati, R&R Films, Regency Enterprises, RKO Radio Pictures Inc., Salem-Dover Productions, Samuel Goldwyn Company, Sargon Film, Scott Rudin Productions, South Australian Film Corporation, Stephen J Cannell Productions, T-D Enterprises, Titanus, Transcontinental Films, Tribeca Productions, TriStar Pictures, 20th Century Fox, 20th Century Fox Television, United Artists, Universal International Pictures, Vanguard Productions, Verona Produzione, Vitagraph Company of America, Warner Bros.

The 1910s-1920s

"I Want To Look Nice When The Ambulance Arrives"

The male figure as a photographed object of beauty only began to take shape a hundred years ago, give or take, a fact perhaps unappreciated or of little concern in an era when obtaining the nude image of a handsome young man takes only seconds...or less.

One hundred years ago may as well be one thousand years ago. As each second of our cyberactive lives seems longer, denser, yet somehow peculiarly shorter, what may be considered the very recent past from an historical point of view fogs into the unfathomable.

Not since the glory days of ancient Greece has the imagery and adulation of male beauty been as culturally deified—outside the specter of Aryan race supremacy marketed by the Nazis—as here at the dawn of the new millennium. So entrenched are the fascist visions of physical perfection that it's almost impossible to just have fun enjoying beauty for beauty's sake without stepping on socio-politically fungoid toes.

It's even called the fascism of beauty. Books are written about it. Sociological tomes and dissertations are devoted to it. Girls are plagued by the Barbie doll culture, it's said, though few boys would say they were brought up to emulate Ken.

Being seen as an object of beauty is by cultural extrapolation a feminine thing. The very concept of a man being gawked at because of his physicality shifts the perspective from a sex once thought to be the looker to the sex not supposed to be the looked at. Disrobing disendows (even while endowing), makes vulnerable, and confuses the sexual identities and gender roles.

Leave it to homosexuals (the reason Athens and then Rome corrupted their greatness, we're told by homophobes) to set things straight. Beauty was not the exclusive attribute of women. Physical beauty could be acknowledged in either sex. That "beauty" itself could be defined in any number of far more profoundly meaningful ways when applied to a person's character, spirit, soul, ugliness, etc. shouldn't preclude the possibility that beauty in its physical form, in its skin-deep sculptural and photographic and artistic representation, could not only be appreciated, but inspirational.

The trick is not to succumb to the cult of beauty. A person who reasons there should be no ugly people in the world, even in jest, has just imagined their own demise; no matter how beautiful they may be, they are ugly for having said it, and the *Twilight Zone* ending reveals a planet of beautiful people where the deformed and elderly and ordinary alike are left to contemplate where their friends and neighbors went.

A couple thousand years after physically idealized boys (with aesthetically small penises—the muscles could be built, not the genitalia) found themselves wrestling one another on Athenian pottery, and a few hundred years after the greatest artists of the Renaissance stroked them on canvas and chipped them out of blocks of marble, the latest representational medium—photography—captured the handsome and the pretty for all to see. What was truly astonishing about this development was its accessibility. By 1890, Kodak had introduced its roll film and amateur cameras were in reach. You didn't have to wait until you were an old man to point at the ceiling in the church or the statue in the middle of the town square and tell disbelievers that once upon a time that was you. You didn't have to wait for that rarest of all opportunities to be chosen to model for a master artist. You didn't even have to write long lost friends and tell them they'd have to haul their cookies across Europe to the palazzo where your bronzed bod stood erect.

Beauty is in the eye of the beholder. Now, everybody could hold your beauty right in the palm of their hand.

Once again, leave it to the queers.

Like Da Vinci and Michelangelo before them, the earliest photographers of the male form—those who comprehended it as physical beauty and worthy of artful rendering—were homosexuals. Love and lust drive all great passions.

5

Properly speaking, the male nude as a photographed image was excused in the mid- to late nineteenth century by its purely commercial and practical applications: as physique studies for practicing artists and anatomists. Much cheaper and far more reliable (if less exciting) than using real models, photographs of nude men and nude women were sold to painters and sculptors, physicians and scientists. Almost astoundingly devoid of sensuality, these still lifes were designed to show form and contour, muscle and motion in suspended animation. Whole series were shot of naked men walking and throwing, bending and lifting, sitting and standing, from many different angles.

When Eadweard Muybridge (1830-1904), a British-born photographer whose photographs of successive motion proved that when a horse runs all four hooves are for a split second in the air at the same time, turned his attentions to human locomotion, he beguiled male athletes from the University of Pennsylvania to disrobe and literally strut their stuff. There were, and are, of course, academic, scientific, and medical applications for this work, but there were and are occasionally erotic implications, too.

Muybridge didn't limit himself to swarthy young men, and much of his work, which was finally published in 1887, is earthy and peopled with ordinary folk, but college boys wrestling one another in the buff (*Two Men Wrestling*, 1885) resonate homoeroticism to this day.

The painter Thomas Eakins (1844-1916), collaborator with Muybridge and both friend and neighbor to Walt Whitman, was able to talk several of his male students at the Philadelphia Art Academy to carouse naked outdoors in front of his camera for both photographic (*Group of Students Wrestling*, 1883) and (then) painted studies (*The Swimming Hole*, 1883).

While several other known photographers were likewise dabbling in the art of photographic representation of the male form, perhaps the most famous for his openly homoerotic content was the Baron Wilhelm von Gloeden (1856-1931), who settled in Taormina, Sicily and took to photographing the local boys in all their nakedness right at the turn of the century. Romanticizing his postcards by having the boys pose as if they were Greek vase art, wearing wreaths around their heads or draped in togas, the images include much male-male contact—holding, touching, embracing—and most of the models had obviously been chosen for the size of their penises rather than their physical beauty, not unlike male porn stars of the 1970s.

Von Gloeden enterprisingly sold these photos to collectors via the mail, as well as to interested male tourists, and before long a nephew (who taught him photography) was successfully doing the very same thing. It's important to understand that these weren't photographs of boys having sex with each other. We're not talking hardcore here. In fact, with their almost singularly dour and bored faces, we're not even talking about joyful expression or enthusiasm here. But in an era of Victorian dress codes, when both man and woman alike wore impossibly layered clothing to hide the flesh, and when even swimwear was designed to cover and conceal, if not also to bundle and facilitate drowning, any representations of nakedness were intensely eroticized.

The turn of the century was a breeding ground for sexual expression, not unlike our own recent turn of the century. For different reasons that brought about similar results, the two eras were rife with proscriptions against sexual activity, hence the creative worlds (literature, painting, theatre, and photography) became the vent for explicit, pent-up desires.

Youth, nudity, a large penis, and male-male physical contact were the stock ingredients then...and the recipe still works wonders today, a hundred years later.

Today's interest in the male body as an anatomic achievement, as something to be appreciated and gaped at, emerged out of the mid-19th century's "physical culture" movement, a predominately German movement that celebrated physical health and physical transformation through diet and exercise. It was the new dawn of bodybuilding, naturism, and nudism.

There had long been exhibitions of strength and acts of brute force, rigged and otherwise, performed by burly, barrel-chested men in tights at circuses and carnivals. But it took Florenz Ziegfeld, Jr., the master showman's son, to realize and then exploit through his father's venues the male physique as it had not been exploited in the West.

After catching the remarkable appearance of Friedrich Müller, a 25-year old German muscleman, in a stage show called *Adonis*, Ziggy brought Müller to papa as an attraction for Sr.'s new Trocadero theater in Chicago on August 1, 1893. Following the standard display of weighty feats, Müller, now stage-named **Eugen Sandow** (1867-1925), the "world's best developed man," stood on the stage and did a very simple, but remarkable thing: he posed.

One might say he posed for posing's sake, not simply to demonstrate what his muscles could do to chain links or steel rods, but how they looked on him, how they made his body appear. Narcissistic, exhibitionistic, and audience-narcotic.

Sneaking a peek at this, that, or the other thing while strongmen heaved and ho'd was one thing, but being asked, then permitted and encouraged to gaze was a whole other body politic.

Ziegfeld signed Sandow the Magnificent for four years and made a quarter of a million dollars on him. The first professional bodybuilder became a filthy-rich celebrity himself, known all over the world. King George V declared him "Professor of Scientific Physical Culture to His Majesty."

You see, it was okay to stare so long as you could come up with a name for it, some way of de-sexualizing it. Sandow was in such extraordinary shape that he would even put on displays for the military in which cadets were invited to run their hands over his sinewed topography, all in the name of inspiring good physical health, of course.

Unlike his sideshow and center ring predecessors, Sandow had cultivated a body that, though highly toned and rippling with muscles capable of dancing to musical accompaniment, was not over-built. A pioneer of the modern bodybuilding movement, he didn't bulk himself to the man-mountain proportions we associate with professional bodybuilding today. If he had, I dare say he would have found himself in a freak show instead of as the main attraction.

Eugen Sandow was an icon of male physical perfection at a time when Western culture had itself cloaked in modesty. The revealed body, long associated with baser instincts and a filthy appetite for sinful thoughts and acts, had to find expression as something that could be purified, beautified, perfected, and attained.

Excuses were ordained and the order of the day if one was to avoid eroticizing the exposure of skin. Boys lost their foreskins because they were thought to contribute to masturbation. Men wore undershirts because the sight of a man's naked chest was crass.

The only way you could get around one of these proscriptions was by telling yourself that there was a good and healthy reason behind it.

Sandow's shows legitimized gazing at the male body as an object worthy of such looks. He even put on ladies-only exhibitions, his body powdered white to resemble marble as he struck statuary poses in the slightest of coverings. If the gals ostensibly went to admire the perfection that could potentially be seen in their husbands, no one need think about how seeing a near-naked man showing them his wares might be contributing to their naughty private thoughts.

What mattered almost more than the desire to see Sandow in naught but a fig leaf (as he was often photographed) was how that desire translated into moola. The unclad male form placed on a pedestal for 3-dimensional flesh and bone perusal was also a moneymaker. The male body as a thing of beauty was also the male body as a thing of commerce. Show business.

In America, 30-year old Bernarr Macfadden (1868-1955), a homely-faced entrepreneur and self-styled self-promoter, published the first issue of *Physical Development* in 1898. Sandow published his own magazine, *Physical Culture*, the same year, and both joined earlier efforts in France and Germany on the newsstands of the world espousing male physical advancement. To be physically fit, of course, was by association to be a more complete man.

In 1900, Macfadden's *The Virile Powers of Superb Manhood* helped cement the association that persists, both positively and negatively today: that musclemen are walking cocks; unable to build that muscle-less dangler between their legs, they outsize each other by making every other part of their body enlarged and showing it off to one another in magazines.

The first bodybuilding exhibition of any scale was organized by Sandow in September of 1901 when 15,000 people gathered to look at the physiques of 60 male contestants in a pioneering pose-off held at London's Royal Albert Hall. Macfadden followed suit in the States in a contest held at Madison Square Garden seeking the "Most Perfectly Developed Man in America."

The muscle movement has long been plagued by ignorant outsiders as the realm of homosexuals and weak men, when in fact it has always been predominantly the realm of heterosexual men. The competition between males to establish dominance has been socially metamorphosed into civilized and uncivilized displays of bigness in all sorts of physical things.

As Jared Diamond succinctly puts it in *The Rise and Fall of the Third Chimpanzee* (1991): "While we can agree that the human penis is an organ of display, the display is intended not for women but for fellow

Nineteenth century glutes on "Sandow the Magnificent." PHOTOFEST

Men develop their bodies essentially for other men, not women. The very notion of bodybuilding is male, long excluding women, though now that we live in a culture of physical beauty, it is attracting women, too.

Beauty, both cultivated and genetic, surely plays into nature's aesthetic for natural selection and survival of the fittest, but unlike nature's design to make the male the more colorful of the species, mating selection also depends upon the mating dance, the female's mood and receptivity, and the need to procreate.

With the human male, selection is based upon power structures more often than it is upon physical perfection. Survival of the fittest doesn't mean the guy with the best pair of glutes. It more often has meant the guy with the best pair of cufflinks.

The act of bodybuilding, of preening the musculature to attain physical attractiveness, is based on the desire to be looked at—to strut—and can't help but be seen in sexual terms, hetero or homo. A man's rippling abs are akin to the make-up women traditionally wear in the modern West to the exclusion of males. Women apply cosmetics to their faces to conform to conventional notions of beauty, while men are now urged to heft iron and do sit-ups to accomplish the same.

Male beauty can be a product of exercise and good nutrition and defined pectorals and a tight butt, but it cannot be exclusively these. Sandow, though somewhat plain-looking in the face beneath his tightly curled hair, and Macfadden, positively ugly in the puss, were modeling below the neck. Their physiques were astonishing and titillating, but they might as well have worn fig leaves over both heads.

Manufactured beauty, or beauty in the can, was the more impressive of hurdles for the culture to jump because contemplating the male physique as beautiful had cultural taboos. But with cameras becoming widely available and no dearth in the production of good-looking lads, it couldn't be long before the twain should meet.

In Sandow's day, health and muscle tone and achieving a developed physique was seen as an attainable ideal and not yet openly eroticized. Even in fig leaf splendor, the guys were showing off their muscles for appreciation not for adoration.

The very concept of male beauty was still repudiated by notions of sissiness. Being seen

George "the Chest" O'Brien as an oversized Cupid. AUTHOR'S COLLECTION

as an object of beauty was strictly the domain of the feminine form. Men showing off their muscles was a wanton display of masculinity, hence its association with ideals of virility and stamina and "manhood." Guys who thought otherwise were pansies.

Lord Alfred Douglas (1870-1945), the pretty boy whose euphemistic "Love that dare not speak its name" unintentionally screamed cultural profanities at Oscar Wilde and helped ensure his public and private descent into hell on earth, was a pansy. Just looking at him made you want to belt him. Or kiss him. Or fuck him.

Exhibitions of physical strength and derring-do increasingly required the doer to display himself. Lard-ass baldies in tights throwing around wooden kegs were a dime a dozen. Now muscles did all the talking. And to see muscles, you had to get the guys out of their tights.

Harry Houdini (1874-1926), the world's greatest escape artist, often appeared in alarmingly skimpy groin straps during his amazing performances. A true showman, Houdini (*nee* Erich Weiss) must have realized the triple threat of such exposure: it showed off his magnificently muscled body, it lent the notion of vulnerability while, practically speaking, it quashed the audience's supposition that he had something hidden up his sleeve, and it provided male and female audiences alike the exploitable appeal of looking at a naked man abusing himself.

Half-naked self-abuse as popular entertainment also has a long history in the squared circle. Boxing was a phenomenon at the turn of the century and spectators went to the fights to see pug-faced scrappers pummel each other. Rarely was there beauty to behold in their mugs, but there was certainly beauty to behold in their bodies. This was the age of John L. Sullivan and the great Jack Dempsey, the latter whom agreed to don a thong (a needless formality given the composition) and become the flesh and blood version of Rodin's *Thinker* for a 1923 issue of *Vanity Fair*. (Seventy years later, Sylvester Stallone would do the same and forego the thong.) It's no coincidence that more pretty boy actors have done boxing movies at one time or another in their careers than any other type of sports picture. Where else can you show off your body while simultaneously engaged in such a thoroughly masculine activity?

And while the fellas went to the fights at night and to work during the day, their wives went to the theatre, both stage and screen varieties. Though the concept is as old as theater itself, the word *matinee* didn't enter the English vocabulary until the mid-nineteenth century. By the turn of the century, matinees were at the height of social popularity. To cater to a mostly female clientele for these midday dramatics, producers staged what they believed the ladies wanted: romances and melodramas.

Matinees were concededly lesser entertainments. All you needed to keep the seats full was a formula: tragic love stories, tragic life stories, and eventual triumphs over all that's tragic. Naturally, every heroine needed a hero. And if he was handsome, well that's where you got your repeat business.

The Matinee Idol was born in the latter quarter of the nineteenth century and by the turn of the century he reigned supreme.

A 1903 *Theatre* magazine piece chided a ridiculed breed of young matinee girls infected with "idolitis": "Sometimes she is at the adorable age of early twenties and then it is hard to forgive her; much oftener, however, she is at the nuisance age of the middle teens. Usually she is in bunches, two or three in a crowd, and invariably she is noisy. All through the play one hears such snatches of conversation as: 'Isn't he just darling?'; 'I think he's the most handsome man I ever saw.'" A scant 94 years later and they might as well be talking about Leonardo DiCaprio as Francis X. Bushman.

Despite such shallow public proclamations, what the vast majority of matinee idols offered their admirers at the time would by today's standards be equivalent to gaggles of young women swooning over Geoffrey Rush. They also looked to be theatrical fops, some no doubt talented, more often not, but they held sway over their female worshippers because they were men shameless enough to play the roles designed for women. It's not unlike poor Frederic in Gilbert & Sullivan's *Pirates of Penzance*: he's only ever seen the hoary Ruth, so he has no idea how beautiful a woman can be.

Of course there *were* handsome men in the plays, and some of them achieved fame of their ilk, but being a matinee idol pretty much meant playing the leading man part and enacting it with aplomb, not just sitting around looking pretty.

John Wilkes Booth was a matinee idol. John Barrymore was a matinee idol. As was Chauncey Olcott. Who, you ask? Precisely. Photos of the star idols of earlier times are as frightening as faces on wanted posters. Middle-aged men with big mustaches and sourpusses were apparently all the rage. It's like looking in your great-grandfather's yearbook and discovering the concept of "it skipped a generation."

9

If, however, you had the good fortune of finding your local matinee idol was also your ideal lover boy, and not just the local master thespian, you no doubt experienced the kind of palpitations that caused shameful swelling of body parts sponsored by impure thoughts. Daily returns to the theatre would then become essential treatment for the ailment.

Unless you were lucky enough to see your matinee idol from the first row, where you could drink in the glittering spray of his spit or the illuminated baubles of his falling sweat in a most intimate theatre of shared bodily fluids, you were likely squinting to make out private details of any sort from elsewhere in the house or glaring through opera glasses that increased your proximity while simultaneously frustrating your desire to hold them still for a good gape.

Movies ended that frustration.

The close-up brought you as close to your beloved as you could ever possibly be—gazing longingly into pores enameled with greasepaint, cavernous nostrils bereft of foliage, and eyebrows groomed like prize ferrets.

Intimacy in the movies was sanctioned by the close-up.

And when the camera got close to **Francis X(avier) Bushman** (1883-1966), he was said to look so much like the Gibson Man that it was proof positive the ideal fella was out there in flesh and blood and not just an artist's rendering in the catalog.

The world of commerce had given birth to ink-limned sexual archetypes. Artist Charles Dana Gibson had drawn a masculine hero for the times, prominent in both nose and chin, and marketed the image for mass consumption in advertising clothes, soda pop, and anything else you might need a man to model in a catalog. His type (and yes, there was a Gibson Girl, too) was copied and mimicked throughout the culture—in newspapers and on dimestore novel covers—and it didn't take long before audiences expected to find him in the movies.

Bushman, a physically robust man who had modeled for artists and been photographed nude for physique studies, signed a contract with Chicago's Essanay Studios in 1911, and made dozens of films, including *The Farmer's Daughter* (1913) and *Every Inch A King* (1914), before signing with Metro in 1915. He was a matinee idol during an era when the screens were smaller and the cigarette smoke in the theatre helped diffuse the close-ups.

Audiences partook of his beef, however, and his initials alone were world famous. A multi-millionaire movie star who was derogatorily nicknamed "the chin," because he tended to gesture with it, was not what we might define as a "beautiful" man today, but he certainly reinforced the nineteen-teen's popularized image of what it meant to be a shapely man and ably held competitors at bay in terms of fame and fortune.

He played Romeo at age 33 opposite 32-year old Beverly Bayne, and the two became perhaps the cinema's first popular male and female movie star team. Unfortunately, foreshadowing an era of public scandal that ruined many a prominent career in silent era Hollywood, Bushman and Bayne's secret marriage became known in 1918 and a feeding frenzy trial revealed Bushman's first marriage and five children, then further alleged physical abuse. The public dropped their idols like hot potatoes. (And in the Crash of '29, F.X.B. lost his millions.)

Audiences may have shirked at the idea that their pre-packaged and romanticized stars were not perfect people, despite being perfect physical specimens, but one thing Hollywood knew how to do from the start was replace a blown spotlight.

After the Bushman scandal, Hollywood's next idol offering was a safer, all-American one. **Wallace Reid** (1891-1923), it is reported, was "discovered" by executive producer Jesse Lasky when the actor was showing ass as a loinclothed Indian in a 1913 production of *The Deerslayer*. Raised in a theatrical family, Reid had the good fortune to be a tall, sturdy, handsome leading man, so when his interests in the technical aspects of motion picture making had him occasionally stepping in front of the camera, the camera liked what it saw.

After appearing as a blacksmith in D.W. Griffith's *Birth of A Nation* (1915), he found himself increasingly in demand, first playing soldiers in patriotic photoplays released during World War I, and then finding it just as easy to take on the role of jazz age playboy, driving his roadsters to exciting heights of youthful thrills in a series of action films exploiting the automobile as boy-toy: *The Roaring Road* (1919; playing Toodles), *Double Speed, Excuse My Dust, What's Your Hurry?* (all 1920), and *Too Much Speed* (1921). Even then, he was the prototype for the clean-cut, decent fellow. Affable, charming, and sweet, he provided

Wallace Reid, seen here in studio portrait, specialized in All-American boys-next-door until his tragic death at age 32. PHOTOFEST
Inset: Reid's shapely rear from *The Deerslayer* (1913). PHOTOFEST

audiences with an idealized vision of what the perfect homebred American boyfriend should be: as one good and one bad twin in *Always Audacious* (1920), in girl's dorm drag in *The Charm School* (1921), as a boxer in *The World's Champion* (1922), and as the reassuringly nice guy in *Nice People* (1922). He didn't often put on airs (he looked silly when he did) and he didn't have the oily sophistication of a stereotyped foreigner. He was your brother. He was your son. He was the polite neighbor boy you enjoyed talking to because he was good-looking and didn't seem to make that an issue.

He actually looked far more attractive when he was younger—writing, directing, and starring in dozens of two-reelers—than he did at his box-office prime, when he sported a little double chin and lipstick had a way of butterflying his lips and making his long face seem longer.

Unfortunately for Reid, a head injury sustained in a train wreck and treated with morphine turned into a horrific addiction. He died at 32 in an asylum.

Neil Hamilton (1899-1984) had the kind of handsome to bring us a light-year closer to the pretty boy male pin-up of the last half of the 20th century. D.W. Griffith cast him decisively in 1923's *The White Rose*, and throughout the rest of the '20s his smooth good looks were put to use at Paramount where he played express rider Nathan Holden in Griffith's Revolutionary War epic *America* (1924), a dashing Digby Geste in the 1926 *Beau Geste*, and Nick Carraway in the '26 version of *The Great Gatsby*.

Hamilton was such a looker that it's said his classic young man's visage was adopted by one of the country's key purveyors of archetypal male beauty in the '20s and he became an "Arrow Collar Man," a pretty boy sold to men and women alike as the epitome of well-dressed youth.

Created by *Saturday Evening Post* cover artist C.J. Leyendecker, the "Arrow Collar Man" was a multi-million dollar advertising hit with the public, most probably modeled for the artist by the love of his life, Charles Beach, though movie heartthrob **Reed Howes** (1900-1964) also gets credit. Looked at today, the ads are conspicuous for their male-male interaction and eye contact at the exclusion of any notice given their female companions. Didn't seem to bother the thousands of real-life female admirers who wrote the Arrow Collar Man fan letters when they had no idea who he was or if he really existed.

Those intrigued by the "whatever happened to?" aspects of our subjects will be astonished to learn that, though he continued acting on screen throughout the '30s and '40s and quickly lost his youthful glow, Hamilton is perhaps best remembered today as Commissioner Gordon from TV's *Batman* series (1966-1968), on which, by the way, none other than Francis X. Bushman made an appearance the last year of his life in the "Death in Slow Motion/The Riddler's False Motion" episodes of April 27/28, 1966.

The screen's biggest male stars of the silent era, its comedians, are today renowned for the enormous personal risks they took to pull off an astonishing array of death-defying stunts. To do that kind of work, of course, you had to keep in excellent shape and there were occasions when audiences got to glimpse the sinew.

The prodigious physicality of their roles lent both **Charlie Chaplin** (1889-1977) and **Buster Keaton** (1895-1966) a sexual dimension, a charisma of physical aesthetics that can render them quite attractive, not unlike the sensual quality Jackie Chan emanates.

George O'Brien (1899-1985), a Pacific Fleet heavyweight boxing champ, became a star in John Ford's *The Iron Horse* (1924). A big guy, nicknamed "The Chest" in Hollywood, he seems an unlikely candidate for a nudie postcard, but he was, striking a pose as a gargantuan Cupid in profile, his massive glutes bared and his tree trunk thigh positioned to obscure his privates. In some ways, it's the quintessential movie star nude of the time, combining the fantasy of a celebrity leading man with the newly permissible display of the naked male physique presented in an aesthetically pleasing and classic pose. Score one for the big guys. Their body type would not long remain in favor.

One of the biggest male stars of the silent era was **Douglas Fairbanks** (1883-1939), a barely handsome but physically powerful and charismatic screen performer whose athleticism and agility made him a safe choice for both men and women to admire. Guys could go to a Fairbanks swashbuckler, such as the 1920 *Mark of Zorro*, without any fear of their lady friends wondering why. He was a thrill to watch—manly and daring—and he was romantic, too, but in an acceptable way, eventually marrying "America's Sweetheart," Mary Pickford, and bringing royalty to Hollywood celebrity.

A popular plot convention hashed over by cultural historians in many of Fairbanks' early films charts

A dashing Neil Hamilton and partner from an unidentified silent. YESTERDAY

the transformation of his dandified self into his man-defined self. Western culture was screwing itself up over fears of inadequacy and Teddy Roosevelt's admonition to "stave off effeminacy" presaged the "Boy Reform Movement." Fearing industrialization's diminishing effects on manliness, society wrestled with fears of breeding a generation of over-domesticated males, the "mollycoddle," singularly speaking.

Boys were being pampered, the argument went, not allowed to be the mischievous little savages nature intended. Too many were being sissified at home by their mothers, who tended to rein in their sons' natural urges to be wild beasts. Physical activity, the outdoor life, camping, hunting, and same-sex bonding were the remedies. To prove it, Joseph Knowles went into the woods in August of 1913 bare-assed and without match or knife. He emerged three months later wearing a bearskin and went on to independent wealth telling his tale to the American male in his best-selling *Alone in the Wilderness*.

It all seems so silly now, but the gender issues being raked over the coals back then were not all that far removed from gender-identity issues we face a century later. (And which Brad Pitt's *Fight Club* takes to extremes.)

Civilization, almost by definition, suggests draining testosterone. Unable to physically accomplish that, what's a civilized guy to do with his natural drives and urges? Repression may lead to venting anger and behaving obnoxiously as a consequence.

Fairbanks' films evidence a way out for the mollycoddle. Either throw a punch in the final reel or lose half the audience.

Fortunately, more women went to the movies than men. And some of those men could not have cared less about a thrown punch, probably because they knew what it felt like to get punched, or at least understood how little provocation it took to be on the receiving end.

Action defined what it meant to be accepted as a man in the movies. But for lots of us, the look of a movie star defined what it meant to accept falling in love with one.

13

The cinema was on the verge of discovering the Pretty Boy as Star. It was time to hook the face up with the body. Beef was beef, but everybody knows it comes in different cuts, and the leaner the better.

The male dancer, particularly as homoerotic import of the Ballet Russe, set the body type standard to be most desired. It was filet mignon up on its tippy-toes.

Vaslav Nijinsky (1890-1950), only occasionally caught looking handsome in some of his photographs, sent shock waves—to use period hyperbole—through Europe with his nearly naked performance as a lusty faun in *L'Apres-midi d'un faune* (1912). The great Serge Diaghilev, impresario extraordinaire, eventually replaced his star attraction in both love and obsession by successively prettier male protégés Massine and Serge Lifar.

The pirouettes, lyrical choreography of body parts, and tights may not have endeared an America getting into the groove of social dance, but the sinew stuffed into those tights—the accentuated curvature of the male buttocks and the full cup of indistinct but omnipresent genitalia—did not go unnoticed or unappreciated.

If the world was to embrace a male sex symbol of the age, I suppose it only makes good sense that he be a dancer, too.

Rodolfo Pietro Raffaelo Filiberto Raffaele Guglielmi, aka "Rudy," remains one of the most famous film stars (silent or otherwise) in history, appearing in 36 films, though his career as a star was a relatively short five years.

Rudolph Valentino (1895-1926), as he eventually became known, may not have invented male sex appeal at the movies, but he was its prime exponent. Thomas Meighan and Charles Farrell dominated the Quigley polls as the cinema's most popular men in the early twenties, but through no fault of their own only their families remember them as male beauties and matinee idols today.

Valentino is an immortal.

And just as he was adored by legions of American women and closeted homosexuals, he was despised by heterosexual American men. How could they ever live up to this Phallus in Wonderland? They couldn't. So they called him names.

He was a "fop," a "fem," a "sissy," a "queer," a "professional male beauty," a "tango pirate," a "flapperooster," a "Latin lounge lizard," a candy-assed "gigolo," a "male butterfly," a "he-vamp," a "taxi dancer," a lazy "wop," a fucking "foreigner," a "powder puff," a "pansy," a "cabaret parasite," a "lady-killer," and a "phony" who invented an equally phony aristocratic past. No wonder. He couldn't hack an honest day's work shoveling shit or laying bricks. Instead, he preened himself in the corner of cabarets and made his bucks preying on their wives and daughters, who—for the love of Pete!—paid him to clutch them close to his serpentine body and then...and then he'd make them dance!

Everybody knew that male dancers were fairies. You didn't have to see Nijinsky's infamous choreographed masturbation to prove it. It just wasn't a natural thing for a man to spend his time doing. Industry was booming, big business was looming, offices needed to be filled and farms needed to be farmed, and if F. Scott Fitzgerald's Jazz Age was upon us, it didn't mean you had to give up being a man's man when you hit the town.

Masculinity was roily, full of self-doubt and apprehension—in fact, in crisis, considering the strides of feminist empowerment. A movie star like Valentino was a perfect cultural match: the male as sex object for the delight of a woman's gaze—beautiful, yes, but still manly enough to get the job done.

He was a perverted ideal. Gay men must have adored him, too.

He was born in Castellaneta, Italy, became a terrible student, a juvenile delinquent in behavior and attendance. He proved a remarkable athlete, however, and there are stories that he learned how to dance by doing so with other boys at his all-male academy.

His veterinarian father died when Rudy was eleven. Hoping to please his mother, he decided to set his sights on becoming an officer in the Royal Naval Academy. He was summarily rejected for having a chest expansion that was one inch too small for admission—not the last time the relative size of his manhood would be called into question.

He studied gardening for a while, then went off and blew his wad in Paris and Monte Carlo before the family put him on a boat, at age 18, for America. He arrived in New York City in 1913.

Disenchanted by a series of manual labor jobs, including dishwasher and gardener (again), Rodolfo wandered in near poverty, but borrowed clothes and tried to put on airs to wiggle his way into higher society crowds, until he was offered his first solid job. He became a dance gigolo at Maxim's restaurant, a trade he excelled at and which would forever change his life. One biographer has Valentino learning the tango from a male acquaintance in front of a monkey cage at the New York Zoo. That's still the way I see it in my dreams, no matter how utterly fictitious.

For twenty or thirty bucks a night, plus tips, the handsome young man in black formals would hang around the restaurant and wait to be asked to cut the rug as partner to women of every size and intent. Strictly speaking, the dance floor romance was to remain entirely on the dance floor, and among the many other things Valentino "authorities" can't agree upon, he was either suspiciously chaste (denoting either gentlemanly or homosexual predilections) or he was quite the bunny humper. If it's true that he was more likely to make spaghetti than make love, it may have been that he was put off by the sexual aggression of these New York women. In this respect he was not unlike many of his most staunch American male enemies. The image of the era's "flapper" and "vamp" was sexy if all you wanted was to get laid, but the trampy behavior was revoltingly unattractive if she actually meant anything to you. Valentino was conflicted by his rather liberal notions of female sexuality on the one hand and his rather Old World sensibilities of a woman's subordinate role in a male-female relationship on the other.

Just imagine, though, how exciting this must have been for these women, bedded or not, to have been caught in the embrace of such a beautiful young man.

Eventually he was snatched by professional dancer Bonnie Glass, who was looking for a replacement for Clifton Webb, her very gay ex-partner who would later find fame in Hollywood as both character actor and enthusiastic advocate of many a handsome young Hollywood hopeful. Professional dancers were quite an attraction, though Rudy never seemed to enjoy the circuit no matter how accomplished he became, and he was regularly finding himself in trouble with the police for the vagabond ways he spent his off hours.

A hoofing partnership with Joan Sawyer lasted until a New York scandal involving a dickering playboy, his dickered wife, and a scurrilous set-up to prove the infidelities implicated a certain "marquis" di Valentina, suitably arrested while wearing a wristwatch (a faggish accessory pre-WWI).

After the trial and yet another brief incarceration for failing to post an excessive bail when charged with being in cahoots with the owner of a house of ill-repute, Rudy joined up with a musical and danced his way to the West Coast. He tried to join the Italian Air Force, but his poor eyesight, not his lack of inches, waylaid that pipe dream. He did meet theatrical agent/actor Norman Kerry, however, who quickly became a good friend and got him $5 a day extra work in the movies to complement the meager income he garnered dancing in hotels—something he still very much disliked.

Because of his dark good looks and America's rampant xenophobia, he was cast in a variety of mustaches playing the heavy in many of his early films, which included such alarmingly autobiographical titles as *The Married Virgin, The Big Little Person, The Delicious Little Devil, The Cheater, The Home Breaker, A Society Sensation, Once to Every Woman,* and *Passion's Playground.*

An exception to his oily bad guy was his pasty good guy in *All Night* (1918). He's utterly without a character to play prior to the formal conceptualization of himself after he attained stardom. In an otherwise dull sex comedy, he injects a little life into the proceedings during a sequence in which he's forced to put on pajamas and go to bed with the woman to whom he's pretending to be married. He feels "trapped" in his pjs and, at one point, wraps his bedcover around him like he was a sheik. He loses that cover while dangling from the roof and lands in a water barrel. When he climbs out, we can see his bronzed legs and a millisecond flash of his well-muscled butt in profile as the waterlogged pjs cling to him.

He's cuter in the film's morning after when his hair is all mussed. "I'm going upstairs and freshen up," he tells his girlfriend after their charade is over and they anticipate all hell breaking loose. "I want to look nice when the ambulance arrives."

Off-screen, Rudy got hitched to actress Jean Acker, an acquaintance of the glamorous Russian-born actress Alla Nazimova—who would play a role in both the neophyte actor's peculiar marriages.

Much to Valentino's agony, Acker slammed the honeymoon door in his face before he even got in it, so to speak, and the marriage was essentially over before it ever got started, unconsummated and unconscionable.

Lacking a definitive explanation for the bizarre wedding night tragedy, though she later sued him for "desertion" much to his incomprehension, suppositions about either Rudy's sexual disinterest (or

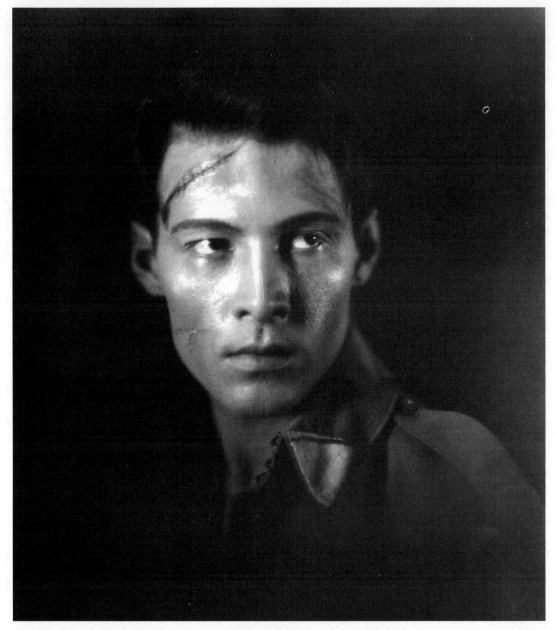

Rudolph Valentino, somehow even sexier wounded, in *The Four Horsemen of the Apocalypse* (1921). PHOTOFEST

inadequacy), or both parties alleged same-sex preferences, were adopted and have become part of the Valentino fairy tale. Valentino eventually won divorce in court based on her desertion of him. Many years later, Acker privately confided that Rudy had told her he had gonorrhea on their way to the honeymoon suite, though we don't know if this was true.

Depressed and back at work, Rudy was cast as "Clarence Morgan, a cabaret parasite," who lures a respectable woman into a compromising situation at a hotel in order to ruin her reputation in *Eyes of Youth* (1919). He's only on screen for eight minutes, but big-time screenwriter June Mathis found herself smitten with all 167 pounds of him and demanded he be cast in the lead of *The Four Horsemen of the Apocalypse* (1921), which she was adapting for Metro.

Playing the "youthful libertine" Julio Desnoyers in this epic WWI melodrama in which two grandsons of the most powerful landowner in the Argentine find themselves on opposite sides of the conflict in Europe, the stereotyped foreigner was about to move from heavy to hero.

Valentino's first appearance on screen as a lead takes place in a smoky café where he's about to dance the dirty dance—the tango—and set our hearts aflame. With his big eyes and big teeth, he's a sexy son-of-a-bitch standing there in his gaucho costume, complete with hat and dangling cigarette. His eyes are almond-shaped, slightly closed in close-ups, almost Asian looking. Very exotic. Very romantic.

When he takes to the floor, throwing his hip into his partner and expertly dragging her along as he struts, he's making love to every woman and gay man in the house. The tango was a truly decadent coupling when it burst onto the scene in the 1920s, ripe with cultural and social taboo.

Tom Cruise danced in his underwear. Rudolph Valentino danced with his stiletto heels on. Both communicated sex appeal to movie audiences and made stars of the handsome men with the moves.

Julio eventually becomes a dandy art student studying in Paris, his cigarette still dangling, and women the "plague of his existence." Mirroring his real life, Valentino's character ends up teaching the Argentine tango, luring in his "many pupils to satisfy his extravagant tastes." He's even having an affair with a married woman in the film, which certainly was morally reprehensible, but had to play nicely into moviegoer fantasy.

As with many of the era's plot developments, the swishy femboy beauty who shares kisses with his lover by smooching the tip of his index finger and then placing it on the other's lips will transform into a much more palatable version of what it means to be a man. With the onset of war, "The Tango Idol was forgotten" the title card tells us.

"Good looks do not count now—all one needs is a uniform." Valentino looks clean and lean in close-up here, as opposed to the slightly puffy features noticeable in some of his other films. And at just 25, he makes a damned fine looking soldier in his helmet and uncharacteristic facial scruff. (Hairiness is, of course, a sign of manliness. A hairless fem becomes a hairy he-man.) Though untrained as an actor, and often ridiculed by critics because of it, he very capably emotes mournful longing on the battlefield despite being saddled with a pet monkey who goes to war with him wearing its own miniature helmet and backpack.

Four Horsemen was the biggest film of the year and Valentino was now a known quantity. While working on *Camille* (1921), co-starring Nazimova, he fell head over heels for her costume designer and set decorator Winifred Shaugnessy, subsequently surnamed De Wolfe, then Hudnut, thanks to her mother's succession of wealthy marriages. Ms. Hudnut preferred to be known as Natacha Rambova. Rudy's near-complete infatuation with her would not only stoke the fires of those red-blooded American males who found him unmanly and thoroughly pussy-whipped (the latter had annoying social implications for all males at large), but her alleged dominance over his lifestyle, attire, personal appearance, career choices, and contract negotiations was unfairly and inaccurately blamed for his subsequent professional failures.

The Sheik (1921) was a lurid sexual shocker in its day, based on a novel apparently so trifling that it could only have become a runaway bestseller because the author of this tale of miscegenation and desert rape fantasy was a woman.

In the film, an adventurous young British gal, who scorns marriage because it is "the end of independence," is captured by Ahmed Ben Hassan, an Arab sheik with wet and weary staring eyes, who repeatedly ravishes her into proper submission before it's revealed in the final reel that he is in fact of English-Spanish descent, a desert foundling.

The film is loaded with sex, but trying to jack a drop of sexiness out of it today is nearly impossible. We're left to wild imaginings of what all the tent histrionics must have meant to audiences at the time. Both Valentino, whose bizarre smile reveals only his uppers and makes him look loony, and Agnes Ayres, whose reactions increasingly resemble a woman about to lose her lunch, are painfully over the top and one begins to fear close-ups.

Still, there is a lot to play with: his excited glare when she's concealing a gun under her wrap; his sneaking into her chamber to bite the head off her bullet, then leaping from her balcony to serenade her from below; the phallic handle of his knife always on display poking up through his belt; talk of "savages" and appellations of "master," "madame," and "sir;" and more sexist intertitles than you can shake a cigar at.

A concoction of florid melodrama and sex-play, it's a forerunner of the afternoon soap opera. Valentino, who glowers and leers and pops up his brows as his eyeballs burst white, gets to order his "helpless captive" around ("Lie still, you little fool!") and force her to be his sex-slave. "You make a very charming boy," he remarks about her stealing into the casino in disguise, "but it was not a boy I saw two nights ago in Biskra."

17

Outfitted in manly, panted attire, our heroine is part of the film's strange sexual politicking in the face of 1920s American male/female sexual role-playing and has the Sheik emasculating the ballsy dame while he, in turn, is masculinized by his association with her.

The film was such a hit that Valentino became a superstar, a sexual icon for the American fairer and third sexes, much to hetero male ridicule and eventually Valentino's own squiggling embarrassment.

Said *Variety* of his performance: "Mr. Valentino is revealed as a player without resources. He depicts the fundamental emotions of the Arabian sheik chiefly by showing his teeth and rolling his eyes." Considering that the reviewer was in all likelihood male, and therefore egregiously prejudiced, his second sentence is spot on.

It's ironic that Valentino's signature role may also be his most awful performance (though he claims he only did what he was directed to do), abetted not only by his silly facial aerobics, but the strange bounce of his knees as he tries on his cape, the noticeably dark make-up on his hands but not his face, and the suddenly distracting wristwatch he wears. (A no-no in porn films, too.)

The only time he approaches anything close to sexy and virile is when he's shown with sword drawn, panting heavily, as he bursts into the bedchamber of the film's true sexual villain. He's here to rescue the woman he's gone limp over now that love has been embraced as nobler than lust. In the end, she gets her sentimental lover and the depraved, bestial foreigner the Sheik appeared to be at the outset has become a doting white guy (though still demonized as a dark guy by the All-American brands).

Whatever his true color, that guy became known as the "World's Greatest Lover." "The Love God," too. Valentino's exotic sexual appeal pumped fantasies into the culture big time. He became famous because he was openly sexual in a way that American men were not.

He married Natacha Rambova in Mexico just after he was announced as the lead, playing the greatest bullfighter in Spain, in *Blood and Sand* (1922).

In a film that acknowledges the cruelty and barbarism of the bullfight and indicts the masses that assemble to cheer on the bloodletting in the name of sport—the original Ibáñez novel was an attack—Rudy plays Juan Gallardo, the "Little Shoemaker." An early amateur bout shows him tenderly kissing the cheek of a handsome fallen comrade, holding him a la *pietà*, after having just slain the beast who fatally gored the pretty youth. Back home, he's a mama's boy with torn britches and a black patch on his bum. Mama darns his trousers while he's still wearing them—him sitting on the table and leaning back, her with an elbow firmly in his crotch as she sews the gaping hole in his pant leg.

Against his mother's wishes, he takes his secondhand toreador's costume and sets out on a career slaying bulls, quickly achieving national fame. While on tour, he's enticed to dance by a strutting hussy in yet another smoky café and he indulges her, leading—as always—with his package. While briefly obliging fans who yearned to see him strut again as he did in *Four Horsemen*, he brings the escapade to an abrupt halt when she tries to kiss him. He snarls and flings her away. "I hate all women—but one!"

Ms. One is his hometown sweetheart, whom he marries. At the reception, he kisses a couple of children who then wave bye-bye. He waves back by wiggling his fingers palm up, as if he were calling them back, or perhaps tickling them under the chin. As an actor, Rudy continues to endear himself to us with these surprising little peculiarities.

The tale's moral dilemma, outside of its animal atrocities, surfaces when a rich dame attempts to seduce the master bullfighter while he's in Madrid. He manages to temporarily resist lust and break it off with a handshake, but then she does something quite remarkable. She vise-grips him: "What wonderful arms you have—your muscles are like iron." Rudolph gives in to the self-appraisal and kisses her. Flattery will get you everywhere with a pretty boy, especially if it's about himself. No, she doesn't reveal more cleavage or drop a hanky and bend over to pick it up in front of him. He would have easily ignored that. To get this boy, all you have to do is grab him and tell him how hot he is...tell him how big his arms are, for lack of further evidence. Call attention to his own body and he'll be yours.

An adulterer who's unhappy as hell, when he next gets his chance to shun her, she fondles his bicep again: "Some day you will beat me with those strong hands! I should like to know what it feels like!" And the audience would, too. What a wickedly juicy invite to S&M and/or a frightfully sexist take on the inevitability of male dominance. Instead, he threatens her with a shaking fist, calls her a snake, and walks out.

Though Valentino was initially quite enthusiastic about playing this coveted role, and was himself a bullfighting enthusiast, he eventually soured on *Blood and Sand*, despite feeling it offered him the best part of his career. Too much studio meddling, the insertion of the gratuitous dance scene, the refusal to film on

18

location in Spain or to pay for a ton of authentic artifacts he wanted to bring back from there for use in the picture, the press playing up his beauty, and the questionably small paycheck for his first lead billing role were all grievances.

For us, as voyeurs who could not have cared less and wouldn't have been otherwise privy to his business and career woes, Valentino is not particularly handsome here, especially in close-ups where his thickened caterpillar eyebrows threaten to meet (and occasionally do). He has strange hair throughout (curly as a youth, then parted at odd places and pan flattened later per the style), though the little pigtail he sports is sometimes looped and makes for a cute, delicate little handle at the back of his shiny head.

There are a few pay-offs, however. He's got a gorgeous smile on display for the members of the all-male press who assemble in front of his dressing screen and rib him while he's being prepped. (His requisite dressing scene, which would be played out more explicitly in later films, included a dashing twirl into his waist sash that unfortunately doesn't appear in the print Kino has transferred to DVD.) And twice, standing tense with his sword prepared to thrust into the bull, he displays an enviable set of dancer's buns.

But Valentino would object to this kind of scrutiny. He abhorred being adored for his beauty, being sold as a moistener. And he let his studio know it in no uncertain terms. He refused to attend the premiere of *Blood and Sand* and his furor prompted studio retaliation.

When Famous Players-Lasky took him to court for not fulfilling his contract, he testified extensively on the subject of his mistreatment. During *Blood and Sand*, he described a makeshift public dressing room without a fourth wall "and without any roof whatever, letting the burning sun shine in, and heating the chair so that I could not sit on it. As my costumes were such that I could not wear underwear and was naked each time that I changed my costume, this condition was almost impossible...When I first sat down on the chair between changes of my costume, I was burned and jumped up and did not sit down again upon it."

In the midst of a flood of lawsuits, personal attacks (including a male-authored "I Hate Valentino" piece in *Photoplay*), and following his jailing on bigamy charges when a California judge refused to recognize the Mexican wedding to Natacha because his divorce to Jean was still pending, Valentino spent huge amounts of speculative cash building his first dream home while friends were swearing in court that he'd only ever slept on the couch when he and Natacha shared quarters.

The new star was proving temperamental and difficult and Jazz Age wacky, eventually getting involved in seances in which an Egyptian named Mesolope and an American Indian named Black Feather were personal spiritual guides. Sexy photos exist of him dressed as a bare-chested Indian and it's assumed he did quite a few "private" photos for friends and admirers—among them, his nearly nude version of Nijinsky's notorious faun, which became public during one of his many trips into court and was explained away as preparation for a role.

For *The Young Rajah* (1922), an inferior project he was contractually forced to make, he's dressed in beads and necklaces and bangles and luxuriating shirtless in a banana boat as a clairvoyant adoptee who learns he's a Maharajah's son and the chosen savior of his people. A revealing shot in the film of Rudy hefting a rowing boat at Harvard, where his swimming trunks indicate it's ten minutes to noon, was used to promote the flick and found its way, no doubt, into the bottom of many a gay boy's dresser drawer.

In a similar vein, Valentino "authored" and was the subject of a number of magazine articles devoted to his physical regimen (among them, "Muscles in the Movies: How Physical Culture Made Me A Screen Star," "Valentino's Bulging Muscles," and "Valentino's Beauty Secrets"), most of which strained to prove he was a real "man's man"—a "he-man"—alongside provocative photos of the skimpily attired star stretching, boxing, and bending over. There was even a film short entitled *The Sheik's Physique* in which Rudy V is seen undressing in his automobile, preparing for a lounge on the beach. Just as he begins undoing his shirt, he looks into the camera knowingly and pulls down the car's window blind. In 1923, his 76-page booklet "How You Can Keep Fit" was published, complete with 30 photos of the shirtless star working out.

At constant odds with a populace apparently divided over his appeal, virtually everything he did was read as the opposite of what he intended, from manly sport pursuits (which only stressed his interest in hanging out with the boys) to griping about the sorry state of the motion picture industry, ostensibly in order to make it better. The young Italian had every right to be pissed at the studios for taking advantage of him, but the highly publicized and nasty court battles hurt his cause with movie moguls.

In some quarters he was seen as a spoiled brat fresh off the boats who was, in effect, publicly railing against the "evil" studios who made him a star and who were already paying him nearly as much as the President of the United States.

Even with legitimate gripes, his grandstanding alienated some of his public, as well as moviemakers, and he found himself effectively banished from Hollywood at the height of his fame. He wouldn't have a new film in release for two years.

Instead, he wrote a collection of poems and had them published in 1923 as *Day Dreams*, a best-seller no less. He also openly admitted to having accepted a "slave bracelet" from his wife, which he proudly wore. In desperate need of cash, the Valentinos were talked into hitting the cross-country rails as part of a $7,000-a-week husband-and-wife dance act in which afterward they hawked Mineralava Beauty Clay to pay off their mounting debts.

Natacha loved to undress her famous mannequin, but she loved dressing him even more. When they finally got back to big screen work in 1924, he was fopped to the hilt in powdered wig, lipsticked and powdered puss, and not one but two beauty marks (in the shape of little hearts) as *Monsieur Beaucaire* (1924). He's actually the Duke of Chartres, Prince of the Blood, a courtier and performer for royalty at the court of Louis XV, looking very effeminate. "The shock of his life—a woman is not looking at him" reads a title card. More shocking still, he shaves himself!

The famed dressing sequence has him powdered and preparing to don a shirt while attended by three dressers and several visitors, including a gentleman who fastidiously applies his lipstick. It actually takes several minutes for Rudy to don that shirt, allowing him to flex a bit and show off his magnificent chest. I get the feeling that the gratutitousness of the display is meant to masculinize him amidst the absurd display of courtly graces. The duration of his shirtlessness is certainly deliberate.

He loses one of his beauty marks after the first scene and, after defying a Court order and escaping to England, he hides out as a lowly barber. Infatuated with the local Belle of Bath, he assumes the persona of a fictional gentleman by the name of Beaucaire and sets out to win her. Some writers have guessed that the film's failure with audiences signaled their rejection of his being effeminized, but I'll bet it had more to do with the fact that the film is overlong, largely a bore, and too obnoxiously class conscious to appeal to American audiences.

As with all foppish movie star roles, he'll prove to be a real man of action before it's all said and done. In an age that fostered the proliferation of the Boy Scouts and the YMCA while the "New Woman" asserted herself, even a guy like Valentino longed to become known as a guy like Douglas Fairbanks, the swashbuckler.

It was a common theme. Two years prior, in *Moran of the Lady Letty* (1922), "Rodolpho" Valentino played a San Franciscan dancer and playboy who's drugged and thrown aboard the "Heart of China," a smuggler's ship in need of a crew. The hardened seamen laugh at the refined and wimpy gentleman with his back-home yacht and no backbone. But he quickly becomes one of the boys after he dons his muscle shirt.

When the scalawags come across the burning Lady Letty, Rudy discovers a salty sea lass named Moran still alive, but unconscious aboard. He rescues her and foolishly falls in love. The gal just isn't interested, though, despite close-ups of him that reveal a streamlined handsomeness and medium shots that show a very nice basket in his tight sailor pants.

"I never knew a girl like you," he tells her. "Never knew a girl could be like you. You swear like a man and you dress like a man—and you're strong. I know you are as strong as I am."

"Believe me, it's all wasted," she says. "I never could love a man. I'm not made for men."

"Nor for other women," he adds, perhaps probingly, perhaps reassuringly—we'll never know without a soundtrack to gauge his inflection.

"No, nor for other women either," she replies. She's not a girl, she adds, she's just Moran of the Lady Letty.

Unfortunately, the film cheats us by ending happily—they even kiss; still, there's a shot of Valentino right before his climactic fight with the captain that should be freeze-framed and turned into posters. Confirming our suspicions about the tightness of his pants earlier, he strikes a pose that attains the level of icon for "gay sailor."

Coming back from one of his many transatlantic trips to Europe, where he was frequently attacked and nearly stripped of his clothing by mobs of overzealous fans, Rudy appeared in physical preparation for Natacha's scripted version of *El Cid*, entitled *The Hooded Falcon*, and sported a manly sprout of facial hair. In a world gone Celebrity Mad, the Associated Master Barbers of America issued the following

Valentino puffs out his chest in *Monsieur Beaucaire* (1924) opposite Anthony Daven, the man most likely of any, say biographers, to have had a relationship with him. YESTERDAY

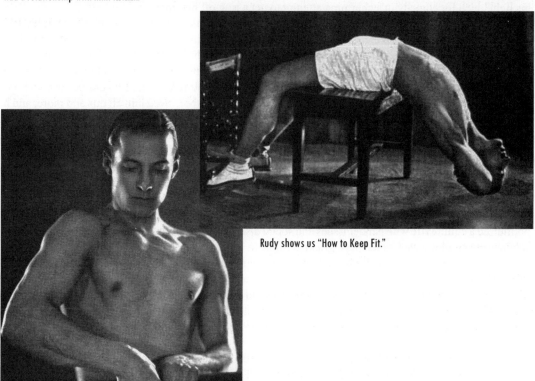

Rudy shows us "How to Keep Fit."

statement:

"Our members are pledged not to attend a showing of Rudolph Valentino's photoplays as long as he remains bewhiskered," fearing public imitation that "would so utterly deface America as to make American citizens difficult to distinguish from Russians."

Valentino was still being ostracized as one of those damn dirty foreigners. It was un-American to fall for the guy, this Latin Loser.

In *Cobra* (1925), another cheap and inferior romance his studio made him do, Rudy demonstrated that he had, at just 30 (but with only a year to live), become the darling of the medium shot. Close-ups were now riskier. He'd become thicker, puffier. In the film's best moment, his eyes fill with tears as he closes a door in pained self-sacrifice—a great shot and a hanky moment for fans.

Cobra marked his last collaboration with Natacha before United Artists insisted upon, and he agreed to sign, a contract banning her outright from having anything to do with his films, thus effectively ending their marriage. He would now be making $520,000 a year and was supposed to see 42% of his film profits over the next three years. Sitting on eight acres of land in the Hollywood Hills, his 17-room, 4-garage, horse-stabled, dog-kenneled Falcon Lair would be Rudy's castle and Rudy's alone. He publicly vowed not to marry until at least after 1930, though rumors flew during his subsequent friendly relationship with actress Pola Negri.

While bowing to kiss the hand of the Czarina in *The Eagle* (1925), Rudy's lieutenant of the Imperial Guard finds the other hand of the horny old broad planted firmly on his slick head, holding him in place. That's 1925 code for she wants him to get it on with her. To his credit, he doesn't, even though it may cost him his life and career.

Hetero men didn't "get" RV's pictures because they weren't made for them. Even his so-called action pictures were low on action and high on romance. His runaway horse-stopping antics in *The Eagle* are delightfully contrasted with his swishy social mannerisms. He waves with an extended hand that bobs at the wrist as if he were a marionette or playing with a yo-yo. Even a dangerous showdown with a captive killer bear in a wine cellar has its rejoinder in the put-upon persona he adopts as Monsieur Le Blanc, effete French tutor to his sworn enemy's daughter.

We can see in *The Eagle* that he was getting better as an actor, too, quite capable of showing audiences his light touch for comedy in a charming attempt to get a ring off his finger.

In 1925, Rudolph Valentino was named the number one male box-office star by the Quigley Poll, despite his hiatus from the screen and all his legal and marital troubles. By 1926, it would be Tom Mix.

Valentino cringed at his dual-edged celebrity. For several years, he had relentlessly pursued his obsessions with fast cars (in which he was wrecked or ticketed regularly), newly acquired and lavish estates, fine clothes, jewelry, expensive trips to Europe to do research for future roles that would never come, rare breeds of dog, and thoroughbred Arabian horses. Fame bought or borrowed him all this and more, and he was usually in steep debt, but the source of the fame made him feel conflicted and perhaps even a bit ashamed: those crazed American girls wetting themselves over him and making them both look foolish in their screeching pursuit.

Would they never let him be? Would America ever let him get past that awful stigma of *The Sheik*? What Valentino couldn't have understood, because he was too close to the subject and had his mind on another career trajectory, was that he was not just an actor, he was an emblem—the movies' first lasting male sex symbol. His Sheik represented a have-it-both-ways sexual libertinism that excited, enraged, and politicized a culture rife with gender issues and social dislocations. (*Thelma & Louise* caused a much more subdued but similarly well-timed psychosexual ripple in 1991.)

Of course it probably didn't help that when push came to shove in 1922, Valentino was all too willing to goad his being a scapegoat: "I blame the American man," he's quoted as saying in the March 1922 issue of *Photoplay*. "He cannot hold a woman, dominate and rule her. Naturally things have come to a pretty pass. He is impossible as a lover. He cares nothing for pleasing a woman." Blaming the American male's attempt to assuage his woman with the leftovers of his preoccupations with business and money, Valentino argued, "In his blindness, therefore, he despises the young European who comes here. He laughs at him, makes fun of him, calls him insulting names." Why? Because the refined European male "shows him up."

On the heels of a *Collier's* interview titled "I'm Tired of Being A Sheik," in which he once again contradicted his legendary sheikdom and made it clear that it was a role opposite his true "farmer" nature and done only for the money, Valentino agreed to star in the sequel in order to pay off huge debts. Surprisingly, he ended up making one of his most entertaining films in the process. It would also be his last.

Anyone clueless as to why Valentino was such a big deal need only see him flaunted in *The Son of the Sheik* (1926). It's all there, baby. Love it or leave it. Determined to hang balls on his lipstick lover boy persona, Rudy cranked up the wind machines, jacked up the pacing and action to balance the lovemaking, and played not one but two roles, both the original sheik—graying and hard—and his spunky young son, thanks to split screen.

In so many wonderful ways, *The Son of the Sheik* is the apotheosis of Valentino's screen image. We first see his face in a dissolve from the face of the film's female star, Vilma Banky, tying together the feminine qualities of both: Valentino's beautiful visage borne out of a longing woman's features.

She's the dancing girl for whom he rides across the desert to see every night, and though she calls him "my lord," it is an important distinction that this young sheik is in love with her, not in lust with her. ("Why fear me, dearest? Love such as mine can do no harm," he tells her, both acknowledging his honorable intentions and making for a nice gay re-reading.) His face may bear the obvious signs of eye shadow and his arms and fingers may be outfitted with jewelry, but he's full of winning smiles and glances, not the silly gloats of the first film.

He's back in exquisite form for close-ups, too, looking radiant and healthy despite his proximity to real-life death. (He would, in fact, die young and leave a good-looking corpse.) He's simply gorgeous, even majestic in profile, such as when he turns away from the dancing girl after he's been fooled into believing she betrayed him.

A 1924 *Photoplay* piece written by Adela Rogers St. Johns that spitefully picked on his physicality and inappropriateness as a moral idol for women decided that "the lure of Valentino is wholly, entirely, obviously the lure of the flesh."

Such allure is amplified in the torture scene. Caught off guard by hooligans while he was making out with his lady after having politely removed his gun because it was getting in the way, he springs into action after affecting a virile stare as sexy as it is heroically masculine. Outnumbered, he is knocked unconscious and bound to a wall, left dangling from his wrists. He makes for an enticing *objet d'fetish* hanging there in his sporty jodhpurs and riding boots, his shirt torn open far enough to expose a nipple. Scourged and whipped, his helplessness at the cruel flogging is made all the sexier by the camera's implicitly voyeuristic subjectivity. This flogging is for our benefit, for our enjoyment, in ways we'd probably rather not contemplate. (A modern corollary is the shock therapy inflicted upon Mel Gibson in *Lethal Weapon*.) His biceps flare, his body writhes, and between lashes of the whip a pony-tailed midget pinches the flesh of his upper arms and stomach. One longs for a *Lawrence of Arabia* subtext to his capture and torture, but no such luck. He's left to be cut down by his friends, a limp Christ figure used and abused, wearing the cuts across his open chest for the remainder of the film.

In truth, the Great Romantic could not have chosen a better vehicle for his swan song in terms of his lasting iconography. He has enormous screen presence here. He looks and moves as an icon, naturally striking poses that instantaneously become classical compositions.

Answering the licentiousness of the first film, he's moral and humanistic, a true romantic whose goal is to save a woman from corruption not corrupt her. His first love scene, among the ruins at night, is tender, sexy, and romantic. The dancer, Yasmin, is unaware of her dreamy lover's name. After a warm and ecstatic kiss, Valentino says to her: "I am he who loves you—is that not name enough?" Like Eastwood's Man With No Name, the film presciently suggests that the image suffice. Valentino is the Lover. Who needs more?

Charming, sweet, gentlemanly, adoring, and infatuated early in the film, Valentino's young buck is tricked into believing his woman is a man-snaring hussy, and the fantasy is knocked up a notch when—like father, like son—he has his way with her in his tent. Confronting her with his suspicions, he raises his arm and its smoothly flexing musculature becomes his displayed sex organ. Now he'll punish her for using him as a sex object; the implications as they relate to Valentino's off-screen connection to his fans are dead-on. In fact, he might as well be talking to his fans, berating them at the very same time threatening disciples all-too willing to be disciplined by their master.

Valentino manhandles Yasmin, shows her the lashes across his chest, then raises his arm again, providing us another heavenly look at his great flexing bicep and naked limb, now engorged, thick, and erect. The girl is kept at his waist level the whole time, groveling and pressing her face into his pantaloons. It's torrid fantasy, a role-playing sex game in costume that culminates in his approaching her, his eyes narrowed to

23

slits, the camera suddenly assuming his point-of-view, before he forcefully kisses her.

"For once your kisses are free!" He's toying with her. She tries to escape. He advances again, his arms outstretched as she backs away and the scene fades out…a fade suggesting he's now going to fuck the living daylights out of her. It's powerful and romantic and sexist and as devoutly wished as the moment Rhett scoops Scarlet up in his arms and charges up the stairs to the bedroom.

What ultimately makes all of this okay, as opposed to the more wantonly lust-driven rape in the original film, is that the audience knows that these characters really do love each other. The betrayal is a lie spread by others. So no matter what they do to each other, no matter how many more reasons he's going to give her to hate him before he's finished with her, the sex is desired by both parties. The audience has been provided an alibi for the sexual punishment—a rape fantasy with a happy ending.

The film concludes with a rousing action sequence that sets father and son flailing swords side by side, and there's even a Fairbanksian swing from a chandelier. The action is meant to masculinize The Sheik, of course, and it does to some extent, but for those of us who could not care less, there's a Valentino so beautiful that he manages to look hot even in a turban.

Valentino: Smoldering appeal. YESTERDAY

The dichotomy between his beauty and his brawn and all of its rancid social implications dogged Valentino until the very end.

Rudy had the misfortune to be in Chicago during the city's record-breaking 1926 swelter, stopping off at the Blackstone Hotel when "It" appeared on the *Chicago Tribune*'s Sunday editorial page of July 18:

"PINK POWDER PUFFS

"A new public ballroom was opened on the north side a few days ago, a truly handsome place and apparently well run. The pleasant impression lasts until one steps into the men's washroom and finds there on the wall a contraption of glass tubes and levers and a slot for the insertion of a coin. The glass tubes contain a fluffy pink solid, and beneath them one reads an amazing legend which runs something like this: 'Insert coin. Hold personal puff beneath the tube. Then pull the lever.'

"A powder vending machine! In a men's washroom! *Homo Americanus!* Why didn't someone quietly drown Rudolph Guglielmo, alias Valentino, years ago?

"And was the pink powder machine pulled from the wall or ignored? It was not. It was used. We personally saw two 'men'—as young lady contributors to the Voice of the People are wont to describe the breed—step up, insert coin, hold kerchief beneath the spout, pull the lever, then take the pretty pink stuff and put it on their cheeks in front of the mirror.

"Another member of this department, one of the most benevolent men on earth, burst raging into the office the other day because he had seen a young 'man' combing his pomaded hair in the elevator. But we claim our pink powder story beats this all hollow.

"It is time for a matriarchy if the male of the species allows such things to persist. Better a rule by masculine women than by effeminate men. Man began to slip, we are beginning to believe, when he discarded the straight razor for the safety pattern. We shall not be surprised when we hear that the safety razor has given way to the depilatory.

"Who or what is to blame is what puzzles us. Is this degeneration into effeminacy a cognate reaction with pacifism to the virilities and realities of the war? Are pink powder and parlor pinks in any way related? How does one reconcile masculine cosmetics, sheiks, floppy pants, and slave bracelets with a disregard for law and an aptitude for crime more in keeping with the frontier of half a century ago than a twentieth-century metropolis?

"Do women like the type of 'man' who pats pink powder on his face in a public washroom and arranges his coiffure in a public elevator? Do women at heart belong to the Wilsonian era of 'I Didn't Raise My Boy to Be a Soldier?' What has become of the old 'caveman' line?

"It is a strange social phenomenon and one that is running its course not only here in America but in Europe as well. Chicago may have its powder puffs; London has its dancing men and Paris its gigolos. Down with Decatur; up with Elinor Glyn. Hollywood is the national school of masculinity. Rudy, the beautiful gardener's boy, is the prototype of the American male.

"Hell's bells. Oh, sugar."

Valentino was outraged. After years of publicly disavowing his sheikdom, he was now being openly targeted as The (foreign) Faggot responsible for the spread of faggotry on US soil.

The editorial was written anonymously, so he didn't have a name to locate on a reporter's desk down at the *Trib* before he broke the offender's nose. Instead, he wrote this response to be published in the *Trib*'s rival, the *Chicago Herald-Examiner*, July 19, 1926:

"TO THE MAN (?) WHO WROTE THE EDITORIAL HEADED 'PINK POWDER PUFFS' IN THE SUNDAY TRIBUNE:

"The above-mentioned editorial is at least the second scurrilous personal attack you have made upon me, my race, and my father's name." [The first offense was a *Trib* writer calling him a sissy for wearing a wristwatch.]

"You slur my Italian ancestry; you cast ridicule upon my Italian name; you cast doubt upon my manhood.

"I call you, in return, a contemptible coward, and to prove which of us is a better man, I challenge you to a personal test. This is not a challenge to a duel in the generally accepted sense—that would be illegal. But in Illinois, boxing is legal, so is wrestling. I, therefore, defy you to meet me in the boxing or wrestling arena to prove, in typically American fashion (for I am an American citizen), which of us is more a man. [Author note: Valentino applied for American citizenship in 1925, but never followed through.] I prefer this test of honour to be private, so that I may give you the beating you deserve, and because I want to make it absolutely plain that this challenge is not for purposes of publicity. I am handing copies of this to the newspapers simply because I doubt that anyone so cowardly as to write about me as you have would respond to a defy unless forced by the Press to do so. I do not know who you are or how big you are, but this challenge stands if you are as big as Jack Dempsey.

"I will meet you immediately or give you a reasonable time in which to prepare, for I assume that your muscles must be flabby and weak, judging by your cowardly mentality, and that you will have to replace the vitriol in your veins for red blood—if there be a place in such a body as your's for red blood and manly muscle.

"I want to make it plain that I hold no grievance against the *Chicago Tribune*, although it seems a mistake to let a cowardly writer use its valuable columns as this 'man' does. My fight is personal—with the poison-pen writer of editorials that stoops to racial and personal prejudice. The *Tribune* through Miss Mae Tinee, has treated me and my work kindly and at times very favorably. I welcome criticism of my work as an actor—but I will resent with every muscle of my body, attacks upon my manhood and ancestry.

"Hoping I will have an opportunity to demonstrate to you that the wrist under a slave bracelet may snap a real fist into your sagging jaw, and that I may teach you respect of a man even though he happens to prefer to keep his face clean, I remain with

"Utter Contempt,

"RUDOLPH VALENTINO

"P.S. I will return to Chicago within ten days. You may send your answer to me in New York, care of United Artists Corps., 729 7th Avenue."

Back in New York, Valentino sparred on the rooftop of the Ambassador Hotel with a sizable boxing aficionado from one of the New York papers and easily held his own against his 200 pound opponent. In fact, Jack Dempsey was a friend of Rudy's, as well as an occasional sparring partner, and knew he was capable of inflicting considerable damage.

The *Chicago Trib*'s pink powder puffoon never came forward much to Valentino's personal regret. (Years later, he was identified as John Herrick, who may have been dying of tuberculosis at the time.) Rudy did in fact return to Chicago to make good on his P.S. According to his close friend and manager S.

25

George Ullman: "That unhappy epithet, pink powder puff, stuck in Rudy's craw. During the few short weeks between the time it was applied to him by this antagonist who was too cowardly to make himself known, and Valentino's untimely death, Rudy repeated the words more times than I heard him utter any other phrase in all the years that I knew him.

"He would repeat them seemingly in agony of soul, as if fearful that, in the minds of some who did not know him, the thought of effeminacy might stick. Whereas I, as his friend, make the statement that no cowboy on the Western plains nor athlete from the Marines could boast a more powerful physique than that of Valentino, nor more truly possess the right to the title of he-man."

In just one of the many examples of gossip being accepted as factual by gay men who'd love to claim another celebrity, Rudolph Valentino's sexual orientation has been the victim of revisionist his-story. Sure, there's tantalizing evidence that his first wife was a lesbian, that his second may at least have had lesbian relationships, and that he may have had trouble with impotence. And there are lots of rumors, hearsay, a trashy British biography, and even fellow celebrity reportage, but I'm still waiting for somebody to document their sources while attesting that Rudy was gay.

Suggestive passages lifted from Valentino's ghostwritten "diaries" from 1923-26, published as an "autobiography," do not a queer boy make. Nor the oft-repeated tale about his giving a lead Art Deco dildo, with his signature on it no less, to Ramon Novarro. Didn't happen.

Do I want Rudolph Valentino, the "World's Greatest Lover," to be gay? Yes. But wanting doesn't make it so. Personally, I'm happy with the ambiguity. Even in what has to be considered the most serious attempt at a sourced biography, Emily W. Leider's *Dark Lover* (Farrar, Straus and Giroux, 2003), the author is confounded by her subject's sex life while acknowledging the desire of all of us to "know the unknowable." For myself, without resorting to post-gay lib constructs of gay or straight, I'd like to think that the most beautiful man in the silent movies was voraciously generous with all comers, boys and girls alike.

Doth the boy himself protest too much? I don't think so. Not for a man of his ethnicity and background. And especially if it wasn't true. Even if it was, you can hardly blame him.

Fortunately, in an unfortunate sort of way, he didn't have long to put up with this latest indignity. On August 15, 1926, Rudy V suddenly doubled over, collapsed in agony, and was taken to the Polyclinic Hospital in New York. The strange abdominal pains he'd been suffering over the past few months, and which he tried to self-treat with bicarbonate of soda, had violently stabbed him in the side. His innards were screaming to get his attention.

He underwent surgery to remove his burst appendix and an acute ulcer, asking his manager upon awakening: "Well, did I behave like a pink powder puff or a man?" Over the next several days, Valentino's condition vacillated from bad to worse to only slightly less worse as reporters and media mobbed the hospital for the latest bedside stats. A nation fascinated by celebrity in crisis, fans or not, charted his wavering high fever and accelerated heartbeat.

During the protracted up and down, "he's gravely ill," "he's feeling better," "he's in serious trouble again" deathwatch, the Hearst papers ran a beefcake photo of the star in shorts, an athletic T, and boxing gloves, offering that he was a strapping young man of "no superfluous flesh" who was well-suited for the "gallant fight" in which he was engaged.

The fight was called on Monday, August 23, 1926. "Rudy Is Dead!" screamed the headlines. The cause: an acute gastric, perforated ulcer complicated by the insidious onset of peritonitis, septic pneumonia and septic endocarditis.

Pre-figuring the death, resurrection, and worship of American Pop Idols to come, such as James Dean, Valentino's abrupt and tragic end, coupled with his now eternal youth, mutated into a stillborn image of sex and death and desire that has become transcendental to the culture. The Cult of the Movie Star was born the day Rudolph Valentino's exquisite chest stopped rising and falling. (So, too, the cult of conspiracy and fan hysteria, from the suggestions of murder by arsenic poisoning or knife blade in logical opposition to a rotten gut in a man of such obviously well-conditioned physique to the non-apocryphal suicide of a few unhinged fans who hanged themselves or slit their wrists and died soaking their Rudy memorabilia.)

The movie industry's media machine worked overtime to stoke the mythology, capitalize on the death, and enshrine the fallen star. On September 7, 1926, for the first time, all the movie studios simultaneously halted production for two minutes, an observance of Valentino's funeral.

And what a funeral! New York City had seen nothing quite like it, nor had the world. Heads of state, yes, but not for a guy who made his living dressing up and playacting in front of movie cameras.

Honoring his peculiar wishes to be put on display for his public, Valentino's body lay for six days under glass (shades of *Snow White*) as nearly 100,000 stood in the rain before being paraded by the corpse. The crowds were so huge and unexpected that police frequently clashed with unruly factions to maintain control and the body had to be moved to alternate viewing rooms at Campbell's Funeral Home because of damage to the facility.

The theatrics included Pola Negri's public displays of grief and fainting, as over-the-top as the worst of silent screen acting. There was also a gigantic wreath on display, allegedly (but not) from Mussolini, and the body was for a time guarded by American Black Shirt fascists, but the staged or real aspect of their presence is undecided, as is the rumor that Rudy's manager was so appalled by the rude behavior and snickering of the crowd that he substituted the body with a wax effigy for the last few days.

Anything but respectful, the showing of Valentino's body for nearly a week was tantamount to a carnival freak show. The Love God was dead. Step right up, folks, and look at an idol mortally idled. The Freudian spin diagnosis is public necrophilia, but it sounds more like revenge by desecration. Morbid fascination mixed with I spit on your grave. (Dead gangsters with bullet-ridden bodies were given similar treatment.) Certainly, it was the show everybody wanted to see. There were easily as many men waiting for a peek as women. Something to tell the grandkids.

The Son of the Sheik opened nationwide after Rudy's death. He would miss the acclaim. Several of his close-ups in that film are suitable for framing and a soft-focus shot of his mournful face, in particular, must have brought tears to the eyes of legitimate fans who had so recently lost him.

Rudolph Valentino was a precocious juvenile delinquent who came to America as a poorly educated working class immigrant with delusions of grandeur, got spoiled by its American Dream riches when he won the celebrity lottery, and felt personally fucked over by the studios he enriched, as well as by a fame and notoriety built on the untoward fantasies of young girls and women, whose adulation was considered at the time to be a sign of the country's moral decay.

Whatever he may have meant to the battle of the sexes in the 1920s, he remains the silent era's sexiest male star. Thanks, Rudy—on behalf of all the fellas who couldn't say so then.

While Rudy Vallee crooned "There's A New Star in Heaven To-Night," each new male lead Hollywood promoted in the 1920s was either tagged "The Next Valentino" or found himself the subject of supposition: "The New Valentino?"

For many, **Ramon Novarro** (1899-1968) was the next best thing, an actor described by one critic as "almost too beautiful to be taken seriously." Antonio Moreno and Ricardo Cortez were active rivals to the Valentino throne, but young Ramón Gil Samaniego was given the seat, like it or not.

He was born in Durango, Mexico, the son of a dentist and the fourth of thirteen brothers and sisters. As a teenager and aspiring singer, he fled the Mexican Revolution in 1916 and re-settled in Los Angeles, joined by most of his family the following year. Blessed with good looks and an equally good singing voice, he whiled away time as a singing waiter and a movie house usher before getting extra work beginning in 1917. He also earned money posing nude for art classes.

After dancing half-naked on a mirrored tabletop in *Man-Woman-Marriage* (1921) and then in a stylish loincloth in the Mack Sennett comedy *A Small Town Idol* (1921), just the kind of thing to get you noticed if you had a nice pair, his big break came in a juicy supporting role as the despicable Rupert of Hentzau in *The Prisoner of Zenda* (1922), directed by Rex Ingram, who had directed Valentino to fame in *The Four Horsemen of the Apocalypse*. In fact, Novarro is out there on the dance floor as a tango extra during Rudy's classic exhibition in that film and can be seen in the "Call to Arms" sequence.

"Ravishing Ramon," as he would be dubbed in the fan magazines, was such a doll in his torn shorts and shirt in *Where the Pavement Ends* (1923) that the studio recalled the original release prints and provided a new finale in which our young hero lives. Audiences not only got a happy ending, but a South Seas islander who, quite conveniently, turns out to be ignorant of the white skin beneath his eternal suntan. He's also a surprisingly authoritative and handsome law student turned incognito actor as *Scaramouche* (1923), who takes up the sword against the tyranny of nobility during the French Revolution.

Novarro was on his way. Every studio on the West Coast offered to buy his services, eager to officially dub him their "Second Valentino." Without being given the choice, he had a niche to fill. And all things considered, the niche would remain unfilled.

Novarro was Rudy-lite, though it's silly to force a comparison. No man could possibly stand up to the legacy Valentino had left behind. The actors were each quite different, and Novarro courted, and amazingly avoided, embarrassing kinship when Rex Ingram threw the sheik duds on him, shipped him to North Africa, and had him play *The Arab* (1924).

No need to worry. He was now being paid movie-star handsomely and was about to stamp his own signature role: the Ben-Hur before the Chuck-Heston. It began as an epic shot on location in Rome with George Walsh in the lead, but the massively troubled production got yanked back stateside, assigned a new director, and outfitted with Novarro in the title role.

At an astonishing $4,000,000 by the time it finally wrapped, *Ben-Hur: A Tale of the Christ* (1925) was just shy of two and a half hours and went on to become the fourth biggest box-office success of the entire silent era.

As the best of Biblical epics do, the photoplay has its share of cruel imagery and sexual suggestion. The slave ship rowing scene has entered the annals of homoerotic cinema (anticipating the very gay readings of the 1959 version) with its bare-assed slave tied to the stock in full view of the tortured men who pull the oars to the beat of the drums. A famous and highly collectible photo of Ramon shows him as a naked oarsman, his pubic hairs either artfully melding into the shadows at the very edge of the photo or "air-brushed" completely away in a cleaned-up version to give the illusion of propriety.

Writing in *Picture-Play Magazine* (June, 1922), Margaret Ettinger described him as "lithe and slender, as most dancers are. Deep brown eyes, well-chiseled features, and a nicely-shaped head are his." All of which, save the color of his eyes, are on display in his greatest role, a dashing young slave who eventually dons a skullcap and challenges his boyhood friend Messala (Francis X. Bushman) to the chariot ride of his life.

Ramon was such a sensation that it's not merely Hollywood legend that for years after he would receive fan mail addressed simply to Mr. Ben-Hur.

The desire to set things "straight," as it were, when it came to hooking an expensive epic on a pretty-boy star made good business sense in the 1920s. When the massive production was reviewed for theatre owners by the trade paper *Variety*, it made a point of stating that in the person of Ramon Novarro: "anyone who sees him in this picture will have to admit that he is without a doubt a man's man and 100 percent of that." If it weren't for the more obvious anti-sissy sentiment behind such a sales pitch, I'd wonder if we haven't come across one of the first examples of outing in Hollywood history.

Novarro was gay.

Unable to rouse interest in him, a seductress tells his Ben-Hur: "If you are as slow in the race tomorrow as you are in love today, Messala may drive snails and win!"

Never a fanatic about his physique, he tended toward the soft side and his nicely-shaped head was more plain and boyish than alluring and sensual. He notably appeared in the non-musical version of *The Student Prince in Old Heidelberg* (1927), then sang the hit "Pagan Love Song" to complement his strolling around in a sarong in *The Pagan* (1929). He would also play opposite Greta Garbo in *Mata Hari* (1931), a talkie in which both ably demonstrate how silent screen histrionics sound.

His generally weak speaking voice—complete with Mexican accent—and effete mannerisms were obstacles enough to his longevity, but his looks were also fading, exacerbated by alcoholism, and his studio cast him in roles he was ill-suited to play, including a college football jock in *Huddle* (1932), a Chinese love-interest in *The Son-Daughter* (1932), and an American Indian in *Laughing Boy* (1934). He would only rarely return to the movies, as in *The Big Steal* (1949), and eventually took guest spots on television shows such as *Bonanza*, *Rawhide*, and *The Wild, Wild West*.

On October 30, 1968, he was murdered in his California home by one of the Ferguson brothers, a pair of hustlers he had invited over for sex. The details have been obscenely and largely fictitiously recounted in print, complete with rumors involving an arty dildo said to be the gift of Valentino being used as the murder weapon. No such item has ever been reported privately or officially (in court, during the trial, in the police report, or elsewhere) and the entire fiction can be traced directly to Kenneth Anger's *Hollywood Babylon*. For a sourced account of Mr. Novarro's life, as well as his horrific death, check out *Beyond Paradise: The Life of Ramon Novarro* (St. Martin's Press, 2002) by André Soares.

John Barrymore (1882-1942), "The Great Profile," started as one of the great matinee idols of the boards. According to his wife at the time, when Barrymore made his entrance in 1919's *The Jest*, audiences

"Ravishing" Ramon Novarro. PHOTOFEST

gasped and men and women alike couldn't help but notice that his tights "left no faint fragment of his anatomy to the imagination." He was hugely successful on screen, as well, and his being stripped, whipped, and put on a roasting spit in *The Beloved Rogue* (1927), even at age 45, provided ample opportunity to exploit the flesh while subjecting it to voyeuristic torments.

Both **Ronald Colman** (1891-1958) and actor-playwright-composer **Ivor Novello** (1893-1951), aka "The British Adonis," had reputable go's as silent film matinee idols, but the type was growing a bit long in the tooth, leaving the mustachioed **John Gilbert** (1895-1936) to close out the era as the cinema's most popular male lover.

John Gilbert in studio portrait, playing down his nose. YESTERDAY

Romantic leads of the decade (and well into the 1930s) were men just as likely to look funny in a sprint as they were to collapse in grief when the girl rejected them, yet Gilbert provided a more robust specimen as silent star. He scored big in *The Big Parade* (1925) and *The Merry Widow* (1925), then tried steaming up Garbo in a trio of popular romances: *Flesh and the Devil* (1927), *Love* (1927), and *A Woman of Affairs* (1928). He had a substantial nose and his voice—legendarily—turned out to be a bit higher and distinctly "thespian" than audiences had fantasized, but it was a tragic drinking problem, the demise of silent screen histrionics, and a loathing Louis B. Mayer that hastened his finish.

A star's alcoholism, affairs, or drug abuse were the kind of things that polite society read about with both glee and virulent disapproval. The royalty of Hollywood became immersed in tawdry scandals in the 1920s and the joyous decadence of the era fueled protests by self-appointed do-gooders and decent citizens all across America who were certain the films were being infected, too. The industry responded by promising to keep things on the straight and narrow. In 1917, the National Board of Review said its members would not allow nudity in the movies, such as that displayed when Annette Kellerman bared herself as *A Daughter of the Gods* (1916).

Ivor Novello, "the British Adonis," was a celebrated playwright, poet, and lyricist, as well as actor.

Ten years later, in 1927, the Motion Picture Producers and Distributors of America set a long, disgusting chain of censorial events into motion when it distributed to the studios—and they adopted—its list of "Don'ts and Be Carefuls," further proscribing nudity ("in fact or silhouette"), cursing, "any inference of sex perversion," and "ridicule of the clergy." An addendum listed 25 subjects cautioned for depiction with an emphasis on good taste, and these included "technique of committing murder," "branding of people or animals," "first night scenes," "man and woman in bed together," and "excessive or lustful kissing, particularly when one character is a 'heavy.'"

Though male nudity and male beauty are hardly co-dependent, the display of the male body on screen and off has an important role to play in the erotic evolution of the male as a thing of beauty. Nudity of any kind in early cinema seems these days to be a surprising revelation, but that just shows how quickly we forget.

You can't even blame it on selective memory. It's more a cultural ignorance exacerbated by explosions of the immediate and an endemic puritanism. Each generation thinks it's the one to discover sex, the one upon which blatant or graphic sexuality has encroached.

Film students, let alone the general moviegoing populace, are constantly astounded to find racy innuendo, lusty plot lines, and full-frontal nudity in films of the sixties, let alone of the silent era. Even

Ralph Forbes, also from the UK, was the son of character actress Mary Forbes, and played John Geste in *Beau Geste* (1926). He's here as an emblem of the many gorgeous silent actors largely forgotten today. AUTHOR'S COLLECTION

Nils Asther has Joan Crawford by the fur in *Letty Lynton* (1932). YESTERDAY

realizing this was a technology that lent itself from the get-go to hardcore pornography (people being people, after all, and film being a representational medium) doesn't prepare the uninitiated for the open sensuality and sexual license afforded an industry forged, let's not forget, as nickelodeon amusements at carnivals. Literal peep shows.

Provocative clothing, shocking violence, and seedy story lines were all employed before and after filmmaking realized it was an art form, though not without moral protest and most of said exposure coming both from abroad and from a broad.

Female nudity has always out-stripped male nudity in the movies. Still, the earliest verified full-frontal male exposure in a motion picture produced for public consumption came in the 1912 Italian production of *Dante's Inferno*. A sweaty prick in hell.

Hell is precisely where proper folks believed Mae West was going after she was arrested and charged with obscenity in connection with her 1926 play *Sex*. "It's not the men in my life, it's the life in my men," she famously quipped while pursuing a drag queen's career. Tiny, yet absurdly curvaceous, West caricatured the liberated woman, an hourglass full of sand at both ends who spoke in double entendre and surrounded herself with beautiful men for personal use and abuse. She traveled for a time in the 1950s with her "eight international Adonises," helping to redress a world in which women were always the sex objects. Her boys were her lap dogs and she made no bones about it in what amounted to cartoonish empowerment. It was okay to ogle the guys for ogle's sake, to acknowledge their physicality without having to fill out commitment papers. At last, men weren't just pricks, they were lollipops. And everyone likes candy when they go to the show.

Perhaps the last pretty boy star of the silent screen to satisfy an audience's sweet tooth was Swedish-born (and gay) **Nils Asther** (1897-1981), a Royal Dramatic Theater student who had been bringing his dark good looks and contradictorily bright face to his homeland's cinemas since the tender age of 17. Tutored by Mauritz Stiller, who discovered and mentored Garbo, Asther came to Hollywood at age 30. He sent hearts aflutter by romancing Garbo herself in *Wild Orchids* and *The Single Standard* (both 1929),

31

though it's unclear whether we should blame our imminent laughter on the acting style or the fact that his facial expressions come this/close to breaking into comedy while conveying his romantic intentions. In *Orchids*, his apple-cheeked Javanese prince looks a bit like Johnny Depp's *Ed Wood* (1994), only taller. Garbo shows her displeasure at his advances by scowling and furrowing her brow. He's a bit on the girly side in mannerism and one has to wonder if audiences of the day found his scoundrel Lothario predatory in a wishful thinking sort of way or predatory in a distasteful sort of way. His greatest screen triumph came post-idolatry as the Chinese warlord who tragically falls for Barbara Stanwyck in Frank Capra's *The Bitter Tea of General Yen* (1933). Irritable and unhappy with Hollywood, Asther begrudgingly married, quite possibly to assuage MGM and its private concerns over his homosexuality, as well as its public announcement that his contract would not be renewed. The studio gave him a second shot post-nuptials, but when the marriage went to pieces in short order so did Asther's career in Tinsel Town.

A common explanation for why some silent stars didn't survive the transition to talkies is that they didn't have the pipes for it; their heavy foreign accents or tweeting voices got in the way. As far as I'm concerned, the era's gorgeous and verbally-challenged brethren remain as good a reason as any for the film industry to have continued making silent features...to this very day. Some actors don't need to be heard to be appreciated. It's enough just looking at them.

Gary Cooper as Enrique, the Llano Kid, goes eye-to-eye with Fay Wray in *The Texan* (1930). YESTERDAY

The 1930s-1940s

"Because I Just Went Gay All Of A Sudden!"

Today, nearly half a century after his death, the media are still looking for the next James Dean. Though an even bigger star in the '20s than Dean was in the '50s, it seemed no one was looking for the next Valentino less than a decade after his own untimely death, when movies were talkies.

The Sound Era had its own ideas about masculinity. Pretty boys would probably have squeaked or lisped, killing their appeal as surely as if they'd stripped their shirts and revealed drooping breasts. Sound added another risk factor to the equation. What if your dreamy-eyed movie boyfriend sounded like a fairy, too?

Gary Cooper (1901-1961) didn't sound like a fairy when he talked. He didn't sound much like an actor either.

Impressionists used to have fun droning out Cooperisms in a monotone matched only by their comatose lack of expression. Cooper was one of those Easter Island sort of actors. Most people who worked with him professionally had doubts about his talent until they saw the image projected back at them. "So that's what he was doing," they'd realize.

Given his screen image as stoic outdoorsman and as a real man's man, it will come as a surprise to some that he was the son of a Montana state supreme court justice, was schooled in an English prep school for boys (both his parents were English), and excelled as an art student, with dabbles in drama, not sports.

He did love the outdoors, though, spent much of his time when he was out of school and stateside in the Montana wilderness, and remained a lifelong American Indian history buff. He would cultivate prototypically masculine interests in cars, guns, and hunting, but was actually preparing to make use of his considerable skills as a cartoonist when he came to visit his folks in Hollywood in 1924.

Though he was painfully thin, he also had extraordinarily beautiful features and knew how to ride a horse, so extra work in the movies beckoned. Among his many silent credits, he's one of the Cossacks in Valentino's *The Eagle* (1925).

An agent dubbed him Gary (he was born Frank) after her Indiana hometown and once he got started in the business there was no stopping him. In 1926, he caught his break when a featured actor dropped out of *The Winning of Barbara Worth* (1926) and Coop was promoted. (More than half a century later, Tom Cruise likewise rose in the ranks when his extra work in *Taps* turned into a featured role vacated by an actor the director felt wasn't working out.)

Despite a reputation as a bit of a loner, Cooper possessed the kind of handsome that couldn't help attracting adoring women (and men). He habitually succumbed to the attentions of several of these ladies, including actresses who would then quite understandably aid his career by getting him roles in their pictures. Clara Bow was an early dalliance and Cooper was right there on the front stoop, showing up briefly as a gum-chewing reporter, when she helped define the 1920s new woman as a girl who had *It* (1927).

Cooper would appear in several films with Bow, who famously proclaimed he had "the biggest cock in Hollywood and no ass to push it with." Handsome movie stars with big cocks are the stuff dreams are made of, but movie stars are also just regular folk subject to the same biological averages as the rest of mankind. Gary Cooper's legendary endowment seems quite indisputable, however, so feel free to think about that the next time you watch him cross a room in medium shot. "He's hung like a horse and can go all night," bragged Bow.

He was, of course, desired by a number of men in Hollywood, too, and there are persistent rumors that he hustled some of them when he first got into town. Others say he steered very clear of such entanglements, perhaps informed by one of his earliest childhood memories: "When I was a little boy in Helena and walking across a bridge, a bearded man came up to me and kissed me on the mouth." That kind of thing is

33

Gary Cooper disheveled in an awfully pretty way in *Doomsday* (1928). PHOTOFEST
Inset: Coop in *The Legion of the Condemned* (1928). AUTHOR'S COLLECTION

bound to get in your craw. Still, he lived for a time with young gay actor and friend Anthony Lawler, who was infatuated with him and reportedly a lover. Honestly, trying to pin down someone's sexuality by slapping a label on its being that way or this way is frivolous without declaration or hard evidence, and even then it's not necessarily definitive. People are sexual beings open to any of a number of possibilities.

By the end of the 1920s, the movie industry was already prepared to honor itself and the first film to win Best Picture (actually Most Outstanding Production) was an epic love story between two guys. *Wings* (1927) is a World War I picture in which Charles "Buddy" Rogers and Richard Arlen, rivals for the affections of Clara Bow (possibly the first movie star to play a fag hag), become far more pre-possessed and affectionate with one another after having it out in a boxing ring than at any time with Ms. It. The pair of Air Force cadets also encounter a stunningly handsome Gary Cooper as a tent mate for one scene. Cooper is their hero, a skilled flyer, who takes a chomp out of a candy bar they offer him before prophesying in subtitles, "Luck or no luck, when your time comes, you're going to get it." Coop's brief close-up is a sigh-maker. Next thing we know he's up, up, and away…and shadows foretell his untimely crash and burn.

A nude swimming scene was filmed for *Wolf Song* (1929), which co-starred the notoriously fiery Lupe Velez, the 5' Mexican spitfire with whom he was involved and whom it has been said made demands to periodically sniff his genitals for traces of other women. Coop's nude swim, shot from afar and waist-up, was cut from the film, but descriptions from stills suggest he is remarkably toned for such an alleged string bean.

In *The Virginian* (1929), his first starring western, he spends much of his time stooped over, uneasy, and particularly awkward while trying to be animated. In fact, he seems drunk at the beginning of the film in which he famously mutters, "You wanna call me that...smile." Coop exhibits virtually no screen presence. He's thin and wimpy, his face powdered, almost chalky looking, and his mannerisms are slightly effeminate. There's no denying he has a pretty face, but he looks goofy when he's emoting.

Cooper often said that *The Virginian* was his favorite film, that he loved doing westerns, but there's no getting around his stiff gestures and stilted body language. He seems very much like the 17-year old boy who suddenly found himself 6'3" and 185 pounds, gangly and unsure how to ambulate. (To be fair, he also suffered from a 1916 auto wreck that permanently affected his gait.)

What's most interesting about looking at the film today is the conspicuous subtextual love "affair" between Coop and Richard Arlen, just the kind of thing that probably isn't there at all but we enjoy reading into all these years later. Note how long Coop keeps his hand on Arlen's leg while Arlen is on his horse. Or the famous scene of Arlen's execution in which both take suspiciously long looks at one another and Arlen jots a note to Coop saying, "Goodbye. I couldn't have spoke to you without playing the baby...Steve." At the moment before the hanging, a whistled signal between the two men is linked to the whistles of two quails, intercut to symbolize their special friendship. During the shooting of the emotional scene, Coop kept blowing his lines, so they were written on the back of Arlen's chaps and he read them from there.

Lots of gay men come across Cooper today only by happenstance, such as when they're completing their Films of Marlene Dietrich library. In *Morocco* (1930), his tall American Tom in the Foreign Legion is caught making hand signals to a woman in the marketplace. His superior officer asks, "What are you doing with those fingers?"

"Nothin'...yet."

He's still stiff and awkward to modern sensibilities, but he's forgiven playing opposite the exotic Ms. Dietrich and they share a classic scene in gender-bending cinema together. A gorgeous but uninspired Cooper comes to life in a smoky café when Dietrich's Amy Jolly saunters on stage dressed in a man's tuxedo and top hat, offering Cooper a flower which he covets and places behind his ear. Dietrich moves on to flirt with a woman in the audience and even plants a kiss on her mouth, much to the shock and surprise of the audience.

Cooper's willingness to show erotic interest in cross-dressing and role reversals adds a welcome touch of kink to his persona.

Kink of another sort adds to requisite male torture scenes in such Cooper films as *The Lives of a Bengal Lancer* (1935), *The Plainsman* (1936), and *The General Died at Dawn* (1936). A recurring theme in this book will be the on-screen torment of half-naked handsome young men in the movies; a sensually-charged subterfuge for exhibiting male flesh under the auspices of non-sexual brutality.

Other choice moments: in *A Farewell to Arms* (1932), he shares a close-up with a bare foot in a bar; in *The Lives of A Bengal Lancer*, he's accused of getting in touch with his softer side; in *The*

General Died At Dawn, he pulls a monkey out of his trench coat; and in all three, Cooper's hairy bare chest is on display but his belly button is conspicuously hidden—another curious Hollywood tradition.

Truth is, his lanky bod looked just as great all dressed up in a tux and he was a sophisticated and knowledgeable dresser off-screen as well. A relationship with a European countess during a short period in which he had burnt out on Hollywood and fled (the studio "replaced" him with Cary Grant) taught him all sorts of social refinements to augment his penchant for big game hunting in Africa.

His connection to Westerns has typified him as an "aw shucks," "yup," and "nope" type of guy, but his laconic, almost deadpan delivery suited itself to comedies and there's a special joy to be had in watching him uncharacteristically mug if the occasion called for it. Being Gary Cooper, though, you don't have to do a whole lot to seem like you're mugging. He could also, by the way, demonstrate an amazing light touch and bring warmth and genuine nuance to scenes. Gary Cooper was soft-focus sensual.

He was the anti-actor whose natural talent manifested itself in what would finally be embraced as "underplaying." A private, even-tempered man who rarely swore, was well liked in the industry, subjugated all signs of ego and seemed truly thankful for his career, Gary Cooper did on screen just what his instincts told him to do. No acting school theatrics. In fact, it might be argued that his sometimes flat and awkward line readings and performance style reveal the deep insecurity, firstly, of a heterosexual man pursuing a career wearing lipstick and powder and playing cowboys and Indians, and secondly, of becoming one of the richest men in Depression-era America doing just that. (A 1930 Norman Rockwell cover for *The Saturday Evening Post* depicts Cooper in full western regalia—big-assed cowboy hat and six-shooter at his side—getting make-up put on his face.)

Gary Cooper, "whose long, lean, tautly modeled face represents," said *Vanity Fair* in 1934, "the epitome of sex appeal," may have almost randomly brought great charm and charisma to the roles he played, but he remains one of the most beautiful actors of the 1920s and 1930s. No wonder they were "tryin' hard to look like Gary Cooper" in the 1930 hit song "Puttin' on the Ritz."

I've an awful urge to liken him to Brooke Shields, but strictly in the sense that she made such a beautiful still image that one wished she'd never spoke or moved on film, because the moment she did the illusion was spoiled. Coop could actually act, of course, as opposed to Shields, but my unorthodox advice: watch *Morocco* (1930*),* *One Sunday Afternoon* (1933), or *Peter Ibbetson* (1935) with the sound off. Even better, try and catch him in one of his dreamy silents—*Children of Divorce* (1927), *Beau Sabreur* (1928), *The Legion of the Condemned* (1928), *Half A Bride* (1928), *Lilac Time* (1928), etc.—and you'll swoon, no matter how awful the flick.

Then go ahead and see the rest of Cooper's classics with the sound on, including *Mr. Deeds Goes to Town* (1936), *Desire* (1936), *Beau Geste* (1939), *Sergeant York* (1941), *Meet John Doe* (1941), *Ball of Fire* (1942), *The Pride of the Yankees* (1942), his Oscar-winning *High Noon* (1952), and the thoroughly charming and playful *Love in the Afternoon* (1957), in which his mid-50s playboy falls for a 30-year younger Audrey Hepburn and you won't get the creeps.

He cracked the Quigley Top Ten Stars poll only twice in the '30s, in 1936 at #10 and in 1937 at #9, but as he matured he became one of the great box-office attractions and landed on the list every year throughout the 1940s.

Clark Gable (1901-1960) had his Düsenberg built exactly one foot longer than the one owned by Gary Cooper. Boys will be boys.

Applying the word "beautiful" to Clark Gable exerts significant strain on the word as I've tried to apply it throughout this text, but we can't ignore this male sexual icon just because he's not a pretty boy. He's too big for that.

In fact, in broad terms, he represents an important transition for us: the displacement of male beauty as a conduit to feminine desires (gorgeous subjects devoted to their queens) by a wanton, wise-cracking, face-smacking masculinity that thumped the notion that men are men and they can live with women or without them. Gable's cocky, earthy manliness seemed to redress the imbalance of gender roles in as primitive a throwback as is suggested by Darryl Zanuck's reaction to his screen test: "His ears are too big. He looks like an ape."

Son of an Ohio oil driller, Gable was dredged through stints as an oil worker, farmer, tie salesman, and lumberman before consummating his love for the theater by marrying an actress fourteen years older and

Clark Gable, the brute as sex symbol, who quickly evolved into the decade's biggest male star with a talent for combining romance, comedy, and no-nonsense action. PHOTOFEST

moving to Los Angeles. To see him in photos as a youth is to see a guy so homely that any talk of being an actor on his part would have to be taken as a sign of mental instability. His ears were the fleshy saucers that seemed cruel when cartoonists caricatured him after he became famous and his teeth were in a severe state of rot. (When he started making money in Hollywood, he had them all pulled and was outfitted with dentures.)

Josephine Dillon was not only his second of an eventual five marriages, but his vocal coach (she stripped his high register down to the famous baritone with voice exercises) and his acting teacher. Having lost his mother to cancer months after he was born, and with a father who never accepted his son's "sissy work" as an actor, even after his success, William (Billy) Clark Gable showed astonishing resilience and determination without the support of family or interest from any of the theatrical companies who kept rejecting him. Every so often he found work as a movie extra. In *The Plastic Age* (1925), he shows up shirtless in a locker room dressing scene.

He also made the occasional stage appearance. In 1928's *Machinal*, a reviewer from *The Morning Telegraph* thought him "young, vigorous, and brutally masculine." Not surprisingly, he found himself playing heavies, but instead of being perceived as a turn-off, he discovered that audiences found his no-nonsense troglodytes sexually intriguing.

His supporting turn as an underworld leader who throws star Norma Shearer into her chair in *A Free Soul* (1931) had politically incorrect audiences wishing for more. And they got it. He smacks Barbara Stanwyck in *Night Nurse* (1931) and threatens Greta Garbo, Joan Crawford, and Jean Harlow, among others in various films, right through Vivien Leigh in *Gone With the Wind* (1939), by which time his forthright masculinity (so ingrained, he didn't want to cry on screen—but did) climaxes in a rape that's perceived as for the spoiled woman's own good.

Gable paved the way for two decades worth of character actors as leading men: guys such as Cagney, Bogart, Muni, Robinson, Tracy, and Garfield. It's not that the movies decided to abandon pretty men as much as the florid romantic of the silent era was largely being replaced during the Depression and WWII years by a rougher masculine ideal. We needed men with backbone, guys tough enough for tougher times.

Social historians have inquired as to whether Gable's enormous appeal represented some sort of masochism in the culture. Here was a manly man just as likely to belt his woman before forcing himself on her as he was to walk away and have nothing to do with her. And this barbarian was embodied by an actor who remained in the top ten most popular stars for eleven years in a row (1932-1942)—in the number two spot six of those years. He didn't always play gruff, though, and it's a distinct pleasure watching him essay a charming softie in *Polly of the Circus* (1932, as a priest, no less), as well as in a quartet of romantic comedies opposite Joan Crawford: *Dancing Lady* (1933), *Chained* (1934), *Forsaking All Others* (1934), and *Love on the Run* (1936). And don't get me wrong, he certainly *was* handsome, perhaps curiously so, dimples and all, and wholly deserved the showbiz title "King of Hollywood" as America's #1 male movie star of the 1930s, an epithet he couldn't stand. Gable never considered himself much of an actor, but as attested by his prodigious success with women, his multiple marriages, and extramarital affairs (he even fathered a daughter with Loretta Young, which was kept an industry secret until many years after his death), he emanated masculine sex appeal and channeled it both on and off-screen.

In *Red Dust* (1932), he's a virile and huffy rubber maker, eventually charming in a surly way. He fancies and then attempts to romance a married woman while he's busy ignoring a wisecracking Jean Harlow. Later in the racist and overrated film (noted for Harlow's bathing in a barrel scene), Gable has Harlow push an iodine-soaked wad through his bullet wound. "C'mon, clean out that hole!"

As every film fan is required to know, when Gable took his shirt off in *It Happened One Night* (1934) and revealed a bare chest instead of the standard undershirt, the sales of undershirts in America plummeted; just how significantly has been debated, though legend would now have us believe that every American male burnt his T-shirt in what would have to be the largest gender-based torching of an undergarment in history, bra-burning included. Trouble is, why this film as opposed to earlier hits? Gable peels off his shirt in front of Harlow in *Red Dust* and he's bare-chested, revealing that bit of hair in the cleft between his pecs. He then proceeds (out-of-frame) to strip completely down in front of her, get into bed and switch off the lights, paying her not the least bit of attention.

Hollywood legend insists that *It Happened One Night* had a noticeable impact on fashion, and thus commerce during the Depression. It's a curious development. When Gable doffed his shirt in that classic romantic comedy, it was a sexy movie star showing skin and defying an institutionalized national cover-up. For men to follow suit and adopt a no undershirt stance *en masse* was to acknowledge in some cultural fashion that there was something "sexy" about their bare chests. But could a Depression-era generation of guys really have collectively decided that not wearing a T-shirt was going to make them sexier to their wives and girlfriends? After all, how many of them could have possibly looked like Clark Gable once they pulled the damned things off? Or were they just reveling in the sudden permission they got from a big time movie star to rid themselves of an extra layer of superfluous clothing? (Cloaking crass and unsightly displays of body hair, nipples, and belly button were the primary duties of the undershirt after soaking up sweat. Incidentally, though his dentures are infamous, Gable's general attitude toward cleanliness is legendary, perhaps in part because of rumored trouble with phimosis.)

Coincidentally, 1934 marked another milestone in the history of men's underwear. The Jockey

John Wayne, with tousled hair and all of 23, hits *The Big Trail* (1930). PHOTOFEST

International Company introduced their white Jockey shorts for men. Like Kleenex, "jockey shorts" have come to represent the thing and not just the brand in most people's parlance. Tighty whities are significant in that their support design meant they revealed more about what they held inside than the traditional boxers or longjohns. No wonder they quickly became one of the more popular gay male fetishes.

The undershirts came off and the underwear came in (less material meant they were briefs) and both eroticized the male body in less than purely utilitarian ways. The addition of the fly-front briefs in 1936 furthered the explicitness. Though it's safe to say that 99.9% of men don't use the fly (it requires more awkward manipulation than men deem necessary in order to take a pee), the accessorizing of a stitched hole called even further attention to what was supposed to be pulled through it. Underwear with a sex.

In my own budding youth, Gable was one of those stars I heard older women talk about as a masculine ideal. My grandmother thought Clark was the most handsome man in the movies and couldn't believe that my own asexual choice for male role model was that "dumb ox" John Wayne. But Wayne seemed such an obvious choice to me growing up in the late 1960s and early 1970s because his manliness was by then ethos for little boys. The John Wayne myth of masculinity commanded awe and respect and possessed palpable power, even virility. It was something a boy wanted to emulate. I spent many hours in the backyard perfecting my "John Wayne walk" and pretending to be him when my brother, sisters, the neighbor kids, and I strapped on holsters and six-guns and played out western movie scenarios. I wasn't yet required to factor a romantic interest in my movie star attachments and thought it must be a girly thing to consider looks before size.

That's why it came as such a surprise to me years later, when my sexual persuasion became clear, to find **John Wayne** (1907-1979) such a hunky young stud when he first started out in movies. Look at his college yearbook photos and you'll wish you had the opportunity to share the USC football team locker room with him. Disbelievers, particularly those who've seen him swinging his rifle during the sweeping out-of-focus close-up in *Stagecoach* (1939) on through his war movies and up through *True Grit* (1969), who still can't fathom that brute being beautiful should check out his Dukedom in *The Big Trail* (1930). Tall and lean in his fringed buckskin, he's a stunning young buck himself, all of 23, with tousled hair and high cheekbones, rushing his lines with that unmistakable drawl caught in a higher register.

If I didn't quite connect with my grandmother's affection for Gable's rugged good looks, and had yet to discover my hero John Wayne as a potential object of beauty, I had no trouble connecting with my mom's schoolgirl regard for **Johnny Weissmuller** (1904-1984).

Weissmuller was doing just what came naturally—effortlessly stroking his way through the swimming pool at the Hollywood Athletic Club—when screenwriter Cyril Hume, also a guest at the club, decided the 27-year old should test for the role of Tarzan in the picture he was preparing for MGM.

Producer William S. Van Dyke had issued a warrant to find "a man who is young, strong, well-built, reasonably attractive, but not necessarily handsome, and a competent actor." Take note of the order of that order, because barring acting chops, "the most important thing is that he have a good physique."

The winner of five gold medals between his world-renowned appearances at the 1924 and 1928 Olympics, Weissmuller had the goods and the physique. He had won 36 national and 67 world swimming championships, was the first to shatter the one minute mark in the 100 meter freestyle, set 51 world records, 94 American records, and was named Helms World Trophy Winner in 1923 as Athlete of the Year, North America. He never lost a race from his very first amateur American Athletic Union win at age 17 in 1921 to his retirement in 1928 after the Olympics in Amsterdam. That's right, never lost. Not once. (Among his many awards, titles, honors, prizes, and long-standing records, the Associated Press named him the "Greatest Swimmer of the First Half of the Century" in 1950.)

What's more, he was a professional model. His $500 a week five year contract with BVD to model their line of swimwear was what finished his amazing career as he went from amateur athlete to a professional with a commercial endorsement.

As a celebrity athlete, he came into his own at a time when Charles Atlas (*nee* Angelo Siciliano), winner of Bernarr Macfadden's "Perfectly Developed Man" contest in 1921, started selling his own course on building the male physique. Johnny appeared in a 1924 issue of Macfadden's *Physical Culture* magazine. It wouldn't be long before someone decided they should capture all six-foot-three inches of him on celluloid.

His first film appearance, in which he played either Adam, Adonis, or himself (sources vary, but they all amount to pretty much the same thing) in 1929's *Glorifying the American Girl*, supposedly glorified him in naught but a fig leaf, though a still shows a foofy sarong draped over one shoulder. It's reported that his sponsors at BVD were unhappy and demanded all of his medium shots and close-ups be cut, which may explain why it's nearly impossible to spot him in this Ziegfeld folly.

Edgar Rice Burroughs' *Tarzan of the Apes (A Romance of the Jungle)* first appeared in the October, 1912 issue of *The All-Story Magazine*. The tale of an orphaned white boy raised by apes in the jungle who educates himself and becomes a multilingual superhero as comfortable in the British aristocracy of his Lord Greystoke heritage as he is among the most primitive tribes of the Dark Continent is the pulp of pulp

Johnny Weissmuller, the silver screen's greatest Tarzan and one of the best swimmers of the 20th Century. PHOTOFEST

fiction and comic books, not the movies.

In the movies, a sensual medium, pictures win over words, flesh over patter. The Tarzan films swung the displaced Anglo-god (Tarzan means "white skin") with a mouthful to say over to a Garden of Eden Adam in pre-apple erotic infancy. This naked, still white savage is a tender savage, a big kid whom we're going to have to teach how to do things. How to talk. How to interact with people. How to lay me down to sleep.

In the very first film version, 1918's *Tarzan of the Apes*, the naked jungle boy fortuitously eyes native grass skirts, and an intertitle attempts to justify the need for "Clothes! At the bottom of his little English heart survived a longing for them." Given the girth of Elmo Lincoln in the very grown-up version of the title role, we can all be thankful for that little Victorian ticker.

Weissmuller was the sixth movie Tarzan, but the first in sound, affording us the legendary yell (which he proudly provided on demand for the rest of his life), the all-purpose jungle command "umgawa," and "Tarzan, Jane...Tarzan, Jane...Tarzan, Jane," without the "me's," thank you very much.

It was none other than playwright and former matinee idol Ivor Novello who wrote the dialogue for 1932's sensational hit *Tarzan, the Ape Man*. It's an atrociously anti-animal adventure for the modern viewer, also tinged with racism, in which the plot involves raiding ivory from an elephant burial ground. Along the way, Tarzan must battle killer hippos, a giant phony crocodile, and not one, but two real lions, with a third on its way. The film climaxes in the village of a tribe of savage dwarves who sacrifice their captives to a giant killer gorilla they keep in a pit. It's a ferociously brutal sequence scored by the frenzied chanting of the dwarves and only gets bloodier when Tarzan comes to the rescue and gorily slashes the face and then gushingly slits the throat of the killer ape, after which its corpse is repeatedly pierced by arrows. Finally, we're treated to what would become a Tarzan film standard, a stampede of elephants called in to level the place, this time destroying the dwarves' village and stomping on them in grotesque close-up.

So where's the beauty? It's there between the action, in the quiet moments, up in the trees. Weissmuller has a stunning, stone-carved profile with exotic, sleepy eyes and a strong brow that belies his Romanian birth. (Fearing he wouldn't be able to compete as an American citizen in the Olympics, his baptismal papers were switched with his one-year younger brother Peter, born in Windber, Pennsylvania, whose middle name was John.) At 190 pounds, it's easy to see he's a big man, and his skin isn't worn skin-tight, if you know what I mean, but it's smooth and sensual and very much on display. After he's been nicked in the head by a bullet and then wounded and fatigued by his knock-down wrestling match with the pair of lions, he's "mouthed" by one of his elephant friends and brought to safety. Carried pietà-like, he's a Renaissance sculpture whose modest loincloth no longer hides his glistening, dimpled buttocks.

Later, in just one of many playfully romantic moments he shares with Jane, beautifully played and played beautifully by Maureen O'Sullivan, he poses near-naked on the shore after proving he can swim faster than she can run. He sits on her boots and then grabs her bare foot and with one swipe knocks her on her ass.

"Tarzan, Jane, hurt me, boy, love it, Jane."

"Darling, that's quite a sentence."

Towering over her as he does, Tarzan can't help charming Jane, and us, with his naivete. Weissmuller excels by not being a trained actor, or much of an actor at all, for that matter. His voice hits just the right childlike tones and unpracticed cadence when he speaks and he has the endearing habit of looking right into Jane's face when he's with her, this/close, staring at her in wide-eyed wonder, curious and unafraid. It's a remarkable tribute to his complete identification with the role that he basically only played one other character (the clothed Jungle Jim) in a career that lasted nearly 25 years. O'Sullivan might as well have been describing Tarzan himself when she said of working with Weissmuller, he's "a big, overgrown kid," a "simple soul."

"I love saying things to a man who can't understand, who doesn't even know what kisses are," Jane says to Tarzan.

"Love it," he says back.

"I dare say you would."

Talk about your grown-up fantasies! Who wouldn't want to get lost in a jungle with this ape man? The enduring power of any storybook is its ability to transport you into the fantasy, to inspire you to trade places with its characters. Tarzan does that. He represents physical beauty, undying devotion, utmost protection, and an uncorrupted innocence open to an education that you provide. He's the ultimate male model.

I'm sure there'd be some drawbacks, but you wouldn't think competition would be one of them when you're sharing living quarters in a tree with a chimpanzee. Cheetah, the gay chimp, was notoriously jealous of Ms. O'Sullivan's proximity to Johnny and attempted to bite her and intimidate her several times. In the film, Cheetah actually whacks Jane twice. The first comes when he slaps her in the head as she tries to get out of the water, the second when she runs to jump back in and he body slams her. He also had the habit of walking around in a state of sexual rigidity between takes, something he reportedly had in common with Mr. Weissmuller.

Tarzan, the Ape Man was a huge box-office hit and Johnny was billed as "the only man in Hollywood who's natural in the flesh and can act without clothes." He had previously been photographed upright in his tight white swimwear by George Hoyningen-Huene, but now posed prone, a golden boy submissive in just a loincloth lying on the sandy beach as captured by gay photographer Cecil Beaton. It's a remarkable photo, a seductive invite to explore a man's sensuality in a pose that's not only prototypically feminine, but jumps across the decades to anticipate the male sex object of today's advertising world.

Of this new Tarzan, "With his flowing hair, his magnificently proportioned body, his catlike walk, and his virtuosity in the water, you could hardly ask anything more in the way of perfection," according to Thornton Delehanty in the *New York Evening Post*. Indeed.

Hollywood was abuzz and a sequel was immediately set into motion. Meanwhile, with his first marriage falling apart, in classic old Hollywood fashion, MGM honchos and publicists must have worried about their side of beef spoiling as an object of desirability and paid the young actress who was Johnny's wife $10,000 to help her move along. Tarzan was now free to be had in the fantasies of every plain Jane from here to Timbuktu. Within a year, however, he would marry the tempestuous Lupe Velez, with whom he was having a none-too-secret affair while he was still married.

As one of the few movie sequels to better its original, *Tarzan and His Mate* (1934) is hotly embraced as the best of all Tarzan films, certainly the best of the even dozen Weissmuller did over his sixteen years in the role.

Besides being well made and exciting, it's a classic because it's sexy no matter what your persuasion. Gay men and straight women could still drool over the smooth contours and primitive sex appeal of Weissmuller and straight men and lesbians could now drool over the gorgeous body and fresh-faced sexuality of Maureen O'Sullivan, whose Jane is outfitted in a midriff-baring jungle bikini.

Tarzan and Jane make an irresistibly sexy and playfully romantic couple. He wakes her up by blowing in her ear, then sweetly, but oddly inflecting: "Morning. I love you." Even the silly, but impressive stunt involving Jane leaping from an impossibly high branch into the open arms of Tarzan down below comes across as the delightful party trick of a loving, trusting couple, and we smile at both the trick and the relationship that came up with it.

Given Weissmuller's athletic prowess, it's no surprise that even his underwater swimming scenes are sensual: his wide shouldered brawn moving through the water with grace and confidence. He's a man in his element. A joy to watch.

When Jane joins him for her famed nude swim—which was removed by censors, gained both mythic notoriety and breathless anticipation over the years, and was finally restored to video prints in 1991—it's romance as underwater ballet, scandalous only when we think about it as being in an "old movie," and yet somehow sexier for that very reason. (Ms. O'Sullivan was body-doubled.)

Tarzan Escapes (1936) was the biggest budgeted film yet. It was begun, halted, and got started again with three different directors (including John Farrow, whom Maureen O'Sullivan would marry), and stepped up the thrills with more gruesome violence alongside oft-replayed action scenes from the earlier films. Nasty encounters with vampire bats, outsized reptiles, and killer pygmies ended up on the cutting room floor when test screen audiences supposedly found them too distasteful. The film did not fare nearly as well as the first two outings at the box-office.

Seventy years after the fact, we forget that the Tarzan films were originally conceived as adult entertainments, hence all the violence and sexual suggestiveness. With the Production Code of the Hays Office firmly in place by 1934, the studios had to clean up their jungle act, diluting the sexual tension between Tarzan and Jane to sitcom cohabitation. Her jungle wear quickly became a cover-up and his loincloth grew by leaps and bounds.

Buster Crabbe to the rescue. Santa Monica, by the way. PHOTOFEST

By the time *Tarzan Finds A Son!* (1939), the series was definitely family fare. Boy, played by curly-head Johnny Sheffield, whom Big Johnny picked out himself, was adopted by the jungle pair after his parents are killed in a plane crash. We certainly couldn't have morally weathered *Tarzan Knocks Up Jane!* (A possibly disenchanted, but assuredly pregnant O'Sullivan vied to have her Jane killed off at the end of this picture, and she was, too, until test audiences again cried foul and MGM added footage resurrecting her. O'Sullivan lasted two more installments.)

A charming piece of trivia is that boy Sheffield couldn't swim, but champion Weissmuller wanted him anyway, reasoning that since Tarzan would have to teach Boy how to swim it only made sense that he should do the same in real life. The two became the best of buddies and Sheffield reprised his Boy in seven more films until he got too big for his lack of britches, at 16, and both the series and Weissmuller had pretty much flabbed out. We'll run into "Johnny, Jr." briefly in the next chapter when he flirts with gay hearts as *Bomba, the Jungle Boy.*

The Tarzan films may have become painfully routine awfully quickly, though we'll revisit the character from time to time during the next six decades as various actors embody him, but I've always had a special fondness for them. Few characters survive on such simplicity. The story of a near-naked man swinging through the jungle is just about all you need to make it work, so long as he's the right near-naked man. No matter what else it pretends to be, and we've seen the series go from politically incorrect to environmentally conscious over these many years, it's essentially a mythical celebration of the idealized guy, both sensitive and sinuous.

A short-term glitch in the character rights allowed low-budget film producer Sol Lesser to make a handful of Tarzan pictures in the '30s, the only one of which I'll mention is *Tarzan, the Fearless* (1933), starring **Clarence Linden "Buster" Crabbe** (1907-1983). Crabbe was also an Olympic Gold medallist in swimming, having won the 400 meter finals in the 1932 games by a tenth of a second. Extraordinarily handsome, his first lead was as Kaspa the Lion Man in *King of the Jungle* (1932), a cheap Tarzan knock-off.

Crabbe was always quick to say that his Tarzan, a serial that was later edited into a feature, was the worst Tarzan film ever made, but it definitely made an impression on me when I saw it on late night TV as a teenager. Buster's vine-swinging ape man was a sight for sore eyes, even more taut than Weissmuller's and wearing the most revealing loincloth I've ever seen on a Tarzan, fully exposing his shapely butt cheeks on both sides. As for the rest of the film, I can't say I remember it.

Buster went on to achieve everlasting fame as a dyed blond intergalactic babe named Flash Gordon in a trio of very popular serials in which he occasionally flashed his first-rate physique in tight space shorts and no shirt: *Flash Gordon* (1937*), Flash Gordon's Trip to Mars* (1938), and *Flash Gordon Conquers the Universe* (1940), as well as a redundant Buck Rogers serial edited into the feature *Destination Saturn* (1939). Once called the King of the Serials, Crabbe played Billy the Kid, later softened to Billy Carson, in 35 low-budget one-hour features between 1942 and 1946.

While there were sixty or so fan magazines devoted to movie stars in the '20s and '30s, actresses had almost exclusive domain on the covers. The few times guys did appear, as we know Valentino did, for instance, I suppose someone could argue feminine beauty still reigned.

The word "beefcake" wouldn't officially be coined until 1949, which shouldn't suggest moviemakers were waiting for Webster's, but a conspicuous lack of just cause for such a term in the 1930s. Maybe that's the real reason Gable's bare chest was such a sensation. The culture was deprived. The Hollywood Production Code encouraged concealment and just about the only places you could find otherwise were when the actors were engaged in physical violence (as boxers), were being punished (as slaves), or were in one of those morally-exempt Bible epics.

If skin on the screen was rare, we can only imagine how sacred a still photograph might have been held. My guess is that any time a shirtless shot of a handsome movie star did make it between the covers of a fanzine, it also made its way between the covers of a fan.

Weissmuller's Tarzan is that rare and exquisite exception to Hollywood's modesty about exposing the male body, because the very premise requires a half-naked ape man. There's something powerfully sensual in watching him march through the jungle with an elephant between his legs.

F.W. Murnau's tragic island romance *Tabu—A Story of the South Seas* (1931) was filmed in Tahiti and captured the physical beauty of Matahi and the other boys of Bora Bora. Though not nude, the fact that Matahi was a native and could have been unclothed was eventually addressed in one of the few exceptions to the 1934 Production Code's no nudity clause, which "shall not be interpreted to exclude actual scenes photographed in a foreign land of the natives of that land," granted we're viewing a non-sexual travelogue. Native, dark-skinned nudity was okay, particularly when provided by African women.

Racism of another kind was on parade in Germany where Hitler's perversion of the physique culture movement espoused the supremacy of the Aryan race. The Nazis blighted the body politic and revealed the ugliness behind their diseased notions of beauty and power. Not all went as expected, either. Jesse Owens was a testament to that. To watch Leni Riefenstahl's magnificent *Olympiad* (1938), an opera of light and shadow covering the 1936 Olympic Games in Berlin, is to celebrate on film the authority and astonishing splendor of the human body—including the male nude—framed and lit to ennoble the aesthetic of the athlete.

We were entering an era in which the male form was not only being recognized as a thing of loveliness unto itself, but was being photographed to that end. No longer an academic record of anatomy on a photographic plate, the male body as subject matter became a full-fledged depiction of beauty. Among the very best photographers devoting themselves to this pursuit: Cecil Beaton, George Hoyningen-Huene,

George Platt Lynes, and Minor White in the US, Kurt Reichert in Germany, Bertram Park and Angus McBean in the UK, and Raymond Voinquel in France. Voinquel's 1939 study of a 20-year old Louis Jourdan from bare mid-chest up is breathtaking. Beaton and Hoyningen-Huene likewise photographed movie stars in addition to their less-famous, less-inhibited subjects.

"The photographs of the 1930s seem more clearly aimed at men who wanted to look at other men naked," writes David Leddick in his hefty compilation of chronological evidence entitled *The Male Nude* (Taschen, 1998). The naked guys being photographed for art and commerce were now getting the Hollywood treatment they deserved. Not just modern day Greek gods, they were the equivalent of glamorous movie stars, and raven-haired **Tony Sansone** (1905-1987) was the paradigm.

Canonized by New York photographer Edwin F. Townsend in two photo collections, *Modern Classics* (1932) and *Rhythm* (1935), Sansone possessed a classically handsome Italian face atop a body so gorgeously sculpted that grown men and women were driven insane by either the painted fig leaf or the spray-painted triangle of pitch black bush used to cover his privates in publications. Even knowing better, I probably would have scratched away at that giant pussy patch until I'd ruined my copy. The very idea that full-frontal nude shots of Tony existed somewhere other than where I could get at them would have compelled me to commit crimes.

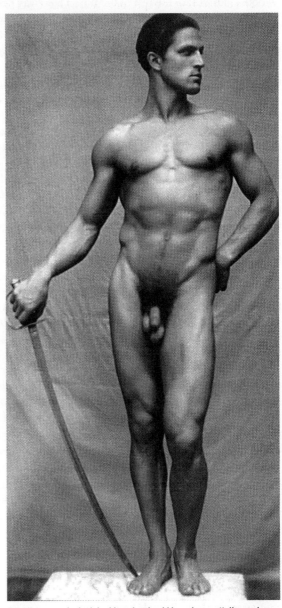

Well-connected collectors could obtain the uncensored versions, and years later they became more widely available, proving that his uncircumcised genitalia was just as handsome as the rest of him. He was a New York lad of Italian lineage who became a physique magazine enthusiast as a teenager and began building his body using the Charles Atlas course. His washboard abs, at a time when washboards were things people actually owned, consisted of an eight- (not a six-) pack, but he achieved everlasting worship because he didn't enlarge himself out of all proportion. He had the good sense to remain lean and juicy; acting a little, dancing a little, and posing a lot. He would end up running his own gymnasiums in Manhattan.

Tony Sansone was beautiful enough to have been a Hollywood movie star; that he came naked and Hollywood movie stars didn't allowed those precious few who had access to him to vicariously satisfy their erotic desires for the Tinsel Town variety.

Professor Kenneth Dutton, in his book *The Perfectible Body* (Continuum, 1995), finds Sansone "the most important figure since Eugen Sandow in the history of the developed male body." Dutton continues: "If Sandow was a Hercules of chiseled white marble, Sansone was a seductive and swarthy Pan. The first was a progenitor of bodybuilding; the second became the prototype of the male pin-up." Our angel is a centerfold.

The Ritter Brothers, Fred and William by name, were a couple of well-built young men who took to photographing each other nude, or as a pair, in various athletic and oiled-up poses and sold the photos by mail-order for a whopping buck apiece during the early to mid-1930s. If Sansone

Tony Sansone, the bodybuilder who should have been a Hollywood movie star.

contributed sheer sex appeal and movie star good looks in poses that were often non-athletic, i.e., "look at me for the sake of looking at me," then the Ritters brought scenario into play. By appearing naked together and, all the more provocatively, by being brothers, the erotic dynamic of the photos was compounded and our role as voyeurs was solidified. We were being made aware that they were photographing each other naked, often in outdoor settings, because they knew an audience wanted to see them that way. Their success was an acknowledgement of an interest in the handsome male nude, an awareness that they possessed something that other people wanted to look at, and a self-conscious means of marketing their nakedness to an audience; it was also exhibitionism laced with the enticing implication of brotherly love.

Collecting male nude photography in the 1930s was risky business, though, and access to the material was beyond difficult for the average citizen. The vast majority of erotically-deprived gay men still had to make do with the guys flashing across the silver screen.

To fall in love with **Cary Grant** (1904-1986) is to fall in love with an image entirely fashioned for celluloid, not necessarily the actor who provided it, though we'd like that, too, despite the very mixed reviews of his off-screen persona. When Grant told the press that he had perfected playing himself, he was right. He was a movie star in the Movie Star sense. Urbane, witty, sophisticated, screwy, seductive, mysterious, even menacing—all and more apply to a Hollywood fiction named Cary Grant.

Born to poverty in England, Archibald Alexander Leach left home at age 14 to join a family of traveling performers. Unbeknownst to him until he was a Hollywood star, his mother, who simply vanished one day when he came home from school, had been placed in an asylum by his father, perhaps falsely—and perhaps she wasn't his real mother anyway, if that matters at all in terms of managing the psychological trauma. It's that kind of a story. He was circumcised as a child, but never knew why. It was not a customary practice in England and could only have resulted in some level of teasing, or at the very least of feeling quite different from his peers. He came to New York a couple of times with his surrogate family of entertainers as a teenaged acrobat and finally stayed, getting a job as a sandwich board on stilts clacking his way through the bustle of tormenting children on Coney Island.

Proof that he was a good-looking kid, if nothing else, he began performing in musicals despite the fact that he couldn't carry a tune. Sometimes he'd stand on stage and mouth the words, his appealing face and lips his entire act, while a singer sang behind the curtain.

The image of Grant as a ventriloquist's dummy is an apt one, because he didn't seem to be much more than that when he first started out in pictures at Paramount, save his sprightly debut as Thelma Todd's javelin-throwing Olympic-athlete hubby in the witty sex comedy *This is the Night* (1932). In *Blonde Venus* (1932), though, he demonstrates a remarkable asexuality. There's absolutely no heat at all in his scenes with Marlene Dietrich, their love lines delivered in deadpan not because they're rank amateurs, but because Marlene was distracted by her director and Cary didn't yet realize he needed to act a love scene. Years later, when asked how she felt about her budding co-star, Ms. Dietrich replied, "I had no feelings. He was a homosexual."

Mae West, who was no stranger to gay men in her act long before she became part of theirs, similarly failed to ignite Cary as her lover boy in both *She Done Him Wrong* (1933) and *I'm No Angel* (1933), though it's hard to blame him. He looks like a live-action *Thunderbird*, one of those Saturday morning marionette TV stars from the 1960s, as though he should have strings attached to his chiseled noggin. Once again, we have two asexual performers playing love scenes together. Part of the problem is West's ego. Grant is left completely without a personality playing an adoring "straight" man to her impossibly unsexy wisecracks; he's the mannequin whom she famously asks, "Why don't you come up sometime and see me?" In *I'm No Angel*, a beautiful boy standing in the audience to the left of the stage makes for a notable distraction just before West saunters out for the first time. He's just an extra, and a mighty green one at that who twice looks into the camera, yet Cary Grant in a featured role is given little more to do than this unknown kid. He's handsome bland.

A hint of life emerged in the notorious *Sylvia Scarlett* (1935), a freak of cinema, in which his Cockney swindler believes that a shrill Kate Hepburn in short hair and trousers is a boy. Shirtless as he prepares to share a bed with the lad, Grant eyes him/her and says, "It's nippy tonight. You'll make a proper hot water bottle!"

His on-screen intro in the film makes him look like he's cruising the foggy train station for boys, a self-proclaimed "gentleman adventurer" and "hawk" who makes a sudden grab for Hepburn's (boy) bod and

Cary Grant, who brought charm, sophistication and wit to the movies, seen here in *Only Angels Have Wings* (1939). PHOTOFEST

declares it a "bit ticklish. Just wondering if there's any more lace in the family." Kate's pop, an embarrassed Edmund Gwenn (*Miracle on 34th Street*'s Santa), is smuggling lace through customs by wearing it beneath his clothes, but—wink wink—we know what that line is supposed to mean. Or do we?

What really hurts from a gay perspective is that despite its cross-dressing themes and its gay star and gay director, it's not even campy. It's crap. Scenes seem barely scripted, with the actors making up their lousy lines as they go along, failing miserably to amuse or charm us in the rambling mess. A bad night at the improv, all involved were right to be ashamed of it.

Amazingly, it was improvisation that at last proved there was more to Cary Grant than oil slick hair, a sing-song delivery, and a baby's butt for a chin. In *The Awful Truth* (1937), a huge hit and the first of his career-defining screwball comedy classics, nervous energy about making a film in which the script was provided almost daily on bits of scrap paper, and sometimes only as ideas, animated him. (In point of fact, he was a natural and quite witty ad-libber with an incomparable sense of comic timing—e.g., the "Excuse me" that follows a Jimmy Stewart hiccup in *The Philadelphia Story* is his.) He tried desperately to quit the film, but was forced by the studio to carry on and ended up establishing himself as an entity with audiences. I'm not sure whether he's got nonsexual sex appeal or pre-sexual sex appeal, but it's something quite novel in a handsome leading man.

Sarcasm and witty asides make him sexy in a safe, playful sort of way. Cary Grant's success as a romantic star is unique because he's a sex star that people don't think about having sex with. (Feel free to disagree.) He appeals to our romantic selves, not our lusty selves. And that's not a bad thing, either, being a hypothetical hunk.

In *Bringing Up Baby* (1938) and *Holiday* (1938), he demonstrates considerable acrobatic skills from his vaudeville days while getting the chance to move from a sexless nerd to the guy we want to get the girl, even if he might not know what to do with her once he's got her. Who cares, at least they'll have fun while he's teaching her how to do the back flip-flop.

Forced to answer the door wearing a woman's frilly robe in *Baby*, he's asked to explain his attire and famously springs into the air and replies, "Because I just went gay all of a sudden!" Doris Nolan, in *Holiday*, describes the first time she met him to sister Kate Hepburn and remarks that "he had a queer look on his face." "I can believe that," says Hepburn. "Gay" and "queer" came with first definition meanings having nothing to do with homosexuality, of course, but their dual nature allows fortuitous interpretations today. Besides, what else can Grant mean when he says he's gone gay?

In *Only Angels Have Wings* (1939), Grant calls Jean Arthur a "queer duck" and she replies, "So are you." Thomas Mitchell tells Arthur in the same film: "The only thing I can tell you about him is that he's a good guy for girls to stay away from." The sole reason he didn't sissify himself to distract us from his horrific pageboy wig years later in *I Was A Male War Bride* (1949) was because director Howard Hawks forbade him to do so. Suggesting or declaring in some way on film, through deception or otherwise, a gay actor's off-screen sexuality makes for interesting viewing and growing curiosity about the motivation. Rock Hudson and Anthony Perkins are two other gay actors who were routinely subjected to the same treatment.

In 1932, Cary met actor **Randolph Scott** (1898-1987), a University of North Carolina engineering grad who befriended Howard Hughes and subsequently began showing up in movies. It's been reported that Scott and Hughes were lovers, as it has of Grant and Hughes, so it seems a bit too tidy to have the actors regularly shacking up together in Hollywood for the next ten years, but that's exactly what they did. After attending many social and public events as an unattended couple, they shared a number of pads throughout years of studio-arranged dates and romances with starlets and society gals, even through marriages. Paramount studio execs were embarrassed by the co-habitation, particularly when Grant and Scott, a handsome couple if ever there was one, posed for fan magazine photos at home together, with Cary in an apron. Another shot has them in just their bathing trunks while sitting on the diving board of their pool—Randy reaching out from behind Cary to suggest an imminent shove, but just as easily suggesting something else. Check out the lover boys paired on screen in 1940's *My Favorite Wife* and pay close attention to the pool scene there. (Or go even further back, if you like, to Grant's first screwball comedy, 1932's *Hot Saturday*, in which Nancy Carroll strikes out to make boyfriend Randy jealous by romping with playboy Cary.)

By the time we get to *The Philadelphia Story* (1941), Grant is in full command of his charms, already evident in comedy, but now there's a dry sophistication to his persona that's very charismatic. Finding him absent from the Quigley Polls as one of the ten most popular stars in the '30s, but on it thrice in the '40s and then from 1959-1966, makes sense when you think about how completely in possession he became of his Movie Star powers as a more mature man in the Hitchcocks of the '40s and '50s (*Suspicion*, *Notorious*, *To Catch A Thief*, *North by Northwest*), as well as in *An Affair to Remember* (1957) and *Charade* (1963). He was twice nominated for Oscars, for 1941's *Penny Serenade* and 1944's *None But the Lonely Heart*, both dramas, but didn't win until given a special award in 1970.

Whatever he failed to do in real life for those few who knew him—let's bypass the bio-hazard stories about his being a cold man with a huge ego and a violent temper, a tightwad, a self-hating homosexual, and a compulsive liar who used LSD for psychiatric reasons, married unhappily far too many times, etc.—he succeeded grandly on-screen for all those of us who didn't. For better and not worse, the man behind Cary Grant deserves to rest in peace. What deserves our attention and everlasting affection is that special feeling you get whenever you hear someone say his name or see it appear in the opening credits of a late-night movie. It has a delicious way of setting off instant nostalgia for "classic movies" of a bygone era, for a certain grace, wit and charm that you don't even have to be old enough to conjure.

The divine curse of movie stars is that their movie selves outlive and even oust their real selves. The Cary Grant I know and love needn't worry. He's as dependable as a favorite novel.

Spangler Arlington Brugh, the only man who could possibly follow Archibald Alexander Leach in this book, never considered himself much of an actor. He was not only pragmatic about his career, but refreshingly realistic and legitimately humble. If there was a place to put credit, he could always point to his face. "I was a good-looking kid and had a good voice, so I got the breaks." Those glorious good looks were taken notice of in a college production of that great boys-in-the-trench war play *Journey's End* in 1932. The music major from Nebraska got himself a screen test and a contract at MGM where he started showing up in small roles as **Robert Taylor** (1911-1969) beginning in 1934.

Within a year, he had become a star thanks to our *Magnificent Obsession* (1935), that Greek tragedy of melodrama in which the drunk who accidentally kills a man then ends up blinding the dead fella's wife in a car accident. Hopelessly intertwined in the mess, he falls in love with the unfortunate woman, who doesn't know his identity, and vows to become an eye surgeon so that he can restore her sight. If the soap opera improbability is too much for your brain, see if your heart can stand the film's uplifting, miraculous finale.

Joan Crawford, *The Gorgeous Hussy* (1936), comes close to delivering Taylor's epitaph as a pretty boy in that film when she remarks, "He's very nice and gay, but... ." The "but" is deliberately left hanging and can be filled any number of ways. For critics, Taylor was very nice and gay, but not much of an actor. For audiences, he was very nice and gay, but his beauty didn't last nearly long enough. For wife Barbara Stanwyck, he was also very nice and gay, their marriage from 1939-1951 widely considered one of convenience for the both of them, though Taylor held the closet door tightly shut and was deeply conflicted about his nature. He would marry again in 1954.

For MGM, Taylor was very nice and gay, too, but also a complete professional and they held onto him for three decades despite his lack of critical praise, his quick fade as handsome leading man, and his testifying before HUAC about communism in the film industry in 1947. In his heyday, though, Taylor landed on the Quigley Poll of top ten stars at #4 in 1936, #3 in 1937, and #6 in 1938.

He beautified a number of films while his looks held out, including *Broadway Melody of 1936* (1935; he sings, but doesn't dance), *A Yank at Oxford* (1938; looking fine in an athletic T), and as a soldier who falls for ballet dancer Vivien Leigh in the romantic drama *Waterloo Bridge* (1940). In *The Crowd Roars* (1938), he's a boxer with a nice body, but it looks like he's afraid of getting hit while unconvincingly mixing it up in the ring. A mobster played by Edward Arnold, who's underwriting Taylor's "Killer McCoy," finds out that the kid is seeing his daughter.

"She's fallen for a face and a body," he tells Taylor. "Wait'll she sees that face all pushed out of shape after the next few fights."

"She'll stick with me."

"That's because she's loyal and decent and straight…qualities you wouldn't understand."

"The Man With the Perfect Profile's" best role may be his Armand Duval opposite Greta Garbo in the smash hit version of *Camille* (1937), the famed Dumas tale filmed several times before, including in 1921 with Valentino playing the part of Duval. In it, Taylor is the boyish, long-faced country boy who falls hopelessly in love with the sickly Marguerite (Ms. Garbo), a selfish society vampire who at last seems to find happiness in his embrace, only to sacrifice it for his sake before dying in his arms.

His strong, clear voice and air of self-confidence obliterates any thought of foppishness despite being saddled with the boyfriend role in a period piece. His face seems to create its own soft-focus effect, complete with the ghost of a cleft in his chin and a neck with room for two bow ties, one above the other. He's the epitome of the good soul, a man of true love and honor. Audiences must have seen him as their dream lover, a romantic ideal who fulfills all roles. His undying love for Marguerite, his forgiveness, and the beauty of his optimistic smile for her in the face of her deathly illness will bring you to tears.

Costume pictures were a reliable source for finding good-looking men. In *Captain Blood* (1935), **Errol Leslie Thomson Flynn** (1909-1959) became a star by default. Robert Donat, Leslie Howard, Frederic March, Clark Gable, and Ronald Colman were all unavailable or uninterested in playing the swashbuckling throwback

Spangler Arlington Brugh becomes Robert Taylor. PHOTOFEST

to the silent era. Maybe it was the English costuming circa 1685. When producer Hal Wallis saw the rushes, he told director Michael Curtiz that Flynn looked like "a God damned faggot." Meanwhile, over at MGM, Clark Gable was whining about his pigtail, velvet kneepads, and silver buckles for much the same reason on *Mutiny on the Bounty* (1935).

Born in Tasmania, Flynn was the son of an Australian marine biology professor and a mother so stern that she repeatedly chastised and beat him as a boy for purely boyish behavior. The psychobabble result was a rebellious, trouble-making kid who was a chronic runaway frequently expelled from school. At 17, he went to New Guinea to find gold and stayed to fornicate with the native girls. His pulp-novel real-life adventures, augmented by a best-selling autobiography heavy on invention, included dynamiting for fish,

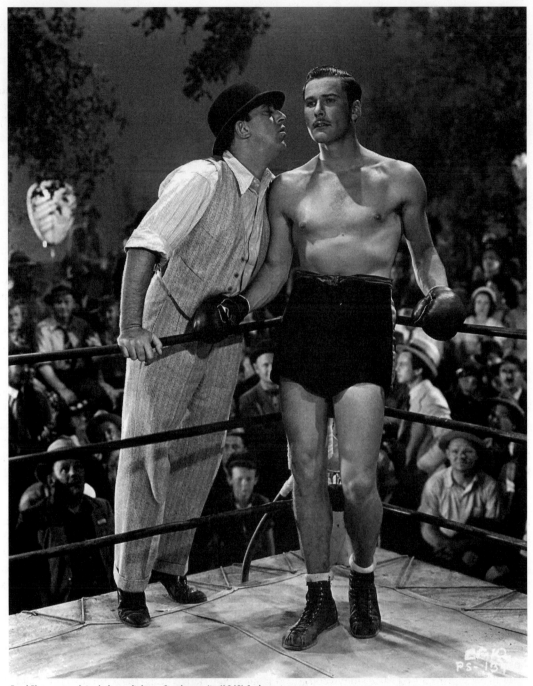

Errol Flynn gets advice before a fight as *Gentleman Jim* (1942) Corbett. PHOTOFEST

fighting off headhunters and cannibals, trading slaves, and being charged with the murder of a native (no body found, no case). By 19, he was a carousing drunk and renowned sexaholic frequently afflicted with gonorrhea.

A job opportunity piloting a British documentary film crew through New Guinea aboard his cutter resulted in his being noticed in the editing room as a startlingly handsome young man with an exquisite bare torso. He was invited to Tahiti to play Fletcher Christian in the low-budget *In the Wake of the Bounty* (1933). He did the role and nothing came of it in terms of professional offers other than sparking his own interest in pursuing an acting career. He embarked on a momentous journey to join his parents in Belfast, where his father had a university chair position, and stopped off to tangle with the Chinese, learn Oriental sex practices, and begin using opium.

All of 23, he joined the Northampton Rep company in Britain on the basis of his looks and shortly thereafter took out an ad in the trades featuring his handsome profile, baited with a list of completely phony film credits. A British studio bit and subsequently cabled Warner Bros. about their find. Warners brought the good-looking lad to Hollywood and immediately set forth promoting him as an Irish star.

Unlike Kevin Costner, whose debut in flashbacks and as the corpse in *The Big Chill* (1983) was scissored (okay, so you see a wrist and an ankle), Flynn's Hollywood debut as a corpse on a slab remained intact, as did a one minute flashback, in the Perry Mason potboiler *The Case of the Curious Bride* (1935). The director was the temperamental Hungarian Michael Curtiz, who would go on to direct Flynn in 12 films, including *Captain Blood*. From dead guy bit player to leading man movie star in a single year after just three films.

Even knowing that Flynn personally tore all the lace from his costume in order not to be seen as a fop, his Dr. Peter Blood is just that when the film opens. A man of peace and moral upstanding who wants his geraniums watered while he's away will quickly turn into a vengeful pirate after he's unjustly found guilty of treason and sold into slavery. The slave auction has him felt up and impetuous, slapped twice for impertinence before being sold for ten pounds to the daughter of his tormentor.

Unfortunately, he's not stripped of his shirt for the prerequisite flogging and the whipping itself is stayed by "the timely interruption" of Spanish pirates. Blood steals the pirate ship and becomes the terror of the Caribbean, briefly allied with pirate Basil Rathbone, who warns us in his mutilated French accent while threatening torture: "It is possible to screw a man's eyes out of his head."

Though the film made a contract player into a star, Flynn nearly seems a contract player in a starring role. It's not an easy task for a neophyte. He's not terribly convincing, but you find yourself staring at his big toothy upper row, that minor cleft, and those darling dimples. Given my choice, I would rather have seen the story of the effeminate Dr. Peter Blood than his rogue alter ego.

He was a rogue, though. Flynn continued to carouse off-screen and quickly gained a reputation as double-edged as Blood's sword. To fellow actors, he was a source of constant frustration, rarely learning his lines, habitually late, the consummate unprofessional. His private life was, by design, never much of a private life. To wife, friends, and the press, he was pusillanimous, pugilistic, and pugnacious. He loved brawls in public, was a vigorous anti-Semite in a town powered by Jews, and dabbled in unpopular politics. Hard to believe, some might say, because he was capable of projecting enormous charm on screen, especially when he approached a role with his winningly devil-may-care attitude.

He shared a pad with David Niven for a time, continuing to pursue the life of a hedonist: drink, opium, sex with untold numbers of women, the bad boy playboy. More precisely, an all-around playboy—a chronic adolescent.

Marilyn Monroe, in a legendary (and some claim entirely fictional) conversation with Truman Capote, recalled going to a party during her modeling days at which Flynn, "so pleased with himself," plunked out "You Are My Sunshine" on the piano with his dick. "Christ! Everybody says Milton Berle has the biggest schlong in Hollywood," she added. "But who cares?" (Mrs. Berle, maybe?)

When a gangly new kid with a big schnozz transferred to my junior high school, the only reason I paid attention to him was because I was assigned to show him around. By the time we got to gym class, however, and he casually revealed possession of the biggest, longest cock I had ever seen, he started to look better to me...in the face, I mean.

I'm not sure the oft-repeated Hollywood gossip about Milton Berle's penis resulted in anyone developing a crush or seeing him as more physically attractive than they had ever thought him before, but it says something about how an envied attribute can change the way you look at someone. It also acknowledges the vast curiosity about celebrity cock size and reaffirms that decidedly male obsession, whether you're a hetero- or homosexual. Of course men compare the size of their genitalia with other guys (if only mentally) and they do fret a great deal over any perceived shortcomings. A big penis transforms most owners. The self-confidence we call "cocky" is aptly-named, because a guy with a cock larger than his peers is usually quite proud of it. It's in his walk, it's in the way he dresses; it's in his pants, but more likely to find an excuse to be out of them than its insecure brethren. If he's got the face of a mule but he's full of flirtatious vim and vigor, he's packing.

So while the artful male nude photography of the era—Tony Sansone, et al—revealed an aesthetic of the body, with "normal-sized" penises and the genitalia presented as part of the whole, it couldn't be expected to negate the baser locker room approach, giggling at whose swings the lowest.

Flynn's has been variously reported as large and small, both conclusions made at full staff, so that should go a long way toward telling us about the reliability of so-called first-hand information. In that same suspect conversation with Marilyn, Truman Capote tells us that he told her he spent an evening with Flynn, but said the only thing memorable about Flynn's equipment was that it was Errol Flynn's. Close friend and biographer Earl Conrad, who said he saw "it" many times, wrote: "It was, if not short, certainly not much longer than that, and rather stout, I thought." We know Flynn put four feet of dead snake in Olivia De Havilland's panties as they sat in her changing room during the filming of *Dodge City* (1939), but it turns out we're talking real dead snake here, not colorful metaphors. Iron Eyes Cody, the crying Indian of the '70s anti-pollution ads, recollected in his published memoir as a Hollywood bit player that he once played a party game with Errol and several male friends in which the winner was the man who could place the most number of quarters side-by-side along the topside of his erection. Flynn won, pants down.

Guys are guys, after all. And what's interesting is that, for the most part, guys are the only ones who find this kind of unacknowledged homoerotic spectacle a real hoot.

Fellow actors of the era whose members make up the Hollywood Big Dick Hall of Fame include Gary Cooper, Humphrey Bogart, Charlie Chaplin, George Raft, and Franchot Tone. Membership is awarded based on erect measurement at or exceeding 10". Corroboration provided by eyewitness, ex-lover, boast, myth, and rumor.

So where does Flynn stuff himself so successfully inside those bright green tights in *The Adventures of Robin Hood* (1938)? Try as you might, especially after reading this, you won't be able to find any telltale signs of hose in his hosiery. He's both well-tucked and precisely skirted by his tunic. Not that that meant he was any less dreamy to all the idolizing gay boys in the audience, some of whom developed a randy obsession with the film and the jolly "bold rascal" whose lively escapades are captured in garish Technicolor. See it too many times and you'll begin to wish they gave the superbly villainous Basil Rathbone more to do, as well as question the wisdom of the archery contest used to try and trap Robin. Flynn didn't enjoy the part—intended for James Cagney, who was in a contract dispute—and felt he couldn't milk anything out of it, but he was wrong. It remains his signature role, from his classic swaggering entrance at Gisbourne's castle with the deer on his back to his plucky, upstart responses to the fey King John and his treasonous courtiers. Flynn had by now perfected the swordplay and action schtick. His rousing "ha, ha, ha" was the sound-era's echo of Douglas Fairbanks' 1922 version. He's also so much more playfully at ease with his romantic self, doing the best job yet believably charming his often-costarred leading lady Olivia De Havilland.

Bette Davis notoriously teamed up with him twice. She made certain the credits didn't read "Errol Flynn in *The Sisters*" (1938), but he's actually quite good as her radiantly handsome, though sexist and alcoholic husband. Second time out, she easily emasculated him both on and off-screen in *The Private Lives of Elizabeth and Essex* (1939), during which she closed her eyes a lot and imagined she was playing opposite Laurence Olivier rather than the rude and sickly Flynn. The man who enjoyed striking journalists and punching the escorts of pretty young women was taken aback when Davis slapped him full on the face during a scripted confrontation. When he loudly complained about the blow, Ms. Davis said she was unable to fake the slap. To her, acting meant playing it for real.

Davis charitably and accurately referred to Flynn some time later "as the most wholesomely beautiful satyr," but the prospect of her playing Scarlett to his Rhett, as was suggested, was too horrific to contemplate. Said the *New York Times* of the pair's Elizabethan effort: "It's Queen Bette's picture just as surely as Mr. Flynn is a good-looking young man who should be asked to do no more in pictures than flash an even-toothed smile and present a firm jaw line." That, my friends, is probably just what he would have done if *Gone With the Wind* had gone ahead with him in the lead. He never took acting seriously and, for that matter, didn't have an even-toothed smile.

A handful of sincere efforts resulted in a handful of good performances: warming up his Robin Hood act with a charming and wisecracking protector of the boy king during the second half of *The Prince and the Pauper* (1937); as a warplane pilot and eventual martyr in *The Dawn Patrol* (1938); another invigorating turn as swashbuckler in *The Sea Hawk* (1940); thoroughly charming as boxer James J. Corbett in 1942's *Gentleman Jim* (he had previously played a scene in the squared circle in the 1937 comedy as *The Perfect Specimen*); as a conspicuously American war hero in *Objective Burma!* (1946); and in sad self-parody as an alcoholic in *The Sun Also Rises* (1957) and a drunken John Barrymore in *Too Much, Too Soon* (1958). But his looks eventually hardened and he rarely seemed interested in what he was doing.

Years of increasing booze and drug abuse, as well as a recurrent case of malaria, weakened his heart and damaged his liver. He was told when he was still in his 30s that he didn't have long to live and famously decreed he would live two lifetimes in the one he was given. There followed multiple marriages and divorces, infamous orgies in his mirrored Mulholland Drive home, nude tennis matches, mansion cockfights, surveillance by the FBI for suspected Nazi alliances (a close friend actually turned out to be a Nazi spy), on and on. Flynn himself, a novelist and playwright, certainly embellished some of his misadventures, aided and abetted by cohorts who helped assure many legends, such as the time the body of Flynn's idol John Barrymore was stolen and propped up for one last drink at Errol's house before being secreted back to the funeral parlor. (Director Raoul Walsh re-told the story many times as a true event in which he conspired.)

Most notoriously of all, however, were the two charges of statutory rape in 1942. Flynn denied the accusations, the first from a 17-year old who said he raped her on his yacht, the second from a 16-year old extra from *They Died With Their Boots On* (1942) who testified he had sex with her while he kept his boots on. The actor was acquitted of both charges after a sensationalized 20 day trial. Thereafter, "in like Flynn" became a sexual euphemism in the pop culture, much to the actor's distaste. In 1950, after cutting the wedding cake on marriage number four, he was served papers again charging him with the rape of a 17-year old. That case was dismissed.

Errol Flynn was a hell-raiser. A love him or hate him kind of guy. He died at 50. Yep, there are at least a hundred years of exploits crammed in there. He also left behind a son, Sean, who was even more beautiful than he was and gave acting a shot in such European fare as *The Son of Captain Blood* (1962), then disappeared while covering the war as a photojournalist in Cambodia in 1970.

Flynn went from obscurity to stardom in three films. It took **Tyrone Power** (1913-1958) five, though he certainly did get noticed in the *Girl's Dormitory* (1936) when he asked "Could I have this dance?" and the audience collectively nodded yes. Movie fans of the female persuasion supposedly wrote the studio asking who the dashing young man with the one line was, but it was two grown men who made all the difference.

Director Henry King and 20th Century-Fox mogul Darryl F. Zanuck practically adopted the young actor who so brazenly walked into studio offices and asked for the lead in their prestige picture *Lloyds of London* (1936). They saw to it that his eyebrows were plucked, gave him fourth billing, and set about making themselves a new screen heartthrob.

Before we even see him, we hear about him. It's 1780s London and he's been arrested. A man and a woman discuss the what for: "It concerns the opposite sex," the man tells her.

"I'll never believe that."

"It does. They arrested him for a peeping tom."

"A likely tale," she says. "I've been trying to make him look at me for a whole year!"

When we finally do see him, he's a lovely sight, despite the blond wig. Beautiful cheekbones. Long black lashes. Dimples. There are times when his face fills the entire screen, inviting us to look into those eyes the same way we would if he were Garbo. The only problem with period movies like this is that even if the leading men are handsome, they aren't allowed to be sexy. They're castrated. So you spend your time listening for dialogue with dual meanings: "I can't imagine anything worse than being in love with someone you can never hope to marry," says Ty, an actor who enjoyed extramarital sexual affairs with both men and women.

His easy acceptance of homosexuality in others may be partly the result of a life lived around the theatre. His father, Tyrone Power, Sr., was an accomplished stage actor and son of famed Welsh actor Tyrone "the Elder" Power. Though his dad pretty much abandoned the family when Tyrone was a young boy, they were briefly reunited while Power, Sr. was playing opposite the studly John Wayne in *The Big Trail* (1930). Tyrone Sr. actively advised his son on the business during this time. A year and a half into their reunion, Sr. suffered a heart attack and died in his son's arms.

While still in his teens, Tyrone, Jr. worked as a movie house usher and kept voluminous notes on the films he saw, as well as written criticisms of the actors' performances. He first appeared on film himself as a plebe in *Tom Brown of Culver* (1932), but the bit wasn't enough to get noticed and he moved to Chicago where he got a job reading comic strips over the radio. He had a great baritone voice.

While in Chicago, he befriended the eccentric and very openly gay Robin Thomas—stepson of John Barrymore and son of the bizarre Michael Strange—whom he subsequently visited in New York. He

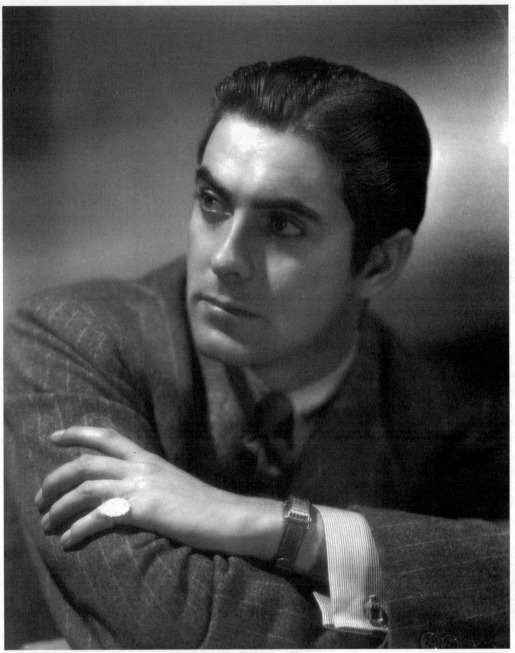
The stunningly pretty Tyrone Power won his first leading role after just four films. PHOTOFEST

immersed himself in theatre and played Tybalt in a production of *Romeo and Juliet* starring Maurice Evans as Romeo and Orson Welles as Mercutio. He actually declined a contract offer to make movies at Universal in 1935 in order to learn his craft on the boards. By the time the famed production reached New York, Welles had been demoted to Tybalt and Power got bumped to Benvolio.

When *Lloyds* proved a big hit, Tyrone proved a big movie star. He consorted briefly with Errol Flynn and David Niven, befriended Cesar Romero (a gay actor in the Hollywood closet who loved him dearly), and learned how to pilot airplanes from director King. He also made a perfunctory, but ravishing leading man opposite Loretta Young in *Ladies in Love* (1936), *Love Is News* (1937), and *Second Honeymoon* (1937), then opposite Sonja Henie in *Thin Ice* (1937) and *Second Fiddle* (1939).

We get a glimpse at his great physique when he comes home and starts to remove his shirt in *In Old Chicago* (1937), the fictionalized story of the O'Leary family and the Great Chicago Fire of 1871. Generally speaking, like most good-lookers in the flicks, Power looks positively glazed over in the stuffy romance scenes. He's much sexier when he's not hooked up yet; lively, fun, and gay until the fateful moment when the life peters out of him because he's had his first glance at "true love." Luckily for us, he turns out to be the bad boy of the brothers and that gives him another shot of vitality while we're afforded several more shots of his great profile.

He signed a seven year contract in 1937 with 20th Century-Fox and his huge success as star of *In Old Chicago* and *Alexander's Ragtime Band* (1938) landed him the #10 spot on Quigley's Poll of the most popular film stars. He would catapult up to #2 in 1939 and finish at #5 in 1940.

Gorgeous in black and white, he's ga-ga gorgeous in Technicolor, especially in the good guy version of *Jesse James* (1939), where his jet black hair stands out wherever it grows: eyebrows, lush sideburns, long-long lashes, even his little mustache. He would meet his lifelong best friend Watson Webb, a messenger boy at the time, during the editing phase of this picture. Ty was known to pine over his women, but he was a loyal and good friend to his male buddies. He had a male secretary, too. Not that there's anything untoward about that.

Power's chosen homosexual affairs were, I hope, exciting and joyous in their discretion and not the fodder for agonizing psychological conflicts, though they were certainly kept under tight wraps. I've always contended that beautiful men should share their beauty with whomever they fancy. Why limit your field of opportunity? It's been long rumored, by the way, that Power was the inspiration for the bisexual film star in Gore Vidal's 1948 groundbreaking novel *The Pillar and the City*, much the same as Cary Grant was said to be the subject of Noel Coward's song "Mad About the Boy."

In *The Rains Came* (1939), Myrna Loy describes him in his Indian make-up and turban as the "pale copper Apollo" and "the one man I've met that I haven't been able to make an impression on." As with *Lloyds of London*, in which he's supposed to be playing the grown-up version of the very British Freddie Bartholomew, and *Son of Fury* (1942), in which he's supposed to be playing a grown-up Roddy McDowall, he doesn't even attempt an accent. Neither did he as the embittered British soldier in *This Above All* (1942). The *Harvard Lampoon's* very first "worst" awards recognized him for his lack of performance in *Rains*, which was little more than a soap opera set-up for some truly amazing earthquake and flood special effects, but I'm less inclined to throw stones.

Tyrone Power was an actor dogged by his "beauty" in nearly every review ever written by another man. Besides, he manages in one smooth motion in *The Rains Came* to delineate the subtle distinctions between handsome and beautiful that may dog critics of this book. After 90 minutes, he finally does away with the turban, runs his hands through his hair, and looks up at the camera, transforming from handsome to beautiful right before our eyes.

He married the French actress Annabella in 1939 and the Powers established themselves as well-liked and very social members of the Hollywood community, hosting parties, and turning part of their property into a small farm, complete with dogs and chickens and goats. He missed out on choice roles at other studios because Zanuck flatly refused to loan him out, but even in that he was difficult to rile. Tyrone Power wanted to please everybody.

He did, in fact, please just about everybody, including his critics, when he planted his tongue in cheek to play the title role in *The Mark of Zorro* (1940), a fun and exciting turn at Douglas Fairbanks fare. The tights are revealing (to the left for both Ty and Basil), the swordplay is first-rate, and Power has even more opportunities to parry between pretty and just plain handsome. If there's a fault, strangely enough, it's in Power's persistently unswishy baritone. He's not quite able to pull off playing the fop with the scented hanky who knows of fashion and perfumes. He's laced too straight. It's a role in which Valentino would have excelled—Rudy longed to do versions of *Captain Blood* and *The Sea Hawk*, too.

While conducting research to star in the remake of Valentino's *Blood and Sand* (1941), Power grew faint at a bullfight. He had once considered starring in a film bio of Valentino, so I guess it's only appropriate he look as unattractive in his flat shiny hair and big eyebrows as Rudy looked unpleasant in the original. Bad acting, bad accents, and silly scenes. It's a sulking and brooding Anthony Quinn who has the sex appeal here.

Ty had sex appeal to spare as far as Judy Garland was concerned when the two of them began a torrid love affair, she at a very awkward 19, he at a very married 28. The result was a genuine split of Power's affections for both the women in his life.

Power joined the Marine Corps as a private in 1942 after the Navy had refused to take him. Following the war, he made efforts to end his too-long relationship with 20th Century-Fox. The prestige pictures were largely gone, though *The Razor's Edge* (1946) was a surprise hit and he successfully talked them into making a daring film noir called *Nightmare Alley* (1947), in which he plays a heartless, scheming carnival barker who connives his way into the mind-reading racket and then falls to the lowest of the low: a sideshow geek who bites the heads off live chickens. It's a grim and callous story with Power as an almost irredeemable hustler. Audiences didn't take to seeing their idol this way. Naturally, it was Tyrone's personal favorite.

A second marriage followed a "goodwill" tour of South America, during which he dined with Juan and Evita Peron in Argentina, but Hollywood kept asking him to play variations on the swashbuckler theme with films such as *Captain from Castile* (1947), *Prince of Foxes* (1949), and *The Black Rose* (1950). He still had a good physique and his smooth chest and hidden belly button showed up in several teasing reminders of his heyday.

He ventured back to the stage in the early fifties to keep himself challenged, married a third time, and gave us a final good performance in *Witness for the Prosecution* (1958). He died shortly after suffering a heart attack while shooting an exhausting sword fight with George Sanders on the set of *Solomon and Sheba* (1959). He was replaced by Yul Brynner.

Tyrone Power may be the most successful movie legend ever to survive on his good looks. He would have been the first to tell you so, as he did a London paper: "If you ask me what films of mine I liked, I can name you about three—and then I have to start thinking. You can't go on always being a knight in shining armor...there are too many young fellows better equipped for that sort of role coming along. You can kid everybody but the fellow you shave every morning."

Tyrone Power IV (1959-   ), the son he didn't live to see, looks good in his Dad's genes—you might just miss him if you blink—as the dark-haired young alien opposite Tahnee Welch (who looks great in her mom's genes) in *Cocoon* (1985).

Sometimes all an actor can hope for is that he'll be remembered for one picture, even if that means falling prey to the criticism that one picture was all he was worth. Charles Hall Locher appeared in several 20th Century-Fox pictures as a contract player, but no one paid much notice. In 1936, he became Lloyd Crane and made another couple of pictures. Still not registering. His uncle was novelist James Norman Hall, co-author of the books that became *Mutiny on the Bounty*. The writer made another fortuitous sale to Hollywood in 1937 as co-author of *The Hurricane*, the film version of which happened to make his nephew, now billed as **Jon Hall** (1913-1979), "Goldwyn's Gift to Women."

The Hurricane (1937) is an exciting South Seas lovey-dovey disaster flick directed by John Ford. The first time we see Hall, he's shirtless and high on the mast of a ship, from which he executes a spectacular dive into the ocean waters. He's a beefy islander named Terangi, a native sailor with a great physique who marries his childhood sweetheart and has his civilized duds torn from him by the wedding party revelers so he can walk around in the more revealing garb of his island home.

He's earnest and handsome as all hell in close-ups, complete with the prerequisite cleft in his chin that so many of the era's pretty boy stars possessed. He's a striking young man in his black first mate's cap, white pants, and bare torso. His belly button, quite unnaturally, is kept hidden, as was the Hollywood custom for most bare-chested men up until the 1960s. I would love to know the rationale, perhaps come across a studio memo about an unsightly outie or a bill for all the treasure trails they were being charged to shave.

Despite the belly button cover-up, we know Hall's an island boy because he's otherwise allowed to bare himself. That skin is the source of trouble when he's incensed by a white racist's comments while in a Tahitian club. He breaks the jerk's jaw and ends up imprisoned, sentenced to hard labor hauling baskets of rocks up a hill under the merciless whip of John Carradine.

A Tarzan-esque escape from the prison island is capped by a breathtaking 131' cliff dive said to be executed by Hall himself, which says something both about John Ford and perhaps about Jon Hall's value as a replaceable face. Acting was never his strong suit, but he was ideally cast in this role.

"I smell a wind coming" doesn't even begin to suggest what's about to blow. The film's famed disaster sequence is one among many impressive special effect blow-outs visited upon audiences in the 1930s. For Hall, the real blow-out may have been his career. Not long after his barefoot *Kit Carson* (1940) uses his toes to play with the fringe on his buddy's buckskins, the actor added a few pounds to his middle

Jon Hall weathers *The Hurricane* (1937). PHOTOFEST

and played and re-played variations on his hunk-on-an-island role in mostly B-movies of the 1940s, including *Aloma of the South Seas* (1941), *Arabian Nights* (1942), *Ali Baba and the Forty Thieves* (1944), and *Zamba* (1949). One of his frequent co-stars was the handsome **Turhan Bey** (1920-), a real smoothie himself when he started out in pictures in his twenties playing exotic villains.

In 1944's cult fave *Cobra Woman*, Hall starred opposite Maria Montez and another guilty pleasure of the era's homoerotic offerings: **Sabu** Dastagir (1924-1963).

Only 13 when he went from a maharajah's stable boy to screen fame as the *Elephant Boy* (1937), Sabu ("Sah-boo," accent on the first syllable) was discovered by a British cinematographer and, once cast, was afforded a movie heroine's close-up as he wakes up alongside an elephant and stretches a good morning. Brought to Britain to finish some of his scenes for that legendary Alexander Korda jungle adventure, he stayed on to achieve international fame as a gorgeous half-naked youth in a series of exotic pictures. He was 16 when he sat in the hand of the genie in *The Thief of Bagdad* (1940) and 18 when he played Hollywood's first live action Mowgli in *Jungle Book* (1942). Photographers habitually posed him as if he were a glamorous movie starlet. Audiences could always count on seeing him in little more than his loincloth in these pictures, so it would be plain prudish of me to ignore his effect on young and old men alike: Tarzan as a twink. Even his sidekick appearances in Universal's Technicolor B-jungle adventures had their secret followings and some, like *White Savage* (1943) and *Cobra Woman*, are camp classics.

He had a beautiful body, a gentle voice, and a winning grin. He was the legitimate article, a real Indian native boy who wandered onto the set of a movie and became its star. In America, he was usually dressed and photographed as if he were an Indian prince. He joined the US Army in 1944 and served as a B-24 belly-gunner. After the war, he found it difficult to find steady work in an industry that had typed him to play a single role, one which required his youth.

Jon Hall, quite fortunately, had prosperous off-screen businesses developing underwater camera equipment (used by the Navy, as well as Hollywood), building boats, and operating a flying school when acting finally dried up for him. Still, an entire generation of kids remembers him as the fully-clothed jungle

Sabu, the maharajah's stable boy who became a Hollywood star in *The Thief of Bagdad* (1940) and *Jungle Book* (1942). YESTERDAY

doctor on TV's *Ramar of the Jungle* (1952-54). Sabu kept his young family supported between shirtless acting gigs by purchasing apartment buildings. Both men died young. Hall took his own life at age 66 after struggling with bladder cancer and Sabu suffered a fatal heart attack at age 39.

Hollywood, it's no revelation, was and is an eating machine. Enjoy your time in the sun, because if they think you wear your talent on your face or your physique, there are a lot of other beautiful boys out there.

When Columbia Pictures went casting for a new star to be their *Golden Boy* (1939), the violinist who becomes a boxer thanks to Clifford Odets, the studio posted a wanted list: Tyrone Power's hair, Errol

Flynn's forehead, Charles Boyer's eyes, Wayne Morris' nose, Cary Grant's chin, Joel McCrea's jaw contour, Robert Taylor's mouth, and Franchot Tone's smile. These days they could probably cobble together all of the above with digital imaging, but back then they got **William Holden** (1918-1981).

It was a coveted role in Hollywood and an entire roster of likely leading men were turned away at the insistence of the director, who had seen 21-year old Holden's screen test and was set on having him. Four days into the shooting, the young actor fell apart under the pressure, walked off the film, and had to be coaxed back by his compassionate leading lady and mentor, Barbara Stanwyck. Holden certainly had the looks and the physique for the role. On top of that, it's a strong performance in a good part: a sensitive boy torn between his love of music, family, and a girl, and his masculine-calculated success as a pugilist. After the war, Holden would emerge as a solid leading man and something of a sex symbol, alternately baring his naturally hairy or studio-shorn chest in *The Bridges of Toko-Ri* (1954), *Picnic* (1955), *The Proud and the Profane* (1956), and *The Bridge on the River Kwai* (1957).

In 1940, a year after Holden's *Golden Boy* had us wishing all our favorite leading men would take up the sport of boxing on-screen, the first Mr. America contest was held. For gay men, bodybuilding's move from a personal fitness program to a competitive sport recognized by the Amateur Athletic Union meant an even steadier and more readily available supply of male imagery. Bob Hoffman's *Strength and Health* was just the first in a long line of muscle magazines featuring bare-chested men that eventually turned up on drugstore shelves. Joe Weider's present day bodybuilding publication empire also blossomed in the 1940s, with *Muscle Builder* and the long-running *Muscle & Fitness* magazine among them.

The "legitimized" bodybuilding movement proved itself a convenient cover for publishers and photographers interested in homoerotic imagery who immediately understood its potential as a commercial vehicle. Bob Mizer founded his famed Athletic Model Guild in Los Angeles in 1945 ostensibly to serve as an agency for young actors and male models, but his personal obsession with photographing them in posing straps fostered an entire physique magazine subgenre targeted at closeted gay men.

Betty Grable's cheesecake photo adorned the barracks of many a soldier in World War II. She and half a million others like her in various states of undress helped remind the guys what they were fighting for, why they were sharing such cramped quarters with a bunch of other smelly men. Poster babes must have been a pretty welcome sight after all the hairy asses one had to endure seeing in the showers. Not that anyone was looking, of course. Then again, some of those hairy asses belonged to Hollywood's finest.

With so many of their biggest male stars serving in the military during World War II, including Gable, Power, Holden, and Taylor, the studios attempted to flaunt stand-ins. Dana Andrews was the slated threat to Tyrone Power's vacancy. Paramount introduced **Sonny Tufts** (1911-1970) in 1943, but the tall, plain-faced blond with the vaguely dirty name (he was born Bowen Charlton Tufts III) could never have caught on and by the 1950s he was the butt of jokes related to his non-acting ability and allegations that he liked to bite showgirls' thighs.

Equally as tabloidish, millionaire aviator, playboy, and movie producer Howard Hughes was battling the motion picture censor's office over the content and marketing of his film *The Outlaw*, begun in 1940. Everybody and their brother-in-law knows that Hughes' apparent obsession with 19-year old Jane Russell's breasts caused quite an uproar at the time. The censors forced him to cut eleven minutes of footage, most of it showing Ms. Russell stooping.

What most people don't know is what all the cleaving left intact: *The Outlaw* (1943) is a gay camp classic as deserving of a following as Joan Crawford in Nicholas Ray's *Johnny Guitar* (1954). Doc Holliday (Walter Huston) is looking for "the cutest little fella you ever saw, mean as mean, but I dote on him like he was pure rock candy." He's "about 13 hands high and cute as a bug's ear." He might as well be talking about Billy the Kid as his stolen horse.

The Kid is played by newcomer **Jack Beutel** (1915-1989), an insurance clerk from Dallas whom the camera occasionally captures as a sultry brunette. Billy learns that Doc's horse will hoof him in the crotch—with no ill effect—whenever he says "shake hands," and while we wonder where the Kid keeps his balls, we revel in the naked truth that Beutel is an amateur actor without a clue as to how to deliver a line.

"He may shoot me in the back," says the outlaw when Sheriff Pat Garrett (Thomas Mitchell) sneaks up behind him in the barn. "They tell me that's the way *you've* given it to some of the boys," replies the lawman. "Well, Sheriff," says the Kid, "if you believe that, here's your chance to do the same to me." The bounty of double entendre commences and variations on "turn my back" find 'hole' new meanings.

Jack Beutel as Billy the Kid in Howard Hughes' gay camp classic *The Outlaw* (1943). AUTHOR'S COLLECTION

The elder Doc befriends the Kid and covers his little backside in order to walk away from the tight situation. Outside the hotel, Billy suggests, "Doc, if you're not already fixed up, you can bunk with me tonight." "No thanks, Billy. I've got a girl." Billy doesn't, though. He doesn't trust them. All he's got is his horse and it's not even his horse.

Guarding the animal in the stable that night, Billy is nearly shot by a stranger in the dark. After a tackled roll in the hay, he ends up atop Rio McDonald (Jane Russell), a raving beauty whose brother was killed by the Kid. She's feisty, gorgeous, and yes, busty. He lets her up, but she tries to prick him with a pitchfork and so he wrestles her back into the censor's darkness and we hear clothing being ripped. "Hold still lady or you won't have much dress left!" is followed by a long, slowed static shot before we fade out.

Then, as if in answer to the question on all of our minds, we hear voices on the audio track arguing, "He did not." "I say he did." The voices belong to a pack of little boys waiting to see the Kid, and ensuing dialogue about how to make a whistle out of a willow stick has inappropriate possibilities.

Billy accompanies Doc to the saloon. "How about a cold hand while we're waiting?" A man interrupts and asks Billy to "go in the back room" with him. He ends up having to kill the guy and then gets wounded himself by the Sheriff before escaping with the Doc to Rio's desert hut. She nurses her rapist and brother's murderer through a month-long delirium, but can't keep her cock out of his face, so she cooks the pesky bird for dinner. During his worst bout with the chills, she pulls off her shoes, tells him, "You're not gonna die...I'll get you warm," then shuts the door and a wave of music swells and crashes for the fade-out, as it does whenever there's an intimation of scandalous passion.

When Doc finds out, he's furious. Aunt Guadalupe, who stays at the hut, too, explains that the Kid's "the devil. He did the same to me. He can charm a bird right out of a bush." "Yes, or a...," says Doc, looking Rio up and down.

Billy and Doc make up that very night when they discover that they're both happy to be sexist pigs, equating the use of Rio to the use of Doc's horse.

A pissed Rio sends the Sheriff after both of them and ends up strung between boulders in the desert with a gag in her mouth, looking all the world like a panel from a Bettie Page fetish magazine. "You know, I think he's in love with you," offers Doc when he finds her.

Finally caught and cuffed at the hands and feet, the Kid chimes in when Rio is told to hurry up and fix some grub. She says she's only got two hands. Well, why don't you use both of them, he wisecracks.

"I'll use one on you in a minute," she sasses.

"I wouldn't put it past ya," he fires back. "Now's your chance, with me all trussed up like a chicken." Between the "all" and "trussed" of that line, Billy launches his legs into the air in submissive surrender and I'll be damned if the angle doesn't provide the sexiest little invite to violate that boy butt good. It's the gayest shot in the flick.

The film moves to an ear-piercing climax that proves it's really the tale of a gay love triangle and, legend be damned, the giant bosom (both in or spilling out of Hughes' own specially designed lifting bra) turns out to be just an accessory, a live-action corollary for twin canteens.

I'm sure straight audiences have a lustier take on the importance of Russell's breasts. Their widespread and controversial exploitation as part of this film's ad campaign undoubtedly resulted in many fond memories for young men at the time. It's apropos, however, that the bisexual Hughes first opened the film in 1943 at the Gaiety Theatre in San Francisco. He did so without the Seal of Approval from the Hays Office, the first to openly defy the censorship board. Without a major distributor willing to touch it, *The Outlaw* vanished again until a 1945 limited release, and then re-appeared in 1950, ten years after Hughes personally took over the direction and had shot 45 times the amount of film he ever used.

Jack Beutel can't be beat, but certainly should have been Billy-clubbed. I like his long eyelashes, the way he blows a beautiful smoke ring out of those wet lips, that sweet cleft in his chin, the way his Billy seems to get dumber as the movie goes along. My only regret is that we don't get to see him shirtless while Rio is tending to his alternating chills and sweats. One of the censor's concerns upon reading the final script was that "care will be needed in this scene of Rio putting the hot stones in the bed. There must be no scene...of her putting them against Billy's thighs." Actually, he looks his most unattractive while shot from a low angle in those bedridden scenes, and there are times when he seems to look best only in medium close-up, but then he'll surprise you with a properly winning screen filler. Of course, it helps if he keeps his mouth shut.

He went into the Navy during the war and it's said that when he got out Howard Hawks wanted him to play the role Montgomery Clift played opposite John Wayne in *Red River* (1948). Sadly for him, but thankfully for us, the other Howard still had him under contract and wouldn't let him do it. He managed to appear in a few B-Westerns and television episodes in the '50s, with his last name interchangeably spelled either B*eu*tel or B*ue*tel, then abandoned his acting career.

Robert Ozell Moseley was still in the Navy when fittingly cast in a small role as a sailor on leave in the Homefront, USA WWII epic *Since You Went Away* (1944). He shot his stint on a weekend pass after being discovered by famed Selznick talent scout/agent Henry Willson, who promptly renamed him **Guy Madison** (1922-1996). Guy was a swell name for a guy who looked like he was snipped out of a dictionary next to

Guy Madison holds Robert Mitchum *Till the End of Time* (1946). author's collection

the definition of, well, a guy. His new last name came off the side of a Dolly Madison truck.

Robert Walker and Jennifer Jones are at the bowling alley throwing gutter balls while a cute-as-a-button sailor ha-ha-ha's them and ludicrously pretends not to be paying attention whenever they look back at him. Walker eventually gets up the nerve to confront the pretty boy and then faints in front of him. They re-group for a conciliatory stroll where the sailor who's a farm boy says "gee" and "swell" and sports a positively huge shock of blond hair that funnels in front of his forehead.

After the nice sailor gets on his bus and leaves, the wimpy Robert Walker character, speaking in a high-pitched voice, says he feels like a fool. He's flustered about the encounter. "He's good-looking, isn't he?" he asks Jones.

"He is? I hadn't noticed," she replies.

"You must have noticed." She says she didn't. But it's just to pump Walker up. I like the fact that his milquetoast, insecure soldier is the one who brings up Madison's looks and appears to have been intimidated by them. Makes the fainting in the bowling alley seem less like fear and more like swoon, no matter how out of context you have to go to get there.

Madison made enough of a visual impression during his four minutes on screen playing "himself" that after his service was completed he was loaned out by Selznick for a starring role opposite Robert Mitchum in *Till the End of Time* (1946), a soldiers-come-home drama showing the difficulty of fitting back into civilian life. He's a gorgeous young man with naturally tousled blond hair, a soft cleft in his chin, and a warm smile that brings out his dimples. He's also an actor afforded reaction shots in which he seems to be waiting for a cue that never comes.

When he talks, you can almost see the words on the screenplay in front of him. Nothing he says sounds spontaneous. The clammy dialogue doesn't help, like when he tries to tell his mom in a delicate way that a foxhole is the equivalent of three men lying down inside a telephone booth and that it really "stunk." He got through it, though, by thinking of her waffles. One of the picture's certainly unintended but unavoidable morals is to be especially thankful if you come back from war in one piece...and still handsome.

He's got a very nice body on him and was even allowed to keep his naturally hairy chest, an almost unheard of accommodation particularly for a young man being marketed as a dreamboat to a young audience. If they imagined taking him to their school sock-hop, however, the dance scene in *Till the End* might convince them to skip the dance and just go parking.

His acting powers never quite caught up with his very pleasant baritone voice and his flat demeanor never quite managed to stir the air when he was on-screen in the late 1940s and early 1950s.

"I'm not made of stone," he says in *Honeymoon* (1947) as Shirley Temple's fiancé, but his delivery and gestures don't convince otherwise.

He was very bland. You find yourself staring at his beautiful face and not paying attention to a word he's saying. Westerns were a natural genre for such a style and he found success as the star of 113 episodes of television's *The Adventures of Wild Bill Hickok* (1951-58), and its radio equivalent (1951-56). He also played Hickok in no fewer than 15 features from 1952-55. In 1960, he began a fifteen year, 25+ film career making westerns and assorted action dramas in Europe.

Being handpicked a filmmaker's protégé was a pretty good way of getting a job. Being his lover could come in handy, too. Poet, painter, playwright, novelist, designer, and all around French cultural hyphenate Jean Cocteau directed nine films and five of them starred his lover **Jean Marais** (1913-1999). *La Belle et la bête* (*The Beauty and the Beast*; 1946) may just be the most poetic evocation of a fairy tale ever committed to celluloid. The blond locks and chiseled face of Marais—an angular handsome threatened by femininity—that are so fully apparent in his roles as Avenant and The Prince, are transformed under the astonishing make-up by Arakelian for his Beast, with his ears twitching and his claws smoking with blood. He is also painfully romantic and sensitive. Marais' expressive eyes and the quiet rasp of his voice enchant us, fill us with his longing and self-hate. By the film's end, in which the heartbroken Beast is reborn as a full-fledged fop, the Prince can't help being other than disappointing. It was Marais' Beast that was the Beauty.

Marais was himself the beauty, a stunning Tristan who prefers to celebrate his engagement to Isolde by wrestling her brother rather than making love to her, in the Cocteau-scripted *L'Eternal retour* (1943). The actor's appeal was literally reflective, even statuary in Cocteau's *Orphée* (*Orpheus*; 1949), playing the poet who must traverse the underworld in search of his wife after a fling with beautiful Death. The extricated still image of his Nordic face pressed up against the mirror in seeming self-love has become an icon for narcissism. Considering he was rejected several times while applying to drama schools as a youth, even Marais, now the inspiration for his lover's creative works, couldn't have predicted the career ahead of him.

He started appearing in films as early as 1933 and eventually matured into one of France's busiest leading men in the 1950s, when his looks hardened and he began to thicken. He's Victor Hugo's title character *Ruy Blas* (1947), a failed poet on a mule who circumstantially rises to great heights in his beloved queen's court; likewise, an anarchist poet come to assassinate the queen he fatally loves in *L'Aigle à deux têtes* (*The Eagle With Two Heads*; 1947); and, dimples and all, is Cocteau's emotionally-ravaged Michel of *Les Parents terribles* (1948), a good son doted upon to the point of collapse by a possessive mother and

Jean Marais as the fairy tale Prince transformed from the beautiful Beast in Cocteau's classic *La Belle et la bête* (1946). PHOTOFEST

her psychosexually dysfunctional family when he announces he is to marry. His final film appearance, at age 83, in *Stealing Beauty* (1996) capped a flurry of activity for him in the 1990s (including playing Prospero and headlining at Les Folies Bergeres) and restored the sight of his exquisite cheekbones to their rightful place on the silver screen.

Louis Jourdan (1919-   ) had both ladies and gay countrymen alike in a swoon while playing the sophisticated and drop-dead gorgeous romantic lead in French films since 1939. He joined the Resistance during the war following his father's arrest by the Nazis. In 1948, he brought his continental good looks and hermetically-sealed persona to Hollywood for Alfred Hitchcock's *The Paradine Case*, as the pitch black-haired and quite sullen valet with whom Alida Valli is dallying. He's given a dramatic entrance 41 minutes into the film, his elegant features masked by shadows when Gregory Peck comes to call. Five minutes later, he's afforded a stunning close-up as Peck pulls open the curtains to the back door of his hotel room late at night and the criss-cross of the window pane quadrisects Jourdan's smooth, angular face. Set up in court to be a woman-hater based on a previous marriage jilt, Jourdan gets tossed a veiled compliment from judge Charles Laughton, who takes into account Louis' appearance and suggests that any woman who left him at the altar might herself be considered "pathological."

More female trouble in *Letter from an Unknown Woman* (1948), in which his splendidly cheekboned pianist screws up his life and everybody else's by failing to remember what Joan Fontaine looks like. He's surprisingly lively as an eccentric artist pursuing client Dana Andrews' wife in *No Minor Vices* (1948), and makes a devastatingly dashing Rodolphe to Jennifer Jones' *Madame Bovary* (1949). He's a half-naked Frenchman finding out the hard way about Polynesian customs and taboos while wooing a South Seas chieftain's daughter in *Bird of Paradise* (1951), an ex-pirate captain conquered by *Anne of the Indies* (1951), quite the engaging ladies' man as Uncle Desmonde in *The Happy Time* (1952), a bore x4 in *Decameron Nights* (1953), Prince Dino Di Cessi in *Three Coins in the Fountain* (1954), and a velvet-toned tutor hopelessly in love with princess Grace Kelly in *The Swan* (1956). *Gigi* (1958), *Can-Can* (1960), *Swamp Thing* (1982), and *Octopussy* (1983) would follow.

Gérard Philipe (1922-1959), like Jourdan, was the son of a hotelier, but unlike Jourdan, Hollywood couldn't suck him across the Atlantic. Philipe quickly became one of France's favorite romantic leads on both stage and film after he lent his comely beauty to the tortured youth romancing a soldier's wife in the controversial *Le Diable au corps* (*The Devil in the Flesh*; 1946). Playing a love-crazed schoolboy of 17, with big hair, dimples, and sparkling eyes, it's easy to see why audiences fell for him, even if the underage love affair and betrayal of the husband caused moral outrage at the time and resulted in its censure and

Louis Jourdan takes a dip into American film stardom. PHOTOFEST

The lovely and tragically short-lived Gérard Philipe.
PHOTOFEST

banning. The film was based on the sensational novel by 17-year old Raymond Radiguet, the boy-beauty who was once Jean Cocteau's beloved and died of typhus at age 20. (The 1986 screen version of the story gained international notoriety for the brief scene in which actress Maruschka Detmers gives young Federico Pitzalis an on-screen blow job.)

Philipe is almost completely unknown here in the States, but was so good-looking he couldn't escape eventually being dubbed the first of many "next James Deans" in France, even though he pre-dates Dean. He actually bears a resemblance to British contemporary Dirk Bogarde in his leading man days. One of Gérard's most popular outings was playing

Philipe and Micheline Presle as scandalous lovers in the controversial *Le Diable au corps* (1946). AUTHOR'S COLLECTION

a vivacious and sexy swashbuckler in the light-hearted *Fanfan la Tulipe* (1951), though the actor developed a reputation for specializing in literary adaptations, having already essayed Dostoevsky's Prince Myshkin in *L'Idiot* (1946). He's delightful as Old Faust turned to young Faust in René Clair's *La Beauté du diable* (*Beauty and the Devil*; 1950). Racing into the street after enjoying his newfound youth at a local café, he stops for a glance at himself in the waters of a fountain. "Merci, Mephisto!" He likes what he sees...and so do we. He's the lively carnival barker who introduces us to *Les Sept péchés capitaux* (*The Seven Deadly Sins*; 1952), as well as humorously shaming our dirty minds with an eighth.

He's Stendhal's tragic hero Julien Sorel, fatally in love with a pair of women while pursuing life in the Church because even kings bow before bishops, in *Les Rouge et le noir* (*The Red and the Black*; 1954); had previously essayed Stendhal's young priest, Fabrice Del Dongo, who covets life as a prisoner of love in *La Chartreuse de Parme* (*The Charterhouse of Parma*; 1948); played a drunken doctor in a small Mexican village faced with an epidemic of meningitis and the love of the woman whose husband brought it in *Les Orgueilleux* (*The Proud Ones*; 1953); sought solace from the drudgery of everyday living as a poor musician by dreaming himself into other time periods in *Les Belles de nuit* (*Beauties of the Night*; 1953); struck a dashing D'Artagnan in *Si Versailles m'était conté* (*Royal Affairs in Versailles*; 1954); and falls hopelessly in love while foolishly pursuing a macho wager to "find favor" with a blonde divorcee from Paris in *Les Grandes manoeuvres* (*The Grand Maneuver*; 1955).

Not surprisingly, his good looks and abundant charms meant he was cast many times over as philanderers and rakes. In Max Ophuls' *La Ronde* (1950), he shows up in the final episode, "The Actress and the Count," to bring Schnitzler's somber play of cuckolds and unhappy lovers full circle. His disenchanted clerk wiles several women in *Monsieur Ripois* (*Knave of Hearts*; *Lovers, Happy Lovers*; 1954), though there's something so infectious about him, even in deceit, that one wishes to make his ledger. Ditto for being counted among his conquests at the boarding house in *Pot-Bouille* (1957).

He followed his acclaimed performance as Valmont in Roger Vadim's *Les Liaisons dangereuses 1960* (1959), an effective modernization of the classic tale of sexual cruelties, with a miscast assignment in Luis Buñuel's *La Fièvre monte à El Pao* (*Fever Mounts at El Pao*, aka *Republic of Sin*; 1960), then died of a heart attack (while battling liver cancer) shortly after completing the project. Gérard Philipe made just over 30 films, as did Valentino, but attained a legendary hold over his audience as a beloved icon of both stage and screen.

Italian director Luchino Visconti, whose eye for beautiful leading men will make him a recurring figure in this text, began his feature film career with an Italian neorealist version of James M. Cain's novel *The Postman Always Rings Twice*. *Ossessione* (1942) starred 24-year old **Massimo Girotti** (1918-2003) as the humpy young drifter who complicates the life of an unhappily married beauty at a roadside restaurant and filling station. Visconti's black-and-white adoration of Girotti in a dirty muscle T prefigured Brando's fashion fetish by nearly a decade. The hair sprouting from Girotti's shoulders and back did not.

The end of the 1940s saw the double-whammy whack at the studios and what has become known as the studio system when Congress mandated them to divest their theater-ownership monopolies and Uncle Miltie's *Texaco Star Theater* had the masses parked in front of their new TVs. If the movies were going to compete, they had to get sexier. And so did the stars. Marilyn Monroe, not quite there yet, was paid fifty dollars to pose nude for that soon-to-be world-famous calendar in 1949. Male actors weren't ready to go that far—at least for public consumption—but the beef in beefcake was close at hand.

The 1950s — Take One

"Live Fast, Die Young, Have A Good-Looking Corpse"

When a skinny young pup named **Montgomery Clift** (1920-1966) holds his own in a fistfight with John Wayne, there's something more than meets the eye. For one great knock 'em down sequence in *Red River* (1948), the new generation of actor takes on the old generation of actor and a lady has the good sense to step in and point out that they're fighting because they really love each other. I'll forego any suggestion that acting styles were combating, because Wayne was a seriously underrated actor and had already demonstrated a facility for giving "natural" performances. Often when critics wrote that "John Wayne was John Wayne," they were paying him a compliment that wouldn't be seen as such for decades.

Clift, who was nervous about going up against such a legendary film icon and making a credible impression, determined that the only way to get noticed alongside the Duke was to underplay. The result is something quite remarkable: a cowboy who commands our attention not just because he's written to capture our allegiance, but because he's beautiful enough to capture our affections. I say that without intending to denigrate the enormity of Clift's talent, but to point out that his physical beauty was a powerful tool for an actor in a medium of images. Hundreds of actors are worth a second glance—that's what this book celebrates—but only a few have what it takes to show you what's under their skin. Monty Clift was one of them.

Edward Montgomery Clift was born in Omaha, Nebraska, the surprise follow-up to his twin sister's arrival. He and his sister and older brother were exclusively raised by their irrepressible mother, known as Sunny, who spent her entire life struggling to be acknowledged as the granddaughter of Union Civil War hero Col. Robert Anderson, a wealthy and noble family tie. A disapproved marriage had led to her adoption and there was resistance and denial ever after. While her husband stayed put and worked to support them, Sunny took her children on frequent jaunts to Europe and saw to it they were tutored in languages, music, theatre, ballet—all the arts. Playmates were not allowed.

The snobbish brood didn't fare well on return trips to the States, where Monty would get beat up in the public schools. Even when the Clifts lost most of their money in the Crash, the children were told to go on as if nothing had happened. Sunny was a stage mother, as in all the world's a stage. She hadn't encouraged her youngest son to act, but when it happened for the first time in an amateur theatre production when he was 13, the reactions to her beautiful boy and the joy he seemed to get out of it convinced her to give him a little push.

He began as a juvenile model for Arrow shirts in New York, work he despised. His mother continued to orchestrate every aspect of his life, fully babying him to the point of rebellion. At 18, critics took notice of him for his sensitive portrayal of a 15-year-old father in the play *Dame Nature*. Off-stage his own sexual nature was at odds. He would have relations with both women and men, but seemed to prefer men sexually.

A trip to Mexico resulted in a nasty bout of amoebic dysentery, a condition that exacted inestimable damage on his long-term well being.

Striving to move out of the clutches of his mother, he would practically be adopted by the famed husband and wife acting team of Alfred Lunt and Lynn Fontanne, who provided an affectionate and life-expanding tutorial in the dramatic arts while the three appeared in *There Shall Be No Night* on Broadway in 1940. MGM offered the gorgeous young stage actor a standard seven-year movie contract to begin with a role in *Mrs. Miniver* (1942), but he turned them down flat, worried that he would be little more than a "slave."

His dysentery meant he was 4F for military service and free to pursue his stage career. He befriended playwright Thornton Wilder, who became a mentor, and starred in his Pulitzer Prize-winning play *The Skin of Our Teeth* (1942) with Tallulah Bankhead and Fredric March. None other than Elia Kazan, the era's

Montgomery Clift seems unsure of his wardrobe test for *The Heiress* (1948). PHOTOFEST

most important director with the era's most profound casting eye, directed the production.

It was also at this time that he met Mira Rostova, the actress who became his acting coach and eventually his acting crutch. He continued to decline offers from "Vomit, California," a place he was certain wouldn't allow him to have the creative input he thrived on. It's a convenient stance for our purposes, as Clift would usher in a new wave of fiercely independent actors at a time when the old studio system was in demise.

Howard Hawks saw Clift in the Tennessee Williams' play *You Touched Me!* (1945), adapted from a D. H. Lawrence short story, and the actor took the offered role in *Red River* because there were no other strings attached. It was a one-shot deal. The film's release was delayed, among other things, by a lawsuit filed by Howard Hughes, who ludicrously claimed literal scene-stealing from *The Outlaw*, so by the time the picture hit the big screen, Clift was working on his third.

His second film, actually his first to make it to theatres, was *The Search* (1948), which he agreed to do only because he was promised creative input. In fact, he enraged the film's screenwriter by re-writing most of his dialogue and improvising extensively; the end result winning the Academy Award for Best Screenplay. He wanted to play real people, not movie people. The film's long, tedious set-up should have been scissored in order to begin with the little Czech boy wandering through the ruins of Berlin and coming across American soldier Clift sitting in his jeep. It's a mesh of old Hollywood corn and sentiment with the fresh face and sparkling eyes of a bright new brand of star. The movie industry sensed something was up, too, because Clift received his first Academy Award nomination for playing the charismatic and self-effacing young Army engineer hoping to reunite the lost boy with his mother.

Clift was literally and figuratively the face of things to come, landing the cover of *Life* magazine as the angelic poster boy for the "new male movie stars" on December 6, 1948. Some of his generation's significant others shared classes with him for his stint as a founding member of New York's Actor's Studio (Brando, Julie Harris, Maureen Stapleton) before he methodically rejected its religious dogma. Clift wanted the freedom to imagine his characters' lives, not give birth to them out of his primordial ooze. Unfortunately, it was his primordial ooze that would increasingly taint his creative juices.

The new male sex star, exploited by magazines as such, hated being the new male sex star. The new male sex star was, in fact, a conflicted homosexual and a heavy drinker whose first glance after a take was behind the camera to his acting guru, Ms. Rostova, who gauged his performance with an approving or disapproving nod. She would provide this "service," much to the horror of directors, on and off for his first seven pictures.

Increasingly insecure about his performances, and often quite vocal about hating them, he became his own worst enemy in the non-reassuring "you're your own worst enemy" sort of way. He really was bad for himself.

I only wish he knew just how good he could be. In *The Heiress* (1949), he is so good that his character's revelatory insincerity is conveyed with a pause and a simple, but brilliantly inflected "Oh, Catherine" after the first time he kisses her. What makes it even more astonishing is that the moment comes with his face turned 3/4 away from the camera. The whole scene is lit for Olivia de Havilland. She is "open" and he is "hidden," but Clift acts through the back of his head.

"Oh, father," de Havilland asks Ralph Richardson, "don't you think he is the most beautiful man you've ever seen?"

"Well, he is very good-looking, my dear. Of course, you wouldn't let a consideration like that sway you unduly."

He signed a three-picture contract with Paramount Studios, of which *The Heiress* was the first, only because he was given an almost unheard-of script approval perk. Meanwhile, he turned down *Sunset Blvd.* (1950), which was written for him. In *The Big Lift* (1950), he's the WWII Air Force pretty boy who's suspicious of the press wanting to use his image to promote something he's not. Walking down a corridor created by the German honor guard out on the airfield, he says he feels like he's getting married to the soldier next to him. Homo-macho was as close a way to kid about your real feelings as you could come in those days.

Immortality first fiddled with Monty when Paramount took a second shot at bringing Theodore Dreiser's *An American Tragedy* to the screen and decided that they should protect the investment and turn the tragedy into a romantic tragedy. *A Place in the Sun* (1951) begins with Monty Clift—dressed in a white T-shirt—boxing swimsuits in a factory. By the time our American Everyman says of Elizabeth Taylor, "I loved you before I saw you," the hook is in and we're all supposed to relate to the desire of a nobody to become a somebody.

If only Clift and the prejudicially thicker Shelley Winters, whom he's knocked up, hadn't chosen the Labor Day holiday to try and get hitched, we probably wouldn't find ourselves out on Loon Lake contemplating her pre-*Poseidon Adventure* glug-glug. Of course, the warnings on the radio about driving and drowning tragedies, pre-accident, don't help.

Clift and Taylor are perhaps the two most beautiful members of their respective sexes to warrant passionate close-ups and for that we can be eternally grateful. Their giant faces—his comes complete with a scar on his right cheek—positively radiate and both have eyes of such expression and beauty that black-

and-white photography can't dissuade you from dreamily guessing their colors, then wishing that the cinematographer would let Monty step out of the darkness, stop shooting his "guilty" character from behind or in profile. James Dean sat through this film over and over again just to study Clift. He was amazed by his every nuance, what *Variety* criticized as "overly-laconic." Monty received his second Oscar nomination.

The problem with this hugely popular "classic" is that the American tragedy is transparent. It's all about figures and symbols. The dream is a nightmare. The goal lost before it's won. Taylor is Angela in white. Monty's crime is too easy to link. Does he want to get caught?

It must be that the idea and not the act goes on trial at the film's end, because pre-*Perry Mason* Raymond Burr's prosecution is too blatant, too melodramatic. And then there's that priceless newspaper headline: "Verdict expected momentarily."

"I chose to be what I am. I believe in what I am. I want you to see things as they are and not go on hurting yourself," says Clift's Catholic priest in Alfred Hitchcock's dreadful *I Confess* (1953). Words that might just as well have been spoken to Elizabeth Taylor, who developed a crush on Clift and a desire to marry him. They remained life-long friends, though "long" seems a bit of a stretch all things considered. Monty was an alcoholic and a rabid pill-popper by now.

He met *From Here To Eternity* (1953) author James Jones at a party and they went to a bar and got drunk together, sealing the personal choice of Clift over the studio's choice of John Derek to play Robert E. Lee Prewitt, the GI bugler with hurt feelings who quits boxing after blinding a guy. The film was a sensational hit and vastly acclaimed by the critics, winning Oscars for just about everybody except third-time nominee Monty Clift. He was pissed by the omission.

He was also piss drunk a lot of the time during the making of the film. Appropriately, his character is a drinker, too. For the scene in which he and Burt Lancaster sit soused on the roadside and Lancaster tells him to seek refuge in another spot, Clift was actually liquored up, humorously defying his personal obsession to minimize the number of lines by ad libbing, "I don't think I coulda got up anyway." Lancaster is clearly acting. You're not so sure about Monty.

The film is most famous for the Lancaster-Kerr smooch on the beach scene with the waves crashing over them, but it's a gelded version of the novel's imputation of the military and you can tell something's not quite right when the flow of dialogue suggests Lancaster's admitting he's got a bathing suit under his dress, too.

Monty registers his trademark calm amidst the variable acting styles of his co-stars, but he's not terribly convincing when it comes to his fight scenes. Great care had to be taken to edit a fighter out of him, because he just didn't know how to throw a punch. He's also been subjected to an aesthetic body shave.

He's so skinny and physically awkward that it's nearly miscasting to have him play a boxer in *Eternity* and then a champion runner in *Raintree County* (1957), the epic-length Civil War opera in need of a lot more opera. Monty's just another half-scorched doll in the collection of spoiled Southern belle Liz Taylor.

In a matter of just a few short years, Monty's health collapsed into chaos. He was seeing a psychiatrist, the now-notorious Dr. William Silverberg, a gay shrink who befriended him, provided him with endless supplies of prescription drugs, fatalistically ignored his debilitating alcoholism, and—some say—encouraged his homosexuality without resolving its conflict. Friends were appalled by the 14+ year relationship and its fall-out and many of them fell helplessly by the wayside to preserve their own sanity when there was nothing more to be done for Monty. He was subject to blackouts, frequent night wanderings through the streets stark naked, chain-smoking, taking barbiturates by the truckloads, insomnia, tantrums, deep depressions, drunkenness, and car accidents.

On the night of May 12, 1956, while following his good friend Kevin McCarthy home from a party at Elizabeth Taylor's, he crashed his car and shattered his face. His two bottom front teeth were lodged in his esophagus and Taylor stuck her fingers down his throat and retrieved them to clear his breathing. After his nine-week hospital recuperation, necessitating a wired jaw but no plastic surgery, he gave the teeth to her.

He predicted that audiences would go to *Raintree County* to see which scenes were pre-accident and which were post. Much has been made of the destruction of his beauty and the contrast of his face from scene to scene, but near as I can tell, without having seen the film on the big screen, the post-accident shots occupy a minimum of screen time.

The damage was done, however, physically and psychologically. A severed nerve resulted in the partial paralysis of the left side of his face. In combination with the damage he was self-inflicting, he now looked much older than 37 and there was a tendency to appear glassy-eyed and staring. He wondered what would become of his career now that he had "lost his face."

He had previously turned down *Shane* (1953), *Trapeze* (1956), and *Bus Stop* (1956), among others. He was already too old for *Raintree* and probably too old for *The Young Lions* (1958), in which Dean Martin asks him "Have you ever had a girl?" and suitably answers himself by saying, "Let us not discuss this sort of topic anymore, let us discuss alcohol." Clift plays the poor Jew who finally gets drafted into WWII to go up against the Nazis and his fellow anti-Semitic soldiers. As in *Eternity*, there's a masochistic streak to the part and he's repeatedly pummeled by the guys who stole twenty bucks from him. Certainly makes you despise the military experience. Clift kept pulling his lines and inspiration from the original Irvin Shaw novel, and not the wishy-washy screenplay, and said that Noah Ackerman was his favorite role. He was mortified when he wasn't even nominated for an Oscar. What he wanted to do was finally win one. (He never would, though he got a fourth nomination for Supporting Actor for his emotional seventeen-minute scene as a mentally handicapped man who was sterilized by the Nazis and provides court testimony in 1961's *Judgment at Nuremberg*.)

"He's the only person I know who's in worse shape than I am," said Marilyn Monroe of him. Monroe, Clift, and Clark Gable, a trio of film legends, co-starred in John Huston's truly strange anti-Western *The Misfits* (1961), and it would prove the last film for two of them. Written by Arthur Miller, whose marriage to Monroe was disintegrating, the film is a weird collision of recognizable movie star talent with an unrefined, almost slapdash style that threatens to turn into a cruel sideshow during its first two-thirds. The famous horse-roping finale, though, whose rigors both contributed to Gable's fatal heart attack and Monty's raw and bloody hands (he didn't wear gloves at first and then couldn't for continuity), belongs to a bona fide American film classic.

Montgomery Clift's physical and mental health continued under siege almost unabated. He fell down stairs, had equilibrium problems, spasms, lapses in memory, was diagnosed with hypothyroidism at age 39, suffered from varicose veins and a hernia, engaged in dangerous sexual liaisons, developed cataracts which required surgery—after which he was sued by the film studio for delaying production of *Freud* (1962), and was largely perceived by the industry as a physical wreck and an insurance liability. Yeah, Monty Clift was fucked up, but he was not without friends and family who cared or companions who did their best to put him back together. The actor who specialized in neurotic, wounded men was living as one, exponentially so. And just like in the movies, nearly everybody who gazed into those eyes felt compelled to reach out to try and help him, protect him, console him. Truth is stranger than fiction. Even Hollywood's brand.

Monty was found dead of a heart attack in the bedroom of his New York brownstone apartment at age 45 on July 23, 1966. He had made only 17 films, but his acting has informed and inspired each and every generation of actors since. Now there's beauty for you.

When the first cut of only eight occurs in Alfred Hitchcock's *Rope* (1948), it's from outside a window to inside the window where **Farley Granger** (1925-) can be seen strangling a man with a length of the title character. Quite unbelievably, the victim is standing, suggesting an agreed-upon experiment of some sort, like autoerotic asphyxia, but in suits. The breathy first lines between the two murderers, book-ending their prey, can't help suggestively comparing the moment of death to the moment of orgasm (the little death).

Famed for its queer style of ten-minute-long takes on a single set, the film is also famed for its queer leads. John Dall and Farley Granger (both gay) were never told they were playing homosexuals—even Hitch didn't bring it up—but everybody knew it, and the roles were loosely based on the notorious Leopold-Loeb murder case in 1920s Chicago in which two young Jewish lovers conspired to kill a pre-teen boy for the sheer intellectual thrill of it.

Granger plays the worry-wart of the two, the one who can't stop directing guilty-as-sin glances at the chest where they've hidden the body. Hitchcock wanted Montgomery Clift to play the instigating other half. Like the distasteful obsession of the two killers, the film is a queer intellectual exercise unto itself. The single takes are meaningless to the material only if you don't think about all the thought that went into orchestrating them—like the perfect crime, a cold attempt to get away with something unnatural. Both are qualified failures.

Granger's brown-suited pianist doesn't eat chicken ("How queer") because when he was a kid he was "quite a good chicken strangler," something he doesn't like to have brought up at dinner parties by his

Farley Granger, playing 23-year old "jail bait," with Cathy O'Donnell, as lovers on the run in the film noir thriller *They Live By Night* (1949). PHOTOFEST

cruel beau. The epithet is a kooky and appropriate one. In gay parlance, a "chicken" is a young man, or a boy.

If you're a good-looking kid who wants to be a film actor, you could do no better than to go to high school in Hollywood. Granger was a 17-year old North Hollywood high school chicken performing on stage at a local theater when a Goldwyn casting director liked what he saw. His angelic, dark-haired beauty was first lent a Soviet youth named Damian in the powerful propaganda film *North Star* (1943), a pro-Soviet vs. the Nazis piece that had to be drastically cut a decade later when the Reds were our "enemies." He also showed up in *The Purple Heart* (1944), as the youngest of eight service men tortured and tried for murder by a Japanese court. Granger then went into the Navy himself.

Fresh out, he was at his best in the film noir crime thriller *They Live By Night* (1949), the first feature directed by Nicholas Ray, who would later helm *Rebel Without A Cause* (1955). He's pretty enough to be playing 23-year old "jail bait," the youngest of a gang of criminals. Lying flat on his belly after he's sprung his back, he wonders why the young lady who has lifted his shirt and is busy rubbing him from behind gives a damn.

"I'd do this for a dog," she tells him.

When he asks her about men folk, she admits she's a virgin who never saw any use in having a fella. Yeah, he knows what that's like. He's a black sheep.

"The only thing black about you is your eyelashes," comes the come-on.

75

The young lovers trying to escape the temptations and vengeful clutches of the crime world make a fine pair at that. When a woman rides by on a horse, Granger goes wide-eyed. "Ain't that some way to ride? Bobbin' your bottom up and down like that?" The observation may have actually helped these dimwitted lovers grasp the mechanics, but the genre won't allow them to get a whole lot of practice despite the revelation of a baby on the way.

As the letter carrier who steals $30,000 from some crooks and regrets it almost immediately in *Side Street* (1949), Farley spills his guts to his wife at the county hospital. She's just had their baby son and, despite their troubles, "he's so wonderful," she tells him. "He's even prettier than I hoped he'd be."

"Boys aren't pretty," says her pretty boy husband.

"Ours is."

Granger was back to wartime duty as the handsome young man with the natural curls on top in *I Want You* (1951), complete with the breath-smelling intimacy of nose-to-nose romance. Hitchcock, surprisingly, came back for seconds and cast him as one of the two *Strangers On A Train* (1951). He's Guy, the celebrity tennis player whom the chillingly psychotic—and perhaps homosexual as well—Bruno Antony (Robert Walker) bumps shoes with on the choo-choo. Bruno wants to trade murders with this "guy" with the beautiful face and long lashes in a theoretical and thematic extension of *Rope*'s morbid fancies.

His butt is dutifully admired by Ann Blyth's precocious kid sister while he's on the roof putting up the aerial in the melodramatic *Our Very Own* (1950), and later we get to admire his hairy chest at the beach. He's a big city wiseacre on his way to elope with a Broadway star, then gets thrown in a rural slammer and refrains from singing, in the MGM musical *Small Town Girl* (1953).

Ultimately fearing the worst for himself as a leading man, what with his studio planting him in "The Gift of the Magi" sequence of *O. Henry's Full House* (1952) and as the ornery choreographer of the Royal Danish Ballet in *Hans Christian Andersen* (1952), Granger bought out his contract and sought work elsewhere.

At MGM, little Ricky Nelson visits a kindly witch in Rome and they conspire to turn him into Farley Granger between the hours of 8pm and midnight in "Mademoiselle," story two of *The Story of Three Loves* (1953). Unfortunately, his pajamas grow proportionally. He then went to Italy to work for Luchino Visconti on *Senso* (1954). Visconti wanted Brando, but the financiers insisted on Granger in the role of the Austrian-German lieutenant who occupies an Italian countess in Venice of 1866. He's the lover who sleeps over in all his buttons and clothes, awaking to tell his girl that he was dreaming: "I was playing soldiers with a wooden sword." By the film's end, he reveals himself a gambler, gigolo, and spy, a heartless user who tricked his lover into arranging a phony medical report declaring him unfit for duty. Generally speaking, actors who get nailed as "pretty" enjoy playing guys who turn out to be rats. "I'm not your romantic hero!" he screams at his Venetian beloved now betrayed. Farley Granger might have been screaming at us, too.

John Derek (1926-1999) moved behind the camera when he got fed up with the roles he was being offered. He's no doubt remembered today more for the films he directed starring his fourth wife, Bo Derek, than he is for a time in which he was himself considered a "10." Derek Harris was the son of parents in the movie biz themselves, which may or may not have been helpful. Everybody in Hollywood talks about how beautiful their children are, but Derek had the face to prove it.

He appeared in bit roles in a trio of Selznick studio films when he was still in his teens, then went off to military service. Upon his return, he officially received his "And Introducing John Derek" credit for the juvenile lead in Columbia's *Knock On Any Door* (1949). Directed by Nicholas Ray six years before he did *Rebel Without A Cause*, the film tells the story of a hoodlum from the New York City slums who's accused of a cop killing. "Pretty Boy Romano Trial Starts Today" read the headlines, identifying our young star by the first thing that comes to mind when you look at him.

Attorney Humphrey Bogart makes sure he loads the jury with women and coaches the dark-haired beauty to turn on that baby-face stare. The story is told in a series of flashbacks as Bogie defends the kid, and we get to see how he first got his nickname when a couple of local delinquents use it and then wrestle him in the alley. Spoiled rotten by all the bad breaks he's gotten in life, the kid even turns on his family. "Did I ask to get born?"

He's full of cracks like that. "All good guys get the dirty end of the stick." "Only suckas work." And most famously, when a stuttering barber warns him about the bad streets getting in his blood: "So it's in my blood? Who cares? Live fast, die young, have a good-looking corpse." (The punch line, an aphorism culled from

Nelson Algren's 1949 novel *The Man With the Golden Arm*.) He enjoys being a thug, pulling off petty robberies, stealing cars, getting slapped in the face by girls, acting the tough guy. Bogie intercedes from time to time to help the kid out, and for awhile he gets his act together, but then everything goes haywire again, ending tragically for the one girl he seemed to care about.

Like most court case flicks, the actual testimony is grossly lopsided, neither believable nor dramatic despite the surprise ending. A sketch artist's rendering of the kid in court looks exactly like an Arrow Collar shirt ad. The single joy of the courtroom scenes is hearing Derek declare under oath, "Yeah, I'm good looking." In the end, we're mercilessly hammered as a society that created this bad boy and ought to be ashamed of ourselves. Not quite an updated *Angels With Dirty Faces* (1938), *Knock On Any Door* nevertheless gave young John Derek a shot at stardom.

After serving little more purpose than a cosmetic one as the handsome adopted son of a political tyrant in *All the King's Men* (1949) and a star high school athlete who learns the hard way about the dirty politics of a college football scholarship in *Saturday's Hero* (1951), Derek got tossed into the usual costume adventures of the day that rarely advanced anyone's career. He played the son of Robin Hood, looking a bit like Errol Flynn but without the accent, in *Rogues of Sherwood Forest* (1950), a returning soldier who dons a black mask and seeks retribution for his father's death in *Mask of the Avenger* (1951), a 16th Century *Prince of Pirates* (1953), the famed Persian barber desired by harem girls in *The Adventures of Haji Baba* (1954), and the younger son and heir to the Shah in *Omar Khayyam* (1957).

There were also westerns, such as *The Last Posse* (1953), *Ambush at Tomahawk Gap* (1953), *The Outcast* (1954), and *Run for Cover* (1955). And there were war movies: *Thunderbirds* (1952), *Sea of Lost Ships* (1953), *Mission Over Korea* (1953), and *An Annapolis Story* (1955). In *Scandal Sheet* (1952), his long black lashes can't distract us from the fact that his and every other character in this indictment of the tabloid press is thoroughly contemptible.

"I know I fill a pair of tights satisfactorily," his mad matinee idol John Wilkes Booth (without accent) tells brother Edwin (Richard Burton, with) in *Prince of Players* (1955). Truth is, he barely does that. He was amazingly vacuous on screen for such a lovely thing.

His last two decent roles came in religious-themed epics. He's Joshua in *The Ten Commandments* (1956), and Taha, the bearded Arab with eyes as beautiful as Paul Newman's, in *Exodus* (1960). Throughout his decade and a half career, he remained as pretty as when he started.

By the mid-sixties, Derek had stopped acting altogether and began writing, directing, and photographing his own films, usually starring a current infatuation of the female persuasion; his nude photos of first wife Ursula Andress made it into *Playboy*, for example. His most successful venture, in terms of box-office, was his horrific re-tooling of *Tarzan, the Ape Man* (1981). Tarzan doesn't show up in the picture for eons, which probably didn't concern heterosexual males drooling over Bo Derek's ample exposure between the endless rants of her father, played by Richard Harris. Tarzan is embodied by model Miles O'Keeffe, after the original muscleman actor was fired because he had a herpes sore on his lip. O'Keeffe is so tragically beautiful, with cheekbones above and dimpled cheeks below his loincloth that rival Ms. Derek's, it's a blessing in disguise that he never speaks. He's there to be ogled.

Bo's first encounter with him, while she fellates a banana, is amateur enough to surrender a monologue befitting an adolescent schoolgirl's romantic crush. There are even more heavenly shots of O'Keeffe's leonine body while he lies unconscious after what seems a week-long wrestling match with an anaconda. Bo is at his side playfully stealing peeks and touches for the rest of us. If only she'd had the guts to remove his loincloth we would be forever in her debt. (The film's weirdest moments come during the end credit "outtakes" when a chimpanzee takes an uninvited erotic interest in Bo and then a lion decides to attack her on the beach. O'Keeffe courageously intervenes.)

In the even more sexually provocative *Bolero* (1984), Derek has his wife playing a "virgin" who falls in love with a matador who's gored in the crotch, rendering him impotent. The film's climactic love scene has Bo giving it (and him) her all. The entire story is predicated on Bo Derek coaxing a hard-on.

Movie subject matter sure had changed since Derek himself was making them in the 1950s. We may have been on the brink of the new sexualized male—the hunk—in moving pictures, but no matter how often we saw Derek stripped of his shirt and that little bit of hair in the middle of his chest (appreciably thicker in *An Annapolis Story* than *Knock On Any Door*), he came off just as ball-less as the rest of his ilk. He wouldn't be the last of his kind, but can be counted among their numbers as a studio leading man sold on his looks but denied his sexual potency. If what we really wanted from Derek was sex and nudity, he

THIS BODY FOR SALE!

MEET THE "KEPT MEN" OF BIG TIME COLLEGE FOOTBALL!

See the body-buying racket...the boy who beat the system...the girl who made him a man...the never-before-told football story —from the wrathful Cosmopolitan serial!

Columbia Pictures presents SIDNEY BUCHMAN'S Production of

SATURDAY'S HERO

Starring JOHN DEREK · DONNA REED

John Derek as "Pretty Boy" Romano in *Knock on Any Door* (1949).
PHOTOFEST
Inset: Derek as jock meat in *Saturday's Hero* (1951).

78

wasn't in a position to give it to us back then. He eventually took control of his own erotic obsessions and understood that the only way he was going to get them on film was if he shot them himself.

So, it's 1947 and Tallulah Bankhead, the grand dame of fuckdom, is out on stage delivering a mind-numbing thirty-minute monologue in Jean Cocteau's play *The Eagle Has Two Heads*. Her poetic lover should be hanging on every boozy syllable, but he's not. He's busy. He's got something in his nose. His finger. His balls itch, too. Might as well scratch 'em.

Marlon Brando, Jr. (1924-   ) scratched and re-adjusted himself for nine or ten more hysterical performances before he got what he wanted: out. Star or no star, and Ms. Bankhead was assuredly the former, Brando was his own little boy, the irreverent prankster, and when she melodramatically opened the curtains on her mink robe one night after a performance and offered her naked self to him, he pointed her towards the window and suggested she jump.

It should make all of us Americans feel very patriotic and proud to know that the greatest actor of the 20th Century was a chronic adolescent who loved fart jokes and habitually dressed like a slob. In later years, he said that memorizing his lines was a waste because people don't know what they're going to say until they say it, so he read his lines off cue cards, cheat sheets hidden all over the set, and his co-star's forehead. Eventually he employed a tiny earpiece and had someone read him the lines while he acted the scene in hopes it would sound even more spontaneous. Most people thought he was just lazy.

If you look in the index to Peter Manso's eight-year-in-the-making, 1118-page *Brando: The Biography* (Hyperion, 1994), you'll find the following revealing entries among the choice stops: "abortions financed by," "anal humor of," "animals loved by," "bisexuality of," "controlling and manipulative behaviors of," "electric eels of," "hygiene habits of," "ice-assisted death scene of," "mooning of," "multiple identities of," "pet raccoons of," "self-contempt of," "slouch of," "stretching equipment experiment of," and "venereal diseases contracted by." This is a guy who sought to be circumcised when he was in his sixties and insisted it be done without anesthetic. (The doc who did the slicing prevailed and a shot was administered.)

He was born in Omaha, Nebraska and raised in various towns, notably Libertyville and Evanston, Illinois, by a pair of dysfunctional parents—a mostly absent father with a flash flood temper, and a mother who was an alcoholic. "Bud" felt generally unloved, unwanted, and unworthy, though desperately connected and "devoted" to his mother. He was a bad boy in school, both academically and otherwise. His father finally shuttled him off at age 11 to Shattuck Military Academy in Minnesota, where he continued to demonstrate his distaste for authority. He flunked out in less than two years.

At age 19, he went to New York and began classes at the New School for Social Research where he came under the inspired tutelage of the now-legendary Stella Adler, who was director of the drama program. He had seriously considered becoming a drummer for a time, and dabbled with the idea of modern dance, but acting quickly became his passion. Adler took him under her wing and into her home during his early years in New York, helping him fight off his natural stammer while in *I Remember Mama* on Broadway. She found in a young and uninhibited Marlon Brando a restless, bold curiosity and he would become her prime cultural exponent of an acting style that would blossom into a revolutionary method of performing.

The so-called "Method," based on Stanislavski's techniques, was a philosophy that induced the actor to give spontaneous birth, digging deep into one's own psyche to tap into the emotional wellsprings of the character. It's a rigorous exploration for emotional truths through improvisations and minimalist exercises, peeling away the layers to reveal the inner you. Characters aren't played, they are lived. (Brando began personal psychotherapy shortly after his stage career got underway.)

He was in attendance during the earliest days of the Actor's Studio in New York, but has always maintained he learned everything about acting from Adler and director Elia Kazan. Adler had helped him land a key role in the NY production of *Truckline Café* in 1946. The play lasted only two weeks, but Brando's turn as a soldier who confesses to having just killed his wife riveted audiences and critics alike. There was an emotional intensity to the confession that jarred the audience out of their just-another-night-at-the-theatre complacency.

When Elia Kazan set out to direct Tennessee Williams' *The Poker Night*, he knew he wanted Brando, not original choice John Garfield, for the role of Stanley Kowalski, the brute man of New Orleans. After meeting him, Tennessee wanted him, too. For the play. What I wouldn't give to have been there December 3, 1947 when Brando, clad in a T-shirt and jeans, took the stage in the re-titled *A Streetcar Named Desire*.

Nobody saw it coming, but Brando's pure, animalistic male figure was so sexually bracing that the play's focus shifted from the pathetic plight of the demented Blanche (Jessica Tandy) to the virile strut and mumble of Stanley. Brando was such a sensation that the show kept playing for nearly two years, though Marlon became exhausted, bored, and easily distracted. He spent some of the time in the theatre basement boxing with stagehands, one of whom smashed in his already blunted profile and broke his nose.

Brando's first film, like Clift's, was agreed to because it was a one-shot deal. In *The Men* (1950), he plays a soldier paralyzed from the waist down in combat who faces the long and difficult process of rehabilitation and coping. As an actor, he already seems well ahead of the game in this pedantic, informational brochure on paraplegic rehab, because you can feel the hurt and anger in him as opposed to seeing it mimicked for you.

It's an old-fashioned, classroom educational film—extremely well-meaning and sincere and even touching—but Brando gives it an edge, not fully appreciated by some critics of the time who thought he made the role unlikable. He doesn't, but Hollywood was waking up to their new angry men and was still a bit groggy. Brando isn't unlikable, he's emotional, depressed, anguished, and explosively angry—the things real people are, not the things handsome young actors are called upon to show off and then get over.

Maybe it was his classical beauty and porcelain-smooth skin that fooled critics into believing that he'd be less challenging. Beautiful boys were (and are) regularly served up as the iconic casualties of war—shown in all their symbolic loveliness with blood trickling out of their mouths—representing lost opportunity, lost youth, lost love. Mourn the young and the beautiful. They're who we're fighting for.

Brando's role in *The Men* required lots of physical exercise and we're afforded generous helpings of his shirtless or tight white T-shirted self using barbells, rope climbing, doing push-ups and sit-ups, and "walking" along the parallel bars. He was in superb physical condition.

The screen version of *A Streetcar Named Desire* (1951) is my favorite film of the 1950s. And Marlon Brando's performance as Stanley is the finest piece of film acting I've ever seen by an American actor. If he went directly from *Streetcar* to *The Island of Dr. Moreau* (1996), I'd still say he's the best American film actor there ever was.

When Stanley first encounters Blanche, he takes off his jacket, revealing a T-shirt soaked in sweat. He absent-mindedly rubs his nipple through the shirt before he pulls the T off and changes to another one in front of her. The crass, earthy, muscled mumbler has just stolen the show the way a gorgeous actress might in another picture. You have to tell yourself that you're watching Marlon Brando, because even though you fully know it, he so completely inhabits Stanley's skin that you'll probably smell the sweat.

Stanley's dumb, but he's absolutely lived-in. Brando illuminates every nook and cranny, finding humor in Stanley's tiny, but precious bit of perverted knowledge about the "Napoleonic Code" (in which the man has a right to whatever belongs to his wife), as well as his having "an acquaintance" of such-and-such expertise that he can always call upon.

As with the stage version (though Brando thought the film version better), we're confronted by the disconcerting dichotomy of the brute, ugly male predator, "the unrefined type," he guesses we call him, who we're drawn to because of his physical beauty, his very maleness. The connection is made clear by the juxtaposition of Blanche telling Stella that she finds Stanley common, primitive, a Stone Age brute, and an animal while a sweat-glistening Brando overhears from outside, looking hot in his little cap, his tight jeans, and his muscle shirt all covered with dirty smudges.

He screeches like a cat. He has a savage temper. He's domineering and prone to violent outbursts. He slaps his pregnant wife in a rage and only after his buddies forcibly throw him into the shower, making his wet T-shirt cling even more to his bulges, does he realize what he's done and weeps like a little boy. He wanders into the courtyard and does his famous "Hey, Stella!" scream and she returns to him. He falls to his knees, crying at the bottom of the stairs, and she sensuously drapes herself over his bare back and they passionately embrace.

In ways far more complex and profound than even Tennessee Williams had imagined when he wrote the character, we find ourselves attracted to Stanley. We, too, want to forgive him, embrace him, have him make love to us. But it's an attraction to danger, a reckless commitment to an abusive relationship. We don't want him to beat his kind and loving wife, of course. We want him to beat us. And then cry and beg us to forgive him.

Even on the eve of his likely rape of Blanche, while his wife is at the hospital about to have a baby, Stanley's powerful sexual urges have a dangerous allure. He strips to his muscle T and shakes up his beer so that it sprays from between his legs, shooting the foam up and into his own hair and mouth. He berates

Beauty, brawn, and the Bard. Marlon Brando as Marc Antony in *Julius Caesar* (1953). EVERETT COLLECTION

and belittles Blanche's affectations, hurling all his inarticulate invective at her with a mocking "Hah-hah! You hear me? Hah, hah, hah!"

Marlon Brando's monumental presence in *Streetcar* was felt by generations of actors to come. His immediate apostles so often imitated him that critics condescendingly referred to the style as "the torn T-shirt" school of acting. About that T-shirt: loose was the fashion of the times, so when costumer Lucinda Ballard fit it for the original play as tight as a second skin and had sopping wet jeans form-fitted on a stark naked Brando (at his insistence), she was dressing a new sort of male sex symbol—the kind that knew his curves were as sexy as hers. He might as well have played the whole thing topless, but then we'd have been robbed of a take-home fetish. He effectively turned an undershirt into a sex object. The opposite of what Gable was said to have achieved.

Those who called him a mumbler were humbled by his ability to articulate Shakespeare as a strong Marc Antony in *Julius Caesar* (1953), and he gave a fiery performance as a peasant ascending to the

Presidency in Kazan's *Viva Zapata!* (1952). *On the Waterfront* (1954) puttied Brando's face into bulldog beauty and provided him with another film classic, but his look in *The Wild One* (1954) became a hallowed image for the American teenaged male.

There's the threat of danger right away as one of the motorcyclists nearly takes out the camera in the middle of the road during the very first shot of the film. We then cut to Brando buzzing down the rear-projection highway on his hog wearing biker regalia—a cap, shades, a leather jacket, and jeans—that looks as queer as Liberace to the modern eye.

The iconic dress was in turn adopted as dress code by a generation of postwar 1950s teens craving to don an attitude. They were punks in sideburns and Levis. The movies often impacted the culture at large—the way we dressed, the way we talked—an infection which television perfected at spreading. Disillusioned youth saw what it wanted to be on film and endeavored to emulate it to achieve vicarious personality. It was us vs. the squares.

The film, based on an inflated real-life event in which a small California town was overtaken by motorcycle gangs, was intended as an anti-gang movie, but like all movie violence and anti-authoritarian fables it can't help being attractive in some ways, maybe even inciteful.

Brando plays Johnny, the taciturn head of the Black Rebels Motorcycle Club, with a full-sized butt and a largely indiscernible bulge up front. There's something "cool" about the way he says things in that sandy tenor voice of his. Maybe it's just the gang's hip lingo. Pops. Daddy-O. Crazy. Thumb me. Give me some skin. Jive. Rebop.

When a gal asks Johnny what he's rebelling against, he delivers the famous "Whattya got?" in self-conscious close-up, but its impact is nearly undone by the girl's need to repeat it immediately afterward to another girl, as if it were a gassy joke instead of the maxim of a generation some purport it to be.

The gang is such a tiresome group of idiots that you'd like them all busted, but the townspeople's vigilante tactics are meant to be seen as equally empty-headed. Brando gets beaten to a pulp and in the midst of it taunts his attackers with "my old man used to hit harder than that." So there you have it, the hurt and abused little boy inside the leather jacket and behind the dark glasses is revealed beneath the anarchic attitude of a punk. Inarticulate youth had a mumblesperson.

Brando broke into the top ten most popular movie stars in the #10 spot for 1954, then #6 in 1955, and #4 in 1958.

He brilliantly plays with his attractive bad self in *One-Eyed Jacks* (1961), a would-be epic western he took over directing after wearing down Stanley Kubrick before the script was even finished. An intriguing tale of revenge, and the last film to successfully exploit his raw sex appeal (complete with a savage flogging at the hitching post), it remains a beautiful and underrated film, providing a fascinating look at the dualities of its director and star's persona. Brando's first cut ran five hours. When the studio mandated he hack it down to size, then insisted on the excision of "crucial" scenes and an altered ending, he all but disowned it.

He openly outed his inner fop as Fletcher Christian in the bloated remake of *Mutiny on the Bounty* (1962), further demonstrating how far we'd come in leading men since Gable was embarrassed by the very thought of being seen as less than masculine in the 1935 version. When a bare-chested Gable has to share the frame with a bare-chested and equally depilated Franchot Tone (both have so little body hair it barely registers under their arms), it's tempered by having girls eyeing them at the beach. Even after a swim that leaves him standing there in a big wet diaper, Gable vainly tries to masculinize the shot by standing with his fists on his sides in what now invokes a Superman pose.

Brando would go on to play the latent homosexual Army officer married to Elizabeth Taylor who enjoys watching young Robert Forster ride bareback bare-assed in the psychologically ripe, but mostly astonishingly awful *Reflections in a Golden Eye* (1967). The role was originally intended for a sickly Montgomery Clift, whom the studio wouldn't approve because of insurance issues until good friend Liz staked him out of her own salary. Fortunately for him, he died before the film got underway.

During *Last Tango in Paris* (1972), the controversial and famous Euro-art sex film, Brando's penis "shrank to the size of a peanut," he tells us in his quirky autobiography *Brando: Songs My Mother Taught Me* (Random House, 1994), and he paced back and forth without pants trying to will his cock and balls to grow. Now that's what all movie star biographies should do: tell it like it is. After all, not everybody was hung like **Rock Hudson** (1925-1985). Certainly few were as beloved, which makes me feel a twinge of guilt about the transition I've written.

Roy Scherer, Jr. was born in Winnetka, Illinois and, at 5.5 pounds stretched out over 27 inches, resembled a log more than he did a rock. Roy, Sr. abandoned his family when Roy, Jr. was just five, during the Depression. An attempt to reunite after two years of hopeful promises that he would see his dad again failed and there's no telling how a kid that age processes such rejection. Mom re-married, this time to a physically abusive alcoholic, and the newly re-named Roy Fitzgerald would later tell interviewers that much of his boyhood was spent trying to keep away from home. He wasn't a momma's boy, though. She exacted her own form of mental cruelty on him. He was left to his own devices.

Shy and intractably insecure, he would become a lifelong nail-biter and rub a deep groove into his thumbnail by obsessively abrading the nail of his index finger into it. The handsomest kid in upscale New Trier High School, he didn't dare let anyone know he dreamed of being an actor, thereby allowing schoolmate Charlton Heston free reign on the stage.

Mom finally dumped the no-good husband during Roy's junior year, but even without that distraction, the poor kid still had to stay an extra semester in order to graduate. He joined the Navy and was stationed in the Philippines, where he failed as an airplane mechanic but excelled in the laundry. He wrote typically macho, profanity-strewn letters to his buddies back home.

Stateside again, his stint as a strapping 6'4" mailman in Illinois who secretly longed to be a movie star seems like something out of a Hollywood B-movie: the kind where impossibly good-looking men are working impossibly mundane jobs and then something impossibly extraordinary happens to them and they manage to live out their impossible dreams.

Roy and his mother moved to Los Angeles, where he worked for a short time trying to sell vacuums for his real dad, then drove delivery trucks and parked them for long periods of time outside of studio lots. He'd get out of the truck, of course. And strike a pose.

He finally got some headshots done and dropped them off here and there. When 36-year old Henry Willson, an agent at Selznick Studios, got a look at him in September of 1947, sparks flew. Willson was well known for at least three things: his taste in handsome young men, his complete disregard of talent, and his penchant for naming names. He created Guy, Tab, Ty, and Troy. And he christened Rock (of Gibraltar) Hudson (River), a name Roy would always hate and wouldn't legally change until five years before his death.

He got his first job from director Raoul Walsh because, if nothing else, "he'll be good scenery." He proved so green and so nervous and so clumsy that only one of his lines remains in *Fighter Squadron* (1948). It took thirty-eight takes to get out "You've got to buy a bigger blackboard," if Hollywood legend can be believed.

He signed on at Universal for a seven-year contract in 1949, got his teeth capped, and began, along with other assembly line stars, such as Tony Curtis, a regimen of voice, dance, fencing, acting, and diction lessons. Some might say you could hardly tell.

The easy joke was that Rock was a rock on screen. Though his billing and screen time slowly grew over his first 25 films from 1948 to 1954, he wasn't exactly the studio's wonder boy. They even seriously considered dropping him. He was still good-looking scenery, though, whether he was a gangster, a cavalry trooper, an Arab, a doorman, a boxer, or an Indian. Of course, he got noticed more when his scenery went undressed. He took a stuntman's dive off a horse when his Indian brave is shot by Jimmy Stewart in *Winchester '73* (1950) and he eventually played the bare-chested title character in *Taza, Son of Cochise* (1954), in which he grunts "Unga bunga wunga" and nearly gets his face scorched by a fellow actor who runs a torch by him too close for comfort. He's oiled up, got gorgeous shaved pecs, and in great shape, enviably so for a man who never committed himself to formal workouts.

Thankfully, Rock Hudson was asked to take his shirt off in a lot of his movies. And he was asked, and obliged, to do the same for countless movie magazines of the time, caught strutting around in tight bathing trunks or fresh out of the shower with a wrap-around towel. He never liked doing it, but true to his personality, he did what his studio told him to do. He wouldn't make waves about being the "Beefcake Baron," as much as he despised it, until after he had attained stardom.

"I find my old movies very embarrassing," he told the press years later. "I was so incredibly bad. I had no experience, no expression, no thoughts. The odd thing is that I thought I was overacting. Now I can see I wasn't doing a damn thing, just standing there, looking helpless."

He starts out looking absolutely dopey as the speed-demon playboy who wipes out his boat at 180 mph in *Magnificent Obsession* (1954). He's the millionaire show-off who's busy huffing on a borrowed

Fresh-faced Rock Hudson the Sailor Boy, 1944. PHOTOFEST

Then as movie star. PHOTOFEST

resuscitator while the good doctor who really needs it (and owns it) is left to die. The widow (Jane Wyman) is a six-month newlywed and when she tries to escape the inappropriate come-ons of Mr. Moneybucks, she steps out of a cab and gets clipped by a car, leaving her blind. Luckily, she's a very cheerful blind woman and Rock is a reforming jerk. He romances her under an assumed name and then goes back to medical school and becomes a neurosurgeon destined to perform potentially sight-restoring surgery on her years later. We see him scrubbing up shirtless for the operation and a poor editing choice has us momentarily believing that he'll be performing the surgery that way. It's unforgivable tripe, but it was a huge hit and, like the 1935 version did for Robert Taylor, it made Rock Hudson a star.

Fully engaged in the arranged social life provided by the studio, Rock was also fully engaged in homosexual liaisons while his mug was adorning the October 3, 1955 cover of *Life* as "America's Most Handsome Bachelor." One wonders how openly-yet-"secretly" gay Rock was considering his sexuality was apparently a foregone conclusion in Hollywood. Was this shy, painfully insecure Midwestern boy who wanted to be a movie star and saw his dreams coming true that carefree (or careless) about his potentially career-wrecking same-sex desires in the puritanical and homo-baiting 1950s? Apparently yes, because he had Universal to protect him, and the studio had to on occasion, as when the scandal rag *Confidential* was looking to expose him as a fag and Universal reportedly hung out another actor's dirty laundry in exchange, i.e., Rory Calhoun's criminal past. Others say hush money was exchanged.

In an interview published posthumously, Hudson himself said he was insulated because there was too much at stake: too many hearts to keep throbbing, too much cash to be made. America simply wouldn't have wanted to know the truth, he reasoned, and no reputable newspaper dependent on the Dream Factory would have printed such a thing.

"America's Most Handsome Bachelor" does sit-ups for the press. Otherwise, he didn't much like working out. PHOTOFEST

He was offered the chance to upstage schoolmate Charlton Heston by playing Ben-Hur, but Universal wouldn't loan him out. They re-united him with Jane Wyman in *All That Heaven Allows* (1956), in which she suggests "you want me to be a man" and he answers: "Only in that one way." *Heaven* is today regarded as a "masterpiece" from director Douglas Sirk, whose striking visual style and airless melodramas are seen as powerful deconstructions of 1950s' social and sexual mores. (Rainer Werner Fassbinder's 1974 film *Ali—Fear Eats the Soul* and Todd Haynes' 2002 film *Far From Heaven* launch from Sirk's critically-revered body of work, and *All That Heaven Allows* in particular.) No offense to Wyman, but you have to wonder what Rock sees in her, especially in *Obsession*. At least in *Heaven*, the matter of choice isn't about his, but about hers. How dare a middle-aged widowed woman take up with her young gardener!

Hudson's on-screen romances were just as arranged as his off-screen ones. He married Henry Willson's secretary in 1955 to help underline the obvious in Hollywood (that she was a beard) and supply the clueless public with clueless visions of hetero-normalcy it didn't know it needed. Rock Hudson was the spitting image of the model husband. That fantasy could sustain itself indefinitely. Remember, studios used to both discourage and hide romantic stars' marriages for fear that their pining fans would abandon them once they were unavailable.

His performance as outlaw John Wesley Hardin in *The Lawless Breed* (1953), which required his character to age over many years (largely amounting to a mustache and gray frosting), supposedly convinced director George Stevens to cast him over other heavyweight leading men for the role of sexist Texas rancher Bick Benedict in Warner's epic *Giant* (1956). It's a great big, flawed, but remarkable film, and we'll talk a bit more about it when we get to James Dean (whom Rock did not care for), but it may be Hudson's best on-screen performance and garnered his only Oscar nomination as Best Actor.

"On *Giant*, Rock felt he was in with the big boys," wrote lifelong friend Elizabeth Taylor for a 1999 *Newsweek* piece. "And he was brilliant in it. But his looks hurt him a lot. It was like being a beautiful woman in Hollywood. If you were considered pretty, you might as well have been a waitress trying to act—you were treated with no respect at all."

But it wasn't just his looks. On-screen, Rock Hudson habitually threatened to bore. It was as if he couldn't shake off that awful thud of a name. He continued to show up in what were considered "women's movies" as their object of matinee idol desire. Douglas Sirk's *Written on the Wind* (1957), Charles Vidor's *A Farewell to Arms* (1958), and Sirk's *The Tarnished Angels* (1958) have varying degrees of trashy and/or painfully melodramatic moments and Rock struggles to make much of an impression. He's so handsome, you're dying to see him actually do something with those looks other than wear them.

He had a damned good role in *Giant*, and it remained his personal favorite, but what he really needed to do was siphon some of his enormous off-screen charm and wonderful sense of humor and put it on screen somehow. Audiences didn't know he had it in him. He loved dirty jokes, he adored telling stories, loved playing pranks, and had a thunderous, hearty, and genuine laugh that came easy and shook the rafters.

He had to be convinced to try his hand at comedy, though, and it took some doing. Thankfully, it was sex comedy. Suddenly he's two inches taller (Doris says he's 6'6") and funny and charming and in a bathtub in *Pillow Talk* (1959), a classic double play on his hetero and homo selves. Rock was so completely identified by the public as the ideal straight man, and was himself a straight-acting gay man who enjoyed pursuing other straight-acting gay men, that one has to wonder how he felt about mocking the gay stereotypes of the time on film: interest in fabrics and recipes, devotion to mother, raised pinkie. Even if we all understand he's just having fun and may himself have held prejudices against effeminate gays, you have to cringe at Doris Day's reaction to his suggestion that her Texas beau might be queer. (That's one of two things they've got down there, you know.)

"What a vicious thing to say!" she protests. "You are sick!"

As filmmaker Mark Rappaport explores in his docu-essay *Rock Hudson's Home Movies* (1992), the actor's films are overloaded with autobiographical insinuations. So many of them are about playing with the duplicity of images—of pretending to be someone or something you're not (but really are, maybe).

Home Movies, which has Rock admitting to falling for Jon Hall in *The Hurricane* when he was nine, is a video catalog of clips and snips from his career revealing overt and covert, as well as cleverly de-contextualized, revisioned, and entirely fabricated examples of homo nudge-nudge.

The possibilities are seemingly endless from his body of work, even upon cursory examination. The most flagrant examples have been cited to death so I won't waste the space rehashing, but you can find this stuff in nearly every film he ever made. *Why* is a question for the cosmos, but it's sure to give gay revisionists multiple orgasms and provide enough material for Gay Studies theses to effect an academic ban.

In *Bend of the River* (1952), Arthur Kennedy warns him: "You're real fast with that gun, kid, but you're soft and someday it'll kill you." "Now if I were the marrying kind...," Rock later ellipses. "His kind never change," someone else says of him. In *Seminole* (1953), his cavalry officer braves quicksand to haul out wounded and handsome James Best instead of the more "important" cannon and we can all empathize with his choice for reasons beyond the purely ethical. In *Written on the Wind*, he tells slutty Dorothy Malone that he loves her like a brother. And he means it. "Don't...please don't waste your life away waiting for me."

Come September (1961), *Lover Come Back* (1962), *Send Me No Flowers* (1964), *Man's Favorite Sport* (1964), and *A Very Special Favor* (1965) were all romantic comedies attempting to start the pillow fight again. Most were very popular. Rock was the #1 male movie star at the box-office in 1957 and wore that crown from 1959-1962.

During one take on the beach with Doris Day in *Lover Come Back*, Rock stooped over and one of his balls popped out of his bathing shorts and then slid back into hiding. Too bad it was discovered during the dailies and snipped. Rock thought it was hilarious and had it played over and over again in the screening room. He was just a big kid.

With the money from *Lover*, he bought his "Castle," his manly inner sanctum where he hosted parties, kept out the press, surprisingly allowed the pilot for *McMillan and Wife* (1971) to be filmed, and eventually returned to die.

As perhaps the last vestige of the old movie star system, a manufactured and groomed star, he found it difficult to keep audiences interested in an era that would foster little Brandos and Deans, Newmans and Nicholsons. His one shot at making the leap was the science fiction film *Seconds* (1966), a disconcertingly stylized black-and-white experiment about the ugly quest to achieve eternal youth through surgical re-birth. It's a weird little film with a brave and odd performance by Rock, who deeply believed in it and gave it his all. It tanked at the box-office and had to wait twenty years before becoming a cult item.

Equally deserving of cult status, though for different reasons, is Roger Vadim's *Pretty Maids All in A Row* (1971), a raunchy black comedy with Rock as "Tiger" McDrew, a high school assistant principal and guidance counselor who's screwing his teenaged students and then killing them. Shy and virginal 17-year old Ponce de Leon Harper (John David Carson) comes to Hudson and confesses to having erection problems: he gets one whenever the wind blows. Rock, whose extra pounds and absence of underwear work well for the role, sets the kid up with substitute teacher Angie Dickinson, who keeps poking her tits in the boy's eyeballs and then glows with pride when he pops a woody in her face. This funny and sick sex comedy was written and produced by Gene Roddenberry.

As everyone knows, when Hudson's rapid physical deterioration was officially linked to AIDS-related complications, it shocked the culture to the core: an image of prototypical masculinity had been shattered. The guy girls wanted their guys to look like and the guy guys recognized as the high standard was suddenly the guy who fooled everybody into believing that he was "normal." These are the hazards of idolatry. Worship an image that also happens to be made of flesh and blood and you're sure to learn a lesson about your own stupidity.

Lots of people felt cheated somehow that Rock was a real person and not just a movie star image: gay men were angry that Hudson hadn't come out sooner and fought the fight that needed to be fought in the midst of the plague-hysteria and then there was a generation or two of women who selfishly (if understandably) felt robbed of their romantic daydreams. "How can we ever watch another Rock Hudson film again without thinking about...you know?"

Only the young and ignorant can sit down and watch an old Rock Hudson flick and avoid mentally deconstructing a passionate love scene with a female co-star. "He'd much rather be kissing..." or "Now that's what I call great acting!" This problem will diminish over time, for even though the revelation of his homosexuality once rocked this world, he will soon, if not already, seem as historically remote to audiences as Errol Flynn or Tyrone Power—one of those old movie stars. Just as likely, he will fascinate inquisitive young gay film scholars who learn of his importance to the cause. There's a twinge of homo-political self-satisfaction knowing that Rock was snatched from heterosexist exclusivity and forced the culture to question its assumptions about celebrity in general and sexuality in particular.

You can't even say his life was his best acting job, as some have tried to oh-so-cleverly suggest. Had the public branded him a homosexual in the 1950s, he wouldn't have had a career as a romantic idol, probably not a film career at all. But had Roy Scherer, Jr. been outed, or came out of his own accord fifty years ago, or magically emerged in an era when such things didn't matter, he still would have been the gay guy most people wouldn't have taken for gay. He still would have been the gay guy who loved sports, women, and chasing blonds.

Blondes did the chasing when it came to Bernie Schwartz. So did brunettes. So did neighborhood Nazi-sympathizers who wanted to beat him up. So might have some pervert who poked his hard-on in the kid's back while he was watching the seals being fed in Central Park. He was an astonishingly beautiful boy. He was also the oldest son of frightfully poor Hungarian Jews who moved their family from tiny apartment to abandoned building throughout Manhattan, Queens, and the Bronx.

Bernard Schwartz is fond of telling people that when he was a little kid fighting his way through life on the streets and in his home, where his mother physically abused him, he dreamed of escaping his private Depression through the movies. He dreamed of one day being **Tony Curtis** (1925-   ) before there was such a thing, and his dream came true.

Though he tells us in his candid 1993 autobiography that the miracle of orgasm was discovered at age eight, he also tells us that he was still a virgin when he entered the Navy in 1943 and that most of his sexual experiences up to that time consisted of coming in his pants. The stubborn fact that he was/is a heterosexual must have been awfully tough on fellow seamen wrestling with either their homosexuality or their ability to cross their eyes just a tad and turn his pretty face into an imaginary girl's.

One look at him wearing his sailor cap in Navy portrait (page 64 in his book) is enough to inspire the warmest feelings in any man. Of course, he would have decked you for trying anything, but you could always look...and I'll bet they did a lot of that. He was inspiring movie star fantasies before he ever made it before a movie camera. Jet black hair (and plenty of it), bedroom eyes, a full lower lip begging for lipstick, and a smooth, sensual face with skin so radiant and unblemished that it looks like a Hollywood publicity photo shot through gauze. That it's just his seaman's shot attests to how beautiful this guy was in real life, without make-up.

He was amazed that he could use the GI bill to pay for schooling as an actor and he happily entered the Dramatic Workshop of the New School. He even got to see Brando doing *Streetcar*. A Hollywood agent took note of him while he was starring as the often shirtless lead in a 1948 production of *Golden Boy* and within three days he was on a plane to Los Angeles with a seven-year contract at Universal.

That's where Rock Hudson was, too. The new kid was thrown face-first into the star-making factory, including all the dancing, acting, and fencing lessons a guy from the Bronx could ever want. Like virtually every other Jew in town, a name change was mandated. He became Jimmy Curtis.

Jimmy never made it to the screen. It's Anthony Curtis who keeps darting in and out of frame while dancing with Yvonne De Carlo 22 minutes into *Criss Cross* (1949). Perhaps it's because he's only afforded a couple of good, but fleeting shots during his two-minute debut that he seems all the more desirous. Glimpses of a boy that beautiful make moviegoers want to find out who he is and when and where they can see him again.

Eight more films, eight more small or minor supporting roles (including in the first *Francis the Talking Mule* picture) before Tony Curtis landed a lead as *The* (shirtless) *Prince Who Was A Thief* (1951), the first of an improbable series of costume adventure films Universal saddled him with despite the incongruity of his Bronx accent.

His legendarily misquoted line—"This is my fahtha's palace and yondah lies the valley of the sun"— from *Son of Ali Baba* (1952) would be used to ridicule him for years to come, touching off painful reminders of his taunted ethnicity. How, though, could you get around that voice?

In *Flesh and Fury* (1952) he plays a boxer, but he's a deaf mute for the first two-thirds of the film, that's how. He was a deaf mute killer in *Johnny Stool Pigeon* (1949), too. It's cruel to suggest that the studio should have somehow figured out how to sustain an entire career having him play cute deaf mutes, because it's not the actor's fault that he was contracted to do costume pictures such as *The Black Shield of Falworth* (1954) and *The Purple Mask* (1955), or westerns such as *Winchester '73*, *Sierra*, and *Kansas Raiders* (all 1950). They are sometimes bizarrely entertaining to watch (and listen to) today, though *Winchester* is an acknowledged genre classic without Curtis' or Rock Hudson's help.

The sensible thing to do would have been to keep him in more contemporary, urban settings. He made quite an impression in *City Across the River* (1949), only his second film, as the white T-shirted gang member who hates Mexicans. And he seems right, if not right at home, in *Six Bridges to Cross* (1954), the

Tony Curtis, in his first lead, as *The* (shirtless) *Prince Who Was A Thief* (1951). YESTERDAY

story of a big-headed career criminal who arranges a heist while using a philanthropic cop as an alibi.

As *Houdini* (1953) in the highly-fictionalized screen bio, he's not near-naked nearly enough of the time for tricks that the real Harry Houdini was and the bogus death scene finale is an insult, but audiences didn't have trouble buying his presence.

Upperclassman Frank Gifford tells him to "kindly assume the angle" for paddling in the win-win-win football flick *The All-American* (1953) and in his only musical, *So This Is Paris* (1954), Curtis is a complete fem with a light, wispy singing voice and a girlfriend with very pointy tits. He and the other two gobs do a locker room dance in their underwear as they change into bathing suits, making sure to keep their belly buttons hidden. During his weird "If you wanna be famous" song to the kids, he does a "Judy, Judy, Judy" Cary Grant impression five years before he suggested it to Billy Wilder and made it his comedic alter ego opposite Marilyn Monroe.

His career points out the dilemma of good looks vs. acting, good or otherwise. He personally disdained the Method and blamed actors who used it for attempting to rip off Brando's personal kinks, which only worked well for Brando. Everybody else was just "jerking off in Macy's window." Curtis, on the other hand, sums up his entire acting technique in a sentence. While playing a bellboy who delivers a telegram to Barbara Stanwyck in *The Lady Gambles* (1949), he was tortured by how he should say his four lines. The director finally took him aside and advised, "All you want is a tip," and the purity and truth of all acting transcended.

My problem is that Tony Curtis never much interested me as an actor. I'd rather look at still photographs—all those great beefcake magazine shots Universal forced him to do when he couldn't say no, hanging shirtless off a sailboat mast or emerging from a swim sopping wet and wearing tight white bathing trunks. Yes, I'm shamelessly lowering the sights.

He was so much hotter in his early, trashy, and awful costume and juvenile delinquent pic days than he was when he understandably fought for better and more challenging roles. He's less beautiful the better an actor he becomes. Certainly not pretty in *The Defiant Ones* (1958), for which he was nominated for his only Oscar, but then still capable of pulling off a cartoonish pretty as the Great Leslie in *The Great Race* (1965).

The less said by me about *Some Like It Hot* (1959) the better, though his choice to adopt a Cary Grant imitation (before there even was a Cary Grant in terms of the film's period) as the millionaire playboy who wants to seduce Marilyn Monroe has some perhaps unintended readings.

"I don't know how to put it," he tells Marilyn, "but I've got this thing about girls."

"What thing?"

"They just sort of leave me cold."

"Frigid?"

Not exactly. "When I'm with a girl it does absolutely nothing to me."

The film has been deified as one of the greatest screen comedies ever despite not being very funny and my opinion thankfully won't diminish the love audiences and critics have for it.

Trapeze (1956) may have been something of a turning point because it was a box-office hit and critics noted his improving dramatic skills in a role in which he's wearing leotards, but it's impossible to see why he would fall for Gina Lollobrigida and risk screwing up his act with Burt Lancaster. "I know how you feel better than you do," Burt tells him.

A year later Lancaster would call him "a cookie full of arsenic" when Curtis' crowning achievement came playing Sidney Falco, "the boy with the ice cream face," in *Sweet Smell of Success* (1957). It's the paramount mesh of pretty boy and slimeball with Tony crossing the t's, dotting the i's, and biting his nails as a sleazy press agent selling gossip and lies to a nasty, ruthless, and powerful newspaper columnist able to make or break careers. A dark and cynical film, it boasts a sharp script and snappy Clifford Odets and Ernest Lehman dialogue from Lehman's own book. Literate slang, you might call it.

Some like oysters, some like snails. Some like *Spartacus* (1960). I prefer *The Vikings* (1958). "And taste is not the same as appetite and therefore not a question of morals, is it?" That according to Anthony Hopkins' flawless mimicry of Laurence Olivier for the dubbed bath scene that was omitted from the original Stanley Kubrick release but included in the 1993 restoration. *Spartacus* is a hugely enjoyable film for reasons other than Tony Curtis, the Roman slave-boy singer of songs whose master uses a food metaphor to let Tony know he swings both ways.

The Vikings is a hugely enjoyable film, though, in no small part because of Tony Curtis. Which is saying something considering half his face is covered in the fungus of a beard. Here, he's a Viking slave-boy in tiny underpants that don't quite cover the bottoms of his cheeks. He's wearing other clothes, so it's not as if he's Baby New Year, but the costume is conspicuously lopsided top to bottom, making us aware that we're supposed to be looking at those lovely gams.

Curtis gets kicked in the gut by the hammy Kirk Douglas and then sics his hawk on him for revenge. The bird bloodily pecks at Douglas' eye, spoiling his "pretty, dainty face" and leaving him with an all-white eyeball for the rest of the film. Kirk isn't the only one who's hammy, though. *The Vikings* is both awful and funny, just short of a camp classic because it loses much of its weird energy after the first half. At one point, Curtis is tied to a post on the beach to be drowned and then eaten by crabs, but the daughters of Odin sing their song and the winds reverse the tide. A fidelity test involving throwing axes at a woman's head while she's trapped in a giant stock is all part of the merriment. And when Tony the Viking gets his hand lopped off and cauterized with a torch, the resulting stump makes his forearm look peculiarly on the long side.

The young man in the curly dark hair and black cap claiming to be a Greek fisherman in *Beneath the 12-Mile Reef* (1953) doesn't otherwise look particularly Greek, and he certainly doesn't sound it, but he does fit the bill in other ways. He introduces himself to both the girl he's interested in and those of us enamored in the audience as "Adonis. My mother named me after a Greek god." He opens his arms and strikes a pose. "I'm a very beautiful young man."

Robert Wagner (1930-   ) was a very beautiful young man indeed. His father was a successful suburban Detroit paint supplier who moved the family in 1937 to Bel Air where he entered the steel business. Robert was a privileged kid, but a restless one. He was repeatedly expelled from private schools (where it was thought he was bored) and began work at a Bel Air golf club where he caddied for Gary Cooper, Clark Gable, and Randolph Scott. He struck up a friendship with Gable, who encouraged him to do some extra work at the studios.

Dad wasn't happy about his son's dalliance with acting, but gave him the fairy tale one year to prove himself or be forced to come work at the steel company. Well, one look at this kid's flawless kisser and you can't imagine somebody somewhere in the biz not making room for him. Almost inevitably, it was boy-crazy Henry Willson (again) who took him to 20th Century-Fox where he was given the standard seven year contract.

He started as a "test boy," playing opposite actresses during their screen tests, including Marilyn Monroe. On-screen at last and even afforded a close-up in Leo G. Carroll's classroom in *The Happy Years* (1950), he moved right up to minor support in *The Halls of Montezuma* (1951), an impressive incorporation of war footage with the studio stuff, where he's so cute he's kissable. He's a baby-faced soldier who comes to the hospital to thank Richard Widmark for saving his life and when he lets loose that smile you feel like fainting. Makes you wish you were a bobbysoxer.

20th Century-Fox production chief Darryl F. Zanuck took note of the young looker in *Montezuma* and had his billing boosted to sixth in *The Frogmen* (1951), even though Wagner has just one line and appears in only a few shots to the right of Gary Merrill on the ship's bridge.

As the gorgeous son-in-law in the divorce comedy *Let's Make It Legal* (1951), he has a long scene standing between the film's two yammering male leads (MacDonald Carey and Zachary Scott) and you find yourself watching him the entire time. Once again, when he smiles, you drop. Even his eyebrows have this sexy way of arching when he's trying to be suggestive.

It was playing a cheerful, then later shell-shocked soldier whom Susan Hayward (as Jane Froman) sings to in *With A Song in My Heart* (1952) that brought the wet fan mail into the studio by the droves. All he's required to do is listen to her and shed a tear, but he does so without any of the usual acted anguish. He cries on screen and he looks like a sad puppy dog you want to hold in your arms and comfort. He's only got two scenes in the film, but they made him a teenage heartthrob.

Another supporting turn as a soldier in John Ford's nixed musical remake of *What Price Glory* (1952) offers him up as the 22-year old Philadelphian who falls for a French teenage girl during a WWI campaign and wants rough and rude American Captain Flagg (James Cagney) to marry them. Someone should have warned them, though, what happens to dreamboat soldiers in war movies. How else would we know war is hell?

As Pvt. Willie Little of the Marine Band, he manages to uncharacteristically survive combat in Cuba and come back with half a leg gone, but ever ready to blow his sousaphone, for the final rousing march of *Stars and Stripes Forever* (1952).

He had by this time begun dating Darryl Zanuck's daughter and subsequently started getting better parts. He wouldn't always have to die, for instance, even if nearly everyone else did. He's the tennis jock with the giant "P" on his sweater in *Titanic* (1953) who befriends Barbara Stanwyck in order to get close to her lovely daughter. (Behind-the-scenes, it's said Wagner romanced Stanwyck herself.) We get to see him sing and dance and clap his way through something called "The Navajo Rag," but it's his moist, plump lower lip that makes it forgivable. With a "yee-hoo" he sends his hat sailing and it falls into the sea amidst some foretelling chunks of ice. As with the phenomenal 1997 DiCaprio version, it's the inevitability of *Titanic* that makes it so heart-wrenching. Those who had no interest because they knew "how it was going to end," missed the boat.

Indignities come in all shapes and sizes for actors struggling to make a name for themselves and even Robert Wagner couldn't escape doing one of those costume pictures. Wearing a pageboy wig that looks just as awful as the one Cary Grant wore in *I Was A Male War Bride* (1949), Wagner forges on with a straight face in the title role of *Prince Valiant* (1954), which proved a surprise hit at the box-office. *Photoplay* named him Hollywood's "Most Promising Star" of 1954.

Fortunately for him, but unfortunately for the rest of us who glimpse a camp classic in the making, his Valentino-esque role in powdered wig as *Lord Vanity* (1954), opposite newcomer Joan Collins, was canned when Zanuck left Fox. All that remains are the frightening costume tests.

He looks good with a little fuzz on his face during the opening of *Broken Lance* (1954) as the angry youngest son of a crusty land baron (Spencer Tracy). The boy takes the fall for his family's squabbles with a mining operation and ends up in jail for three years. He's half Comanche and half Irish and falls in love with a white woman, adding racial strife to the familial war between his father and his ornery older brothers, all of whom have been treated like lowly ranch hands instead of sons. Wagner looks gorgeous in his blue suit, black hair, and red tint, but his voice has now fully given over to an affectation evidenced as early as in *What Price Glory*. I'm not sure if it's just his natural style of delivery or the result of vocal training, but the effect is something like that of a put-on "radio voice," an almost unnatural lower register that borders on monotone. Mix it with his trademark cadence and you've got the voice Rob Lowe easily recreates as the younger #2 in *Austin Powers: The Spy Who Shagged Me* (1999).

Robert Wagner keeps in shape poolside circa 1950s while running the risk of exposing his belly button, a studio no-no. PHOTOFEST

Playing against type, Wagner is the see-through bad guy in *A Kiss Before Dying* (1956), based on Ira Levin's novel about a beautiful opportunist whose marriage-into-riches plan is foiled by his girlfriend's two-month pregnancy before they get to the altar. He decides to get rid of her now that she's of no use to him and when a stumble down the bleachers and a poisoning scheme fall through (his shock at seeing her still alive is as overplayed as the film's score), he lures her to a fourteenth story rooftop and gives her the ultimate kiss-off. It's a pretty cold-blooded, shocking, and evil act despite our knowing it's coming, but there are too many lapses in logic and plausibility throughout the rest of the film to keep us tingling, even as her sister investigates the "suicide" as a homicide while unknowingly dating the killer.

Unfortunately, it's not a juicy role for Wagner because it's so transparent. He's just a good-looking bad guy without the psychological quirks that might make this fun. The whole plot unravels too easily. He even uses the same name both times. This would have been so much more delicious had the filmmakers played us for fools, like with Rob Lowe in *Masquerade* (1988) or Skeet Ulrich in *Scream* (1996).

His bigoted Southerner learns the errors of his ways while sequestered on a hill with the Japanese approaching in *Between Heaven and Hell* (1956), but his most truly unlikable character during this play-against-type year was as Spencer Tracy's much-much-younger brother in *The Mountain* (1956). After an Indian passenger plane crashes in the French Alps and a rescue team fails to reach the site, Wagner's angry young man, resentful of his entire empty life, cruelly forces his elder brother to make the climb with him so that he can pilfer the plane and corpses for treasure.

Tracy, in a marvelously restrained and touching performance as a legendary mountaineer who gave up climbing years ago after a fatality, is hopeful that this one last climb will enrich his thankless brother's spirit and not his pockets. After the arduous ascent, however, the runt turns even uglier when he comes across a sole survivor and greedily plans to pick her nose of a diamond stud before letting her languish and die. Though he's awfully cute in his little blue cap with the ball on the end, Wagner's character is such a one-note jerk that you want Tracy to take him over his knee, give him a good spanking, and then boot his red butt right off the mountain.

Off-screen, Wagner dated and then married Natalie Wood, a star in her own right, whose career eventually eclipsed his own and whom he was re-married to at the time of her tragic death in 1981. As with the romance and marriage of stars Tony Curtis and Janet Leigh, the studios were openly against weddings involving romantic idols, but both young couples didn't pay them any mind.

The True Story of Jesse James (1957) wasn't any truer than when Tyrone Power filled the role, despite Wagner's Jesse clearly going bad, but he and Jeffrey Hunter make such a handsome couple as outlaw brothers that truth would probably only further tarnish the fiction.

The international espionage plot of *Stopover Tokyo* (1957) was widescreen dull, but at least we get to see him in a towel at the bathhouse. Strangely, the hair we saw at his neckline earlier in the film is completely shorn in the steam room, making his chest look slightly sunken. His posture isn't great either, but two shots of him in recline are suitable for CinemaScope framing.

With *The Hunters* (1958) and *In Love and War* (1958), the studios were telling Wagner they didn't know what more to do with him. A stab at song and dance man, though he's playing an unlikable sleaze, in the Bing Crosby pseudo-musical *Say One For Me* (1959) didn't energize new opportunities, though it's kind of fun to watch him try something fresh. Instead, he began playing leading-man versions of the supporting roles in war movies that started his career. Elsewhere, he's embarrassingly bad giving a 1940s performance—stilted, phony, and with a permanent stoop that betrays his discomfort—as a Chet Baker-ish jazz trumpet player who gets dirt-poor Natalie Wood pregnant in *All the Fine Young Cannibals* (1960). In *The Longest Day* (1960), he really was back to playing a supporting role in a war movie; though, to be fair, so was everybody else in this epic Hollywood call-to-arms to recreate D-Day, including Sal Mineo, Jeffrey Hunter, Tommy Sands, Fabian, and Paul Anka.

Dissatisfied, he moved to Europe for a stint (played a playboy for DeSica in 1962's *The Condemned of Altona*), then went blind for three weeks after the detergent used in the bathtub scene of *The Pink Panther* (1964) lacerated his corneas. Friends Paul Newman and Joanne Woodward cast him here and there in their movies, but it was television that finally came to his rescue: *It Takes A Thief* (1969-70), *Switch* (1975-78), and *Hart to Hart* (1979-84).

In the mid-1950s, Humphrey Bogart was asked to comment on the new crop of young actors and had this to say about Wagner in particular: "He's the boy next door, but who the hell is gonna pay a buck to see the boy next door?" Heterosexual movie stars just don't get it. For my money, it all depends on what the boy next door looks like. And if he looked like RJ Wagner, I'd be willing to pay a whole lot more than a dollar. If there's an injustice, it's that he came to prominence at a time when men's fashions dictated baggy trousers.

John Ericson (Joachim Meibes; 1926-   ) was on his way to becoming a dentist at his father's behest when he changed gears and pursued the manly art of acting after a roughneck friend of his shared his own intention to do so. "The kids I grew up with thought acting was for sissies," Ericson told author Richard Lamparski years later.

Fellow classmates Grace Kelly, Jack Palance, and Don Rickles joined the beautiful blond in his stint at the American Academy of Dramatic Arts, all the necessary ingredients for a Hollywood movie right there. While in rehearsal for a bit part on TV's *Studio One*, Ericson was called to an open audition for a feature film and within three days was in Italy starring opposite studio discovery Pier Angeli in *Teresa* (1951). He's a pretty-boy soldier emotionally stunted by a smothering mother and a jellyfish dad. He's jellyfish, jr. Sweating buckets throughout the film, Ericson is put through the psychological wringer while trying to conquer his weakling anxieties and become a stable husband to the beautiful young Italian girl he brings back from war-ravaged Italy. It's as if a shirt model was given the lead. You're inclined to conclude he's not much of an actor, but you're equally inclined not to object.

MGM offered him a contract, which he turned down in order to take the lead in the Broadway production of *Stalag 17*, which ran for 688 performances. When he returned to Tinsel Town, he was the better-looking half of Elizabeth Taylor's musical infatuations in *Rhapsody* (1954), the Count in *The Student Prince* (1954), Grace Kelly's younger brother, whose search for emeralds ends in a rock slide, in *Green Fire* (1954), and the young buck who sweats a lot with the baddies, but ultimately lends a helping hand to one-armed Spencer Tracy in the classic *Bad Day at Black Rock* (1955).

He's one of Barbara Stanwyck's *Forty Guns* (1957), a lowdown cowboy bully named Rocky who thinks he's Brando's *Wild One* in the Old West and cowardly uses her for a human shield. He made a handsome addition to westerns of the period, ambling in tight pants as the hotshot gunslinger in *The Return of Jack Slade* (1955), as a wimpy county sheriff in *Day of the Bad Man* (1958), and as an Army lieutenant with Indian trouble even when he's trying to support their cause in *Oregon Passage* (1958).

Ericson was always a welcome distraction—lead or not—but he didn't like what Hollywood had to offer, turned down several scripts, and effectively ended his big time movie career.

He's shirtless for the first fifteen minutes of *Pretty Boy Floyd* (1960), but the low-budget film is cheesy beyond belief. "I don't know whether to clout you or kiss you," he tells a dame. "Well, just kiss me...*hard*...pretty boy." He slaps her. It's both weird and backward to see him doing this kind of crap a decade after he'd starred in his first studio film. He still has his incredible good looks and shapely physique, so it's not as if he let himself go to pot, and yet he displays all the thespian gifts of an investor's son-in-law calling a favor. After he's shot dead and lying out in the field, a farm widow runs a hand across his handsome cheek and laments: "What a waste."

The *7 Faces of Dr. Lao* (1964), spaghetti westerns, TV appearances, dinner theatre, and painting awaited, as did an inexplicable appearance at age 47 in the January, 1974 issue of *Playgirl*, in which he's a bare-assed Tarzan cavorting about California's Lion Country Safari and holding a yowling cub in front of his crotch.

Tarzan himself swung through his fourth and into his fifth decade at the cinema by morphing from the handsome and beefy **Lex Barker** (1919-1973), who made five appearances in the role from 1949-1953, into the even beefier **Gordon Scott** (1927-), who did the next five from 1955-1960 before exporting his prime cut to Italy for a series of Samson films.

The move from Weissmuller's large, but sexy ape man to a progressively muscular and asexual comic book cutout mirrors the rise of the commercial bodybuilding movement in 1950s Americana. Bulging muscles were proudly displayed as inspiration for good nutrition and exercise, especially true on kiddie matinee Tarzans whose other bulges were now hidden under panels of canvas large enough to take all the loin out of loincloth.

Muscle fetishists were thusly inspired while the rest of us wondered where all the un-pumped meat went. In the glorious Tarzan movies of the early 1930s, audiences came loaded with sexual expectation. The Tarzan flicks of the 1950s offered far less in the way of sensual thrills, though there must have been some degree of anticipation when a new young actor was announced in the role and you went along to conduct that very first physical. If he was your "type," great. If not, you could always while away the afternoon paying attention to the continuity gaffes as his nipples went from soft to hard to soft again in the same scene.

For a single guy over the age of twelve, going to see a Tarzan movie, even expressing interest in going to see one, had its risks. You might have to answer that telltale question brimming with homosexual taunt:

John Ericson snuggles Elizabeth Taylor in *Rhapsody* (1954). AUTHOR'S COLLECTION

"Why?" So just imagine our brave brothers of the 1950s who had the balls to go see *Bomba* movies on their own.

Johnny Sheffield (1931-) made his Broadway debut at age seven in the original cast of *On Borrowed Time*. His father, actor Reginald Sheffield, picked up his *Hollywood Reporter* one day and saw a piece that queried: "Have you a Tarzan, Jr. in your backyard?" Why, yes, he did. The seven year-old who could sink (not swim) was promptly screen-tested and handpicked by Johnny Weissmuller for the role of Boy in the literally titled *Tarzan Finds A Son!* (1939).

Eight Tarzan films and ten years later, as a shapely teenager with tight curls, he was rescued from his post-Boy casting crisis when low-budget Monogram Studios signed him on to play *Bomba, the Jungle Boy* (1949). He ran around showing off his fine young physique from ages 18-24 in no fewer than twelve Bomba installments between 1949-1955, sporting a leopard-skin loincloth slit at the sides and far more revealing than what the new Tarzans were wearing. All this in spite of the fact that Bomba is reportedly Swahili for "small package."

As he matter-of-factly explains in *Bomba and the Jungle Girl* (1952), he's "just a white boy who was left alone to grow up with the animals." Basically, Sheffield gamely gives the same two-note performance throughout the entire series. He's either action Bomba or static Bomba, and everyone else is either a "bad man" or a "good friend." He occasionally smiles (without the benefit of movie star teeth), delivers his lines and tromps through the jungle with all the conviction of a dry run rehearsal, and has an endearing way of wobbling as he swings through the trees on those convenient vines.

Still, he's the whole show, since the series is otherwise occupied by routine storylines, boring dialogue, and hundreds of feet of repeated stock footage inserts from African wildlife documentaries. As with the early Tarzan films, there's a blatant disregard for nature and cruelty towards animals in the wild, with far too many killings of beasts simply behaving as they ought to be behaving.

Bomba never gets the girl, isn't even interested. He always returns solo to the jungle to be with his friends. "Sometimes at night I sleep between their feet," he tells us of his giant buddies in *Elephant Stampede* (1951). (Nobody ever claimed he was smart.) In *Bomba and the Lost Volcano* (1950), he befriends a little white boy whose parents think Bomba is an imaginary friend until they come face to leopard skin with the loincloth junior was given by Bomba, who has the boy change into it during their playtime in the jungle. Bomba is such a nice fella, though; he even obligingly keeps his hands behind his back to facilitate his captors tying his wrists—despite having been knocked unconscious.

The cutest moment in the series' first entry, *Bomba, the Jungle Boy*, has Peggy Ann Garner accidentally tearing her skirt and then asking Bomba if he has a leopard skin she could wear. He immediately reaches down to take his own loincloth off, but she quickly stops him. "Oh no, Bomba, you keep that one."

He began as the *Jungle Boy* and finished as *Bomba, the Lord of the Jungle* (1955). And is that my imagination or do we get to see a flash of Bomba's left nut during the fight with the would-be elephant shooter four and a half minutes in?

They were, of course, B-grade entertainments, but they were beloved by a generation of young and old men alike. Johnny may not have had a pretty face, but he had plenty of appeal below the neck for an afternoon's ogling. He was even allowed a light sprinkling of chest hair in some entries, most notably in *The Lion Hunters* (1951), where it's distinct enough in close-ups but looks like a rash in medium shots. Sheffield's dad tried extending his son's beefcake career by producing and directing an unsold television pilot in the mid-1950s called *Bantu*, in which the jungle teen rides a zebra and wears a matching loincloth, which must have given the animal some cause for concern.

A perfect Tarzan for the 1950s would have been Henry Herman McKinnies, the strapping young man discovered by agents during a 1950 production of *All My Sons* at UCLA. Then again, he may have been overqualified. He had a BA in Speech from Northwestern University and went to graduate school at UCLA where he studied radio.

Several studios were interested in him, but it was 20th Century-Fox that signed **Jeffrey Hunter** (1925-1969) to his first movie contract and graduated him to main title billing and secondary lead roles within a year. His first part, as The Kid in *Call Me Mister* (1951), illustrates a slight, but consistent career difficulty in seeing this fully grown 6'1" man in his mid-twenties playing roles that called for physically slighter, younger guys. He's just too big to have anybody call him "son" or "boy" (which might be why he plays his sole scene in *Mister* lying on his army bunk), and you never believed it when the other guy, whoever he was, kicked his butt in a fight.

Johnny Sheffield: Tarzan's "Boy" graduates to *Bomba*, the Jungle Boy, in an even dozen Saturday afternoon features through 1955.
PHOTOFEST

A baker's dozen into his film career, you'd have realized that you'd go to see him in anything. Even if he never made a classic, you'd have the satisfaction of spending the afternoon or evening with him, waiting for him to come on screen and marveling at how handsome handsome could be.

He spends much of *Sailor of the King* (1953) without his shirt on, displaying an attractive physique that comes both with chest hair and a belly button thanks to the production being British. Besides that, after a lifeless 15 minute prologue without him, the film proves a natural for Hunter's physicality, credibly playing a Canadian signalman in the British navy who, armed with nothing more than a rifle, single-handedly holds up a German battleship's timely repairs.

He's stunning without his turban as a 13th Century Arabian prince in *Princess of the Nile* (1954), perhaps the liveliest and most enjoyably swift (at 71 minutes) of an epidemic of Arabian misadventures

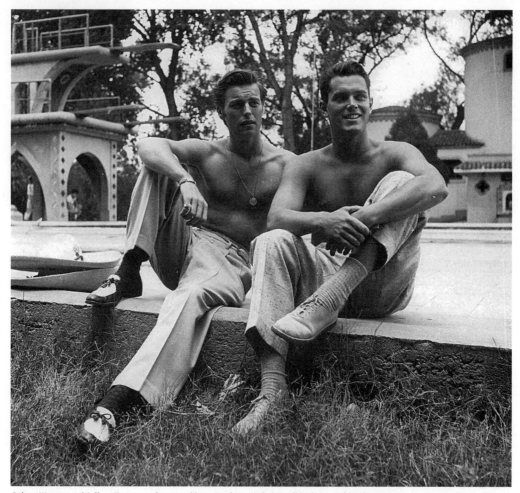

Robert Wagner and Jeffrey Hunter made seven films together. Wish they all had scenes like this. PHOTOFEST

that studios were forcing their male beauties to appear in at the time. Even Rock Hudson did one: *The Golden Blade* (1953).

Jeffrey Hunter had an almost classically masculine face: dark locks, strong chin, movie star teeth, perhaps—if one was to nit-pick—a smallish nose, but it was his blue eyes that fans fell into. Their supernatural hue diffused across the rest of his features and left handsome in the wake of beauty.

He's often as beautiful as Monument Valley on the horizon in John Ford's western classic *The Searchers* (1956). He's afforded an entrance befitting such beauty, seen from the doorway as he rides in and jumps off his still galloping horse into silhouette. His character is one-eighth Cherokee, a foundling rescued by racist Ethan Edwards (John Wayne) after the boy's parents were massacred. "It just happened to be me. No need to make more of it," his benefactor grumbles.

As with other roles, he's a little tall in the saddle to be playing such a big dumb kid. Caught in a washtub when the girl predictably walks in on him, he panics and she calmly reminds him that she's got brothers. "You talk as if a feller should run around naked!" he protests.

His character is written more juvenile than he looks (even with a shaved chest), perhaps more appropriate for Wayne's own gorgeous boy, **Patrick Wayne** (1939-   ), who shows up for a scene as a cavalry lieutenant. ("Just funnin', son," the Duke says to him on-screen.)

Hunter made seven films with Robert Wagner, all of which are worth watching to test your allegiances and choose your favorites among friends.

Both Wagner's and Hunter's names come up first in the credits and with promising little red lips next to each of them for *A Kiss Before Dying* (1955). The title inspires its own romantic fantasy, with the terminally ill Wagner kissing young neurosurgeon Hunter on the way into the operating room before the

98

revelation that the hospital had mixed up the X-rays. No such canned luck.

Hunter is plain awful as a pipe-smoking and bespectacled college math tutor who will eventually help figure out the obvious: that Wagner is a cold-blooded killer dating his first victim's sister. The math nerd is played like a math nerd. There's not a flesh and blood character there, leaving Hunter to fool with his glasses. You can tell that he's not used to them because he handles them like a prop; so much so, that he's actually a bit better in the film when he doesn't have to wear them.

A veteran of westerns, Hunter was 32 when he played momma's boy Bless Keough in *Gun for a Coward* (1957), but was still playing one of the younger brothers and looking too big to pull it off. What helps is that older bro is Fred MacMurray and youngest bro is a very cute and precocious Dean Stockwell, thesping as if he's the only begotten son of Clift and Dean.

The problem with Bless is that he's soft. He's afraid, shaky with a gun.

"I'm not even sure what kind of a man I am," he tells elder brother Will. "I don't fit."

"There's a lot of Ma in your ways, Bless, and that's part of your fight."

Make love, not war. If you have to fall for a wimp, best he should have eyes like Jeffrey Hunter's.

And after a solid decade of film work, you'd think he'd deserve better than a "co-starring Jeffrey Hunter" credit for playing the *King of Kings* (1961). Nicholas Ray's *I Was A Teenage Jesus*, as it was

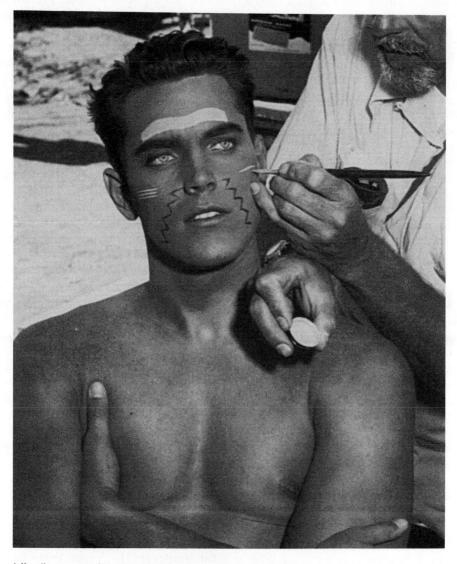

Jeffrey Hunter getting his make-up for *White Feather* (1955). AUTHOR'S COLLECTION

occasionally chided in the press, is an epic-length rehash of the story of the Christ that opens with the Romans marching into Jerusalem. You can see the rubber tips of their spears wobbling as they go.

We first meet Jesus at age 32 as he stands before John the Baptist, the blue of the Savior's eyes so penetratingly alluring that they inspire sinful thoughts. Probably not the best way to get started.

Unfortunately, though in some ways it would become his signature role, Hunter's Christ is pretty-by-the-numbers, not inspirational. In films as early in his career as *Red Skies of Montana* (1952), in which he plays the embittered son of a killed forest fire fighter, he demonstrated he could both credibly command the screen and be parenthetically beautiful without an argument, but Jesus drains all the life out of him. The difficulty in translating Biblical stories to the screen is magnified by their distinct lack of humor. They're solemn, serious, and sacrosanct. If you're Cecil B. De Mille, you can lather them in violence, sex, and special effects, but you can't make them warm, funny, or the least bit joyful.

At first glance, while he's being scourged, the fact that they shaved Jeffrey Hunter's underarms in *King of Kings* ensures that subsequent close-ups of Christ on the cross won't have his holy countenance sandwiched between his unholy armpit hair in 70mm Super Technirama. Though fully capable of growing a beard, the Son of God has been spared additional secondary sex characteristics. It's weird and definitely calls attention to itself (rather than not), but possibly the smooth underarms are meant to accomplish an iconic effect. Without the hair, he looks more like an actual crucifix. (The "style" may have been Hunter's own personal preference, by the way. He's similarly depilated playing wooden Indians: as Cheyenne warrior Little Dog, whose friendship with cute white surveyor Robert Wagner turns ugly in 1955's *White Feather*, and as Matuwir, the pony-tailed grandson of the chief, in 1955's *Seven Cities of Gold*.)

He's even more beautiful in *No Man Is An Island* (1962), the true story of Navy serviceman George W. Tweed's nearly three years hiding out from the Japanese on the island of Guam. Hunter's last starring role in a major studio film, it's marked by a strange mix of brutal realism and old Hollywood war movie shtick. In that sense, it's emblematic of the demise of the old studio system and the increasing difficulty studio-bred stars had making the transition from their style of acting to the grittier, more realistic approach post-Brando.

Some suggest the actor had been typecast as Christ (Hunter never believed this; how can you be typecast as God?) in order to explain his rather sudden difficulty finding quality work when he still looked so good. He starred as the title western lawyer on NBC's *Temple Houston* (1963-64), then made a number of films in Spain when his two-year contract with Warner Bros. expired in 1965. After that, there were occasional guest shots in American films, most embarrassingly as a fig leaf-wearing Adam to Phyllis Diller's Eve for a dream sequence in *The Private Navy of Sgt. O'Farrell* (1968).

Sci-fi fans know him as Captain Christopher Pike, the original captain of the USS Enterprise in the 1965 television pilot of *Star Trek*, which wouldn't become a series for another year. The producers were ready to go with him until a screening of the pilot was requested and Hunter's second wife—and she alone—came to see it. She bluntly told them that her husband was a movie star not a TV star…instantly killing his career, though she could hardly have known she was doing so and was understandably unimpressed by what she saw. Much of his footage would be used in a two-part episode entitled "The Menagerie," which aired during the first season in November of 1966 (and is available on DVD). Hunter's second near-miss at eternal TV cult fame was as Mike Brady on *The Brady Bunch*. He was deemed too pretty.

A pitiful decline into Z-movie trash being filmed abroad was his fate and the actor fought with depression and alcoholism. He was seriously injured during a special effects explosion on the set of *Viva America* (1970) when the window of a car he was driving was accidentally rigged to blow in and not out. Hunter began suffering from neurological ailments upon his return to Los Angeles in 1969, requiring hospitalization. Somewhat mysteriously (and suggesting a stroke), he fell down a three-stair staircase in his home, fracturing his skull on the banister, leaving him unconscious and requiring emergency brain surgery, during which he died at age 43.

In *The Sea Chase* (1955), John Wayne is improbably cast as the German captain of a freighter docked in Sydney at the outbreak of WWII. He's such a good German, though, such a thorough anti-Nazi, that he doesn't even have an accent. "Owf weeder zane, Sydney," he says as they head out of the harbor. There's only one man on his entire vessel who looks the part: blond, blue eyes, impossibly handsome, with a well-chiseled face. It belongs to **Tab Hunter** (1931-   ), born Arthur Andrew Gelien (Kelm) in New York City. He moved with his mother and older brother to San Francisco when he was two, then down to LA three years later.

At 15, he lied about his age on his application to the Coast Guard and served a year alternating on both coasts. While on leave, he became enchanted by the stage plays in New York City, and when he joined his mother back in San Francisco a year later, he decided he wanted to give acting a shot. He had no plans to go to college, was working as a sheet metal worker in a factory, and spent much of his off-work time participating in competitive sports: riding horses and ice skating.

His two word line, "Hi, Fred," got snipped out of *The Lawless* (1950), but he's still credited in the picture with the name dreamed up by a conversation between his best buddy and his agent. Tab Hunter was now a commodity.

When director Stuart Heisler, who was second unit director on *The Hurricane* (1937), went looking for someone to play a half-naked Marine stranded on an island with Linda Darnell, the newly christened Tab Hunter was offered and accepted.

Island of Desire (1953), a British production known as *Saturday Island* in the UK, afforded audiences drool-inducing shots of Tab walking around in a tight homemade loin wrap cut high enough to afford us peeks at his bundled package. (He's similarly unclad throughout 1954's amateur-hour *Return to Treasure Island*, where his belly button and descending treasure trail are on full view because it wasn't a studio picture.) As with *The Blue Lagoon* (1980) nearly three decades later, the simple plot is an erotic excuse to have the attractive leading players show off their bodies in Technicolor. Like Christopher Atkins, Tab Hunter had no real acting experience before he landed this gig and it's easy to see that thespian abilities were not high on the list of casting priorities. His line readings are painfully amateurish and delivered as if someone were squeezing his nuts. "We'll lick the whole cockeyed world!" he declares with a squeal. He's got a gorgeous physique, though, and an even more beautiful face. He's a Golden Boy all right. Darnell relents to his year-long case of blue balls, but proves herself stir crazy when she has to make a choice between Tab's "Chicken" (that's his character's nickname, no fooling) and a handsome RAF pilot who crash lands and breaks up their little party.

Tab Hunter, as "Chicken," takes a hold of shapely Linda Darnell while stranded on the *Island of Desire* (1953). PHOTOFEST

Mainstream audiences and teenyboppers didn't discover him, however, until two years later when he starred in the box-office hit *Battle Cry* (1955). He's a 19-year old "All-American Boy" from Baltimore drafted into service in 1942. Despite its success, the film has to be one of the most inconsequential war stories ever committed to the screen. It begins as a blatantly stereotypical look at the process of inducting young men, putting them through basic training, and trying to make them into soldiers, then veers off to follow a handful of stilted relationships between the guys and their gals.

Tab goes for a hayride with an older woman and has to take his shirt off in her apartment. "Sorry, I felt kind of itchy," he says as she comes into the room and he puts it back on. She gives him a little Scotch, then suggests a dip in the pool. Her tits are pointing like rockets out of her red-glare sweater. He doesn't have a suit, so she gives him a pair of her husband's shorts, which are gigantic. "Wait a minute, not so fast. I'm liable to lose these!" If only he had. The problem is he's being forced to play a nice boy, not a real character. It's stock work.

When he and his true love from back home are out necking and romping at night, you wish a Gill Man would come out of the lake, kill her, and abduct him. That's the movie I wanted to see, but there were plenty of boys and girls who fell for him anyway.

Stardom had arrived, further proven by his making the scandal sheets. *Confidential*, which would plague the industry for at least two more years, ran an item in 1955 about his arrest at a "limp-wrist pajama party" on the night of October 14, 1950. They were busy digging up anything they could under his real name.

So long as Tab kept showing off his body, that's all that mattered to most of us. We see him shirtless and sweaty chopping wood in *The Sea Chase*, as well as wearing just his shorts and preparing for a morning swim with a handsome buddy. He's also got a shirtless scene and some nice CinemaScope close-ups in the routine western *The Burning Hills* (1956), the first of three films he would co-star in with Natalie Wood. In one publicity photo of the fictional off-screen duo, Tab lays over Natalie's lap as she prepares to give his behind a spanking. He's also the cover boy in swim shorts for an issue of *Tomorrow's Man—The International Magazine of Bodybuilding*. A headline next to his photo asks, "Are We Too Preoccupied With Sex?"

He wasn't very happy with what Warner Bros. was giving him in the way of money or parts, however, and he infuriated the studio when he allowed himself to be talked into cutting a single for Dot Records without their permission or financial interest. "Young Love" was marketed to the bobbysoxers and became a smash hit, topping the charts in March of 1957 and selling over a million copies. Could a musical be far off?

First, though, he had to play an angelic-looking American delinquent who joins the French Air Force before the U.S. got into the war in *Lafayette Escadrille* (1958). He's shirtless several times, we catch him in his boxers, and he shares the bunkhouse with a lot of cute young guys, including Clint Eastwood, Bill Wellman, Jr., Jody McCrea, and Tom Laughlin.

After striking an officer and finding himself beaten and imprisoned, he's afforded an escape thanks to his pals and has to spend the rest of the movie with an ugly putty scar trailing from his right eye. The film's thematic highlight comes when he's forced to go to his French girlfriend's madame and get a temp job as a male prostitute. At least that's the way it plays on-screen, though director William Wellman writes in his 1974 autobiography that the guy's real job was acting as a pimp. Hunter's movie-version gigolo is subsequently picked up by a general for a hotel tryst, but can't help confessing his life story on the ride over.

"They don't put medals on you for poking an officer" suddenly has a whole new meaning. Astonishingly, the officer has a kind heart and sees to Tab's salvation without even getting what he came for.

Tab finally got his musical with *Damn Yankees* (1958), playing the 22-year old reincarnate whose deal with the Devil means a short career as a star baseball player. It's corny, but he's cute. His beautiful, blond, buzzed head only has to warble a bit of one song. Otherwise, he slouches, chews Juicy Fruit, and, unfortunately, wears bright white baggy boxers in the locker room. One of his dopey teammates is trying to finish a crossword puzzle and asks: "What's a three letter word for a sticky substance?"

He eventually bought out his contract at WB for $100,000. At Paramount, he was the soldier boy "old enough to do anything" with Sophia Loren, because she was *That Kind of Woman* (1959). The subtleties of a performance may have been missing, but he's got one of the all time great jaw lines when it comes to photogenic smooching. Good roles were getting even harder to come by. He joined Frankie Avalon and

Tab in his loinwrap from the same film, also known as *Saturday Island* (1953). YESTERDAY

Gary Crosby in *Operation Bikini* (1963), which sounds like a beach party movie but isn't, then ended up in one anyway with *Ride the Wild Surf* (1964).

Tab did TV, too. He starred in the original version of *Fear Strikes Out* on the tube shortly before Anthony Perkins, who was a boyfriend for awhile, did the film version in 1957. *The Tab Hunter Show* lasted just a single season in 1960-61 with Tab playing a cartoonist whose autobiographical comic strip is called "Bachelor-At-Large."

Cult film fans know him from at least two of his three unlikely teamings with Divine in the 1980s. He plays drive-in guru Todd Tomorrow in John Waters' "Odorama" classic *Polyester* (1981), then produced and starred with his 300 pound amour in *Lust in the Dust* (1985). Their final teaming came in *Out of the Dark* (1988), a horror film about murders at a phone sex company which features a non-drag Divine. Tab's also the bespectacled sex education teacher who leads the gang in a dorky, but catchy song about "Reproduction" in *Grease 2* (1982).

A 1957 teenybopper magazine devoted entirely to Tab Hunter had this to say about his long-term potential: "On the screen, Tab reveals a freshness that is as exhilarating as the first smell of spring in the air. His clean cut looks, his typically boyish smile, and the aura of wholesomeness that pervades the film once he makes his appearance, have become synonymous with a new trend in Hollywood. The movie makers are subtly replacing the great unwashed, who sniffle, scuffle, and muster their way through a plot, with the more appealing 'boy next door,' or 'why, he could be my son' identification." Tab Hunter certainly qualified. He worked all the prototypical jobs of the era: soda jerk, delivery boy, gas station attendant, and movie house usher. You can just picture him doing any one of those things and then paste that picture in a magazine or newspaper ad of the day.

Maybe that's why some people feel the need to jokingly conjure his name as an example of one of those pretty boy non-actors churned out in the 1950s. It's a typically mean-spirited response to the pop in

Tab Hunter, seen here in a studio portrait from the 1950s, announced in 2003 that he was writing his memoirs, chronicling his years in Hollywood as a closeted gay actor. PHOTOFEST

pop culture. There was room for Tab Hunter in the 1950s and he gave the movies and his fans his best shot.

How could the teenybopper magazines, which traded on selling American teenagers clean-cut, nice boys, have known that what we really wanted was "the great unwashed, who sniffle, scuffle, and muster their way through a plot?"

The 1950s — Take Two

"Hey, You Wanna Come Home With Me?"

James Byron Dean (1931-1955) liked to sign his name "James (Brando Clift) Dean." He was cocky that way. He pestered both of those actors, whom he adored and worshipped as gods, with persistent phone calls and both thought it was kind of creepy. Director Elia Kazan was said to have told Monty: "He's a punk and a helluva talent. He likes racing cars, waitresses—and waiters. He says you're his idol."

Clift found the frequent calls to his unlisted New York number weird. The kid had nothing to say, he just wanted "to listen to the sound of my voice."

If Clift was Dean's emotional touchstone as an actor, Brando was his method. In an era when every young actor was attempting to mimic the star of *A Streetcar Named Desire* (1951) and *On the Waterfront* (1954), James Dean was attempting to mimic a life, swallow it whole. He took up such Brandoisms as playing the bongos and the recorder, cultivated a careless and carefree attitude about his appearance, visited the set of *Desiree* (1954) to study his idol's every move, and generally made it no secret that if Marlon did it, he wanted to do it, too.

Brando tried to discourage the flagrant copycatting, even telling Dean to go pick up his coat and hang it up like a nice boy after Jimmy had rolled it into a ball at a party and ceremoniously dumped it in the middle of the floor. Some say Marlon was a little miffed at all the attention "the kid" was getting doing his act, as opposed to all the other hopeless wannabes who couldn't pull it off, and that he made efforts to ignore and otherwise discourage his acolyte from friendship or mentorship. In his own book, Brando says he now understands that Dean was copying him out of youth and inexperience and that by the time he did *Giant* (1956) he had found his own chops and probably would have gone on to be one of the greats. He said he knew that the guy had psychological problems and he encouraged him to seek professional help.

Jimmy was born in Marion, Indiana, the first and only child of Winton and Mildred Dean. Son and mother developed a close and special relationship—the kind that you see in movies and immediately know disaster lies ahead. Shortly after a move to California, Mildred was diagnosed with cancer and languished for a year before she died. Jimmy was just nine years old. Unable or unwilling to care for him, you can guess which the little boy grasped, Jimmy's father sent his young son back to Indiana to live with his aunt and uncle in the tiny farming community of Fairmount, Indiana. The boy rode the train back. His mother's body rode back with him.

From ages nine to eighteen, Jimmy Dean grew up in Fairmount, halfheartedly working on his uncle's farm and wholeheartedly buzzing around town on his motorsickle. He attended church where he gave a speech on temperance one afternoon and went to Fairmount High, where his academic record was only average but he excelled at sports and dramatics. He was extremely nearsighted, as well as on the short side, so it seems almost inconceivable to find him crouching there among the basketball team in school photos, but there he is. The gangly kid in the number 3 jersey whose glasses kept flying off during games was actually a star player by his senior year.

Under the guidance of drama teacher Adeline Brookshire (later Nall), Jimmy appeared in numerous school plays and took his delivery of "A Madman's Manuscript" (from Dickens' *Pickwick Papers*) to first place in the state forensic league finals. He went on to the national competition in Colorado where he placed sixth, an achievement that nevertheless left him bitterly disappointed.

Almost as if Dickens himself were writing his life story, Jimmy came to befriend a revered and trusted local preacher by the name of Reverend James DeWeerd. The degree to which they were friends and the exact nature of their relationship has been reported with great variation over the years, particularly since DeWeerd's homosexuality has been acknowledged. Before we go any further, it must be said that there is an enormous amount of literature on the subject of James Dean and, as with Elvis and Marilyn, who complete the Trinity, as many versions and interpretations of the text as suitably Biblical. [My personal

105

The soft side of James Dean in *East of Eden* (1955). EVERETT COLLECTION

advice to the uninitiated or just plain confused looking for a good place to start: *James Dean: The Biography* (St. Martin's Press, 1995) by Val Holley.]

A month after his high school graduation in May, 1949, Jimmy moved to Los Angeles to live with his dad, but the move was a familial disaster. He enrolled at Santa Monica City College where he got involved in sports and plays again. After a disillusioning year, he managed to transfer to UCLA as a pre-law student, though the theatre department was his real goal. He was accepted into the Sigma Nu frat, for which his singular personality and wildly independent spirit was not well suited. In the entertainingly awful documentary *The James Dean Story* (1957), which plays like one of those 16mm specials you were forced to watch in high school on the "Story of Aluminum," a frat brother tellingly refers to the dead movie star as "Dean" and points out that an examination of the frat records shows "Dean" left them owing $45, which, logic dictates, they won't get now.

His embarrassingly peppy be-bop Pepsi commercial appearance in late 1950 at least got him his actor's union card and he made his first dramatic television appearance in 1951 as St. John the Apostle in "Hill Number One," where he's afforded several nice close-ups and proclaims his few lines of dialogue in a deeper register than we'll ever hear him use again. He had the flu.

He bailed out of UCLA, took some acting classes, and had a generally miserable and unsuccessful time getting noticed by the studios. While parking cars at a lot next to CBS, he caught the eye of radio director Rogers Brackett, who took a shine to him and got him some on-air work. Brackett's homosexuality was undoubtedly a factor, but besides giving the kid a few breaks, he became his surrogate father, mentor, and patron. As with nearly all of Dean's friends and confidantes, the relationship had an expiration date unknown to the friend or confidant.

Nearly as many doors were being slammed as were being opened, however, because of Dean's personality quirks, his cocky insolence, and bad personal habits. He was already acting the part of a star, though in truth, he was just a bit player with delusions of grandeur. He has two lines at the very end of the excellent Korean War film *Fixed Bayonets* (1951), then a single line—but at least more screen time—as an attendant to Jerry Lewis' boxing opponent in the smash hit comedy *Sailor Beware* (1952), and the recitation of one rather long line of desired ingredients for a mega-malt at the soda bar in *Has Anybody Seen My Gal?* (1952).

When Brackett took a trip to Chicago to direct a show, he paid for Jimmy to come along, too, then financed the kid's hometown stop (during which Dean was given the ego-stroke opportunity to lecture his alma mater about Hollywood, etc.) and a fortuitous move to NYC thereafter.

It was while in New York that the insecure, but occasionally charismatic young actor began making some important contacts with Brackett's friends and a circle of fellow showbiz hopefuls. He did a few television shows and even performed a stint as a stunt tester on *Beat the Clock*. His 1952 audition of an original piece by and with duet partner and friend Christine White for Elia Kazan and Lee Strasberg at the Actor's Studio resulted in his acceptance. He subsequently performed something called *Matador* in front of the class and Strasberg tore both the piece and the actor to shreds, or so it must have seemed. The remainder of his involvement with the famed school of modern acting consisted of sour non-participation. He was highly sensitive to criticism and felt rejected and angry if it wasn't in his favor.

His Broadway debut in *See the Jaguar* (1952) lasted five performances, during which he played a teenaged mountain hick who ends up in the cage intended for the title wildcat. It's more than rumored that he landed the role by insinuating himself onto the yacht belonging to the show's homosexual and married producer while it was being cast.

In his next show, a 1954 stage version of Andre Gide's novel *The Immoralist*, James Dean was the Arab houseboy Bachir who seduces a married, but tormented gay archaeologist (Louis Jourdan) by performing something called the Scissors Dance. The play was intended as an examination of repressed and self-denied same sex love, but underwent a thematic change when a new director came in and suddenly the gay married man started to appear corrupt and deviant instead of anguished and empathetic.

Dean reportedly poured on the effeminate and made quite a sensuous spectacle of himself despite not looking remotely Arabic even with all the dark make-up. I'm sure he stirred the loins of many a married man in the audience who found themselves personally playing out the drama on stage from their seats. The actor butted heads with the new director and his co-stars, though, never doing anything the same way twice, and he gave his two-week notice after the opening night's performance in New York.

Before he quit trying to seduce the irritated and cardboard-cutout Jourdan on stage, though, Dean managed to seduce the sensibilities of director Elia Kazan, who caught a performance and then met with the 23-year-old to feel him out for the key role in his next picture. For once, the actor's carefree, slovenly, little punk demeanor enchanted instead of repelled. Kazan knew he had his star.

East of Eden (1955), based on half of John Steinbeck's novel, was originally to have starred Brando and Clift as Caleb and Aron, but both were otherwise preoccupied and director Kazan had his heart set on the wily James Dean. After Steinbeck met and took an instant dislike to him, too, he also knew the film had its quintessential Cal.

The first words spoken to James Dean in his first starring role in a motion picture are "Hello, pretty boy," and they come from a hefty black harlot smoking her cig while parked on the front porch of a neighboring whorehouse.

Wracked by the lie his Bible-beating father has told him all his life—that his mother is dead—Cal has resigned himself to being the bad boy.

In his best film, Dean literally embodies the tortured emotions of being a teenager who has felt unloved all his life. His body language has him huddling, ducking, hiding, hanging. He's the proverbial little boy lost. "Talk to me, father. I gotta know who I am. I gotta know what I'm like." His father Adam (Raymond Massey) doesn't know how to help, maybe can't. In the film's most heartwrenching scene, Cal tries to give his father a birthday present of money made on bean crop prices that soared during the war and the gift is catastrophically rejected.

Dean turns moaning toward Massey and in a moment of inspired improvisation caught on film embraces his father in anguish. Massey had no idea this was going to happen. He was one of many seasoned professionals who worked with Dean and didn't at the time appreciate his selfish experimentation. Earlier in the film, Massey's character grows increasingly perturbed when his son deliberately reads Scripture improperly. For Massey's reaction shots, Dean inserted profanities in his Biblical recitation and infuriated Massey for real. Just one of the "new school" tricks that the old school didn't get.

"I don't want any kind of love anymore. It doesn't pay off," says Cal, speaking in his beautifully tortured way to the darkness inside all of us. James Dean may speak to generations because he made discontent, teenage angst, and self-hate beautiful. Misery loves company and projecting it via an image sanctified by beauty has a powerful appeal. He's the wounded young man you want to take in your arms and console. In addition to the film's classic images showing him huddled in his sweater atop a moving freight train, standing aloft the old mill angrily shoving the ice blocks down the chute, and lying in the field watching the bean sprouts sprout, he appears outside Abra's window and when she says he looks "terrible," in reality, he looks postage stamp gorgeous. It's not a prettified conceit on the part of the actor, either. Dean's chronic insomnia tended to give him horrendous bags under his eyes and he could easily look ten years older than his boyish self, but there he is, his flaming hair at perfection, his soulful eyes, high cheekbones, and mournful face classically framed, at one point pressing up against the house as if he was embracing a lover.

Angst wasn't his only specialty. It was his sensitivity, his access to all his emotions that made him a new kind of teen idol and movie star. It's a joy to see Cal smile during the short time he's happy in the film, capable of a boyish giggle so genuine that you wonder whether Dean knew it was coming. When his spirits are up, he even giggles at his father's unfunny comment about needing his glasses looked at and the quiet laugh comes across as subtle psychological encouragement. He wants his dad to know he's capable of being a good boy, of connecting with him.

The story's designated "good boy," Cal's brother Aron, is played by young looker **Richard (Dick) Davalos** (1935-   ), a movie house usher spotted by Kazan in New York, who beat out Paul Newman, among others, for the part. He's a full-faced pretty boy, complete with dimples, who's clueless that he's his father's favorite in *Eden*. Aron genuinely loves his brother Cal and even says so.

A famous still exists of the brothers from a scene that was cut from the final print, supposedly because of homosexual connotations. The still—which became a popular postcard amongst gay men—shows a shirtless Davalos lying in bed in the background looking at a shirtless Dean sitting in the foreground with a phallic recorder at his lips. As a still, it's got overtones galore, but I sure would like to see what the scene looked like on moving film that caused such problems. A black-and-white test of the scene survives, and though it's staged completely differently, with Dean hidden in the shadows through much of it and Davalos outfitted in pajamas, the dialogue has Aron trying to convince a dejected Cal how easy it is to show their father that he loves him. It's a touching exchange and even if they were both nude I would wonder what was remotely "homosexual" about it. Davalos himself says (or has been talked into believing) that it was snipped because of gay overtones.

Homoerotic overtones, undoubtedly, because both of these beauties are half-naked, but that should have been a thematically harmless and welcome box-office draw. My goodness, even half-naked Dead End Kids in the original *Dead End* (1937) have their homoerotic moments, but that's only to say that there are moments which are perceived as erotic by the audience, not by the characters themselves. Why should two brothers talking in their bedroom without their shirts on signal any more objectionable eroticism than two sisters wearing their nighties doing the same thing? I understand the cultural fantasy divide (hetero men like to fantasize about two women), but I'm not buying the homophobia in *Eden* (even if it is the McCarthy '50s) until someone can show me the finished scene or the notes that led to the cut. (Remarkably, 1955 also saw Davalos as a Sicilian accused of homosexuality and shockingly kissed full on the mouth by Van Heflin in Arthur Miller's one-act play *A View From the Bridge*, which played briefly on Broadway before becoming a 1962 film with Raf Vallone smooching Jean Sorel.)

Davalos' most beautiful shot in *Eden* has him lying on the grass out front of the house during a discussion about the war. But the scene that brings me to tears every time I see it is when Aron angrily accuses Cal of starting the fight in the German's front yard, as well as fooling around with Abra, and Cal slaps and then punches him—twice. Davalos was so overwhelmed by the emotion of the scene and Dean's genuine rage that he left the set immediately afterwards and was said to have cried for hours.

It has been reported that Davalos and Dean didn't get along well together, but it has to be remembered that Dean was a tough guy to get along with even if you were his best friend. The two actors were shacked up for a time in a one-room apartment across from the Warner Bros. lot and their strikingly different living habits understandably caused tension. I think that's just exactly what Kazan was hoping.

A bloodied Richard Davalos in his best-known role, as Aron to James Dean's Cal, in *East of Eden* (1955). PHOTOFEST

In addition to *Eden*, Davalos appeared in two other films that year. In *I Died A Thousand Times* (1955), the CinemaScope and color retread of Bogie's *High Sierra* (1941), he has one scene as the dancing beau of the 19-year old ex-clubfoot whom Jack Palance helped pay to have surgically corrected. Dennis Hopper does the mambo with Shelley Winters in the same scene. Ornery Jack hates these damn kids and their wild ways and almost comes to blows with Davalos, who has a very prominent mole or beauty mark next to his right eye.

In *The Sea Chase* (1955), Davalos plays Sam the seaman and he looks downright cherubic beside shipmates Claude Akins, James Arness, and Alan Hale, Jr. A morning dip with Tab Hunter, both in their swimming shorts, has Davalos getting munched by a shark, then rescued and forced to undergo amputation. He suffers a couple of bare-chested, sweaty fits in bed before making the most dramatic decision of his life.

He was one of *All the Young Men* (1960), a Korean War melodrama with racial themes (Sidney Poitier is reluctantly put in charge of his troop), but five years after starring opposite James Dean, he was now lost among the very very supporting cast. He played the tempestuous younger brother who fights for the South while his older brother fights for the North in the one-season television show *The Americans* (1961), then only occasionally made film and television appearances after that: in the pointless reworking of *The Cabinet of Dr. Caligari* (1962), as the only actor without a definable character to play in *Cool Hand Luke* (1967), in notorious exploitation filmmaker Jack Hill's racecar flick *Pit Stop* (1969), and as the gun crazy Pvt. Gutowski, who fires the first shot from the bell tower as one of *Kelly's Heroes* (1970).

You look at Davalos and Dean together on screen and you can only hope they tested the waters with one another off it, if for no other reason than to validate a wishful thinking theory I have that beautiful men are more likely to experiment with other beautiful men because they're, well, men, and they're beautiful. James Dean said it best when he responded iconoclastically to a query about his sexuality by saying: "Well, I'm certainly not going through life with one hand tied behind my back."

And though his relationship with Pier Angeli came dangerously close to marriage, and shouldn't be discounted, Dean expressed a great deal of curiosity about homosexuality. Considering the misdirection of the debate over his sexual orientation these many years, which pits the fools who deny his homosexual experiences against the fools who write about them in sperm shooting detail, the fact that gay men played key roles in his eventual ascent is unsurprising. I can't imagine a queer alive who wouldn't have wanted to help this beautiful young man get somewhere. Certainly Rogers Brackett was just one of many who did. A legendary quote attributed to Dean has him admitting that he'd had his "cock sucked by five of the most powerful men in Hollywood."

It's widely guessed and reported from intimates that his rejection for military service was on the basis of his declaring homosexual tendencies, though his terrible eyesight could just have likely been a factor.

So much has been made of the sex life of James Dean that one hardly knows how to nail it down. At the very least, his bisexuality is doubtless and that in itself lends to his appropriation by both women and gay men as an *objet d'sex*. Not having lived quite long enough to face journalist interrogations over his supposed "homosexuality," Dean's revealed private life has done the trick in absentia, and that is where his legend assumes ironic significance in the scheme of things: With only fleeting examples of hinted homosexuality on-screen, and those—most notably Plato's in *Rebel*—were directed at him not from him, it was Dean's intimated off-screen life that legitimized him as a gay icon.

For decades an infamous is-it-him photo of a nude "James Dean" perched in a tree holding his hard-on had been served up as a foggy antique in the occasional adult magazine, but it found an illustrious home for all to see in Paul Alexander's *Boulevard of Broken Dreams* (Viking, 1994), a bio whose purpose is not only to assert that the actor was gay, gay, gay, but to recount his sexual encounters in such impossibly intimate and graphic detail that you'd think someone had them on film somewhere. This may be the culture's most tawdry assimilation of a star: his sex life rendered as gay porn.

A surprising number of naked movie star photos, many from the 1950s and '60s, have circulated among private collectors and along gay "underground" circuits. In addition to the Dean shot, there are nudes purported to be (and in some cases confirmed to be) Burt Lancaster, Victor Mature, Roddy McDowall, Yul Brynner, John Saxon, Vince Edwards, George Maharis, even Pat Boone. There's the legendary photo alleged to show Brando in profile sucking dick and a less-famed, but highly collectible shot claiming to show Tab Hunter sucking his own. For years these photos were only whispered about and very hard to come by. Today, they appear in magazines, on the Internet, and for purchase from gay memorabilia shops alongside an enormous inventory of fakes facilitated by easy-to-use imagery software.

The Dean photo is extremely grainy, and you certainly have to wonder what the circumstance was for such a pose, yet it's not beyond the realm of possibility that he allowed himself to be photographed that way. He didn't have a reputation for being a genital exhibitionist, but he had few inhibitions about nudity. The guy in the photo certainly looks like him, though it looks like lots of other guys, too. Would someone say, "My God, that's James Dean," if they were shown the photo without being told who it was? I'm not so sure.

East of Eden was the only starring film James Dean lived to see play in theatres. It arguably contains his best performance, for which he was nominated for an Academy Award as Best Actor. But it was as Jim Stark in *Rebel Without A Cause* (1955), wearing his red windbreaker and blue jeans, that James Dean became a 24-year-old teenage deity and cultural icon.

The perpetual new kid on the block, whose parents moved him the last time after he beat up a kid who called him "chicken," Jim Stark is lying in the street drunk when we first encounter him. Since James Dean is playing him, though, drunk wasn't nearly enough. He had to be playing with a little mechanical monkey, too. Dean always worked in layers. Which is why he giggles as if he's being tickled when the cop frisks him at the police station. You won't find that subtle and ingenious piece of business in any copy of the script.

Dean was an organic actor. His character's body does things subconsciously, reactively. Consider the way he reclines on the family couch, the way he seems to be humping his car when he leans onto the hood while keeping both hands in his pockets during his nighttime rendezvous with Judy (Natalie Wood), or the way he puts a cigarette in his mouth backwards.

He often kept his fellow actors waiting as he went through his private preparations in his trailer, antagonizing lots of people who found his selfish behavior unprofessional and rude. He prepped for an hour on everyone else's valuable time before coming to the set for the scene in which he violently punches the desk of the juvenile officer played by Edward Platt. Dean did the scene in a single take and injured his hand in the process. If you watch closely, you'll notice that even though he's about to explode into rage, Dean uses his index finger to make sure Platt's leg is out of the way before he lets go his punch. There's something vaguely heroic about watching an actor do a scene in which you know the pain he's inflicting on himself is real. He also got sliced in the neck during the switchblade fight at the Griffith Park Observatory.

"If I had one day when I didn't have to be all confused and didn't have to feel that I was ashamed of everything…if I felt that I belonged someplace, ya know?" There he was speaking for generations of teenagers to come, even those who didn't have bossy mothers or pantywaist fathers who made lists and wore aprons.

He looks too old to be a teenager, but the image is such a cultural paradigm that it's hard to imagine there were such things as "teenagers" before the 1950s. Dean's projected image is so classical, it's like watching a myth in motion. When Plato (Sal Mineo) talks to him after the lecture at the observatory, instead of a halo, Dean's supernatural hair looks like the flame of some great torch. It irradiates from his head.

When he and Judy and Plato form their nuclear family during the film's last half hour, Judy says she wants a man who "is gentle and sweet, like you are," but it also means a man who would befriend a boy like Plato when no one else would. She's speaking for gay men and women alike. We all wanted a friend like Jim Stark when we were kids, maybe still do. We can accept his heterosexuality, not just because he's beautiful, but because he's beautiful and he's sensitive and he's smart enough to accept us for who we are. He's also not afraid to show the hurt.

Jim Stark's agonizing plea to his parents and to society at large is that they listen to him, take time to hear what he's got to say, consider his feelings, and recognize him as an individual. What began as a black-and-white B-movie about the harsh realities of teenage gangs and delinquency became a full-color widescreen declaration of independence. "I got the bullets!" Stark screams after Plato is shot by the cops and the camera Dutch tilts. The script may be melodramatically and self-servingly loaded by that point, and the film really has no ending to speak of, but Dean's wrenching cry out to the cops has reverberated for half a century. Talk to a troubled kid before you shoot one.

He was nominated for his second Oscar as Best Actor in his next and last film, *Giant* (1956). Jett Rink is actually a supporting role, showing up 23 minutes into the film, dragging on a cigarette and watching from the sidelines with his cowboy hat cocked over his eyes. He's incredibly beautiful to look at in the first

Jimmy (with glasses) trusses up Elizabeth Taylor, who unconvincingly pleads for Rock Hudson to intervene, between shots of *Giant* (1956).
PHOTOFEST

half of this Texas ballad based on Edna Ferber's best-selling novel. He's seductively low-key and seems to sidle into his accent and the forever-and-a-day landscapes effortlessly. He moves in slow motion.

When he does make efforts, such as his playful pre-occupation with his lasso, he's using it to cunning effect, not just showboating his acting quirks. The lasso scene comes when Jett is being buttered up by friends he never had in order pay him off, so it's a brilliant piece of character work to have him appear to be inattentive and unaware. He's demonstrating a trick of his own just as surely as they're trying to pull one over on him.

Besides, what Dean does in moments like these is create a weird rhythm, an almost improvisational style that unbalances fellow cast members' more conventional approach and makes the moment seem unpredictable and vital. You never know what or when he's going to say something and if you look at the actors he's doing his scenes with, neither do they. Sure, it's a bit studied in *Giant*, but it's damned effective. He's in complete possession of his character, making an unforgettable impression in a role that few other actors could have made so peculiarly memorable. It goes beyond the fact that we know we're watching Dean, the legendary dead movie star, in his last role. Even if this was the first and only performance we'd ever seen, we'd never forget him: the way he lounges in the long car with his hat on his boot, the way he looks like a little kid playing a game while marching off his property line, or the grandiose way in which he climbs the windmill and very deliberately sets himself down and crosses his arms, hunched over like Quasimodo surveying Paris from high atop Notre Dame.

All is fine and good until the film's leap from Jett's "I'm a rich'n" revenge at age 19 to his oil tycoon self at age 46, where the make-up doesn't hold up and it's all too easy to see where he's had his hairline butchered. He's certainly not in any way "dreamy," as teenaged Carroll Baker refers to him. If anything, his bizarre looks, somewhat abetted by his insomniac's baggy eyes, provide a creepy and ugly portrait of a man corrupted by wealth and power.

Dean didn't get along with director George Stevens, who chewed him out in front of the cast and crew, so he may have gotten even more careless than his usual carefree self as the film progressed. Actor Nick Adams ended up having to dub part of Jett's pathetic and drunken speech to himself after the ballroom is empty because Dean's recording was too garbled. Adams' voice is distinctly different from Dean's, but Jimmy couldn't come back to do it. He was dead.

On September 30, 1955, while driving to a racing event in his silver Porsche Spyder 550, dubbed "The

Little Bastard," James Dean was killed when his car was hit by an oncoming Ford sedan making a left turn across his lane of traffic. He was 24 and remains so to this very day.

He starred in only three films, but few people know that Dean made appearances in at least 30 television shows throughout his short career, a growing number of which are available for the home market. Of the ones I've seen, they certainly run the gamut in terms of quality, but even the worst of them—where he's in eternal hunch, so bent over that the microphone has trouble picking up his lines—make one long for the days of early TV. The scripts were so bad and the acting so amateurish, you get the feeling that the high school actor in you could have shared the screen with great stars if you'd only been born earlier. There's such cornball charm and innocence there. Then, it was every man for himself. Just awful...and fun.

For a young man who died before his fame kicked in, James Dean was the subject of a staggering amount of photographic documentation, almost as if he and everybody else who met him knew he was going to be a legend. That legend continues to grow and prosper with each new detail unearthed, with each collection of photos reprinted, despite the fact that not a single one of his followers would have liked him had they really known him. The fantasy advantage of hindsight infatuations is that you think you know the object of your infatuation and can adjust accordingly. That's star power. Fans willing to change their own personalities to mesh with that of their dream boy's. If we understand what upset him, they reason, we can avoid upsetting him—we can comfort him and become the best friend he never had, never mind that we can't really help him.

I count myself devotedly amongst his cult. Every attempt to demystify him, to show his faults, to reveal him as a lonely, insecure kid who was night-and-day moody, overly-sensitive, and a bit crazy only ends up feeding the legend on which his legacy is built. The portrait of a rebellious, temperamental young man who quit things when he was criticized, who didn't show up to rehearsals, who held up the shooting of movies, who lived fast and dangerously, and who was his own worst enemy is apparently intended to humanize the demigod, make him a real person with real flaws. It backfires in a very peculiar way, because, in retrospect, these are the very things that make James Dean appealing to us, to everyone who has ever felt like an outsider: lonely, unwanted, or different. Okay, so that's all of us. Long live the little bastard.

Our surrogate and, in many ways, our conduit for expressing how we felt about James Dean came in the form of **Salvatore Mineo, Jr.** (1939-1976), who nabbed an Oscar nomination at age 16 for doing it in *Rebel Without A Cause* (1955).

Like a girl, Plato notices Jim Stark while looking in a little mirror inside his school locker where he has a picture of Alan Ladd pinned up. At the Griffith Observatory, watch how Plato looks Jim up and down when he leans in to talk to him from the row behind. After the presentation, he gripes about the lecturer and his philosophical topic: "What does he know about Man alone?"

In case you couldn't figure it out, Plato is the first gay teenager in a Hollywood movie (as near as I can tell) and he sure picked the right one in which to show up. Buzz calls him "chicken little" when he asks him where Jim is for the famed chickie run. The terms intertwine quite deliberately. The 1950s covered both threats abroad and threats at home when it coined "pinkos." Queers were deviants and perverts—pretty much always had been—but now they were also suffering from a devastating mental disease that could be psychologically explained and medically treated.

So while we're eager to embrace him as one of us, we also have to face his demonization. He's the sensitive little boy with absent and separated parents and he's been left alone on his birthday. His real name is John Crawford and he's about to meet two of the most important people in his life at the police station, but not because he's thrown a rock through a church window or was caught hanging around in the men's room at the bus station.

"Do you have any idea why you shot those puppies, John?" the officer asks him.

He's such a doe-eyed, cute little kid that the crime he's accused of committing just doesn't sit well. I try to forget it for the rest of the film, because he's just a puppy himself and no sweet gay boy, no matter how tortured, could ever shoot one, let alone a whole litter.

Not that he isn't a bit odd in an endearing, hero-worshipping sort of way. He lies and tells Judy that he's friends with Jim, that Jim is going to take him hunting and fishing, and that when Jim teaches him stuff he won't get mad at him if he goofs. He even tells her that though his "friend's" name is James and he prefers Jim, "if he really likes you, he lets you call him Jamie."

Is he coming in loud and clear?

113

"Hey, you wanna come home with me?" Plato asks his Jamie. "I mean, there's nobody home at my house. Heck, I'm not tired. Are you? See, I don't have too many people I can talk to." And he doesn't stop there, bless his little pumper. He wants Jim to stay the night and have breakfast with him in the morning. Like a dad. "Gee, I wish you could have been my dad."

I'm not sure what audiences at the time were thinking about this dark-haired kid with the dimples and sad eyes fawning over James Dean, but a generation of closeted gay teenagers were up there on the screen with him heart and soul. When Jim gives Plato the red jacket he's been coveting, the younger boy even seems to sniff it. It's that palpable.

I'm not pretending to know if it was any of the various writers' intentions to sacrifice Plato because he was perceived by the audience as a queer, and thus expendable, but I wonder how many people understand Jim Stark's agony when it happens. What is it about this lonely boy (whose one red sock and one blue sock point out a glaring continuity error involving his shoes) and his senseless death that we're to take away from the film? The climax is so strange that you wonder if he's getting cut down strictly for the melodrama. Sure, the moral of his death has something to do with fucking up our kids by not listening to them enough, not loving them enough, or not keeping our marriages together, but I don't think Plato is the messenger. Does anyone in the audience besides gay men and bobbysoxers really care that he's dead or do they just feel bad for Jim because he keeps trying to do the right thing and adults keep mucking it up? Oh, and by the way, he also tried to help out a screwed up kid on a motor scooter who killed puppies and was delusional enough to imagine that his new teenaged friends could be his adoptive parents.

Conversely, from a gay perspective, Plato's death has an almost mythological certainty to it. James Dean was the only one willing to reach out and try to help the kid, try to be his true friend. Adult society wasn't ready to help. They killed lots of gay teenagers who were afraid of their own feelings or were taught to be afraid of themselves. Dean's rebel had many causes after all.

And Sal Mineo had himself a career by association. He was born in Harlem, the third son of a Sicilian-immigrant casket maker and his wife who shortly thereafter moved the family to the Bronx. Sal looked exactly like his mother. When he was nine, he and his younger sister were scouted right off the streets to train as dancers while he struggled to stay out of fights with all the older kids at school who enjoyed teasing him.

The publicity mill that would eventually turn out stories about his childhood nicknamed him "The Switchblade Kid" and reveled in tales of his hard-knock life and juvenile delinquency. Family members recall it differently. He was a gentle and kind boy, not a juvie, and was more often being chased by neighborhood jagoffs and having to defend himself than he ever was knocking heads of his own accord. That wasn't his personality.

His cute-but-bruised Italian kisser earned him a walk-on at age 11 dragging a goat across the stage and reciting "The goat is in the yard" in Tennessee Williams' *The Rose Tattoo*. He continued taking his dancing quite seriously and eventually landed a coveted gig as understudy to the Crown Prince in the original Broadway production of *The King and I* with Yul Brynner. At 12, he began playing the role himself for what amounted to 900+ performances over two years.

Brynner was an inspiration and acting was Sal, Jr.'s newfound love. He studied it passionately and won the role of a young Tony Curtis in the first 14 minutes of the Brink's Heist drama *Six Bridges to Cross* (1955). He's a juvenile delinquent gang boss who gets his balls shot off by a rookie cop. Sal was sent to Hollywood to re-record some of the soundtrack for that film and ended up playing the young Colonel at a Catholic all-boys military academy in *The Private War of Major Benson* (1955).

Amazingly, *Rebel* was next, only his third film and he was already an Academy Award nominee. He also appears in *Giant* (1956), walking in at the 124-minute mark in his brown uniform as the first Mexican soldier from Reata to enter the war. Appropriately, his name is Angel. "That boy's the best dang man on the place," says a drunken Rock Hudson, whose own boy has disappointed him. Sal only says four words, actually "thank you" twice, but his memory augments the newspaper headline of his coming home and the powerful image of the train going by to reveal a flag-draped casket on the platform.

He was supposed to be reunited with Jimmy Dean in *Somebody Up There Likes Me* (1956), the Rocky Graziano story, but Dean was dead and Paul Newman was tagged to play the part. Sal appears only a half dozen times in the film, playing one of Graziano's two-bit thief buddies. He's the symbolic kid, sickly and running a bookie operation, who never made it out of the slums.

In *Crime in the Streets* (1956), he's the wimpiest member of the Hornets. Hateful gang leader John

Sal Mineo gets a squeeze from Yvonne Craig in *The Gene Krupa Story* (1959). YESTERDAY

Cassavettes calls him "Baby." Sal's best moment, and the best scene in this overwrought jd film, comes in a close-up during which he tries not to cry while his father makes an impassioned plea for him to quit the streets and be a good boy.

Teen superstardom was not to elude him, though.

He reprised his Emmy-nominated TV role as *Dino* (1957) for the big screen, where he's described by his parole officer as "that real intense kind of quiet." Sal plays a 16-year old recently released from reformatory incarceration after his involvement, at age 13, in the murder of a night watchman during a gang robbery. Sent to social worker Brian Keith, Dino is all tough guy body language and says he knows the routine. "Did your mother smack me when I was little? Do I like girls? All that crazy stuff." (An interesting subtext considering the era of electroshock therapy we were in at the time.) Keith says he only wants to make the troubled teenager feel better. "So why don't you give me a rubdown?" Sal cracks.

Dino's mom greets his return from the reformatory by telling him, "I guess you're too big to be kissed," and walks right by him. Later, his abusive father belts his defiant son's face bloody. We learn that Dino used to get "ganged" in the reformatory for making too much noise because of chronic nightmares.

Only his little brother, a gang-banger wannabe whose posse is called "The Silk Hats," has any sugar for him. They embrace like two lovers and Sal paws the kid so passionately you expect him to kiss him full on the lips. (The actor is actually Sal's older brother Michael.) Little bro's affection won't last, though. He's as pissed and ashamed as any of the gang when it turns out that his older brother has become a reformed chicken.

Sal is like a junior Brando in *Dino*, a taut poser in his skintight T-shirt and pained histrionics. When he finally breaks down and cries on the shrink's couch, admitting in a fit that his father never gave him bear-hugs, he turns his back to the camera in anguish and it lingers on an image that looks remarkably like a modern day jeans ad. Meanwhile, all the gay boys in the audience are thinking the same thing: Sal's got a great little butt.

He's referred to as a "big fella" no fewer than six times during the first twenty minutes of *The Young Don't Cry* (1957), but that's orphanage parlance separating the little boys from the bigger boys. His Leslie Henderson is a defender of the little guys, though, and he's so sweet and soft and affectionate when comforting a crying kid that you have to wish that crybaby could have been you. And I don't mean anything untoward by that. Sal's a great comforter. He's an older brother and younger brother all combined into one.

He walks around the grounds of the Southern orphanage with his shirt open, which may seem a little too much like baiting when you consider the chain gang of convicts working on the adjoining property. Once again, all the adults turn out to be idiots, and you want Sal and his skinny friend Jimmy Brown to sail their little boat off together and make a new life for themselves.

Something possible to do with all of Sal's teen movies is imagine that his characters' root problem is being a closeted gay boy growing up in the repressive 1950s. Even in *The Gene Krupa Story* (1959), when Yvonne "Batgirl" Craig saucily invites him to a weenie roast and swim party and then steals his necklace and drops it between her boobs, he just turns her upside down and shakes it out of her. He's otherwise completely disinterested.

In the unusually violent Disney film *Tonka* (1958), Sal puts a spin on his coming-of-age roles by falling in love with the title horse. "From now on you walk with the women and dogs," orders his nasty older cousin Yellow Bull after the boy takes and loses a prized rope trying to catch the wild horse with it. Poor White Bull. Nobody will give him a break.

"No longer will they call you the mother of a son who does not know how to be a man," he defiantly promises his disappointed mother, and off he goes to capture Tonka and recover the tribal heirloom. He does just that, of course, and more, but forgive me if I can't take my eyes off that incredible body of his: those pointy brown nipples on well-defined pecs and that lean torso. He became a regular workout queen in those days and the fan magazines were full of luscious shots of him going through his regimen. There are even some naughty shots of him all soaped up in the shower, cut off at the pubic hair line.

All the skin comes early on in *Tonka*, because then it diverts to a Cavalry subplot and we find ourselves heading toward the massacre at Little Big Horn, which features a surprising amount of on-screen violence. Combine the bloodshed with the neck-breaking roping scenes and a vicious and very real horse fight and it's little wonder that Disney hasn't marketed this title aggressively in their family video collection.

During the musical numbers in *A Private's Affair* (1959), the voice looped to Sal Mineo's mouth doesn't sound a thing like him. Which is a little strange, because the boy could sing. He cut a single called "Start Movin' (in My Direction)" which sold a million+ copies, had "Lasting Love" after that, and even released an album called *Sal* that did measurably well as he became thoroughly ensconced in the surreal world of teen idoldom. *Private's* is a ludicrous excuse for a movie, but handsome Barry Coe makes a nice distraction, along with a potato peeling scene in which the guys are filmed from a low angle with their legs spread and there's something anatomically interesting about the way their pants bulge.

Sal Mineo was such a teen sensation that he demanded and got $100,000 to play *Aladdin* on a 1958 television special—a musical version written by Cole Porter and S.J. Perelman. The guy was so popular that after Bob Hope made a joke about kids in the Bronx having a school holiday the next day because it was Mineo's birthday, hundreds stayed home.

He had the lead in *The Gene Krupa Story* (1959), playing the famed drummer who went from Chicago speakeasies to New York clubs before getting blacklisted for possession of marijuana. It was one of Sal's personal favorite roles, which you might guess when you see how maniacally he plays. It looks like he's having seizures. Krupa himself laid down the drum tracks we hear, but you have to wonder why considering how absolutely convincing Mineo is without cutaways. Unfortunately, the film is a Hollywoodized bio, pretty much

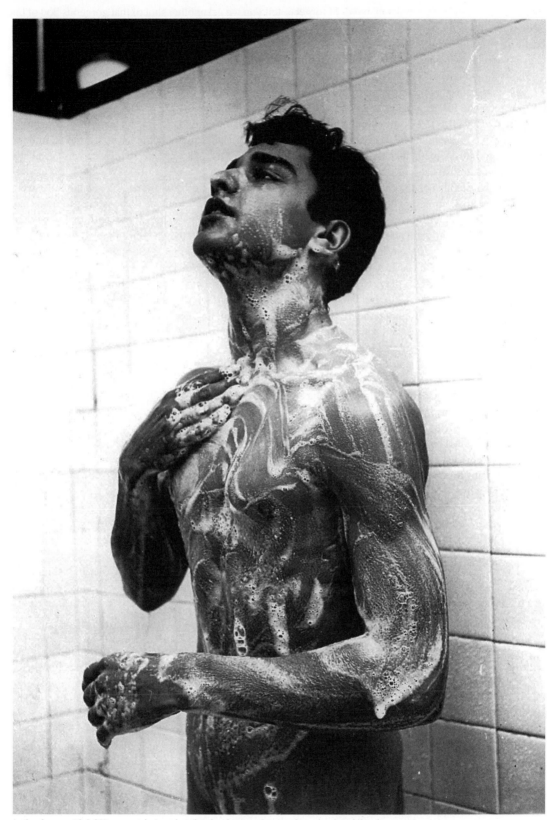

In the shower with Sal Mineo, wondering what else the photographer may have developed that day. AUTHOR'S COLLECTION

by the numbers and rather dull. Oh, but did I forget to tell you we get another shot of that gorgeous bod of his as he wakes up in the diva's bed wearing only his shorts? (Sorry, I just can't stop harping about Sal Mineo's beautiful physique. FYI: At age 23, he posed for artist Harold Stevenson's work "The New Adam," an oil-on-canvas nude study in nine sections, which was completed in 1962. The work measures 8' high by 39' long and serves as a monumental introduction to a mythical movie star's genitalia. What's more, Sal even talked to *Playgirl* magazine about doing a nude photo shoot in the mid-70s.)

He received his second Oscar nomination—and hoped to win—for his role as a Jewish rebel with a cause in *Exodus* (1960). His street tough attitude is a front for a young man who, we learn in a devastating scene, survived Auschwitz by working for the Nazis shaving heads, taking bodies from the gas chambers, collecting gold from teeth, then dynamiting holes for mass burials. In return, we're told, he was "used" by the Nazis, like a man uses a woman.

Though he landed on the cover of *Life* magazine in January of 1960, Sal's dark skin and ethnicity were said to eventually hamper his ability to be cast in leading roles, while others say that casting problems had a lot to do with his insistence on having family members run his career for him instead of Hollywood agents. When he finally did employ a professional management outfit, they weren't much help either.

He's back playing an American Indian in John Ford's *Cheyenne Autumn* (1964), but the film proved a troublesome shoot for Sal and he had numerous difficulties with Ford, who kept calling him "Saul." Outfitted in pigtails and a red shirt, he plays Red Shirt, the wily brave whose most thrilling moment comes when he dramatically bares his chest, looking the epitome of the young Indian brave holding his rifle and wearing a single feather sticking straight up out of his head. Most of his dialogue and additional scenes were cut by Ford, who complained that Saul sounded too much like he was from the Bronx.

After being healed by Jesus in *The Greatest Story Ever Told* (1965), he slipped on a pair of his tightest underpants and made obscene phone calls to Juliet Prowse in the truly bizarre cult item *Who Killed Teddy Bear* (1965). The first four minutes of this low-budget black-and-white rarity, in which all we see of Sal is his torso and his tight underwear, is like watching an underground or experimental film. It's almost Warholian, except for the cutting. We first see him as he turns off a gratingly loud alarm clock. He's sitting on the bed, rubbing his side, the lighting showing off the musculature. He gets up and goes to a mirror on which there are pin-up girls, and he stands there for a bit sensuously rubbing his stomach. We still haven't seen his face. Then he goes to the bed, lying down again so that his torso and hip and upper leg are landscaped across the screen. He rubs his upper leg and hip just below his underwear line as he makes his first dirty phone call. His eraser-tip nipple is caught in the chiaroscuro.

"You see, in some of the shots while I was on the phone they wanted to sorta suggest that I was masturbating," Sal told gay *In-Touch* magazine, "but I couldn't be naked...so I was just wearing my jockey shorts. It turned out that that was the first American film where a man wore jockey shorts. They always hadda wear boxers on screen."

The second time his character calls in the film, we get a close-up of his torso and you can just glimpse the hair at his belly button. There's a nice transition from a normal framed view of the object of his affection to a binocular-view. The calls are fairly explicit and certainly creepy.

Just when you find yourself drooling over the seedy premise and the promise of camp appeal, the film turns out to be serious in its consideration of perverts and degenerates. Detective Jan Murray specializes in the stuff, listening to graphic audio recordings that can be overheard by his 10-year old daughter in her bedroom, and warning club girl Prowse about the hyphenates: sado-masochists, voyeur-masochists, etc.

Of course we know all along that club busboy Mineo is the perv, but the film decides to officially clue us in at 41 minutes when he lights a match in his dark bedroom and the frame freezes for a moment. The whole film comes off as a censure of sexual libertinism, the corrupting power of pornography, and the destructive force of explicit sexuality on the psyche of children exposed to and abused by it. Mineo has a demented sister he's protecting, he's shown wandering the night in and out of sex clubs, and looking physically ill at the lingerie window displays on New York streets. We get gratuitous, indicting shots of the American public's new accessibility to sexual materials, such as bookstore racks carrying *Fanny Hill*, *Naked Lunch*, and *Last Exit to Brooklyn*.

Elaine Stritch appears as the lesbian manager of the club who puts on Juliet Prowse's coat and declares, "I dig fur." She takes advantage of Prowse's emotional breakdown over being stalked and tries to get something started until Prowse suddenly realizes what she's up against: another "sick" pervert. Peculiarly, after Stritch is killed (sorry to spoil it), Prowse doesn't seem fazed in the least considering she's partly responsible. If anything, she's cheerier. Probably because the character was just an old dyke as far as the script was concerned.

Sal's herky-jerky movements in the club when Prowse cajoles him into dancing with her look as dopey and awkward as the sex act, if you think about it. Both make you feel great, but neither look particularly pretty.

We can only be thankful that Sal wasn't playing a gay psychopath, though he was increasingly interested in exploring his homosexual identity without hush-hush and seemed to enjoy shaking people up and shocking them. When he decided to produce and star in an LA stage production of *Fortune and Men's Eyes* in 1968, he also decided to put on stage what had previously been dealt with off stage; namely, homosexual rape in prison. The cover of the play's highly collectible souvenir book pictures Sal "mounting" from behind a terror-stricken and shirtless young actor: a University of Kansas drop-out named Don Johnson.

Johnson told interviewer Marvin Jones in 1973 that the play's homosexuality wasn't so much a problem as his concern that it might give people the wrong idea about him. "After all, back in the Midwest, on the farms, it's more or less taken for granted that boys will be boys," Johnson said. "And while they're growing up they're going to start checking out each other's wee-wees." No big deal. But that didn't mean he was lining up to bend over for anybody in Hollyweird.

Johnson and Sal ended up getting along just fine and the graphic and brutal play was well-received. Only in his thirties, Mineo's film career had pretty much dried up. So much so that he agreed to appear unrecognizable under all the make-up as Dr. Milo in *Escape From the Planet of the Apes* (1971), only to get choked to death by a gorilla in the film's first fifteen minutes.

Sal Mineo was murdered on the night of February 12, 1976 in West Hollywood when he was returning from a rehearsal for the play *P.S. Your Cat is Dead*. The exploitation press theorized everything from a dope deal gone bad to a sadomasochistic ex-lover, but the awful truth was much simpler. He was being robbed. He was stabbed once. It took two years before a man was arrested and convicted of the crime. He was paroled eleven years later, still vowing innocence, then reportedly confessed when he was arrested for yet another crime.

Sal cultivated the image of the baby-faced punk, perhaps as a defense mechanism because of his short stature, but to everybody who knew him he was a helluva nice guy. The dichotomy is fitting for the young man who came to symbolize gay youth in the 1950s. You had a role to play if you were to avoid getting your head knocked off. It's nice to know the real Sal got a chance to live the life he preferred, even if Hollywood and the world weren't quite ready for him.

Sal Mineo got lead billing in *Rock, Pretty Baby* (1956), a dull precursor to the AIP beach movies, but it's pretty boy **John Saxon** (1936-) who plays the teenage band's lead singer and guitarist as if all he had to bank on were his dark good looks. With a guitar in his hands and a pulse in the air, Saxon does a surprising thing for a young film star playing a rock and roller: he shuts himself down. Unlike the deer caught in the headlights, Saxon seems to know exactly what kind of trouble he's in and can't hide his discomfort for the life of him.

What's worse, they even made a sequel. Mineo didn't return, but Saxon and Rod McKuen and Shelly Fabares did and *Summer Love* (1958) followed the further adventures of the band at summer camp. Two year's worth of interim acting experience should have prepared him, but he still looked uninhabited when he played, as if he was in on a private joke—rock and roll isn't real music, it's just lookin' pretty and whackin' off a beat.

He's a drum player in the delightful sex comedy *The Reluctant Debutante* (1958), and though he displays a measurable degree of personal charm as the American boy with a bad reputation who turns out to be a very nice boy with nothing but honest intentions, just as soon as he's playing those drums or beating those bongos, he's a cigar-store Indian again.

Born Carmine Orrico in Brooklyn, he got involved in dramatics while in high school, but it was a dreamy still from a modeling shoot that caught the eye of an agent and the soon-to-be renamed John Saxon, all of 17, became a contract player at Universal.

He's the "Boy Watching Argument in Park" in *It Should Happen To You* (1954) and the "Premiere Movie Usher" in *A Star is Born* (1954). Universal then threw him in among his first gang of teenaged juvenile delinquents in *Running Wild* (1955).

A handsome studio portrait of John Saxon, mid-1950s. PHOTOFEST

He made quite an impression when the studio cast him as the darkly handsome high school quarterback stalking music teacher Esther Williams (in her first non-swimming role) in *The Unguarded Moment* (1956). Universal was hoping to fashion him into something of their own James Dean. His bad boy role is tempered when we meet his tyrannical, quietly menacing father, who hates women because his own wife ran out on him years ago. Pop doesn't allow his "minor god" of a son to see girls and threatens to "break every bone in your body" if he does. It's the flip side of Dean's dad in *Rebel*, but the bad parent = messed-up kid theme is paramount.

A flashlight serves as phallic symbol during one of Saxon's threatened rapes and a cop describes Esther's flight out of the boys' locker room after an assault by reporting "she came out of there like she'd seen a snake."

Saxon handles the dual-edge of his violent and vulnerable selves quite well and the first half of the film is especially well-written and acted, taking advantage of his beauty to play against type. At the film's end credits, we're treated to Saxon posing on the set and flashing his pearly whites while a title informs us:

"You have just seen a new personality. John Saxon."

Debbie Reynolds finally begins to see more than just his personality after she's sorted out her crush on charming actor Curt Jurgens, whose personal secretary she becomes, in the early Blake Edwards' comedy *This Happy Feeling* (1958). (Troy Donahue has a non-speaking bit as the new breed of actor whom Jurgens feels has usurped him.) It's nice to see Saxon in full color and with a smile on his face, because more often than not he was being cast as a troublesome teen, and increasingly of an ethnic persuasion other than his own. The exception: he's the good boy who falls for the scandalously illegitimate Sandra Dee in *The Restless Years* (1958), "the story of a town with a dirty mind." But he's cast as a Puerto Rican gang member failing to go straight fresh out of the can in *Cry Tough* (1959), an Arab prince during the conversion of Simon-Peter in the Disney-produced Bible-epic *The Big Fisherman* (1959), a Mexican gunfighter in a juvenile delinquent Western version of *The Wild One* called *The Plunderers* (1960), and an American Indian who goes by the name Johnny Portugal in *The Unforgiven* (1960).

Johnny Portugal is "the one with no whiskers" who throws a knife and then hangs his hat on it. He tells a horse he's about to gently bust that "it ain't gonna hurt much...not after the first time anyway." Saxon is given disappointingly little to do in this Burt Lancaster western, which is a shame because he's got a cool name, a flashy way with a blade, and the red tint of his make-up does wonders alongside the jet black of his hair and the gleaming white of his teeth.

The film nearly makes up for its slight of Saxon by offering us the equally bright white teeth of a very cute and 25-year young **Doug McClure** (1935-1995) as the little brother itching to go to Wichita to meet a woman who only has one name. In the background of an early scene, he's sitting bareback on a white horse while his pals repeatedly jump up and slam into him from behind. Looks like a lot of fun. And McClure's impossibly narrow and beautiful blond head looks like it's still squeezed while everyone else's is unsqueezed in the Panavision widescreen process.

Saxon relaxin', 1958. PHOTOFEST

In *Posse From Hell* (1961), Saxon plays Seymour, the bank employee, who ain't used to ridin' a horse cross country. Audie Murphy has him go behind a rock and take his pants down, then pours alcohol on Saxon's saddle sore ass and tells him to rub it in good.

He shows up as the dry college professor in black swimming trunks who has read *Moby Dick* all the way through in *Mr. Hobbs Takes A Vacation* (1962) and as an insane Korean War soldier in the low-budget *War Hunt* (1962). In the first third of Otto Preminger's bloated religious soap *The Cardinal* (1963), Saxon is a half-hearted Jew who knocks up priest Tom Tryon's little sister (Carol Lynley) so that a grotesque predicament involving morality and faith can be exampled. B-movies (such as 1965's *Bloodbeast from Outer Space* and 1966's *Queen of Blood*), European movies, and American TV appearances (including as Dr. Ted Stuart on *The New Doctors* from 1969-1972) mark a long career that numbers over 100 feature films. People who don't remember him in his young leading man prime do tend to know him from such roles as Chuy in *The Appaloosa* (1966), Luis Chama in *Joe Kidd* (1972), the white guy in the Bruce Lee kung-fu classic *Enter the Dragon* (1973), and Lt. Donald Thompson in the original *A Nightmare on Elm Street* (1984).

Sidney Poitier (1924-   ) had been making films for four years before Dorothy Dandridge pulled off Harry Belafonte's belt and rethreaded it through the loops of his pants while he was still wearing them in *Carmen Jones* (1954). It's probably the single sexiest moment in that film and, for most historians, it wasn't until this controversial revamp of Bizet's classic opera that black actors were allowed to be sexy on screen. Dandridge is feisty and hot-blooded, but eventually we can see that Carmen is not worth having. Belafonte sings a (dubbed) song with his shirt off and later blows on Carmen's toes to help the polish dry.

Meanwhile, Sidney Poitier, who would quickly become the premiere black actor of his time and the first culturally-allowed black film star, had to wait fourteen more years before he got a legitimate love scene: a coyly nude, but quite-in-bed coupling in the romantic comedy *For the Love of Ivy* (1968).

Through no fault of his own, but with a profound sense of responsibility, the very handsome and sometimes pretty Poitier was much too busy contending with his role as a "noble" and "dignified" symbol to so much as flirt with the threat of being a sex symbol. "Quiet dignity," "noble," and "sensitive" is how reviewers described him from the get-go. He's fourth billed in his very first film, *No Way Out* (1950), but he plays the lead character, a new doctor who encounters the virulent racism of a white crook (Richard Widmark) who blames him for the hospital death of his brother after the two are brought in with gunshot wounds.

He controversially initialed a document making him producer Zoltan Korda's property in order to play a minister caught up in the hateful politics of apartheid when *Cry, the Beloved Country* (1952) was shot on location in South Africa. His first line in *Red Ball Express* (1952) comes in reply to a "minstrel show" comment made by a racist white soldier (Hugh O'Brian) in a subplot assigned to Poitier's presence in this otherwise routine WWII drama.

Strangely, but fortuitously, Sidney was cast as a 31-year old teenager in the sensationalistic youth melodrama *The Blackboard Jungle* (1955), where his intrinsic better nature is eventually rallied in support of abused teacher Glenn Ford in this nasty indictment of juvenile delinquency as a disease on the rise. He was then paired piggyback riding atop Rock Hudson as grown up childhood friends on opposite sides of the political fence during the Kenyan Mau Mau rebellion in *Something of Value* (1957). It may be the first of his films to exploit his physical beauty—he's shirtless quite a bit early on—but it's a shockingly violent and grim story.

He gets third billing, after Clark Gable and Yvonne De Carlo, in the painfully acted, horribly written, and shamelessly trashy Southern Gothic plantation melodrama *Band of Angels* (1957). Gable doesn't show until nearly a half hour into the running time and Poitier another ten minutes after that; they had good reason to stay off the screen as long as possible. Gable is a wealthy plantation owner in the Civil War South who was once a ruthless slave trader. De Carlo discovers she's the "issue" of a slave woman and is subsequently bought by Gable, while Poitier is Gable's educated financial advisor and accountant, who sings (dubbed) "Blow the Man Down" as a thunderstorm brews. He eventually vows to kill his boss-in-sheep's-clothing.

After nearly a decade in the business, Poitier finally managed to clinch his movie stardom by being shackled to white racist and fellow escaped convict Tony Curtis in Stanley Kramer's *The Defiant Ones* (1958). Pale in terms of real character development or hard-earned drama when looked at more than four

Sidney Poitier was the first black actor embraced as a sexy leading man in American cinema. EVERETT COLLECTION

decades later, it was nonetheless an enormously important film in terms of subject matter and billing, and earned both Poitier and Curtis Oscar nominations as Best Actor. (They lost to David Niven in *Separate Tables*.)

Very probably blacklisted for a time in Hollywood for his friendships with Paul Robeson and other politically charged black artists, Poitier returned to the stage whenever film work was sparse. His acclaimed Broadway performance as the frustrated son of a poor black family in a city tenement who schemes to get out in *A Raisin in the Sun* was later recreated with the original cast for the 1961 film adaptation. *Life* magazine said of him when reviewing the stage version: "He is already accepted almost without question as the best Negro actor in the history of the theatre."

No small praise for a young man born to utter poverty in Florida while his tomato farmer father and very pregnant mother were making a crop-selling trip from their home on Cat Island in the Bahamas.

Sidney was child number eight for the couple, and he worked hard labor in the island fields while growing up isolated from white men and much of the modern world. They lived in a hut without electricity or running water, all ten of them. Sidney didn't see his first automobile until he was ten years old.

The Depression sent the family to Nassau on the island of New Providence. Sidney was a poor student, dropped out of high school his first year, and went into a life of thievery and petty crime with peers. He was sent to live with his brother Cyril in Florida to escape the likely fate of prison, and it was in the white neighborhoods of Miami that he learned firsthand about a prejudice he had never known. He had a pistol jokingly put to his head by a white cop. Eventually he made his way to New York City where he got directions to Harlem, a job as a dishwasher, and lived for months out of a men's room stall in the Greyhound bus terminal. Numerous manual labor jobs followed, as well as a failed stint in the Army.

While looking through the papers for yet another job, he saw an ad in the *Amsterdam News* that caught his eye: "Actors Wanted. Apply the American Negro Theatre." Deciding it might be fun, he auditioned and was advised to find a dishwashing job. His West Indian accent was nearly impenetrable and he had no idea what he was doing. Still, the insult of the rejection fueled an obsession to become an actor and prove them wrong. He listened to the radio and practiced reading the newspapers aloud to slowly break through his accent. He discovered he could imitate broadcasters' voices and diction.

He returned to the American Negro Theatre six months later and this time won a spot in the company with his improvised audition piece. They were also painfully short of men. He appeared in several productions at ANT, including *Days of Our Youth*, starring a new young actor named Harry Belafonte.

Does it occur to you how you couldn't possibly make a movie about how Sidney Poitier became a movie star without it seeming completely fanciful and purely the fiction of Hollywood hacks? It's a truly extraordinary story.

So what is Sidney Poitier doing here in the 1950s if he didn't really become a star until the 1960s? And where is the spate of juicy and juvenile descriptions of how hot he looks with his shirt off or in a tight pair of pants? Am I just being respectful because it's Sidney Poitier, for crying out loud?

He's here in the 1950s because he made a dozen film appearances in the decade and just because he wasn't permitted to be sexy in them doesn't mean he wasn't a damned fine-looking man and worth our admiration. When Paul Newman gets to play a long morning-after scene shirtless in *Paris Blues* (1961) opposite Joanne Woodward, Sidney doesn't get the same opportunity for exposure opposite Diahann Carroll. Even when he did have occasion in another film to remove his shirt, one reviewer was compelled to reassure potential audiences that Poitier was "gentle" in the scene.

He is, though, wearing a pair of very nice tight white pants that hug his behind and let us know for perhaps the first time in his screen career that he has a shapely butt in the otherwise respectful and beloved *Lilies of the Field* (1963). You can tell this low-budget story about a traveler who gets rooked into building a chapel for a group of German nuns is an old-fashioned fable because in the real world Poitier should have (and would have) simply moved on to greener pastures after the Mother (Lilia Skala) proved to be so ungrateful. The film was a major hit at the box-office and won Poitier an historic Oscar as the first black Best Actor. "It is a long journey to this moment," he said at the podium. *Lilies* is also one of a very few films in his career in which his race is not a factor of the plot.

Poitier's reserved and low-key acting style frequently resulted in the same kind of reverence/bewilderment associated with Gary Cooper's performances. The actor doesn't seem to particularly resonate most of the time that camera is on him, but he also doesn't have to do much in the way of emoting to seem as though he's on the verge of hysteria. He's serious but somehow detached standing by as witness to a nuclear foible in *The Bedford Incident* (1965), trying to avoid romancing a blind white girl in *A Patch of Blue* (1965), or gamely attempting to talk Anne Bancroft out of killing herself while keeping her on the phone through the running time of *The Slender Thread* (1965).

He's so low-key at the start of *In the Heat of the Night* (1967) that he doesn't say a damned thing during his false arrest as a murder suspect in a small Southern town, though his silence is both plot-driven and characteristically intelligent. We're not supposed to know yet that he's a cop. Only that he's a black man arrested with a wad of money in his wallet after a wealthy man is found dead on the early morning streets. Gum-chomping hick sheriff Rod Steiger is none too happy about the mistaken arrest, but even more incensed at the man's expertise and monthly paycheck. He thinks "Virgil" is a funny kind of name for a cop. He wants to know what they call him back in Philly.

"They call me Mister Tibbs" comes the famous response in this classic interface of race and prejudice against the backdrop of a small town murder investigation. Poitier delivers the line with stern rebuke, barely raising his voice but still able to punch it with enough dramatic impact that capital letters and an exclamation point were necessary when they titled the hapless sequel *They Call Me MISTER Tibbs!* (1970). A third entry for Poitier's Tibbs character, *The Organization* (1971), denigrated the role to routine TV cop drama.

Once blasted by his fellow black actors and the NAACP for agreeing to play the role of Porgy in the film version of *Porgy and Bess* (1959), Poitier was later criticized by some African-Americans for playing it safe for white Hollywood. In 1967, Poitier was the number one male box-office star, with leads in the three biggest hits of the year: *In the Heat of the Night*, *To Sir With Love*, and *Guess Who's Coming to Dinner*, and not a single Oscar nomination for his work among them.

He deserved an Oscar for *Heat of the Night*, while *To Sir* was a well-meaning, if equally unbelievable British update on *The Blackboard Jungle* (1955). Sidney plays the new teacher for a rebellious class of blue-collar misfits who all learn to love him by the end. *Guess Who's Coming to Dinner*, the biggest hit of the trio, is one of those watershed movies that cannot be fully appreciated outside the context of its time. A populist exploration of racial prejudice among an aging white couple (Spencer Tracy and Katherine Hepburn in their last film together) whose daughter is engaged to a black man, it yields some sparkling dialogue and a final, rock-solid performance by Tracy. Criticisms that Poitier's affluent doctor role was a whitewash of the issue because he was picture perfect were addressed by director Stanley Kramer, known for his "social issue" films, when he replied that the character had to be otherwise flawless so that his race was the only objection.

Poitier eventually became conflicted by his role as spokesperson for a race of people, having already quite successfully paved the way for a new generation of black actors in other than black exploitation flicks. The incessant focus on his race and its attendant political dimensions associated by the media during the Civil Rights movement became tedious and tiresome. He began directing his own projects as early as *Buck and the Preacher* (1972), a comedic western opposite Harry Belafonte, then a trio of very successful comedies with Bill Cosby: *Uptown Saturday Night* (1974), *Let's Do It Again* (1975), and *A Piece of the Action* (1977), as well as the Richard Pryor/Gene Wilder hit *Stir Crazy* (1980).

He returned to acting in the late 1980s, co-starring with River Phoenix in both *Little Nikita* (1988) and *Sneakers* (1992), and in 2002 received an honorary career-Oscar.

Young actors with extraordinary good looks don't always grow up to be older actors with extraordinary good looks, and even if they do, audiences are too fickle and the industry too hungry for new meat to sustain such an actor if he doesn't also happen to have extraordinary good luck.

Paul Newman (1925-) would be the first to tell you that he has had such extraordinary good luck. His family was well-off and ran a very successful sporting goods store in Cleveland, Ohio, just the kind of place you'd hope to run into a salesman who looked like Paul Newman. But sporting goods wasn't in his blood. His pre-college military career was compromised by his short stature and his being color blind to red and green, so he became a back-seater in a torpedo bomber. Frankly, he saw more action in the streets back home, where he was habitually teased and beaten by bigger kids at his Shaker Heights' high school. He was a late bloomer.

He got booted off the football team at all-male Kenyon College for participating in a barroom brawl and landed in the drama department, where he appeared in a succession of school plays. His appetite whetted, he traveled to the Midwest for summer and winter stock theatre and met his first wife while a member of the Woodstock Players in Woodstock, Illinois during the 1949-50 season. He returned home shortly after his father died to run the sporting goods store, but was restless enough to do a local TV commercial and shortly thereafter made the commitment to move his family to New Haven and enroll in the Yale University School of Drama.

Only a year into the three-year program, he was urged to give NYC a try and easily found regular TV and stage work. His first professional acting gig was in the 1953 Broadway production of *Picnic*, for which he won rave reviews and met future wife Joanne Woodward. He landed a spot in the Actor's Studio that same year and Warner Bros. offered him a five-year movie contract.

In May of 1954, Paul Newman stood opposite James Dean for a screen test: Paul in his little bow tie and Jimmy in his open collar. The director tries to get their attention: "Hey, you two queens, look this way."

"I don't want to look at him," Newman says of Dean. "He's a sourpuss."

"Oh, he's only doing his job," pipes in the director. "Turn the other way then."

Now it's Jimmy's turn: "I don't like him either."

They're told to look at each other but can't do it without breaking up.

"Paul," asks the off-camera director, "do you think Jimmy will appeal to the bobbysoxers?"

"I don't know. Is he going to be a sex symbol?" (He gives him a quick appraisal.) "I don't usually go out with boys. But with his looks, sure, sure, I think they'll flip over him."

"What about you, Jimmy? Do you think the girls will like you?"

Classic Dean half-giggle, then: "Sure. All depends on whether I like them."

When asked again to size Jimmy up for the girls, Newman uncomfortably looks him over and Dean says, "Kiss me." Without missing a beat, Newman replies, "Can't here." They both bust.

The awkward improvisational test proved uneventful for Newman, vying for the role of Aron in *East of Eden*, but the consolation prize was a starring role in his very first motion picture. It was a part that James Dean was asked to play, but didn't, and when the picture began a nightly showing on television in 1963, Newman famously took out an ad in *The Los Angeles Times* saying, "Paul Newman apologizes every night this week."

The Silver Chalice (1955) is a painfully dull pseudo-religious epic in which a young man, dubbed Basil after being bought by Roman nobility, is betrayed and sold into slavery to deny his inheritance. He's eventually commissioned by Christians to carve the heads of the apostles and Christ himself on a chalice in which the cup of Jesus will rest. It's a gigantic snore and Newman shouldn't have been any more ashamed than anyone else. He's certainly no worse. Jack Palance provides the single best moment in the picture as a magician in First Century wizard's cap who's employed to outdo the so-called miracles of Jesus in order to subvert the cult of Christianity. Engorged with self-importance and outfitted in a superhero's red leotard with giant black sperm cells all over it, he climbs to the top of a precipitous tower before all of Rome and intends to aviate. A watching Caesar says it best: "He didn't fly."

Newman's film career might have been over before it started, because not even his Roman-carved face and lovely gams make the film bearable. He immediately returned to the stage in *The Desperate Hours*, then to television where he successively excelled in Gore Vidal's teleplay *The Death of Billy the Kid*, 1956's televersion of *Bang the Drum Slowly*, and nabbed a much better role intended for James Dean, a boxer in the television adaptation of Hemingway's *The Battler*.

One Dean boxer role led to another Dean boxer role, now that he was gone. Newman plays Rocky Graziano in *Somebody Up There Likes Me* (1956), and as much as I would have liked to have seen Dean play the part, Newman gives it a good shot, even with his New Yawk affectations. It's a great part: a physically and mentally abused kid from the slums, a violent thug who fights anybody who gets in his way, a poor, uneducated mug who only knows how to talk with his fists and then becomes a renowned prize fighter. When told to have the locker room attendant give him a cup, he answers without a rimshot: "That's all right, I don't need a cup. I'll drink out of the bottle."

Beneath the rough exterior, of course, is the Newman face and physique. When Rocky gets married (to Pier Angeli, no less), and they eventually have a baby, a trainer says to Rocky, "It looks just like you." "How can it"? he replies. "It's a girl."

The first film to capture the special incandescence of his surreal pale blue eyes also had the smarts to make him a pyromaniac. His Ben Quick in *The Long, Hot Summer* (1958) also comes equipped with a bronzed body that looks especially fine in his workman's T-shirt, all dripping with sweat. Actually, Newman's incredibly toned torso sets something of a precedent in leading men. There's a definition that Clift, Brando, or Dean didn't have. (Brando was muscular, but beefier.) If you need any proof, just check out the six-pack on this guy in *From the Terrace* (1960). He's got a pre-Brad Pitt body that looks particularly modern in its lean aesthetic compared with the more traditional leading men of the day: Victor Mature, Kirk Douglas, et al. It's little wonder that Joanne Woodward finally comes around in *Summer* to seeing there's more to this macho-man than the "prize Blue Ribbon bull" and "big stud horse" her monstrous papa sees and that she's only been fooling herself dating gay mama's boy Richard Anderson. (Woodward and Newman married in 1958.)

According to legend, Paul Newman's Billy the Kid was supposed to be gay as written by Gore Vidal, whose teleplay became *The Left-Handed Gun* (1958). Billy is given a "lady" horse by the name of Buster at the outset and he's portrayed as a sensitive kid who, when he was 11, killed a drunk who said bad things about his mommy. Now an ornery adult, he's befriended by a book-reading Englishman who doesn't carry

Decade after decade, one of the most beautiful men in the movies. Paul Newman in *Cool Hand Luke* (1967). EVERETT COLLECTION

a gun and who ends up getting murdered by the local sheriff and his gang. Billy vows revenge. Still, for a trigger-happy punk, he looks awfully cute wearing his hat set way back on his head. He's got two hick friends, one blond, the other brunette, and when he visits them, one guy's goofing in the washtub while the other cavorts in his long johns and snaps a towel on Billy's behind. Later, when the Kid's recovering from a serious burn, the pair brings him a pet horny toad.

"There's nothing wrong with you that a young girl can't fix," says a señorita to Billy, telling him to dance with one of them at a party. He doesn't.

"Gee, I'd sure like to see your gun, mister," Billy says to a lawman while looking at his pearl inlay revolver from Chicago. It's about as subtle as John Ireland's Cherry Valance lovingly comparing guns with Monty Clift's Matthew Garth in *Red River* (1948). The only difference is that Cherry is actually in love with Matt, while Billy is cleverly scoping out and outwitting potential enemies. He's a wired little guy, a real firecracker who thinks he's invincible after surviving an otherwise deadly blaze. In the end, he can't love anyone, even himself, so he draws on Pat Garrett from an empty holster.

Yet another would-be homosexual character gets his wings clipped in the filmed version of Tennessee

Williams' play *Cat On A Hot Tin Roof* (1958). Brick Pollitt breaks his ankle while trying to drunkenly relive past glories on the high school football field. He's married to the cat, Elizabeth Taylor, but they have a mutually disagreeable agreement imposed by him: no sex. She wishes he would get fat and ugly so she could stand his disinterest in making love. Instead, she says, he's gotten even better-looking since he's become an alcoholic.

"People like to do what they used to do after they've stopped being able to do it," Brick tells a little girl who wonders why he was trying to jump the hurdles on the old football field in the middle of the night. Might as well be talking about something else.

The root of his "disgust" for "mendacity" has something to do with the night his high school best buddy and football hero Skipper jumped out the 11th floor of a Chicago hotel after Brick had hung up the phone on him, but the suggestions of a homosexual relationship are whitewashed. Disappointingly, in the end, Brick is finally ready to fuck the cat again.

For the scene in which he locks himself in the bathroom, Newman decided to play a joke during one unused take and slip into Taylor's nightie, which hung on the inside of the door, reciting "Skipper, Skipper!" over and over again. Nobody laughed or stopped him. They thought it was a Method moment.

Newman received his first (of seven career) Oscar nomination(s) for *Cat*, but Warner Bros. wasn't convinced they had a star and were royally dicking him on money they were making lending him out to other studios. A chronically private man, Newman made his gripes with Warners public after he completed *The Young Philadelphians* (1959) and immediately went off to appear in the Tennessee Williams play *Sweet Bird of Youth*, directed by Elia Kazan.

His agent convinced him to buy out his contract at Warners for $500,000 in 1959 and the studio agreed. They had no idea what they had when they had him.

When it came time to do the film version of *Sweet Bird of Youth* (1962), the censors castrated the script as surely as they removed the castration of Chance Wayne that was the play's climax. Instead, the Hollywood star wanna-be who makes the mistake of returning to his pissant hometown has his face smashed with a cane. "No woman will ever again pay to love that."

He's a gigolo, the "whatever your name is" pretty boy behind those dark sunglasses who's hauling around an aging, alcoholic, and drug-addicted movie star (Geraldine Page) so he can blackmail her into arranging a screen test for him. In a slow-motion flashback, we see him execute a swan dive into the pool. His body is in superb shape and we even see him doing a few inclined sit-ups to keep it that way. He's a self-centered beauty and he knows it, but he's also a fool who may only end up one of those "nameless bodies" used and abused while chasing pipe dreams.

It's interesting to me that Paul Newman finds it difficult watching his own performances and that, among his self-criticisms, he finds himself a much too-serious and overly studied actor in his early work. In fact, he feels he didn't start to loosen up until *Slap Shot* (1977), a film in which he got to say "cocksucker" more than once and we got to see Michael Ontkean do a strip down to his jockstrap out on the hockey rink.

There is something airless about Newman. He's gorgeous, but sometimes he's not fully formed, not come into his own. Early critics harped on his appearing to imitate Brando and Dean, but they harped on every new young actor for doing the same thing. To some degree, it must have been a sincere form of flattery...to Brando and Dean.

The Long, Hot Summer and *Cat On A Hot Tin Roof* were both set in Mississippi, both hot and humid, both about failings to sire family, both had rich, fat, and cantankerous daddies, and both had Paul Newman playing against type but not quite defining himself beyond the confines of his characters.

Hud (1963) changed all that. The second of his 4-H classics (*The Hustler*, *Harper*, and *Hombre* being the other three), *Hud* may contain the best performance Paul Newman ever gave, as well as the best part he was ever asked to play. Once criticized for lacking sexual threat while essaying blatantly sexual roles, he reeks of it as the swaggering "man of no principles" who's determined to drive his cattle ranch pa to the grave. If there's Method here, it's of the transcendental sort, making the promotional ads declaring "Paul Newman is *Hud*" an accurate assessment of the way he lives the role.

He's a first-class shitheel who consorts with married women, loves to fight and drink, attempts to rape the housekeeper (Patricia Neal), and doesn't give a good goddamn about anybody, least of all his father. The single time the first-rate storytelling falters is when Hud tells Neal he's sorry about attacking her and she suggests that sooner or later something would have happened anyway because he looks pretty good with his shirt off. Maybe she's just offering him a tidbit because she knows she's leaving, planting a seed she hopes will grow in her absence.

In a rare case of beauty giving depth to character, Newman's face and body and eyes—provocatively captured by James Wong Howe's Oscar-winning black-and-white cinematography—make the shallow, deeply angry, and contemptible Hud a man we're both attracted to and repelled by. The film's final shot says it all.

Paul Newman's unabated beauty continued to make hearts throb through five decades of film work; he was a legitimate sex symbol through each one of them, though he'd find that fact demeaning. He was consistently a top three or better box-office draw through the late '60s and early '70s with such favorites as *Cool Hand Luke* (1967), *Butch Cassidy and the Sundance Kid* (1969), and *The Sting* (1973). He finally got his Oscar for *The Color of Money* (1986), but deserved it four years earlier for *The Verdict* (1982).

Sal Mineo, who worked with Newman on *Exodus* (1960), called him "a great looking ice cube." Maybe that has a lot to do with his personality. For someone who has made his career as an actor, he struggles with conveying emotions. Off-screen, it's said he rarely shows them, preferring to mask them, keep things to himself. Even his famous self-deprecating and wisecracking sense of humor suggests a self-defense mechanism. He became one of those bigger-than-life movie stars, famous for being famous, as well as for film directing, car racing, political and social activism (civil rights, gay rights, women's rights), nuclear disarmament debating, and running his recreational camp for seriously ill children.

He refuses to sign autographs ever since he was asked for one while he was using a urinal, he takes great offense when people ask him to take off his sunglasses so they can see his baby blues—likening it to asking a beautiful woman to show her tits—and he's made more money developing, marketing, and lending his likeness to salad dressing, popcorn, and an assortment of Newman's Own products than he ever has as an actor—and he gives it all to charity. The company logo: "Shameless exploitation in pursuit of the common good."

When **Elvis Presley** (1935-1977) was a movie house usher in Memphis, Tennessee, his dream was to be up there on the big screen—an actor not a singer. In 1956, the dazzling year of his rock and roll ascension, studios showed interest and he told his family and fans that he was about to make a movie and, no, he wouldn't be singing in it. He didn't plan to sing in the movies at all. His acting screen test was for a scene in *The Rainmaker* (1956), with Burt Lancaster and Katherine Hepburn. He thought it was going to be his first picture.

MGM had other ideas when they picked him up for 2.3 million dollars for seven films over seven years, though they were slow to realize them. What exactly do you do with a rock and roll singer who wiggles? Seems obvious to me, but they loaned him out to 20th Century-Fox for *The Reno Brothers*, playing the youngest of four Texan brothers, and the one who marries his eldest bro's betrothed because it's believed he's been killed in battle. He hasn't, and his return eventually curls hero-worshipping Elvis' lips into a snarl. The opportunity for a straight acting shot was short-lived. The studio inserted four songs to be sung by their young star and retitled the picture *Love Me Tender* (1956). Elvis wasn't happy.

"Appraising Presley as an actor, he ain't," wrote *Variety* of his inaugural effort, a jibe that would echo throughout his 33 film career and a particularly vapid criticism considering how quickly Hollywood robbed him of all opportunities to show us whether he could or not.

If you're at all unsure, because the culture teeters back and forth between embracing his enormous contributions as a musical icon and abusing him as a bad joke, early Elvis movies are the way to go. If his hair gets out of control, bouncing into spikes that defy gravity, sit back and watch. If it's a coifed helmet, move on.

Back at MGM, *Loving You* (1957) was written specifically for him as a plea to the older generation to accept rock and roll. It showed him as a regular guy, a lonely delivery boy who borrows the name Deke Rivers from a tombstone and gets baited into show business by an enterprising publicity gal who orchestrates the career of "the one with the jumpin' beans in his jeans." He gets pissed when the bandleader jokes that maybe they should change his name to "Tab or Rock."

Every film guide identifies a different title for "Elvis' best movie," so I'll add my two cents and nominate *Jailhouse Rock* (1957). It's essentially another juvenile delinquent picture of the period, but it's one of the few to flirt with his dark side. He beats a woman-beater to death in a local café and serves time for manslaughter. He even gets a "shocking" haircut. A television variety show beamed from the jail nets

129

him a bag of fan mail. After his release, he meets a young record promoter (Judy Tyler) and bullies his way into controlling his own record company, doing television, and making movies for the aptly-named Climax Studios. He succeeds in alienating everyone along the way and an ex-con friend gives him the licking he deserves, punching him in the throat and knocking his Adam's apple loose.

Elvis' astonishing good looks dress up a kid with a real chip on his shoulder, a temperamental bad boy who's both rude and dreamy at the same time. When he roughly plants a kiss on Ms. Tyler and she chides him for using such tactics, he explains, "They ain't tactics, honey, it's just the beast in me." And we believe him. He seems actually capable of sexual threat here, unlike the castrated sex symbol he would become in his movies of the 1960s. "What'd they do, cut Elvis' balls off?" asks Kevin Dillon playing the Catholic school punk circa 1965 who sneaks into a theater to see *Blue Hawaii* (1961) in *Heaven Help Us* (1985). Pretty much.

Fittingly, for a male sex symbol, he's given his own punishment scene in *Jailhouse*. The cops tie him shirtless—arms over head—to a pipe and subject his back to the whip. The close-ups, cropped at mid-torso, complete with his writhing, look like something out of an S&M fetish loop. It's a very brief scene, but the impact on audiences inestimable. By the way, Elvis tended to drip quite a bit, and longer close-ups of him reeling in pain (or below-frame ecstasy) show the perspiration beading and running from his underarms, so they were cut.

He's particularly fetching in his black sweater and pants for the poolside number "Baby, I Don't Care." Then there's the famous choreographed title number where they have the good sense to dress him in black jeans with white stitching outlining his fly. It also has that lyric about #47 thinking #3 is "the cutest little jailbird I ever did see."

Watch even a few early Elvis pictures and you'll notice he's alive and charming and sexy as all get-out when he sings, but when he walks off the stage he loses the smile and broods. What gives? Well, he noted, Brando and Clift and Dean—his heroes—didn't smile, so neither would he. He suffered from pout envy as a result. When asked about the late James Dean on a live television program, Elvis said, "I would never compare myself with James Dean, because James Dean was a genius in acting."

King Creole (1958), based on Harold Robbins' boxing tale *A Stone for Danny Fisher*, was intended for Dean, but pummeling became crooning when it was re-fashioned for Elvis. He was afforded a two month deferment on his draft notice in order to finish it. The director was Michael Curtiz, the feisty Hungarian who made Errol Flynn a star and helped turn a B-movie called *Casablanca* (1942) into a classic.

Once again, Elvis gets the chance to play a bad boy. He's a poor high school kid whose mother died three years ago in an accident, leaving the parenting to his wimpy dad, *ala* Jim Backus in *Rebel*. The kid comes to the aid of a vixen being manhandled by a couple of mugs and soon gets involved with the wrong crowd after he's subsequently denied his high school graduation for being "a hoodlum or a hustler."

This being an Elvis film, however, he's quickly discovered as the busboy who can sing and becomes a star at the King Creole, a New Orleans nightclub. Rival club owner Walter Matthau proceeds to make life hell for the kid in order to get him to headline at his joint. It's strictly melodrama, but Elvis may just look his most beautiful, in part thanks to the gorgeous black-and-white cinematography of Russell Harlan.

Elvis had a smoldering beauty. His eyes had that sleepy, heavy-lidded quality, his bee-stung lips were prone to curl up on one side, and his boyish, apple cheeks came out whenever he treated us to a smile. He was a very pretty boy indeed. And good to his mother.

His overt sexuality, a strange but intriguing body language of convulsions, tics, and spasms, was unlike anything we'd ever seen before from a white guy and was immediately condemned by moralizers as demonic possession. Perhaps so, with one devil wrestling for control of his shoulders while the other twisted in the opposite direction at his hips. On top of all that, the poor boy was fighting off a spectral dog trying to hump his left leg.

The rhythmic thrust of his pelvis, the quivering legs, and the shimmying shoulders were all the natural phenomena of his feeling the music, but they came to symbolize the intoxicating and hypnotic power of "rock and roll," a southern euphemism for the sex act. A handsome young man shaking his booty and whipping his body into a frenzy in front of impressionable youth was a real cultural powder keg. The male sex symbol as Elvis Presley was the male sex symbol as vibrator.

His 1950s' movies seemed to know that, too. In *Creole*, he takes a nice girl he's just met and attempts to beguile her into an empty motel room. She stands outside the door, suddenly aware of his intentions,

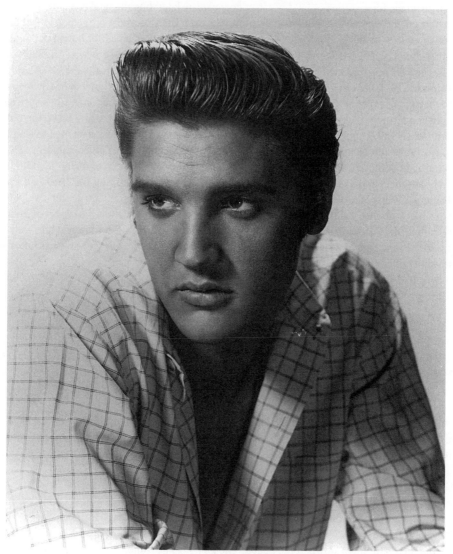

Elvis didn't like it when the studio inserted songs into his debut film and retitled the western *Love Me Tender* (1956). PHOTOFEST

and begins to weep. He wonders why. The lonely gal admits she'd like to see him again and wants to know "if *that's* the way." With adroit critique of Presley's own power over his fans, she tearfully speaks for legions of them when she admits: "I like you more than anyone I know and I don't even know you. That's why I'm crying." In *Jailhouse*, the first fan letter he reads is from a 15-year old girl who includes her measurements and phone number. [Check out *Elvis—That's the Way It Is* (1970) for a revealing documentary look at this kind of celebrity worship; beware the 2001 re-edit, however, which completely removes the fans from the film in deference to more of the star in rehearsal and in concert.]

Long-circulated photos of Elvis standing around in his undershorts during his Army induction do nothing more than attest to what his movies already prove: like most of us, he looks sexier with his clothes on. The movies gave ample opportunities to see Elvis without his shirt. He was one of the few celebrities allowed to keep his body hair (which is several shades lighter than what's on top, because he was a natural dirty blond who dyed his luxuriant Tony Curtis do ink-black), but he had an "average" physique, particularly to our eyes today, spoiled as they are by years of buff advertising. Even when he gets to wear tight shorts while in Hawaii, he's constrained by even tighter and shorter shorts hidden underneath.

After he was released from the service, his return to the movies almost immediately took a turn toward the routine, much to his personal disappointment. *GI Blues* (1960) is enjoyable fluff and we get to see him loading

131

his songs with all the funny little tics he'd use in concerts years later: bugging and crossing his eyes, pouting, surprising himself, then letting that million dollar smile take over. Elvis packed more acting, inflection, and story into his songs, especially the lively ones, than the scriptwriters ever conceived for him in dialogue.

Flaming Star (1960), one of his personal faves (perhaps partly because it was originally written for Brando), has him playing an American Indian half-breed and there are no songs after the first six minutes. That proved a nice diversion for a singing star who still had hopes of being an actor, but it didn't do well at the box-office. No thanks to "Colonel" Parker's carny management and boss-man swindling, Elvis suffered through increasingly bad formula flicks. There were three Elvis movies released every year (excepting only a pair in 1963) from 1962-1969. Dumb songs were born out of dumb plot contrivances, so he had to sing lyrics like: "There's no room to rumba in a sports car," and "I'm a kissin' cousin to a ripe pineapple, I'm in a can."

Eventually he indulged in self-parody and, as emperor of his own empire, surrounded himself with a group of big laughers and yes men who helped warp his perspective, tainting his already damaged self-image. Tellingly, in his last film, *Change of Habit* (1969), he plays J(ohn) C(arpenter), a doctor healing children in a black ghetto, fighting corruption and rapists, and finding himself the object of affection to an undercover nun (Mary Tyler Moore). In the final scene, the nun reaches an epiphany while watching Elvis singing in church, learning to transform carnality into spiritual devotion as the filmmakers intercut shots of Elvis with shots of Christ on the cross. The Kings of Kings.

He never had the chance to fully realize his potential as an actor, but Presley was one of the most highly paid in the business, and his off-screen life was every bit that of a full-fledged and completely whacked-out movie star. As a kid, I connected with Elvis through my dad, who liked him, and I remember the tremendous anticipation of the *Aloha From Hawaii* concert in 1973, the first-ever satellite broadcast to a billion and a half of us watching at home. Arguably, he was at his most beautiful for the NBC-TV "1968 Comeback Special," but even from *Hawaii*, I was struck by the ritual of women clawing at each other to get a silk scarf drenched in his sweat. His curse: he survived to see himself a legend. Despite all the wealth, it couldn't have been an easy thing to stomach.

Polaroid introduced their self-developing film in 1950 and the dirty picture market must have exploded. No more having to send the film out to process. Your beloved could pose and feel safe about your capturing the moment. Until, of course, the first argument, or heaven forbid, the break-up when those private pictures had the darndest habit of disappearing.

Who knows how many intimate moments were made public after the fact.

The world was a lot less connected in the 1950s than it is today. If you were a young man looking to make some extra cash, perhaps one of a trillion or so aspiring actors giving Hollywood a fleeting glance, you might just run into a guy who says he's interested in helping you out. Maybe you met him at the bus station, in the men's room, or down at the beach. The guy says he thinks your looks could land you in the movies, but you'll need pictures. He happens to be a photographer who runs a modeling agency and he'd like you to come around his place and pose for some snaps. Sure, you reason, I can handle myself. If the guy's legit, it just might be the start of a beautiful relationship. If he's a creep, nobody's the wiser. Hell, if I need the cash that badly, maybe I'll even show off a little skin. Only degenerates will ever see the photos anyway.

For nearly half a century, **Bob Mizer** (1922-1992) photographed and filmed thousands of near-naked and completely naked men showing off their toned, glistening bodies on his property at 1834 W 11th Street in Los Angeles. Started in 1945 as a photography referral service for male models and actors, his Athletic Model Guild (AMG) would become legendary as both portrait studio and film production house, making boy-next-door models available by mail order to gay men of the Eisenhower era and beyond through publication of his *Physique Pictorial* (*PP*) magazine, begun in 1951.

The men came from all walks of life: beach bums, runaways, street kids, hustlers, actor-wannabes, military men, displaced WWII and Korean War vets, bodybuilders, and physique enthusiasts. Mizer brazenly sought out his models from every nook and cranny and brought them to the home he shared with his mother where he took photos of the guys wearing tiny posing straps, sort of G-string affairs. Ostensibly, the business that he began was on the up-and-up and the subject was the male figure offered for artist's models, acting agencies, and health-conscious appreciation.

The straps were present only for legal reasons, but you weren't supposed to be staring at what they were filled with anyway. You were supposed to be admiring the body aesthetic, the musculature, the symmetry. Still, the all-male nature of the magazine, as well as those provocatively drawn covers and illustrations, seemed pretty faggy. And is that or isn't that a line of curlies I see peeking out of the top seam of that kid's pouch? Mizer went from dropping a few copies of the mag off at the Cahuenga newsstand off Hollywood Boulevard to building a mailing list of interested clientele and selling them via US Post.

The first few years were slim as far as making much of a return, but Mizer also didn't have the Internet to help him spread the word. What he did have was the beefcake.

Montana-born boy-beauty **Steve Reeves** (1926-2000), who won the title of "Most Healthy Baby" of Danials County in his first year, then the Mr. America contest before he was 21, was featured in the November, 1951 issue of *PP* and served as model for artist Kenneth Kendall's homoerotic rendering of Ganymede in the June, 1954 issue.

Working here and there on the stage since 1947, his first film acting gig was for legendary bad movie maestro Edward D. Wood, Jr., who cast him as Det. Lt. Bob Lawrence in *Jail Bait* (1956). As wooden as the rest of the cast, Reeves manages to provide a three second glimpse at his incredible body when he walks into the frame carrying his shirt for a scene at the cop shop.

"Bob, why don't you do your shaving at home?" the inspector asks him.

"I'm never home long enough to do it," he answers, slipping his shirt on in such a way that we can see his chest and armpits are completely bare. Full body shaves do take more time, you know.

The inspector intends to warn him about making a visit to a suspected killer's house while reminding him that the killer's sister is quite a babe. In classic Ed Wood wordsmithing, he's told: "And Bob, being a pretty girl, don't take chances. Don's a killer."

Legitimate Hollywood didn't know what to do with this statuesque beauty with a waist as sutured as Vampira's, so he went to Italy, grew a beard, and became the international star of a series of sword & sandal films, starting with *Hercules* (1957) and *Hercules Unchained* (1958).

Eighteen-year old bodybuilder **Ed Fury** (1934-   ) was a *PP* favorite throughout the 1950s. He managed a handful of uncredited walk-ons in Hollywood films (the December, 1953 issue pictures him with Susan Hayward), as well as a featured role in *The Wild Women of Wongo* (1958), before following in Reeves' footsteps and achieving a modicum of fame in Italy as Ursus, son of Hercules.

Movie stills of Tony Curtis and Guy Madison graced the back covers of *PP* compliments of their respective studios while all sorts of bit players showed up in its pages donning posing straps and nothing else: Jerry Ross, Lars Anderson, Richard Harrison, Richard Barclay, Roger Devereau, Bruce Mars, and Sammy Jackson. Not exactly household names outside their own households, but there's the rub—queer studio execs or casting agents might get an eyeful and an "audition" while the models' families would never be the wiser.

Not that modeling for physique magazines was necessarily improper or illegal. They were popping up all over the place. *Tomorrow's Man, Vim, Man's World, Body Beautiful, Adonis, Jr. Mr. America*, the *Grecian Guild Pictorial*, and more were all competing for the attentions of the queer buyer alongside the more mainstream bodybuilding magazines. But *Iron Man* published an anti-homosexual rant in 1956 and Weider Publications, the muscle mag giant, declared it would no longer accept ads from agencies that offered photos of models in other than full-cut swimming trunks. The physique magazines were coming under increasing scrutiny by legal agencies, the postal service, and the courts for courting with homosexual obscenity.

Generally speaking, *PP*'s artwork by Quaintance, Bob-Art, and Tom of Finland, among others, was much queerer than 99% of the photos between its covers during the 1950s. Drawings and paintings of butt-naked, but not frontally-naked groupings of men carried titles such as "Washday in the Navy" and "Game's Over." Another depicts a pair of carpenters on the job with the first busy pulling splinters out of the second's bare backside.

That being said, *Physique Pictorial* was, in its way, the *Playboy* of the American closet, bringing gay men a host of near-naked boys to the relative privacy of their mailbox while editorializing a steady stream of invective at the government censors who harassed all publications of its ilk. Mizer's tiny-print editorials were a relentless source of protest and propaganda on everything from capital punishment (anti), police brutality, personal rights and freedom, the ACLU, censorship, smoking (anti), homosexuality and bodybuilding, juvenile delinquency, vice squad arrests and sting operations, as well as the rumored practice of competitors stuffing their models' shorts—either with something called a "dildoe" or with a sock. "Frankly, we feel that an athlete sporting an exaggerated artificial 'bulge' looks as ridiculous and unaesthetic as a boy sticking out his tongue."

Steve Reeves, the "Most Healthy Baby of Danials County" grows up. PHOTOFEST

Then there was the issue of nudity. Mizer had enough run-ins with the cops and the court system to be wary of Big Brother, so while he made it clear that AMG had no moral qualms about nudity and the beauty of the human male body, he also made it clear what the legal climate was for such displays. AMG said it didn't shoot or offer nudes (they did shoot them, but kept them hidden for years until it was "safe") and warned buyers of the dangers of dealing with studios who did. In 1958, a New York studio was busted for offering nudes and hard-ons and its mailing list was confiscated. By contrast, the first penis to make it into *PP* belonged to a statue in a drawing called "The Wrestlers," featured in the Spring, 1959 issue.

The real thing would have to wait nearly another decade to show up in *PP* despite earnest justifications from readers, like the one who lamented that his alma mater, Boston Boys High School, no longer allowed the 15-17 year old boys to swim nude. Seems a teacher got into trouble for spanking a bad boy who wasn't wearing a suit at the time and a swimming trunks cover-up was instituted, leading to "an unnatural curiosity and lewdness in the showers and locker room, and because a finger cannot be lifted against them, juvenile delinquency is on the rise." Of all the things blamed for juvenile delinquency, the lack of nude swimming by high school boys seems the likeliest culprit to me.

Nude or not, the little physique magazines were now stigmatized as the pedophilia press. In 1959, the Los Angeles AAU barred all physique mags other than *Strength and Health* from covering the Mr. LA contest. Mizer wasn't happy, but he also wasn't quite competing with them anymore. He offered his subscribers more than just super-pumped muscleheads.

Mizer loved pissing off the mainstream bodybuilding publications, as well as the few clueless heterosexual men who still subscribed to *PP*, by also featuring average to slightly built boys amidst their beefier brethren. Fools would write in and complain about the fact that a kid didn't have any definition, completely ignorant that what he did have was a cute face and a cheeky way of fashion-modeling a jockstrap.

"Thousands of letters have convinced us that the average collector [who we later learn was male, between the ages of 25-35] is more interested in the more moderately developed body than in the extremely muscular type."

In the Fall of 1957, AMG announced its first film and would soon go into production not unlike one of the Hollywood majors, developing its own particular style and house specialties. Silent, both black-and-white and eventually color, these 8mm and 16mm films provide fascinating glimpses into a world of homoerotic celebration during an era of severe social reproach and conservatism. They look like home movies made with friends in the backyard, yet there are slave boys at Roman auctions, frat initiations complete with pledges to be paddled, and confrontations between juvenile delinquent greasers and cute (barely older) "cops" or butch bullies.

In a typical and very popular title, "The Bathroom Athlete," a narcissistic jock in a jock admires himself longingly in the mirror. A juvenile delinquent younger brother and his pal, wearing only jockstraps themselves, have surreptitiously put itching powder in the self-obsessed boy's shorts and watch from around a corner as he goes wild. They're discovered of course, and get a powder puffing themselves before each is turned over big brother's knee and spanked. Hollywood has clearly run out of ideas of its own these days, so if they're looking for a great re-make opportunity this should be their first choice. Skeet Ulrich as Narcissus and Ashton Kutcher and Ryan Phillippe as the two little dickens.

Readers were encouraged to send in script ideas for films and you could win a free copy if your idea was used. A drawing of a group of jockstrapped boys force-washing a stinky stud in a tub was published in the Fall, 1958 issue and subscribers were asked to let AMG know if that was a good idea for a movie. Works for me. Get the guys from N'Sync on the phone. The 1990s' boy band heyday may be over, but that's no excuse not to keep busy.

The male Teen Idol was born in the 1950s. And cultural taboos about eroticizing him were being broken, if not quite as frankly as AMG was doing with their unknowns. *16 Magazine* debuted in May of 1957 and was the brainchild of three enterprising middle-aged men who invented an editor-in-chief named Georgia Winters to camouflage their gender. It was an answer to the popularity of *Seventeen* and a savvy business decision to market young male stars to an ostensibly young female audience. In 1958, a real woman was given the job of editor-in-chief and former model Gloria Stavers shaped, wrote about, photographed, and occasionally slept with the defining generation of teen idol pin-ups. An ambitious woman and great publicist who marshaled *16* for seventeen of its years, Stavers fed teenage America what it wanted without allowing her subjects to be pictured smoking a cigarette, holding a beer, or getting any dirtier than the playfully romantic and gushy article titles allowed. Sex was out of the question. Love and romance, crushes and sweethearts were all the rage.

The most prized pages were the pin-ups. Long after the groovy articles and publicity-positive interviews began to reek of repetition, and even after you'd outgrown the lovey-dovey nonsense and "My Fantasy Date with Paul" schlock, you could still covet the photograph. Pictures didn't lie. Sure, he may be posed and smiling because he's being paid to, but isn't he just to die for? It was like having your own full color snapshots of your favorite big and little screen stars to hide and study, then dream and fantasize about without anyone having to know. It was taking the fantasy home with you...to bed with you.

Boys had a devil of a time getting them, too. All the teen magazines to come (*Teen Beat, Tiger Beat,* etc.) seemed aimed at girls, but that's only because they had so many boy pictures in them. The magazines professed they were meant for all young people, and they certainly didn't want to alienate potential revenue, but a stigma was definitely there. Teen magazines were for girls. Why would a guy be interested in looking at a picture of **Ricky Nelson** (1940-1985)?

Perhaps because, at just 17, he was one of the most beautiful young men on the planet. A generation had heard him growing up as the youngest son of the real-life showbiz family *The Nelsons* on the radio, then watched him do it in 435 episodes over 14 years on television's *The Adventures of Ozzie and Harriet* (1952-66).

Plenty of gay men remember the strong and often self-defining and self-revealing crushes they had on TV stars, with Billy Gray of *Father Knows Best* (1954-63), Tony Dow of *Leave it to Beaver* (1957-63), Paul Peterson of *The Donna Reed Show* (1958-66), Luke Halpin of *Flipper* (1964-68), Davy Jones of *The Monkees* (1966-68), Burt Ward of *Batman* (1966-68), and David Cassidy of *The Partridge Family* (1970-74) being particular hotbeds of homosexual infatuation and awakening. Some men do, in fact, trace their earliest clues to orientation by recalling the way they felt about cute male TV stars prior to their own adolescence and sexual maturity.

"I don't mess around, boy!" was little Eric Hilliard "Ricky" Nelson's trademark crack, and as a little boy, his ego was being stroked with all the funniest lines. He had a real charm and lively spirit about him. Growing up under the microscope of fame, as well as under the stress and strain of being a child mandated to work and spend nearly all his living and breathing time with his real (and somehow unreal) family, he started to withdraw. The wiry little kid became what appeared on screen to be an increasingly shy and apathetic teenager.

His line readings went flat, and so did his affect. He might even seem a bit troubled, haunted, or sad in retrospect. Whatever it was, in combination with his supernatural beauty, he began to smolder. Maybe it was that fat lower lip or the way his eyelids blinked in slow motion and never seemed able to completely uncover his gorgeous eyes, giving him a perpetually sleepy look. His face alone would have been enough to inspire devotion, but it came atop that high school athlete's trim frame, already revealing plenty of hair at his open collar when he was just 16. Ricky Nelson was hot hot hot, and then, on April 10, 1957, he cagily wiggled his leg and sang a song and assured himself immortality.

He'd done a gag, but affectionate impression of Elvis on an episode of *The Adventurers*, then cut a record with the help of his enterprising dad, but when Ricky Nelson crooned "I'm Walking" on the "Ricky the Drummer" episode of that April '57 *Ozzie and Harriet* show, a star was re-born. And he was no flash in the pan. He had 27 Top 20 hits over his career, including "A Teenager's Romance," "I'm Walking," "Poor Little Fool," "Lonesome Town," "It's Late," "Travelin' Man," "Hello, Mary Lou," and "Teenage Idol," a tune whose lyrics he disliked because he thought they were self-pitying. He loved singing and did so on the TV show frequently, quickly moving beyond the boyish delight of being up on stage to soulful, even gloomy interpretations.

He had appeared as a youngster twice in the movies (*Here Come the Nelsons* and *The Story of Three Loves*) before his Teenage Idoldom, but when he did *Rio Bravo* (1959), he was the "It" boy, the "Teen-ager's Top Throb," according to the cover of *Life* magazine. You can drive a herd of cattle between the register of John Wayne's voice and the pitch of Ricky Nelson's. As the young buck, Colorado, Nelson brings along his beauty as well as his ethereal acting range. He's so lightweight and unexcited that when he makes a gesture, such as putting his finger alongside his nose like Monty Clift did in *Red River*, giving a wave as he walks away from the Duke, or bringing a cigarette to his lips, it seems operatic.

Though he ended up in a classic western, I would have preferred seeing him as Mississippi, the role played by James Caan, in *El Dorado* (1967), the lightweight reprise of *Rio Bravo*. Dramatic was not his

Cowpoke Ricky Nelson on the set of *Rio Bravo* (1959). PHOTOFEST

strong suit, though his flat roles in *The Wackiest Ship in the Army* (1960) and *Love and Kisses* (1965; as Buzzy Pringle) don't take him appreciably further in the other direction.

Much to his vocal opposition, he was obliged to croon two songs he hated in *Rio Bravo*. In the first, he chimes in on a little duet with Dean Martin called "My Rifle, My Pony and Me." On the second, his bouffant hair is in full sheen and out from under that cowboy hat as he's forced to sing: "I wish I was an apple, hangin' in the tree, and every time my sweetheart passed she'd take a bite of me." There's more: "Cindy hugged and kissed me, she wrung her hands and cried, swore I was the prettiest thing that ever lived or died."

Across the Atlantic, in Great Britain, Laurence Harvey's motormouth talent agent would never have put up with such tripe...unless he was paid handsomely for it. Harvey finds a toothy, chipmunk-faced teen idol bouncing, singing, and beating his bongos in a local teen hangout and promptly markets him as a new sensation in the energetic and self-aware comedy *Expresso Bongo* (1959). Indian-born Harry Rodger

Webb was already a Teen Idol singing star named **Cliff Richard** (1940-) by the time he played Herbert Rudge, the cute drummer who gets turned into a singing heartthrob named Bongo Herbert. It's a loopy and funny film, and despite Richard's being upstaged by the brilliant Harvey and perhaps being a bit more cherubic than beautiful, he strikes some very attractive poses. A scene where he's sunning himself on the terrace wearing his little striped swimming suit has an ass-end shot that looks like it was pulled right out of an AMG loop.

The desires Teen Idols inflamed in their fans probably scared parents—no matter what side of the Atlantic, no matter how seriously or not seriously they were taken—more than anything those idols were yet permitted to do on screen. The newspapers, magazines, and television reports were full of stories and accompanying pictures of sobbing, hysterical, hormone-ravaged youths fainting, bawling, screaming, and rampaging at the sight (or even anticipated sight) of their objects of desire. These were the concerts where no music was heard over the din of shrieks. And the personal appearances where beautiful rock and movie stars were frighteningly clawed and pawed and stripped of their clothing in a frenzy like something out of Tennessee Williams' *Suddenly Last Summer* (1959), in which Montgomery Clift finally learns of Sebastian's fate. The long, lean, anonymous man in white who had been preying upon the street youth in a small coastal town in Spain was finally attacked by the other children, who tore him to pieces and devoured him.

Teen Idols were boy candy. Their fans wanted to eat them alive. Still do.

Teen idol Fabian (right) makes his film debut in *Hound-Dog Man* (1959), with Stuart Whitman (center) and Dennis Holmes along for the ride.
PHOTOFEST

138

The 1960s

"People Who Are Very Beautiful Make Their Own Laws"

The young man getting off the boat is being watched. An older man is looking at him through a telescope while the young man carries a bag identifying him as U.S. Mail. His real name is Merle Johnson, Jr. He was nearly re-named Paris, but they settled on **Troy Donahue** (1936-2001), and *A Summer Place* (1959), the film in which he's being watched, would make him a star.

He was a journalism student at Columbia University whose tall frame and boyish good looks were welcomed in college and regional theatre. Universal-International was his first home, where he appeared in juvenile bits and supporting roles in 13 films during 1957-59, including a single ugly scene in *Imitation of Life* (1959) where he brutally beats girlfriend Susan Kohner after he discovers that her mother is black. Warner Bros. gave him the standard contract treatment in 1959, but now he was playing leading roles. By 1961, he was voted #1 Male Star by the teenage readership of *Ingenue* magazine...presumably female.

He starts out rather plain-looking in *A Summer Place*. A shrill Sandra Dee has reached her sexual maturity and needs someone to try it out on, much to the abject horror of her puritanical stepmother and the free-spirited delight of dad. She admits to daddy that she used to torture the neighbor boy by deliberately undressing while he watched from his bedroom window. She also wants to know if she bounces when she walks, because her evil stepmom intends her to wear a cast-iron support bra. Pop seems a bit creepy during all his speeches about the healthy side of sex, but maybe that's because he's played by Richard Egan, who scared the hell out of me as a kid when I saw him in *The House That Wouldn't Die* (1970) on afterschool television.

"As for you Troy Donahue, I know what you wanna do," goes the famed lyric in *Grease* (1978), and he does look prettier and quite do-able in close-ups. He's Johnny and she's Molly.

"Are you bad, Johnny?" she asks while they snuggle on the beach. "Have you been bad with girls?"

"No, I just don't exactly know what that word good means." They should have clipped his answer right there. It would have fermented well over the years and helped make this sexploitation soap opera a classic. Instead, he rambles on before coming to the second punch line: "I think all of you is good. I know your lips are good."

Good enough to get her pregnant. They lie to their parents about wanting to go see *King Kong* at the local movie house—maybe they'll sit through it twice—so they can rendezvous for sex. The famous "Love Theme from *A Summer Place*" is more memorable than either of them.

But there must have been just enough steam and hinted at raunch to make audiences sit up and take notice. Warner Bros. cast him as Sandy Winfield II, one of three handsome private dicks on a Miami houseboat taking on the ladies and nabbing the crooks, in ABC Television's *Surfside Six* (1960-62), just one of many carbon copies of Warner's *77 Sunset Strip* (1958-64).

My favorite Troy Donahue film, and the one I recommend to all initiates, is *Parrish* (1961). Claudette Colbert ended a six year retirement from the silver screen to play Troy's mom in this adaptation of Mildred Savage's novel set in tobacco country. The cinematography is gorgeous, the actors are all earnest and slightly hammy, and the story is just campy and soapy enough to be a musical, which it isn't.

Troy plays Parrish, a Boston blondie who gives up his gig deckhanding on a ferryboat to travel with his mom to a tobacco plantation where she's got a job trying to rein in the wildebeest temperament of beautiful Diane McBain. Meanwhile, Troy falls for migrant worker Connie Stevens, who invites him to her backwoods family home. He'll sleep in the attic right over her bedroom.

"It ain't much, Parrish, but we could have a lot of fun together," she tells him while showing him his sleeping quarters. She gives him a tour of one of the tobacco sheds and confides that sometimes she sleeps there. And you wanna know what else? "When it gets too hot, I sleep raw."

"Gee, Parrish, I went ape over you the minute I saw you, don't you know that?" she tells him. "Wow,

Troy Donahue: "I think all of you is good. I know your lips are good." PHOTOFEST

I never knew it would be like this. You sure know how to kiss."

Their consummate encounter takes place when Troy contracts tobacco poisoning after his first day in the fields. He's shirtless and has a red rash all over his shoulders and back. He doesn't know what it is, but Connie knows just exactly what to do. She brings in a bottle of calamine lotion and starts to dab.

"Feel better?"

"Mmm-hmm."

"It feels cooler still if you blow on it." And she does, bless her heart. "You put this on during the night, or if you want me to put it on, just stamp on the floor. I'll come up and do it for you anytime."

During an idyllic walk, Troy hurls a rock (not a pebble) and it hits the water with an unromantic *ka-thump* despite the mushy music and their on-cue kiss. Later, a gong clashes when Connie uses the word "pregnant."

Donahue has gorgeous blue eyes and the costumers like to dress him in prime colors (with the occasional stripes thrown in) to accentuate his blond good looks. He's quite dashing in either his blue coat, his red sweater, or his black formals and white tie.

Those good looks don't always know what to do, however. It's funny watching him not react in the least to Colbert when she lectures him about women, trying to discourage his relationship with Connie because she's an available habit. It's as if he doesn't realize he's on camera. He eventually responds that he likes the gal because she's "free and natural."

"That's the longest shower I've ever listened to," says the lovely McBain as she moves in on him in his re-located bedroom at the plantation's main house. He's the romantic interest of no less than three gals in the movie, while his gold digger mom inexplicably and unbelievably marries tobacco tyrant Karl Malden.

Fatherly advice from Dean Jagger comes in the guise of a lecture about men needing poles to hold onto—all men have poles—while an "erect" test tube is used to represent "man, or you." Parrish finally leaves to join the Navy as a submariner and comes back looking exactly the same as he ever did, despite Jagger's noting that it's obvious he's "left the boy" behind him. Yes, agrees Troy, his boy got separated from his man "one night under the ice of the North Pole."

"How'd you like me to saddle up your old boyfriend?" Troy asks Connie Stevens in her titular role of *Susan Slade* (1961). He's referring to her horse. Troy is the writer and stable boy in red and white who stays true to his love even when the truth about her unwed motherhood comes out after the baby sets fire to itself.

Rome Adventure (1962) was director Delmer Daves' fourth Troy Donahue flick in a row. Little more than a picture postcard tour of Italy without the tourists and most of the citizenry, this boring travelogue outfits Troy in his red sweater and white pants (again) from *A Summer Place*. Ex-girlfriend Angie Dickinson reminds him he nicknamed her Frigid Brigid. "You said if I sat on an iceberg it wouldn't melt." (Shouldn't that have been ice *cube*?)

Donahue joined Connie Stevens for the last season of ABC-TV's *Hawaiian Eye* (1959-63), yet another detective show knock-off of *77 Sunset Strip*, though he wasn't one of the detectives. Stevens and the show's other lead, Robert Conrad, then joined Troy on the big screen in *Palm Springs Weekend* (1963), for which Troy crooned "Live Young" over the opening credits. It's a mundane beach movie without the beach concerning a busload of football jocks on a resort outing. Mr. Donahue, looking a bit long in the tooth even for college, is out-cuted by spoiled-rotten rich boy Conrad.

The September, 1962 issue of *McCall's* magazine featured a Judith Krantz story called "The Night They Invented Troy Donahue." The invention wasn't meant to last. Emblematically, also in 1962, Troy became one of the first celebrities to be replicated ad infinitum by Andy Warhol on canvas. The biting lyric in 1975's *A Chorus Line* claimed that if "Troy Donahue could be a movie star then I could be a movie star," but Donahue's starring role days were over. His career took a nosedive. Married and divorced four times, he battled for years with alcoholism—was even homeless in Central Park for a spell—before re-emerging in low-budget schlock, and a small role as Talia Shire's beau Merle Johnson (his real name) in *The Godfather Part II* (1974). He was also unrecognizably cast as Mink Stole's chain-smoking wreck of a husband who wheels her into the courtroom in her iron lung in John Waters' juvenile delinquent send-up *Cry-Baby* (1989).

Johnny Depp's Cry-Baby Walker looks a lot like **Fabian** (1940-), a slightly more cherubic mini-Elvis. Fabian Forte was a South Philly teen plucked off the front stoop of the family home by a drive-by talent agent because he thought the kid had the right look. The same agent was handling a young singing star by the name of Frankie Avalon.

Fabian, whose father had recently succumbed to a heart attack, was painfully shy, all of 14, and had no designs on show business. By 18, he had eight albums milked out of him, including *The Fabulous Fabian*, which went gold, and two gold singles: "Turn Me Loose" and "Tiger." He was also starring in his first feature film. *Hound-Dog Man* (1959) has him wearing the same pair of tight blue jeans throughout the entire film. He's wholly jumpable from the first time we see him, lazily laid out at the bottom of a haystack. "I'm growin' up and feelin' like a man," he sings later during his all-male trek into the woods on a hunting expedition. The perfect afternoon hee-haw matinee, the plot is simple, there are plenty of forgettable songs, and Fabian is so fucking cute that any and all criticisms of his being a factory-made product, a teen-idol clone, end up an endorsement of the manufacturer. He may just be the perfect litmus test for gay youth.

Unfortunately, the real-life Fabian Forte felt a lot like a product. He was hustled, bought and sold to an audience, set up on phony dates, forced to live the life of a teen idol in the public eye, and subjected to gratuitous and painful personal attacks for being one.

In *North to Alaska* (1960), he's an eager-for-beaver 17-year-old in tight pants and a teenybopper

141

Fabian and a girlfriend poolside.
EVERETT COLLECTION
Inset: A dreamy Fabian collectible.
AUTHOR'S COLLECTION

hairdo playing Stewart Granger's little brother in Nome, circa 1900. He's wide-eyed and baby-faced, a boy-man who has been told to play a virginal, love-crazed teenager until it hurts. He gets to sing a little ditty with a squeezebox and have John Wayne grab him by the seat of his pants and toss him into the drink.

Co-starring with Bing Crosby as college students in *High Time* (1960), he's briefly glimpsed as a bare-chested swimmer, gets to throw the winning basket in a basketball game, and looks hot sweating it out in his open shirt as his chums grill him before senior finals. He's a Coast Guardsman horning in on Tommy Sands' girl at the beach house in *Love in A Goldfish Bowl* (1962), joined John Wayne, Robert Wagner, Richard Beymer, Jeffrey Hunter, Paul Anka, Sal Mineo, et al in the D-Day epic *The Longest Day* (1962), and spent *Five Weeks in a Balloon* (1962) with Red Buttons, Barbara Eden, Peter Lorre, and Chester the Chimp.

When *Mr. Hobbs Takes A Vacation* (1962), he's Joe, the cute cat Jimmy Stewart pays five bucks to dance with his daughter, who's ashamed of her braces. Like a good boy, he returns the money after the dance because he really and quite sincerely likes her. Later, at the pizza parlor, he's got some unsightly fuzz growing on his chin and inexplicably sings a duet with her that begins and ends: "Cream puff, shortcake, sweet stuff, jelly roll; gum drop, milkshake, girl come and be my baby doll."

A notorious Robert Altman-directed episode of ABC TV's *Bus Stop* (1961-62), called "A Lion Walks Among Us," in which Fabian played a teenage psychopath, "was widely denounced for its explicit violence and sadism and was cited in Congressional hearings on violence in television," according to Brooks and Marsh's *Complete Directory to Prime Time Network TV Shows*.

He's joined by a spray-painted blond Peter Brown and an incongruously brunette Tab Hunter in *Ride the Wild Surf* (1964), in which he looks a little like a young Martin Sheen. He's a bronzed surfer from California named Jody who's given up on his dreams (and school) to become a Hawaiian surfing star until Shelley Fabares helps set him straight and he conquers the big one. His chest was hairy at 17, but with so much skin on display here, he's been demurely de-furred. He's admittedly short in stature, but he's got a nice bod and tweakable nipples.

Things kind of went to hell career-wise after he was knocked off as #10, therefore the first to go, of Agatha Christie's *Ten Little Indians* (1965). He's a cute, but obnoxious American squirt singing star who proudly recalls running down a young married couple with his car while driving fast and drunk after a party. I'd have killed him, too. But probably not before a protracted torture and punishment scene. Career punishment had him running from Vincent Price's exploding fembots in *Dr. Goldfoot and the Girl Bombs* (1966), and he subsequently found himself one of low-budget American International Pictures' resident stars. He did race car movies for AIP (*Fireball 500, Thunder Alley, The Wild Racers*), a 1970 gangster picture (*A Bullet for Pretty Boy*), and most entertaining of all, the so-called *Reefer Madness* of the 1960s: *Maryjane* (1968), in which he plays a high school art teacher trying to keep his kids off weed. Much to its credit as camp entertainment, it's played as deadly seriously as you'd hope.

Little Laura and Big John (1973), a home movie version of Bonnie and Clyde-like gangsters, is so feraciously amateur that you expect to see Ed Wood's name in the credits. Or footage from your sister's third birthday party seamlessly integrated.

In the September, 1973 issue of *Playgirl* magazine, the shy former Teen Idol dropped his drawers and posed for a not-quite full-frontal, but definitely nude layout, joining a number of former stars shamelessly (and thankfully) looking for a boost after the sensation caused by Burt Reynolds' centerfold in a 1972 issue of *Cosmopolitan*. We'll briefly look at that phenomenon in the next chapter.

The Idolmaker (1980), in which a temperamental and driven talent agent played by Ray Sharkey transforms a handsome young waiter (Peter Gallagher) into his new teen idol, knocking his current boy wonder down a notch, is essentially a reworking of the Fabian vs. Frankie Avalon franchise of Bob Marcucci.

Gallagher's eyebrows are almost as thick as his armpit hair, but his Cesare and the real-life Fabian have something in common. They're both beautiful young guys whose talents are taught and whose images are manufactured. Both are set up to appeal to an audience as nice, clean-cut, sweet boys, but that kind of one-note act is going to play out quickly. In *The Idolmaker*, Cesare gets his shirt torn by a mob of scary fans and then re-groups, conquers his fear, embraces his power, and goes back out on stage and tears the rest of it to shreds while he sings, driving his fans even wilder. Fabian needed that kind of abandon. Even in his boyish innocence, there was sex appeal lurking behind that big white grin. For a short while, in his prime, his sterility must have fed the fantasy. Man, it would have been fun to tear that boy's clothes off just to watch him squirm.

British physique photographer John S. Barrington (1920-1991), whose personal obsession with same-sex encounters and photography began when he was just a teenager (as these things often do), met **Alain Delon** (1935-) at Cannes in 1958 and photographed him shirtless sprawled across a hotel room bed.

Five years later, when Delon was now a recognized international sex symbol, Barrington put one of his pictures on the cover of the Spring, 1963 issue of *Man-ifique* magazine, incurring the displeasure of Delon and his managers, who threatened legal action.

There may or may not have been a touch of homosexual panic in the public works, because Delon surely knew he was as likely to attract men as he was women. He was also no stranger to same-sex relationships, but enjoyed an on-screen ambivalence.

Born in Sceaux, France, Delon endured a difficult childhood shuttled between foster homes and his mother's custody after the divorce of his parents when he was just four. He was expelled from at least a dozen schools (mostly Catholic) and stopped going altogether at the age of 15. He joined the French marines at 17 and was a parachutist during the Dien Bien Phu campaign in Indochina in 1954, a clash that would prefigure the American conflict in Vietnam. Years later, he played a paratrooper in Indochina at the beginning of *Lost Command* (1966).

Working at an assortment of jobs when he got out, including porter and waiter, he began to socialize with a number of actors and theatre folk. He was persuaded to attend the Cannes Film Festival with actor Jean Claude Brialy, placing his incredible beauty in the proximity of an industry built on looks. A Selznick talent scout (reported to be our old "friend" Henry Willson) spotted him, talked him into a screen test, and was told to offer the kid a seven-year contract in the states, but the novice wasn't ready to make such a move when there was plenty of local talent eager to put him before their cameras.

Simone Signoret's husband, director Yves Allegret, cast him as a junior assassin in *Quand la Femme s'en mele* (1957). Delon's career duality of pretty boy doing evil deeds was apparent from the start. In *Sois belle et tais-toi* (aka *Just Another Pretty Face*; 1958), he's Loulou, one of a gang of young smugglers who finds out that a fortune's worth of stolen jewels are hidden away in one of the cameras he's trafficking. By the film's end, the lovely Loulou will have to team up with the inspector to rescue their respective girlfriends from a mobster known as Charlemagne. Still operating in the moral gray zone, it took only three more films before the perfect match of man and material was made.

Plein Soleil (*Purple Noon*; 1960) is a movie classic based on the first of Patricia Highsmith's series of books about the "Talented Mr. Ripley." As stunningly beautiful as the Italian coast, the 24-year old Delon plays Tom Ripley, a sexually ambiguous opportunist who has been sent by a friend's father in San Francisco to retrieve his wayward son in Italy. The two had at least a fleeting friendship as teenagers (Ripley tells Phillippe: "I worshipped you"), but it's evident that it was a one-sided relationship. Phillippe enjoys having Ripley around to play mind games with and belittle in front of Phillippe's girlfriend.

Unlike the 1999 revision of the material (*The Talented Mr. Ripley*) starring Matt Damon as Ripley and

Alain Delon and Mylene Demongeot in *Faible femmes* (*3 Murderesses*; 1959). AUTHOR'S COLLECTION

Jude Law as the friend, repressed homosexual longing and rejection is not offered up as a psychological rationale for murder. Delon's Ripley is all the more chilling because we're not explicitly aware of why it is he's doing what he's doing. We empathize with Damon's murderer because Law is so gorgeous and charismatic that we can understand his wanting to have him, but Delon is the pretty one in *Purple Noon* and his crimes seem motivated by status-envy not penis-envy. Damon clearly wanted "Dick"ie Greenleaf. Delon wants to "Phil"lippe Greenleaf's shoes. Both are interesting, but very different takes on the original story and would make a fascinating, if long, double-feature for discussion.

There are reflecting pools inside Alain Delon's beautiful blue eyes and the sun is shining. Like cut jewels, they seem faceted—the purity of the color is broken up by light, making them incapable of penetrating stares even as you're drawn to them. When Delon looks at you, you go to him, not vice versa.

Turns out he's just as lovely in black-and-white. In *Rocco e i suoi Fratelli* (*Rocco and His Brothers*; 1960), mama calls him an "angel" and the girls at the laundry where he works for a stint refer to him as "Sleeping Beauty." The middle of the five Parondi brothers, Delon's Rocco is the saint among them in Luchino Visconti's epic tragedy of a family of rural southerners relocating to Milan at the behest of their

144

recently widowed mother.

Rocco follows his bad seed elder brother Simone into the boxing game, but hates nearly everything about it despite becoming a local champ. A prostitute works her way through three of the five siblings and eventually sets their lives on end, inciting jealousy, rape, and murderous rage. Throughout, Rocco is sweet, forgiving, and painfully unselfish. After suffering the wrath of Simone, Rocco is still able to turn his face to the woman who was violated and tell her she must go back to him—she is the only one who can save Simone. It's an incomprehensible suggestion to the rest of us, but the tears falling from Delon's eye as he says it reveal both a character and an actor capable of unexpected dimensions.

There are ample opportunities to gaze upon Delon's smooth and taut physique in both *Purple Noon* and *Rocco* (both from gay directors), but there's quite a bit more than meets the eye. In *Purple Noon*, he's so beautiful that you actually want him to get away with the murders and deceit, providing yet another level to the complexity of our personal reaction to the material and indicting us to the point of complicity. In *Rocco*, the most beautiful of the brothers is weakened by his untenable belief in the goodness of his brethren. He becomes a champion doing something which he hates doing and martyrs himself for what seem to us wrong reasons. There's a quality of sadness in Rocco that goes beyond simple naivete. It seems preordained.

L'Eclisse (*The Eclipse*; 1962) was the third in a trilogy by Michelangelo Antonioni devoted to the emotional ennui of Monica Vitti. Though he's in fine form as the workaholic stock trader and nail-biter, Delon is caught up in the zombie-like malaise of Vitti's worldview: dull, gray, and lifeless. "Who has time to go out with call girls?" Delon jokes during one of the few seconds he's allowed to lighten up. When it comes to dining out with investors, "I'm the one who is a call girl."

He looks great in his tight little swim trunks as an ex-con pretending to be a playboy in *Any Number Can Win* (1962), and his hustler in dark shades gets himself hustled when a gig as a chauffeur turns into a job as Jane Fonda's trophy lover in *Joy House* (1964).

Reunited with Visconti for *Il Gattopardo* (*The Leopard*; 1963), he shows up in Burt Lancaster's shaving mirror as the nephew to the Prince of Salinas (Lancaster) in this 3-hour and 20-minute chronicle of the end of the aristocracy in 1860 Italy. Nearly every frame is a painting, though Delon's role as a revolutionary

Alain Delon for lunch. *Purple Noon* (1960). PHOTOFEST

turned army boor and romantic lead is not one of his most charismatic. I like the scene, though, where a black Great Dane sloppily mouths his wrist and leads him to say his goodbyes to the members of the palace.

At last ready to give the American and British film industries a go at him (he was reportedly highly considered for the lead in *Lawrence of Arabia*), he played a very brown Italian gigolo posing as a street photographer who romances an uncultured gangster's moll (Shirley MacLaine) in story two of *The Yellow Rolls-Royce* (1964). He's particularly cute in his little white cap, and again there's a nice sequence with him running around in his tight wet swimming trunks, but true love ends up giving way to self-sacrifice amidst the beautiful locales. He's married to Ann-Margret and brother to Jack Palance in *Once A Thief* (1965), an over-the-top crime drama in which he's unwillingly recruited to pull off one last big job before settling down with his family as a fisherman. Things don't exactly work out that way. Best of all, he's a cheek-kissing and cheek-slapping Spanish Duke in the Old West opposite Dean Martin and Joey Bishop in the slight, but enjoyable comedy *Texas Across the River* (1966). These turned out not to be the kind of projects to win over American audiences, however.

Returning to his homeland, where his notoriety as a ladies man (even while married) was coupled with a distaste for his "traitorous" contract with MGM just when he had become France's most highly paid actor, Delon connected with what would become something of a signature role. Wearing a face no longer golden with youth, but a beauty glazed with approaching age, Delon could almost be accused of donning a mask as hired killer Jef Costello in Jean-Pierre Melville's *Le Samourai* (1967), earning him the epithet "Ice Cold Angel." It's a somber film-noir meditation on a hit man's empty soul during the last flicker of a career.

In what turns out to be a surprisingly enjoyable buddy film, Delon is coupled with Lino Ventura in *Les Adventuriers* (1967), both head over heels for the lovely and lively Joanna Shimkus. The trio end up heading down to the Congo to retrieve sunken treasure, and before things get too heavy there's a lovely and extended montage of their "vacation" together. Alain is shirtless for much of it and looks very sexy in his facial scruff, a beard that doesn't have the genetic imperative to fill in on the sides. Probably unwilling to cover up such a face.

He's beside himself in Louis Malle's 35-minute segment of *Histoires extraordinaires* (*Spirits of the Dead*; 1968), loosely based on Poe's *William Wilson*. As a sadistic medical student with peculiar ideas about live vivisections, he's thwarted by his doppelgänger.

He's another sort of demon in Jack Cardiff's psychedelic curiosity *Girl on A Motorcycle* (*Naked Under Leather*; 1968), which stars Marianne Faithfull as an unhappily married young woman who receives a motorcycle for a wedding gift and uses it for frequent jaunts to be unfaithful. A political sex flick with the fetishistic motorcycle metaphored as the female body instead of the male, the film wrestles with her confused identity as a woman with one foot in her heterosexist shoe and the other in liberated leather.

She wants a *real* man to tell her to shut up and keep her from being a bitch, she explains to us in voice-over. Delon is a Swiss intellectual with Clark Kent glasses, a pipe-smoking professor who lectures his boys about free love. "You get to eat the biscuit without having to buy the packet," observes one of his students.

During a winter tryst outside their cabin, Faithfull undoes Delon's black coat and pulls up his white sweater to kiss his chest. His big red nipple matches the big red ball on the top of his black ski cap. A post-coital scene has him gesticulating in bed as scenes of motorcycle races and wipe-outs are intercut. A pot of red roses hide his genitals in another scene; at one point in their lovemaking, Faithfull bites his shoulder and he reaches out and grabs for the flowers, sending the film into psychedelic colors. Afterward, he kisses her foot, telling her, "Your toes are like tombstones."

In a circus fantasy, ringmaster Alain gets to whip her velvet-lined leather suit right off her. And in yet another of the originally X-rated scenes, there's a particularly spicy shot of him as he lifts her up and then uses his teeth to unzip her suit. It looks like cunnilingus. *Girl on A Motorcycle*, which was diluted in some markets, was based on Andre Pieyre de Mandiargue's novel. The author's *La Marge* (*The Streetwalker*) would be made into a sex flick in the 1970s with Joe Dallesandro and Sylvia Kristel.

While Delon was in St. Tropez filming *La Piscene* (aka *The Swimming Pool*; 1969), his sometime double/valet/bodyguard Stefan Markovic, a Yugoslav hustler, was found shot in the head, wrapped in mattress cover plastic and burlap, and dumped in a garbage heap. A tabloidish feeding frenzy ensued with the press theorizing that, as reported in *The New York Times*, Markovic "had been organizing sex parties for prominent people, taking photographs of participants and later trying to blackmail them." Delon and his wife Nathalie were raked over the coals by press and police alike, particularly after the murdered man's brother surrendered a letter in which Markovic called the actor "a stupid and sick man" and wrote: "For all the unpleasant things that happen to me and for all my troubles, you should hold Alain Delon 10,000 percent responsible."

Another of Delon's bodyguards, also a Yugoslav and the man who introduced the actor to Markovic, had been found shot to death in the states two years earlier while Delon was there filming *Texas Across the River*. Fearing for his life, and saying so in a nationally published letter written to the President of the Republic, Delon became the focus of much scrutiny and criticism over his friendships with underworld figures dating back to when he got out of the service. The Markovic case was never solved, the Delons were no longer under official investigation, but the marriage was over in 1969.

If anything, as horrible as the murder/sex scandal was, it provided the actor with a dimension of real-life character that transcended his pretty-boy looks.

He even started to play gangsters, quite successfully in both *The Sicilian Clan* (1969), with Jean Gabin, and *Borsalino* (1970), with Jean-Paul Belmondo. *Borsalino* was, in fact, a smash hit produced by Delon himself, putting his Adel Productions on the map. By 1979, he had produced nineteen films. He also decided to join a generation of young actors who were baring it all in the 1970s when he stripped and went for a full-frontal romp on the beach in *Traitement de choc* (aka *Shock* or *Shock Treatment*; 1972). He's as long and lean as the rest of himself. Within a year of the film's release, paparazzo shots of the actor sunbathing in the nude appeared in the Italian women's magazine *Libera*. The *Los Angeles Times* reported that the photographer was "disguised as a beach boy."

Alain Delon remains one of France's most famous film stars nearly a half century after his serendipitous discovery, defying those who chose to see him as nothing more than a pretty face and justifying the faith of a handful of gay directors who knew they had something more. Among his many roles, he's the gentleman bandit and poofy poof in a low-budget *Zorro* (1975), an embarrassed and first-billed Capt. Paul Metrand in *The Concorde: Airport '79* (1979; the disaster series' worst entry), a foppish Baron de Charlus in a Van Dyke, busy eyeing all the servant boys, in *Swann in Love* (1984), and the proud business entrepreneur of a line of AD (Alain Delon) products, including his own brand of cigarettes, cognac, perfume, cologne, and men's underwear.

Criticized for his politics in recent years, as well as deservedly or undeservedly burnt by ex-lovers' memoirs and the documentary *Nico Icon* (1995), Delon is also unavoidably a controversial figure. All doubts about his acting ability, however, were irrevocably shattered by *Mr. Klein* (1976), director Joseph Losey's masterpiece with Delon troubled once again by a double. Opportunistically purchasing artworks owned by persecuted Jews in France during WWII, his character suddenly finds himself mired in just such persecution when he's suspected of being a Jew who shares his name.

"You go home to your mother and father and grow up to be strong and straight" is Shane's advice to his hero-worshipping Little Joe in the classic 1953 western. Young **Brandon de Wilde** (1942-1972) may or may not have taken that advice to heart, but he surely added "beautiful" to the list.

Andre Brandon de Wilde ("da-willda") was born into a theatre family and was all of seven years old when he debuted on Broadway as inquisitive neighbor boy John Henry in *The Member of the Wedding*. Watching the 1952 film version, it's impossible to tell that this little boy had previously played the role for 492 performances. He's astonishingly spontaneous and completely natural alongside the powerhouse performances of Julie Harris and Ethel Waters in this must-see drama chronicling the painful coming-of-age of a confused and anguished 12-year old Southern girl. John Henry is a priceless member of the ensemble. He recalls how cute he thought a circus pinhead was, sympathetically tells Frankie (Harris) that he doesn't think she smells bad, and even dolls himself up in drag as a fairy princess.

No wonder director Fred Zinnemann knew he had his Little Joe for *Shane* (1953), a performance so good that the 11-year old was nominated for an Academy Award as Best Supporting Actor. In a 1964 interview, to help illustrate the troubling chasm between his parents' encouragement of his acting life and their rampant desire to ensure he didn't develop an ego, he claimed he wasn't even informed of his Oscar nomination until four years after the fact.

He starred in his own television show, *Jamie* (1953-54), on ABC, in which he played Jamison Francis McHummer, an orphan boy who finally finds a friend in his Grandpa. Back on the big screen, he played a backwoods lad abusing a laughing, crying, and rat-catching mutt in *Goodbye, My Lady* (1956), then

Brandon de Wilde sees his uncle Paul Newman for what he really is in *Hud* (1963). EVERETT COLLECTION Inset: Brandon, gone too soon. PHOTOFEST

showed up as a youngster in the Jimmy Stewart/Audie Murphy western *Night Passage* (1957), and as a 15-year old orphan on the run who's hassled by Lee Marvin in *The Missouri Traveler* (1958).

When the Broadway play *Blue Denim*, which dealt frankly with the subject of teen pregnancy and abortion, was bought for the movies, inevitable changes were made. Several of the key cast members from the play would be retained (among them, Carol Lynley and Warren Berlinger), but the shocking and tragic finale would be altered and the male lead would be replaced by 17-year old Brandon de Wilde.

The 1959 film's trailer was hosted by that paradigm of parenthood Joan Crawford, who assures us that "these are not juvenile delinquents. They're nice kids. Nice kids in trouble." The film's sets look like TV sitcom sets and TV dads and moms populate them. Brandon's mom knits and doesn't know what "biology" is, which squarely lays the blame on the parents if you ask me.

Brandon plays a nice young man who hangs out with his fast-talking buddy in the basement, where they play poker, smoke cigarettes, drink beer, and swear—playacting the parts of little men. Brandon's girl (Lynley) stops by and finds a copy of his *He-Man* magazine, which he wrestles away from her. If only he had stuck to those physique magazines, they might not be in this mess.

As the younger brother to a heartless gigolo played by Warren Beatty in *All Fall Down* (1962), he's cute enough to wish we'd see him get into a little trouble before deciding that his role model is just a big jerk. Still, it's primarily a dress rehearsal for *Hud* (1963), where he's Paul Newman's nephew. We never believe that 17-year old Lon will turn out like his reckless uncle, but we need his coming of age to validate the film's morality. Selfishly, we're also made aware that Brandon has grown into a very beautiful young man and we enjoy looking at him. When housekeeper Patricia Neal tickles him awake, he flirts with her like any teenage boy would, telling her he can't get out of bed just yet because he sleeps in the raw. Sure, he's got pajamas, but they strangle him. It's just one brilliantly realized scene in a film filled with riches. (Another of which is watching Paul Newman carry de Wilde over his shoulder and into bed.)

At 22, in Disney's *Those Calloways* (1965), we get our first chance to see him grown up and in full color and he looks quite the Golden Boy. His voice is well-modulated and masculine considering the sing-song of his pre-adolescence.

He's so smooth-faced, handsome, and geometrical in the WWII film *In Harm's Way* (1965), with a haircut that's as perfectly clean-cut as it is immovable, he looks like a marionette. To estranged papa John Wayne: "You look like your mother." He's an uppity little brat mixing with the wrong crowd at first, but by the time he's a lieutenant under the command of his admiral dad, he's seen the error of his ways and straightened out. There's a disturbing lack of information when dad has to tell son about the death of a nurse, suggesting that Brandon's to blame, but the point is that they've reached some sort of unspoken understanding and the handsome young man can go on to fulfill his destiny as a heroic casualty of war.

Weary of the limited roles he was being offered to play, de Wilde "retired" from acting in 1965 to study music. He eventually made two more films, *The Deserter* (1971) and *Wild in the Sky* (1972), as well as a 1971 appearance in an episode of Rod Serling's *Night Gallery*, opposite Vincent Price, which are rare enough to be highly sought after by his cult of fans. Brandon de Wilde was only 30 years of age when his vehicle hit a truck during a torrential thunderstorm while he was on his way to perform in a stage production of *Butterflies Are Free* in Denver on July 6, 1972. As with James Dean, he left an indelible image of suspended beauty for his fans. We saw him grow up on screen. We saw him become the good-looking, kind, and dreamy boyfriend we wanted to have in our own perfect little dream world, and suffered with the sudden loss of him in our fantasies.

Horst Buchholz ("book-holts;" 1933-2003) dubbed foreign film actors into German before making his own debut in *Marianne de ma Jeunesse* (1955) and being honored at Cannes for his role in *Himmel ohne Sterne* (*Sky Without Stars*; 1955).

Die Halbstarken (1956), a German juvenile delinquent picture, opens at the public pool where Horst and his buddies are scheming in their tight swimsuits. He starts a ruckus because he's smoking and it's verboten. Er, forbidden. With the export potential to the US market of a teenage gang movie, the production company decided to shoot the entire thing in English.

It was released as *Teenage Wolfpack* (for some markets as *The Hooligans*) in the US and Horst was Americanized to Henry Bookholt. He dresses in black, with black leather pants that match his ink-black hair wherever it appears. He's the bad older brother who works in a filling station by day and roams with his wolfpack by night. He's got great cheekbones. You're required to notice them, because he and his whole gang are such rude little bastards that you'll want to slap them silly and you wonder whether cheekbones like that will screw up your hand.

There's a dance scene in a little café and Horst struts and bobs like a chicken. When he wants his gal to clear out, he barks, "Sissy, go make me pancakes, I'm hungry." He barks a lot in this film. In fact, barking is one of Horst's trademarks: a sudden and ferocious explosion of audio accompanied by facial histrionics and a flash of his big white teeth.

The nicest thing he does in the film is adopt a cute dachshund puppy, but he's still too much of a jerk to win over his good-guy younger brother. Little bro doesn't like Horst's mean streak and tells him so, though he won't look at him. "Why won't you look at me, John? Most people like my face."

149

453-63/26

Horst Buchholz and his *Fanny* (1961), Leslie Caron. PHOTOFEST
Inset: Horst plays a juvenile delinquent up to no good at the pool
in *Teenage Wolfpack* (1956). YESTERDAY

I certainly do. *Teenage Wolfpack* may be an awful, boring little movie, but Horst was too much a force to be stopped by a mere exploitation flick. All he needed was the right material: *The Confessions of Felix Krull* (1957) was adapted from a Thomas Mann short story about the adventures of a nobody who becomes a somebody while working his way up the ranks of a posh hotel in Paris.

In voice-over, Felix (Horst) admits he comes from "seedy people." Facing military service, he devises a way to be declared unfit so he can go on with the rest of his life. At the induction office, he asks the examiners if he can put his shirt back on because he's embarrassed by his own nudity. He

150

twitches his way out of service by falling off his chair (revealing he's still wearing his undies), thus managing to be declared epileptic and exempt.

In Paris, he becomes a lift boy at the hotel under the assumed name of Armand. A dishwasher calls him pretty boy, introduces him to a life of petty crime, and kisses him on the forehead whenever he sees him. Eventually, he becomes the plaything of a rich woman who writes romance novels. She dresses him up as Hermes in a bed sheet and poses him. She calls him all sorts of names (fool, blockhead, chump) and wants him to engage in a variety of role-playing games with her, pre-figuring Joe Dallesandro's objectification in both *Flesh* (1968) and *Trash* (1970).

One of the three hearts that beat for him in the film belongs to a man, an older gentleman who wants him as his private butler in Scotland. "Come with me. It is the wish of a lonely heart." Felix diplomatically declines, because he chooses "not to deviate from the course I've chosen." Felix Krull is a gigolo and a hustler, even conniving a rich and jealous man into allowing him to travel under his identity in order for that man to stay and carry on a relationship with a girl whose parents don't approve of him. That double identity may just cause the crafty lad to leave his "well-shaped corpse" on a slab.

Felix Krull was a widely-acclaimed success and a star-making performance for Horst Buchholz in the international community. It was *Tiger Bay* (1959), however, that brought him to the attention of American filmmakers. Starring alongside Hayley Mills, in her film debut, Horst plays a Polish sailor who returns to England to find his girlfriend has moved on to another relationship. Bitter and angry, his reaction is noted by the precocious Ms. Mills, who has been spying through the mail slot. The unlikely pair subsequently strike up a charming relationship in this first-rate suspense drama, which alerted Disney to the enormous potential of Hayley Mills and sent Horst Buchholz to be counted as one of *The Magnificent Seven* (1960).

He's the intense, taunting epitome of youthful belligerence and egocentricity, humiliated by not being able to put a pistol in between a Yul Brynner handclap. He's perfect for the role, a muscle-knotted upstart and show-off who's over the top in almost every way, grandstanding his youth. I particularly like the way he pets his fish when he catches them in the stream, and the way he hangs off the side of his horse to get a drink and wet his face. He sees a scrawny bull and tries to act the part of matador, but it just drools.

Famed Broadway stage director Josh Logan had seen him in *Tiger Bay* and knew he wanted him to play Marius when it came time to bring the musical version of Pagnol's *Fanny* to the big screen. Only the studio was nervous about musicals, so *Fanny* (1961) would only get made if it wasn't one.

As a 19-year old bartender in a little café in Marseilles, he dreams of sailing off on one of the many ships that comes into port. But wouldn't you know, when he gets his chance, his lifelong friendship with the fishwife's daughter, Fanny (Leslie Caron), blooms into romance. They are to be married in spite of his growing desire to sail the seven seas. Tortured by his two loves, but certain he'll embark the next morning, he has a touching scene with his pop, the owner of the café, bidding him goodnight and then tenderly adding: "I like you very much." It's as close to "I love you" as he can get, and Horst delivers it with the perfect inflection.

He's beautiful in Technicolor. He has a wide face, accommodating a distinctive bone structure. His eyes are almost beady, barely more than slits with black centers. Sometimes they don't seem to be quite symmetrical, and they photograph black, not brown or dark blue or dark green. They peer his jet-black hair, a luxuriant mop that always looks best slightly or severely mussed. When he returns from his voyages in *Fanny*, he makes a stunning figure decked out in clothes that match.

As East German Communist Otto Ludwig Piffl in Billy Wilder's charming and fast-paced comedy *One, Two, Three* (1961), he's mussed from head to toe. No socks, no undershorts, a permanent scowl on his face, and nearly every line he speaks is spat with invective. Coca-Cola distributor James Cagney (in his last film role before retirement, save *Ragtime* 20 years later) has been put in charge of the boss' wild daughter while she's in West Berlin, only to find out she's been sneaking off to see a cute Commie.

The first fifteen minutes can be grating, what with Cagney's compliance to shout all his dialogue and more than a handful of flat jokes, but the film gets cooking with the arrival of the daughter (Pamela Tiffin), the jokes start hitting, and the dialogue begins to crackle and pop. There are several verbal and visual allusions to Cagney films of the past, including the threat of his pushing a grapefruit in Horst's face. The two have a number of fun exchanges: "I spit on your money!" barks Horst to capitalist Cagney. "I spit on Fort Knox! I spit on Wall Street!"

"Unsanitary little jerk, isn't he?"

Horst practically foams at the mouth over the stench of capitalism, saying it's "like a dead herring in

151

the moonlight. It shines, but it stinks." Forced to be outfitted in the finery of a royal name Cagney has bought for him from a bathroom attendant, Buchholz is embraced by his adopted father and comes away from the coupling wearing the other man's monocle. It's a silly moment, but his reaction when he suddenly thinks one of his eyes has gone bad is classic mugging. Required viewing.

Back in Europe, he played the uninspired artist who faces *The Empty Canvas* (1964) and a blonde-mopped Bette Davis as his mom. Davis said she had no idea why she was asked to do the film, thought the script horrible, the part terrible (the blonde wig and incompatible Southern accent her ideas), and Horst difficult. An infamous scene has her walking in on her son while he's in her bedroom decorating his mistress' nude body with 10,000 lire banknotes. She doesn't bat an eye. "Please put the money you don't want back in the safe. I don't want the maid to find the room in this curious state."

He showed his own bare ass in *Come, Quando, Perche* (*How, When and With Whom*; 1968), then went full-frontal in 1971's *Le Saveur*. He worked steadily in French, Italian, and German cinema throughout the '70s and '80s, did a few lousy American films (*Avalanche Express, Sahara, Aces: Iron Eagle III*) in between, then showed up memorably as Lessing, the Nazi doctor with a thing for riddles, in Roberto Begnini's Academy-Award winning *Life is Beautiful* (1998).

Whatever else **Henry Warren Beaty** (1937-   ) may be prolific at—making love, making enemies—it's not making films. Forty years in the business and he has yet to crack 25 features. Not that size necessarily matters, but even the notoriously troubled Monty Clift managed 17 during his 16 years in the industry and it took Warren 20 to reach that number. Could politics and women possibly have taken up that much of his time?

He dropped out of Northwestern University's School of Speech after the first year and went to New York to study real-life drama while his older sister, Shirley MacLaine, was making her screen debut in Alfred Hitchcock's *The Trouble With Harry* (1955). He nabbed a few television roles, including a regular slot on the 1959-60 season of *The Many Lives of Dobie Gillis* (1959-63), and appeared on stage in a production of *Compulsion*. It wasn't even one of the lead roles, but beauty like Beatty's couldn't be beat. Producer Josh Logan saw the play and courted him for the lead in his new film *Parrish*. Warren was flown to Los Angeles where he screen-tested opposite Jane Fonda. Logan ended up backing out of *Parrish* because he didn't like the final script, and so the part went to director Delmer Daves' boy ingenue Troy Donahue.

Logan then considered Beatty to star opposite Fonda in *The Tall Story* (1960), an entertaining and silly college flick that has her falling for a school basketball star. The studio insisted that Logan use an actor of their choice, so it was Anthony Perkins who got to share a cramped mobile-home shower and awkward make-out scenes with Fonda.

Playwright William Inge had also seen Beatty in *Compulsion*, in turn compelling him to cast the dark-haired young man in his new play *A Loss of Roses*, which flopped and closed after 25 performances in 1959. Beatty had enough time to demonstrate, however, that he was cocky, arrogant, and impudent. Co-stars and director alike barely managed to put up with him.

When you were a "difficult" young beauty it seemed that only one man of the era knew what to make of you. Elia Kazan made Warren Beatty a star in his film debut in *Splendor in the Grass* (1961). Set in 1928 Kansas, it's the thinking teen's teen-sex movie and a genre classic. It was also written for Warren by William Inge, the you-might-have-guessed gay playwright who makes an ironic cameo in the film as the minister.

Warren plays Bud Stamper, who has his back to us when we first see him at the waterfall because he's busy sucking Natalie Wood's face. Natalie's Wilma Dean Loomis ought to know better, but she doesn't. Her sex-hating mama explains to her that "a woman doesn't enjoy those things." It's a virtual template of teen sex movies to come: the lovers are from two sides of the tracks (Beatty wealthy, Wood poor); Beatty's gimp-legged, super-macho pop has big plans for his football star buckaroo ("Don't disappoint me, I got all my hopes pinned on you"), but the son can't get a word in edgewise to let him know he wants to do something different with his life; Bud's a sensitive boy, so dad wants to make a man out of him by procuring a prostitute. The kid's also got an out-of-control vamp for an older sister (Barbara Loden) who's destined for disaster; meanwhile, Wilma's puritanical mother drives her insane with the sin and filth of it all. Literally insane. Before the movie is over, Wood's character will have spent two and a half years in an institution. The moral could be that not enough sex will drive you nuts.

Beatty makes a rather stunning debut in this tale of a what a man is expected to want, what he's expected to get, and how he's expected to get it. He's the sensitive rebel in the James Dean tradition. No wonder Natalie has her little shrine to him on her bedroom mirror. He has a great smile—dimples, too—bites his fist a lot, and seems to be having an orgasm while he works through his decision to go to Yale after all in exchange for a promise that he can marry Natalie when he returns.

While the two lovers cuddle on a rock along the falls, it's Beatty who's topless with Wood on top, rubbing and kissing his chest, instead of vice versa. (There are a couple of eerie water scenes involving Oscar-nominated Wood, who died by drowning in 1981.) During an argument, Beatty forces her down on her knees in front of him and the staging couldn't have been more obvious to teens in 1961 than teens in 2001. That's paying it a compliment, too. *Splendor in the Grass*, which did well at the box-office, is an aching love story like all love stories should be. Only in real life do two genuinely nice lovers ever end up together. In the movies, it's just another cliche.

If you're interested in Warren Beatty's playboy love life, which gained notoriety from the get-go with the romance of his *Splendor* co-star while she was married to Robert Wagner, I'm sorry to disappoint you,

Warren Beatty lost in *Lilith* (1964), but bored viewers could always count his eyelashes. PHOTOFEST

153

but there will be precious little of that here. Mr. Beatty's reputation with a long list of celebrity beauties precedes him and has been well-documented elsewhere.

I'm more interested in the fact that his second movie has him playing a gigolo created by yet another gay playwright, this time Tennessee Williams. In *The Roman Spring of Mrs. Stone* (1961), Vivien Leigh tells the Contessa: "People who are very beautiful make their own laws." She's right, you know.

With his tan from a can, Warren Beatty is a lacquered beauty as the conniving, self-centered, self-obsessed Paolo. The brown of his face contrasts with the white of his tall teeth. His eyelashes have been dipped in black ink. Paolo's not quite hateful, despite the peculiar accent, but he's never really likable either. A stroll on the terrace while he's wearing tight beige pants, with his hands thrust in his pockets making them tighter, reveals skimpy underwear lines and a not very attractive ass.

Gigolos should have heavenly butts. Vivien Leigh's "older" actress should get what she's paying for, and maybe she does. She's cruelly referred to as a "chicken hawk" at one point. When she's screening home movies, Beatty shows up as a sunbathing beauty in one of them, a sunning boy on his belly wearing black trunks and filmed from behind with his rear-end slightly raised and his legs spread. His bod is what's on display. You can't even see his face is the joke, compounded by the Countess immediately identifying him. "Ah, there's Paolo!" Both the joke and the butt ogling are surprisingly frank and especially rewarding. The pose looks like something out of an AMG film. You can easily transpose the body language to gay erotica and an open invitation. Beatty then gets up, his butt still to the camera, and runs off down the beach. The shot is that much more provocative considering it's supposed to represent Leigh holding the camera.

All Fall Down (1962), adapted to the screen by William Inge, has its moments, especially from Angela Lansbury as Beatty and Brandon de Wilde's histrionic mother, but Warren is too busy working on his James Dean and one aches for vanilla de Wilde to at least dabble in his reckless brother's lifestyle before deciding it's wrong. As with *The Outsiders* 21 years later, the film has our perspiring 16-year old hero coming of age while keeping a journal and being forced to say his brother's silly name over and over again. (It's Berry-Berry, as opposed to Ponyboy or Sodapop. Or Motorcycle Boy, for that matter, since the younger brother's worship of his older brother also calls to mind Hinton's *Rumble Fish*.)

Beatty is served up as a selfish, suicidal pretty boy, morally unhinged and jailed twice for whacking his women. Completely self-involved, he's a step toward acknowledging the callous hustlers and gigolos to come. He quite rightly claims ignorance of his effect on women (he's just a stud), but it's interesting to see how the film uses his attractive image to subvert his character. (*Hud* would do the same thing with Newman in 1963.) Lonely dame after lonely dame succumb to his look. They do not, importantly, fall for his charm, because he's not charming in the least. This is purely about sexual attraction. A middle-aged teacher stops at the gas station on her way to Louisville and ogles the good-looking attendant reflected in her car door mirror. Should have been rearview. She admits to wishing she had a young man who could be her companion on the trip and before she can believe it he's negotiated extra cash, hotel room expenses, and climbed into her car. Some days later, after she's been used and abused, she whines about his behavior at a seedy café while he chomps down food and guzzles his drink, completely oblivious to her pathetic attempt to make him human.

Sometimes it's a bitch being so good-looking that you end up getting everything you want without ever really getting anything worth having; in this case, we've a cautionary fable about a mama's boy coddled and doted upon to the point of emotional vacancy. A strangely sensual kiss between mother and son (accentuated by its being cut away from at the last second) suggests an even darker relationship, the result of which is her undying devotion and his subterranean hatred.

Good looks are not enough. The privileges are as likely to lead you to despair as they are to happiness. Being identified as a sex object, willingly or unwillingly, means possibly being used as one, gal or guy.

His good looks get him the job as a nurse who wants to "be a direct help to people" in the psychodrama *Lilith* (1964). He has returned to his hometown after an unexplained war injury, or "something like that," and falls in love with the title's beautiful and perplexing patient played by Jean Seberg. A gray, dreary, mostly lifeless film, it nevertheless revels in its recurrent water themes (waterfalls, reflections, blood as water, Beatty buys an aquarium) and has our handsome young man swirling into his own madness after dabbling with this disturbed woman. She has a lesbian lover in the institution and he follows them to a barn and roughs her up, calling her a "dirty bitch."

Beatty is laid-back, almost lying down. He doesn't seem focused enough to be brooding when he needs to be, though he tries. His face is too smooth, however. His brows arch and his eyes cast down and search the ground when he feels the need to emote. He's pretty and pretty vacant, too. Perplexed, bordering on Tony Perkins. Maybe it's withdrawal we're seeing. He managed, once again, to infuriate all his co-stars and the director while the film was being shot.

Nobody much cared for him while they were making *Mickey One* (1965) in Chicago either. Are we starting to understand why this guy has made so few films? He's had to produce almost every picture he's acted in since 1975. And he's either lost or refused roles in *The Leopard, Butch Cassidy and the Sundance Kid* (with Elvis as his Sundance), *The Way We Were, Ryan's Daughter, The Sting, PT 109, The Great Gatsby*, and *Last Tango in Paris*. There may never have been a Robert Redford if it wasn't for Warren Beatty's disapproval ratings.

Years before *Ishtar* (1987), he's an unfunny and jangled-nerves mess of a stand-up comic in the artsy-fartsy *Mickey One*, directed by Arthur Penn. He's busy avoiding Detroit gangsters by hiding out in seedy joints in Chicago, trying to get a gig at a weird club owned by foppish Hurd Hatfield, the actor who played eternal youth in the 1945 version of *The Picture of Dorian Gray*. Tellingly, Hatfield can't bring himself to cut Beatty's beautiful face with a broken perfume bottle. It's an attempt at American New Wave filmmaking, with strange angles, odd rhythms, and abstract dialogue, and so worth a look. Is Beatty just awful or perfectly awful? You decide.

Promise Her Anything (1966) is just awful without debate, probably the most inexcusably vacuous film about a pseudo-pornographer ever made. *Kaleidoscope* (1966) isn't much better. Leslie Caron was the excuse for both. And not a good one.

Without a single hit film to his credit, Beatty went on the offensive to get a pet project financed, a throwback to Warner Bros. gangster flicks. *Bonnie and Clyde* (1967) is a watershed film, an occasionally arty, anti-establishmentarian send-up of celebrity with the kind of bloody violence America was unaccustomed to in their color movies.

The original script gave Clyde Barrow a homosexual slant, but Beatty wouldn't play it and everybody involved thought it would be a mistake if the idea was to have the audience on his side. So, they made him impotent.

"I ain't much of a lover boy," he tells Bonnie Parker right off. "There ain't nothing wrong with me. I don't like boys."

"Your advertising's just dandy," she retorts. "Folks'd never guess you had nothing to sell."

The film was not a critical or box-office success upon its initial release. Reviewers lambasted it for making heroes out of a couple of low-life murderers and bank robbers. (This many years later, viewing the film in a different sociopolitical context, it takes considerable effort to see these people as heroic in any respect.) But then Pauline Kael wrote a chapter-length review praising the film to the high heavens, causing others to take a second look. "How do you make a good movie in this country without being jumped on?" Kael asked in *The New Yorker*.

Time magazine put *Bonnie and Clyde* on its December 8, 1967 cover, headlining: "The New Cinema: Violence...Sex...Art." A re-release in February of 1968 (less than a year after it opened) caught on like gangbusters and it went on to garner ten Oscar nominations (winning only two), became the 15th largest grossing movie of the decade, and the number one moneymaker for Warner Bros. of the 1960s.

Warren Beatty had reached his zenith playing limp. By 1975, he was ever-ready hard as a listless hairdresser looking to get his own shop and trying to figure out which of the many women he's bonking he should take seriously. Unfunny for the first hour, *Shampoo* (1975) finally realizes its potential at the halfway point and succeeds in its portrait of the American male playboy who went to beauty school "to fuck 'em all."

That's right, "I don't fuck anybody for money. I do it for fun." The blunt, racy dialogue was considered very adult when the film was released, famously culminating when a drunk Julie Christie tells a wealthy man at a political fundraising dinner who offers to get her anything she'd like, that, "Most of all, I'd like to suck *his* cock"—pointing to Beatty. She gets up and spills a drink on Warren's lap and then feels him up while wiping it off in front of the guests. She even ducks down under the table to make her wish come true, reciting "who's the greatest cocksucker in the world?" as she goes.

There's convenient suspicion that Beatty's "gay," a "fairy," a "queer," a "faggot" (all are used), but the film resists turning into a primer for the TV sitcom *Three's Company*. *Shampoo* has a perfect ending to the playboy's fantasy. It also has (I'll mention parenthetically) a few seconds glance at a beautiful young brunette wearing only a towel. The lean boy-beauty with a single line to utter and too much hair around his face to see him say it is **Andrew Stevens** (1955-   ).

By the mid-1960s, the male physique magazine market was booming. *Male Figure, MANual, Mars, Big, The Young Physique, MuscleBoy, Champ, Butch, Mr. Sun, Tomorrow's Man, Muscle A' Go-Go, Go Guys, Grecian Guild Pictorial, Photozique, Tiger, Trim,* and good old *Physique Pictorial* were being stuffed into maleboxes across America at various times throughout the decade.

Some of them went belly-up, pressured by competition or by governmental harassment, while others fought the competition by lowering the posing straps and taking their oppressors to court.

The U.S. Post Office seized a trio of publisher Herman Lynn Womack's physique titles (namely, *MANual, Grecian Guild Pictorial,* and *Trim*) in 1960 as obscene and he successfully took the case to the Supreme Court in 1962, where it was ruled that "these portrayals of the male nude cannot fairly be regarded as more objectionable than many portrayals of the female nude that society tolerates." The Court didn't like what it saw, but they failed to find it "patently offensive."

MANual vs. Day's 1962 decision was a landmark case for the physique industry, seeming as it did to allow the male nude consent to hang free in their pages. Not everyone was convinced.

Bob Mizer, for instance. In 1962, he reported having to edit a wrestling film down to choppy bits and pieces in order to avoid censorial proscriptions about visible pubic hair on one of the models. He also boasted that AMG now had 60,000 photos available.

Ingeniously, if only in the sense of mythmaking, Mizer devised a cryptic hieroglyphic code that he began placing next to each boy's picture in the February, 1963 issue of *Physique Pictorial*. These symbols indicated, so he said, "a subjective character analysis of the models." Considering how critical and blunt he already was about his boys in the text accompanying their photos—for example, offering that so-and-so was "so difficult to work with that we got very little of value" or that an AMG editor felt they'd really "scraped the bottom of the barrel" on this guy—it's curious to imagine he'd need to code anything.

He even noted their deaths—homicide, suicide, or Vietnam—when such a thing happened, and detailed numerous models' thievery and vandalism of the AMG property alongside a photo of the butt-naked delinquents. The July, 1964 issue has a whole list of excommunicated boys and a litany of their sins. The January, 1970 issue includes a full-frontal of Paul Ferguson—one of murdered silent film star Ramon Novarro's assailants—and by the time we get to the 1980s there seems to be a killer model in every issue.

A helpful clue sheet to the hieroglyphics was eventually made available to regular subscribers for the cost of a self-addressed and stamped envelope in mid-1965, but Mizer warned that the key was far from complete and suggested you combine it "with your knowledge of astrology, European traffic signs," and your own intuition to decipher the meanings.

Though several of the symbols have been revealed over the years, the complete key remains to this day the most sought after piece of AMG memorabilia. Mizer continued offering it as late as the mid-1970s, noting that the FBI was trying to use it to crack what they believed to be a male prostitution ring in which a model's sexual orientation, availability, and perhaps even criminal aptitude were being secretively conveyed to potential customers through the magazine.

The October, 1964 issue was sort of a Hollywood edition, with appearances by a host of would-be actors, including a couple who were: Gary Conway and Glenn Corbett. A studio publicity still of Ty Hardin made the back cover of June, 1965.

By 1965, AMG had so many 8mm films available that they were offering one a week for the next ten years! They were filming at least one posing loop on every boy who wandered into the place. Wrestling boys became an AMG movie staple and the single activity most associated with the studio outside of showering. Posing strapped wrestlers. Jockstrapped wrestlers. And eventually nude wrestlers. It didn't matter. What was most important for the audience was to see two or more well-built guys mix it up. Mizer's trademark couldn't have been a more appropriate one, even if he did personally find it a bore. Interested from the very start in the exhibition of the young male form in all its physical glory, he invoked an Olympian sport and dared to eroticize precisely what the Greeks openly celebrated—ancient Greek wrestlers did so in the nude—and intuitively flirted with a sexual tension between men joked about even today, and probably the major reason true wrestling has no life of its own beyond the Olympic circle.

Besides, what boy—straight or queer—hasn't felt the twinge of sexual excitement when forced to wrestle his classmates in junior high or high school? It's a rite of manly passage as potentially awkward and humiliating as having to wear a jock for the first time in front of a locker room full of boys. In the wrestling match, you're called upon to reach for and grab your same-sex peer in places you'd be punched silly for

doing so in any other public setting. Your opponent's crotch and those hairy underarms are unavoidable axes when you're looking for a place to gain leverage. AMG brought all of these unspoken tensions to life for gay men who couldn't share those feelings with anybody else. Sexual nostalgia, you might say.

Physique Pictorial (*PP*), in its prime (roughly 1951-1970), was a directory of guys who made no pretenses about an identified sexuality. They were neither gay nor straight, both gay and straight; they were simply guys who were willing to get paid to take their clothes off and have a picture snapped. In fact, the likelihood that most were undoubtedly heterosexual made the magazine even sexier for many gay readers because it mirrored their own closeted sexual fantasies about the boy next door or a fellow teammate and added that dimension of capturing them in forbidden, albeit sometimes oblivious, sexual display.

The secret to the success of Bob Mizer's AMG stills and studio-made films is that he tapped into the homoeroticism of growing up male—gay or straight—not just the skin, muscle, and bones of it. For the delighted subscriber, AMG might as well have been MGM. Every time he got an issue of *Physique Pictorial* or one of those 8mm mini-movies, he could see favorite stars (and rising stars, too) who were the equivalents of Sal Mineo, John Saxon, Troy Donahue, Ricky Nelson, and Fabian, stripped and giving him an eyeful. Where Hollywood only teased, AMG delivered.

And though pubic hair started making a much more definitive and less shadowy appearance in *PP*'s pages in mid-1966, it was in Vol. 16, #3, the September, 1967 issue, that *PP* favorite Brian Idol was listed as "An AMG natural model," which meant, it turns out, that AMG had frontal nudes of Mr. Idol available.

Another "natural" model in the 9/67 issue was a young man of Italian and Norwegian descent by the name of **Joe Dallesandro** (1948-   ), whose session of 86 photos was taken when he was on the lam in California in 1965. Joe and a fellow teenaged buddy were trying to make a go of it as runaways from NYC and had made their way to LA after spending a couple agonizingly long weeks living inside a cave just outside of Juarez, Mexico.

The invitation to pose came while he was hanging out at an LA bus station. Of the 73 photos I've seen from the session, all of them are nudes, though there is now some debate as to whether all of these were in fact taken by Mizer. (Mizer regularly featured the work of a great many other physique photographers in his publication.)

In 1967, Directory Services Incorporated (DSI), a major distributor of male nude physique magazines and assorted homoerotica, was facing 29 obscenity counts in a Minneapolis courtroom and its owners were subjected to a parade of anti-homosexual propaganda squeezed out of "gay" witnesses. The case was tossed out on its bare ass by the judge, who found the gay-baiting irrelevant.

Though it wasn't a federal case, the DSI decision seemed to finally convince Bob Mizer it was safe to take *Physique Pictorial* into full-frontal territory. Even then it took him two years, though he began selling frontals by mail-order to customers stating they were 21 or over beginning in 1968.

Vol. 17, combined Issues #2-4, of January, 1969 had a full color cover of sweltering blond Al Wyant in full-frontal glory. In a 1969 update to his editorial on "The Big Basket Fraud," in which he had accused competitors of stuffing models' pouches and photographically enlarging their genitalia, Mizer now said that the all-nude norm in the physique mag industry had caused some boys great anxiety about being "ungifted." Nudes were okay, but tumescence was not. Once again, Mizer held off taking the next step until long after his competitors went stiff. (The first stand-up hard-on appeared in the December, 1979 issue of *PP*, during a time when the magazine was focusing almost exclusively on wrestling and guys in chains and the quality of models had plummeted. Long averse to porn, Mizer eventually specialized in "anal-erotic" photos—ugly buttholes on ugly models—to keep selling his wares in a market now dominated by gay hardcore magazines.)

Joe Dallesandro is also featured in the first full-frontal issue of *PP*. He would represent a month in their 1969 AMG pocket-size calendar and show up as the Jack of Diamonds in the AMG playing cards deck offered in December, 1971. Imagine that, to be one of 52 in 100,000.

Joseph Angelo D'Alessandro III came from a broken home. He and his younger brother Bob saw their "Wonder Bread years" in New York City foster homes. A bit on the short side, Joe eventually became good at making sure the other kids knew he was capable of walloping asses twice his size. He was also a chronic runaway with a nose for trouble.

He was permanently expelled from school for socking the principal in the nose for making a disparaging remark about his father and started stealing cars for kicks and whatever money he could get for parts. While driving a stolen vehicle across state lines because the buddy who nabbed it was too drunk to drive it, he blew off a toll stop and drew a squadron of police who also drew their guns and opened fire. Joe was hit once in the leg, just above the right kneecap, managed to escape, but then got nailed when his dad took him to the hospital for the wound.

The teenage delinquent was sent to a boys rehabilitation camp for three months where he earned fifty cents a day cutting down trees and had a friend help him draw a tattoo on his upper right arm that would become part of his legend: "Little Joe" was emblazoned in India ink with a needle and thread, both a nickname and a moniker to be immortalized years later by Lou Reed in "Walk on the Wild Side."

After his dalliance with physique photographers on both coasts, D'Alessandro settled into an unsettled married life back in New York while still a teenager. One fateful day in 1967, while visiting some friends in Greenwich Village, he literally walked into a future he could never have imagined for himself.

Andy Warhol and Paul Morrissey were shooting footage for an 8-hour long film in the apartment complex where Joe was visiting and they had left the door open, allowing Joe and his buddies to walk in (while the camera was running and facing the door) to see what they were doing. Not much of anything, it seemed, to director Paul Morrissey, who suggested to Warhol that they have the handsome kid who stopped by come into the scene. Everything was improvised anyway, so it didn't matter.

Joe agreed to do it, certain that motion picture history was not being made. It looked like home movies. So, with only the set-up that he was a college wrestler who should show the other actor some moves, the gorgeous young man did in fact enter motion picture history, stripping down to his underwear to wrestle the incomparable speed-queen Ondine.

"Next to your chest, your tattoo is dreary," flirts Ondine, clearly interested in this soft-spoken young man with the gorgeous body who's willing to play along. Joe is disarmingly sweet and honest, worried that because he doesn't know what to say he'll make the film boring. He's completely oblivious to the volumes his near-naked body is speaking to us. He's the sex symbol, the film's ingenue.

He scoffed when asked to sign a release for his 23 minutes of screen time. Who the hell will ever see this? When the ads went into the *Village Voice* in August of 1968 for the 86-minute feature-length excerpt now called *The Loves of Ondine* (1967), Joe Dallesandro (as he was now Americanized) was at the epicenter, sitting on a stool wearing his jockey shorts.

Not only was Joe's sex appeal being used to lure in art house audiences in New York, it was his male sex appeal and homoerotic sex appeal that was being openly marketed for consumption. Said *Variety* of the kid who couldn't imagine this thing playing in any real theatre where people would plunk down money: "This boy, Joe Dallesandro, is good-looking and natural-acting enough to have a showbiz career beyond Warhol."

He was working at a bookbinding factory when Warhol and company recruited him to play their Little Joe in *Lonesome Cowboys* (1968), which they were shooting in an old movie ghost town in Arizona. Still shy around talkers, he looks ill at ease during the scene in which fellow cowpoke Eric Emerson teaches him to do pliés next to the hitching post because they'll put meat on his buns and help hold up his holster when he gets a gun.

He's not the film's sex star, perhaps because Andy Warhol was still behind the camera and didn't realize that potential in him yet. Instead, a gorgeous surfer boy named **Tom Hompertz**, who's even more ill at ease than Joe, is the object of everyone's affection in this virtually all-male, improvised send-up of westerns that started out as a variation on *Romeo and Juliet*. Hompertz can barely bring himself to say a word, let alone a sentence, but his beauty does all the talking necessary and his best scene is an extended solo in which the camera watches him wash up. There's an intent to this prolonged bit of business that radicalizes the kind of physical subjectivity reserved primarily for women in the movies. Straight audiences tolerate undramatic and unnecessary fillers in which beautiful women carry out everyday activities—especially preparations for bathing or bed—because it's understood that men enjoy looking at beautiful women and they're being encouraged to fantasize.

Tom Hompertz is fulfilling that very same purpose as he stands at that washtub and washes. As with the best of Warhol and Morrissey, the simplicity of the image reveals its complexities. Handsome boy washes himself for several minutes communicates not only an awareness and an appreciation of the young man's beauty, but an awareness and an appreciation of the male as a transmitter of desire and fantasy in a context that had been culturally defined as feminine.

Lonesome Cowboys, which wouldn't be released until 1969 and even then caused homosexual panic in civic and law enforcement that resulted in banning, an FBI probe, and the arrest of an entire audience in Atlanta, was heralded as "the story of men among men and the woman who tried to interfere." It's a gay western about a band of brothers who seem also to be lovers and the discontent visited upon their macho, self-loving way of life when they encounter a woman and her flaming queen of a nurse in a desolate town.

It is also something of a watershed for a generation of gay men coming out and coming to terms with society during the country's sexual revolution. Gay porn was still a few years off in terms of its accessibility and certainly in terms of its being produced feature length and shown in adult cinemas. For many gay men eager to find homoerotic imagery at the movies, *Lonesome Cowboys*, at least in the big cities where it played, acknowledged their desires and provided fuel for their fantasies: boys fighting over sleeping with other boys, a morning pee, a young man persuaded to take off his pants, and Little Joe in tight white trousers energetically bucking away to "Magical Mystery Tour" on the soundtrack. It is fondly remembered as one of a generation's firsts.

Tom Hompertz and Joe Dallesandro were also in *San Diego Surf* (1968), the only Warhol feature never to get a theatrical release. A hodgepodge of improvised scenes in and around Cliff Robertson's rented beach house in La Jolla, California, it was deemed a throwback to the more "primitive" experiments of Warhol and Morrissey's considering that it wasn't even edited until after the release of the film that made Joe Dallesandro a Warhol Superstar: Paul Morrissey's *Flesh* (1968).

Shot on 16mm for as little as $1,500 over a few weekends in late summer of 1968, *Flesh* was in a New York theatre by the first of October and played for seven straight months. The idea germinated while Morrissey, Joe, and other Warhol players stood around bored to tears between set-ups for the "underground film party" sequence of *Midnight Cowboy* (1969). Warhol was intrigued to learn from Morrissey that the Jon Voight film's subject matter was male prostitution, something the two had fiddled with three years back in *My Hustler* (1965), with Paul America. Gee, thought Andy, why couldn't we do a movie like that again using our kids and get it out before theirs?

Warhol was still recovering from the near-death and life-altering experience of having been gunned down by Valerie Solanas, so Morrissey was at last given full reign and knew he wanted Joe Dallesandro as his star.

159

Flesh is quite simply a day in the life of a hustler, bookended by lengthy static close-ups of Joe's face as he sleeps. Roused from bed by his shrill wife (Geraldine Smith), he's being asked to head out onto the streets and make $200 to finance her girlfriend's abortion. Joe doesn't want to go. He's sleepy, a bit irritable, and not very motivated. Oh, and he's also completely nude.

Flesh delivers what it promises. The flesh of the title is Joe's flesh and we will see plenty of it before this day is out. An elderly gentleman will pay to sketch it while pontificating on the politics of "body worship" and lending a helpful hand to pose him like classical statuary. A gym buddy will try to seduce Joe right out of his underpants after popping a zit on the young man's face and reading excerpts from a dirty book to him. A dancer will give him a blowjob while two transvestites read movie magazines and then discuss the pros and cons of breast implants.

It's somehow appropriate that the first extensive full-frontal nudity by a man in the movies should come from a man whose beauty is objectified and desired by all who see it. It's also instructive that it can be yours for a price.

Joe Dallesandro was not only the first actor (to become even somewhat famous) who unashamedly walked about naked on film, but he also seemed completely unselfconscious in doing so. He seems, if you will, like a regular Joe...albeit a beautiful one. For gay audiences, the first gorgeous naked man they could lay eyes on at the cinema was also a liberating icon. With Joe there was a slight androgyny, but a distinct ambiguity about sexuality.

In one scene, he meets two young men on the street who are new to the trade and ask him for advice. (The quiet one with his back to the camera is Joe's brother Bob.) In response to a question about sexuality, he tells them: "Hey, nobody's straight. What's straight? It's not a thing of being straight or being not straight. It's just...you just do whatever you have to do." After all, when it comes to the johns, "he's only gonna suck ya peetah," and then you're out of there.

Joe's famous peetah is so important to the movies that in the very first scene in which it appears, it not only gets semi-erect, but the wife insists on tying it up with a ribbon. Today, there may not be a glut of movie penises, but the movies have had their share if you've been paying any attention for the past three decades. Imagine then a time when there were only glimpses of male backsides at the cinema and you'll have an inkling of how profound an impact Joe's dick had on a generation of both gay and straight audiences. Add further into the equation the fact that the young man attached to that dick was just the kind of beauty that—if you saw his face on the poster—you'd pray to see the rest of him, and you'll begin to understand why he became a gay icon.

Another reason Joe resonated so deeply with audiences was because of the assumption that he was playing himself. This was no actor pulling a stunt by dropping his britches and pretending to be a hustler, this was a non-actor, a kid right off the streets who was making up his lines as he went along. He's as real as the day is long. His name is Joe. He's got Joe tattooed on his arm. And there's a remarkable sweetness to him, especially during a silent segment early on in the film when he's naked and feeds a cupcake to his baby daughter before heading out onto the streets.

For all its remarkable achievements, and there are many, it must be remembered that *Flesh* was not likely to be playing at a theatre near you if you didn't live in a big city. We've largely lost our sense of limited access in this age of multi-multiplexes and widespread video/DVD availability. It played at art houses and on some college campuses, but its most significant critical and box-office success came from bookings in Germany. *Flesh* was unknown to American mainstream audiences. At most, it was one of those dirty, X-rated underground movies made by the guy who painted Campbell's Soup Cans. (Andy Warhol presents...*Flesh*, but it's Paul Morrissey's film, let's remember.) It did, in fact, beat *Midnight Cowboy* (1969) to the screen, though the famed Jon Voight/Dustin Hoffman picture is often credited as being the first to tackle the subject of male prostitution and it remains the only X-rated film to win the Oscar for Best Picture.

For Dallesandro, who was now employed at the Factory as bouncer, occasional elevator operator, and assorted all-tradesman, the success of *Flesh* wouldn't sink in until he was treated like royalty on the German tour two years after the film's American debut.

By then, his hair had grown long and he had already shot his second starring feature: Paul Morrissey's *Trash* (1970). It began as a project called *Drug Trash* and chronicles the tragicomic story of a couple living in squalor on the Lower East Side: he's an impotent junkie named Joe, forever fixated on getting his next fix, and she's a sex-starved collector of trash whose goal in life is to be perpetually supported by Welfare.

As the girlfriend, Holly Woodlawn nearly steals the film—once again shot without a script, only brief instructions from Morrissey. Joe, whose bare ass is the first image we see in the film, is chronically lethargic and mortally limp. The same dancer who gave him a blowjob in *Flesh* can't resurrect the dead. His flaccid penis looms in the foreground like another character in the scene and gives a damned good performance. So does its owner.

The comic irony of Joe's role in *Trash* is that he's the young man whom everyone wants to fuck, but can't. The dancer says she'll give him some money if he can fuck her. He tries, but fails. She tells him that sex gets her high and he seems momentarily interested. How, he wonders.

"When you came, wasn't it so beautiful that you just..."

"No," he interrupts. "It was over."

An LSD-freak, played by the incomparable and tragic Andrea Feldman, watches him shoot up in excruciating detail (thanks to Morrissey's close-ups), then berates him into attempting rape, which he also fails to accomplish.

Sheepishly, Joe buckles up and tells her: "If you took dope, you couldn't get a hard-on either."

"Sure I could," she says.

While attempting to rob a house, he's caught by a snooty young newlywed played by the equally incomparable Jane Forth. She decides to have him stick around and act out a rape fantasy. Clearly not up to it, and then interrupted by the arrival of her husband, Joe does manage a shower and shave, but with nosy Jane right there the whole time. She sits on the closed toilet next to the completely naked Joe ("Oh my, you're rather large"), telling him bizarre stories about the first time she ever saw a penis, asking him if he likes to give rim jobs, and inviting him to join in a *ménage à trois* with her hubby.

Everybody wants a piece of poor Joe, even his girlfriend's very pregnant sister, who insists it won't hurt the baby. Holly catches them in the attempted act and goes berserk. In priceless response, Joe says he was "just practicin'." Earlier, at Joe's suggestion, Holly had to make do with a beer bottle.

Trash was an even bigger hit than *Flesh*. At last, American critics were starting to take note, and Germany heralded it a masterpiece, dubbing Joe the "Valentino of the Underground." *Trash* helped bring the underground overground, if you will. In the broil of the sexual revolution, rampant drug experimentation, political and civic unrest, and a renewed interest in cinema on college campuses, *Trash* had a little something for everyone. What most people didn't know was that director Paul Morrissey was a staunch conservative politically and his so-called underground films were meant as social comedies condemning the youth culture's free love and free drugs mentality.

Audiences may or may not have understood what the films were saying, but they knew what they meant to them. Letters came into the Factory imploring Joe to get off the drugs and clean himself up. They truly cared for this kid. They wanted to lend a hand, invite him into their lives. They had no idea that he was married, had children, and a full time job at the Factory. One magazine interviewed him and called him a "closet bourgeois."

In *Heat* (1972), the last of Morrissey's Joe trilogy, he is a former child actor trying to get his career going again by schmoozing with a has-been actress (Sylvia Miles) in seedy Los Angeles. He's probably in the prime of his physical beauty, with a long ponytail, busy hustling anyone—man, woman, or otherwise—who he thinks can help him out. There's less nudity this time, but he has at last become the callous hustler and it's his least empathetic role. He allows himself to be pawed by the motel landlady while he's wearing just a jockstrap so he can get a break on the rent and he lounges in the sun unconvincingly protesting as his lover's whacked-out daughter (Andrea Feldman in her final performance) suckles on one of his nipples. "I can do anything my mother does."

Joe followed Paul Morrissey to Italy in early 1973 to star in a pair of films to be shot back-to-back. *Flesh for Frankenstein* (1974), which became known as *Andy Warhol's Frankenstein*, has Joe as a horny shepherd with an anomalous (and therefore quite funny) New Yawk accent whose best friend gets his head lopped off by the necrophiliac Baron (Udo Kier) who's building a male zombie to mate with his female. X-rated at the time of its initial release, the film boasts insane performances by Kier and his sidekick (Arno Juerging), outrageous utilization of gore, and the opportunity to see Joe's bare butt in 3-D! The scene in which Monique Van Vooren sucks on Joe's armpit is one of the funniest sex scenes ever filmed.

Blood for Dracula (1974), which became *Andy Warhol's Dracula*, casts Joe as an entirely incongruous Marxist handyman, a crude, sexist, and mean-spirited hunk who deflowers the DiFiori daughters before they can be sucked on by the sickly Count (Udo Kier again). The vampire must have virgin blood or he

161

goes into crimson vomiting spasms. Both of Morrissey's Italian monster comedies are funny and Joe contributes by sticking out like a sore thumb and delivering his lines flatter than pancakes.

Tired of the Warhol scene, and frustrated by the perception of their ownership of him, Joe stayed on in Europe where he had offers to make movies and somehow hoped that those productions would do for him what European films had done for the careers of Eastwood and Bronson.

There are those who will argue that after he left Morrissey and began to make movies for other directors, requiring a non-actor to learn lines and repeat them instead of speak only when he had something to say, he lost his spontaneity and charm. He would make 18 highly variable films while in Europe throughout the rest of the 1970s. His baptism into a movie world without Warhol was having a woman squat and pee on his face in the sex-farce *Donna e bello* (1974). He played a sexy young man on his way up the crime ladder in *L'Ambizioso* (*The Climber*; 1975), a mute who has fathered a gaggle of children with his sister (Alexandra Stewart) in Louis Malle's bizarre dreamscape *Black Moon* (1975), a family man from the country who's corrupted by Parisian prostitute Sylvia Kristel in *La Marge* (*The Streetwalker*; 1976), a New Yorker looking for his kidnapped girlfriend and running from knights on horseback in Jacques Rivette's *Merry-Go-Round* (1978/1983), a dead bisexual husband whose wife drinks a vial of his sperm and has a baby boy by him in *Queen Lear* (1978), and a selfish American actor in Catherine Breillat's *Tapage Nocturne* (1979).

The best of his European films, and his personal favorite of all his work, is *Je T'Aime Moi Non Plus* (1975), writer/director/composer/cult figure Serge Gainsbourg's sexually provocative riff on his famed international hit song. Joe plays a gay garbage truck driver who falls in lust with a flat-chested café waitress, played by the beautiful Jane Birkin (Gainsbourg's wife), because she looks like a boy from behind. The only way he can consummate their relationship is by entering the backdoor, but every time he attempts to do so her screams of pain bring unwelcome intervention.

Sexy, strange, symbolic, beautifully scored, and well-acted, *Je T'Aime* is a cult classic waiting to be discovered.

Joe Dallesandro is a cult classic waiting to be re-discovered. He has worked only sporadically in films since his return to the states in 1980, most notably as Lucky Luciano in Coppola's *The Cotton Club* (1984). Ambivalent about his fame as a Warhol Superstar, he cannot escape the power of his allure in those films. As the first overtly-eroticized male sex symbol of the movies to walk naked across the screen, he not only transcended the convention of being an actor, but he spoke to our fantasies and liberated the male nude as an object of beauty in the cinema. He likes to tell interviewers that all he ever had to do in a Warhol/Morrissey film was show up. He's right. He's a natural.

Joe Dallesandro was born out of the so-called underground film movement, an imprecise and somehow all-encompassing term used to designate films that were not made for commercial exhibition, but personal exploration and experimentation. It was film as a fluid art form.

Homoerotic imagery and themes were endemic to the underground film long before the "underground" had been tagged as such in New York, Paris, and Los Angeles, where venues for exhibition blossomed in the '50s and particularly the '60s. Two film study classics are Kenneth Anger's *Fireworks* (1947), a homoerotic incantation made when the filmmaker was all of twenty, and Jean Genet's *Un Chant d'Amour* (1950), a quilt of evocative homo imagery set in and around a prison.

Film was yet another medium for the homosexual artist to express his fantasies, desires, self-hate, or emancipation. Jack Smith, Gregory Markopoulos, and Andy Warhol, among others, made films in which a queer subjectivity found a highly varied, but provocative voice.

Warhol's male beauties included Gerard Malanga, Tom Baker, Joe Spencer, Tom Hompertz, and Joe Dallesandro, all of whom to one degree or another were successfully objectified by their proximity to heterosexuality. Their ambivalent identification as "straight or not straight" broadened their sexual appeal in ways that flaming queens would have limited. They reached a wider spectrum of gay desire as trade.

The beauty of the male body and face in the mainstream cinema was largely appreciated by fantasy and projection. As an audience member, you took whatever you could get and played out the rest in the privacy of your head. The underground film allowed the beauty of the male body and face to be appreciated as interactive voyeurism. As an audience member, you were given the raw material and the only issue of privacy is what you did with it. You didn't have to imagine homoerotic content, it came right at you, and everybody else in the audience was subjected to the same: we were being asked to respond to the male body as an unambiguous purveyor of sexual desire. Underground films encouraged neurotransmission on a direct route from brain to crotch.

In Jim Bidgood's underground 8mm classic *Pink Narcissus* (1965-71), the pants on comely teenager **Bobby Kendall** are so tight that they go up the crack of his ass, making his pockets look as if they're stitched right on his buttcheeks.

A 65-minute wet dream, the film has our young god posing before mirrors that become urinals in a men's room where he plays matador to a leather-clad biker. His fat cock and balls are well-defined in the excruciating tightness of his pants, then get a little breathing room when he peels them off at the 16-minute mark.

He's shown bare-bottom nude, humping the wet grass, before the first of his formal mirror fantasies begins. As a Roman slave-boy, he's felt up by "himself" as the emperor. The undies come off at 21 minutes, but the exquisite tease continues when he dons a mid-length robe and the sash covers his genitalia. An extreme close-up of his nipple as a blade of grass is played over it and then on down to his belly button furthers the eroticism by nearly abstracting it.

During an erotic daydream, he mythically holds a twittering butterfly over his crotch as he lies in a field, followed by the suggestion that he has urinated over his hands and is now sucking on his fingers. An Arabian fantasy has him appearing as an exotic dancer wildly bucking his veil-covered erection in slow-motion. An extreme close-up of a penis ejaculating into the camera lens (our faces) ends the segment.

Naked, but still wearing white booties, he next imagines himself in a bizarre city street sequence, very Fellini-esque, with all the men in their work uniforms but naked below the waist. We even see a sailor or two beating off in the background as ugly characters mill outside a bar called Cissy's. By now we've seen plenty of penises in the film, but still can't wait to see Kendall's. We get a glimpse of it as he luxuriates naked in a thunderstorm, confirming by comparison the semi-tumescence of its earlier appearances through fabric. An extreme low angle shot of him walking toward mythological immortality reveals his shapely ass and the dangling of his once-again impressive genitalia.

You can see the not quite as impressive outline of Jim Morrison's dangler through the tight leather pants that became as much a part of his iconography as his music. The chronically unhappy pudge who wrote poetry in high school and didn't get along with his parents did manage to convince them to let him leave college in Florida and enroll at UCLA in 1964 to study film.

Jim Morrison (1943-1971) was interested in making his own "underground" films, but he got a D on his first-year film project and promptly dropped out. He immersed himself in the drug culture, washed it all down with alcohol, and during the summer of 1965 lost 25 pounds. LSD turned Jim Morrison into one of the most beautiful men on the planet.

Morrison's terrific flash in the pan was immortalized by Joel Brodsky's photo session, which captured the rock god in Christ-like poses, arms spread, shirtless, pouting, with a mane of unkempt hair framing his beauteous countenance and high cheekbones. Selling his newfound beauty and cultivating his Dionysian image, even to teenagers (thanks to an affair with *16 Magazine's* editor Gloria Stavers), Morrison quickly grew to hate his creation.

A self-abusive martyr, he was also depressed, violent, usually drunk or stoned (notice how huge his pupils are in most photos), and enjoyed nothing more than berating, insulting, and inciting his audiences. He laced his songs with obscenities, couldn't dance, sometimes could barely stand, and saw his beauty bloat and disappear within two years.

By the time he got busted at a 1969 Miami concert for indecent exposure (though it's debated to this day among attendees whether he did or didn't whip it out), he was out of shape and the poster boy for wanton self-destruction. His personal legend—outside of the music of The Doors—wouldn't likely amount to half so much after his intangible death on July 3, 1971 if it weren't for the power of his beauty and the manner in which it was cultivated in antithetical melancholy. Jim Morrison was less a pretty rock god than he was a dark angel. His saturnine poetry set to haunting reverberations came packaged in irresistibly carnal wrapping.

Morrison considered himself an "erotic politician," and I mention him here not just because he was beautiful, but because he's a talisman for the 1960s youth movement, a symbol of the shaking up of sexual mores and the indulgence in sexual experimentation. Whether he exposed himself or not isn't the point as much as that he made headlines for doing or not doing it. Though not homosexual, he was one of the first

Christopher Jones, a star in ascent circa 1968. He made six films and then all but vanished. PHOTOFEST

to simulate fellatio on another band member during a gig and was said to have rubbed himself into perceptible erection inside his leather pants while performing.

Perhaps it should come as no surprise that the first male nude in a major motion picture was the first male nude in creationism. John Huston's *The Bible* (1966) doesn't get beyond the first 22 chapters of Genesis, but those who came to see it were only interested in the first five...the ones with the naked people in them. All the ads, trailers, posters, and billboards for this astounding bore had one thing in common: an image of 27-year old Michael Parks, as Adam, rising from out of the dust. His genitalia are kept discreetly and frustratingly obscured from view, but we do get to see his bare ass in the film. And his belly button, which is an odd thing if you think about it.

That belly button had a trail of hair running down into his pants the year before when Parks played the title role in *Bus Riley's Back in Town* (1965). His kid sister and her girlfriend swoon over him, agreeing that he's more gorgeous than Rock, Cary, or George Maharis. He isn't, but there's a nice shot as the camera pans across the room and we see his clothes strewn all over, and then his bare feet come into view as we find him sleeping. The camera continues on its trek and encounters his legs spread, with only a blanket to cover his loins. Unfortunately, after he's roused from his slumber, we find out that he's still wearing his boxers.

Never heard of Michael Parks? That's okay. The point is that as the movies began to dare to bare, they needed a whole new crop of actors willing to go the distance. Throughout the early to mid-1960s, the biggest male stars at the box-office were Rock Hudson, Cary Grant, Tony Curtis, John Wayne, Elvis Presley, Jerry Lewis, Frank Sinatra, Jack Lemmon, Paul Newman, Richard Burton, and Lee Marvin. Sean Connery rounds off the list at an even dozen thanks to Bond, who almost gets his wee-wee lasered off by *Goldfinger* (1964) and whose bare buns and erect gun (in an illustrated graphic) made for an enticingly neo-sexist ad for *Thunderball* (1965) in an otherwise retrogressively sexist series.

Masculinity through much of the 1960s was eroticized in terms of bulk. Kirk Douglas, Burt Lancaster, Anthony Quinn, and Charlton Heston were the fetishistic models in epic tales of bare-chested adventure, but where were the equivalents of Jim Morrison in the movies? Where were the beauties of long-haired youth who were prepared to greet the Woodstock generation after the summer of love?

One was driving across country in a stolen car. William Frank Jones was born in Jackson, Tennessee, and lost his mother when he was only four when she was committed to a state mental hospital for the rest of her life. William and his older brother were eventually raised at Boys Town in Memphis.

The executive director of the facility handed the boy a copy of *Life* magazine one day during his early teenage years, telling him that he looked like the subject on its cover: James Dean. Almost 16, the boy left Boys Town to live with his father, who had re-married. Shortly thereafter, he joined the Army, but the regimentation proved too much for him and he went AWOL after two days.

While on his cross-country trek in a stolen car, he visited Fairmount, Indiana, the hometown of James Dean, where Jimmy's aunt and uncle warmly received him. New York City was his ultimate goal. Once there, he turned himself in to the military and spent six months imprisoned on Governors Island.

Back on the outside, he met Frank Corsaro, a one-time mentor to Dean, and an acting coach at the Actor's Studio. Jones gained admittance as an observer, even performed a scene for Lee Strasberg, who found him personally intriguing as an actor, shapeless enough to warrant curiosity about who he was. He got a role as a Mexican beach boy in Corsaro's 1961 Broadway production of *Night of the Iguana*, starring Bette Davis. There was already a William Jones registered in the actor's union, so he was billed thereafter as **Christopher Jones** (1941-   ).

He befriended co-star Shelley Winters, who in turn introduced him to Susan Strasberg, the beautiful daughter of the aforementioned Actor's Studio guru. Christopher and Susan began a relationship that did not win favor with her father, and in 1963 the young lovers went to Los Angeles. They later married and Strasberg chronicled the abusive relationship in her 1980 autobiography *Bitter Sweet*.

Christopher Jones won the title role in ABC TV's *The Legend of Jesse James* (1965-66), in which he proved both instantly popular with writers of fan letters and instantly temperamental with the demands of television production. He absolutely refused to have his hair cut for the role and found it difficult to play the fame game. The series lasted a single season.

He got to play the title lead in his first movie, too. *Chubasco* (1968), which means "hurricane," opens with Jones getting busted during a fight with motorbike punks under the pier at a teen pot party. In the midst of a make-out session with his girlfriend Bunny (Strasberg, who was now his wife), he makes a run for it after tussling with the cops and they shoot at him. Bunny calls out to him in the darkness and he staggeringly returns, wet and looking a lot like James Dean. Is this his *Rebel Without A Cause*?

Not quite. His real name is Anton Rosie, he's got a record, and he's about to get flushed by the system. His only chance is to sign on for a job at a tuna cannery catching fish on a clipper, where he's tormented by the other guys on the boat who want to give him a haircut. He lands a job on another vessel and elopes with Strasberg, whose mean old dad (Richard Egan) is also a fisherman. By fateful circumstance, Jones and dad get booked on the same boat and don't know it until they're well out to sea.

Chubasco isn't much of a movie, but Jones looks pretty hot in a vest and there are some nice Panavision close-ups of his bare chest as he's caught like a fish from shark-infested waters and they use a respirator to revive him.

He signed a three-picture deal with American International Pictures, the exploitation factory, and starred in the film that would assure him a place in cult movie history. *Wild in the Streets* (1968) is the story of Max Jacob Flatow, Jr. (Jones), who makes LSD in his basement and plans to blow up his dad's treasured car with dynamite. The much-abused son of a tyrannical mother (Shelley Winters), he destroys his parents' bourgeois Middle American home (complete with plastic covers on the furniture) and writes "screw you" on the mirror for good measure.

End of Max Flatow. Beginning of Max Frost, the handsome young rock star he's transformed himself into now that he's free of the constrictions of suburbia. He's a multi-millionaire at 22, "a leader of men and little girls." His band includes a trumpeter/guitarist with a hook, and a drummer played by Richard Pryor— author of the *Aborigine Cookbook*. There's also a completely accepted 15-year old gay boy genius who plays the guitar and does Max's taxes.

With 52% of America under the age of 25, congressman Hal Holbrook has decided to lobby the youth vote for his bid to be senator. He asks Max to play at his televised rally. Frost will only do it if the congressman in turn announces a promise to lower the voting age to 14. The hedonistic lifestyle of Max Frost (who wears a very strange ponytail) is eventually institutionalized and before long the fogies in Congress and over-35s throughout the land will be doped up thanks to an LSD-tainted water supply and kept in retirement camps where they will continue to be drugged. The dark satire of the film ultimately reveals its anti-youth stance by making the movement fascist-totalitarian. With everything backfiring, Holbrook is seen tearing down his own teenagers' pop posters, including James Dean, and screaming, "From now on you read *Winnie the Pooh* or you don't read anything!"

More than a run-of-the-mill juvenile delinquent movie, *Wild in the Streets* could have been a call to arms. Even with the rousing "14 or Fight" song, and enough "groovy," "chicks," "the fuzz," "cats," "hippies," and "heads" references to make it very much of its time, the film is pretty sedentary for a youth flick. It's a great, fun idea, and it touches on a lot of important social politics (Vietnam, sex, drugs, celebrity-worship, ageism, even the shooting of 12 teenaged troop members by police during a demonstration), but the direction is uninspired and even the Oscar-nominated editing job doesn't save it from being square when it needs to be funky, wild, sexy, psychedelic...trippy.

"I don't want to live to be 30," says Max. "30's death." At times, Christopher Jones in his signature role sounds like Jim Morrison. Jones is very good in the film, but isn't given the full opportunity to exploit his charisma. He deserves a better movie. *Wild in the Streets* doesn't live up to its legend (primarily built over the years on its scarcity), but in its time it did very well at the box-office, helped assure Jones a loyal following to this day, and reportedly had Chicago Mayor Richard Daley nervous enough to secure the water supply during the tumultuous 1968 Democratic convention.

Three in the Attic (1968), the second of his three-picture deal at AIP, has Christopher Jones playing Paxton Quigley, "one of the first casualties of the sexual revolution." With an all-male college and an all-female college set one mile from each other in Vermont, there's bound to be intermingling. Quigley is so irresistibly cute—he also has a thing for heinies—that he's busy diddling three ladies at the same time. The first is a blonde feminist whose ass he compares to a hovering hummingbird. "You have nice hair," he tells her at the local bar. "It fits the mood of your butt." I don't know what that means, but I like the look on Chris Jones' face when he says it.

The second is an African-American painter who has him pose butt-naked while she busies herself at the canvas. Once we've had a pleasant and awe-inspiring eyeful of Mr. Jones' beautiful rear-end, we discover it's not what she was painting. So why was he naked?

"I just wanted to take a little peek. Because fair is fair." And there you have the ostensible rationale for a decade to come of male nudity in the movies.

The third young lady is a Jewish psychedelic with magic brownies who paints marigolds on his back and tickles his armpit. He tells her he's as queer as a three dollar bill, something to do with his junior high school swimming coach. It's an effective ploy to getting her in the sack.

"Thank God for faggots," he tells us in voice-over. "I sometimes think that faggots make it with more chicks than guys do. Did you ever think of that?"

An hour into the film and the trio discover his cross-pollination and lock him in the sorority house attic. The plan, if you can believe it, is to use him as a love slave, each taking their turn to sap him of his precious bodily fluids. It makes no sense why he can't get out, but the concept is certainly interesting.

Off-screen, Jones was himself quite the ladies man. I find it refreshing when a gorgeous young movie star acknowledges his desirability and enjoys sharing the wealth. Pauline Kael, writing about *Three in the Attic* in *The New Yorker*, found him "the American as a young dog. In a sense, he's the American as enemy—the unredeemed, self-centered, carnal frat boy."

He was seeing Jim Morrison's girlfriend, Pamela Courson, when he went off to England to make *The Looking Glass War* (1970), based on John Le Carre's novel. He gets top billing over Ralph Richardson and Anthony Hopkins in his first prestige production and would never look back to making a third low-budget film per his agreement with AIP.

Christopher Jones never looked sexier on screen than he did in *The Looking Glass War*. When we first see him, he's shirtless, bouncing a ball off the wall of a holding room where a trio of British agents will interview him. His belt is unbuckled. His pants are undone at the top. He invokes James Dean when he leans over to get a light for his cigarette from Hopkins. Later, the beauty of his face and high cheekbones will be upstaged by documented proof of possession. Christopher Jones' eyebrows *are* James Dean's eyebrows.

Jones is playing a Pole who jumped ship and is being detained by the British because they want to use him for an operation in Germany in exchange for allowing him to stay in the country where a British girlfriend is about to have his baby.

Jones has perfected his body language, smoldering with on-screen charisma as he poses, and effectively making use of his accent for the role. After a prolonged knock-down scrap and scuffle with Hopkins during his tutelage, the young scamp plants a full-lipped smooch on one of his elder male trainers. It's an epiphanic moment for gay men circa 1970.

He remained in Europe and took up with *War* co-star Pia Degermark, with whom he made *Una Breve Stagione* (*Brief Season*; 1969) in Italy. What should have been his most fortuitous film opportunity came when David Lean saw dailies of *Looking Glass War* and decided to cast him as the wounded British soldier in his epic production of *Ryan's Daughter* (1970).

In the most gorgeously photographed, but horrific little town in coastal Ireland, Ryan's daughter (Sarah Miles) marries the much-elder Robert Mitchum, hoping that the "satisfaction of the flesh" will transform her into a different person. It doesn't.

One hour into the three hour and twenty-four minute marathon, a truck drives off and reveals a lone figure (Jones) standing like a wooden soldier on the horizon, appearing strange, epicene, and waxy. He also has a limp. A shell-shocked British soldier with an ugly scar that looks like a mascara run down the outside corner of his left eye, he's pale and zombie-like, suffering from battle flashbacks and spasms.

I'm not sure there's much of a role to play there, but Jones seems to be making no effort at all. He's barely audible the few times he speaks, feeding but not quite confirming a rumor that his voice had to be dubbed. If he's haunted, he's not haunting. He's vacant. He manages to make love to Miles in the forest (without the benefit of music) and brings her to her first orgasm. His scar also seems to disappear during their second go at it.

The production of *Ryan's Daughter* was a difficult and lengthy one. Jones didn't flourish during the interminable set-ups and multiple takes despite having new girlfriend Olivia Hussey occasionally by his side. At the time, director Lean found the young actor exceedingly difficult and not at all shy about saying "no" to a given direction.

"This clearly irritated David," said producer Anthony Havelock-Allan in an interview years later. "Someone who ostensibly was a professional actor, but when asked by a director to act, expressed himself as being absolutely incapable of doing so."

At one point during the shoot, a frustrated and free-wheeling Jones went on a joyride in his new 1969 365 GT Ferrari and crashed and rolled it after speeding by a nun. He also got the horrifying news that Sharon Tate, whom he had recently befriended in Italy, was among the victims of a mass murder back in Los Angeles on property belonging to his manager and at which he had once stayed.

The agony of Tate's murder and the grating and unfulfilling task of acting the part of an automaton in Lean's epic took their toll. Jones returned to Los Angeles, living in the guesthouse of the Benedict Canyon estate where the Manson murders took place. Within months, he left the guesthouse and his film career behind.

He went into an even deeper depression upon hearing of the death of soul mate Jim Morrison in 1971.

Martin Potter (left) and Hiram Keller (right) prowl the streets of Rome to find their mutual lover boy in *Fellini Satyricon* (1969). PHOTOFEST

After just six films, Christopher Jones walked away from the industry and entered the realm of Hollywood folklore as the mysterious star who vanished into a fog of whispered rumors. He was alleged to be everything from a street hustler to a crazy homeless person to a drug addict to an inmate at an asylum to dead as a doornail.

He was, in fact, alive and in Encino. There would be marriages, children, hard financial times, turbulent relationships, family scandals, and chronic health problems, including a debilitating and near-fatal bout of bleeding ulcers in the late 1990s, but he has survived. Quentin Tarantino offered him a thankless and ugly role in the Bruce Willis S&M sodomy torture sequence of *Pulp Fiction* (1994), which he wisely declined. He did, however, say yes to an old friend who was directing a film called *Mad Dog Time* (aka *Trigger Happy*; 1996), and thus 26 years after *Ryan's Daughter* he played a hired assassin who takes on Gregory Hines and then coolly faces Jeff Goldblum in a sit-down showdown. Two scenes. That's all.

There's an undeniably appealing side to the mysterious Legend of Christopher Jones, a beautiful young actor who seemed to say "fuck you" to the movies while on the precipice of his career. There's also something quite human about that decision. We tend to get caught up in the trajectory of movie stars' lives, second-guessing their every move as if the script was already written. None of us knows what Hollywood would or wouldn't have done with Chris Jones if he had stayed with it. He was courted for *Dillinger* and would have screen-tested for Michael Corleone, along with the rest of the industry's young leading men, but his managers may have set up an additional stumbling block by making his minimum asking price $500,000.

Part of Jones' legacy, believe it or not, and you'd believe it if you were growing up in the sixties, was that coy nude pose in *Three in the Attic* (1968). We weren't yet used to having our handsome leading man drop his drawers for our approval. And we liked it. A lot.

Franco Zeffirelli tastefully acknowledged a night of star-crossed love by having his Romeo, the beautiful 17-year old Leonard Whiting, wake up buns to the sun the morning after in *Romeo and Juliet* (1968). It's a bold and judicious move, as are the multi-colored codpieces sported by his cocky, bawdy, and easily roused male players.

With a cultural revolution that gave birth to flower children, hippies, and the body beautiful, the arts were ready to flash back. *Hair*, *Oh, Calcutta!*, *Dionysus in 69*, and other stage shows were luring patrons with onstage nudity the year of the Stonewall Riots and the death of Judy Garland.

The movies had adopted a ratings system that was supposed to guide parents concerned about content, but decades later still acts as a censor. *Women in Love* (1969), a British import based on D.H. Lawrence's story, got an "R" largely for a scene in which Alan Bates and Oliver Reed strip naked and wrestle each other in a dark sitting room. There is enough light to see their pee-pees, so it remains something of a landmark film in terms of commercial exhibition. (Remember, Joe Dallesandro was an art house phenomenon.)

Fellini Satyricon (1969), a free adaptation of the Petronius classic filled with ugly/beautiful imagery and something of an attack on the hedonistic youth culture of the late '60s, stars two unknown lads worth knowing: American brunette **Hiram Keller** (1944-1997), an Actor's Studio pupil from Georgia who was hot off the original Broadway production of *Hair*, slinks onto the screen from out of the darkness wearing only a loin wrap as the lusty Ascyltus. He wrestles with Encolpius, played by dyed-blond Brit **Martin Potter** (1944-   ), who has the loveliest iridescent blue eyes this side of Paul Newman.

The two young friends are former lovers now at odds over the gangly and barely pubescent Giton (Max Born). Had Fellini found Björn Andresen, later of Visconti's *Death in Venice* (1971), for the part, we would have really had something here. As it is, the odd rhythms, dubbed lines and laughter, and disconnected storyline give us precious few opportunities to savor these two. Potter is contorted into a compromising position during a wrestling match aboard Lichas' ship, during which the elder Lichas seems to bend over and put his nose into the young man's armpit at the victory. Lichas will claim Encolpius as his bride and give him a full mouth kiss at the ceremony.

Later, a reunited Encolpius and Ascyltus will wrestle in a shallow bath with the female slave left behind in an empty palace. They share her kisses and touch each other, but we witness no consummation. When Encolpius admits in yet another segment that "my sword is blunted," he has his bottom caned with reeds and visits a witch with a fiery cunt to find a cure.

Keller also appeared in writer/director Catherine Breillat's first sexually explicit coming-of-age film,

169

A Real Young Girl (1975), which was banned in France and went unreleased until 2001. Potter made the rarely seen *Goodbye Gemini* (1970), playing one half of an incestuous brother/sister act interrupted by the affections of another man.

Male sexuality had come literally out of the closet by the end of the 1960s. The penis had been liberated, if still something to be frightened of. Filmmaker Pat Rocco was successfully filling Los Angeles' Park Cinema with a steady stream of male nudie flicks, including *Yes* (1969) and *A Very Special Friend* (1969). It wouldn't be long before feature-length gay porn was upon us, i.e., *Boys in the Sand* (1971).

Hollywood and the movies quickly learned to oblige the interest in male exposure. While writer-gay erotica historian Tom Waugh tells us in his superb book *Hard to Imagine: Gay Male Eroticism in Photography and Film from Their Beginnings to Stonewall* (Columbia University Press, 1996) that a collection of male movie star "crotch shots called *Basketfuls of Goodies*" played at an LA venue in the late 1960s, the studios were about to make male crotch shots all in a day's work.

Leonard Whiting's bare-assed Romeo checks on his Juliet (Olivia Hussey) the morning after in Franco Zeffirelli's *Romeo and Juliet* (1968).
PHOTOFEST

The 1970s

"Tell Him To Take Off His Sweater And Look At The Camera"

There was a time in the 1970s when **Charles Robert Redford, Jr.** (1937-   ) could have walked into a gay bar and easily gotten lost in the crowd. Redford's mustachioed Sundance Kid in the enormous hit *Butch Cassidy and the Sundance Kid* (1969) was, for nearly a decade, the paradigm of butch in gay iconography. The look was a dime a dozen, differentiated only by the color of the hanky and which pocket it hung from. There were at least 75 variations on the Hanky Code, with that many again depending on which side you wore it on, signaling to others your particular sexual desire or fetish.

Redford would have worn silver lamé on the right. He was a celebrity.

A golden boy from Santa Monica, he dropped out of the University of Colorado as a sophomore and spent a year in Europe studying painting, after which he came to New York as an art student at the Pratt Institute. A notion to become a theatrical art director led him to the American Academy of Dramatic Arts, where he learned it was acting that he loved most of all.

Television work included *Alfred Hitchcock Presents* and *The Twilight Zone*, but it was his appearance on Broadway in 1963's *Barefoot in the Park*, a role he would repeat for the big screen in 1967, that brought this blond good-looker to the attention of producers. He had already done a solid turn in his first film, *War Hunt* (1962), playing a soldier who tries to lure a Korean boy away from a demented American warrior played by John Saxon.

He was reluctantly cast as a "gay" film star in *Inside Daisy Clover* (1965), which garners interest because the reticent Mr. Redford at long last settled on the idea his character was "bisexual." He's cute and charming and even a little fey as Wade Lewis, whose real name is Lewis Wade, but the studio made him flip flop it because they said it sounded sexier the other way.

"Your husband never could resist a charming boy," quips Katherine Bard to newly married and abandoned Natalie Wood. The "hetero" movie star who's really a bisexual gigolo whom everyone falls hard for is an intriguing premise. Still, Redford's essentially asexual, which might be said of his entire career. The Golden Globes, meanwhile, named him "Star of the Future."

Not since Cary Grant has a major sex symbol been so unfuckable. He's attractive, though certainly less charismatic than Grant, but he's likable and safe, and almost transparent, as a movie star. In *The Chase* (1966), his Bubber Reeves, a potentially dangerous prison escapee, sure comes with shiny clean hair, and there's probably something about Redford's own impending celebrity to be read into the badly staged attempt at recreating the Oswald killing for his character's demise at the end of the picture. (Sometimes you can be famous for doing bad things?)

Robert Redford was very good-looking, but only occasionally sexy, which likely suited him fine. It wouldn't even be an issue for a serious actor if it weren't for his face. Some actors ooze sex. Some completely untalented actors smolder with sex appeal. Robert Redford was either so oblivious to or completely aware of his beauty that he ignored it. The camera could see what he had, but he frequently refused to animate it.

Besides, I don't think he enjoyed playing romantic roles. He looks good in a white uniform, but has the right idea early on when he falls asleep atop Barbra Streisand in the repetitively uneventful *The Way We Were* (1973). Buoyed by the sentimental, haunted quirks of his undying love for Daisy, he finally looks his best when he's floating in the swimming pool and about to be tragically scapegoated as *The Great Gatsby* (1974). He preferred to play thieves [*Butch and Sundance* (1969), *The Hot Rock* (1972), *The Sting* (1973)] and adventurers [*Downhill Racer* (1969), *Jeremiah Johnson* (1972), *The Great Waldo Pepper* (1975)], even a target [*Three Days of the Condor* (1975)], as opposed to drawing room mannequins. There's something ethereal about Redford's beauty, though. It's tangible only in terms of its packaging, not for what's inside. Which is why he's perfect as the naive politician who learns how politics and image are

Robert Redford makes his film debut as a new recruit who hopes to separate a Korean boy from the company of a psychotic American soldier in *War Hunt* (1962). EVERETT COLLECTION

marketed in *The Candidate* (1972) and why he's ostensibly little more than an aesthetic alternative to Dustin Hoffman's mug in the classic *All the President's Men* (1976). (Behind the scenes, however, Redford was the one who bought the rights to the story, produced the film, and was vital to its vision and success.)

Redford is clearly his own man, in the sense that his passions about politics (he was #19 on Nixon's enemies list) and the environment, independent film and filmmaking, life and lifestyle, are more successfully roused off screen. He's not the first actor to be cursed by his looks, but he's certainly one of the biggest movie stars to have achieved that status without a defining role or performance. Sure, you can point to films that put him on the map, and to which he made major contributions, but he's not single-handedly responsible. To his unusual credit, given that he works in an industry that exploits image over content, Redford seems to require a strong co-star—male or female—to help carry a film.

After *The Sting* (1973), in which he was Oscar-nominated but Paul Newman was not, Robert Redford was the number one male box-office draw from 1974-1976.

The Electric Horseman (1979), a charming romance, proved a big hit, and then he surprised the hell out of everybody by directing *Ordinary People* (1980), an American classic about familial dysfunction, for

172

which he won the Academy Award. His legendary good looks were by the 1980s institutionalized and his name couldn't fail to turn up in polls enumerating the sexiest men alive year after year. For some, his giving Meryl Streep a shampoo on the veldt in *Out of Africa* (1985) brought sighs, but the cleverest casting was having him offer Woody Harrelson cash for one night with Demi Moore in *Indecent Proposal* (1993). The tables had turned.

The original casting duo for *Butch Cassidy and the Sundance Kid* had Newman as the Kid and Brando as Butch. Then it was Beatty as the Kid and Elvis as Butch. Then it was Beatty as the Kid and Newman as Butch. Then it was Steve McQueen as the Kid and Newman as Butch. It's hard to imagine any of those pairings resulting in the chemistry that Newman and Redford brought to the roles. For my money, it's the most believably romantic film Robert Redford ever made.

"Basically, I guess, I'm an exhibitionist," **Don Johnson** (1949-   ) told interviewer Marvin Jones in 1973. "I'm very proud of my body. I'm pleased with the way I look and the way I carry myself. I feel that it's all there to be used—the looks and everything. Some people have great minds, and they were given them for a reason. I've never been accused of having that great a mind, but I do have my looks."

The University of Kansas dropout came to San Francisco in 1968 at the age of 18 to be an actor after successfully auditioning for the American Conservatory Theater. He wasn't there two weeks before he was given the lead in a musical called *Your Own Thing*. Sal Mineo then nabbed him for the pretty-boy jailbait who gets raped onstage by a fellow inmate (Mineo himself) in Mineo's shocking production of *Fortune and Men's Eyes*.

Numerous stills of the slim young pup in his white briefs being threatened by a gruff Mineo from behind were used to sell the play and bare ass shots of the pair appeared in Issue 1 of *IN* magazine. Just in case folks didn't catch on, some of the publicity stills had Mineo quite obviously sizing up Johnson's butt and still others featured a close-up of Don's face twisted in excruciating pain. The idea of baiting an audience to a play about the brutality of prison by using a cute young man in his underwear getting plowed is just one of the ideological curiosities of the production and the time in which it was staged.

Needless to say, Johnson was an instant hit with gay audiences. He was sold as chicken feed and pecked at with delight.

He also spends time both in and out of his underwear in his first feature film, *The Magic Garden of Stanley Sweetheart* (1970), as a cute blond college junior in New York City perplexed with himself. He occasionally fantasizes alternate versions of his daytime events, but is otherwise stricken by self-doubt, confusion, sexual obsession, and identity crisis characteristic of a young man who doesn't know what he wants to do with the rest of his life. At his apartment, he lies around in his underwear swatting at flies, masturbates in the bathtub, and considers making another 16mm underground film.

Stanley's films are adolescent preoccupations with sex. He entitles his latest effort *Masturbation* and invites the chubby best friend of his recently deflowered girlfriend to get drunk and climb over him into the bathtub to diddle herself. He'll end up experimenting with drugs and liquor and three-way sex, experience guilt, regret, and momentary joy before emerging into the daylight of the city streets again. He'll even bolt from an encounter at a local café where a stranger talks to him about pussy before making a desperate plea to discover the size of Stanley's cock.

Johnson is charming and uninhibited in the role. He's comfortable in his skin. His teeth haven't yet been fashioned movie-star perfect, but a star couldn't have played Stanley Sweetheart. It's a role meant for a novice, a new face, a new body.

When Matthew (Don Johnson) asks cowboy John Rubinstein "What are you lookin' for?" in *Zachariah* (1971), the handsome young man replies: "A friend. Got a light?" It probably doesn't have anything to do with the fact that Johnson is standing there shirtless in a blacksmith's smock, but the hope that the homoerotic possibilities of this exchange will turn it into the first gay western since Andy Warhol's *Lonesome Cowboys* (1969) keeps your fingers and toes crossed.

Before there was *The Electric Horseman* (1979) there was this "Electric Western." Zachariah (Rubinstein) proudly shows his mail-order gun to Matthew, who declares it "far out." Rubinstein, with his big floppy head of curls, and Johnson, with his sandy blond helmet of hair, both with their big white teeth and smooth red lips, make a good boy-boy team.

At a local watering hole, a nasty bad guy refers to Matthew as Zachariah's "girlfriend" and belittles his shiny new gun. "Look what the tough little boy has in his pants," he jeers. The brilliant touch is that

Don Johnson actually glances down at his partner's crotch.

The film immediately loses energy when Johnson is left behind because, like all love stories, it desperately needs the boy/boy sexual tension. Rubinstein's Zachariah goes off on a *Pippin*-ish quest to find himself (Rubinstein would play Pippin on Broadway) while Johnson's Matthew becomes Zach's alter ego. He's the pretty boy bad-boy wannabe in black with silver bracelets around his biceps and a broad-rimmed coal-black hat. Will the two come face to face? What will it take to get the other to strap on his gun? And what about that single silver bullet that Matthew made for Zachariah, but now wears on a necklace? I would have been happy with a long, wet kiss. Don Johnson's fat lips were made for chewing on.

The Harrad Experiment (1973) is a softcore porn flick masquerading as a hip, post-sexual revolution lesson in free love. James Whitmore, the esteemed actor and "Miracle Grow" spokesman, heads up "a controlled group experiment in premarital relations" that encourages college co-eds to engage in sexual intimacy. You can change roommates once a month, but no sooner, because that's the minimum required to get to know someone. This virulently heterosexist new age hooey was based on a best-selling sex book

Mop-topped Don Johnson in *Zachariah* (1971), the "electric western." PHOTOFEST

by Robert H. Rimmer (oh, that name!) and co-adapted for the screen by Ted Cassidy (Lurch of TV's *The Addams Family*), who appears at the counter of the local café.

Don Johnson, looking skinnier than ever, has the distinction of stripping off his shirt before he even gets his name out, then lowers his jeans for a butt shot on his way into the john. He emerges from the bathroom shower in front of his female roommate (and still complete stranger) holding only a towel, flashing his genitalia and considerable pubic hair. He sleeps in the nude. And everybody exercises in the nude...together. They swim nude, too, including a young Gregory Harrison. Then the whole group of kids sit naked in a big circle and pass "zooms" around as the film trips into a free-love, anti-marriage propaganda flick. It's a freaky hippie movie scored with funky '70s porn music, which subverts hippie ideals for a horrifically sexist design based exclusively on male fantasies.

Johnson, with his mop even more helmet-like and his bangs hanging right down to his eyebrows, always has great big sweat stains under his arms, but I'm attributing that to embarrassment of the material, not the fact that he's being asked to get naked with Laurie Walters (later of TV's *Eight is Enough*) or Bruno Kirby, or must sustain the shock of being ordered to screw Tippi Hedren on the lawn in broad daylight. (Fourteen-year old Melanie Griffith, Ms. Hedren's daughter, who Johnson would later marry, appears as a clothed extra.) Don also sings the song "It's Not Over" over the credits. Not a bad voice.

Johnson escaped appearing in the follow-up, *Harrad Summer* (1974), but made an equally dull sequel to a bad movie with *Return to Macon County* (1975). He and Nick Nolte (in his feature film debut) play a pair of rambunctious hicks named Harley and Bo on their way to the Grand Nationals drag racing contest in California. A wacky gun-wielding ex-waitress in 1958 rural Georgia fouls up their plans. Harley's most endearing quality: he can't get it up in bed because he's only ever had sex in a car.

Johnson's other low-budget film that year was *A Boy and His Dog* (1975), set in 2024 AD and some time after a five-day WWIV has left the planet looking like a desert. He's a wandering 18-year old who wants his wisecracking dog Blood (played by Tiger of *The Brady Bunch*) to sniff him out a chick so he can get laid. Vic, as he calls himself, is known as Albert to Blood, whose thoughts the young man can hear as clearly as if the canine was saying them aloud.

Johnson is baited by a crafty female who lures him to an underground society where white-faced survivors are bent on building a facsimile of Topeka, Kansas. All of their men are sterile, so Johnson's young stud is bathed, outfitted as a farm boy with straw hat, overalls, and a plaid shirt, and readied for duty. He's feisty, all right, and squeezes his crotch once he's told why he's there. "You mean you want me to knock up your broads?" he asks. "You talked me into it. Line 'em up." Unfortunately, they intend to pump it out of him the no-fun way.

It would be another decade of multiple TV series guest appearances (he's cute as all hell as a shirtless Indian brave in a 1973 episode of *Kung Fu*) and TV movies-of-the-week (including one as Elvis in 1981's *Elvis and the Beauty Queen*) before he at last found the vehicle that would make him famous. Michael Mann's *Miami Vice* (1984-89) was to the 1980's what *Charlie's Angels* was to the 1970's: an embarrassing media microcosm of a decade's trash culture. *Vice* was a phenomenal hit, influencing for better and worse both real-world fashion and television cop shows, making Don Johnson a bona fide star 20+ years after he began in the biz, and irradiating all that now seems pompous and silly about the Reagan era of false prosperity and greed. Slickly formatted, shot among gorgeous locales, peppered with "Top 40" song interludes, and featuring horrifically "stylish" clothes, cars, boats, shades, and two-day stubble, the show has aged badly, but still has its flock of devoted followers. A decade later, *Nash Bridges* (1996-2001) proved another popular television vehicle for Johnson.

A successful movie star career has pretty much eluded him, not improbably due to the difficulty audiences have paying to see something different from an actor they can see just as they like for free.

In the early 1970s, Don Johnson was cute enough to make the transition to Hollywood studio films, but all his experience was in low-budget flicks and his core audience was largely made up of a gay constituency. He appeared on the cover of *In-Touch for Men* magazine (May, 1974) in a bathrobe, leisurely looking out the window with a cup of coffee in his hand. Johnson was extremely gay-friendly and gay-thankful. Nude stills from his films, as well as some cheeky originals taken all in good fun, were regularly printed in gay magazines and are traded among gay men right up to the present.

In-Touch was the first gay magazine of its type, an openly homosexual publication courting advertisers, doing celebrity interviews, offering lifestyle pieces, and featuring photographs of nude men intended for same-sex consumption. Issue 1 went on sale in October of 1973. At a time when the gay movement was making its way through a haze of increasingly visible politics and even the American Psychiatric Association finally (though not overwhelmingly) voted homosexuality off its list of mental disorders in 1974, *In-Touch* was tapping into the sexual liberation of gays and the liberal leanings of some of Hollywood's stars.

Among those who granted interviews (though only occasionally touching specifically on gay issues) over the next decade, or were subjects of lead articles: Nick Nolte, Beau Bridges, Glenda Jackson, Shirley MacLaine, Robert Morse, Tab Hunter, Ann-Margret, Elton John, Barbra Streisand, Elizabeth Taylor, Sal Mineo, Martin Sheen, Russ Tamblyn, Warren Beatty, Bette Midler, Robert Redford, Jan-Michael Vincent, David Bowie, Timothy Bottoms, Burt Reynolds, Michael Ontkean, Van Johnson, Steve McQueen, Robert Mitchum, John Travolta, Henry Winkler, Keith Carradine, Kris Kristofferson, Jon Voight, Ryan O'Neal, Perry King, Robby Benson, Alan Bates, Richard Gere, and Christopher Atkins.

There they were, hawking their latest movie accompanied by studio-provided stills between a six-page color layout of a mustachioed hunk named Bob and an advertisement for Accu-Jak featuring a guy with a vacuum pump on his dick.

In-Touch kept in touch with Hollywood, regularly featuring campy and tantalizing spreads on movies and the stars, including "The Films of Crotch," a pictorial of movie scene "big baskets." But a fun and entertaining series that printed nude photos purported to be of "Celebrity Dicks" ran afoul of at least one real-life celebrity in the mid-1980s and threatened lawsuits led to the magazine's complete about-face on the subject.

The 1970s were an otherwise great time to enjoy the sexual objectification of men in the media, most of it originating from gay filmmakers and photographers and fashion designers, but then swallowed whole by the popular culture with the April 1972 edition of *Cosmopolitan*. The sight of a naked Burt Reynolds lying on a bearskin rug might give you the willies, but it's the absence of his willie that made it so effective as pseudo-feminist propaganda.

Burt has a friendly smile on his face to let all of us know he's in on the joke and perfectly agreeable to the turnabout. He's also got his forearm casually laid across his genitalia, fully obstructing any and all glimpses of his fleshy particulars while still showing enough pubic hair to convince us he's really nude. It's the kind of centerfold you can feel comfortable showing your grandmother. In its own way, it's nearly sexless, a castrated and very safe approach to the male nude with which to tantalize the masses, who wouldn't have wanted to see an inch more of Burt no matter how sexy they thought he was.

I'm not saying that plenty of women and men weren't disappointed that Burt didn't show all, only that it was the savviest and most practical approach to reach the widest possible audience. The issue was an instantaneous sell-out. Two years later, John Davidson and Jim Brown would do similar poses for *Cosmo*, followed by Arnold Schwarzenegger in 1977. Tellingly, by 1990, when David Hasselhoff posed, he's not only the most covered of all the guys, but he's covered by a Sharpei puppy. How cuddly and "safe" and yet somehow unsexy could you get?

The impact of Reynolds' sensational centerfold was multifold: a well-timed boost into superstardom in conjunction with the release of *Deliverance* (1972), a cultural debate about packaging the male as sexual consumer goods, and a spate of copycat exposures in other magazines, most notably in a brand new one calling itself *Playgirl*.

Playgirl hit the stands in May of 1973, the Los Angeles reincarnation of a failed Indiana venture with the same title. The magazine was marketed to and "understood" to be enjoyed by heterosexual women. Not unsurprisingly, gay men made up a significant, and largely unacknowledged, share of its readership, fostering an occasional bitter denial by the magazine's editors and betraying a love/hate relationship.

The popular wisdom is that women aren't particularly attracted to nor excited by photos of naked men. They might admit to liking the look of a well-formed tush (even the word is de-sexed, and heaven forbid, keep those cheeks closed), or they might say that "he's got a nice chest, pretty eyes, or sexy arms," but add the genitalia and rumor has it that 98% of the female audience could take it or leave it. Not that they're necessarily anti-meat and potatoes, just that they could get the same buzz or better without having him take off his jockey shorts. "Leave something to the imagination" translates to "leave *that* thing to the imagination." Though I once wrote that I'd wager just as many boys were secretly disappointed that Ken had no shiny plastic genitalia as girls were relieved to discover the same, I have been adamantly informed that's untrue. So while I cringe at reducing the subject to blatant generalization, I have to note there does seem to be some social evidence that concurs. *Penthouse*'s dabble in nude male photography was the short-lived *Viva*, suggesting that demand for more than one heterosexual source was and remains limited. In the 1990s, *Glamour* magazine asked readers if they thought there should be more male nudity in the movies and 86% responded yes, but only half said it would be reason enough to see the film. (Today, the availability of male nudity on the Internet is likely providing an outlet for interested women, but three decades of skin magazines and only one directed at the ladies managing to survive is both conspicuous and curious.)

In the 1970s, *Playgirl* featured coy poses (and occasional head-on frontals) of Steve Bond, Jim Brown, Gary Conway, John Ericson, Fabian, Christopher George, Sam Jones, Peter Lupus, George Maharis, Don Stroud, Lyle Waggoner, and Fred Williamson. Bond and Jones hadn't yet achieved their fifteen minutes of fame, and Conway and Ericson weren't household names, but all attained some level of celebrity and agreed to market themselves by stripping off and stepping into the fair-play pages of *Playgirl*, which ran and re-ran and ran-to-death their photos.

Personally, it wasn't the Burt Reynolds centerfold that helped clue me in to my own diverging sexuality. And I was still a couple of years away from finding my first issue of *Playgirl*. However, as sure as a guy's heterosexuality could be inferred by the ubiquitous presence of Farrah Fawcett's nipply swimsuit poster in the 1970s, I was a homo transfixed by a poster of Mark Spitz.

He won a record seven gold medals at the 1972 Olympics in Munich, but was likely unaware of the enormous sexual impact he had on adolescent gay males as he stood there in just his red, white, and blue speedos with the stars running down the front, wearing his gold medals around his neck and posed with his hands on his hips like Superman.

I pored over his poster—that smooth and wide chest, that bit of hair discernible below his belly button—to find even a single exposed pubic hair or a telltale bulge that would distinguish his thing from his thingies.

And just as I was at the point in my young perverted life to enjoy looking at the underwear ads in catalogs, staring at the airbrushed pouches of handsome smiling men, it happened. On page 602 of the Fall/Winter 1975 *Sears Catalog*, out of the left leg hole of #4 boxer shorts peeked the tip of one handsome smiling man's penis. At least that's what it looked like to me and several other excited and/or upset crotch gazers. Looked at today, the photo is tragically less likely to be what I positively knew it to be when I was 13 years old and willfully naïve. Sears claimed all along that the "thing" was just a printing blemish or watermark on the original artwork. They're probably right. The gentleman in the photo would have to be quite well hung to hang that far (even though the waistband is riding awfully high) and it seems further unlikely that he would be unaware of his exposure during the shoot even if he was a long fellow. The photo has become something of an urban legend, but was plainly and wishfully taken for real by me at the time, validating the intensity of my past and subsequent, though vain searches.

In 1977, the book *Looking Good: A Guide for Men* by Charles Hix suggested not wearing underwear to avoid crotch odors, but said nothing about how your pants would subsequently smell…or stain, just how embarrassing it might be in an emergency. More important than his unorthodox advice were the striking photos of partially dressed and undressed (but not full-frontal) men by photographer Bruce Weber, whose work would be instrumental in the mass media popularization of the sexually objectified male in advertising. Hix went on to do several other glamour guy guidebooks in the 1970s and 1980s, most notably *Working Out: The Total Shape Up Guide for Men* (1983), which I bought strictly for the Ken Haak pictures.

Typically, one pointed to Europe for examples of a less-puritanical, sexually open society where nude imagery was much less sensationalistic and never naughty. I'm so glad I grew up in America. The fact that I was the product of a zippered culture (despite being post-Kinsey, post-*Playboy*, and post-Woodstock) meant the discovery of nude imagery held unimaginably contradictory and exciting pleasures. Guilt-laced lust is a powerful thing. (The effects of a generation raised on Internet porn, however, are frightening to imagine and we will all pay the price.)

European films may have featured more nudity than American product, but eventually it mattered who it was had their clothes off.

Helmut Steinberger was an Austrian lad of 22 when he anxiously showed up on one of Luchino Visconti's sets and admitted to the aging director that it had been his dream to meet him. Visconti was instantly taken with this gorgeous blond acolyte and invited him to his home, beginning a tempestuous, loving, and mutually abusive relationship that would last until the great filmmaker's death twelve years later.

Helmut Berger (1942-   ), as he was abbreviated, became Visconti's protégé. He's a waiter in Visconti's installment of *Le Streghe* (*The Witches*; 1967), but even that proved difficult for him. He was incredibly nervous and said to visibly tremble when the lens of the camera set its eye upon him.

His entrance in *The Damned* (1969), Visconti's controversial hit about the internal conflicts of a powerful German industrial family amidst the rise of Nazism in 1933, may be the director's idea of a cruel joke, because it's the entrance of a star...and the star is in drag. Fishnet stockings and garters *ala* Dietrich, with a second pair of eyebrows etched on in pinpoint liner, his appearance is a grotesque and decadent birthday performance from impudent grandson to steel tycoon grandfather. The only thing that stops its complete delivery is the news that the Reichstag is burning.

Helmut Berger posing as a modern *Dorian Gray* (1970). EVERETT COLLECTION

Because of the effeminate drag act, and Visconti's known homosexuality among his critics, many contemporary reviews wrongly assumed that Visconti's new boy was playing a homo, but he was not. Berger's Martin is, in fact, a hetero momma's boy loaded with psychosexual perversions. He's a pedophile whose latest victim is a little Jewish girl who hangs herself, but spoke his name in delirium the night before she committed suicide. The Nazis are willing to overlook this indiscretion (her Jewishness means the act isn't even a crime) so long as they can broker a deal with him now that he's become president of the family's steel mills.

Morally weak and a drug addict, Martin is dragged through the murderous and power mad corruption of his family and attempts to ward off a coup by his mother and her conniving fiancé (Dirk Bogarde). "I will destroy you, mother!" he screams at her. "You are the vurst!" He blames her for introducing him to wigs and lipstick as a child, then proceeds to strip and bed her. At last, a perverted heterosexual.

Berger gives a strong performance in a key and very difficult role. It's the kind of performance that an unknown actor might be afraid of giving for fear that an audience would never forget or forgive him for it.

On the queer-baiting front, *The Damned* certainly has its share of handsome servant boys, but will forever be remembered for its "scandalous" version of the Night of the Long Knives, a sequence in which the all-male partiers of the SA are homoerotically conjoined and, in some cases, drunk and naked atop one another as Hitler's murder squad moves in and machineguns them.

Dorian Gray (1970), aka *The Secret of Dorian Gray*, aka *The Evils of Dorian Gray*, is such a juicy subject for a modern allegory starring a pretty boy that it's a travesty someone talented didn't come up with the idea. Helmut makes a lovely blond Dorian, and there's something chic and antique about his posing for his portrait shirtless, yet wearing a blue silk kerchief knotted around his neck. He's wearing blue jeans with a big ol' belt buckle, too, with his thumbs latched into the front pockets, causing the rest of his fingers to frame his crotch like a Santa Monica Blvd. hustler.

The film is a low-budget, English-language affair, with Helmut re-dubbed even though he's already saying his lines in English. We see him in a blue speedo, dropping soap in the shower, taking a nude swim, cruising a black man at the public urinals, and lounging in the sauna, but he's inexcusably deliberate about covering himself. We deserve more, and he deserved a better version of this classic tale, something that lived up to the film's tantalizing advertising tagline: "Youth is the ultimate perversion."

In *Un beau monstre* (*Love Me Strangely*; 1970), he's cast as a freaky bisexual whose mom was a prostitute, which may or may not have something to do with why he can only have sex with a girl if she's been drugged unconscious. Tab Hunter had similar problems in Curtis Hanson's ultra-low budget schlocker *The Arousers* (1973). Tab's sexual psychopath was traumatized in his youth by his momma's whorin' ways, witnessed in all their ugly detail while he was stowed away in her bedroom closet. Now a high school boys' gym teacher, he's murdering all the gals who discover him to be impotent. The only way he can get his nut is by hiring a prostitute to dress up in his mom's old hat and veil and lie on the bed with her eyes closed. He can then disrobe her, lay his head on her bare breasts, and masturbate.

Like Tab, Helmut wasn't always appreciated as the most accomplished of actors, but at least he was still able to mix the schlock with some important films. He plays the small role of the Jewish son who eventually doesn't venture out of the family mansion anymore in Vittorio De Sica's classic *The Garden of the Finzi-Continis* (1971), symbolically chronicling the rise of fascism in Italy among a wealthy family of Jews who fail to grasp the evil before it's too late.

Fans who could not have cared less about his acting chops enjoyed his nude scene in *Les Voraces* (*The Voracious Ones*; 1972), but it was his mentor who offered him the next opportunity to play a great role. He is Ludwig II, the so-called "mad" King of Bavaria, in Visconti's 4-hour epic detailing the peculiar life of a beauty made king at age 19, who then became an eccentric recluse and obsessive patron of the arts, especially of composer Richard Wagner. The king shirked wartime responsibility because he abhorred war, though managed to rule for 22 years before politics framed him as "mad" and sent him to a sanitarium. It was there that he was either promptly murdered (perhaps shot) or took his own life (his body was pulled from a lake along with that of his doctor).

Initially stiff and apparently weighted down by his new responsibilities, Ludwig is played by Berger as a romantic whose romance is with the arts, not with the kingdom. Even in love he is thwarted. Almost predestined to romance a beautiful cousin, he can't go through with it; instead, he mans his palace with handsome servant boys and even follows one of them late at night to catch him taking a nude swim. Ludwig, we're told, has the problem that all "sensitive" boys have, but most grow out of. His Catholic priest explains that one body is as warm as another in the dark; therefore, the devoutly religious king should go ahead and marry a woman and reject his temptations.

Easier said than done. Tortured, disillusioned, and subject to melancholia, the king grows hairier as the film goes on. His teeth blacken. His face bloats. Helmut Berger starts to look like Mr. Hyde.

Ludwig (1972) is a film in which people exit a room only to have them seen entering another. It's long, probably too long, but at its center is a performance that grows on you in a surprising way. Berger demonstrates once again what he can do for the man who both loves and hates him behind the camera. The elaborately detailed project was a difficult undertaking for the aging and increasingly frail Visconti, who suffered a debilitating stroke during the production.

Though partially paralyzed, Visconti would direct his Helmut in a film once more, putting him in duds by Yves St. Laurent and having him take a shower in front of Burt Lancaster. *Conversation Piece* (1974) is, on the surface, about a lonely old professor (Lancaster) whose solitary life is needlessly complicated by a suspiciously aggressive family and their pet hustler (Berger).

Helmut wears his pants very tight and sounds funny saying things like, "The apartment bullshit, sweetheart!" and "If he breaks your ballz, send him up to me and I'll break his beak." Even "cunt" sounds wrong. They shot both English and Italian-language versions, but I think I prefer the English only because it's even further removed from Helmut's native tongue, upping the entertainment factor. *The Damned* was shot in English, too, but at least there his accent seemed right. Here, his impertinent explosions of temper sound comical, even a bit amateurish—the fault of the dialogue more than the performance. Then again, the performance by Claudia Marsani as the 18-year-old who believes in free love is beyond amateur, with line readings that require a new expression for every sentence uttered.

Class, left/right politics, intellectualism, and a half-dozen other interesting themes get touched on, despite the acting, but the simple premise of the retiring professor surrounded by his painting, music, and books who throbs into messy, complicated life because he fancies the young troubled hunk who rents the upstairs apartment is all I really wanted. Helmut's frontal nude scene would have been conversation piece enough for me.

Back in clothes by Yves St. Laurent in *The Romantic Englishwoman* (1975), Helmut is once again the hustler. He claims he's a German poet. A vacationing Glenda Jackson asks him "to go down" when she meets him on an elevator and he deliberately takes her to the wrong floor. She's unhappily married to a snobbish novelist, played by Michael Caine, who has been employed to write a screenplay. Helmut shows up on their English doorstep months later and charms his way into staying.

At the outset, the film is enjoyably self-aware of its set-up and even allows Caine open commentary on its plot. Caine decides to keep the slightly effeminate Berger around the house as his paid secretary because he wants to study him for a character he's developing. Everybody realizes the lad is just a sponger. We've seen this kind of thematic arrangement before and expect Berger's presence to seduce the entire household *a la* Terence Stamp in *Teorema* (1968), Michael York in *Something For Everyone* (1970), or Sting in *Brimstone & Treacle* (1982).

It's too bad then that Berger's character is so paper thin. He's handsome, yes, but neither complex nor even plainly radiant. His handsomeness and his delivery conspire to make him rather common instead of seductive. He's not even tempting. His silhouette (against the hallway door at night) is sexier than his flesh and blood self.

Worse yet, he was cast as a Nazi in the degenerate *Salon Kitty* (1976), a grotesque, creepy, and unclean sexploitation film directed by Tinto Brass, who would later helm *Caligula* (1980). Recommend a double bill with Pasolini's *Salo, or the 120 Days of Sodom* (1975) to people you want out of your life.

In 1990, Berger showed up as Frederick Keinszig in *The Godfather Part III*, and in 1993 he reprised his role as the mad king in *Ludwig 1881*. His blip on the pop culture scene was registered as the answer to a trivia question in a Quentin Tarantino movie. In *Jackie Brown* (1997), Samuel L. Jackson asks if the guy in the movie he's watching on TV is Rutger Hauer. "No," answers Bridget Fonda, decisively enough to be an all-knowing vidiot via Tarantino's script, "Helmut Berger."

On film, **Bruce Lee** (1940-1973) was invincible. Twenty-five guys could circle him and it would never cross your mind that he wasn't going to crack all their heads and walk away. The joy was in the anticipation of the inevitable, of watching the odds get bigger and bigger and then waiting for the master to unleash his fury. No holds were barred. He'd kick, he'd punch, he'd chop, he'd bite, he'd grab you by the nuts and crush 'em, not just give 'em a squeeze.

Born in San Francisco in the Year of the Dragon, Lee Jun-Fan got into movies almost from the start—he played a baby girl in *Golden Gate Girl* (1941). His father was an actor in the Cantonese opera, which is what brought him to the states in 1940. He would return to Hong Kong with his wife and infant son in 1941.

The charismatic youngster had already made at least two films in Hong Kong before starring, at age 10, as *Kid Cheung* (1950), the only film in which both he and his father appeared together. Several more films followed over the next few years, culminating in his playing a Chinese version of Pip as *The Orphan Ah-Sam* (1958) in a plot right out of Dickens' *Great Expectations*.

A rowdy teenager with a nose for trouble who went to several different schools as he grew up and enjoyed the camaraderie of a gang, he ventured back to America in his late teens. He lived above a restaurant owned by a family friend in Seattle and waited tables. In 1961, he enrolled at Washington University in Seattle as a philosophy major. He also began teaching self-defense and the martial arts to fellow students. His own lessons had begun at age 13 back in Hong Kong.

While still in school, he opened the Jun Fan Kung Fu Institute in 1963, then a year later opened a second school in Oakland. He married in 1964 and moved to California, where an impressive exhibition at an international karate championship brought him to the attention of *Batman* producer William Dozier.

Nicknamed "the Little Dragon" as a child actor, his interest in the profession hadn't waned as he'd gotten older. He was offered the role of Kato on ABC-TV's *The Green Hornet* (1966-67), he joked at the time, because he was the only Chinese actor the producers could find able to properly pronounce the name

Bruce Lee seizes icon status in *Enter the Dragon* (1973). EVERETT COLLECTION

of the Hornet's unmasked character Britt Reid.

The show lasted only a season, but those 23 episodes, as well as a March 1967 appearance as Kato on *Batman* ("A Piece of the Action/Batman's Satisfaction"), provided him with a forum to display his wares and make connections throughout Hollywood. He served as karate advisor for the final installment of Dean Martin's Matt Helm series, *The Wrecking Crew* (1969), and steals the whole show in the first of his two scenes in the otherwise dry detective retread *Marlowe* (1969). He walks into James Garner's office to hand out some friendly persuasion and proceeds to completely destroy the place while Garner sits at his desk and watches.

On ABC's *Longstreet* (1971-72), he was given the rare opportunity to play himself and not a comic book character as self-defense instructor to a blind insurance investigator played by James Franciscus. Lee's off-screen connections were growing and his enormous talent and philosophical approach to the martial arts made pupils of many of Hollywood's leading men, including Steve McQueen, James Coburn, and Lee Marvin.

With a big-screen career hoped for, but questionable in the states, and the international appeal of *The Green Hornet*, especially in Asia (though it was the French who compiled several episodes of the series into a 1975 theatrical release), Lee accepted an offer to star in a Hong Kong feature called *The Big Boss*. By the time it arrived in America in 1971 as *Fists of Fury*, Bruce Lee was nothing short of a sensation in his homeland.

The martial arts film, or "chop-socky," became popularized in Hong Kong as early as 1949, but the genre established itself internationally at the hands of Bruce Lee.

He wears his dead mother's locket to remind him of his promise to her not to fight in *Fists of Fury*, but then his cousins start disappearing from their jobs at the local ice house and we know it won't be long before he discovers that the big boss is smuggling drugs in the ice blocks and that his cousins have been cubed, too. Struck twice by adversaries, he still won't put up a fight.

Finally, nearly 45 minutes into the film, he can no longer help himself. Like a scorpion sting, he delivers controlled strikes and methodically levels his opponents to the sounds of Three Stooges-like slaps dubbed onto the soundtrack. He fights for keeps.

He also enjoys munching on snacks while killing the factory manager's guards. When he gets to the big boss man himself, in a nice touch, he frees the bad guy's caged bird before the main event gets underway.

During the fight, Lee's white shirt gets torn half off, so he tears the rest of it off to get it out of the way. It's a ritualistic baring, further celebrated by the blood that will soon flow from him. In all of his martial arts films, Lee will display his body, seemingly tensed into a single band of sinew, and it will inevitably be slashed before he attains his assured victory.

That's the ritual. And the rub. He bares himself for violence; at the very same time his etched physique is sending out sexual signals, he's preparing to use it for battle. It's a close enough commingling of sexual response and violent satisfaction to make you wonder whether or not it constitutes a form of S&M.

In *The Chinese Connection* (1972; confusingly, *Fist of Fury* in Hong Kong), the ritual is sanctified when he gets his chest sliced open with a sword. Visually, *Chinese Connection* is a considerable step up from the film that made him a star. It's a colorful period piece, set in Shanghai of 1907, with Lee handsomely outfitted in either all white or all black as a Chinese boxing student whose master has mysteriously died in full health. A rival Japanese school stops by to insult the Chinese and call them chickens. Their teacher wouldn't condone the violence, so they stand there and take the abuse until one among them steps up to the challenge.

And he doesn't just take on one of the bozos. Bruce Lee takes on the entire school, and doffs his jacket to reveal a naked chest to do it properly. With his bare hands and feet, the guy is unstoppable, but give him a pair of nunchuku (two sticks conjoined by a chain) and it's as if he has bolts of lightning at his command.

Chinese Connection gives Lee his best role, a student out to avenge the murder of his master, while getting to wear a variety of disguises in order to learn the designs of his enemies. In one outing, he's cute in his cap posing as a rickshaw boy who lifts his passenger into midair, rickshaw and all, before tossing him down the alley. In another, he plays a scene as a simpleton telephone repairman with thick glasses who overhears a plot to have himself killed and witnesses a demonstration of strength by the Russian recruit hired for the job.

When he finally gets to fight the Russkie, he does it bare-chested, naturally, and director and cinematographer have made sure he's beautifully lit and framed. His fighting style is as unique an expression of self as he intended the martial arts to be in his teaching. Poised, reticulated, and graceful, his body fluidly assesses the dangers around it, and then—zap!—his fist flashes into action, often staying frozen in space after contact, vibrating with power as if still expending lethal energy.

He's more like a snake than a dragon.

His style, an amalgam of disciplines combined with his personal philosophy, instead of the dogma of one school or another, became known as "Jeet Kune Do," or "The Style of the Intercepting Fist."

Even with a few more appearances on *Longstreet*, and both Paramount and Warner Bros. interested in having him star in a TV series (he wanted to do a western called *The Warrior*, which later became *Kung Fu*), he couldn't pass up the potential opportunity to use the Hong Kong films as a springboard to success in the West.

Besides, he got to write and direct *The Way of the Dragon*. Unfortunately, it's the worst of his completed films. It's known in the States as *Return of the Dragon* (1973) because it was released after *Enter the Dragon*, his last film.

It's a shame it isn't better, because the basic set-up couldn't be simpler and the idea suggests a character he could have trademarked in future movies. Lee plays a sweet and smiley cousin sent to Rome to help relatives who own a restaurant that the syndicate wants for real estate purposes.

He's such a gentle guy that the relations in Rome aren't sure what good he'll do them...until he has his first fight. Though his opponents are all out of shape or unskilled—and Lee has been criticized for never giving himself a worthy foe in terms of skill or physique—when one pair of nunchuku is met by the arrival of a half dozen more men, he pulls out a second pair and astonishes us by twirling and then wielding both at the same time with equal speed and ferocity. It's one of the few times in which he allows a little humor into his combat.

A key bad guy is also a flagrant fruit who looks Bruce up and down and tucks in his belt for him, but it's Chuck Norris who ultimately takes on Lee inside the Coliseum for the film's climax, refereed by a kitten. Even with a world-ranked karate champ like Norris, Lee never seems in trouble, though the moment when Bruce rips a handful of Chuck's chest hair out by the roots is a highlight.

The opening fight in *Enter the Dragon* (1973) has Bruce Lee in nothing but a pair of black undies. That's what they look like anyway. Talk about immediate gratification. In perhaps the most famous martial arts film ever, due in large part to the Americans co-producing in order to capitalize on the craze, Lee plays a martial artist hired by the British to infiltrate the drug and prostitution business of an international criminal by entering his exclusive island tournament.

Also on the island are John Saxon, avoiding $175,000 in gambling debts, and Jim Kelly, an African-American harassed by white bigot cops whom he puts in their place. If it can be imagined, Lee is even leaner here than in his previous films, but he's also not allowed much in the way of a character. He's the strong, silent type; the only guy of the trio who refuses a woman or four when provided by their evil host.

In fact, for being a sex symbol, the only time Lee appeared in a sex scene, he was passed out. In *Fists of Fury*, he drinks more than his giddy fill after being promoted to foreman by the corrupt boss, who also provides him with a woman. All she can do is stroke the incredible hard contours of his bare chest while he's unconscious. Of course that's not all she can do, but the scene doesn't dare to go further. It's a great, sexy fantasy—the idea, I mean, of having such a god lying there at your mercy.

The entire island is at his mercy in *Enter the Dragon*. The actor sliced up one of his hands during a . fight in which his opponent wields a broken bottle, everybody remembers the hall of mirrors battle at the finale. The lead villain, who in Bond-like form has a thing for white cats and wears a gloved metal hand, outfits himself with a steel bear claw and then a four-bladed vegetable slicer for the showdown.

Lee gets his face slit, then his belly, from which he tastes his own blood in one of those inspired moments of odd genius that make legends even more legendary. His chest gets the quadruple slash next and then we're treated to the artsy and visually rich multiple imagery of Lee as he makes his way through slivered reflections of himself, a concept as cool in its own way as the mirrored climax Orson Welles orchestrated for *The Lady From Shanghai* (1948).

Lee only saw a rough cut of *Enter the Dragon*. He began suffering from a series of headaches and inexplicable blackouts in April of 1973. On July 20, 1973, while in Hong Kong, he reportedly took some medication to arrest a headache before a business dinner, laid down, and never regained consciousness. The official cause of death was cerebral edema, or a swelling of the brain.

In what works out strangely enough to be a tribute to his unique gifts, his considerable status as a cult figure was already assured. He didn't have to die young to earn it. But since he did, the conspiracy theories mingled with the books and documentaries and feature film biographies that inevitably followed. His own writings, interviews, personal correspondence, and martial arts instruction and philosophy have also been published.

Six years after his death, ten minutes of fight footage he had shot for a film that was put on hold—because the deal for *Enter the Dragon* had been signed—was tacked onto the ending of *Game of Death* (1979), which used jarring and unmatched clips of Lee from previous films mixed in with work by an obvious double in large, dark sunglasses. The new Lee footage was formerly worth fast-forwarding to for fans, but can now be appreciated, along with much more of the master at work, in the documentary *Bruce Lee: A Warrior's Journey* (2000), which concludes with a fascinating reconstruction of Lee's original intent for the film. Prior to the release of this material, you had to sit through the awful *Game of Death* to take in Lee's 5'7" awkward combat with a 7'2" Kareem Abdul Jabbar, who's outfitted in short-shorts that reveal the straps of his jock whenever he tumbles to the floor. Lee is attired in a snappy yellow jumper with black stripes and when he pulls out his nunchuku, it's nice to see they're color-coordinated. In another one of those special moments that Lee affords each of his films, he inexplicably licks the ends of his weapons as he prepares for battle.

Even weirder than seeing all the inserted clips and, at one point, what looks to be an actor holding a cardboard cut-out of Lee's face in front of a mirror, *Game of Death* has the Lee character playing a martial arts film star and there's a re-creation of the finale from *Chinese Connection* in which his character runs toward a line of men aiming guns at him. One of the extras, in reality a syndicate member, takes out the blank from his weapon and puts in a live round, resulting in Lee's character being shot in the face and a subsequent faking of his death through the world media to allow him to seek revenge.

You must know where I'm going with this, because you can't watch the film without thinking about it. Lee's only son, **Brandon Lee** (1965-1993), who was on the verge of achieving his own level of fame as an American action star, was fatally wounded while shooting a scene in *The Crow* (1994) in which a live round was accidentally left in the barrel of a prop gun that was aimed and fired at him by another actor.

Bruce Lee never made a good film. But he was never less than an artist of great physical presence and prowess in those which he graced. He once told an interviewer that motion pictures meant "motion" to him, that dialogue should be kept to a minimum. Like a silent film star or a ballet dancer, Bruce Lee could express himself with the sound off. He showed us physical beauty manifested in physical violence, an emblematic paradox of the cinema.

"Tell him to take off his sweater and look at the camera," director Luchino Visconti instructed the boy's grandmother. Little else was apparently said...or required.

Death in Venice is a tale so precariously on the brink of pederasty that it is more often read as a tale of morality than one of mortality. Like Scripture, it is many things to many people. It is about homosexuality and it is not about homosexuality. It is about a search for purity and beauty and inspiration and it is about the corruption of purity and beauty and inspiration. It is about supreme self-sacrifice and it is about pathetic suicide.

It is also about "a dirty old man chasing a kid's ass."

That's how the American studio committed to financing the 1971 film version reportedly saw it. They wanted to change the teenage boy in the story to a teenage girl. Tadzia instead of Tadzio. Europeans might be willing to stomach the degenerate, but America still liked boy/girl stories even if they had to be man/girl stories. A middle-aged married man falling head over heels at the sight of a 14-year old girl may not have been proper, but it was certainly more palatable than the alternative. If there was a saving grace, unlike all the problems with *Baby Doll* and *Lolita*, in this story the man would only pine over the girl, not molest her.

The classic story has inspired operas, ballets, plays, short films, videos, and poems. It has become a *Cliffs' Notes* critical reference overused by reviewers whenever they find themselves confronted with the older man, younger man love story, most recently in connection with both *Love and Death on Long Island* (1998) and *Gods and Monsters* (1998). It's the politically correct literary reference to safeguard male-male March/November romances from more hostile, prejudiced, and improper accusations.

Björn Andresen (1955-   ), a Swedish boy all of 15 whose grandmother brought him to director Luchino Visconti's European casting call for the perfect Tadzio, had no idea what the film was about. He had made one appearance on film prior to this, but the idea of starring in another one didn't appeal to him until he was assured his salary would cover an electric guitar and a motorbike he coveted.

Though Björn was actually found by Visconti in Stockholm on the first day of his heralded search, and Visconti knew he had his boy, prior commitments meant the director had to at least go through the motions of an international scouting and auditioned hundreds more hopefuls before returning to his original choice. An unsubstantiated entry in *Guinness* for the largest disparity in actor salaries between two leads reports Björn was paid $5000 while star Dirk Bogarde managed exactly 100 times that amount.

In a 1978 published memoir, *Snakes and Ladders*, Bogarde recounts a nervous Warner Bros. slashing Visconti's budget because of his refusal to cast someone other than Bogarde in the lead. A big chunk of change then went to securing the rights after the project was underway and they discovered someone else owned them. The actor said he was paid only $40,000 for the five-month shoot along with a percentage that he never received. He probably would have accepted even less. The role was the pinnacle of his career, his "Hamlet," and he knew it.

Thomas Mann's 1912 novella was based on an amalgamation of 72-year old Goethe's infatuation with a 17-year old girl and Mann's own infatuation, at age 36, with a Polish youth while vacationing in Venice in 1911. He also knew of the similar lamentations of composer Gustav Mahler, whose death he learned of while abroad on that trip, and who became the cinematic doppelgänger in Visconti's film version. The original story follows a middle-aged writer named Aschenbach, vacationing in Venice, who suddenly and quite unexpectedly finds himself enamored of a teenage boy on the beach. His contemplation of the boy's beauty in Socratic and Platonic inner dialogues play on his intellect and ultimately bring about his demise. Inspired by the young man's beauty to write again, he cannot find it within him to leave for safety once it is clear that cholera is spreading throughout the city.

Aschenbach's "eyes embraced that noble figure at the blue water's edge, and in rising ecstasy he felt he was gazing on Beauty itself, on Form as a thought of God, on the one and pure perfection which dwells in the spirit and of which a human image and likeness had here been lightly and graciously set up for him to worship."

In the film, the writer is a composer, Gustav von Aschenbach, brilliantly played by the aforementioned British actor Dirk Bogarde, made up to resemble Mahler amidst a soundtrack steeped in the composer's work. This wasn't Bogarde's first trip to gaydom, either. Ten years prior he had distinguished himself playing a married barrister blackmailed for his relationship with a young male lover in *Victim* (1961), the first film to use the word "homosexual" and one of the earliest attempts to portray such men as people, not perverts. There are also varying degrees of gay overtones, muted and overt, to Bogarde's roles in *The Spanish Gardener* (1956), *The Singer Not the Song* (1961), *The Servant* (1963), and *Modesty Blaise* (1966).

Critics almost equally split over the 130-minute *Death*, a lavish, slowly paced, largely non-verbal work. Debates raged among those who saw it as a masterpiece, a cinematic work of art, and those who felt Visconti had done little more than reduce Mann's greatest literary work to a pathetic portrait of homosexual lust.

That's the crux of art. No two people see it quite the same way. If on the printed page Mann's story transcends physical longing and provides a powerful metaphor for creative and intellectual ascent and descent, on film, Visconti could never have satisfied those who prefer to believe Mann's intent was entirely ascetic. Visconti spoiled his film for them the moment a protracted panning shot across a crowded room connected a middle aged man's gaze with the image of an epicene youth in a sailor suit.

I could not care less. *Death in Venice* is potentially all of that philosophical wax (and more), but it is also quite specifically a tragic and mournful self-realization of homosexual desire. Desire for lost youth, lost opportunities, and lost love, too.

It is also about the accursed awakening of a desire to have lived a life one has failed to live—that awful brew of inspiration and resignation every time you see an attractive young couple walking hand in hand down the street. It makes you feel romantic in ways you know you'll never share with someone else. You smile at the thought while your heart sinks into gloom. Those kinds of relationships are for other people. In the film, Aschenbach is shown to have been a happily married man with a beautiful wife and daughter. Tragedy strikes and they lose their child. His inspiration lost, his foolish love of life gone, he grows increasingly cold and bitter, reducing his work to calculated mathematics. The crowds boo his latest symphony. He's lost it. His health is precarious. He needs a rest.

Confronting Andresen's Renaissance beauty is to confront an androgyny so metaphysical that a gay man can't help but contemplate the potential of a subverted attraction to girls at some time or another in his life. He's almost preternaturally effeminate, his long blond locks flowing around his face as if he'd stepped out of a Pierre-Narcisse Guérin painting and pointed headlong toward Leif Garrett's and Taylor Hanson's teenybopper stardom on the way to Calvin Klein supermodel Travis Fimmel.

With his straw hat, he is Donatello's David. At the end, a dying Aschenbach watches his beloved Tadzio humiliated by a boy friend on the beach. The rejected youth then steps out into the sea. One arm poised on his hip, he inexplicably points into the distance and Aschenbach succumbs. The composer had gone to the local barber earlier in the day and indulged the stylist's attempt to make him look young. He dies a grotesque figure, appearing more like a white-faced corpse with ghastly red lipstick, clownish rouge, and rivulets of black hair dye running down his face.

All cast members other than Bogarde were reportedly told not to read the novella, but young Björn finally managed to get a copy and is said to have told Bogarde: "Now I know who I am. I'm the Angel of Death, right?"

Off screen, the teenager was fond of his black chewing gum and the Beatles, Bogarde tells us, but on screen, he was an ethereal beauty asked to do little else but sit and pose without expression. As the film progresses, the boy begins to acknowledge his suitor in subtle ways, ably balancing the suggestion that he might have an inkling of what is going on, and therefore teasing the older man, with the possibility that he is also acknowledging the man's attentions the only way he can, with a glance from across the dining room, a turn, or a smile.

"You should never smile like that...you must never smile at anyone like that," says an anguished Aschenbach to himself after passing the boy and passionately taking note of an ambiguous grin. "I love you!"

I remember showing the film to a friend, foolishly confessing that whenever I watched it I was reduced to tears, only to have him find the sight of Tadzio's blank face and Mona Lisa smiles goofy in their repetition. Wouldn't it have been more interesting dramatically if the kid were in on the whole thing, if we

Björn Andresen as Tadzio, "the Angel of Death," who bewitches a middle-aged composer in Visconti's *Death in Venice* (1971). YESTERDAY

Tadzio promenades before Dirk Bogarde's Aschenbach in *Death in Venice* (1971). YESTERDAY

knew he was tormenting this fellow, he suggested afterwards, as I searched for reviews from well-known critics to bolster my emotional commitment to it.

Visconti had it just right. Aschenbach can never believe that Tadzio could actually have reciprocated in any way. Tadzio is an archetype (a "twink" in modern gay parlance), only desirable in the agony of being unattainable. Tadzio is, indeed, Beauty sculpted as a Boy, a simultaneously life-affirming and life-extinguishing ideological conceit, all at once nourishing and depleting emotion and intellect.

As the boy comes into closer and closer proximity to the man (once across the room and across the beach, now sharing an elevator), the strain becomes almost unbearable. Coming upon the boy wearing his form-fitting striped swimsuit while walking under a canopy toward the beach, Aschenbach is stunned and brought nearly to a faint as the young man playfully and deliberately promenades before him, crossing in front of the old man's path then circling each of the canopy's support poles before stepping in front of him again. Visconti has played out the tease, the dance, the unspoken relationship of the entire film for us in microcosm.

Deciding to leave Venice for his physical and mental health, the fuss-budget, cranky composer is suddenly rejuvenated when he realizes that his luggage has been misrouted and can be used as an excuse to return to Venice, where he now knows a plague is arriving on the winds of the sirocco. He willingly returns to a place fraught with death and decay in order to once more lay eyes upon the object of his desire.

As Goethe suggests, and Visconti paraphrased to Bogarde, "If you ever look upon perfect beauty, then you must die."

Flushed with music, including Beethoven's "Für Elise" (a tune chosen because Andresen could play it on the piano, it links both the boy and a whore whom Aschenbach fails to make love to in flashback), the film is a triumphant marriage of the stunning visuals, both interior and exterior, photographed by Pasquale De Santis, with Mahler's 3rd and 5th symphonies. They are paintings set to music, a masterful opera of imagery and orchestration.

As for the boy Thomas Mann was obsessing over that summer of 1911, he would later be identified as Wladyslaw Moes (1900 – 1986), nicknamed "Adzio," whose cousin gave him the book in 1924 after she noticed its amazing likeness to his family. He saw the film version in 1971 and contacted his dear friend, the other boy on the beach, by letter. For more, read *The Real Tadzio* (Carroll & Graf, 2003), Gilbert Adair's biographical sketch and essay, which falters only when ludicrously attempting to argue that a time will come when Björn Andresen's beauty "will seem just as frumpy as his turn-of-the-century model."

To gaze at Tadzio on that beach is to gaze into the soul of every gay man inspired by Beauty but painfully aware that it can never be had. When I see him (on film, on a street corner, in a coffee shop), I can't help but see my entire youth lost to keeping a secret. Falling in love from afar and having to make do with that. Settling for a momentary glance or an illusory smile.

As for young Björn, rumors of his death have been greatly exaggerated. He appeared in a half-dozen other Swedish films, including *En Kärlekshistoria* (*A Swedish Love Story*; 1970), which saw re-release in Sweden in 2003, and had a starring role at age 22 in *Bluff Stop* (1977). He married in 1983.

Björn Andresen couldn't have been a teen idol, even though that's exactly what he was, because the source of his idolatry was a grown man. Of course, the source of all teen idolatry is rooted in some aspect of potentially unwieldy desire.

Teen idol boys and teen idol girls are sold to their peers on their desirability, their cuteness, their sexiness. They're kissable, huggable, sizzling, hot, and adorable. You can learn their intimate secrets, twenty things that turn them on, and what they look for in the opposite sex all by turning to the pages of your favorite teen mag.

The teen magazines that flaunted their teenybopper idols' half-naked flesh with such abandon presumed to know that we all wanted to see them that way. Opposite sex or otherwise. The idea is that the teen actor is being "sexy" for a presumed teenaged girl readership, but what is it that girls are looking at when they see a skinny boy with his shirt off? Musculature? Or development? And what kind of development?

Could it be about nipples? I doubt it. Too gender non-specific. Belly buttons? Perhaps. Especially if a trail of hair descended from it into the idol's tight pants. How about armpit hair? Possibly…in a generally unacknowledged and perhaps unconscious way. Only in an evolving commercial photography aesthetic that began in the 1960s and flowered in the 1970s (fashion, advertising, motion picture—oh, and skin magazines) did the male armpit attain its rightful place as erotic signifier and sexual transmitter in the modern age. What other possible purpose could there be for a male model to pose in an advertisement with one or both hands at the back of his head than to show off his armpits? Armpit hair is sexy…that's why. Okay, so maybe not on your Uncle Lou, but it is on a streamlined model like Joel West. Check out West's famous late 1990s ad for Calvin Klein's *Escape* and you'll note that his armpit and its terrific splay of black hairs are actually the center attraction. His face and chest and washboard stomach are all supporting players. Armpit hair is, after all, a secondary sexual characteristic (just like pubic hair), so it has irrevocable ties to sexuality that for many have been subverted by the deodorant industry.

At one time in their life, believe it or not, guys are actually proud of their armpit hair, even if they won't admit it. ("I remember when my friend Sal first sprouted underarm hair," said Johnny Depp to a magazine. "We were about 11, and I was very jealous. I still hold a grudge.") Boy band N'Sync's first hit video in the late 1990s included a teen-dreamy shot of star boy Justin Timberlake reclined in bed with one arm up and over his head, affording a glamorous framing of pretty boy face (feminine) and hairy armpit (masculine—see, I'm a man), as classical and deliberate a sensual composition as the Hellenistic full nude Barberini Faun of 200 B.C.E.

Even as a kid, I wondered what girls thought of when they looked at these shirtless boys. I knew what I thought was sexy, but was it the same for them? I remember standing in the hallway in my high school one late afternoon when the guys were coming in from practice out on the football field. A trio of girls was already in place for the event and watched from the windows, where I joined them under the pretense of school pride. One of the players was an amazingly handsome young man who also, as it turned out, was such an early bloomer that by the time he got to high school he had quite a bit of manly hair on his chest and a pronounced trail of fur running down the center of his belly and into his pants. "Whoa, look at all the hair on that guy!" one of the girls squealed to her friends. They all giggled and I gloated in silence. I now realize that there wouldn't have been a different response if we were all adults at a strip show. Women tend to joke and laugh and have fun. Men tend to stay quiet and carry out inner imaginings, unless they're socially masking their interest in gross displays of macho hooting and hollering. For me, the minor event left a lasting impression. I enjoyed hearing the girls talk about the guys' bodies like that. I wanted to join them.

As with *Playgirl*, even more so, teenybopper magazines were also purchased (or stolen) by gay teenagers (and, dare I mention it, lonely gay men). So what is it exactly that these shirtless shots of teen stars are preparing their female readers for? More of the same in *Playgirl*? I fondly recall the days when 1970s teen star Leif Garrett's skintight pants habitually revealed the exact location and distribution of his genitalia, and the appearance of Bruce Penhall's scrotum out the seam of his short-shorts in a hotly sought-after teen magazine of yesteryear that I used to own but cannot for the life of me find.

If girls like to see boys with their shirts off, even if it's just the pure pleasure of bare skin exposure, then so do other boys who happen to be gay. I longed for an episode of *The Partridge Family* (1970-74) in which Keith would take off his shirt. That turned out to be such a rarity, but I was always hopeful. The episode (#43, "I Am Curious Partridge") in which Danny starts the rumor that Keith (David Cassidy) has a heart tattooed on his derriere was a particular favorite, especially when some of the guys in his gym class try to sneak a peek while he's showering. Clever Keith—he's wearing a towel.

Before someone caught on and changed him into thicker jeans for the second season, it was always a pleasure to watch the earliest *Partridge* episodes for glimpses of Keith's impressively well-defined bulge. It was about this time that I learned what "dressing to the right" meant. Later, there were the constricting pants worn by Sweathogs on *Welcome Back, Kotter* (1975-79), especially Laurence-Hilton Jacobs, and then John Schneider of *The Dukes of Hazzard* (1979-85), a show I never had any interest in, and still don't, outside of periodic checks to see if things below Bo Duke's belt are as I remember them.

David Cassidy, under enormous pressure and teenybopper image strain, tried to put a wicked spin on his candy ass image by posing nude and talking about his fans' wet panties for an infamous issue of *Rolling Stone* (5/11/72), but it backfired into scandal. The cover photo by Annie Leibovitz is surprisingly unattractive, a weird effeminization of her subject, making him look like a French actress with unshaved pits lounging on the lawn. The centerfold is much more aesthetically pleasing, though it injudiciously cuts off after a slim border of revealed pubic hair. Reprints of the image in subsequent books show even more bush, but not even a hint of the big cock that led his siblings to nickname him "Donk" (for donkey).

In his 1994 book *C'Mon Get Happy*, Cassidy states at the outset that he's not going to get trashy, but thankfully ignores his own censure. We learn that he was an early bloomer, that "I walked around with a hard-on all day. At 13, all I did was play with myself. That's all I can remember—thinking about getting laid, getting blown." He was fixated on women sucking him off. And he even posed for Gina Lollobrigida's private book of cock photos, surely among the most wanted books in the history of printing.

Buster and Billie Jo have decided to go skinny-dipping, though you have to wonder why because the rushing water looks like pure sludge. Billie Jo has got her back turned and Buster's watching her from behind a tree, sitting on a stump. He smiles at us, almost as if to acknowledge what's on our dirty little minds, stands up, and then casually pulls down his pants and underwear. The camera follows his peel just enough to catch his pubic hair, and the sight shocks us upright in our seats.

A cut back to Billie Jo still readying takes only a moment and then—good God!—there he is, **Jan-Michael Vincent** (1945-) matter-of-factly stepping out from behind the tree and into full view naked as a jaybird! Our prayers had been answered. And a still frame of the moment from *Buster and Billie* (1974) would be enshrined in *Playboy*'s "Sex in the Cinema" (an anxiously-awaited annual source for the occasional male nude shot from the movies) and reprinted hundreds of times in skin magazines and celebrity nudie rags in the decades to come, far outreaching the number of people who saw or even heard of the film when it was in theatres. (Bruce Weber managed to put the clip back up on the big screen as part of his 2001 docu-scrapbook *Chop Suey*.)

It was a big deal. Bigger, in many ways, than had Marlon Brando persuaded his dangle to make an appearance in *Last Tango*. Why? Because Jan-Michael Vincent was a beauty, because Jan-Michael Vincent was so hot that you'd already fantasized about what he'd look like naked, and because Jan-Michael Vincent was a known entity—a mini-movie star, not a relative unknown like Don Johnson or an urban legend like Joe Dallesandro. (All three had been featured in various states of undress in *After Dark* magazine, the only place that treated star and chorus member with equal reverence for the way in which light and shadow played across their respective bare bums.)

Born in Colorado, but raised in California, Vincent grew up surrounded by extended family criminal activity, though his strait-laced father was an ex-Army pilot who had a billboard business in Hanford. The blond good-looker lasted a year and a half studying art at Ventura City College before drifting to Mexico and the beaches, leaving a wife and daughter behind. Back in the states, he joined the National Guard and worked on helicopters in order to avoid being drafted.

An advertising agent noticed Jan-Michael's high school swimming team physique and astonishing good looks while at the billboard shop and recommended him to gay talent agent Dick Clayton, who had handled James Dean's Hollywood career in 1954 and '55.

At 19, he began his dabble in acting, first in *The Bandits* (1967), shot in Mexico and starring Robert Conrad, which led to a contract with Universal, though it wasn't even released until 1979 as *Crossfire*. TV gigs in Hollywood included three episodes of *Lassie*, two on *Bonanza*, another on *Dragnet*, and a live-action adventure film series shown as part of *The Banana Splits Adventure Hour*.

He's billed as Michael Vincent in both *Journey to Shiloh* (1968), a Texan Civil War drama in which he plays Little Bit Luckett alongside Harrison Ford's Willie Bill Bearden, and *The Undefeated* (1969), the less-than-momentous teaming of John Wayne and Rock Hudson in a post-Civil War western. He's Bubba Wilkes, the shiny young suitor of Rock's daughter, but she's smitten with Wayne's "adopted" Indian son Blue Boy and Bubba gets left with nothing to do.

He played the teenaged son of Lana Turner and Kevin McCarthy on the short-lived (three and a half months) ABC-TV drama *The Survivors* (1969-70), based on a Harold Robbins literary stew. Also on TV, *Tribes* (1970) found him as a long-haired "hippie" drafted into Darren McGavin's Marine Corps. As with most military basic training films, the incessant hollering (though without the expletives for television) makes for boring by-the-numbers drama done to death. Watching rows of men being insulted, humiliated, and degraded just doesn't do it for me no matter how tantalizing and campy it sounds. Perhaps because I was spared military service, I don't get the same knowing chuckle out of the whole process that several generations of men experienced as part of their ritualized coming of age in America. Regardless, *Tribes* hit the small screen in the midst of Vietnam, so it was a timely, if not particularly compelling look at the military mentality and hippie pacifism.

Jan-Michael then played Robert Mitchum's teenage son in a dark drama about a wife-killer who tries to reconnect with his boy whilst a load of songs interrupt on the soundtrack in *Going Home* (1971). An even more macho teaming was as the crooked and inquisitive son of a murdered crime boss who weasels his way into a job as an associate to Charles Bronson's *The Mechanic* (1972), an underworld term for a hit man.

Writer John Lewis Carlino, who would later direct Rob Lowe in a scene in *Class* (1983) with the actor outfitted in red panties and bra, wrote the screenplay of *The Mechanic* as a gay love/hate story between two male criminals. Hollywood didn't want to make that story, though, and nobody wanted to play it. George C. Scott was the original choice for the Bronson role and he turned it down flat. Bronson and Vincent reportedly agreed to go forward only if the homosexuality was excised, which it was, though several critics still managed to sniff it.

Years later, Vincent appeared in a controversial installment of the ABC series *Hotel* (1983-88) in which he combats a group of fag-bashers on behalf of a gay soldier, but then walks away from his former friendship because, he explains, "I was brought up not to accept this sort of thing."

A pretty boy himself who peaked in the movies at a time when movies were being made—for better and worse—more openly about homosexuality, Vincent was a prime candidate for just "this sort of thing." He was considered for a time to play the killer in a version of Gerald Walker's novel *Cruising* when it was being mulled over in 1973, and, on the flip side, was being touted as an ideal candidate to play the young Olympic hopeful who falls in love with his track coach in the often talked about, but never realized film version of Patricia Nell Warren's 1974 gay "classic" *The Front Runner*. Paul Newman was thought perfect for the part of the coach, and a Newman/Vincent love story would have had a meaningful impact on the gay movement's cause in the 1970s.

I tried to watch *The Mechanic* as if it really was about two gay men and I thought it might work when Vincent's first shot is from behind as he walks into frame and we see his ass in blue jeans before we see anything else of him. But it doesn't hold up much after that, even if Bronson lives alone in a beautifully decorated house in the hills, listens to classical music while he plans his assassinations, and one of their hits involves Vincent hijacking a "Chicken Lickin'" delivery van. He's the chicken we should be lickin', but it's an ugly, heartless film. Both actors are deadpan serious to the point where Vincent's being cute doesn't occur to you anymore. I can't imagine the film being much less than the *Cruising* (1980) of its era had it been done "gay," anyway, so the "Bang, you're dead" finale is the nicest surprise it has going.

Leave it to Disney to lighten the mood and put Jan-Michael Vincent back where he belonged: in a loincloth as *The World's Greatest Athlete* (1973), a film for which I have some personally significant memories. I was 11, now fully certain that I was attracted to boys and not girls, and I remember the thrill of watching this young blond, nearly naked god running through the jungle. It was as close to sex as I was going to get in a G-rated movie and Jan-Michael Vincent was probably the first movie star that I distinctly recall responding to in a sexual way; that is, his body, his sheer physical beauty, and the anticipation of seeing it, was reason enough to sit through the rest of the silly movie.

Essentially *A Boy and His Tiger*, the film even has a romantic slow motion run through the meadow that shows Nanu (Vincent) passing the open arms of Jane only to collide and roll around with Harry, his tiger, who, in other moments, enjoys licking Nanu's arm and, most frighteningly, taking his throat in his mouth during a scene in which Vincent playfully wrestles with him. Why, oh why, oh why, though, does Nanu sleep in pajamas while he's here in the US? I remember wondering that even when I was 11, though I certainly missed any inkling of queer thought concerning the young lady's decision to tutor Nanu on Ancient Greece right after his biology lesson.

The World's Greatest Athlete was a big box-office hit in 1973, all the more reason that Jan-Michael Vincent's full-frontal in his very next feature film, *Buster and Billie*, was such a profound event. It was even his idea. He acknowledged the fact that women always had to get naked in the movies and wanted to do likewise because it was just fair play.

He also liked the script a great deal. It starts out as something of a cousin to *Summer of '42* (1971). It's a crude, though likable period piece set at Greenwood High School in 1948 Georgia. We meet Buster at the urinal trough in the boys' room. It's a movie preoccupied with sex in purely in-and-out terms. Buster's got blue balls big time and can't get his gal to let him sow his oats. Jeez, didn't anybody know what a hand-job was back then?

"If a man doesn't reach a climax every time that he gets excited, he's liable to develop kidney trouble and die young," says Buster to Pamela Sue Martin, claiming to cite a *Reader's Digest* article written by a doctor. Her answer to that predicament is to stop doing even what little they have been doing so he won't get himself excited.

"I always said you can't believe everything you read," he quickly adds.

Jan-Michael Vincent is so fucking cute in this film, especially during a lamp-lit bedroom scene he shares with future Freddy Kreuger and real-life close pal Robert Englund. Then there's the way he wears his little cowboy hat at the beach…and then again to the picnic where he meets Billie Jo. And he's got an adorable habit of wearing those shirts without sleeves.

The only thing I can't understand is why he cares about Billie Jo, the plump and mildly retarded girl abused by the local boys and forced to have sex with them. It's not that he shouldn't care, it's just that the film never convinces us why he does. They go to a drive-in and see a Johnny Weissmuller Tarzan movie. Billie Jo becomes a transformed woman, reading Buster his Captain Marvel comic books and tending to him when he's sick, but we all know this is leading towards something very ugly.

Echoing *Last Summer* (1969), the powerful and controversial teen flick that ends with the shocking rape of an unpopular girl by boys who were her "friends," *Buster and Billie* also portends the tragedy of another Billie Joe, *Ode to Billy Joe* (1976), in which a Southern teen played by the lovely and omnipresent Robby Benson engages in a freak act of homosexuality and subsequently jumps to his death from the Tallahatchie Bridge.

With *Buster and Billie*, you have to wonder what the point is to the film's uncompromising turn to viciousness. It would have been more dramatic to have the two young lovers say "fuck you" to everybody and go off together. As it is, the film has a brutally dark end that, I'll selfishly and narrow-mindedly admit, ruins all the scenes of sexuality before it, even rendering them creepy—like the first unflattering p.o.v. shot of Billie Jo after Vincent's full-frontal, which moves in on her chalky white body like a stalker in a slasher film.

There's a little of *Walking Tall*'s (1973) Buford Pusser in Vincent's Carrol Jo Hummer of *White Line Fever* (1975), the story of one honest trucker's refusal to haul contraband and the violent consequences of that decision. Next, he's teamed as the good brother of butt-ugly Kris Kristofferson in the gratingly bad *Vigilante Force* (1976), in which a small town harassed by undesirables hires bad boy Kris to come in with his gang of criminals and clean up. They end up taking over the town. Excitement comes from the anticipation that at any moment some straight-lipped drone might break loose and resemble a performance. Vincent is as flat a board as Kristofferson. During the climax, younger bro decked out in overalls runs around shooting at older bro decked out in a city band uniform.

Just when it looked like all he had left in him were drive-in flicks, he co-starred with Gene Hackman, James Coburn, and Candice Bergen in *Bite the Bullet* (1975), the story of a 700-mile horse race. His character, Carbo, is the hotshot boy looking for a reputation who gets his kicks out of provoking fights and punching a jackass. It's too bad he's so unlikable instead of just a cocky squirt. Regarded by some as something of a classic, the film has a plot and characters too thin to sustain the running time.

He's unbelievably rejected from the Marines for being uncoordinated in the low-key *Baby Blue Marine* (1976). How they could toss out such an obviously able physique is a quandary of the script when you cast a specimen like Jan-Michael Vincent. He plays Marion Hedgepeth, a doe-eyed, sweet, and soft-spoken young man who gets sucker-punched in an alley by a burnt-out 20-year old Marine Raider played by Richard Gere in snow white hair. Uniforms are exchanged and Vincent is suddenly seen as a Jap-killing war hero during a stop in a small California town where he falls in love with a local girl. Folks get suspicious because he's the softest Marine anybody's ever seen.

He's fighting giant scorpions and hordes of man-eating cockroaches in the low-budget sci-fi flick *Damnation Alley* (1977), then part of the stunt man fun of Burt Reynolds' *Hooper* (1978). He followed with a character close to himself in painful ways, playing a drunken young surfer in *Big Wednesday* (1978).

The film visits three best friends at four different junctions of their lives from the summer of 1962 to the spring of 1974. Ironically, considering the enormous problem with alcohol that would plague Vincent's personal life, he's drunk from the get-go. Miraculously, the ocean revives him. His buddies are played by off-screen buddies Gary Busey, who willingly and curiously gets basted with warm butter during a party, and William Katt, still awfully cute in his post-*Carrie* (1976) days and heralding a curly-headed Christopher Atkins yet to come.

As for Jan-Michael, he's a shirtless Adonis whose physique looks positively carved out of marble— tanned marble. He's got a divot in his sternum that makes his chest look like it was assembled out of plates perfectly pieced together at the factory. Turn him upside down and I'd bet you'd find a trademark stamp and date of manufacture.

Gorgeously photographed, *Big Wednesday* is a mythological surfer's romp and macho rite of passage that quickly turns into the shattering of innocence in the face of Vietnam. By 1965, Vincent is a bum, causing trouble on the beach where Katt is now a lifeguard. All he ever wanted to do was surf with his friends, but times have changed and they've grown up to be very different people. Vincent's given the opportunity to become a local celebrity but says he's not interested in being in magazines for kids to look up to because "I'm a drunk and a screw-up." Only Katt will enlist in the service. The others contrive entertaining ways of trying to avoid it.

By 1968, Vincent runs a swimming pool service. Still recognized as one of the originators of the hot-dogging modern style of surfing, he's invited to a film that includes him in its documentary footage. It's there that he realizes he's just a ten-second footnote. Only Big Wednesday, the great swell of the spring of '74 which swallows surfers and spits out their boards, can redeem him as the three best friends reunite.

The film was not a hit. You might not have expected the once hot actor, at age 32 and succumbing to alcohol and drug addiction, to get another chance. In 1983, he played Robert Mitchum's son once again, this time in the hugely popular television miniseries *The Winds of War*. Vincent then landed the lead in CBS television's action-adventure series *Airwolf* (1984-86), playing a crafty pilot who steals back a high-tech helicopter from a foreign power and then uses it to carry out missions while forcing the US government to search for his brother, a Vietnam MIA.

The show was a hit and Vincent was paid handsomely. But after the first season, his drinking worsened and put the show in behind-the-scenes jeopardy. The series was canceled after a shaky second season. Even at the height of his moneymaking rebirth, the personal burdens proved too self-destructive.

Jan-Michael Vincent's off-screen traumas compounded in the 1990s, a decade during which he was involved in DUIs, alleged spousal abuse, and multiple wrecks. He famously showed up on the set of *Red Line* (1996) only a few days after a devastating motorcycle accident and the horrifying proof is captured on film, since he insisted on doing the job. His mangled, stitched, and puffy face simply became a part of his character's recent past. He even makes ad-libbed mention of looking like Frankenstein, "with zippers in my lips."

Another crash, this time in a car, in August of 1996 resulted in his breaking his neck. This, too, he would recover from without paralysis, making a shocking appearance on Howard Stern's show, and then finding himself the subject of magazine, TV entertainment, and news show pieces on how the beast destroyed his beauty. Many of them showed pathetic footage of the actor stoned into oblivion while trying to film a scene in one of the low-budget specials he kept busy at in the '90s. The director has trained the camera on Vincent's face, then sits next to him and speaks aloud, one by one, the lines he needs Vincent to simply repeat. Dazed and completely disoriented, the actor responds to hearing his line by asking questions in answer to it, and gets frustrated and irritated because he doesn't know what the guy sitting next to him is talking about.

It's the sad antithesis of the leonine beauty streaking across the projected rear-screens at Disney Studios in 1973, once again pointing out the difficulties of reconciling a fanciful image of beauty on-screen with the human being that comes in three dimensions off it. It seems to me just as potentially trivializing to celebrate the beauty as it does to recount published and rumored misfortunes, but I take no pleasure in presenting the latter. I note this only to suggest how selfish a task I had originally envisioned for this book. I would have preferred beauty without the beast. But you can't always have it both ways. Just ask Jan-Michael Vincent.

Once it broke through the diluted cultural taboos and the revised rating system, male nudity in the movies (and on stage) peaked in the 1970s, so much so that handsome male celebrities couldn't give interviews without having to address the issue of whether they would or wouldn't.

Two of the most important sources of the era for male nude photography, evidence of its ever-growing place in the arts, and barely disguised worship of male beauty in the entertainment spheres were *After Dark* magazine out of New York and *Films and Filming* out of London.

After Dark, The National Entertainment Magazine, debuted in May of 1968, and though there has been much debate about whether it was or wasn't a "gay" magazine, it was. It catered to, advertised to, and openly courted the "single" guy with a large discretionary income and an interest in film, theatre, ballet, art, dance, music, opera, late night parties, and naked men.

An awe-inspiring array of nude and near-nude studies of actors, dancers, and performers of every ilk graced its pages thanks to such immensely talented photographers as Kenn Duncan and Jack Mitchell, both of whom brought grace and style and sensuality to their subjects. *After Dark* would soon be joined

Jan-Michael Vincent showed off a lot more than just his cheekbones in *Buster and Billie* (1974). PHOTOFEST

and then surpassed by Andy Warhol's *inter/View* magazine—less overtly gay, but distinctly queer friendly.

Films and Filming, whose title doesn't suggest anything but an industry trade, exhibited a remarkable interest in male beauty in the 1970s and issue after issue featured the sexiest stills of movie stars and would-be stars to illustrate a story or cover a new film.

There was an increasing number of sources to pull from; not only were Joe Dallesandro, Don Johnson, Alain Delon, Helmut Berger, and Jan-Michael Vincent dropping trou, but so did these guys in the 1970s, all willing to show more than just their heinies: Michael Margotta in *Drive, He Said* (1971), Perry King in *Mandingo* (1975), Tom Berenger in *In Praise of Older Women* (1977), Jon Voight in *End of the Game* (1976), Sylvester Stallone in *A Party at Kitty and Studs* (aka *The Italian Stallion*; 1970), Rutger Hauer in *Turkish Delight* (1973), Gerard Depardieu and Robert De Niro in *1900* (1977), Peter Firth in both *Equus*

(1977) and *Joseph Andrews* (1977), Rudolph Nureyev in *Valentino* (1977), Donald Sutherland in *Don't Look Now* (1973), Roger Daltrey and his gigantic veined member in *Lisztomania* (1975), and an impressive assortment of handsome guys in both the films of Pier Paolo Pasolini—notably, *The Decameron* (1970), *The Canterbury Tales* (1971), and *Arabian Nights* (1974), and Derek Jarman—*Sebastiane* (1976) and *Jubilee* (1978).

Despite that list, movie nude scenes rarely meant baring it all—there are far more ass-enders—but they were evidence of a growing acceptance and the spilling over of homoerotic imagery into the mainstream. (Years later, in 2000, Matt Damon was such a "hottie" that even the cartoon character he provided the voice for in *Titan A.E.* got a butt shot.) Ever wonder why they call it "homoerotic" when men get naked as opposed to hetero-erotic? Me, too. The suggestion is that a naked man would appeal only to a fairy. It's erotic to the Greek homo (the same sex, as in homosexual), not the Latin homo (man, as in homo sapiens). By this definition, *Playgirl* is homoerotic, the *Sears Catalog* men's underwear pages are homoerotic, and so is your sister's boyfriend every time he takes his clothes off before hopping into bed. Isn't it just like a male-dominated culture to define what might just as well be considered as something "for the girls" as something for the queers?

When an otherwise indisputably heterosexual character like the one Dennis Quaid plays in *Breaking Away* (1979) lies shirtless sunning himself on a rock alongside his buddies—his incredible abs throwing shadows on themselves—is he an object of hetero or homo desire? Both is the easy answer and the correct one. If Dennis Christopher was lying next to him and decided to twirl the fur trail beneath Quaid's belly button, then you've got yourself homoerotic, even if the gals find it a turn-on, too.

Who does Peter Hinwood's beefy blond Rocky in *The Rocky Horror Picture Show* (1975) appeal to: gay men or women? And what about John Phillip Law's blind angel in *Barbarella* (1968)? Michael Beck's open-vested gang leader in *The Warriors* (1979)?

When I was in my teens, Robby Benson's habitually shy, wispy-voiced, and interchangeable characters were sexually attractive to me, and on TV, once David Cassidy was gone, it was Lance Kerwin [of *James at 15* (1977) and *James at 16* (1978)] who I thought should have been the gay poster boy for adolescence in the 1970s. In the 1983 TV movie *A Killer in the Family*, Robert Mitchum gets busted out of jail by his three angelic teenaged sons: James Spader, Eric Stoltz, and Lance Kerwin. I wanted to live next door to that seriously dysfunctional family so that I could convince the boys to run away with me.

In the December 7, 1978 issue of the *SoHo Weekly News*, in an article called "Menswear in Style," photos appeared of Jeff Aquilon, the captain of the water polo team at Pepperdine University. The photographer was Bruce Weber. The model was modeling underwear: briefs, boxers, an athletic T-shirt; he was lounging in bed, even holding a teddy bear. More importantly, a few months prior, thanks in large part to gay art director Donald Sterzin's decision, Aquilon was caught in Weber's reverential photos emerging from the pool in his speedo—shot from behind—in *GQ* magazine. The decade was on the verge of mainstreaming the male form as overt sex object, something you could already find in the pages of *After Dark*, as well as in its advertising: the close-up crotch shots selling all varieties of "fun"derwear were just a few years ahead of their time. An ad with a guy in his jockey shorts shouted "gay" to advertisers and consumers alike, but that limited appeal wouldn't last for long.

The 1980s — Take One

"Well, I Guess I'll Have To Go Queer Now"

All you had to do was watch the first twenty minutes or so of *American Gigolo* (1980) to get what the 1980s had in store for the American male. **Richard Gere** (1949-   ), a cocky, self-assured, but artificial advertisement for the union of a fashion model sensibility extended to men, strolls through his chic apartment, playing music and jigging just a little as he expertly lays out a week's wardrobe on the bed and matches ties to shirt and coat.

A single guy doing that in the movies prior to 1980 would have been seen as a homo, but the 1980s were eating gay culture up by the butt-full and hetero men were expected to look like catalog models and dress for success. It was all about appearances. Young American men were dressing up and showing off.

Don't think that Gere's playing a male prostitute detracted one bit. Men were being invited to role-play as sexual objects, to make themselves desirable with washboard stomachs and designer suits. Besides, as Gere's Julian Kay makes it perfectly clear in the movie: "I don't do fags."

It's the lean, clean style of Julian's apartment that matters. The paintings, the pottery, the closet full of assembly line clothing, the car, the Blondie song, the blue shorts, those fucking blinds, and the inversion boots. Gere inverts his sublime physique and predicts a cottage industry of home exercise machine infomercials that make viewers think there's hope of replicating the rippling bodies of the genetically-endowed demonstrators.

American Gigolo only succeeds, in retrospect, as a symbolic indictment of a mentality. Here was the American male all sexed up and with nowhere to go. As a film, it's dull, homophobic, and perversely uninvolving and routine, considering the subject matter. Writer-director Paul Schrader's behind-closed-doors sex scenes are ugly, cold, and creepy, but don't seem to serve a higher purpose if that's how he intended them to be seen. Even Gere's famous full-frontal, which requires significant squinting, hasn't got the balls to be anything other than an artfully rendered optical illusion, during which he drones about having to take three hours to bring a woman to her first orgasm in a decade.

Born in Philadelphia, Gere was an accomplished high school trumpeter and varsity gymnast who received a gymnastic scholarship to the University of Massachusetts, where he majored in philosophy. He left after two years to pursue music, writing, and acting in the theatre, getting his first big break as understudy for the role of Danny Zuko in the 1972 Broadway production of *Grease*. He headlined as Zuko in a London production, then made his big-screen debut as a pimp in *Report to the Commissioner* (1975), followed by a scene as a shell-shocked, white-haired soldier who coldcocks Jan-Michael Vincent in *Baby Blue Marine* (1976).

Years later, after stardom, he would tell Andy Warhol that it was seeing Warhol's improvisatory film *Bike Boy* (1967) that first made him realize he wanted to be an actor. Warhol could have outfitted Gere for the flashy role that finally made audiences sit up and take notice. He's a hyperactive coke dope and hot-to-trot hustler offering first grade teacher Diane Keaton the "best fuck of your life" after hitting on her at a seedy joint in the homophobic *Looking for Mr. Goodbar* (1977). She eventually takes him home and he does calisthenics and a weird, predatory dance holding a glow-in-the-dark knife while wearing nothing but a jockstrap. Later, they have a nasty slap fight when she makes it clear she's her own woman and she wants to *use* a man, not be responsible for one.

On Broadway in Martin Sherman's award-winning and highly-acclaimed *Bent*, as a man imprisoned by the Nazis for being homosexual, the pretty boy actor found himself the subject of predictable speculations about his own sexuality. "Yes, I'm gay when I'm on that stage," said Gere. "If the role required me to suck off Horst, I'd do it." The inane rumors and speculation would surface and resurface over the next two decades. Famously, when a female interviewer asked him in the early 1980s, "How do you feel about being a sex symbol, or are you gay?," he responded by standing up and dropping his pants. I'm not sure what

Richard Gere warms up for his role as male sex symbol of the 1980s in *Bloodbrothers* (1978). EVERETT COLLECTION

In full swing as an *American Gigolo* (1980). PHOTOFEST

she thought his answer was, but I admire his style. Perhaps, since that was what she was reducing him to, she was supposed to ask his dick. (As in that great speech from Bill Sherwood's 1986 low-budget film, *Parting Glances*, in which Adam Nathan tells Steve Buscemi about coming out to his parents when he was sixteen: "When you reach puberty you don't fuckin' decide which sex you like; you ask your dick. You say, 'Hey dick, what do you like?' Okay. All right. Then you go for it.")

Gere is just one of many pretty things in Terrence Malick's *Days of Heaven* (1978), a gorgeous pastoral of rural life eventually beset by adultery, revenge, and locusts, which was cast and filmed before *Looking for Mr. Goodbar*. The antithesis of *Heaven*'s classic beauty is *Bloodbrothers* (1978), which should have been called *Dumb Fuck Brothers*. Based on Richard Price's novel (which ended differently), this is a horror film in which the monsters are your noisy neighbors. Packed wall to wall with loud, repellent characters, drunken idiots, and brawling ignoramuses, the story has Gere finally escaping his repulsive construction worker family for life anywhere-but-here with his abused, anorexic little brother. Someone should have mercy, cut out everything except for the several scenes in which Richard has his shirt off, and get the running time for this atrocity down to fifteen barely excusable minutes.

He's a short order cook from Tucson who dreams of one day owning a chain of motels in the WWII drama *Yanks* (1979). He's just handsome enough to make that dream sound like a nice one, too. Unfortunately, his British girlfriend is engaged just when his romance with her is at its sweetest. Luckily, the beau is plain-looking and off to war, clearly giving Gere the cosmetic and thematic advantage.

An Officer and A Gentleman (1982) was an R-rated throwback to the kind of romance pictures "they used to make," and went on to become the fifth biggest film of the year (right behind *Porky's*). The fact that Gere and co-star Debra Winger didn't get along is said to have put the fire in their love scenes.

Newsweek magazine explored "The Male Idols: Hollywood's New Sex Symbols" and put Richard Gere in properly bulging blue jeans on the cover of its May 23, 1983 issue to illustrate the point. As the "reigning new sex symbol of the 80s," he was about to flirt with sex-symbol self-parody as the dopey car thief with a thing for the Silver Surfer and singing in the shower in the pointless 1983 neon remake of Jean Luc Godard's 1960 landmark *Breathless*.

The performance is annoying and cocky, bordering on completely self-aware, but it must have meant something to fans when their idol promenades nude in the shower while singing "C'mon, baby, don't be shy," and then later breaks the shower door while screwing his gal before flopping naked onto the bed.

One of the few arguments outside the realm of a male stranglehold on studio control as to why there are fewer actor full-frontals than actress full-frontals has to do with the mythological power of the phallus vs. the physical reality of the penis. Movie stars are the equivalent of mythological beings in pop culture; the potency of male movie stars' masculinity has much to do with the assumption of what they have between their legs—the idea of it—rather than the reality of it. Show John Wayne's penis and he shrinks in stature; not because he was or wasn't well-endowed, but because it can never live up to the myth. He just becomes one of the boys.

Combine the penis with the rest of a physically attractive body and its perceived length (short or long) and girth (skinny or fat) become the actor's distracting assessment, not the character's. No actor or actress gets naked in a movie without the audience pulling out of the drama and becoming hyper-aware of the celebrity baring his or her flesh, no matter how principled the actor who said he or she would only do nudity if it was important to the character or an integral part of the film.

Richard Gere's approach to on-screen nudity seemed to be as casual as Joe Dallesandro's. "The characters are not coy about their bodies," he told *Newsweek* of *Breathless*. "In a way it takes the voyeur aspect out of it, having them just walking around the way they do." He's right. There should have been lots of full-frontal nudity in *Breathless*. It was right for the character, whose exaggerated machismo would have been suitably humbled by his unimposing, bouncing wee-wee. It was also right to want to satisfy fans' curiosity about what the actor's genitalia looked like. And it was true that Richard Gere's flaccid penis was the perfect organ to demythologize what *Time* magazine declared "The Year of the Hunk." Not destroy or corrupt it, mind you. Just bring it down to size. (In the 1930s and '40s, "normal sized" penises were routinely featured on physique models and considered as merely part of the aesthetic whole. As movies developed masculine mythos and pornography infiltrated the culture, we became increasingly cock-obsessed and projected our own manic insecurities about size onto our depiction and evaluation of the male nude.)

At the height of his youthful powers, he was just 33, Gere's career derailed within a year of *An Officer and A Gentleman*. Unfortunately, he didn't stop making movies in the '80s, making us suffer through

197

Beyond the Limit (1983), *The Cotton Club* (in which he blows his own trumpet, but can't blow life into a stillborn attempt at airless acting; 1984), *King David* (probably the worst of the lot; 1985), *Power* (1986), *No Mercy* (1986), and *Miles From Home* (1988).

I was fully prepared to give him my blessing to pursue the important humanitarian, environmental, and political causes that marked his off-screen role as a Buddhist and celebrity activist, but a surprisingly rewarding and savvy back-to-back combination of *Pretty Woman* (1990) and *Internal Affairs* (1990) demonstrated that he could be legitimately charming, in deference to playact charming, and legitimately creepy, instead of "hey, look, I'm playing a bad guy" creepy. He also gave strong and/or winning performances in *Primal Fear* (1996) and *Dr. T and the Women* (2000). Plus, prematurely gray and all, he was still damned sexy.

Eric Roberts (1956-   ) managed to do what lots of pretty boy actors wish they could do. He went from being a dark and gorgeous leading man to a dark and damaged character actor in one fell swoop. As with Montgomery Clift, legend marks the painfully obvious turning point with a devastating car accident, but the damage to his face did not destroy Roberts' leading man good looks. A performance did.

He was robbed of an Academy Award nomination for his spine-tingling, thick, and creepy portrayal of Paul Snider in Bob Fosse's *Star 80* (1983). It's one of those once in a lifetime performances in which the actor seems to meld with the character; in this case, the slick and sleazy hustler who charmed Dairy Queen girl Dorothy Stratten and ushered her to the edge of sex-siren stardom as a *Playboy* centerfold before going into an insanely jealous rage, murdering her, and then taking his own life after defiling her body.

It's not a pretty sight. And no longer was Roberts, who chewed up the scenery in *The Pope of Greenwich Village* (1984) and *Runaway Train* (1985), the latter for which he was finally Oscar-nominated. This isn't to suggest that Roberts got ugly, only that he was now a character actor who fit less the mold of his earlier promise.

He's still strikingly handsome in *The Coca-Cola Kid* (1985), a charming and offbeat tale about a soft drink salesman up against a local soda pop monopoly Down Under. For some reason, he's had his hair dyed a copper blond and the incongruity with his features doesn't backfire.

He was a member of his father's acting school and troupe of players in Atlanta from a very early age. He was attracted to theatre because the memorized lines helped him overcome a serious stuttering problem, for which he was mercilessly teased by peers. As a teenager, his parents went through a major rift and an ugly separation. His sisters (including Julia) went with mom. Eric with dad.

His father sent him to the Royal Academy of Dramatic Arts after the boy graduated from high school at age sixteen, then enrolled him in the American Academy of Dramatic Arts in New York upon his return two years later. In 1976, he found work as Ted Bancroft on a single season of the soap *Another World*. He quit the Academy after less than a year because he wanted to get out there and act, not merely prepare to do so.

I still remember the newspaper ads for his first film. Each week the image of a necklace hanging against a bare chest showed more and more of the young man wearing it. When we were finally introduced to *The King of the Gypsies* (1978), the dark street-punk beauty was a newcomer afforded the entrance of a star.

As David, the young gypsy who will become embroiled in family politics no matter what his personal dreams, Roberts doesn't enter the film until nearly the 40-minute mark. He's being chased by the police. David runs insurance scams to make a living, like getting hit by taxis or slipping on eggs at the supermarket. When the doctor examines him after his latest pratfall, the physician repeatedly pets the pretty boy's head. It's a strange thing to do, but completely understandable.

Roberts has an urban, pugilist beauty. His David wants to be a surgeon. He defies his family heritage, dates a blonde white girl, and works as a singing waiter. You want to see the boy make it, but the script (based on a novel) has other designs, including having papa send some thugs to slice open his pretty face.

King of the Gypsies was not the kind of film to launch a star as it turned out, but Roberts survived his debut with a good performance. He followed it with something even more depressing. *Paul's Case* (1980), based on the 1905 story by Willa Cather, is a 55-minute featurette made for PBS television and introduced by Henry Fonda. Roberts, with dimples, high cheekbones, and with eyes so dark they look permanently eye-shadowed, plays Paul, a teenaged dreamer in trouble at school for being inattentive and temperamental. He's not really much of either, just a hopeless romantic who falls in love with paintings, with art, and the

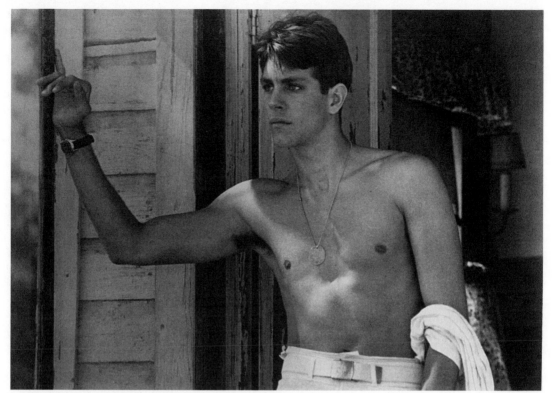

Eric Roberts as the sweetest sailor you'll ever meet in *Raggedy Man* (1981). YESTERDAY

theatre. The paintings transport him, underlining Cather's theme about the absence of art and spirituality during the Industrial Revolution.

The only reason to watch this progressively depressing short is to see how radiant Roberts can be even in his darkness. He's got a face tailor-made for black-and-white photography and sometimes he seems to be black-and-white, pale as a vampire, with a single red carnation reminding us that the film is in color. There's a particularly nice moment when he's in the middle of the woods, accidentally stumbles in the snow, and then heaps it onto his face and chomps on a mouthful. It's playful improvisation that seems completely natural. Too bad his character couldn't have found himself a wealthy patron to give him a reason to live.

My favorite Eric Roberts performance clocks even shorter than the one just described. He's only in *Raggedy Man* (1981) for 49 minutes, but once seen, you'll never forget the sight of him as the sailor who comes in out of the rain to use Sissy Spacek's phone in little Edna, Texas, circa 1940.

Teddy is on a four day liberty when he learns over the phone that his girl has up and married someone else. Fresh out of boot camp in Texas, he's a fresh-faced Oklahoma boy destined to become a gunner's mate. Sissy is scandalously divorced and has the formidable job of telephone operator, as well as mother to two adorable boys, Henry and Harry. Teddy stays on at the house during his leave, which creates plenty of local scandal in itself, and ends up falling in love with the whole family.

Dressed in his white T-shirt and white pants, offset by the coal black of his hair, he is as beautiful as beautiful can be, and the nicest, sweetest, most well-intentioned, and romantic young man you're likely to dream up. He plays with the kids, takes them to their first picture show (a John Wayne war flick, complete with blood-spewing enemy pilots being gunned down, prompting the boys to ask, "Is that what happens?"), gets into a bloody scuffle to protect the youngsters from two local cretins, and buys sheer hosiery for mom.

He steps out onto the front porch without his shirt ("half-nekkid") on the morning after, only to be seen by two local busy bodies. I'd never have him put his shirt back on. Fuck Edna.

It's heartbreaking to see him leave on Day 3 at the request of the woman he has come to care so deeply for; selfishly, I wanted to keep him around, too. His goodbye to the boys will put a lump in your throat (*ET*'s Henry Thomas is a first-class crier as Harry), and I will forever remember the handsome young sailor walking down the road reciting "Henry and Harry, Henry and Harry," because he's named his shoes after each boy and recites them aloud with every step.

On June 4, 1981, Eric Roberts' jeep hit a tree on the drive down from actress Sandy Dennis' home in Connecticut, leaving him in a coma for three days. *Star 80* was next, and if you can believe him, director Bob Fosse chose Roberts after seeing him in *Raggedy Man*.

Dogged by a near lifelong commitment to marijuana, contentious family squabbles, a couple unfriendly run-ins with the police, and a bad boy temperament, Roberts and his career went into a rocky slide in the late '80s and early '90s and he appeared in dozens of low-budget thrillers and direct-to-cable/home video specials.

There have been highlights along the road, however, and no doubt more to come. "If you're looking for a beat-up ex-pretty boy, I'm right up there, because I'm pretty beat-up," he told *The Advocate* in 1996. He's excellent as a designer with AIDS who decides to chuck it in and take his own life after one last get-together with friends in *It's My Party* (1996), directed by Randal Kleiser. The occasionally soppy melodrama and nearly thankless sound bite appearances by a host of recognizable celebrities (including Roddy McDowall, Lee Grant, Olivia Newton-John, Christopher Atkins, George Segal, Greg Louganis, and a frightful bitter queen act from Bronson Pinchot) won't prepare you for Roberts' agonizingly emotional farewells.

I wanted Matt Dillon to be gay, though I knew all along that he was too straight to ever be able to admit it himself. Now that he seems assuredly heterosexual, my interest in him hasn't dimmed. Gay actors have long been entreated to stay in the closet so as not to spoil their bread-and-butter hetero appeal. I'm happy to prove the inverse true. Knowing Matt Dillon is straight hasn't fazed this overgrown gay boy in the least. I'm used to getting my male sex symbols packaged for my sisters' consumption. I've rarely felt excluded by that fact either. Most guys identify as straight. Most of us live in a "straight" world construct. I've adapted without a sense of self-betrayal.

In-Touch magazine, the oldest gay nudie mag on the market, managed a decade and a half of exciting flirtation with Hollywood celebrities before threatened lawsuits over purported celeb nudie photos dried up their resolve to tease us with Tinsel Town. When Coppola's Zoetrope went belly-up in the mid-'80s, the studio auctioned off props and costumes from their warehouse and Collector's Bookstore in Hollywood snatched up a number of items.

"If you've ever wanted to lick Matt Dillon's boots, sniff Rob Lowe's armpits, or taste Tom Cruise's crotch, now's your chance," announced *In-Touch* (#92) of Collector's acquisitions from *The Outsiders*. Hurry now and you might just get a piece. Any fantasy I may have momentarily held about the news was destroyed by the accompanying photos of the magazine's editor molesting the memorabilia. In one of the trio of shots, the guy is clenching the crotch of Tom's jeans between his teeth.

The prizes no longer held any allure. The thought of receiving a pair of Tom's pants hermetically sealed in plastic with the hopes of taking a drag off choice perimeters of denim (especially since fellow cast members complained of Cruise's refusal to shower during his entire stint as a greaser) was violated by a silly photo showing that someone else had already beat you to it. Who wanted a pair of celebrity pants previously masticated over?

[*Inches* magazine subsequently offered its readers Arnold Schwarzenegger's jockstrap from *The Running Man* (1987). What made this offer even less tantalizing was the intimate nature of the garment. The likelihood of finding a stray pubic hair was actually extremely high, but the chances of it belonging to the star were nil. You can bet those boys at *Inches* are still telling friends about the day each of them got to try on Arnold's jock.]

From the same Zoetrope auction, *In-Touch* managed to procure Matt Dillon's makeup-stained tank top from *Rumble Fish* and offered it as a contest prize to readers. In 25 words or less, you had to write why the undershirt should go to you. I found myself poised with pen in hand.

Ultimately, there were so many entries, including 180 from the same guy, that the magazine drew a winner at random. Some of the responses: "Rob Lowe is my favorite actor and Matt knows Rob." "My tongue is tired of licking Matt's photo in issue #70." "It would go well with my Scott Baio pajama bottoms!" "Maybe they will forget to take him out of it." "He makes my gun smoke." "He's Jesus." "My throbbing cock has awaited each release of his since the underwear scene in *Little Darlings* and to wear his 'T' would be the ultimate ball popper." (27 words—should have been disqualified.)

My entry: "I'd have to return it." Not terribly witty or original, but a loser, too.

A few years later I came face-to-fly with Matt's jeans from *The Outsiders* at a Hollywood memorabilia museum and risked being ejected by reaching out and copping a feel.

Matthew Raymond Dillon (1964-   ) was born in New Rochelle, New York, the second son in a family of five boys and a girl. One of his great uncles was Alex Raymond, the creator of the *Flash Gordon* and *Jungle Jim* comic strips. Another great uncle, Jim Raymond, drew the *Blondie* strip for many years. And Matt was not named after James Arness' character on *Gunsmoke*. Glad we got that standard trivia in the MD bio out of the way. As to the storybook story of his discovery, it has been told so often that just two years into his career he was refusing to relate it again, saying that it had been chronicled so many thousands of times that whenever he saw it in print it was like looking at words spit out of a computer.

Dillon was characteristically bored to death by the recounting of how he was caught cutting math class at Hommocks Middle School by two casting recruiters. He was asked if he would be interested in trying out for a movie, didn't quite believe them at first, but agreed and went to the cattle call the next day.

Casting agent Vic Ramos, who was testing teenagers to fill out a roster of troubled youth for a film called *Over the Edge*, was instantly taken by the 14-year old Dillon's wiseass, carefree attitude. He famously wrote on his notepad: "*Is* Richie White. Should be a movie star."

Dillon played Ben Franklin in a fourth grade production of *The Imaginary Child of George Washington*, but spent the rest of his grade school and early teen years playing the off-stage role of tough guy. It was an unlikely dress rehearsal for stardom.

Fortunately, Matt Dillon was Richie White, or vice versa, and Dillon's swagger and punkish persona negated the need for acting lessons that would have spoiled him into learning unnatural behaviors. In front of the camera, Matt Dillon was a complete natural.

Over the Edge (1979) opens with the ominous factoid that in 1978 there were 110,000 acts of vandalism by arrestees under the age of 18. In the isolated community of New Granada, where a quarter of the population is under the age of 15, the dopey adults have built a community resting all its hopes on corporate development and have completely forgotten about their kids' welfare.

The only place the kids have to hang out is a rec center made out of a Quonset. Thus, they spend their days engaging in sexual activity, getting drunk, taking dope, and wreaking havoc while the adults get frustrated and don't seem to have a clue as to what's wrong.

Richie White is one of the town's baddest apples. He wears his hair shoulder-length long (as was the style for many boys then), struts around in a sleeveless half-shirt, and looks as pretty as a girl. Intended or not, there's even something right about the fact that his character's name is "Richie" White in the credits and all related print media, but the black flag flapping from the back of his bike says "Ritchie," with a "t." It's unlikely that Richie would know the difference.

The town's jagoff cop gets a BB in the window and comes across Richie and his friend Carl hiding in the brush, though they weren't the perpetrators. "You got any special reason for hiding in there?" the cop asks.

"Yeah, we heard you were horny," cracks Richie.

The cop frisks him and finds a pocketknife, and he foolishly asks about the blade's length. Dillon's Richie again: "Three inches. Almost as big as your dick."

Dillon has a way of spewing these lines so that you're on his side even as you're glad you're not the adult on the other end of his insults. Later, when another cop grabs hold of him to take him out of the room, Dillon gripes, "Get your hands off me, you pinhead."

He's a kid you'd like to slap silly, but he's also so gorgeous and so charismatic that you know he'd only have to flash his puppy dog brown eyes beneath those jet black brows at you and you'd be giving him another chance. The chance to rob you blind.

Taking target practice with a stolen pistol, wearing jeans and a black vest with no shirt, Dillon makes a hot poster boy for the street punk, just in case they were looking for one. I like the fact that Richie eventually comes across as a boaster, an even more immature version of the tough guy Dillon would play in *The Outsiders*. Both characters protect themselves by pretending to be big time hardasses. Dillon's remarkable debut at age 14 lasts just 55 minutes.

As a social allegory, the film lays it on pretty thick, what with all the kids on booze and acid finally trapping the adults inside a town meeting and setting the place ablaze, but it has its effective moments and the image of Matt Dillon standing defiantly atop a police car had the potential for Rebel With A Cause status.

Matt Dillon, the prototypical New Yorker, plays a 1949 Texan farm boy with ease in *Liar's Moon* (1981). PHOTOFEST

Unfortunately, with sporadic inner city gang violence in movie theaters associated with the release of *The Warriors* (1979), the distributors got nervous and *Over the Edge* was shelved for a few years.

Controversial not for violence, but for sex, *Little Darlings* (1980) was battered by the press at the time of its release because the plot hook had two teenage girls (streetwise Kristy McNichol and spoiled rich girl Tatum O'Neal) in a contest to see who could lose her virginity first during a summer at camp. What the over-excited critics failed to see was that this so-called "teen sex comedy" was actually a responsible and thoughtful coming-of-age film written by two women.

The film memorably opens with a cigarette smoking Kristy McNichol (the tomboy love of my life) being approached by a teen boy who asks her to "slide me somethin' nice." She smiles that beautiful, wicked smile of hers and then kicks him so convincingly hard in the crotch that I'm at a loss as to how they did it without sending the actor to the hospital.

I wasn't a regular follower of McNichol's TV series *Family* (1976-80) until re-runs years after I saw *Little Darlings*, delighting in her gifts as an actress on that show and her character's short-lived but heart-thumping relationship with a boy swimmer played by Leif Garrett.

There was a time when Kristy could make my heart ache and my tears flow faster than just about any other actress. On top of that, she was so incredibly cute. I'd almost have had to reconsider my sexual orientation if it wasn't that I quickly realized that she was the mirror image of Matt Dillon, a boy with features so soft and beautiful that he hardly has a profile. (Dillon's mother was famously quoted in *Rolling Stone* as saying, "I didn't think Matty was our best looking kid.")

Kristy plays Angel Bright ("Don't let the name fool ya") and Matt plays Randy (ditto), the dumb New Yawk teen with long black hair to match his sexy black muscle T. Kristy first sizes him up from behind, the camera moving up his jeans and stopping at his butt, causing her to raise an eyebrow of approval. Randy's so dopey that when she paddles her canoe over to the boys camp and yells his name, he answers, "Who? Me?"

He's only wearing his cut-off jeans when she takes him to a cemetery out in the woods in hopes of getting him drunk and getting it on, but he passes out instead.

Their second shot at it comes at night in an empty boathouse, with Matt peeling down to his briefs while Kristy has second thoughts and makes excuses. It's a well-played, difficult, and awkward scene that ends up with Randy angrily thinking Angel is just a tease. The next night, back at the boathouse, they do end up having sex, and if the rumors are true that more "graphic" footage of their first time exists somewhere out there, I'm glad they didn't use it.

A rollercoaster of mixed emotions (hurt, anger, sadness) are played out in their dialogue after the event. Angel admits, "it wasn't what I thought it would be," while Randy sweetly, but dumbly says, "I don't know, I think I love you." "You don't have to," says Angel, capping the scene by saying quietly enough to nearly qualify as a whisper: "God, I feel so lonesome."

Little Darlings isn't a "just say no to sex" movie any more than it's a "get it on" flick. Tatum O'Neal can't muster the kind of support that would have made the girls' revelations to each other while sitting on the tire swings truly classic, but Kristy is so incredibly brilliant and heartbreakingly real that it doesn't matter. The mix of pain and regret and honesty on that actress' face as she tells Tatum about what happened with Randy raises the film's gimmicky plot to whole new dimensions. It's the girls' coming-of-age film that girls don't get from male filmmakers.

Though it was R-rated and controversial, *Little Darlings* was sold to and hyped at a teenage audience, and so was Matt Dillon. In a carefully crafted plan, agent Vic Ramos, who was now Dillon's personal manager, deliberately targeted the teen magazines in order to fashion himself a movie star, just as agents and managers used to do with the movie magazines in the Golden Age of Hollywood.

The result was an almost immediate frenzy of success. Matt Dillon was on the cover and between the covers of every teen magazine on the market, posed holding teddy bears, reading the latest issue of *Tiger Beat*, signing love and kisses to the fans, and endlessly baring his shirtless physique so that you could trace his adolescent development one belly button or chest hair at a time. He was generating thousands of fan letters a week. Soon *People*, *US*, and even *Playgirl* were doing stories on the teen star. However, there were no official Matt Dillon posters, no network TV show guest appearances or series, no manufactured record deal, no dolls, and almost no commercials. Ramos wanted to launch Dillon as a film star using a base of fans his age, but he did not want the actor to flash in the pan of teenybopper stardom, here today, gone tomorrow. Matt was seriously considered for *The Blue Lagoon* (1980) opposite Diane Lane, but they would never have been able to talk him out of his clothes. His screen test included this classic and very to-the-point remark: "I ain't showin' my dork."

For Dillon, the teen idol phase was an agonizing and degrading experience, something that he rarely speaks about on the record. He has always hated giving interviews anyway, and most of them comprise writers struggling to get him to talk like anything resembling a movie star. Painfully uneasy at first, and then understandably suspicious and even resentful of journalists as he became seasoned, Dillon is my kind of guy—refusing to be anyone other than himself.

He has third billing in *My Bodyguard* (1980), the charming comedy-drama about a rich kid who befriends a school outcast after hiring him for protection from a gang of jerks who extort lunch money from all the students. With his long hair finally chopped off only to be slicked back like a '30s gangster, Dillon is perfect as the school bully Melvin Moody, a skinny, tough-talking punk so pretty that I would have deliberately not paid him so I could be beaten daily and find myself on the receiving end of those dreamy and intimidating stares. Who would have thought eyebrows could be so sexy? They're nearly as thick as Groucho Marx's mustache.

"Physical appearance isn't anything, but you know, it helps," Dillon either flubs or improvises to himself while primping in the guy's john and talking about girls. His lean physique is well-displayed in a tight blue shirt when we first meet him and a very complimentary red number for the big fight at the film's exciting finale. He's also, thank you very much, a "skin" when it comes to a rough game of basketball in gym class.

His first starring role came in *Liar's Moon* (1981), set in Noble, Texas in 1949. He has no problem adopting the accent, and he sure as hell looks good in his blue jeans and dirty muscle T-shirt. He enters a greased pig contest, smooches a pretty girl at a carnival kissing booth, and runs around in his boxer shorts at the swimming hole, but everything goes to hell (the movie, too) with a weird plot twist about the possibility of his being closely related to the girl he's just married and about to have a baby with. It's his first bad movie, and I'm tempted to say it's the curse of his being finally talked into taking acting lessons, but it's not his performance that's to blame. Not even an alternate ending helps.

Tex (1982) wasn't a box-office hit for Disney, but it eventually found an audience retroactively when other of novelist Susie Hinton's popular books about teenagers in Oklahoma became junior high school staples. Hinton couldn't believe that Dillon was being cast to play her sweet 15-year old, but changed her mind about whether he was right for the part shortly after meeting him in the flesh. Not only was Matt exactly the kid for whom she was writing the books, but he seemed to have stepped right out of them.

Sweet and not quite book-smart Tex lives with his older brother Mason in a house that should be occupied by their father as well, though he's on the rodeo circuit for long periods of time and this time seems to have practically forgotten the boys. Mason sells Tex's horse Rowdy to pay some bills and put food on the table, setting off a conflict between the two brothers in which Mason assumes the tough role of father and Tex becomes even more the prankster at school.

A classic scene has the two brothers being interviewed on local TV after they narrowly avoid being killed by a deranged hitchhiker. Mason clearly thinks the questions being asked are stupid, but Tex is enjoying the hell out of the whole thing, saying that he doesn't think all hitchhikers are bad because sometimes even he does it. When a female reporter improbably asks the glowing youth where he got his dimples, Tex lights up and tells her, "Well, God gave me my face, but He let me pick my nose." The astonishing thing about Dillon's performance (and Jim Metzler is excellent, too, as Mason) is that he doesn't seem to be acting in either situation: as the kid answering the question knowing he's on TV or as the wide-eyed kid later watching himself on the tube at home. Tex tells Mason that "you look pretty cool. I sound funny, though." And then the scene ends with Dillon throwing a pillow at Metzler that careens by his head and knocks over a table lamp, causing the bulb to blow. The accident of that moment is as real and spontaneous as the rest of the scene.

Kristy McNichol (this way), Matt Dillon (that way).
AUTHOR'S COLLECTION

Tex is a sweet, well-written, and beautifully acted movie about growing up, brotherly love, and forgiveness. "Matt Dillon radiates a mysteriously effortless charm," wrote Pauline Kael in *The New Yorker*. "Dillon has a gift for expressing submerged shifts of feeling—we may feel that we're actually seeing Tex's growth process."

Susie Hinton found Matt to "be a genius, though not a verbal one." If you're one of the few to have seen *Wild Rides* (1982), a 30-minute short in which Matt wings his "narration" while standing alongside several of the most exciting roller coasters in America, and then rides them, you'll know what she meant. So how can you possibly say that one of the things you love about the guy is his unpolished, off-the-cuff delivery and not sound like you're insulting him or calling him inarticulate? (For that matter, how would any of us fare if confronted with our teenage selves in print?)

"I've felt pretty crazy when it comes to chicks," said an 18-year old Matt to *US* magazine in 1982. "But it only lasts a while. If worse comes to worse, I just break up. Half this world is male and half is female—there's got to be something else out there."

See, you know what he means, but it doesn't come out quite right. Here's a kid who has fallen out of high school (not finished it) and into the limelight where guys and gals with tape recorders ask you silly questions and record every syllable as if you're reciting dialogue. Here's a kid whose passion for music (the boom box was made for Matt Dillon) informs his world in ways that answering questions about being famous ("I've been recognized at a urinal a few times. That's pretty weird.") does not.

Dillon cemented his fame with generations of teens to come, but who will have missed his teen idol media blitz, by playing Dallas Winston in *The Outsiders* (1983). All it took was 78 signatures from eighth grade students at a Fresno, California junior high school and a letter from the school librarian to convince *The Godfather* (1972) and *Apocalypse Now* (1979) director Francis Ford Coppola to make their favorite book into a film.

S.E. Hinton, whose name was thusly abbreviated by her publishers because she was writing books about teenaged boys and they didn't want the readership to know she was a woman, was only a high school student herself when she wrote the novel. It tells the story of two disparate groups of teens in Tulsa, Oklahoma: the gritty, wrong side of the tracks Greasers and the well-off, other side of the tracks Socs (so-shis; for socials). Both sides clash after a drunken soc is accidentally killed by a baby-faced greaser during a fight.

Today, the film is known more for its stellar cast of future movie star and movie-star-near-misses than it is for anything else. Among the Greasers: Patrick Swayze as Darrel Curtis, Rob Lowe as Sodapop Curtis, C. Thomas Howell as Ponyboy Curtis, Ralph Macchio as Johnny, Emilio Estevez as Two-Bit, Tom Cruise as Steve, and Dillon as "Dally" Winston. Among the Socs: Diane Lane as Cherry and Leif Garrett as Bob. All beauties, though Garrett was well past his teen idol stage. Even the store clerk who shoots Matt Dillon is played by **William Smith** (1934-   ), the once-gorgeous young actor who played Joe on television's *Laredo* (1965-67) and then grew up to be Clint Eastwood's gruff and beefy bare-knuckled opponent in *Any Which Way You Can* (1980).

If you're not careful, you might miss the best performance in *The Outsiders*, a film whose script and green actors can't fill the wide-screen aspirations of its famous director's vision to poeticize the tale into a 1950's teen epic. Matt Dillon is all strut and swagger and mannerism as Dally, but that's exactly who the character is, not merely the uninspired shtick of a young actor who thinks he's playing a hood. Besides, it helps that Dillon's own natural walk has an attitude of its own and earned him the nickname "Bounce" long before he was doing it on the silver screen.

When Ponyboy and Johnny come to Dally after the knifing, he's all attitude. He doesn't even ask for details and doesn't flinch in the least when he hears what happened. He just sees it as his being mixed up in a murder rap. For the first time in the movies, hair is visible on his chest and he strikes a match on his necklace to light his catch-stick. Dally's living the B-movies he's seen at the local theater in Tulsa. Catch-stick, heater, hideout. He's got the lingo, the moves, the half-baked philosophy about not getting involved with anyone or anything because you can only get hurt if you do. He stands by while the other two youths help a group of kids get out of a burning church, eventually assisting a little, but only from the outside. Ponyboy and Johnny are the heroes who get burned, but it's Dally and Johnny who end up in the hospital. Why Dally is admitted is anyone's guess, other than he now wanted to be a part of the story. (S.E. Hinton, who showed up as a typing teacher in *Tex*, is the nurse Dillon is harassing from his hospital bed in *The Outsiders*.) And, of course, it's Dally who comes completely unhinged after Johnny's death because he's unequipped to deal with real life emotions and tragedy.

Matt Dillon's "bounce" is just about at its bounciest in *Rumble Fish* (1983), the third Hinton adaptation in which he appeared and the second "boy movie" directed by Coppola. This time Coppola set out to make an art film for teenagers, filming in arresting black-and-white (because of a key character's literal color blindness), using time-lapse imagery, fantasy sequences, symbolism, smoke pots, dramatic lighting, muted and echoing sound effects, and a tribal score by Stewart Copeland.

Rusty-James (Dillon), always in a form-fitting T-shirt, is the thuggish younger brother to the legendary Motorcycle Boy (Mickey Rourke) who once reigned over the gangs before succumbing to inner demons of darkness and depression. Rusty-James has romanticized the gang era, since ruined by dope, but dreams of its eventual return and his ascension. He thinks he will grow up to be just like Motorcycle Boy, but he doesn't stand a chance. He's just a fucked up kid worshipping an idol; an idol whose last wish is to put the Siamese fighting fish from the pet store into the river and then have his younger brother follow the river to the ocean, a place he never got to see.

205

Rumble Fish is one of Dillon's personal favorites and remains a fascinating film to watch. There's something more than pathetic about Rusty-James' misguided adoration of the Motorcycle Boy and something poignant and sweet about his being completely unaware of the message his ghostly brother has brought back since his recent trip to California to see their mother, whom Rusty-James was told had died. "I wish you would talk normal," he complains to his drunken dad when the words "acute perception" are used to describe the Motorcycle Boy. An earlier exchange between brothers which amounts to little more than "hey"s and "why"s is just as incomprehensible to Rusty-James. Let's hope he understands the meaning of what he sees in the film's last frame.

Matt Dillon displayed a light touch in the rarely seen anymore PBS production of Jean Shepherd's *The Great American Fourth of July...and Other Disasters* (1982), but the performance he ended up giving in *The Flamingo Kid* (1984) was an astonishing change of pace and image. The tough guy and brooder whose brows threw shadows over his eyes suddenly had light shining on that face and beneath those brows. At the expense of his classically high cheekbones, every nook and cranny was illuminated and his refreshing, big smile and perfect white teeth made him even brighter. Not plastic movie star brighter, thank goodness, just brighter by contrast, making way for hands-down handsome, not just pretty. No wonder one of his customers keeps missing his back pocket when she tips his white pants while he's working parking cars. He's gorgeous.

Set in 1963, this hugely enjoyable comedy tells the story of a good-looking Brooklyn boy who temporarily succumbs to the self-aggrandizing and selfishly materialistic philosophies of a rich car dealer and card shark over the sensible, hard-working advice of his plumber pop. Dillon is so good in this film—it may be a perfect performance—that any and all bets about his range and/or acting abilities were off. The material may not be Shakespeare, but he completely owns the role, displaying an innate sense of comic timing, endearing awkwardness, and tender romance. His scenes opposite Hector Elizondo (as his dad) are classic.

Bad choices and bad movies and bad performances dogged him for five years until he accepted the lead in Gus Van Sant's *Drugstore Cowboy* (1989). As jittery Bob Hughes, head of a ragtag group of fellow dopers and society fringe dwellers in 1971 Portland, Dillon is brilliant showing us an addict who seems quite satisfied with his life out of a prescription drug bottle, even if it means that he's become inordinately superstitious and uninterested in sex. "You won't fuck me and I always have to drive," complains his wife. Eventually, Bob decides to make a clean break of it, get on the methadone program, and face life's sober challenges, "like tying your shoes."

It's a performance that deservedly won the actor reams of critical praise, as if this was the first time they realized he was now both a very good actor and a grown up one.

The 1990s brought him his first box-office hit, doing a goofy supporting turn as the sleazy detective hired by Ben Stiller to find Cameron Diaz in *There's Something About Mary* (1998). He could also be seen enjoying a threesome and then briefly stepping off his mark to reveal Kevin Bacon's weenie in *Wild Things* (1998), and as the Oscar-winning actor who dedicates his award by outing his high school acting coach in *In & Out* (1997). At age 38, he directed his first feature film, *City of Ghosts* (2003), one of the few films shot in Cambodia since the mid-sixties.

Matt Dillon may, in retrospect, be the longest-lived and most successful actor to work in the movies after being marketed as a teenybopper heartthrob, and then a known quantity, without a starring hit movie to his name. Just another reason to love the guy.

Christopher Atkins Bomann (1961-) had recently signed with the world-famous Ford Agency and completed a jeans ad when he was sent on a cattle call to audition for Columbia Pictures' *The Blue Lagoon* (1980). The 18-year old's dreams of an athletic scholarship had been dashed after a serious high school sports knee injury and he was making a living as a lifeguard and sailing instructor in New York before a dabble in modeling got him, of all things, the cover of a corporate annual report. His original trajectory was to go on to college to study sports medicine.

From a sea of 2,500 or so lovely lads, Atkins was plucked, had his naturally straight hair set in curls, much to his concern, and found himself shipped off to Fiji to get an "all-over tan." Legend has it that the arduous screen test consisted of Christopher standing in front of a camera in bikini briefs without having to utter a syllable. Not true, though he didn't get the part until months after his first test because they didn't like his hair on the original audition tape and the producer was slow to realize they could just re-style it.

Director Randal Kleiser insisted that the neophyte actor sleep beneath a poster of his co-star Brooke Shields (to inspire wet dreams perhaps), but Chris admits that the lovely Brooke, already a media-sensation as controversial child/whore in Louis Malle's *Pretty Baby* (1978), was only 14 going on 15 and not attractive to him in that way.

The impact of *The Blue Lagoon* on a generation of young filmgoers can't be properly registered simply by recalling a time when its provocative tanned-teen billboard caused gaper's blocks and gnarled traffic outside of the Cineramadome in Hollywood—nor its exposé in the August 11, 1980 issue of *People*, one of their top 10 best-selling covers even twenty years after the fact, in which the subject of child pornography masquerading as R-rated Hollywood entertainment was sensationally brewed. Pauline Kael called it "Disney nature porn" in *The New Yorker*, remarking that watching the two young actors was "about as exciting as looking into a fishbowl waiting for guppies to mate."

It's less a sign of the jaded, seen-everything times than it is a remarkably easy-to-grasp reality check that watching *The Blue Lagoon* today you wonder what all the fright was about beyond the excuse to sell magazines employing the very same teencake imagery used to sell the movie. It's a lushly photographed fantasy of innocent sexual awakening, a playful South Seas adventure of young love.

It also cost less to make (4.5 million) than it did to promote (6.3 million). Brooke Shields had been shamelessly sold as a teen (and pre-teen) sexpot, and that was controversial enough before she managed to grow into her eyebrows. With *The Blue Lagoon*, prurience played a major role in the film's marketing and box-office. Contemplating a barely teenaged girl as a sexual object rightly raised ugly inquiries into the propriety of children packaged as erotic properties. But the film proved to be quite innocent in its own way. Playful, yes, and teasing, yes, but certainly not explicit as far as Brooke's exposure went. She goes through the film with her long hair taped over her breasts and has time to duck out and be replaced by an older woman for a breast-feeding scene shot without a cut to make the audience believe they've seen Brooke and not a body-double. Same goes for the swimming scenes in which any evidence of female nudity is silhouetted in the water to barely disguise the fact that it's not Ms. Shields.

The tease would work again for *Endless Love* (1981), in which audiences lined up to see how sassy Brooke's manager/mom would allow her to get in yet another R-rated "sex" film. Once more, Brooke kept her clothes on and her male co-star, Martin Hewitt, was the one who bared his buns for the camera. Even Tom Cruise, in his first film role at all of 60 seconds or so, takes his shirt off. As with *Lagoon*'s Kleiser, *Endless Love*'s director, Franco Zeffirelli, is gay.

I have a theory. Find a film with lots of male nudity, especially frontal stuff, and you're damned likely to find a gay director, out or not—the favor serendipitously extended to the opposite sex. This isn't to suggest that gay directors are preying upon their male stars any more than hetero directors are preying upon their female stars, just that only gay men are sweet enough and thoughtful enough to think about their brethren out there in the dark waiting for that extra-special moment to take home with them. The lopsidedness of male vs. female exposure in the movies is an indisputable fact and for a legion of teenaged female moviegoers *The Blue Lagoon* was their first opportunity to see a guy naked. And what a guy. A golden Adonis in the altogether flesh.

Based on a 1908 novel, and filmed once before in 1949 with Jean Simmons and Donald Houston (who?), *The Blue Lagoon* is the story of Richard (Dick in the novel) and Emmeline, two young cousins shipwrecked on an exotic little island who become the Adam and Eve of their castaway paradise. They grow up, discover sex by happenstance, manage to have a baby of their own, and then are rescued while on the verge of death, lolling adrift in a homemade boat. The film was gorgeously photographed by the great Nestor Almendros, who was Oscar-nominated for his work here.

There's a potent rite-of-passage quality to the experience of watching these kids discover each other that transcends health-class horror movies. Though the pair are incredulous as to how they ended up parents, their sensual coupling and tender play titillated audiences.

Puberty never seemed so easy a transition, so clean and natural, as when these naked little forms swimming in translucent blue-green waters suddenly reveal themselves splendidly enlarged, turning into the full nude forms of a young man and woman gliding through the water like beautiful sea creatures.

Shields is spared the natural fact that she would be sporting hair under her arms and on her legs in order to maintain her Westernized appeal, while Atkins is displayed to accommodate full-scale ogling. When he does adorn his loincloth, it's no Tarzanesque flap designed to simulate a Ken doll's lack of equipment. It's barely more than a supporter, with things to support in it. Atkins is sleek and golden and sexy, a fantasy figure who

He's going to need a bigger boat. Christopher Atkins in *The Blue Lagoon* (1980). PHOTOFEST

knows nothing about sex. Who wouldn't love to teach this boy the facts of life?

Brooke's first period, her developing "buppies," Chris' wondering why "all these little hairs are growing on me," his getting caught playing with himself. their frequent nude swims: Human Sexuality 101, Hollywood style. Kael again: "The film has an inevitable, built-in prurience. All we have to look forward to is: When are these two going to discover fornication?"

There's more to it than that. There's also tremendous charm in these non-actors' occasionally awkward performances. Atkins actually fares better than Shields, especially when she finds that insistent monotone when she's mad at Richard, but they're a lovely pair on screen and they work very well together. There's a sweetness to their recitation of half-remembered Christmas carols or when his "Our Father who art in heaven" ends with "and liberty and justice for all."

The film was shot on Nanuya Levu island and Atkins says day after day of filming in that kind of heat and amongst those exotic surroundings made walking around naked in front of 30 people feel quite natural and not embarrassing in the least, though he was slightly concerned about the possibility of getting aroused in front of a very innocent Brooke. The biggest hazards he faced on the shoot were multiple cuts and scrapes from the coral, bruises on his behind, and the grief of parting with the cast and crew when the project was finished. It remains his favorite film. Probably because, he admits, it was his very first and such a rewarding experience.

Though it may be hard for some readers to fathom, *The Blue Lagoon* was released before the widespread advent of the VCR, so the only way you could see dear Christopher was to go back to the theatre, pay again, and sit through the whole movie again. No fast-forwarding, slow-moing, or freeze-framing. You had to see everything you wanted to see at 24 frames per second, so with a movie as packed with good stuff as this, you had no choice but to see it over and over just to make sure you saw what you thought you saw or what you thought you may have missed or what you wanted to see more clearly now that you knew where to look.

One could certainly buy the teen magazines for some pretty provocative stills of Mr. Atkins, and, at age 20, I wasn't above doing that if the cashier was an old lady and there was no one else in line, but *Playboy*'s treasured "Sex in the Cinema" issue was the only place you could find him in all his glory. They

So he's got a bigger boat. Christopher tries to launch Brooke Shields, leaving the island to the two of us. PHOTOFEST

209

had printed a color shot of him and Brooke on the water slide, with Chris up front and completely nude at a perspective that may not have lent itself to flattering proportion, but was an accurate freeze-frame of a very fast on-screen moment. For now, that would have to suffice.

I was smitten with Christopher (just a year older than myself) and my infatuation turned July of 1982 into one of the longest months I have endured. No personal tragedy experienced. No special birthday coming up, anniversary, or longed-for coming out. Nope. I had just perused the latest copy of *Playgirl* at the local dimestore by using the "I'm looking at *Time* magazine" overlay technique when I came upon the "In Our Next Issue" last page which promised a Christopher Atkins celebrity centerfold. My heart raced. A thrill of anticipation flushed through me and I must have gone several deeper shades of red than usual. My God, he's going to appear naked in a magazine! In thirty days, he'd be mine.

I visited the store too often not to be suspicious that agonizingly long month, daydreaming about Christopher's eventual unveiling. After weeks of longing and numerous mental bouts during which I fought the rush of excitement by attempting to think about other things because there was nothing I could do until it actually showed up, I walked into the store and my eyes immediately caught a reconfiguration of color denoting a new cover. The September 1982 issue was on the stands with Chris' bright smiling face and gorgeous green eyes there to greet me. "Celebrity Nude: *The Blue Lagoon*'s Christopher Atkins Takes Off His Loincloth." With only slightly more hesitation than in the past because the stakes were now considerably higher, I secreted the issue into my jacket, paid for a copy of *Time* magazine, and walked out of the store. Had there been surveillance, I would have been nabbed right away. Even though it was evening, I had no sooner stepped into the parking lot than I pulled the issue from my jacket and flipped through it with an earnestness made appreciably thicker by the tension in my hands.

I devoured the spread in seconds, just enough time to realize he had no penis. He didn't have the heart to show his dick.

I returned to one shot injudiciously cut off just below a tease of pubic hair, then turned to a full page beauty, likewise lopped, but this time even higher than his short and curlies, though I strained to see them where the little fuzz trail beneath his belly button fell off the page. Then again to the centerfold. Chris standing in a pool, his body awkwardly torsional at the waist so that his buttcrack could be seen, but still only a bit of hair up front. I tried to make out his penis or some semblance of it in the ripple of seemingly clear water in front of him, but the photo had been too artfully rendered to obscure. It might as well have been Burt Reynolds' famed spread in *Cosmopolitan*, but I was glad it wasn't. I was disappointed to be sure, but eventually adjusted and made do. That frustrating centerfold was even extricated and prominently featured on the refrigerator door of my first apartment in Hollywood. Out on my own for the first time, it was liberating to hang a naked man on my fridge. Of course now I wish I hadn't chopped up the issue.

The Blue Lagoon made Christopher Atkins a fixture in gay men's bedrooms, as well as on their refrigerators. Professionally, he was signed to a four-year contract with Columbia, but 20th Century-Fox eventually bought him out to do *The Pirate Movie* (1982), a "*Pirates of Penzance*" mod musical so awful that it's a must-see, especially for the scene in which Atkins is asked to don a loincloth and a deep-sea diving helmet while Kristy McNichol sings the catchy tune "Pumpin' and Blowin'." The new studio made no bones about what they had bought: not just this hot young actor, but more specifically, *The Blue Lagoon* boy, full head of unnatural white-blond curls and all.

The very first shot of him has him shirtless and getting his chest fondled by a gaggle of gals. Later, he'll treat us to a shirtless flex and pose.

"A terrible disclosure has just been made," he tells Kristy.

"Then zip it up."

Television work included a turn as a Mormon hunk rejecting polygamy in *The Child Bride of Short Creek* (1981) and a sexy, but short-lived stint on *Dallas* (1983-84 season) as Linda Gray's Peter. A lifeguard love-interest on the series, he was usually shown to great advantage poolside and was once accused of stuffing his speedo with a sock by a production company exec concerned about the clarity of the actor's manhood on the small screen. (Typically, *Playgirl* ran some of Chris' photos again in the December, 1983 issue when he was *Dallas*' new heartthrob.)

Such clarity reached its zenith in *A Night in Heaven* (1983), a surprisingly trashy and therefore assuredly guilty pleasure from *Nashville* (1975) writer Joan Tewkesbury and *Rocky* (1976) director John G. Avildsen. Tapping into the male stripper trend of the early '80s, the film hoped to exploit that fad and throw in a simple twist. A career rocket scientist whose own rocket doesn't fly finds out that his lonely wife, a teacher played by Lesley Ann Warren, is having an affair. One of her students, a cocky young thing named Rick (for Richard or Dick), turns out to be a male stripper at club "Heaven," where a very shy and embarrassed Warren finds herself with friends. Garbed appropriately in an astronaut suit and introduced as Ricky Rocket, Atkins bucks his Teflon bulge in his teacher's face. The student/teacher fantasy is a porn loop staple and it's nice to see that Oscar nominee talent in Hollywood didn't feel the need to elaborate much.

At a suspiciously scant 83 minutes, *A Night in Heaven* was either seriously chopped by a nervous distributor or they just couldn't scrape up any more usable footage. The film remains legendary in its own way not only for its subject matter, but because it offered Atkins his most gratuitous exposure since *Lagoon*. A pair of bright yellow shorts nicely packed to the left with a roll of quarters and a hacky-sack is only a hint of things to come from spunky young Christopher. The piéce de resistance is a hotel room love scene between Atkins and Warren. (The actress recalled that Chris was a "great kisser.") When he places her trembling hand on his crotch, every gay man in the audience was cupping a hand in Pavlovian response. As his pants are coming off, the audience begins a frantic search for some telltale sign of "it" before the camera cuts away in the long tradition of cinematic tease. Astonishingly, the shot lingers and catches his cock bobbing into view in what appears to be a semi-excited state! It's brief, but it's irrevocable. It's also a surprising revelation given major studio reluctance to feature male frontal nudity, and that much more surprising given the fact that Atkins was no longer an unknown. If an actor does show his all on film, it's usually early on in the career, rarely after he's been established as a name. (It's also worth noting that a man, director Avildsen himself, was the editor. So it was his decision to lengthen where others have shortened. He operated the camera, too. Lucky devil.)

Of course, Atkins' name was synonymous with nudity by this time, so perhaps the filmmakers were just being kind enough to give the audience what it wanted. Still, the exposure is landmark. A celebrity dick sighting is an important event whenever and wherever it occurs, but what makes this one extraordinary is that it looks to be on its way up. (The only other tumescent member I've come across in an R-rated film is John Canada Terrell's bedroom hard-on in Spike Lee's *She's Gotta Have It*.)

Christopher has often been asked about appearing nude on film and the disparity of male nudity in relation to female nudity in motion pictures, but from his perspective, he half-jokingly says, the disparity is a myth because every movie he's done he's been asked at one time or another to peel.

Twelve years after *The Blue Lagoon*, he dropped his shorts and sauntered butt-naked down the beach in *Wet and Wild Summer* (1992), but mostly he's tried to branch out and play villainous roles in low-budget, direct-to-video films, such as *Dracula Rising* (1993; actually, his vampire isn't the bad guy) and *Die Watching* (1993). He found some success doing features in Australia and has twice appeared in period western/Civil War era projects with Martin Sheen. He was even Broadway-bound in the 1980s in a revival of Tennessee Williams' *The Rose Tattoo*, starring opposite Gina Lollobrigida, but the production was scrubbed well into rehearsals after the untimely death of the show's producer. And in 1995, he briefly reunited with *Lagoon* director Randal Kleiser to play a young man dying of AIDS in Kleiser's autobiographical *It's My Party*. There was persistent talk of a sequel to *Lagoon*, but there probably wouldn't have been much interest unless the young couple had decided to become nudists when returned to Victorian society. (The unofficial follow-up, *Return to the Blue Lagoon*, released in 1991 without the original stars, was a PG-13 retread with virtually no nudity, bigger loincloths, and decidedly less combustion.)

As for his own queer fans, Atkins has been aware of them since day one. Not only has he been genuinely untroubled by the attention, but he has even embraced it to a degree. From the get-go of his career, he granted a friendly interview to the oldest gay skin magazine, *In-Touch for Men*, the year he was "The Creature from the *Blue Lagoon*," complete with a half-dozen loinclothed stills provided by Columbia Pictures. Married since 1985, and with children, Atkins has shown himself to be quite open to his extended family of fans. He was reportedly very gracious at a signing in the mid-'90s in West Hollywood when a long line of middle-aged men, some hefting scrapbooks devoted to him, patiently waited their turn for an autograph and a picture. Among those photos he happily signed were nude stills (even frame blow-ups) from *Lagoon* and a piece of pure beefcake from his *Playgirl* shoot that included a swatch of pubes incomprehensibly clipped from the magazine's version.

Christopher Atkins was the tenderloin icon of the new decade, a golden boy whose loinclothed image invited the world to contemplate his beauty as a male in erotic terms. Not long after Nastassja Kinski's famed Avedon nude appeared in which she was provocatively draped in naught but a python, Atkins was asked to do the male equivalent and didn't hesitate. An actor concerned about being objectified as a male sex symbol and perhaps undermining his integrity would undoubtedly have passed. To his credit, Christopher thought it was a great idea and just went with it. He was right to do so. It's a sexy photo and a refreshing example of an actor with insight into his own image who's willing to have fun with it. Years later, still in great shape, Christopher finally obliged with up-front nude studies in Greg Gorman's photobook *As I See It* (2000).

It little matters if critics or even audiences think he is an accomplished actor. He embodied male sexuality at the cinema at a time when acknowledging such beauty for beauty's sake was just beginning to become acceptable. You hear men described as being "beautiful" all the time these days, but that wasn't (and perhaps isn't) always considered a compliment. With Christopher Atkins it sure as hell was. What's more, he had the good sense to be flattered by it and enjoy all the attention.

"I'm completely straight," he told a gay publication many years ago. "I'm still too busy looking at girls to think about guys. But," he shrewdly added, "I don't want to turn anybody off." Spoken like a true gentleman and a savvy leading man.

The first on-screen kiss **Mel Gibson** (1956-   ) unleashes in his movie career is square on the lips of another man. And he smiles about it.

Lucky for him, virtually no one saw the film at the time. *Summer City* (1977) is a god-awful drive-in movie, a plotless ramble about four obnoxious guys driving and driving and driving around with surfboards on top of their car, stopping only to drink, be rude, and mutter apparently improvised dialogue that's nearly inaudible. Gibson is shirtless when we first see him, and his lean physique is beautifully cut, topped off by a blond dye job. He has trouble improvising why he loves surfing while black flies dot his face, arms, and bare chest. None of the other blokes are any better at it. Some of the made-up lines are repeated over and over because the actors can't think of anything else to say.

Okay, so acting wasn't his first choice. It wasn't even his choice at all. Born in Peekskill, New York, he's the sixth of eleven kids raised by traditionalist Catholic parents. His father worked on the railroad until suffering a serious back injury and then carted his family off to Australia in 1968 partly in order to remove his oldest boys from possible draft into Vietnam. The trip was largely financed by dad's appearance on TV's *Jeopardy* game show, where he won $21,000.

Mel's older sister Mary, perhaps sensing her brother's potential for a life of pub-stool mediocrity, filled out an application on his behalf to audition for the National Institute of Dramatic Arts and he got in. *The Summer City* job came up while he was studying performance and appearing in numerous productions, including playing Romeo to Judy Davis' Juliet.

After graduating, he went on to the State Theatre of South Australia. The indigenous after hours pub life and his pretty face assured him trouble and it was fortuitous that he was still recovering from a good smashing when he went to audition for *Mad Max* (1979). Otherwise director George Miller might not have seen the potential.

At first glance, *Mad Max* looks like a drive-in flick, especially circa 1979 in the US, where the film had all its Australian dialogue replaced by bad American dubbing. (Finally, in 2001, the DVD edition returned the Australian soundtrack.) But its low-budget and crashing cars, flying metal, screeching tires, and crunching bodies are the kinetic elements to a dark and cynical story that's surprisingly visceral and intense. "Just a few years from now...," Max Rockatonsky, an interceptor for the Bronze, loses one of his closest friends on the force at the hands of a marauding gang of bikers called the Glory Riders.

A disturbed and angry (not quite yet mad) Max quits the force despite a superior officer setting him up by telling him, "they say people don't believe in heroes anymore. We're gonna give 'em back their heroes." Max escapes to a slice of countryside bliss with his lovely, saxophone-playing wife and their adorable baby and family dog. We know their idyllic existence will be short-lived. And we know that once Max gets Mad, there will be no rest for the wicked until the guilty explode onto grills of oncoming semis or burst into flames while contemplating using a hacksaw to hew through their own ankles.

Mel Gibson was born to play Max. In many ways, it's a supremely enviable role for any actor faced with a face like his. He's so incredibly good-looking that we're instantaneously attracted to him, whether we're full-body leather fetishists or not. In or out of his kit, he's gorgeous. Gibson is blessedly unaware of his looks, though, and you sense that, so there's never a threat of his spoiling his image with ego. He's an actor first and foremost, and the scene in which he's running down the highway in absolute desperation in order to rescue his wife and baby, only to realize he's too late, is a dramatic and powerful moment for the

Mel Gibson finds himself the object of Captain Bligh's desire in *The Bounty* (1984). PHOTOFEST

actor in him. Devastated and drained of emotion, with his family destroyed by social violence, Max becomes a shell of a man. Gibson's face glazes over, but he doesn't become vacant. Like Clint Eastwood, he possesses the ability to emote through his mask, and I'll wager it's harder to do when looking out through a pretty face than a leathery one. We are ever aware of the pain behind Max's increasingly broken, beaten, and bloody facade. Vengeance never looked so beautiful.

In the equally low-budget *Tim* (1979), based on a novel by *Thornbirds'* author Colleen McCullough, but with a plot set-up that suggests a porn flick back in the days when they had plots, Mel plays a 24-year old retarded man who gets a job working as a yard boy for a lonely older woman. Tim is earnest, cute, sweet, and genuinely endearing, but he's also inescapably hot in his tight cut-offs and black muscle T. He's got arms like other people have got legs. But he's got legs, too. And shiny thighs after a day's work. And a tantalizing smattering of chest hair between eraser-nub nipples. Mary, the older woman played by Piper

Laurie, invites Tim to the beach, but calls and asks his dad for permission first. Tim's decked out in a pair of tight blue Speedos, but he doesn't want to go swimming all by himself. He uses his puppy dog face to plead with Mary. Their friendship isn't particularly developed in the film, but it's still touching because—can you believe it?—it's not really sexual.

A series of utterly ridiculous death scenes materializes to complicate matters and teach Tim what "die" means, though that's a real stretch of ignorance for a 24-year old. The whole movie should have been 25 minutes long, having the good sense to end with the scene showing the happy couple running along the beach together. I selfishly would have preferred the sweet to the sour. Gibson won Best Actor from the Australian Film Institute for his performance.

Mark Lee (1958-   ) is the face that fills the screen at the beginning of Peter Weir's *Gallipoli* (1981). We may have been expecting Mel Gibson's, and he'll get his own introductory shot when the brim of his hat lifts to unveil the face of a star, but unsuspecting viewers will be just as pleased with Lee's. Coached by his father to run "as fast as a leopard" on legs made of "springs, " Lee's Archy Hamilton is a blond boy of 18 eager to run and join the fight his countrymen are putting up against the German-allied Turks on the

Mel Gibson and Mark Lee (right) are best of buddies signed up to fight the German-allied Turks in *Gallipoli* (1981). PHOTOFEST

peninsula of Gallipoli in 1915.

Before he joins up, he races a drifter named Frank (Gibson) who has no interest in joining the fight because "it's not our bloody war." Archy and Frank define a handsome couple. Archy is blond and wears white clothing. Frank is brunette and wears dark clothing. They ride the rails and get stranded in the middle of nowhere, deciding to defy odds and trek 50 miles through the desert to get to the next town. When Archy joins the Lighthorsemen, thanks to Frank's pasting some hair on his baby face, Frank decides he might as well have a go, too. Anything but infantry, but infantry it is. The two will meet again during training in Cairo and carve "Frank + Archy" into a pyramid. They'll carouse with friends, go skinny-dipping together (one butt as perfect as the other's), and find themselves in the trenches during an ugly diversionary campaign that's supposed to allow the British to make a landing.

One of these beautiful lads will act as communications runner. The other will be part of the next wave of young men to face the enemy machineguns. An order to send the next group out onto the field is being "reconsidered," but it will have to be delivered by a runner to an officer who has just received conflicting orders. There will be two runners at the end of the film and a final image you will never forget.

Gallipoli is a love story between two men in every way except sexual. It also becomes in its last half-hour or so a lyrical ballad about war...not just this war, but the war of your choice. It possesses the ambient thickness of a poem whose tone turns inexorably to dread. It's self-fulfilling in a way, because we know where we're heading but we can't turn back until its last word...its final, haunting symbol.

Mel Gibson went on to *The Road Warrior* (1981) a bona fide Australian film star. Mark Lee, a former model and coffeehouse singer, has only appeared sporadically in films since the enormous critical success of *Gallipoli*. *The Best of Friends* (1981), *The City's Edge* (1983; as an unpretty addict), and *Emma's War* (1986) were Australian films that barely strayed from Australia, but *The Everlasting Secret Family* (1988) had some quirky cross-over appeal.

Arthur Dignam, who had trouble as a Brother keeping his eyes off the Catholic school boys in *The Devil's Playground* (1976), plays The Senator, a man of wealth and power and breeding who cruises Saint Michael's Private School for Boys one afternoon and picks out The Youth (Lee). He's got the blond boy-beauty naked in his hotel room in under seven minutes. The young man with the impossibly smooth and golden skin says he wants Creme de Menthe and to watch the telly before they finally embrace on the bed and kiss for the fade out.

The Youth is quite aware that he's part of a long tradition of boy-playing and decides to take full advantage of what he's got—even talking a clerk at a men's store into letting him try on a pair of bright white undies before buying them. The Senator thinks the boy should enjoy his station as the personification of youth, but the Youth wants more. He gets out of line at a restaurant and is punished for it. He responds by calling the Senator a "fag." Later, the older Japanese man he's forced to couple with at a queer party stops by the fish tank to pick out a live crab to take into the bedroom with them.

At first, Lee looks just a little bit too old for the role. The *Gallipoli* Lee would have been perfect, but the odd screenplay has somewhere to go; namely, fourteen years later, when the Youth strikes up a relationship with the Senator's son—they sunbathe at the beach together. The actor playing the son has a nice body, but he should have been prettier. He actually looks older than Lee, which is slightly the point, since the Dorian Grayish Youth has undergone experimental and secretive medical treatments to remain as boyish-looking as possible.

Those of us awed by his natural beauty in *Gallipoli*, and thankful for the way in which he deepened our emotional connection to that story by virtue of his looks and acting skills, could only have wished that we could one day see Mark Lee: changing positions butt-naked in bed, sucking on a pair of fingers, going down on a guy in the backseat of a limo, threatening to use the belt around his waist for discipline, forcing a high court judge to lick his shoes, stripping down to a pair of tight black undies in the doctor's office, dragged up in make-up and garters, or walking around the house in just a shirt and asking us if his "bum has dropped." *The Everlasting Secret Family* came damn close to fulfilling all those wishes.

If Lee couldn't be prolific on the big screen, though he still shows up from time to time on the Aussie little screen, then we should all thank our lucky could-have-been-stars that we got the chance to see him shine even just a little.

Mel Gibson was awarded Best Actor, again from the Australian Film Institute, for his work in *Gallipoli*. He followed it with another classic. *Mad Max 2*, which America knows as *The Road Warrior* (1981), is the action film as mythos. The story is narrated to us as history after a third World War (importantly, non-nuclear) has taken its toll on the planet, leaving disparate bands of survivors to clash over hoarded supplies of gasoline. One such community bargains for the mercenary assistance of a lone Road Warrior (Gibson's Max) to fend off a roving army of freaks and geeks, outfitted in the leftovers of punk rock and professional wrestling, so that they can travel to a picture postcard paradise 2,000 miles away and start over.

Its action sequences, which rivet because most of them appear to be playing out in actual time, literally hurl you into the mayhem. Gibson, with his scarred and weather-beaten face, displays an intuitive sense about why Max is now The Road Warrior, a mythological being who comes out of the desolate landscape as a Dark Angel and is left standing in the middle of the highway against a murky dark blue and misty sky. Max is one of the movies' great anti-heroes.

The Road Warrior was a huge international hit at the box-office and propelled Mel Gibson to stardom. Predictably, another sequel was made in 1985, *Mad Max Beyond Thunderdome*, but turning the character into a franchise was a mistake. Having the Road Warrior rescued by a monkey in the desert doesn't even begin to detail what went wrong. Nearly a decade later, Gibson reprised the role again in *Mad Max: Fury Road* (2004).

Reunited with *Gallipoli* director Peter Weir on *The Year of Living Dangerously* (1983), Gibson plays the temperamental foreign correspondent sent to cover the political strife in 1965 Jakarta. It's a powerful film, and though some have suggested all he's got to do is play straight man to Linda Hunt in her Oscar-winning performance as Billy Kwan, he once again demonstrates a screen presence that transcends his good looks. On the basis of his work here, I'm not sure Gibson is capable of just showing up as a pretty face. He's always got something going on behind those gorgeous green eyes.

"Ain't the size that counts, youngster," says a boatman to Franchot Tone when he looks upon his ship in the 1935 version of *Mutiny on the Bounty*. "It's the salt in the lads that matters." Mel Gibson is a salty lad. He tells us that if we look closely we can find the shot in his version of *The Bounty* (1984) where a nasty beating by three bozos in a pub brawl the night before necessitated his being photographed from only one side of his face. His brawling and drinking and reckless nights out also put fear into co-workers on *Mrs. Soffel* (1984), whose scenario glances on the weird dynamic of handsome criminals before careening into unbelievable romance—even if it is based on a true story. He boiled his *Hamlet* (1990) down to an angry young man and put quite a few asses in seats to watch Shakespeare that hadn't before.

Early on in *Lethal Weapon* (1987), Gibson climbs out of bed and walks across the room butt-naked. It's a handsome butt. A very fine specimen indeed. Extremely well shaped. And utterly exploited. It doesn't look much older than when it had a scriptural reason for being bared in *Gallipoli*, but not many people saw *Gallipoli* and *Lethal Weapon* was designed for the masses.

The abominable *Bird on a Wire* (1990) gave the masses a second look—in close-up—and it wasn't nearly as pretty. "I didn't realize I was that furry on my back end," said Gibson to one of several media magazines that cheekily asked him about showing his heinie. "My bum's got a fair carpet, doesn't it?"

I was sure that the close-up of Mel's butt in *Bird* was a stunt-butt, because it's not seen connected to anyone in particular, but then you have to wonder why someone would stunt-butt a star so poorly. "It's kind of gross," said Mel to another magazine. "When I saw a rough cut, I said, 'Aw, c'mon, you've got to cut that out,' and they did cut some of it. Of course, now that the movie's on video, viewers can freeze-frame it, I guess."

It's hard to believe that when someone yelled, "I'm ready for my butt close-up, Mr. DeMille," that the star or his make-up people didn't ensure that everything was picture perfect back there. Not everybody's ass can stand the rigors of close-up photography, mind you, but I'm still unconvinced that we're looking at Mel in that scene. In *Lethal Weapon*, where the moss may be camouflaged by the distance, there's no mistaking that the behind belongs to him because the rest of him comes with it.

So, in addition to sitting and shitting, it turns out that Mel Gibson's ass has many jobs. It also has a sexual occupation. Women love looking at it, and made no secret about admiring its appearance in *Lethal Weapon*, whereas gay men must have enjoyed the flash, too. Straight guys who blanched at the sight, but knew it was there for the benefit of their girlfriends, sisters, and wives, had no trouble settling back and watching the rest of the badly made crowd pleaser with its whacked-out heartthrob as a suicidal cop prone to fits of Curly Howard.

In the long tradition of torturing the homoeroticism out of good-looking leading men (Valentino, Novarro, Barrymore, Flynn, Power, Hall, Ladd, Mature, Newman, Presley, etc.), Gibson is trussed up and has jolts of electric current shot through his bare torso while being doused with water. The audience squeals in associated pain, but there's a bizarre sexual undercurrent to the scene that you don't have to be an S+M/B+D practitioner to appreciate.

Both scenes, the baring of his ass and the lingering on his bod as he's tortured, have the same purpose: star-fuck titillation. They're both blatant examples of eroticizing Mel Gibson's "Sexiest Man Alive" movie star image to the masses, though he would be the last to admit it.

How could his ass mean anything more to audiences than it does to him? In 1992, the crude and very honest Mr. Gibson gave an interview to *El Pais*, a Spanish newspaper, in which he was asked in some form or another about gays and responded by rising, pointing to his behind, and announcing, "This is only for taking a shit." Furthermore, it's said he admitted that it upsets him at times that people assume he might be gay because he's an actor. "Do I sound like a homosexual? Do I talk like them? Do I look like them?"

No. No. Yes. (Just kidding.)

Suddenly no upstanding member of the gay community—whatever that means—could admit he found Mel Gibson sexy anymore. A decade before, you'd have to squeegee the floor after mentioning his name. Look at *Mad Max* or *Tim* or *Gallipoli* and you have to walk pretty far around the subject not to come to the conclusion that he is a most lovely example of manhood.

Do I have to agree with what an actor says off-screen to enjoy what he has to offer on-screen? I don't think so. It may not help fuel my desires in the same way when the fantasy becomes tainted by an outside reality, but I'm a big boy now and I think people are entitled to their opinions. Not everybody who doesn't understand or accept homosexuality is an evil homophobe. Gibson has suggested that his comments were misunderstood jests; he has a notorious sense of bad humor and enjoys the filthiest of jokes. So who knows?

Well, Mr. Smarty-pants writer, who apparently will apologize for any asshole celebrity so long as he's "beautiful," how do you explain what Gibson did with *The Man Without A Face* (1993)? The original book has a homosexual subtext that was entirely eliminated by the adaptation Gibson approved and directed and it's reported there was an attempt to have the novelist write out that particular aspect so that the book could be republished as a movie tie-in. The author refused.

And what about the scene in his Academy Award-winning *Braveheart* (1995) where he has the king throw the faggy prince out the window?

The easy, but doubtless unsatisfying answers are that all book adaptations are just that; they're not the book. Producers, studios, and directors make all sorts of decisions about how they want to tell their story to reach a desired audience. The operative phrase is "based upon." As for *Braveheart* (1995), a monumental achievement in updating an old Hollywood studio epic—like the rousing kind Errol Flynn used to make, but with a shocking sense of what steel really does to flesh and blood when they meet on the battlefield—I suppose you could argue that thousands of innocent people were slaughtered so why pick out one? Since when does medieval history show us that purported homosexuals were protected from acts of wanton cruelty?

Enough already. Even post-*The Passion of the Christ* (2004) weirdness, I'm not quite ready to condemn him. If anything, his proclivity for ritualistic depictions of physical punishment unleashed on the male body is more troubling at this point. Should we really take his sudden flaming faggot hairdresser act in *Bird on a Wire* as proof that he's out to get us? Perhaps he's just a true-blue heterosexual, married only once and with a small army of kids, whose subscription to a Catholic sect manifests moral and religious beliefs that don't coincide with yours or mine. He's also likely among that percentage of straight men who cannot imagine in their wildest or most desperate dreams one iota of erotic interest in another man, which otherwise would clue him into the vast spectrum of sexual attraction and complexity in the human animal. He's not alone in that feeling. There are plenty of gay men who can't muster likewise for a woman, though it's true they'd be hard-pressed to deny its occurrence in the species.

Is it so difficult to admit that who you dreamed about and lusted after all along up there on the movie screen was never more than a fantasy anyway? The knee-the-jerk reaction from some segments of the organized gay community to Gibson was not entirely unlike the plot of *The Bounty*, in which Anthony Hopkins' gay Captain Bligh is so taken with the strapping young (and often shirtless) Fletcher Christian (Gibson) that when it turns out the fellow is really interested in a native girl rather than seamen, the Captain throws a scorned tantrum and makes life miserable for everybody. The punishment won't go on for long, though, because Mel and his hetero mates mutiny and set the scowling queer and his lackeys adrift in this superb re-thinking of the famous story.

If you can't help your politically correct self, throw Mel Gibson overboard with a hiss and a raspberry into the arms of straight women, precisely where he thought he was making his mark all along. For the rest of us, gay and straight alike, there's no denying he was once a real babe.

"Homosexuality always openly celebrated male beauty, and there's little doubt that the general acceptance of a gay subculture has encouraged an outspoken appreciation of masculine sexuality in the mainstream culture," reported *Newsweek* magazine in May of 1983 as it took on "The Incredible Hunks" that seemed to be popping up everywhere we looked.

Boston Orioles pitcher Jim Palmer had been successfully standing around in his Jockeys since 1980, but the celebrity sports figure as good-sport sex symbol was what sold the posters and ad space, not the design or daring of the airbrushed and asexual images.

It took an "unknown" Brazilian pole-vaulter standing 45' x 48' on a billboard in Times Square to seal the deal between what America was too embarrassed to admit it desired and the gay culture was too pre-occupied with to ignore. Bruce Weber's historic composition for Calvin Klein Underwear in the fall of 1982 rightfully belongs in a museum somewhere. The Male Idol was born again.

Lounging somewhat stiffly against a simple white stone sculpture, with the bluest of clear blue skies shouldering the image, a deeply bronzed **Tom Hintnaus** aloofly models his blazing white Calvin Klein briefs and there's no mistaking that he's got something in them. As profoundly important as that is, he's also got something pouring out of them: the rest of himself—a lean, hairless body with well-defined pectorals and strong, sturdy thighs. His face, with its turned-up nose, is unmistakably handsome, and the black hair lends striking contrast, but the stroke of genius was to have his eyes closed. Is he resting? Is he posing? Does he know we're looking at him? Does he care? Is he inviting us to admire his body? In other words, he's all things to all people. The image invites a mental dialogue, inspires a scenario. It tickles your fancy and triggers fantasy.

As an icon unaffiliated with a specific celebrity, which would only have engaged presupposed personality and the problem of narcissism, the Hintnaus billboard for Calvin Klein sparked a sweeping cultural acclimation to male beauty as both pleasurably inoffensive and highly desirable. Hintnaus, by the way, shows up in the show-stopping locker room number in the camp classic Village People musical *Can't Stop the Music* (1980). Along with the sights of Olympian Bruce Jenner in very tight and very short shorts, and even Steve Guttenberg managing to make an impression in the front of his tight white trousers, you can catch Hintnaus as the smiling beauty in the Speedo next to the smiling blond in the jockstrap as bust-bursting Valerie Perrine and the gang crash the Y.M.C.A.

The impact of Bruce Weber's photos on fashion advertising, television, the movies, and a cultural sensibility about fitness and desirability was enormous and influential to this very day. Neither Weber nor Calvin Klein can claim to have invented the aesthetic packaging of male beauty, but they were certainly pioneers in the commercialization of it. Even John Travolta, whose naturally hairy and less-than-muscle-bound physique shown off in tight black undies or dressed up in white polyester didn't stand in his way of becoming a huge male sex symbol in *Saturday Night Fever* (1977), was forced to reconfigure to the new aesthetic. Director Sylvester Stallone put Travolta on a torturously rigorous training program to build up all his vein-popping and unnatural potential, then had the actor's body shaved to show it off in the horrific sequel *Staying Alive* (1983).

While it was nothing new to have gay men model as "straight" for *Playgirl* magazine, the men of gay porn, who had been paying meticulous attention to their bodies for years, were suddenly being "secretly" tapped to pose as the modern woman's new ideal. Mr. September, 1980, "Jean Carrier," with a hard-on nearly as wide as it was long, had been working in both straight and gay porn as "Johnny Harden," famed for his ability to suck his own dick and ejaculate in his mouth. I clearly remember seeing him under another phony name on a *Donahue* show in the '80s about male gigolos. He was basically playing it straight for the Midwest crowd, but one curious member of the audience asked to see the copy of his *Playgirl* spread that Phil was waving around and the camera didn't cut away quite fast enough before she'd opened to the centerfold and her mouth dropped in shock. We didn't see what she saw, but we could tell something was up.

In his essay on "The Gay Decades" for *Esquire* (11/87), Frank Rich recalls being outsized by the Hintnaus billboard that "had the androgynous Studio 54 waiter look...It was a shocking sight at first—I couldn't decide whether the image was more threatening as a homoerotic come-on or as an unrealizable heterosexual physical ideal that women would now expect me and all men to match." Going on to perceptively criticize the negative aspects of the obsession with male beauty as pseudo-Fascist and, in the gay community at least, a form of cruel prejudice against those who lack it, Rich notes the telling names of exercise machines called "Bringing Up the Rear" and "Butt Attack." We could add "Buns of Steel" and others to the list. "The ass, that prime receptacle of male-male sex, was the new king of erogenous zones."

He's right. The culture at large didn't talk about guys' butts, or how "cute" they could be, until the gay '80s. What, after all, does a woman want to do with a guy's butt other than squeeze it? Is it merely an aesthetic, something to show off but left otherwise unexplored? Heterosexual men also have big hang-ups about their asses when they're not alone. But slap Bruce Springsteen's in jeans on the cover of *Born in the U.S.A.* (1984) and look out.

The exercise infomercial for men was born in 1984 when a little company called Soloflex hired 20-year old college dropout and ex-gymnast **Scott Madsen** (1964-   ) to be their poster boy. Blond, boyish, and beautiful, Madsen possessed a face and body so flawless, and artfully photographed by Aaron Jones and Lis DeMarco, that they connected the viewer to the lush sensuality of skin and the erotic harmony of muscle tone. This was Tadzio grown up.

Rolling Stone said Madsen did "for exercise machines what Brooke Shields did for designer jeans." Simon & Schuster published the oversized *Scott Madsen Poster Book* in 1984, featuring 18 increasingly gorgeous and increasingly less-clothed tributes to this Adonis with his streamlined and perfectly symmetrical porcelain body, his sparsely haired underarms, and his peculiarly sexy and anatomically suggestive belly button.

Books about pretty boy models and pretty boy models doing books about fitness were a sign of the times. Madsen's own fitness book, *Peak Condition*, with a cover that invites us to lean in and sniff his sweaty armpits, was published in 1985. But it was the cover of his poster book that said it all about the collision of gay male erotic imagery and its incorporation into the mainstream. Seated on a bench, with his legs spread to either side of it, Madsen rests one hand on the top of a thigh and has the other arm raised up and resting on his head. He's all shiny, and in full color, and you can see the beads of sweat (real or sprayed) on his bare skin. The only clothing he wears is a pair of off-white, almost sheer-looking exercise pants and the unmistakable bulges of his crotch will cause your eyes to cross trying to burrow through the thin fabric and determine what is what and where is what.

Madsen's successor to the Soloflex beefdom was Olympic Medallist **Mitch Gaylord** (1961-   ), just one of many enticingly handsome and cute male athletes the world was treated to at the 1984 Games. (A statue of a male nude torso, including uncircumcised genitalia, bookended a nude female torso at the Olympic Games that year, but the media was apparently afraid to show it. The model, by the way, was Olympic athlete Terry Schroeder, captain of the U.S. water polo team.) We may shy away from saying it, but the often astounding combination of beauty and athleticism we're treated to every four years at the Olympics ritually satisfies our appreciation for athletic excellence and our appreciation of the human figure in perfect form.

"A hard man is good to find" read the ads when gymnast Gaylord was Soloflex's spokesbody, but the homoerotic probabilities of the Madsen ads and his substantial gay following were tempered and broadened by the addition of a female arm coming from off frame and resting on Mitch's shoulder. With a name like Gaylord, you can guess the heterosexual athlete and the enterprising company wanted to make sure there were no misunderstandings.

Gaylord, who was privately traumatized at the Games because of a high bar performance he couldn't forgive himself for in spite of team medals, was cruelly suckered into the Hollywood meat grinder and "promised" a career like Tom Cruise's. He played a chain-smoking and troubled gymnast in the awful *American Anthem* (1986), helmed by the director of *Purple Rain* (1984), and was devastated by its failure. His personal life spiraled out of control until he met a woman who didn't know who the hell he was and they happily married and raised a family.

The 1980s saw the rise of male strip clubs and the Chippendales became nationally famed for their hard-bodied and often long-haired hunks who were ready and willing to disrobe for trendy female attention and the thrill of having a throng of screaming and giggling ladies stuff dollar bills into their thongs. Christopher Atkins played a stripper in *A Night in Heaven* (1983) on the big screen, while **Gregory Harrison** (1950-   ) and **Jon-Erik Hexum** (1957-1984) did it on the small screen in *For Ladies Only* (1981) and *The Making of A Male Model* (1983), respectively. Hexum was a devastatingly handsome 25-year old man with a beautiful face on a solid, thick, and nicely haired (and groomed) body. He went from calendar man to a failed TV series (*Voyagers*) to impossibly gorgeous poster boy before tragically and accidentally killing himself while fooling with a .44 Magnum loaded with blanks on the set of CBS-TV's *Cover Up* series in 1984.

Even heterosexual men got in on the testosterone fest of the decade by making Arnold Schwarzenegger, Sylvester Stallone, and Jean-Claude Van Damme huge and bare-chested action stars. Van Damme, who once told *Movieline* magazine—which was evidently interested enough to ask—that "I've got a normal dick" size-wise, found himself in the New Releases section of the video store on the cover of *Monaco Forever* (1984) after he'd become a big screen star. It still gives me a twinge of righteous pleasure to think about all the beer-swilling boys who rented the thing thinking they had just come across a brand new action flick starring the Muscles from Brussels. Instead, three minutes into this obnoxiously bad 28-minute short, they saw their hero in a red sports car pick up a male hitchhiker, feel his passenger's leg up, and then grab the guy's crotch. The car comes to a halt. "Come on faggot!" the hitchhiker taunts, to which Jean Claude, after asking if they can just talk it out, peels off his top and executes a series of face-shattering, near-miss twirling kicks. The hitchhiker runs away as Jean Claude Vandam, the Gay Karate Man (as he's billed), flexes his mighty biceps and calls him a "sissy boy." In 1991's *Lionheart*, a thug tells Van Damme: "You're kind of pretty. I don't know if I want to fight you or fuck you."

In the vernacular of show business, underwear has legs.

Risky Business (1983) would have no doubt been considered a very good film and done more than reasonably well at the box-office without it, but I'm not sure it would have come to be recognized as a great film and a huge box-office success had **Tom Cruise** (1962-   ) not danced in his underwear.

It was a single line of action in the script, but a frightfully serious young actor like Cruise was encouraged to embellish and the resulting 68 second riff on freedom to the tune of Bob Seger joined Rick and Ilsa at the foggy airport as one of cinema's classic scenes. Think I'm kidding? I'm not.

Risky Business is *The Graduate* (1968) of the 1980s, a shrewd and sarcastic view of the American Dream served up as a coming-of-age film. "The dream is always the same," intones Joel Goodson (Cruise), the cute white boy destined for corporate affluence with a foot in the office door thanks to his wealthy suburban parents and his participation in the school's Future Enterprisers program. The dream, as he describes it, is of the classic high school anxiety variety. He finds himself at a house in which a naked woman taking a shower invites him to wash her back, but then loses her in the steam and relocates himself in school with only two minutes to take his college entrance exams.

Left on his own by his white bread parents while they visit Aunt Tootie, the young man mixes Coke with his Chevis Regal, doesn't know enough to heat his frozen TV dinner, and when backing his Dad's off-limits Porsche out of the garage, he stalls it and the soundtrack music stalls, too…until he restarts it.

Tom Cruise has a butt that does something to a pair of soft, lived-in jeans. The sight makes you want to move in. So when he cranks up the off-limits stereo and slides into mid-frame across the wooden floor wearing only his socks, a pair of white briefs, and a pink shirt, you're certain that even if the rest of the film degenerates into crap, you've been rewarded with a moment of greatness. Wisely, the film's trailer included generous footage of the undie scene—an instant seller. No one really knew who Tom Cruise was that summer of 1983, but they would definitely know him thereafter.

Fortunately, the rest of the film is as brilliant. The underwear dance wasn't about sex or lust or cheap exploitation of a young male star. It struck a chord because it was liberating. It was charming and sexy and funny; completely abandoned and real. Audiences were treated to a playful moment of adolescent exhilaration with which they could all identify.

Risky Business is a comedy that finds layers in any number of seemingly genre-specific ideas. Horny teenager movies are a dime a dozen, but Joel Goodson has to go to the bank to cash a bond his grandparents gave him as a child in order to pay for the gorgeous hooker he had in the living room, on the staircase, and in front of the "Star Spangled Banner" on TV last night. Joel Goodson gets a crash course in American business and becomes the ultimate Future Enterpriser by agreeing to turn his folks' Glencoe home into a whorehouse to service his needy schoolmates. Joel Goodson is going to Princeton not because he has the grades, but because he showed himself to be an impressively savvy entrepreneur.

There has been criticism that writer-director Paul Brickman caved in to studio pressure to change the original ending of the film because it was considered too dark. In that version, Joel made his $8,000 in a night, but he wasn't going to Princeton. He had failed. Yet the new ending doesn't seem to be any "lighter," and I can't imagine anything much more appropriate than the closing we're given. The boy becomes a man over a weekend and all his folks notice is a small crack in the interior of mom's artsy-fartsy knick-knack egg. Joel gets what he wants by trading in sex, but the gains are superficial. He even wonders if Lana (Rebecca DeMornay) and Guido have played him all along. Joel's relationship with Lana is pointedly ambiguous, as is their final exchange.

As fitting testament to the film's mixed messages about materialism and self-worth in the '80s at the expense of relationships, the Ray-Ban Wayfarer sunglasses Cruise wears when he adopts his role as cigarette-smoking pimp sold 330,000 pairs after *Risky Business*, an 1800% increase over sales from 1981. Teenaged boys even started wearing pink shirts.

Thomas Cruise Mapother IV was born in Syracuse, New York, but was constantly on the move from town to town right up until he became an actor, and then he traveled even more. He was raised almost entirely by his mom (after a divorce from dad) in a house populated by women. His three sisters used to bring their girlfriends home from school and let the young ladies practice their kissing techniques on Tom while he sat on the kitchen sink.

Ever the new kid in school, he was challenged by dyslexia and sought to make friends by playing sports. He briefly considered the priesthood while at a Franciscan seminary. After suffering a knee injury while running stairs as part of wrestling team practice at Glen Ridge High School in New Jersey, he was encouraged by a teacher to go out for the school play in order to keep active.

He was cast in the lead as Nathan Detroit in the high school's production of *Guys and Dolls* (would have loved to hear him sing) and it was there that a very Hollywoodish thing happened. A casting agent saw the play and asked him whether he thought he might want to be an actor. He didn't have to ask twice. The kid even skipped his high school graduation to get a jump-start on his newfound career.

He worked for only a day or three on *Endless Love* (1981), the Brooke Shields' epic of young lust and madness, during which director Franco Zeffirelli was said to have felt up young Tom's chest. Cruise appears in just a single scene, but it's a speaking role and an important one. He runs into frame wearing a pair of cut-offs after chasing a soccer ball and then pulls off his sweaty blue shirt to join a conversation in the schoolyard. In high register, he boasts about having been an arsonist at age eight and unknowingly gives the idea to Martin Hewitt to set fire to Brooke's house and then save her, pretending to be the hero.

From Day One of his chosen career, Tom Cruise had a single overriding character trait: he was deadly serious about the work. He was cast in a very small role in Harold Becker's military drama *Taps* (1981), but exhibited such selfless determination and tenacity during the off-screen boot camp preparations for the film that when it came time to replace an actor in a supporting role who wasn't working out, Becker went straight to Cruise and asked him to play the part.

Tom's remarkable politeness got in the way. He felt bad for the actor who was fired and had mixed feelings about taking it. Becker set him straight. And Cruise made his first impression on audiences as a short, beefy powder keg named David Shawn, a red beret at a military academy forced with closure until violently taken over by its cadets. Shawn becomes the symbol of the macho, gung-ho military mind-set who skipped everything in the training manual that didn't have to do with combat. Timothy Hutton is the well-intentioned cadet making a series of wrong decisions to uphold immature concepts of honor and tradition and Sean Penn makes his impressive film debut as the moral conscience of the piece.

Teen psycho roles in horror movies were offered to Cruise after his ballistic turn in *Taps*, so he decided to fight off the possibility of typecasting and agreed to star in a low-budget coming-of-age film whose title was crassly, if understandably, changed for marketing purposes from *Tijuana* to *Losin' It* (1983). No one would have believed it was the same actor. Doughy to the shirt collar, he plays Woody, the nice guy who goes with three friends down to Tijuana to dip his wick. To its supposed credit, the film wants to be more than just a teen-sex movie, but maybe would have been a lot more fun had it ignored its aspirations. Cruise appears visibly embarrassed, and it's not just coming from his character. He and "older woman" Shelley Long check into a seedy motel room and have sex (off-screen), but it isn't at all clear as to why. In fact, it's weird given Woody's personal morals and the rest of the plot. Too bad cute John Stockwell (aka John Samuels IV in *The Andy Warhol Diaries*), who appeared to better advantage in *Christine* (1983) and later directed *crazy/beautiful* (2001) and *Blue Crush* (2002), gets thrown in jail before he can fully exploit his physical charms on our behalf.

Continuing his chameleon-like physique changes from film to film, Cruise built up his biceps, took a cap off a chipped front tooth, and refused to shower for a week at a time to play the small role of greasy

Greaser Steve Randle in Coppola's *The Outsiders* (1983), assuring him entry into the teen magazines as one of a juicy line-up of hunks. It's nearly impossible to imagine that when Cruise flew in to audition for *Risky Business* he would have been seriously considered for the role. Good actor or not, he was surely the wrong physical type. That's what director Paul Brickman thought, too, until he had him read. Fate must have played a hand, as did a promise from Cruise that he would re-shape his body in time for filming. The muscle gelled into high school P.E. class fitness wrapped in a thin layer of role-appropriate baby fat.

Risky Business made Tom Cruise a star in August of 1983, and like the hard-working Hollywood player under contract he resembled, he still wasn't done. *All the Right Moves* (1983), an earnest and grimy drama about a high school football player hoping to land a sports scholarship to get out of a bleak Pennsylvania steel town and earn an engineering degree, was Cruise's fourth film release in a single year. The baby fat was turned back into muscle thanks to weeks of rigorous football practice with a high school team before shooting began.

The solidly acted and well-intentioned film is probably better known to non-sports aficionados as the movie in which you can glimpse Cruise's dick as he shucks a pair of jeans in a nipple-to-nipple love scene with Lea Thompson. As pleasantly surprising and curious as the close-up of a film star's genitalia is, there's a lovely context and a tenderness to the scene in which it appears here; my awkward way of saying that I fully appreciate the look (and paid admission three times in a single day to see it again and again), but find it all the more extraordinary because it's part of a sexy scene in which two characters are expressing love for one another, not lust.

Tom Cruise was such a huge star in such a short time that he could have burnt out in a hurry, but even after two years absence from the screen, when the legendarily troubled *Legend* (1985) opened, the box-office showed significant interest…at least initially. Wearing his hair down to his shoulders and decked out in a tunic, he's Jack O' the Green, a friend of the forest, who teams up with an assortment of little people and fairies to save the Princess and the world of light from the big, nasty, red demon of Darkness (Tim Curry), hell-bent on sacrificing a unicorn. Amazingly, considering all the lush botanical sets amounting to forests built on soundstages, the glitter in the air, and the fairy tale trappings, Cruise still manages to give off sexual vibes. The long hair works well with his face (a romance novel cover boy without all the exaggerated girth) and he's got the shapely legs of a dancer.

Buzz off the long hair and give him his sunglasses back, then put him in a cockpit wearing a US flag on his uniform and look out world; America is suddenly 5'10" with a mile-wide smile and capable of kicking ass along that highway to the danger zone. None of Cruise's legendary research and role preparation mattered when it came time to playing Maverick in *Top Gun*, the biggest hit of 1986. There wasn't even a character to play. Just a symbol. Cocky, arrogant, sexy, brave, sensitive, hero-boy.

In terms of action, the goods in *Top Gun* are all aerial. The down-to-earth stuff is paint-by-numbers and increasingly silly, though two sequences are worth mentioning. First, the brief volleyball game in which half-naked, sweating he-men glisten and grunt while their muscles flex and reverberate and half the audience knows this is the best part of the whole movie. Second, the love-making scene which begins in bluish silhouette. Cruise is standing there shirtless with the flaps of his pants open. In the era of AIDS, straight America staunchly reassured itself with what has to be the most explicit French-kissing between film stars ever seen in a PG movie; the fact that the tongue exchange is also in silhouette makes it even more startling. Parents who cringe with their kids next to them when any love scene begins had to be stunned when the tongues came out. My advice to nervous future generations wanting to share the film: tell your little guys to pay attention to how Cruise gets taller then shorter then taller again from scene to scene. That ought to keep them busy.

Top Gun is a weird movie. A thrilling entertainment in some respects, but wide open to ridicule. Cruise and Val Kilmer (as Iceman) both have teeth so big and white that you wish they'd take big juicy bites out of each other. Quentin Tarantino's famed gay deconstruction of the movie in *Sleep With Me* (1994) was an exaggerated joke, but you have to legitimately wonder what's behind the moment when director Tony Scott skootches his camera back to show Cruise standing at the mirror in his tight white jockey shorts—affording us a breathtaking wide-screen view of his handsome butt—when the emotional context of the scene is Cruise's mourning the loss of his best friend Goose.

For all the bashing that Cruise would eventually take as a control freak pretty boy with little or no acting range—a favorite cheap shot at actors dubbed "pretty boy" is that *ipso facto* they can't act—you only have to look at his follow-up to *Top Gun* to see cracks in the popular criticism. Cruise dons a ridiculous

Tom Cruise as a star quarterback, ominously shadowed by coach Craig T. Nelson, in *All the Right Moves* (1983). PHOTOFEST

wedge of Tony Manero hair and plays a dopey flake opposite Paul Newman in *The Color of Money* (1986), Martin Scorsese's update on Newman's pool shark Fast Eddie Felson from *The Hustler* (1961). Audiences who had turned him into a hunky poster boy of an American ideal in *Top Gun* weren't nearly as patriotic when he showed them that what he really was was an actor. An actor acts. He plays all sorts of parts. He's not afraid to look like a goofball if the script calls for it.

Cocktail (1988) almost seemed like a concession, though. If this is what you really want me to do, then I'll do it. It was a gift to the fans who dated him in their minds. He took that strikingly handsome image and lacquered it in Reaganomic yuppiedom in *Rain Man* (1988), though we all knew he'd finally cave in and love Dustin Hoffman just like the rest of us who don't show an ounce of equal compassion or understanding toward real people in our lives.

Born on the Fourth of July (1989) saw him outwardly unattractive and wheelchair-bound playing to the hilt the real-life story of Ron Kovic, who patriotically went off to fight in Vietnam, came back paralyzed from the waist down, and became a vocal protestor of the conflict. Cruise was Oscar-nominated. And he continued picking his projects in a fashion that mirrored his diverse choices as a young actor when he wasn't in a position to pick and choose.

Days of Thunder (1990) is a pandering summer movie with few thrills beyond guessing what Cruise has in his pants for that close-up in which a female police officer frisks him as part of a practical joke. We were also eager to see what was under the bowl he had resting over his privates as he lay naked and provocatively unconscious in bed in *Far and Away* (1992). Then-wife and co-star Nicole Kidman got to peek for us. If it's any consolation, he wasn't wearing anything.

A Few Good Men (1992) and *The Firm* (1993) weren't particularly impressive in terms of acting challenges, but his wholly controversial casting as Lestat, the long and lean and very blond bisexual vampire in the much-heralded screen version of Anne Rice's *Interview With the Vampire* (1994), was, according to Rice, like casting Edward G. Robinson to play Rhett Butler.

Rice would later recant after seeing the film, and I give Cruise all the credit in the world for having a go at a role everyone said he was wrong for, but *Interview* is a serious bungle and Cruise looks like a blond Tiny Tim. True, vampires of ancient lore, and certainly pre-nineteenth century, were monstrous demons, not fops in formal wear, but there's too much needless gristle and gore in the film, clotting the rich possibilities for a gothic romance between Cruise and Brad Pitt. When Cruise first puts the bite on Pitt, an epiphanous, operatic moment that carries them both aloft among the sails of a docked ship on the Mississippi, the hot and heavy spell is quickly broken by everything that follows. The second visitation, in which Lestat munches on Louis and gives him the choice of dying or living on as one of the undead by munching back, should have been erotic, but it's just gory. You have to wonder why the hell Louis says "yes" to the invitation to prolong his personal misery by becoming a creature of chalky countenance, with fat blue veins and irritating contact lenses.

There are those who devoutly believe vampires are metaphors for gay people because they are "different," are ostracized as "monsters," and are essentially misunderstood. Each represents a netherworld of attitudes and desires that seem foreign or even perverse to the vanilla-straight populace. Each are feared and hated because they fall outside the norm. Gay people have been effectively demonized as creatures of the night by a society blinded by self-righteous sunlight.

Horror and eroticism are inextricably linked in literature and the vampire has long been regarded as a sexual creature. That his desires are perverse and that his very life is sustained by the ingestion of blood has further commingled the connection between the undead and the unstraight. "The blood is the life," remarks Count Dracula to Jonathan Harker by way of circumnavigating his own bloodlust through quoting Scripture. The blood that was considered the life ever since mankind took notice that his brother stopped moving after all that red stuff ran out of his head became medically and literally metaphorical to semen just about the time that science identified the sperm cell and literature blushed at the idea.

To drink blood—to drain away "life"—is to ingest semen, of course. Once fully drained, the victim of a vampire becomes one of the Undead, joining his brethren in their unnatural quest for more victims. Death in the biological sense, in the sense of finality, only comes to those inconsequential one-night stands whom the vampire never sees again (the connection works wonders since the stigmatization of AIDS as a "gay disease"). They have fulfilled their purpose, to feed the vampire's desires, and are now of no need. But the others, those whom he cares for or falls in love with, they are destined to rise from the dead and join him for all eternity infecting others. The so-called gay initiate is in for the same kind of undeath. His natural life dies (sometimes including job, family, and friends) and his unnatural life begins in association with those who are just like him. The comparisons are nearly endless, as are the extrapolations and compensations and leaps of logic that are employed to justify the association.

But the real question is: why?

What is the advantage of gay people identifying themselves with demons of the night and why are some people so insistent on the marriage? The truth is that vampires have been linked with homosexuality in literature and the cinema because vampires are unnatural, deviant, evil. Gay men and women have conversely found a resonant, even erotic connection because the vampire's aberrant nature allowed the expression of perfectly normal same-sex attraction to the almost exclusion of it in other contexts. It was an empowerment amidst repression, and there was a viable and once understandable connection made between the demonized and misunderstood and often quite sad creature of the night and the world that shunned him or her. But vampires don't have to be evil. Neither do gay people have to be feared and reviled. I love a good horror story as much as the next guy, and I've always been interested in the sexual aspects of vampires, but I'm tired of all the half-baked homo-metaphors. Give me two lovely lad protagonists, live or undead, and I'm always going to be hopeful that they fall into each other's arms.

Since first reading *Interview with the Vampire*, I have maintained that my primary interest in the story, aside from my own adolescent fascination with vampires, was in its sensuality. Rice's lush prose and overabundant descriptions of room interiors and draperies was just too much frosting on an already rich concoction of physical transformation. Lestat's "love" for Louis sustained me throughout and the tension was palpable along the way. I forged on through the tale hoping against hope that Lestat would finally take Louis in his arms and make wild passionate love to him. Many would argue that that's exactly what he did when he bit the kid—the bite, of course, being the obvious metaphor for penetration and the exchange of bodily fluids. But sex as biting has never made any sense to me except in the driest and most academic of literary senses. Why would vampires forego the pleasures of the body just because they find sustenance in sucking blood from their victims? The blood is food, and though food and sex have ancient connections and can be a lot of fun when properly mixed, they are two very separate needs that can be entirely independent of one another. Even leeches, which are hermaphroditic, have sex once in a while. And why not bite a guy in his hard-on? Lot of blood there.

Tom Cruise was smart to make it clear in publicity interviews for his role as Lestat that the piece wasn't about homosexuality, though the media was ravenous about connecting the sexual connotations of his character's falling for Brad Pitt with the rampant and insistent rumors about Cruise's own sexual orientation.

In two *Mission Impossible* movies, the 2000 sequel even worse than the 1996 original, he trumped an industry fixated on his adherence to Scientology and his all-consuming control of every aspect of his films by satisfying the box-office with big numbers and proving that the image of Tom Cruise suspended in mid-air by wires or hanging by his fingertips from a mountain precipice was reason enough for the masses to go to the movies.

At the same time, he could use his movie superstar powers for good. *Jerry Maguire* (1996) was a refreshing return to commercial success and a winning performance (Oscar-nominated, too) in a Hollywood movie, while *Vanilla Sky* (2001) explored the psychological agony of (movie star) facial disfigurement and *Minority Report* (2002) posited a future in which I would have been arrested by Tom Cruise for things I imagined doing to Colin Farrell. He also agreed to sleepwalk for two years through Stanley Kubrick's thick and deliberately unsexy *Eyes Wide Shut* (1999), and then turned in a knowing and self-immolating performance as a consumer-culture perversion of the male sexual animal reclaiming his manhood at the end of the 20th century in Paul Thomas Anderson's epic *Magnolia* (1999). As an infomercial guru shamelessly worshipping the cock as the almighty symbol of male superiority, Cruise skewers celebrity, misogyny, the male ego, and about half a dozen other topics—identity, father/son relationships, empowerment seminars, male anxiety, and male penis envy, among them.

It was a film in which, once again, audiences wondered just what it was he had inside his underpants.

Robert Hepler Lowe (1964-) has probably done more for his gay fans as a straight film star than any actor of his generation, a not insignificant claim considering his contemporaries include Matt Dillon and Tom Cruise.

Born in Charlottesville, Virginia, but raised until adolescence in Dayton, Ohio, Rob was the oldest of

225

four boys, though you might forgive someone for thinking that the Lowes had three sons and an older daughter. He's just that pretty. Beautiful, in fact.

And like many male beauties, he had great difficulty with the way in which his extraordinary, crippling good looks made up other people's minds about him. He was both an object of desire and an object of derision.

His mom and stepdad moved the family to Southern California when Rob was about 12, almost as if they knew a boy that photogenic should be near an industry built on images. He went to high school at Santa Monica High, where his classmates and friends included Sean and Christopher Penn, Charlie Sheen, and Emilio Estevez. The future generation of highly divergent movie talents spent afterschool hours goofing off and making dozens of Super 8mm home movies together. (A compilation of these indie efforts would be a blast to see, should the group ever sanction it.)

Interested in theatre since he started seeing and then appearing in plays back in Dayton, Rob pretty much knew it was acting that he wanted to do more than anything, even though he has been completely deaf in his right ear since infancy and some might have considered that an occupational disability. He landed a few commercial jobs in L.A. and found work in a pair of ABC Afterschool Specials: *Schoolboy Father* and *A Matter of Time*. In 1979, he was cast in the ABC sitcom *A New Kind of Family*, but the show lasted only six aired episodes before getting canceled.

He did an admirable job playing a skinny boy with a defective heart in Hallmark Hall of Fame's *Thursday's Child* (1982), but he was fortunate to get his first feature film assignment co-starring with a gaggle of talented would-be names in Francis Ford Coppola's *The Outsiders* (1983). Rob plays Sodapop Curtis, the only greaser of the Curtis' that has a right to be greasy; he works at the DX (dicks) gas station with Tom Cruise. At least he knows something about personal hygiene. It's a welcome sight to watch Sodapop emerge from the shower wearing only his towel while surrounded by so many other good-looking guys.

The Outsiders could have been a huge break for the pretty kid without a lick of acting school training, but the studio forced Coppola to cut his three hour epic into less than half and most of Sodapop's scenes went down the drain. (A couple were added back in for the non-premium cable TV airings of the film, but the scenes are just as awkward and unimpressive as what was left in.)

So how come he's almost entirely lost on the cutting room floor in his first film and then he's given lead billing over Jacqueline Bisset and Cliff Robertson in his second? Because *Class* (1983) was a teen sex comedy with a surefire teen sex star. Bisset may be a key plot device in the film, which has her playing Rob's slightly deranged and sex-hungry mom, but the script drops her like a boat anchor after she's served her purpose. She's left to an off-screen psychiatric institution after picking up and bedding Lowe's new best friend at prep school, a teenager her son's age played by Andrew McCarthy.

Class is about the boy-boy friendship anyway, so I selfishly ignore the "you screwed my mother and now she's nuts" gimmick and just enjoy the hell out of the rest. Lowe is a clean-cut, but devious, wisecracking, and fun-loving yuppie-in-the-making named Skip Burrows. His first act of friendship is removing his robe to reveal a tanned, slim physique in red bra and matching panties. Even on the big screen, I couldn't imagine where the filmmakers (let alone the actor) had stuffed his naughty bits to effect such an unoccupied presentation. We may not have had it at the time, but hard evidence that Mr. Lowe came handsomely equipped was forthcoming and makes the visual effect all the more amazing...and possibly Oscar worthy. The trail of dark fuzz descending from under his belly button and into those panties seems to lead to nowhere.

Alas, Skippy has not come out of the closet, though Lowe takes a quick look "down there" when McCarthy, the humiliated victim of his new roommate's practical joke, pulls off his own black panties. Straight guys coming of age, even at the behest of their roommate's mother, are nowhere near as tantalizing as "straight" guys coming to grips with each other.

"You still owe me a blow job," quips Lowe to McCarthy after a joke about his helping the latter get accepted into Harvard. I would have definitely re-written the film's ad copy thusly: "The good news is that Jonathan is having his first affair...The even better news is that it's with his roommate." The film could still have ended the same way, with the two beating each other up, wrestling around, and bloodying each other's noses until McCarthy knees Rob in the nuts, they fall to the edge of the bed next to one another, and then break out in laughter. Time to make up.

In interviews over the years, Rob Lowe admitted that being called a "teenage heartthrob" angered him to the point where his stomach would burn. Everybody talked about his looks, judged him on his looks, wrote about his looks, asked him about his looks, and looked at his looks. He was fuel for the teen magazine industry and, though it may have irked him, he posed shirtless and provocatively for countless articles, color pin-ups, and posters, just like the rest of the boys. Redford, Beatty, and Newman were his early interview heroes for having successfully transcended the outer curse of their physical features to reveal inner resources as good actors capable of playing more than hood ornaments or window dressings.

Lowe's beauty may have cost him the leads in both *WarGames* (1983) and *Footloose* (1984), but landed him in *The Hotel New Hampshire* (1984). John Irving's unfilmable novel was put on film by veteran British director Tony Richardson, whose career included *A Taste of Honey* (1961), *The Loneliness of the Long Distance Runner* (1962), *Tom Jones* (1963), and *The Loved One* (1965).

Hotel is one of my guilty pleasures. Rape, incest, lesbianism, homosexuality, suicide, murder, prostitution, terrorism, interracial marriage, a plane crash, a child who has stopped growing, Nastassja Kinski in a bear suit, and a terminally flatulent dog named Sorrow don't come close to completing a list of its contents. It's a weird, awkward, throw-it-at-the-fan kind of movie that struggles to inhabit a literary alternate reality. Lowe said he certainly felt like he was in an alternate reality while he was making the film.

Rob plays handsome John Berry, our narrator, #22 on the high school football team, and the brother who loves his foul-mouthed and ballsy sister Franny (Jodie Foster) in a way that a brother isn't supposed to love his sister. The unflappable, thoroughly eccentric Berry family transform a broken-down seminary into a hotel and the fiery redhead maid catches John during a morning run in the rain. The way he's panting, "I don't know if you're dyin' or tryin' to cum." She invites him into her room, waives a kiss because of all the germs, and then drops down below his waist. Rob takes Andy Warhol's old film *Blow Job* (1964) to new heights, crossing his eyes in ecstasy as she goes to town.

"And thank God you're taking an interest in your body," says Grandpa to John, the latter whom we see during regular work-outs throughout the film: lifting a barbell while the camera looks up a gaping leg hole in his white shorts, punching the boxing bag while shirtless and shiny with sweat, and doing sit-ups in our faces.

After the family moves to Vienna to open a second Hotel New Hampshire, John catches sister Franny getting it on with Susie the Bear (Kinski). "Well, I guess I'll have to go queer now," he tells his queer brother Frank, who assures him he doesn't think that's the way it works.

The Hotel New Hampshire uses a bizarre cast of characters and situations to capture some of the craziness and unpredictability of life, where tragedy and comedy coexist. For all its death and sorrow, it celebrates the wild journey. Franny realizes that to rid themselves of temptation they must indulge. She calls her brother to her hotel room and he jogs over in lightning fast motion, takes a shower, and jumps into bed with her. She tells him his balls are still wet. "What's wrong with wet balls?" asks John, but it's Rob Lowe whose balls are wet and he's in bed with Jodie Foster and they're supposed to be brother and sister and there's something suddenly quite rewarding about the wonderful world of movies that got them there.

How the hell were the teen magazines going to sell a moment like that to their constituency? "*Class*y Rob and *Freaky Friday* Jodie play a brother and sister with very strong feelings for one another."

Rob was perfect casting for this kinky role, easily the best part of his young career. He's so incredibly pretty that even when he manages to get Susie out of her bear suit and make love to her, you know that she can remain confident in her lesbianism.

In *Oxford Blues* (1984), he's a brash Vegas parking attendant whose real-life brother Chad, playing a computer geek in one scene, gets him into Oxford by hacking into their online admissions system. Rob's Nick DiAngelo is obsessed with Lady Victoria (Amanda Pays) when we know all along he'll end up with Ally Sheedy. He's incredibly hot in his blue jeans strutting around campus, but even hotter in his black sleeveless rowing shirt and white shorts as the sculler sitting behind Julian Sands for the film's climactic rowing competition.

St. Elmo's Fire (1985), a disastrous attempt at mixing *The Breakfast Club* (1985) with *The Big Chill* (1983), has him playing a horny sax player with big hair who finally realizes what a jerk he is and gets the chance to explain what the title means by using a lighter and a can of hairspray.

Youngblood (1986) is second only to *The Hotel New Hampshire* in capturing Rob Lowe's beauty and exploiting it. It's one of those deeply homoerotic sports movies in which the sport is only the excuse for getting straight actors interested in doing it. Sports movies are also locker room movies, and if gay men are traditionally stereotyped as being non-sport enthusiasts, the locker room has never lost its heady appeal.

An irresistible invitation to climb into bed with Rob Lowe, seen here in *Masquerade* (1988). EVERETT COLLECTION

With few exceptions, sports films are to be judged on the basis of their locker room scenes, not their ball play. No matter how inept you were in gym class, how dopey you thought phys ed was, or how humiliating, it was all made worthwhile by the dressing and undressing parts.

So many gay men have rooted their early erotic awakenings to the high school locker room that virtually every aspect of the experience has become fetishized, from showering to towel snapping to secret glances to gym socks, gym shorts, and, most potent of all, jockstraps.

Hoping for just a glimpse of Rob in his jock, even willing to accept a millisecond flash that would have to remain burned into memory until the video release and stop-motion could blurrily remind you how little you saw or how much you missed the first time, no one could have prepared us for the lingering spectacle so graciously provided in the hockey movie that put newcomer Keanu Reeves into the same locker room as Rob Lowe.

The tease begins with a freshly battered Rob getting a slash near his eye stitched up in bloody, thread-pulling detail, just the kind of macho that makes the pretty boy seem remotely manly and more akin to Rambo, who sewed up his own arm. We can just make out the top band of his jock at the bottom of the frame and hope for a wide shot despite the need to go in closer and closer toward his grimacing face.

In the most homoerotically-charged scene in the film, all of his jock buddies initiate the new kid on the team by grabbing him while he's half-naked in the locker room, sprawling him down onto a bench, his biceps helplessly flexing against the pinning hands of his teammates. Team captain Patrick Swayze, sporting a jockstrap over the lower half of his face in lieu of a surgeon's mask, holds up his instruments—a straight razor and a can of shaving cream. While Rob tenses and the black hairs of his armpits offer corollary evidence to his state of manliness, Swayze pantomimes below-frame the shaving of Rob's scrotum, a particularly sexy rite of passage that's curiously unexplained. Removal of his "man hairs" serves what purpose in the ritual? Perhaps it's to separate the men from the boys...with the new kid symbolically returned to boyhood so that he'll understand his place among the pack. Sort of, he'll have to do more than show up with pubes to prove that he's a man. The only thing I can think of more exciting than the scene itself would be spending the day on the set as they worked it out, talked about it, and then filmed it over and over.

The film's crowning achievement, however, comes fairly early on, after a particularly nasty thug doesn't make the team and grumbles and tosses things around before marching out of the locker room. Rob, draped in a white towel and carrying a hockey stick, goes after the guy in a hopeless display of machismo. Hockey is, after all, about guys smashing guys' faces. The spoiled sport is gone before the encounter ensues, but Rob's towel has casually dropped from around his waist and he now finds himself standing in the hallway in nothing else but his jock, something he takes no notice of, but we can't ignore. To maximize the moment, the coach's cute daughter (Cynthia Gibb) walks up from behind just in time to catch him and she picks up the towel, asking him if he's lost. Rob turns to her—a handsome specimen in his athletic undergear, with noticeable peeks of hair from either side of his pouch—and manages a nervous, slightly embarrassed smile as he tries to escape through a couple of doors that prove locked. Resigned to his fate, he coyly covers himself with the paddle of his hockey stick. Ms. Cutie-Pie points out the direction of the locker room and he decides he's got no other way out. Grabbing his towel as he passes her, he heads down the hall back to the locker room, but with the towel over his shoulder, offering her (and us) a final look at the sashay of his strap-framed buns.

Just when there were those of us fully prepared to accept Rob's fate as the star of bad movies who took his clothes off for us, he made a few good movies and still showed us his butt.

"I refuse to go out with a man whose ass is smaller than mine," says Elizabeth Perkins of Rob in *About Last Night...* (1986), based on David Mamet's one-act play *Sexual Perversity in Chicago*. It's an in and out and in and out and in and out and in love story between two dolls named Danny (Rob) and Debbie (Demi Moore), with sarcasm and crass punch lines provided by sidekicks Perkins and Jim Belushi. It's an attempt at a modern young couple's slice-of-life, aided by the sincerity of the actors and the beauty of the two leads. There's lots of good skin exposure, too, and whether he's stepping out of the shower, standing naked at the fridge, or going for the morning paper in his jockey shorts, Rob makes the domestic situation look fairy-tale desirable even in the face of all the silly arguments. Most folks would be happy to have silly arguments over "Sandwich Night" with that face and body lying next to them in bed.

"You know what your problem is?" Belushi rhetorically asks Lowe at a local bar. "Your face. You're too good-looking. They get nervous. These girls go out with you and they feel dumpy. They don't want to compete. The best thing that could happen to you Danny is an industrial accident."

Rob was nominated for a Golden Globe as Best Supporting Actor for his role as a fiddle-playin', red-headed retarded boy who plays house with Bible-thumpin' Winona Ryder in *Square Dance* (1987). She catches him bein' fornicated upon and he feels so bad he takes a pair of haircuttin' scissors and tries to "cut off his thing." Playing against expectations allowed him to be seen as an actor, not just a face.

Even with the face, he was smart to play against type in *Masquerade* (1988), another of my guilty pleasures. A glistening, butt-naked Rob stands in front of actress Kim Cattrall and hands her a gift. The real gift had to be right before her eyes, but she doesn't give it a second glance, instead forging ahead with the scene in which she opens the box he's given her and discovers it's lingerie. Does he want her to put it on? Close-up of Rob Lowe's face. "I can't bite 'em off if you don't."

The moment is near-camp—in fact, the whole movie is, especially with John Glover mincing as straight and enough clever boy-boy schemes and plot twists to conceivably turn the thing into a gay conspiracy. What's with that scene in which Rob comes to visit cute blond Doug Savant (who years later played the token gay guy on TV's *Melrose Place*) and blondie stands there the whole time in his bright white jockey shorts? Fuck political correctness. A Lowe/Savant/Glover love triangle would have been a real treat.

Rob gets to undulate convincingly atop Meg Tilly, who was too embarrassed to be completely naked like her co-star. Rob laid there between takes *au naturel* and quietly joked with Tilly to keep her at ease. She said he couldn't have been more professional or gracious given the situation. "Believe me," she told *US* magazine, "murdering my baby in *Agnes of God* was much easier compared to this." Huh?

After becoming the scapegoat for simply being a good sport and participating in producer Allan Carr's kitschy opening number sketch singing to Snow White on the 1989 Oscar show (a moment contractually forbidden to ever be re-broadcast because there was no licensing agreement with Disney), Rob plunged headfirst into a magnum opus sex scandal that many thought had instantly destroyed his career.

Mr. Lowe, practicing unfortunate judgment, allowed two young ladies the opportunity to steal a videotape from out of his camera, $200 out of his wallet, and a bottle of prescription medication with his name on it out of his Atlanta hotel room and into the night. Rob was in town stumping for the 1988 Democratic National Convention and got hooked up with the 16-year old and her 22-year old "known lesbian" friend. The trio went up to the room where Rob enjoyed directing the two in a fantasy sex scene.

On the same 39-minute tape was a sexual encounter in a Paris hotel room in which Rob and a male buddy teamed up with a consenting adult female and performed a variety of sexual acts with her. Whether she knew that the camcorder on the dresser was aimed at the bed or in the record mode isn't made clear from the video alone.

What was crystal clear to the mother of the 16-year old when she saw the tape was that a movie star was engaging in sexual activity with her daughter. Ten months after the incident took place, and after the tape had been handed over to authorities, The Rob Lowe Sex Scandal broke loose with a frenzy. The case split open like a rotten cantaloupe as the press moved in on the gynecological details: a punky hair salon that employed both young ladies, a pre-publicity history of bragging by the girls—complete with screenings of the video for friends, an implied threat to extort a couple of million dollars out of Lowe in exchange for the tape, a mother going through a nasty divorce case who brought the tape to light by including it in her grievances, and the following desperate charge in the face of Georgia's age of consent being 14: Rob Lowe "used his celebrity status as an inducement to females to engage in sexual intercourse, sodomy and multiple-partner sexual activity for his immediate sexual gratification, and for the purpose of making pornographic films of these activities."

Worse yet, depending on your point of view, the Parisian episode was duped and almost instantly available on the "black" market, as well as in highly edited and highly profiled segments on national tabloid and entertainment news shows. Here then was one of the most beautiful men of the movies caught in the act, and unfortunately for the actor there wasn't quite enough loss of resolution to avoid impressive silhouettes of his enthusiasm. And even though it fulfilled a prurient fantasy beyond one's wildest dreams by offering such first-hand knowledge of the sex life of a gorgeous movie star, it couldn't escape the stigma of real-life attached to the viewing of it. There was perhaps a bit too much reality at work. Readers may find it hard to believe, but I think the *Rob Lowe Sex Tape*, as it came to be known, was a horrific invasion of privacy. It was never intended to be seen by anyone other than whom Lowe may have purposely shared it with, if he shared it at all. If there was "moral" wrongdoing, or criminal culpability, then those charges should have been dealt with entirely in a court of law. The tape itself was evidence, and as such, shouldn't have been allowed out of responsible hands. But videotape is videotape, after all. Highly reproducible. And even the most principled among us couldn't deny an overwhelming curiosity once it was bootlegged. People were paying up to $5,000 to view it before it became as easy to purchase as commercial porn. Lowe was eventually sentenced to community service, but the tape and the scandal threatened to do something truly bizarre, and yet strangely predictable, for him.

The sex tape gave Rob Lowe character. Not necessarily character that he didn't have, but definitely character that people pre-occupied with his pretty boy image would never have looked twice to see. Everybody knew he was something of a playboy, with a long line of dalliances and romances with famous femmes such as Nastassja Kinski, Fawn Hall, and Princess Stephanie, but behind-closed-doors playboy and naughty sex video playboy are two different things, if only in superficial terms of image.

Cast and crew alike took to wearing T-shirts on the set of *Bad Influence* (1990) emblazoned with an answer to the question everybody was asking: "The video scene was already in the script." And Lowe, quite truthfully, had already been signed to the glorified B-movie before the scandal hit.

Lowe's first film after the humiliating and personally mortifying experience of the sex scandal had him playing a psychotic Lothario named Alex (the same name as *Fatal Attraction*'s harpy) who mysteriously gives James Spader, playing a mouse with ulcers, a set of man-balls. Early on in their relationship, Spader awakens in his apartment to find Rob watching a home video of a drunken Spader having sex with a woman he's miraculously picked up at a bar.

"You make a very funny face when you cum," observes Alex, who also manages to have the tape played at Spader's engagement party. Later, Alex will use videotape to complement a dastardly deed he carries out at Spader's apartment, easily the creepiest and most powerful scene as orchestrated by director Curtis Hanson, who later directed *L.A. Confidential* (1997). There's even a sex scene in which Rob is naked in a room where two women are in bed together.

Alex asks Spader early on, before everything goes to hell, what he wants more than anything else in the world, and I wish he would have just said, "you," because the film is in painful need of some sort of motivation. Written by David Koepp, who wrote a better first draft of this story for *Apartment Zero* (1988), *Bad Influence* is so afraid of homoeroticism that it's entirely devoid of sexual tension. It comes off as a vacant exercise whose plot is essentially inexplicable. There doesn't seem to be any meaning behind their relationship. And okay, so once again it's probably not the best solution to make this a gay psycho flick, but wouldn't it have been great if Spader was forced to deal with his closeted homosexuality because of his attraction to Lowe, only to find himself torn when the object of his affections turned out to be both a fucking nut and straight?!

Even *Saturday Night Live* knew enough to predictably play around with the homoerotic appeal of Rob Lowe, as it does with virtually all its good-looking guests in the tried and true theatrical tradition of extracting cheap laughs by having "straight" boys flirt with queer possibilities. Today, it's most often employed to both defuse straight audiences' suspicions of an actor's "silence" on the subject, as well as show how hip and casual actors are to playing with their hetero-personas and demonstrating that they're good sports and open-minded, but certainly not really gay. For an appearance broadcast live on his birthday in 1990, Rob takes a tingling verbal lashing from Dana Carvey's Church Lady for his recent behavior, then willingly submits to having his jeans-clad ass paddled while the delirious Church Lady shouts into his rear at point-blank range and commands: "Get out of his buttocks, Satan! Leave his buttocks!"

Another skit has Lowe thrown into a prison cell with a paunchy hard-ass played by Phil Hartman. It isn't long before the brash daddy is complimenting the new kid on his "nice, tight butt...the ladies, they like a tight little butt." Turns out that the big oaf just wants some tips on getting into shape for the gals on the outside. Rob says he can help. He wants to know if the guy has ever heard of the Lambada? It's the forbidden dance, of course, and Rob is suddenly at his cellmate's behind, bucking his hips into the worried big guy's backside. Then, draping an arm awkwardly across Hartman's chest and managing a leer, Lowe adds: "Ya know, it's not just the ladies who like a tight ass... ." Hartman breaks away and screams at the bars while Rob cackles to himself in a final frame worthy of a gay EC horror comic.

Rob Lowe stopped boozing in 1990, quite happily married in 1991 (and has children), played the Monty Clift role in a Great Performances production of *Suddenly, Last Summer* (1992), and appeared on Broadway as part of the National Actors Theatre's mounting of the French farce *A Little Hotel on the Side*. He has made a barrage of low-budget and direct-to-cable movies—wrote and directed some—and did regular cameos in Chris Farley and Mike Meyers movies. He received unanticipated critical accolades for his role as Deputy Communications Director Sam Norman Seaborn on NBC-TV's *The West Wing* (1999-), though contract negotiation difficulties and hurt feelings resulted in his leaving the show in 2003, and striking out on his own in *The Lyon's Den* (2003-). He did a dead-on impression of Robert Wagner's #2 in *Austin Powers: The Spy Who Shagged Me* (1999), though his in-bed-with-himself scene (Wagner and Lowe together at last) was chopped out of the theatrical print...only to show up in the DVD version extras.

Mike Meyers would use his "cream of some young guy" joke in a scene with Lowe ordering Chinese food in *Wayne's World* (1992). That the oily cartoon villain Rob plays would also get stopped by the cops and subjected to a rubber glove-snapping full body cavity search is the price to pay for being that good-looking. Straight audiences find it funny when men are threatened with anal invasion, because it's such a basic fear. It's perceived as emasculating, first off, and then, on some level even beyond its humiliation, it's satisfying in an almost sexist way. Getting something shoved up your ass is akin to giving men a dose of their own phallicentric medicine. "See how you like it, asshole!" Something tells me Rob can handle it.

I haven't found him yet in *Skatetown, USA* (1979), but I'm looking. And in *Xanadu* (1980), it's impossible to tell that he's playing Gene Kelly as a youth in a ghostly flashback because it's a long shot that never moves in for a close-up. Oh, but there he is when Michael Beck and Olivia Newton-John take Kelly to go clothes shopping. He's the second from the right, at the top of the screen, wearing yellow pants and a green muscle shirt, as one of the window mannequins who comes to life. His hair is greased back like Bela Lugosi's. Then there he is again, center screen for a second or two, right after Kelly punches the bumper on the giant pinball machine. He's wearing a revealing light green top that looks like its been cut out of a hammock.

When Olivia Newton-John comes up the steps to start singing the Xanadu finale at the club, he's in the red jacket over her shoulder on the left side of the screen. We'll see him undulate rather nicely in a later shot and then he's the cowpoke with his head lowered whom Olivia struts up to, touches his face, and then tips his hat.

Matt Lattanzi (1959-   ) takes male beauty to just about as far as it can go in any direction without undergoing a sex change. The eldest of ten children from Portland, Oregon, Matt was thinking about becoming an engineer when he got a taste of drama class outside the confines of his all-male high school. He went to community college in Portland and appeared in plays, studied acting and dancing, and then high-tailed it to Los Angeles at age 20.

An active outdoorsman, fisherman, hiker, and the like, he had a body in as incredible shape as his face was naturally flawless. He was too pretty to be real, but he could dance and model and found work doing both. As a skating extra who could also hoof, he was a natural for Allan Carr's megacamp musical *Xanadu*, whose climactic club opening is done on roller skates. The kid also found himself pleasingly paired with star Olivia Newton-John as the dancing stand-in for Michael Beck. Rehearsals soon turned into quiet romance, though rumors were flying that Newton-John was involved with an extra who was ten years younger. That would be him.

Older women would become a persistent theme in the young man's career. Fifty-three minutes into *Rich and Famous* (1981), he makes himself available on the street to Jacqueline Bisset, whose character had just railed against the culture's obscene obsession with young flesh: "It's like eating green cantaloupes."

Back at her hotel room, he slowly takes off his shirt and glides towards her. She's seated on the bed, watching him. "How old are you?" she asks.

"Eighteen," comes the response as his bare torso is within licking distance and he peels down his tight, tight pants to reveal an ass as smooth and kissable as his kisser.

"Showing my buns on camera was a big decision for me, " Lattanzi once joked, "but I decided to do it for the sake of art."

New Yorker critic Pauline Kael, who knew of legendary film director George Cukor's homosexuality, seemed to allude to it when she curiously wrote: "Bisset's affairs with young men are creepy, because they don't seem like what a woman would get into." We can all beg to differ.

Years later, when author Boze Hadleigh interviewed Cukor, whose career spanned many classics over a half century, and asked who was the most handsome actor he ever worked with, he mentioned Robert Taylor and John Barrymore. "More recently, the chaps in *Rich and Famous*...the one who did the strip."

Not bad company, even if he didn't remember his name.

Lattanzi didn't even have a supporting role yet—his appearance as "The Boy, Jim" in *Rich and Famous* amounted to only six minutes screen time—but lots of people were taking notice. He was regularly invited for all-nighters by prospective producers and directors who may not have known or cared that he was Olivia Newton-John's boyfriend. He told *Drama-Logue*: "You'll sit down for an interview and they'll say, 'I just want to get right to the point' and they'll hit you with it. The way I deal with it is that I play so naive I pretend I don't even know what he's talking about. Even in Portland I had to deal with it. I feel I am more experienced than most young actors because I've been hit up so many times that way. I remember people, whose names you hear all the time, inviting me over to their house."

Gorgeous Matt said he never surrendered to the casting couch, "but I'll never be rude, because I respect everyone's sexual preference. We all have them so you can't condemn somebody for that."

He's billed as Brad in the second of his now-camp classic bad movie musicals, *Grease 2* (1982). Like

Matt Lattanzi, as "The Boy, Jim, "who gets his pants taken down by Jacqueline Bisset in *Rich and Famous* (1981). PHOTOFEST

Xanadu, the film is awful enough, but the music is catchy enough to sustain repeated viewings and I think someone should market one or both as the new *Rocky Horror* on the cult circuit. If nothing else, both liven up gay parties considerably.

One of the games you can play while watching *Grease 2* is "Spot Matt Lattanzi," whom I've personally located at least 25 times in the film. It's a lot of fun trying to find him in the background or just walking by: wearing his red-lettered white sweater in the opening number; leading the pack of track runners; front row on the aisle during the infamous "Reproduction" song sung by sex-ed substitute teacher Tab Hunter; the middle man of the "Mr. Sandman" trio who enjoys practicing in the boys' locker room shower (unfortunately, fully clothed); the boy "Brad" who wears black Chinos "with a cute little buckle that fastened in back" in the twins' duet; a dancer in white shorts around the pool at the luau, only to appear in the very next shot as the bare-chested boy up front and on the right carrying Adrian Zmed and Michelle Pfeiffer into the pool of enchantment; and then over Maxwell Caulfield's shoulder on the right side of your screen for graduation.

Ready for his first lead during Hollywood's wave of teen-sex movies, Matt stars as Bobby Chrystal, the high school virgin who flunked his French final and gets himself a sexy pedagogue in *My Tutor* (1983), not to be confused with the similarly-themed *Private Lessons* (1981).

Those of us already following his career couldn't wait for the ripe exploitation the premise promised.

An early tease as we see him briefly shower, emerge in a towel, and apply his deodorant before he and his two goofball buddies seek out prostitutes is pretty much all we get, though, as things go wrong for the dopes and Bobby, disappointingly attired in a pair of blue boxers, passes out in the enormous chest of a very large woman. These idiots can't even get laid in a whorehouse.

Hope hasn't abandoned us altogether, of course, since the tutor has yet to arrive, but we already have to make an adjustment when it comes to our beautiful lead: his remarkably high voice. You can hear it giving ammunition to those who must have teased him about his pretty face, but it's refreshingly unique and one more reason to adore him.

My Tutor may be a low-budget teen-sex movie, but it's easily a par above its cruder brethren and it finally offers us a chance to gaze at that lovely visage in "awww"-inspiring close-up. His blue-green eyes look bluer off his blue shirt. The long black lashes and eyebrows play off his jet-black hair. He possesses the kind of beauty that allows him to wear a pink shirt or, better yet, a skintight pink muscle T and make it seem sexy in the way that professional fashion models do with clothing they don't wear much off the runway either.

Bobby peeps on his tutor, played by Caren Kaye, as she takes nude midnight dips in the family swimming pool. He's supposed to be into stargazing, a budding astronomer with prop eyeglasses on hand for a single scene to prove it. They don't go well with his black T-shirt and tight and very high-cut tan shorts, though.

Eventually, the kid gets caught peeping and ends up in his tutor's bedroom. My then-21-year-old heart was throbbing in my throat during the close-up in which Kaye's fingers run down along Matt's shirtless bod, past his rippling abs, and then open his pants. But the tortures of the damned were soon visited upon me as the "love scene" degenerated into a perfunctory and unsatisfying series of overlapping fades. We don't even get a butt shot. What kind of pay-off is that for a film whose title song contains the lyric: "You show me how to squeeze it, I'll squeeze it 'til it screams?"

Comparing his two most famous love scenes for *Drama-Logue* in June of 1983, Matt revealed: "In the scene with Jackie, I was totally nude, but in *My Tutor* I wore a cup. They taped it on with duct tape. If I ever do a scene like that again, I'm going to be nude. The duct tape was excruciating. But Caren Kaye felt more comfortable if I was covered up. Now Jackie—she didn't mind. We did two takes of the scene where I pull down my pants. The first time I got into the scene, all of a sudden I saw the camera and I thought, I'm taking my pants off. I broke totally away from it. The second time I looked at her, she looked at me and I got into that. When they yelled 'Cut!' it was like a shock."

In 1984, Matt Lattanzi found himself as the alarmingly hot cover boy for Karen Hardy's trade paperback *Boy Crazy: An Intimate Look at Today's Rising Young Stars* (Plume). He also married Olivia Newton-John and appeared on her television special *Let's Get Physical*, a family-friendly take on her 1982 hit album. Interestingly, her MTV-aired video for the song "Physical" featured a work-out room full of fat sweaty men who eventually morph into taut-bellied hunks with defined pecs and bulging biceps. The video's final joke has all the guys going off with each other instead of paying any attention to Olivia, the only female in the place. It was a clever wink-wink at the notion of male bodybuilding being a gay preoccupation, or at a reach, bringing about a narcissism that could result in homosexuality.

Three years later, when Matt was being considered for the coveted role of a gay track runner who falls in love with his coach in the umpteenth attempt to film Patricia Nell Warren's *The Front Runner*, it was Olivia who reportedly told the *New York Daily News* that her husband was definitely not interested. "It's not good for his image." Truth is, had he done it, he would likely have secured himself a following until the end of time.

He replaced the silly red moped he was forced to buzz around on in *My Tutor* with a more fitting set of wheels and a career as a hot-rodder in *Catch Me If You Can* (1989). Essentially an AIP teen flick of the 1960s, the film deals with a high school due to be shuttered if it doesn't come up with $200,000 in two months. Lattanzi is a long- and wild-haired dragster with a headband who gets the heroine to use school fund-raising cash to bet on his races. Matt is supposed to be tough and mean, but he's unconvincing. The whole thing made me wish they had stolen the money scheme used in *Campus Man* (1987), based on the Arizona State University beefcake calendar that set off the trend in the 1980s. Instead of the full-sized swimming trunks Matt wears at the pool for a scene, they should have had him decked out in a Speedo (or less) like blond beauty Steve Lyon in the other flick.

Wishes sometimes do come true. Matt Lattanzi has numerous scenes wearing nothing but a tight red

Speedo in *Diving In* (1991), the story of a young diver working to conquer his fear of heights. Cute and shapely Matt Adler plays the comely lad coached by a hot "older" woman and our Matt shows up as the incredibly sexy villain—a long-haired bad boy diver who's the man to beat at the big competition. The scene in which bad-Matt tries to scare good-Matt in the locker room with a story about "choking" has a shot of Lattanzi with his arms up over his head that compels freeze-framing. The persistence of camera angles looking up at the divers as they walk to the edge of the high diving board in their wet Speedos is also much appreciated.

You can catch Matt sporadically in Blake Edwards' *That's Life* (1986) and as one of the hapless firemen in the immensely charming *Roxanne* (1987), but few other places. In the rarely seen *Blueberry Hill* (1987), he's all attitude and overacting in close-ups as a 1956 teen with his hair greased into a Superman curl. He's awfully busy performing his part, so it's refreshing to see him without dialogue—even if it's from behind—as he emerges from the swimming hole in his wet, clinging jockey shorts. He all but bowed out of the acting game in the early '90s and concentrated on a construction business, though he showed up briefly as the "older guy" in the Australian soap *Paradise Beach* (1993). Matt and Olivia have a daughter and amicably called it quits in 1995. He remarried in 1999.

If while playing the "Spot Matt Lattanzi" game during *Grease 2* (1982) you forget to check out the background once in a while, it's probably because of who's in the foreground. **Maxwell Caulfield** (1959-   ), who plays Michael Carrington, the handsome cousin of Sandy (Olivia Newton-John) from the first film, has a face that's hard to ignore. Clean-cut, sweet, with perfectly shaped sideburns and a silky soft voice and British accent, Caulfield is a dreamboat among all the other 30-somethings playing high schoolers. He's cute, he's dorky, he's absolutely lovely to look at, and he's trapped in a bomb for his first Hollywood movie.

The Carrington name is uncomfortably close, too, since he played a stint among the Carringtons as Miles Colby on *Dynasty* in 1981, then joined *The Colbys* spin-off (aka *Dynasty II*) from 1985-87. He was part of the *Dynasty* reunion in 1991 and also played Pierce Riley on ABC's daytime soap *All My Children* in 1996.

Born in Scotland, Caulfield began on the boards as an actor and dancer, and there are several gorgeous photos in existence of a young nude, but non-frontal Maxwell posed for Kenn Duncan's famed camera. Showing off his buff bod in the buff became something of a specialty for the actor. He appeared on stage in little more than a diaper in a production of *The Elephant Man*, got felt up in his undies while perfectly cast as the ambiguously bi leather boy who becomes the mutual property of a wacky sister and brother in Joe Orton's *Entertaining Mr. Sloane*, and then walked around for the first forty minutes of *Salonika* completely naked.

"I started seeing the same faces every night in the audience," he told the Hollywood Kids, a gay gossip columnist duo. "People who only came to see my wild thing."

Can you blame them? What's particularly nice about a hunk like Maxwell Caulfield is that he's been perfectly willing to show off what he's got. He keeps himself in exquisite physical condition, samples of which can be seen as "late" as *The Real Blonde* (1998) or during a guest appearance as a stripper on a 1998 episode of TV's *Veronica's Closet*.

He's been in quite a number of films, mostly low-budget and direct-to-video, such as *Animal Instincts* (1992), or in supporting roles, such as in *Gettysburg* (1993). Back in 1980, he married actress Juliet Mills, of *Nanny and the Professor* (1970-71) fame, whom he met on the first day of rehearsals for *The Elephant Man*.

In *The Boys Next Door* (1985), the little-seen juvie horror show from *The Decline of Western Civilization* (1981) director Penelope Spheeris, Maxwell joins Charlie Sheen as a pair of high school losers who decide to blow graduation and head to LA to make trouble. Caulfield's pop is a beer-drinkin' TV zombie who lives in a trailer park and the boys are destined to start worthless factory jobs on Monday. Caulfield's character, Roy, has got "stuff inside" him. He wanted to join the Marines so he could kill guys.

Instead, the pair enjoy violent cartoons, beating up people, throwing beer bottles at an old lady, and never get around to acknowledging that what's wrong with Roy is that he's a self-hating homo in love with Charlie. Spheeris shoots Caulfield lying shirtless in bed posed as a muscle god, a blond turn-on who predates Brett Easton Ellis' *American Psycho*. Later, Roy "seduces" a lonely gay man, then beats and shoots him to death. When Charlie is having sex with a girl, Roy commits a violent act

"I want a cool rider." Maxwell Caulfield, pumped for his role as Michael, the Aussie bookworm turned motorcycle leather boy, in *Grease 2* (1982). PHOTOFEST

of *coitus interruptus* and kills her, too.

It's the most disturbing and pointless use of a beautiful actor imaginable. All that Roy needed to straighten himself out could easily have been found in the San Fernando Valley. The guy had the body of a porn star, thanks to Maxwell Caulfield, and a lucrative job in the skin factory could have been his on Monday. Think of the lives that could have been saved.

"I have no control over that. It's demeaning when people talk about my looks. I think I usually look like shit, and most people would probably agree."

A chain-smoking **John Christopher Depp II** (1963-   ) was answering a question put to him during his 1996 *Playboy* interview. The interviewer wanted to know how it felt "to be so handsome that women yank out their pubes for you." Amongst the 10,000 letters a month he was getting at the height of his detested teen idol phase, some of the gals thought that sending along samples of their pubic hair was somehow going to get them noticed. What they evidently didn't realize is that you're not a blip on the teen idol map until you've received several dozen such packages. It's no big deal, just a disgusting reminder of how sad and bizarre the cult of celebrity. The real genius would be the reverse marketing to fans of authenticated celebrity pubic hair, because if the celebrity was at a loss as to what you imagined he was supposed to do with yours, he could be assured you'd find a hallowed, if unspeakable use for his.

Depp was the youngest of four kids in the family, born in Owensboro, Kentucky, but raised in 25 to 30 different homes and locations along the way during his parents' separation and eventual divorce. His teenage years were spent in and around Miramar, Florida, where he indulged in alcohol and drugs and fell in love with a $25 guitar. He taught himself to play, formed a number of bands with peers, and dropped out of high school at age 16.

While with The Kids, the band opened for headliners like Iggy Pop, The Ramones, Chuck Berry, and The Pretenders. At 17, he got the prominent Indian head tattoo on his arm in tribute to his great-grandmother, who was full Cherokee. It was the first inked entry in what he has referred to as the "journal" of his body, which took on "Betty Sue" (his mom's name), and then years later the famed "Winona Forever" (for one-time fiancée Winona Ryder, which was then abridged to "Wino Forever"), various other symbols, and a series of self-inflicted gashes marking significant events.

At 20, he was married and on his way to California with the band. The marriage wouldn't last, but the young actor his ex started dating—some guy named Nicolas Cage—suggested the good-looking Mr. Depp try his face at auditioning. Not even a closet actor as a kid, Depp went out on a call for a little horror flick titled *A Nightmare on Elm Street* (1984), read in the presence of the director's teenage daughter, and won the part of the script's big blond football jock. That Johnny wasn't either brawny or blond didn't matter in the least. He was adorable.

Regardless how painful it may be to reduce him to his parts, he's actually damned cute: tightly packed into his blue jeans when we first meet him, and then outfitted in one of those darling half-shirts (his #10 on the chest) and sweat pants for his memorable death scene. It's too bad that he can't manage something as simple as staying awake while his girlfriend wanders through her dreams looking for Freddy Kreuger. His half-shirt reveals the sexiest little trail of hair under his belly button and into his pants. He's a multi-pop-culture-infused child of the '80s, listening to his tunes on a headset while balancing his TV set on his lap waiting for the appearance of Miss Nude America on the late night boob tube. Instead, he gets swallowed by his bed and regurgitated in a crimson fountain. (Seven years later, in *Freddy's Dead: The Final Nightmare*, he shows up for a 16-second spoof of the famed anti-drug ad campaign that likens your brain on drugs to an egg frying in a pan. Freddy pops up and wallops Depp with the pan.)

"I was sucked into a bed and spewed back out as tomato juice," Depp told *InFashion* magazine, "so I had to find another job, which was a movie I won three Academy Awards for called *Private Resort* (1985). It's about two guys who go to a resort and try to get laid. It's not like anything you've ever seen before."

If interviews are any indication, Johnny regards this teen sexploitation flick with more derision than any of the feature films he's done, despite the fact that *Nick of Time* (1995) and *The Astronaut's Wife* (1999) are far and away worse.

Of course, he has every right to hate the film, but I highly recommend it. I think it's great that he made one of these kinds of flicks before he got principled and in a position to be choosy. It's a silly, but enjoyable AIP beach movie update and, at just 78 minutes before credits, has enough gags and legitimate laughs to make it one of the better entries in the sub-genre. (I'll never forget Hector Elizondo yelling, "You moron, that's a faggot barber and he's got my diamonds in his tits!")

Johnny is such a doll that when he enthusiastically pulls off his shirt and then peels down his boxers to unveil his squeezably soft bare butt, he's fulfilling the kind of fantasy that sexy film stars can't possibly admit they owe their fans. Johnny Depp shows us his butt, not his ass, mind you, for those capable of grasping the distinction. It's an interactive butt, too. With some movie stars, you look at their ass and say, yep, there's his ass. With Johnny Depp, you look at his butt and along with the picture comes the warm, soft, and smooth feeling of it cupped in both your hands.

You have to look for him in Oliver Stone's *Platoon* (1986), since his supporting role as the unit's translator mostly ended up on the cutting room floor, but it wouldn't be long before he could be seen with all the regularity of a weekly TV show.

Depp signed a six-year contract with fledgling Fox-TV for a high school/undercover cop series called *21 Jump Street* (1987-91) that he was certain wouldn't last more than a season. For the next four years, with no-secret wriggling to get off it (he even offered to work a season for free in order to be let go), Depp went through teenybopper hell as boyish Officer Tom Hanson. Molded by the publicity department into a "stay in school and don't do drugs" poster boy, the actor was anguished by the pretty boy marketing and the complete hypocrisy of his unwanted role as spokesperson and teen role model.

"Really, things are very bad when kids have to write to an actor for advice. I can't tell anybody what to do. I'm just as screwed up as the next guy," he told *Cosmopolitan* in 1991.

Even after finally breaking free, he refused to mention its name, calling it only "that show," and condemning its student-posing cops busting teenagers in high school premise as "fascist."

Still, it was Depp's cutie-pie omnipresence in teen magazines that brought him to the attention of John Waters, the famed director of such gutter classics as *Pink Flamingoes* (1972) and *Female Trouble* (1975), who recently had found commercial success with *Hairspray* (1988). He was preparing a musical riff on the juvenile delinquent films of his youth and found the bad boy of his dreams in Johnny.

Wade "Cry-Baby" Walker, the dreamy Drape with greased locks who's eventually found "guilty of rampant juvenile delinquency," sets Depp's own teenybopper stardom on its ear by lampooning the image circa Elvis and Fabian. A sensitive, deeply emotional, and polite young hood, Cry-Baby hangs with a gang of loveable misfits and falls for a beautiful Square (Amy Locane). He's got an electric chair tattooed on his hairless chest and earned his nickname for his habit of oozing tears that leave glycerin-trails over his magnificent cheekbones. "One single salty tear is all they'll ever suck out of this Cry-Baby," he avows, and then his girlfriend has the decency to lick it off his cheek. (She'll drink from a jar of her own tears later in the film, causing audiences to gag.)

When he dismounts his motorcycle, he has the most endearing way of digging into the denim of his crotch and rearranging himself. As an orphan with "special needs," he'll hotly initiate a French-kissing scene that spreads to all the other couples at the Turkey Point dance and then later lasciviously licks at the glass separating him and his girl during her visit to the jailhouse. Prison guard Willem Dafoe gets a kick out of giving a resounding slap to Cry-Baby's butt. During an attempted escape through tunnels, the juvenile delinquent's striped prison pants get snagged and come off, leaving Depp to scuttle through the rest of the scene in his dingy jockey shorts.

Cry-Baby (1990) is an entertaining send-up of an already self-mocking sub-genre, but Depp is priceless, endlessly cute and sexy while he's exploiting the exploitation of a teen idol image from the era in which it was invented.

"I don't necessarily want to always play the leading man," said Depp, finding himself having to state the obvious to the press. "I'd like to shave my head and sew my eyeballs shut."

His eyeballs aren't sewn shut, but the rest of him is sewn together and not quite finished in Tim Burton's *Edward Scissorhands* (1990), the first of three films the actor would make for the director before the new millennium. Tom Cruise was nearly set to play the part, say some sources, but legend has it that he wanted to meddle with the ending and turn the freakish Edward into a prince Edward.

Johnny Depp would have none of that. In fact, he was so instinctively in tune with the role of the sad and innocent boy, who lost his father/creator before his razor-sharp scissorhands could be replaced with the fingered variety, that he convinced Burton to cut out much of Edward's dialogue from the original script. What remains, despite the probably unintentional similarity between Edward's bizarre hairdo and clothing and the fashion of a wave of '80s rockers, is a touching performance of sweetness and simplicity that reaches back to the days of silent film.

The burglary that sets Edward's banishment into motion seems like a weak plot device considering the extraordinary beauty and classic imagery that keeps showing up in the film. Burton's plotting reveals a practical side to the fairy tale he's telling (with Edward gardening, grooming the dogs, and doing the ladies' hair in suburbia), though I have to say I prefer the mythical and lushly romantic touches, such as having a lyrical snowfall where snow had never fallen before.

Johnny Depp and the *21 Jump Street* pout. Or is that pang? PHOTOFEST

He's a New York harbor fish counter forced to attend his wacky uncle's wedding in Emir Kusturica's *Arizona Dream* (1991), belatedly released in the US, but a treasure if you're in the mood for something odd. In a darkly comic tapestry of weirdness, you won't soon forget the inexplicable image of him squatting wrapped in a sheet, propelled by some unknown conveyance straight down the hall and into a wall while clucking like a chicken. It's even funnier on the return trip.

Who better to take care of your slightly disturbed, pyromaniac sister than a slightly disturbed, long-haired movie freak who worships Buster Keaton and comes dressed in hat, coat, vest, polka-dot tie, and cane? As played by the magical Johnny Depp, Sam sits in trees, on top of mailboxes, and makes grilled cheese sandwiches with the clothes iron in *Benny & Joon* (1993). No matter how this well-meaning romantic shtick hits you, there's no denying the classic image of Johnny swinging to and fro outside the window wearing his crumpled top hat.

The entirety of *What's Eating Gilbert Grape* (1993) is classic. It's a flawless, beautifully-written, beautifully-acted, beautifully-made film about a young man's stalled life in the little town of Endora, Texas. Tied to his needy family, which includes a retarded younger brother (Leonardo DiCaprio) and a

600-lb. mother (Darlene Cates), Gilbert (Depp) is further depressed after the arrival and anticipated departure of a young woman on her way across country. When all the details are right, when every scene strikes a chord, when you find yourself welling up with tears or smiling at some little piece of business or perfect touch (like Gilbert lifting up a neighbor kid to the windowpane so he can see the enormous woman inside), all you can do is tell everyone you know to see it. And don't ever talk to them again if they say they don't like it. It's a litmus test for friendship.

Depp was going through a very difficult time in his personal life while making the film, so it's one he rarely talks about. As for seeing it, he won't. He can't stand watching himself on film and rarely ever has. For a guy who jokes that all he does is get "paid to make faces," here is pure evidence that film photographs far more than light, texture, and movement.

Upon first viewing of Tim Burton's *Ed Wood* (1994), I heard little more from Johnny Depp than one note held for two hours. I was also mightily distracted by the fictional profanity coming out of Bela Lugosi's mouth. A lifelong Lugosi devotee, I was disturbed by the film's cheap shot at having the elderly, drug-addicted, and alcoholic film star curse up a storm for comic relief, no matter how affecting the rest of Martin Landau's Oscar-winning performance. Once over the shock, I had a better time of it with *Ed Wood* the second time around. Seen as a fairy tale homage to a fascinating misfit—the supremely untalented transvestite director of *Glen or Glenda?* (1953), *Bride of the Monster* (1955), and *Plan Nine From Outer Space* (1959)—suddenly Johnny's relentlessly optimistic and gleefully zealous performance resonated. And like in a fairy tale, it made sense that Ed Wood should talk movies over a drink with Orson Welles in a neighborhood bar.

He's a predictably demented young man who fancies himself *Don Juan DeMarco* (1994) and predictably teaches psychiatrist Marlon Brando a thing or two about embracing life in an unpredictably charming film. Then he's a bespectacled accountant named William Blake who circumstantially becomes an outlaw in the Old West and a better shot after he loses his eyeglasses in Jim Jarmusch's fascinating and hypnotic feature-length poem *Dead Man* (1995). The first word of dialogue isn't uttered until nearly five and a half minutes in. Close-ups of Johnny's face in the gorgeous black-and-white photography of Robby Müller call to mind soulful frames of stars from silent films.

In *L.A. Without A Map* (1998), he comes to life inside the one-sheet for *Dead Man* hanging on the lead character's apartment wall, then shows up as himself to offer advice and some fried chicken in a cemetery.

Johnny Depp is noted for his oddball characters and praised for his offbeat career, but it's the choices that he's made that makes his career unique, not that he's the only leading man out there who'd rather play character parts. He turned down the Swayze role in *Point Break* (1991), Keanu's roles in both *Bram Stoker's Dracula* (1992) and *Speed* (1994), Aramis in *The Three Musketeers* (1993), a title shot at *Chaplin* (1992), the Brad Pitt role in *Legends of the Fall* (1994), and Lestat in *Interview with the Vampire* (1994).

His few "commercial" choices, other than the superb *Donnie Brasco* (1997), reveal a curse associated with his playing mainstream. Any grown man who wishes he had three mouths so he could smoke three times as much, takes pride in his numerous cavities and bad teeth, collects bugs and lizards and weird paraphernalia (he proudly owns a 9' cock, but it's the kind that crows), trashes a ritzy New York hotel room and gets dragged off to jail, gets engaged at least thrice, has been known to beat off paparazzi with a stick, and relishes the wide wonderful world of all things stinky, has my complete devotion. Quite in spite of *Fear and Loathing in Las Vegas* (1998), I look forward to each and every thing he does. He has directed several short films, co-wrote and directed *The Brave* (1996), about a guy so in need of cash to support his family that he agrees to do a snuff film, and gave Tim Burton's *Sleepy Hollow* (1999) just the right chicken-hearted touch.

He appeared in two Oscar-nominated films in 2000. In *Chocolat* (2000), he's a charming Irish gypsy who casts a romantic counter-spell on fairy tale chocolatier Juliette Binoche. And in *Before Night Falls* (2000), he's peculiarly asked to play two brief roles: the first, a full-buttocked drag queen named Bon Bon who's known for her capacious derriere; the second, a Castro-regime military lieutenant who tests prisoner Javier Bardem's (as author Reinaldo Arenas) resolve to denounce his homosexuality by flagrantly rubbing his own crotch to see if the writer will bite.

Whether dorked out in a blond mop, sideburns and bell-bottoms as the suspiciously likable source of America's cocaine addiction in *Blow* (2001), foiled by history from revealing the labyrinthine conspiracy behind Jack the Ripper's crimes in *From Hell* (2001), or eye-shadowed and playfully fey as Jack Sparrow in *Pirates of the Caribbean: The Curse of the Black Pearl* (2003), Johnny is an actor you're willing to follow just about anywhere.

He's a rare breed; a beauty whose looks draw us inside his characters instead of stopping us at the surface. Just because he doesn't think he's beautiful, by the way, hardly compels the rest of us to agree.

Johnny Depp as juvenile delinquent *Cry-Baby* (1990) Walker. PHOTOFEST

The 1980s — Take Two

"I Could Love Someone Even If, You Know, I Wasn't Paid For It"

In Gus Van Sant's script for *My Own Private Idaho* (1991), Mike Waters and Scott Favor sit around a campfire and Mike asks Scott if he ever gets horny. Of course, he does. Scott tells Mike that two guys can't love each other. There's a pregnant pause, and then Scott calls Mike over to him and holds him in his arms. He tells Mike that he only has sex with other men for the money. Mike goes into his pockets for some. Scott says he can't take it. A pause. "But we can be close friends."

Then it's "next morning," and there's nothing to suggest that anything resembling sex took place.

In the film version, Mike (River Phoenix) wants to know what it is he means to Scott (Keanu Reeves). Scott tells him, "you're my best friend." Mike thinks that's great and all, but...

"I only have sex with a guy for money," says Scott, catching on.

"Yeah, I know."

"And two guys can't love each other."

"Yeah...well, I don't know. I mean, for me, I could love someone even if, you know, I wasn't paid for it. I love you and you don't pay me."

"Mike."

"I really wanna kiss you, man."

Squatting on his haunches, speaking with quiet sincerity, and unable to look the boy he's in love with in the face while he confesses his feelings for the first time, Mike Waters has revealed a tenderness, sweetness, and honesty that makes this otherwise perfunctory stop along his journey a pivotal and heartfelt moment. And it's due entirely to **River Phoenix** (1970-1993), whose improvisation fleshed out an ambiguous character and instantly connected him to every member of the audience.

Scott takes a moment to realize what has been said. Out of pity, or semblance of friendship, he invites Mike to lie down next to him. They hug.

Passion for the scene among gay audiences has reached such a pitch that it has even inspired mass hysteria. In both printed sources and from the gay boy on the street, you'll learn about the kiss between Keanu and River that culminates the scene, but no such kiss exists. The wishful thinking of a generation of gay men have put those two boys' lips together and let no man tear asunder. It's almost sacred enough a delusion to deem canonical.

I had to see the film again in theatres in 1991 to make sure that I didn't miss the excruciatingly anticipated smooch. I was disappointed that it didn't suddenly appear on a repeat viewing, but it still took me a half dozen more viewings of the film to uncloud my perception of Scott Favor's acquiescence. Though I knew Scottie would soon transform into a three-piece schmuck and turn his back on all the other street urchins, and even though I knew he was basically straight and just being a bad boy, I had continued to falsely veil his invitation for Mike to join him around the campfire with the possibility of a glimmer of self-revelation, or even just the momentary warmth of friendship. Well, they don't call him Favor for nothing.

My Own Private Idaho was the most anxiously awaited release of 1991 as far as I was concerned. From the moment I heard that River Phoenix and Keanu Reeves were starring in a film about male hustlers, I was as privately atwitter as a 13-year old girl with tickets to see her favorite boy band. So what if I was nearly 30?

To understand the enormous contribution the actors made to Van Sant's American classic, and the level of creative collaboration, all you have to do is read the script. It's almost entirely devoid of poetry. All the great emotional themes of the film are missing. And it has a completely fucked-up ending. Mike tells us in voice-over that the road is his home, that sometimes he feels like God isn't smiling on him, but other times does. Passed out on the road, he's picked up by a driver and that driver turns out to be Scott.

Van Sant was working on three different screenplays at the time, two of which had the B-52's song title "My Own Private Idaho," the other a slice-and-dice version of Shakespeare's *Henry IV*. He collaged all three, mixed in liberal doses of Welles' *Chimes at Midnight* (1966), and shot the film in sequence, allowing his actors and non-actors free reign to improvise.

Mike Waters, a gay street hustler, is prone to narcoleptic fits during moments of stress or, conversely, moments that remind him of his long-lost mother. He's been on the streets for three and a half years with his best friend Scott Favor, the son of Portland's mayor. Favor will run headlong into his "inheritance" at the age of 21, just a week off. He's been busy rebelling against his father by working the streets, wallowing in drugs and sex, and being mentored by homeless Bob Pigeon (William Richert), a Falstaffian oaf who's in lust with him.

Characteristic of his mosaic approach to the material, Van Sant's film is at times a dreamy, hallucinatory evocation of Mike's narcoleptic worldview, a hodgepodge of truncated and altered Shakespearean dialogue right out of *Henry IV*, and even streetwise documentary. Real young men whose lives and experiences were used as research and background for the actors appear in a café scene to tell their first time hustling horror stories. Mike Parker, who Van Sant also used in a scene in *Drugstore Cowboy* (1989), was the basis for Mike Waters. He tells us about being raped with a wine bottle. Scott Patrick Green, who's also listed as assistant to the director, tells us about having to finish a date with a hugely-endowed john he was hoping to get money from and skip out on.

As in the script, Mike's frequent narcoleptic seizures serve as unique transitions, allowing us to move from one scene, time frame, or even country, simply by having him wake up somewhere else. After a fit in Seattle, brought on by the lovely home of an older woman who reminds him of his mother (Phoenix even has Mike re-buttoning his shirt in her presence when she wants him to be taking it off), he reawakens in Scott's lap and arms, a la *pietà*, in Portland under a statue that marks "The Coming of the White Man."

Mike's first seizure in the film, while he's out on a lonely road with its "fucked up face," parallels his twitching convulsions with the moment of orgasm as a greasy fat john finishes sucking him off. At the height of his climax, with his eyes closed, we see a stretch of country road as an old barn falls from the sky and crashes into pieces. Sheer poetry.

Speeding vistas of clouds, hazy home movie footage of Mike and his mom and his older brother, and shots of salmon jumping against the river torrent to return home to spawn are as iconographic as the tinkle of "Home on the Range" and the twang of "America the Beautiful" on the amazing soundtrack—which, unfathomably, has never been available for sale as its own entity.

Two sex scenes are presented in *tableau vivant*, the actors posed as statues and filmed, instead of using still photography. In one remarkable journey into an adult sex shop, the covers of the gay porn magazines come to life. Scott's lean and shirtless physique, with pants undone, graces the cover of *Male Call*, where, with black cowboy hat, he's a homo on the range. It's the perfect place to deliver his philosophy about making his ass available for cash only, either on the cover of a gay mag or in the sack, but warning about the danger of "growing wings" and becoming a fairy while he's addressing Mike, who's lounging nearby in a sarong on the cover of *G-String*.

Much was made in the press at the time that two teen idols were risking their careers by playing hustlers, possibly gay, in a movie, but both wisely took offense at the idea that they weren't allowed to be actors. Privately, Phoenix supposedly said that *Idaho* was the project that would at last get him off the cover of *Tiger Beat*. Besides, the film wasn't about homosexuality. Both were mature enough to see that aspect as subordinate to the film's central theme: the search for home.

River Phoenix was born in Madras, Oregon in 1970 to hippie parents John and Arlyn Bottom; thus he was River Bottom—actually River Jude Bottom, the River from Herman Hesse's *Siddhartha* and the Jude from The Beatles. The mythological Phoenix came about only after the family split from their missionary roles in a religious cult called the Children of God, which dwelled commune-style, had River and little sister Rain singing on the streets of Venezuela for money before they were five, and reportedly introduced the children to communal sex acts. The Bottom family set out on its own, reborn as Phoenix, in Florida, where River was entered into talent contests. The Phoenixes were hell-bent on making their musical children stars. A call to one of Arlyn's old classmates, Penny Marshall, brought the family to Southern California, where River auditioned for talent agents and played guitar on the streets of Westwood. He was cast at age 12 on the short-lived CBS television series *Seven Brides for Seven Brothers* (1982-83), where his objection to wearing a leather belt as part of his costume caused backstage friction.

Coming as he did from a family of devout vegans and strident environmentalists, it wasn't easy to adapt those deeply held views to the commercially driven TV and film industries. That's why the children stopped doing commercials—too many animal by-products—and focused on acting. River did several other TV projects, including playing Robert Kennedy, Jr. in the TV miniseries *Robert Kennedy and His Times* (1985).

His feature film debut came as the least likely of *The Explorers* (1985), playing the brainy, sensitive nerd with glasses who constructs a flying machine from the plans provided in one of his dreams. Dyslexic and without any formal education, River would surprise fellow actors, directors, and friends alike throughout his short life with his lack of cultural or historical knowledge.

He was, though, a natural performer. Evidence of his talent, thoroughly untainted by acting school training, is on full display as Chris Chambers, one of four cigarette-smoking, foul-mouthed 12-year olds who "set out to find the body of a dead kid" in *Stand By Me* (1986). Despite the Stephen King-based tale's insistence on having all parents and siblings save one (and he's dead) be drunks, abusers, depressives, or assholes, the central coming-of-age story is beautifully realized by the four young actors.

River clearly stands out as the compassionate friend who knows Gordy (Wil Wheaton) has a gift as a writer and is destined for something special. The scene under the tree in which he breaks down and confesses his fear that his family's reputation as low-lifes has cursed him is a real heartbreaker and a spontaneous and genuine outpouring of emotion. "I'd like to go someplace where nobody knows me" is as achingly poignant as if James Dean had said it.

Unfortunately, the appearance of a switchblade and a handgun for an unnecessary showdown with a group of older bastards mars the film and robs it of a perfect ending. In fact, it's not unlike the bad ending that Corey Feldman's Teddy suggests after Gordy has already told the perfect story about the infamous blueberry pie-eating contest. We don't need, "Suck my fat one you cheap dimestore hood." For that matter, we shouldn't have been shown the face of the dead boy. His stockinged feet would have sufficed.

In *The Mosquito Coast* (1986), director Peter Weir's powerful film version of the Paul Theroux novel in which an inventor (Harrison Ford in the film) hauls his entire family into the jungle to start from scratch, then begins to lose them to his egomania, River played a role that must have felt close to him in some ways. He had lived like this before. He had seen a life built on pure ideals and simplicity go to hell at the behest of religion and the ego's need for stroking. Martha Plimpton's character, daughter to a missionary, memorably tells River as she saunters away from him: "I think of you when I go to the bathroom."

That, evidently, is what Hollywood wanted lots of young girls to do. River started appearing in the teen magazines. He was next cast, and miscast at that, as a 17-year old stud trying to get money to go to Hawaii and evade talk of college in William Richert's *A Night in the Life of Jimmy Reardon* (1988). (Richert would go on to play Bob Pigeon in *My Own Private Idaho*.) A near-complete fizzle, the film has the too-boyish and inexperienced looking River, in a jiffy-pop hair-do circa 1962, getting the sexy once-over by older woman Ann Magnuson. Though I certainly lodged no complaints as she lounged over his golden bod, both River and his family had concerns about the film's sexuality and how it would affect his image.

As would become increasingly clear, his image was something River Phoenix worried a great deal about. As his fame grew, so did his interest in keeping secrets about himself, while openly advertising those interests he felt were important to his fans and the public. He was a vocal animal rights activist, did television spots for PETA (People for the Ethical Treatment of Animals), was a vegan, and a no-nuker who ritually lied to the nosy press about aspects of his childhood as part of a cult, his drinking, his sexual experiences, his smoking, and his drug use. A squeaky-clean naturalist to the media, he even objected to a line about getting drunk in one of his films, saying he was afraid how it might influence other kids.

His work in *Running on Empty* (1988) was judiciously Oscar-nominated for Best Supporting Actor. River was just 17, but his beautiful performance as the teenaged son of Vietnam War protesters, who bombed a napalm lab in 1971 and have been on the run ever since, is all the proof you'll ever need that he was one of his generation's best actors. After years in the business, he was still a complete natural, capable of making us feel the pain and heartache of a kid torn between his allegiance to his family and the limitless potential of a life without them. You will never forget the film's last ten minutes.

He's perfect as the young Indiana Jones, from whom we get to see how Harrison Ford's grown-up version got his fear of snakes and that scar on his chin, in the 12-minute prologue to *Indiana Jones and the Last Crusade* (1989). He's the loyal Devo, who reads runes, is deeply in love with Tracey Ullman, and

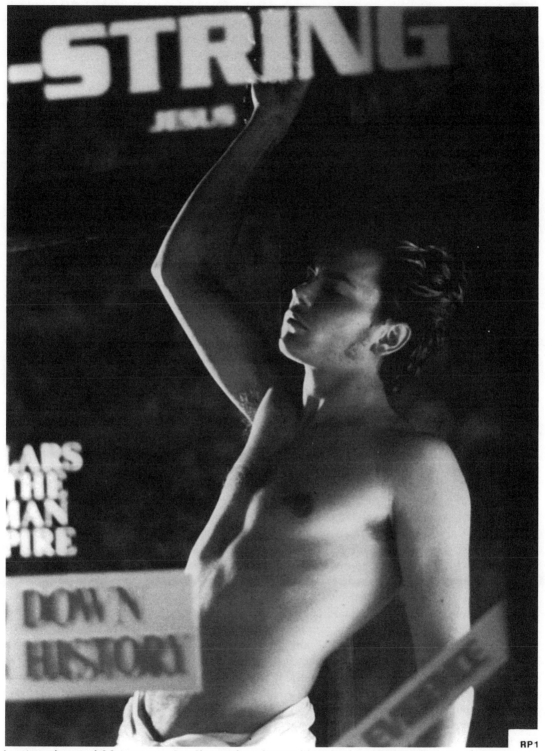

STRING

RP1

Lounging on the cover of *G-String* magazine, River Phoenix subverts his teen idol image and openly embraces his gay fans in *My Own Private Idaho* (1991). AUTHOR'S COLLECTION

hires dopey William Hurt and even dopier Keanu Reeves to finish off Kevin Kline in the black comedy *I Love You To Death* (1990).

Pumped up and shaved down to play a conniving, foul-mouthed jarhead in *Dogfight* (1991), he reveals a sweet and awkward young man once he gets past the god-awful contest in which he and his pals compete to bring the ugliest girl into a bar for a drink. The relationship between River and the wonderful Lili Taylor makes this one of the best romances you've probably never heard of.

River despised his status as teen idol pin-up, forced to primp and pose for magazines alongside phony, glamorized stories about his life. In rebellion, he started to show up for interviews dressed slovenly, his long, unkempt hair hanging in his face. He also began letting down his guard, fucking with a *Details* magazine interviewer by saying that he'd lost his virginity at age four, "but I've blocked it out." If there was creepy and tragic truth behind what he was saying, the interviewer and reader couldn't be sure. Asked whether he'd date a woman who eats sausage, he responded: "I wouldn't want to lick her juices if they were made up of her metabolism's version of all that shit that goes in a sausage. But she could eat my sausage—lick it, put it in her ear, up her nose, I don't care." How does he change his "consciousness without drugs or alcohol?"

"Blowjobs...and music."

Having realized his parents' unreasonable dream that at least one of their children make it big in Hollywood, and thus becoming a spokesperson for causes they held dear, River resolved to live away from the decadence of Los Angeles and moved his entire family to Gainesville, Florida in 1987, where he supported up to a dozen family members, friends, and other hangers-on. He justified his career and the money he was making by giving generously to environmental charities, at one point purchasing 800 acres of rain forest between Costa Rica and Panama in hopes of preserving them. It was in Florida that he also began working and performing with his band, Aleka's Attic. Music was still his first true love.

Doing a bit in a commercial film like *Sneakers* (1992) was only a way to keep the money flowing so that he could pursue the kind of projects he was increasingly attracted to after the critical and personal success of *Idaho*, for which he was awarded Best Actor at the Venice Film Festival. He's not particularly memorable in a supporting role in the weird western *Silent Tongue* (1993), but resonates as a remote and sullen country and western singer/songwriter in *The Thing Called Love* (1993), his last completed film.

Sadly, considering its vital place in his body of work, *My Own Private Idaho* was also the film on which it's said that he truly began falling apart, willfully indulging in booze and drugs. Dario Scardapane, who visited the shoot in progress and wrote about it for *US* magazine, reported: "Frankly, there's not much difference in his performance when the camera is rolling and when it is not." There's a suggestion that Phoenix got too close to his character's lifestyle while working on the film, that this was Method gone mad.

During the making of an earlier landmark film in his career, *Stand By Me*, he was introduced to cigarettes, booze, and marijuana, and re-introduced to sex. Should we blame the film? He was a 14-year old kid who suddenly had access to all the sorts of things that 14-year old boys are exposed to, and he partook. He had access to even more drugs while on location in Belize making *The Mosquito Coast*. *My Own Private Idaho* was just one more stop on this tragic boy's journey of reckless self-abuse, experimentation, and addiction.

He was at work on a film called *Dark Blood* (1993), for which he had already filmed a death scene, and had been announced to play the rather uninteresting role of interviewer in *Interview With the Vampire* (1994), when he went to The Viper Room, a club co-owned by Johnny Depp, on October 30, 1993. He had brought along his guitar to play.

A bad mix of heroin and cocaine sent him into convulsions on the sidewalk out front of the club. His last words, reportedly, were "I want anonymity." Peering up through the haze of activity over him, he apparently made out the dangling cameras of two paparazzo photographers who had come to his aid—neither of whom was snapping pictures.

River Phoenix was 23.

His death was a shocker.

Family and friends and co-workers had known about his drinking and drug problems for some time, and there was sufficient word out in the industry, but his fans and the public at large were clueless. We were sure that he was the smart, no chemicals, clean living actor that he wanted us to believe he was. In truth, he was a troubled young man whose natural ability to hide and keep secrets translated into a handful of unforgettable performances before he took some bad junk and died.

In the wake of River's death, there were stories of his own private homosexual experimentation (namely, a diluted reference reported in *Esquire* that he had allowed a male extra on *Dogfight* to go down on him as "research" for his role in *Idaho*), of possible confusion over his true sexual nature, and that was just enough to create a martyr in some segments of the gay population. The thought that he could have been one of us, struggling to come out and then lost to us in the process, assures his future deification as a junior James Dean. Unlike Dean, whose early tragic death has been repeatedly served up in pop cultural parallel to Phoenix's, there's no real evidence yet that River Phoenix was gay or had homosexual tendencies, but his empathetic and deeply felt performance as Mike Waters has secured him a revered place as an icon to gay youth. Outside of his many passionate environmental and animal rights causes, it may be the only honor he could ever have accepted with pride in the unreal world of celebrity.

Watching William Parry's 24-minute short *This Road Will Never End* (1996), made up of interviews with gay, lesbian, and bisexual UK fans of River's and, in particular, his role in *My Own Private Idaho*, I am convinced that it's near impossible to ask people to talk about beloved film stars in any personal context without making the interviewee appear in need of mental health services. It's something of the same risk I run writing this book. It compels many people, and critics, to invoke "get a life."

If a book can change your life, if a painting can impact your life, if a song can score a life moment, then damn it, a film and a film star can do the same.

Was River Phoenix a pretty boy? Sure, if you confine yourself to the teen idol cosmetics of *Little Nikita* (1988) or *Running on Empty*. But he also had a weak chin, an insistently lazy eye, and an upturned nose. He had the distinction of quickly growing out of his boyish good looks, and must have been glad to do so.

River Phoenix wasn't pretty when he made *My Own Private Idaho*. He was beautiful. He carried with him the baggage of a one-time teen star whose extraordinary natural talent insisted he had more to give than just another face among a sea of other faces on a magazine cover. But it was precisely because he was River Phoenix and wanted to play a gay character in love that lent it an element of affirmation and cultural empowerment to gay men, young and old alike. He has inner beauty as Mike. He yearns for us to reach out to him on the screen and take him in our arms...to love and care for him. Like a child, he chuckles while he watches *The Simpsons* on a motel TV screen, then embraces the john like he would a father—reaching out for a simple hug—but sadly unable to sustain the moment.

Our love for Mike is so strong that the film's "ambiguous" ending doesn't seem the least bit ambiguous in my mind. I've decided that the young man who picks him up off the highway is going to help him find his mom. No question about it.

"This is a nice home," Mike tells the older lady who hires him early in the film. "Do you live here?"

"Yes."

"I don't blame you."

On a quest for home, for a place to belong, Mike Waters is a sweet, confused kid that any other kid can identify with; as a gay young man on that same journey, thanks entirely to the inspiration of River Phoenix, he is also a soul mate.

"My daughter's a real big Keanu Reeves fan and she would just love to have this," said Dad, pointing to the life-size stand-up displayed in the suburban Chicago laserdisc store. The cardboard Keanu was caught in mid-run from *Speed* (1994), the action movie that introduced the rest of America to his rather stoic charms—buzz-cut, biceps, and all. "How much do you want for it?"

The deal was made. Keanu was carted off. Dad had succumbed and bought his little girl a piece of her fantasy. She could proudly display it in her bedroom, invite jealous friends over to gaze upon it, sneak a little peck on his cheek from time to time, and say goodnight to him just before she turned out the light.

If Rod Serling had written the scenario, the cut-out would have come to life in the dark of that teenage girl's bedroom and the implications would have been rife. In a way, Keanu did just that.

Dad brought the taciturn star, still running, back to the store the very next day. "She doesn't want him," he explained.

Too big? No place to put him? Mom didn't agree?

No. "She found out he's gay." True story, circa 1995.

Well, excuse me, sweetheart, but that's just the news I'd been waiting to hear since I first caught him sharing Rob Lowe's locker room in *Youngblood* (1986).

Keanu Reeves (1964-   ) was born in Beirut, Lebanon, where his Chinese/Hawaiian father met and married an English showgirl. Keanu (kee-ah'-noo) means "cool breeze over the mountains" in Hawaiian, as anyone will tell you, whether it's literally true or not. The parents divorced when Keanu and his sister Kim were still quite young. The children and their mom moved to New York, where mom married a stage and film director, then up to Toronto, and at least four other cities (including a jaunt in Australia) following the second divorce less than a year later.

Back in Toronto, where his mom was working as a costume designer and husband number three was a rock promoter, the Reeves' home played host to any number of offbeat celebrities, including Alice Cooper, who tied up Keanu and a male friend as a joke.

Keanu started showing an interest in things other than hockey, which he loved to play as a skilled goalie, while a junior in high school. Acting held real appeal and he was a nut for Shakespeare from the beginning. He successfully auditioned for the Toronto High School for the Performing Arts, but was tossed out after a year, reportedly for attitude problems.

He finally decided to forego finishing high school and concentrate on specifically educating himself as an actor. He joined Leah Posluns Theatre School for training, hoping to concentrate on Shakespeare. Instead, his first professional break came when he was cast as a young beauty in a psychiatric hospital who becomes the victim of a deranged boy. The kid thinks he's some sort of werewolf and ends up sucking the blood out of a knife wound in Keanu's chest.

The weird play's appeal was considerably enhanced by a series of homoerotic close-up photographs of Keanu and co-star Carl Marotte, wearing white T-shirts, caught in provocative sweaty embrace, and even a near-kiss, that were then used for publicity purposes, understandably drawing a large gay audience. Years later, after *Speed* made him a huge star, the tabloid and mainstream press alike would reprint the 1984 *Wolfboy* photos to help fan the flames of rumors that Reeves was gay.

"Hey lady, can I use the shower?" was his first (and only) line while making his TV debut in an episode of a series called *Hangin' In*, and he did commercials for both Coke and Corn Flakes. With Hollywood, especially medium-budget Hollywood, taking advantage of the variable countryside and lower cost of shooting in Canada, Keanu soon found himself plenty of opportunities to audition for work. And he was getting cast.

He was billed as KC Reeves for a short time (the "C" for his middle name of Charles), because people were telling him that his own name was strange and unpronounceable. You have to look for him in the locker room in *Youngblood*, because his character isn't much of a character, but he demonstrates an ability to walk a line with a roll of tape balanced on his head and he can howl with the best of his testosterone-infused teammates. He may also have been the only one of them who could credibly play the game.

He drove his 1969 Volvo down to Los Angeles in the summer of 1985, moved in with his stepdad—director Paul Aaron—and set about getting himself an agent.

He's in no less than five made-for-TV or made-for-cable flicks in 1986, including as alcoholic Andy Griffith's son in *Under the Influence*, the 17-year old version of Robert Urich in *Young Again*, Kiefer Sutherland's main pain as a vigilante jock in *The Brotherhood of Justice*, and Drew Barrymore's peppy Jack Nimble—hear him sing "Cincinnati"—in *Babes in Toyland*. He shows up 73 minutes into HBO's *Act of Vengeance* (and gets billed as "Keannu Reeves") as a young thug hired to wipe out union reformer Charles Bronson and family in what has to be the most depressing use of his talents ever.

His first starring role came in the prehistorically bad *Flying* (1986), a teen gymnast variation on *Flashdance* (1983), in which he plays the friend who's in love with the girl, but doesn't think she knows he's alive. During a love scene, you can get a glimpse at his shirtless torso a couple years before it would be permanently scarred in a motorcycle wreck.

River's Edge (1986) sounded like an answer to the spate of teen-slasher and teen-sex flicks that dominated the 1980s. It was a gloomy indictment of teenage emotional disconnect based on the ugly real case of a California teen murdered by a classmate, whose body is seen by several other teenagers, none of whom think to call the police for several days while it lies out in the woods. The bleak and pretentiously serious film seizes on the worst impulses of director Tim Hunter's previous screenplay for *Over the Edge* (1979) to demonize the kids, heavy metal music, and drug use. It remains a horrific disservice to the real incident and a contender for the worst film of the year. That being said, Keanu's low-key, scruffy-faced Matt is the only one who shows signs of a conscience and at least he's sweet to his baby sister. Crispin Glover's completely whacked (and somewhat brave) performance is in desperate need of a David Lynch film. The rest is phony and atrocious.

River's Edge has its staunch defenders, including Reeves, and it was an important film in terms of his defining a niche for himself outside the realm of the John Hughes' teen flicks his contemporaries were doing. A more impressive performance in its own way than the slightly, but permanently buzzed kid in *River's Edge* was his high school novice guitar player whose best buddy (the handsome Alan Boyce) inexplicably commits suicide in *Permanent Record* (1988). The deed moves Keanu's character centerstage where his growing anger and personal struggle to deal with his friend's desperate act is palpable. There's a particularly powerful scene in which Keanu nearly runs down Boyce's kid brother while out drinking and driving. Unfortunately, the film's end degenerates into a soppy movie-of-the-week moment.

The punked-out Matt Dillon mop he's sporting as *The Prince of Pennsylvania* (1988)—a dead air movie with a dumb and uninteresting plot—fills out and gets pulled back into a ponytail for his next project. He's a most surprising casting choice for *Dangerous Liaisons* (1988), in which his doe-eyed music teacher finds himself easily lured into the wicked sexual scheming of Glenn Close and John Malkovich. "Like most intellectuals, he's intensely stupid," remarks Close of Reeves' effete character, who's seen weeping at the opera in his very first shot. He has the hots for virginal Uma Thurman (neither of them can sing), but ends up in bed with Close and, most importantly, on the lunging side of a sword while dueling Malkovich's satyr.

The role in *Liaisons* would be the first of an amazingly eclectic body of work for an actor who struggles to this day with critical and even public recognition of his relative gifts. Pre-*Matrix*, Reeves' legacy was his Ted "Theodore" Logan to Alex Winter's Bill S. Preston, Esq. from *Bill and Ted's Excellent Adventure* (1988) and its sequel *Bill and Ted's Bogus Journey* (1991). The original, made in 1986, sat on a shelf for two years before finding unexpected popularity with legions of mallrats who may or may not have realized its pandering celebration of stupidity. Bill and Ted, two San Dimas, California dopes who at least got that way without using dope, are ingratiating innocents who travel through time in a phone booth collecting historical figures for a school final. They're playful caricatures of the Valley Girl as teenage boys, looking for babes, flailing on their guitars as a band called The Wyld Stallyns, and riffing on their adventures in contagiously quotable Bill-and-Ted-ese.

"Be excellent to each other," indeed.

Keanu played right into the hands of his future critics by nailing the lovable airhead Ted. In a sense, he was too good at playing this charming, buoyant idiot. In the films, we learn that in the future Bill and Ted are worshipped as gods. Their simplicity has an appealing philosophical side, sort of like Chauncey Gardner's gardening tips in *Being There*.

Once you've played a god, where can you go? The sequel was un-shockingly unfunny, other than a few gems provided by Death, but Ted became Keanu's signature '80s role, like it or not. He told an interviewer that even with a long career, in the end, they'll write on his tombstone: "He played Ted." (Not to worry post-Neo.) Director Gus Van Sant asked Keanu how he was going to approach playing the character in the sequel. He responded somewhat profoundly: "Basically, Ted is a lot dumber this time."

When Reeves climbs out from under Martha Plimpton's bed in *Parenthood* (1988), wearing just his jockey shorts, you can see a huge eviscerating scar that bisects his belly from up out of his underwear to his lower chest, evidence of a serious injury. At the time the actor found out he had won the role in *Liaisons*, he was recuperating from a nasty motorcycle spill on Topanga Canyon. The accident ruptured his spleen and left many of the gouges and scars that map his body.

Martha says he's got a cute ass, and he makes a pitiful attempt to wiggle it, before climbing on top of her and announcing that he's brought a camera so that "we can record our love." He's another dope, and he's another lovable dope, who gets the classic opportunity to explain to Dianne Wiest that her troubled son (played by Leaf Phoenix, who then changed his name back to Joaquin years later) has been "slapping the salami" after getting his first boner a few months back. The kid has been suffering the pangs of guilt ever since and needed a guy like Keanu's Todd to set him straight. "I told him that's what little dudes do."

If it seems that Keanu is just delivering another Ted as Todd, you're not paying attention. The guy's thinking about what he's doing. Todd shivers his way out of a semi-profound thought about society requiring licenses for everything else, "but they'll let any butt-reaming asshole be a father."

Half his head is shaved as the even more brain-dead Marlon (of Marlon and Harlan) in *I Love You To Death* (1989), the film in which he first worked with River Phoenix. Joan Plowright shows Marlon a clipping from a tabloid about a kangaroo giving birth to a human baby and he asks, in lethargic seriousness:

Unkempt, but utterly washable. Keanu Reeves in *River's Edge* (1986). PHOTOFEST

"Is that legal? You know, having sex with a kangaroo?"

There's a reality to the stupidity Reeves endows his stupid characters; a reality that makes them somehow all the more sweet and endearing.

His Scott Favor is anything but stupid. As the cold and calculating son of Portland's mayor in *My Own Private Idaho* (1991), even his rebellion is cold and calculating. He becomes a male prostitute, turning the occasional trick and posing nude for gay magazines, teasing the affections of a fat street tramp whom he calls his real father, and then showing up in his actual father's office wearing an open leather vest with no shirt and a dog collar.

When the mayor sends the cops out looking for his son, they find him noisily faking a hump atop Mike Waters (River Phoenix). Keanu tweaks the moment by playfully plucking at the hairs around River's nipple, though River slaps his hand for doing it. Later, in sex scenes caught in still-life tableaux, Udo Kier

250

(*Andy Warhol's Dracula*) is variably posed with his nose in Keanu's armpit, with River's fingers in his mouth, with Keanu applying a C-clamp to his nipple, and then sucking on Keanu's toes. The fractured, fetishized images relay both an emptiness and absurdity to the behaviors, but also play out like memories faint with erotic charge. Later, in Italy, Keanu will again find himself nude and in still-life as he makes love to an Italian girl who will become his wife. The parallel is clear. Even the second event is more about posing and business than it is about sex and giving of yourself.

It's too much wishful thinking that if we were to have seen Mike and Scott have sex that night around the campfire that they would have been shown in full motion up until the moment of orgasm, when Mike would have fainted dead away.

The timbre of his voice and the iciness of his pallor set against the coal black of his hair and brows eventually conspire to turn Keanu Reeves' exotic beauty into the slick shit that he at last becomes in *Idaho*. I always feel the deepest regret for what happens to Scott, who he ends up becoming of his own design, less because I'm confused by his choices, but more because I can't help feeling what a waste. Good lord, that boy is beautiful, even when he's torturing Bob by suggesting he'll have a job for him one day after he's come into his inheritance, and does so by dramatically running his hands down the front of himself until he's boxed in his crotch.

There are those who will be put off by the Shakespearean dialogue more than the decision to have the boys drink Falstaff beer, but I enjoy the odd rhythms it creates, the audacity with which Van Sant injects a classic coming-of-age tale into a contemporary piece. It speaks to the idea of *Idaho* being a filmed poem, or perhaps, a filmed song lyric. Reciting Shakespeare has been both a pastime and a ritual exercise for Keanu since he was in high school. He's often mentioned as mumbling a bit of this or that of the Bard while journalists visit his sets, appeared in *The Tempest* on stage (in which his Trinculo's necessity to say "Excellent" at one point brought warm laughter from Ted-heads), and famously turned down the sequel to *Speed* so that he could appear as *Hamlet* in a sold-out three-month engagement on stage in Winnipeg, Canada in 1995.

He plays one of Shakespeare's least written and motivated villains, the permanently scowling Don John, as part of Kenneth Branagh's purposely eclectic casting of *Much Ado About Nothing* (1993). The published screenplay indicates that Don John is lying butt-naked during his on-screen massage. For reasons quite indefensible, that's not the way it was filmed. He does, however, cut a striking figure in a beard and black leather pants.

He shows up uncredited as Ortiz the Dawg Boy, who then runs out of the film chasing a squirrel, in friend Alex Winters' loony, but crude and funny *Freaked* (1993). Then he's got a handful of minutes as an Indian watercolorist in a plaid jacket, red pants, a gold cumberbun, and pork chop sideburns in Van Sant's bizarre adaptation of *Even Cowgirls Get the Blues* (1994). He has an asthma attack immediately upon meeting giant-thumbed Uma Thurman and gets dragged off to a swishy penthouse surrounded by New York society freaks.

In Bernardo Bertolucci's *Little Buddha* (1993), he's no less than Prince Siddhartha himself, introduced 28 minutes into the film and looking every bit as beautiful as Liz Taylor in *Cleopatra* (1963). Reeves may seem like one of the last choices you'd ever consider to play the Awakened One, but he devoted himself to the challenge, immersing himself in Buddhist thought and shedding a dangerous amount of weight to appear as thin as a reed growing beneath the Tree of Enlightenment. His simplicity works well no matter how out of place he seems.

That he went from what seemed an unlikely Buddha to what seemed an unlikely action star and pulled both of them off is rather astonishing if you think about it. Those who were blown away by his presence in *Speed* (1994), though, might have seen an earlier inkling of such possibility in the stylish and exciting *Point Break* (1991).

A boy's movie directed by Kathryn Bigelow—who includes a horrifically graphic and over-the-top scene of violence, as she did in her stylish 1987 vampire flick *Near Dark*—*Point Break* has Keanu all wet, in a black T-shirt, and toting a shotgun as FBI special agent Johnny Utah. Even Keanu loved the name. In interviews about why he wanted to do the part, it seems the name was all it took. It sounded so fucking "cool." He is not "young, dumb, and full of cum," as an asshole superior officer labels him at the outset. Instead, he's an intense and hard-working ex-jock who reluctantly surfs into a kinship with a gang of surfers who also happen to be a gang of bank robbers. He has pointy nipples that show up nicely in T-shirts, and even through his wetsuit, making a sexy fashion statement six years before Batman and Robin's

251

costumes were outfitted with exterior likenesses.

As for *Speed*, it's a macho thriller replete with sexual innuendo and phallic doublespeak about an FBI agent's attempts to defuse a bomb on a passenger bus that will blow sky-high if it drops below 50 mph. Variously, a character has "blown his wad," possesses "all the balls in the world," describes a bomb as "a pretty big wad...brass fittings," invites us to "Fuck me!" when he gets a load of how much explosive has been rigged, is "somewhere jerkin' off" while tethered under a moving bus, has "got some big, round, hairy cojones," is "a little prick," "has a hard-on for this bus," and rescues a bunch of people out of an elevator shaft. If that wasn't enough, the villain is missing a thumb and his gun is rendered impotent when beauty-struck by Keanu's face. When it finally comes time for the bad guy, who refers to the detonator he's carrying as his "stick," to die, he loses his head in a big spurt.

With a pumped bod thanks to two intense months of Gold's Gym workouts, a bullethead haircut that was his own idea, and a gun, a girl, a Jag, and a speeding bus numbered 2525 (so that we can note how cleverly they add up to 50), Keanu Reeves is not only good-looking and set to go, but he's engaging and heroic and can even manage to suggest a shade of romance by flashing a smile that bleats through the physique. His substantially hollow voice and limited vocal range suit hotshot Jack Travern to a T. Even the pulsing veins in his impressive biceps are in on the act.

Speed is chockfull of ludicrous moments, bad dialogue, completely illogical and unbelievable events, but it was a rollercoaster ride summer action flick that raced across the big screen with a kinetic rush. It begged us to *feel* it, not think about it. It's a big dumb American movie, but it was a huge hit and will probably one day (if not immediately) be seen for what it is: a spoof of testosterone flicks.

While trying to remind Sandra Bullock that Dennis Hopper is the bad guy, that "*he's*" the jerk, Reeves' enunciation clips the "h" and we hear him say with all sincerity: "Ease the asshole, Annie."

Sounds like damn good advice to me.

For Keanu, it was the film in which his (heretofore elusive) appeal reached its zenith. The guy became a movie star. Talented or not, genius or joke, he has a face the camera loves and he's able to corral a physicality and a screen presence and sexual charisma that makes debates about his skills as an accomplished actor nearly moot.

As with any actor who stumbles into a blockbuster hit, the ensuing media frenzy was enough to put a guy off his privacy. Everybody wants a piece of you. You might like to think the crowd is showing up because they want to hear Dogstar, your glorified and hard-working and steadily improving garage band, but most of the people are there to stare at the guy playing bass—you. Ted.

There was a time when Keanu was eminently quotable. At 22, in September of 1987, he told author and photographer Karen Hardy, who was profiling *The New Breed: Actors Coming of Age* (1988), "I feel like a young pubic hair—you know, I keep getting checked out and played with sometimes." The goofy, disheveled young actor who obliviously poses in a squat that reveals a gaping hole in the crotch of his pants and proof that he occasionally wears underwear, takes a question about what actress he would most like to work with and flip-flops it into who he'd most like to shtup. "Meryl Streep...because even if I wasn't good, she could fake it the best." In 1989, he talked to *Rolling Stone* about doing movie love scenes with strangers: "You have to say to them, 'Excuse me if I get excited,' and 'I'm sorry if I don't.'"

His open, good-natured, boisterous self would soon sour into internal monologues, bouts of moodiness, and a general antipathy toward the whole celebrity profile media machine. He wanted to talk about serious issues, or didn't want to talk at all, becoming distant, aloof, uncommunicative, and famously uncooperative when approached for interviews or profiles. Too many years of having his words, or his struggle to articulate them, slap him in the kisser as writers wrote about his eccentric disdain for the face-to-face and then chronicled what he wore, how he smelled, and how often he used "wow," "dude," and "man." Besides that, the press started to mess with his family and private life.

In late summer of 1994, with *Speed* the number one flick on the planet, a London tabloid carried an item that openly gay film and music mogul David Geffen reportedly took Keanu on a shopping spree for clothes in Beverly Hills. By December, a French magazine claimed that the two had actually gotten hitched in LA in a secret gay marriage ceremony and the US press picked up the tale before the New Year. Despite the fact that Geffen and Reeves had never even met, the rumor took on the proportions of an urban legend and a year's worth of good-natured, then tired denials by both parties in the press still couldn't completely stamp it out.

The gay community, meanwhile, thought it needed Keanu Reeves to be queer. It was looking for

Homoerotic photos advertise the 1984 stage play *Wolfboy*, featuring a teenaged Keanu Reeves and Carl Marotte. PHOTOGRAPHY BY DAVID HLYNSKY. POSTER ART DIRECTION (LOWER RIGHT) BY RANDY GLEDHILL.

another Rock Hudson and wanted to pull him out of the closet before, heaven forbid, he got sick, or ate the pavement somewhere up on Mulholland Drive. Please, please, *please* tell us that you're gay! Tell the world. Screw the bigots; declare yourself one of us.

The urge to co-opt a pretty young star by an increasingly proactive gay movement was and is strong stuff to contend with—no matter that in the real world such an admission would still jeopardize his career. The effort to liberate Keanu came on the heels of a volatile and well-publicized scare tactic called "outing," in which certain members of the gay community thought it politically and socially-expedient to force closeted men and women, as well as only rumored-to-be homosexual politicians and celebrities, out of the closet by publicly labeling them gay. The idea was that coerced admission or exposure of sexual orientation were necessary means to break down stereotypes and compel a dialogue with a prejudiced society in an era of virulent homophobia and the AIDS crisis.

There doesn't have to be an ounce of homophobia or self-hate in a gay actor's decision to keep his sexuality quiet, contrary to politically correct theories about self-love and acceptance. He owes his gay brothers and sisters nothing in the matter of his private sexuality and it makes bad business sense to cave in to the pressure. Sure, if you're a leading male actor who's gay and you want to come out on your own accord, then more power to you. But you do so expecting, at least for the foreseeable future, to literally assume an alternative lifestyle, beginning with calls from your creditors, followed by requests to do the TV talk-show circuit, gay pride parades, and then as fund-raiser poster boy.

As long as the movies engage the mind, stir the loins, and excite the senses sensual, an openly gay hunk compromises his entire career by billboarding his off-screen sexuality. No longer able to simply play a role that audiences are asked to get emotionally involved with, he is destined to repeatedly jar them out of the fantasy and back into reality each time said gay actor makes goo-goo eyes at his romantic co-star, who will be of the opposite sex a good 99.8% of the time.

If your livelihood depends on creating a fantasy rapport with your audience, then the last thing you want them to think about every time they see your character putting another in an amorous clutch is your imagined off-screen proclivities. Too much reality has a nasty way of kicking fantasy right in the nuts.

This is not to say that knowing Rock Hudson was gay necessarily spoils the fun of watching his movies. Not at all. But nobody looks at them the same. No one can help but think about...other things; for better or worse is not the issue, it's the thought that discounts. Besides, Hudson has the distinct advantage of hindsight. America didn't know he was gay simultaneous to his being our dream boy. It all came after the fact.

Being openly gay when you're a matinee idol means asking the audience to accept, affirm, and yet deny your sexuality all at once. So while it seems that mainstream America is more comfortable with us (or more precisely, with our TV selves), and while economic and pop culture assimilation have even resulted in a growing segment of "Who cares?," where will the poor out-and-proud stud-muffin Hollywood actor be when liberated America doesn't show up to see his movies? Not because they have a problem with his professed sexuality, only that the knowledge doesn't do much for them between either ears or legs—both vital territories for a flickering fantasy vying for attention on the silver screen.

When a straight actor plays gay, and inevitably announces he has no problem with it, even his apparent liberalism doesn't short-circuit the "yeah, but he really likes girls" safety mechanism that ensures his ability to play future heterosexual roles. The openly gay leading man can't make the same transition. Accepted or not, if you declare you belong to only 10% of the population in a business forever seeking to tap into the wallets of the masses, your subsequent casting couch chases are sure to become marathons.

The topic smacks a kinship to a debate waged in gay skin magazines over the true sexual identity of certain "gay" porn stars. Here again, the questions being asked reveal an absurd need for adherence to an identified and exclusive sexual desire. The fantasy is that much richer, so the argument goes, if you know that the men fucking on screen really enjoy fucking each other and aren't doing it just for the money. True, it can add a politically satisfying dimension to know that a porn star, such as the late Joey Stefano, proudly identified himself as gay and was interested in the man-to-man sex he was paid to perform. However, interest doesn't assure a great performance each time out, nor does personal disinterest necessarily translate to bad on-screen sex.

If porn stars Jeff Stryker and Ryan Idol were haughtily branded as "trade" and yet they got naked and had sex in their respective videos because men found them attractive and wanted to watch them do that, then someone needs to explain how these guys were not keeping up their end of the deal.

Every time a "gay" porn star gives an interview in which he says he's straight, it seems a small segment of the audience tunes him out as a traitor and the rest figure he's a liar. (Shows how much we know about sex. Anybody can suck a dick. It doesn't mean you're queer, you know.) The point is, how important is it that the fantasy also be the reality and how completely goddamned silly is it of us to expect that the two will ever correlate?

When is a hunk no longer a hunk? For card-carrying queers and little girls alike, it seems, it's the moment you find out you don't have a chance to climb into the sack with him.

The boys in the skin magazines have the virtue of not talking back to their audience and nobody much pays attention to the tiny disclaimer usually hidden somewhere in the masthead that states appearance in the magazine doesn't equate to the sexual orientation of the models. If only movie stars wouldn't give interviews they might maintain the same unbridled worship lavished on the centerfold boys. Of course, they'd also be replaced in a month.

The completely cool thing about Keanu Reeves' appearances on the magazine racks at the height of the gay rumors was that he didn't outright deny being gay. It's meaningless, this gay, straight, bisexual business. We're all humans, he said. Nice work, Keanu.

"Well, I mean, there's nothing wrong with being gay, so to deny it is to make a judgment," he explained to *Vanity Fair* during his post-*Speed* press blitz. "And why make a big deal of it? If someone doesn't want to hire me because they think I'm gay, well, then I have to deal with it, I guess. Or if people were picketing a theater. But otherwise, it's just gossip, isn't it?"

In fact, Keanu was such a good sport that he did inestimable service to his own rumors by having answered a flat-out query about his being gay in *Interview* magazine several years before with a "No" followed by a "but ya never know." It was a playful tease on his part that he couldn't have guessed would come back to haunt him.

It's said the only reason he finally decided to conclusively answer the question with a "no" was at the behest of his agent, who figured putting the issue to bed, so to speak, was a good idea. Where he's done this, outside of remarks from his agency, is unclear, since even his appearance on the July/August, 1995 cover of *Out* magazine's "Straight Issue" failed to include a proclamation of any sort within its pages.

Sex comes loaded with enough sociopolitical issues without having to subject those politics to a vote. Nobody should give a damn about whether Keanu, Brad, Tom, Matt, Leonardo, or Johnny are really queer. Admission would only rob us of the juicy mystery of it all. It doesn't matter if Keanu Reeves and Brad Pitt aren't sleeping together. All that matters is that they might be...there's the *frisson* for friction.

And believe me, for some of us, it doesn't take much, like reading an interview with the director of *Feeling Minnesota* (1996) in *Movieline* magazine and finding out that during the love scenes, "the most difficult part was keeping Keanu's thing inside the jock. If it fell out, he'd put it back and go on." True, his bathroom sex scene with Cameron Diaz is a showstopper that even brings a tear to Keanu's eye, but there isn't a shot in the sequence that looks as though it would require him to wear a jockstrap, let alone the opportunity to fall out of one. All the more reason to appreciate the behind-the-scenes details. (Incidentally, it looks as though he might be wearing a jock when he gets out of the steamy car in the middle of the street and hitches up his pants during their second go-round.)

Minnesota is a dark and funny play on the cruel relationship between brothers whom have only ever gotten along by beating on each other. All hell breaks loose when younger bro Keanu, perfectly cast and played, takes off with his fat-head brother's token wife (Cameron Diaz). Vincent D'Onofrio is inspired as the idiot older brother who later wrestles with Keanu and bites off a chunk of his ear.

Some would argue that as a pretty movie star you're little more than a collection of your body parts. Close-ups of Keanu's eyes, belly, lips, and an armpit were featured in photographer Matthew Rolston's 1991 collection *Big Pictures* (Bulfinch). An actor has many of his parts photographed over a career, but if you're also a sex star, you're expected to show a little more of yourself. Like many leading men, Keanu has been captured in stunning sessions by a who's who of great photographers. Particular favorites include a series shot by Brad Fierce in which Keanu is playful in and out of a black leather vest, as well as in a pair of tight black leather pants into the front of which he's not afraid to dip a hand. Then there's the famed Greg Gorman session, which appeared in the U.S. in once hotly-sought copies of the May 1993 issue of *Detour* magazine. "Much Ado About Keanu" is an 11-page spread of gorgeous images (oh, and an interview), including a scampish crotch grab, a shirtless Keanu in suspenders, then posing in a giant black sweater, appearing suitably classical in an open, billowing white shirt, allowing detailed study of his nipples, a full-page (and quite heavenly) head-to-toe look at his bare backside, and a coltish peek at a swatch of coal-black pubic hair. (A quartet of these photos can also be found in Greg Gorman's *Inside Life*, a 1997 coffee-table photobook.)

With Valentino and with DiCaprio, it was the femininity of their beauty. With James Dean, whom Keanu was asked to substitute for in Paula Abdul's *Rebel Without A Cause* "Rush Rush" music video, it was the denial of his homosexual affairs. There's always some reason why a segment of the population abhors the popularity of a given star, especially a beautiful one. With Keanu Reeves, it's the completely ludicrous perception that he's a dope. Both the movies and television are far more forgiving, and deliberately accommodating, in fact, of hunks who don't have much upstairs. The "himbo" is the cute guy with the great body who cannot be allowed to be smart as well. Nobody's that perfect. So with good looks and sex appeal in the forefront, make him a dummy and the audience will find him endearing and fuckable instead of narcissistic and completely out of their league. There's a long history of dumbing down beautiful women in order to effectively objectify and disendow them. Some of the boys get the same treatment, whether it's the cute, but stultified football jock, the self-obsessed and air-headed muscleman, or the drop-dead gorgeous boytoy who's as dumb as a stick, e.g., Sasha Mitchell on *Step by Step*, Thomas Haden Church on *Wings*, Ashton Kutcher on *That 70's Show*, and Joey Lawrence on *Blossom* (TV); Brendan Fraser as *George of the Jungle*, Matt Keeslar in *Waiting for Guffmann*, Robert La Tourneaux in *The Boys in the Band*, Ivan Sergei in *The Opposite of Sex*, Rex Smith in *The Pirates of Penzance*, Mark Wahlberg in *Boogie Nights*, Paul Walker in *Meet the Deedles*, and Ashton Kutcher (again) in *Dude, Where's My Car?* (Movies).

Does anyone really think Keith Partridge would have any trouble living the orgiastic lifestyle of David Cassidy if it weren't for the writers' weekly humiliations and blows to his intellect and ego on *The Partridge Family*? For that matter, does anyone really believe that Chris Klein was still a virgin trying to get laid in *American Pie* (1999)? Even his enormously sweet (and dumb) jock in *Election* (1998) is managing to get blowjobs from a lesbian and knows enough to thank God in his nightly prayers for giving him an enormous penis.

Those most vociferous in their dislike of Keanu Reeves not only think he's a bad actor (and seem to openly resent his making a living), but seem to think his stardom is an affront to the intellect because he's obviously such a Ted. Even if he is (he's not)—and I can't imagine how they presume to know—I can't see what the hell that has got to do with anything other than how unwittingly they've succumbed to the brainwash of multimedia. If you think he's a bad actor—and he'd be the first to admit that "I'm not the best actor in the world; I know that"—so be it. If you hate him because you think he's a bad actor and he's stupid, then it has to be because his beauty freaks you out. Those who see success founded on beauty as pointless and intellectually insulting at least partly do so because beauty is in and of itself not considered an accomplishment. It's a culturally and temporally protean attribute that encourages superficiality, corrupts values and self-esteem, and disenfranchises those who either don't possess it or waste their lives foolishly pursuing it. Beauty is supposed to be in the eye of the beholder, but it seems to have been usurped by the eye of the fashion photographer and the shallowest of physical characteristics. Those who struggle daily to conform are vain, while those who spend a lifetime in depressed sublimation to it are ruled by envy. (See, we've already got two of the seven deadlies covered.) Those who have it are placed on a pedestal, handed opportunities, and held in ludicrous esteem simply because they've got razor's edge cheekbones, abs you can grate cheese on, and a butt so pretty that most of us would gladly shave it and proudly spend our lives walking backwards.

To some degree, all of the above complaints about looks are valid. But none convince me that Keanu Reeves is to blame. It's the beauty pageant argument. Should we hate the women who participate or the contest that ogles them? Marilyn Monroe's showbiz persona would become fodder for certain feminists, as if she were doing blackface. The reduction of a performer to just his or her parts can be degrading—no doubt about it—but beauty is not inherently anti-intellectual. Smart people pretending to know someone based on an image are dumb people. Keanu Reeves is not Ted. But for some, he will always be the winner of an offensive pageant.

In 1994, the Art Center College of Design in Pasadena, California made headlines by offering an accredited course entitled "The Films of Keanu Reeves," a serious study of sixteen Keanu titles augmented by readings from Nietzsche, Hegel, and Foucault. For many, it was a sure sign of the Apocalypse.

Clearly, however, there is more to Mr. Reeves than just his exotic beauty, though I must admit he looks great in his worker's singlet and flapping his butterfly wings in the well-intentioned and pleasantly old-fashioned romance *A Walk in the Clouds* (1995). He's vacuous on purpose as *Johnny Mnemonic* (1995), the guy with a computer chip in his head whose true purpose in the sci-fi source material got mindlessly reprogrammed by a studio that decided the character should be looking for his erased past.

One of the many things I like about Keanu Reeves, and find fascinating about his career, is his personal resolve (and casting success) to take on a wide variety of characters and acting challenges, whether it's playing Suh-thun as a clean-cut and smiley-faced radio newsman in 1951 Detroit in *Tune in Tomorrow* (1990), or as "the One," our cyber-age savior Neo in *The Matrix* (1999) and its sequels.

The Matrix is a dense sci-fi-martial arts religious parable that stands as a watershed hybrid of genre and technique for cinema in the new millennium, alongside *Fight Club* (1999) and *Magnolia* (1999). It was a huge box-office hit that thrilled while it commented, spiking its mixture of high-tech violence and philosophical treatise with a disturbing need for "guns...lots of guns." Reeves looks ultra-cool and iconic dressed head to toe in black, sporting shades and wielding an endless array of weaponry. The violence looks cool, too. It's superhero chic, and the innocent cops and security guards that get needlessly blasted away can be slaughtered because they're not "real," just the unreal lives of human battery cells—killing as a catharsis for saving all of humanity. Despite some initial "huh's?" when the film overwhelmed us on the big screen, it's neither indecipherable nor terribly complex, just rich in exploitable ideas and a potent source of media-age mythology. It's not often that an action film gives us those kinds of opportunities, and a younger generation of filmgoers embraced it as their *Star Wars* (1977), praising it to the high heavens and tripping on its "complexities."

Thankfully, just as the *Matrix* phenomenon threatened to take its mass media brainwashing metaphor too literally and attempt to legitimize itself as a new religion, the first sequel, *Matrix Reloaded* (2003), lowered the sights and happily indulged in its true pulp sci-fi comic book nature. It will be interesting to see how the series holds up over the years, particularly whether the first film's vicarious and kinetic violence will be understood as extended social commentary on a video game mentality that celebrates carnage as it dehumanizes victims and not just the source for a cutting-edge series of great action sequences that have been imitated to death.

Putting in a rare guest appearance as himself in *Action* (2000), the short-lived TV spoof of Hollywood politics, Keanu sits in a movie theatre during a premiere, staring down at his crotch and wriggling in his seat. The camera moves back to show us that Ileana Douglas has her hand down his pants. "I'm a big fan," she says. He looks back down at his pants, then at her, and replies, "I'm getting to be a pretty big fan of yours, too."

There's a point at which you risk becoming an apologist for an actor based on selfish devotion to his sex appeal and, if you haven't figured it out by now, I'm guilty of that and then some. You'll get no arguments from me over *Bram Stoker's Dracula* (1991), *Chain Reaction* (1996), *The Devil's Advocate* (1997), *The Watcher* (2000), *The Replacements* (2000), or *Sweet November* (2001). But I'll never miss a Keanu Reeves film. That's the point.

"I'm a visceral experience," he told the *Los Angeles Times* in 1988. What's more, as co-star Charlize Theron once pointed out to *Movieline* magazine: "Anything naked with Keanu is a good thing."

The squat, dark-haired kid of Irish extraction who's playing Jose, a Brazilian gang member in *Mixed Blood* (1985), is telling the undertaker that he wants a wall full of red and green flowers when it comes time for his own funeral. "I'm afraid there's no such thing as green flowers," the man replies.

And without a blink of an eye and barely a beat, the kid says, "Get 'em."

One of the things I enjoyed most about watching **Rodney Harvey** (1967-1998) was that I always knew what I was going to get. He had the same unique personal style and complete disregard for conventional acting in his first film as he did in his last. I guess you might call him a guilty pleasure.

Director Paul Morrissey, who discovered Joe Dallesandro nearly two decades before, saw the 16-year old Harvey hanging out on the streets in Times Square trying to finish a deal to buy a knife. Morrissey was looking for kids to play gang members in *Mixed Blood*, a seedy, often darkly funny story about a drug war between a German operative and his gang and a horde of Brazilian youths mothered by Marilia Pera in Alphabet City. Morrissey called Harvey's mom to make sure it was okay.

He got one hundred bucks a day and graduated to a key supporting role. He's the first person we see in the film, crawling through a hole in a graffiti-ridden wall, behind which the Maceteros bunk on the floor. He's got puggish, tough guy looks, with black hair and thick eyebrows that may momentarily distract you from the possibility of beauty that his streetwise face possesses. His character has got a nasty mouth on him, and as with other of Morrissey's actors over the years, there's the appealing suggestion that the kid isn't much different off-screen. He seems authentic.

Not that Rodney Harvey ever sold white babies on the black market or abstained from drugs (a defining Morrissey theme in all his urban pictures is a disgust for drugs), but there's a no-nonsense attitude and an almost deadpan delivery that doesn't feel acted or affected, just real.

Unfortunately, Harvey's life story turned out not to be a pretty one, though it's as fascinating and tragic as anything he'd ever have the chance to play on screen. His father was an absent dad and his mom re-married when Rodney was just two. Beloved by his friends, Rodney grew up in South Philly as a fighter and a troublemaker, a scrappy little boy who was teased about his size and good looks and made anyone who did so sorry. When nearly a teenager, he contacted his real dad by phone and was rejected, traumatizing his sense of self-worth and making life at home with his stepfather even more difficult.

Mom and husband eventually abandoned their two boys (Rodney and an older brother), leaving them to fend for themselves until the house was boarded up. In one of those possible to believe, but impossible to dramatize life moments, a friend remembers Rodney watching a *Superman* movie on TV and suddenly announcing that he wanted to go to Hollywood and become an actor and play Superman's son.

He dropped out of high school in 1984 and was on one of his frequent train ventures into New York City when Morrissey saw him and ended up putting him in the movies. A talent agent who attended a screening of the film signed Harvey on and began getting modeling and acting jobs for him.

In the execrable softcore teen-sex flick *Delivery Boys* (1984), made after but released before *Mixed Blood*, Rodney plays Rodney "Fast Action," the manager of the title morons who work delivering pizzas but also happen to be one of the hottest break-dancing teams in the city. The sexcapades along the way to the Brooklyn Bridge BreakDance Contest include an old guy demanding glory hole service from one of the

The beautiful and tragic Rodney Harvey, here from *Salsa* (1988). PHOTOFEST

boys in drag, a pizza boy who's given a constant and enormous woody after being injected with a blue liquid by German mad scientists, and a naked delivery boy standing in for a broken sculpture at an art exhibit who passes gas, urinates in some champagne glasses, and has his mother recognize his hairy butt from across the gallery. Fortunately, Rodney isn't at the center of any of the above. In fact, he doesn't have much to do at all.

During a stint in Los Angeles, he landed a gig for a day's shoot on a music video. He's running and jumping and twirling in his bright yellow 1/4 shirt, black shorts, and matching bright yellow headband in Menudo's "Hold Me" (1985), and he seems to like piggyback-riding in the background of several shots in which all the extras are screwing around and generally being joyous while little Ricky Martin and company dance and sing in the foreground. In *Mixed Blood*, which includes a shoot-out in a store that sells exclusively Menudo merchandise, a character makes a derogatory remark about the 1980s all-boy group that contractually ejected members when they reached the age of 17. Rodney pipes up in defense and says,

"Menudos ain't no pussy." The gang's matron, Rita La Punta, adores Menudo, too. They lose many boys...just like her.

In 1987, Rodney started showing up in the photographs of Bruce Weber, the premier eroticist of beautiful young men in commercial photography. A controversial and very sensual series of photos of Rodney and a model named Lisa Marie appeared in a denim fashion spread in the May 7, 1987 issue of *Rolling Stone*. In one particularly hot shot, Rodney is shirtless, has his overalls pulled down around his waist, and Lisa Marie has a hand tucked inside the front of his undies.

Lisa Marie became Rodney's girlfriend. He had her name tattooed above his own on his arm, then later removed it one letter at a time with a lit cigarette.

Weber also shot a series with Rodney in the arms of another handsome young male model and those photographs are probably the most beautiful ever taken of him. He's aware of the camera, gazing into the lens, outfitted in a black muscle T, a cigarette dangling from his mouth. The other man is shirtless, caught up in serious adoration, running his fingers through Rodney's hair. Weber would also pair Rodney with Madonna for *Life* magazine and include him both in his Academy-Award nominated documentary on Chet Baker, *Let's Get Lost* (1989), where he can be glimpsed butting bumper cars with Baker and later cheering him on before a performance at Cannes in 1987, and in vintage footage getting smooched on the lips by another beautiful boy as part of the mix in *Chop Suey* (2001).

Rodney is one of a pair of oddballs in Tony Bill's marvelously strange and dark *Five Corners* (1988), set in The Bronx of 1964. In a quirky subplot, he's a stogie-smoking street mug partnered with a German sidekick who inherit a pair of giddy gals after they're given five bucks to take them off another fella's hands.

No one does a line reading quite the same way as Rodney Harvey. The South Philly accent and deadpan delivery do wonders with: "Listen, someone murdered our teacher, so we got the day off...you wanna go for a ride?" The boys' idea of a date is stepping onto the tops of two elevators temporarily parked on the 10th floor and necking as they glide up and down through the shaft while a sampling of Delibes' *Lakme* romances the hell out of this completely unexpected and beautiful sequence.

He was exported to Australia to star in *Initiation* (1987, aka *Zoomstone*) as a Brooklyn teenager facing the elements after his drug-smuggling dad's plane crashes. It's nice to see him in the lead, and there are some stunning landscapes, but the coming-of-age, trial-by-fire story meanders and fails to create legitimate drama. Back stateside, a sexy CK Obsession for Men television commercial provided ample exposure and industry interest.

He's ex-Menudo star Robbie Rosa's best friend in the rarely-seen, but has-to-be-seen dance movie *Salsa* (1988), in which we briefly witness Rodney do a little bumping, grinding, and mock-humping to a spicy beat. For his part, hyper-Robbie cavorts in a towel and does a dance number with his girlfriend that has her grabbing him by the weenie and pulling him along as part of the choreography.

Always the best friend or sidekick, despite his looks, but perhaps because of his size (barely 5'6"), Rodney's also there to lend support to a young boxer in Paul Morrissey's *Spike of Bensonhurst* (1988).

Spike Fumo is as lean and meaty as the porterhouse steaks he shoplifts into his sweatpants thanks to the tall, lanky, and very buff physique of **Sasha Mitchell** (1967-   ), who studied acting in New York at the National Improvisational Theatre. As a dreamy summer romance in the 1986 TV-movie *Pleasures*, he's a boy who only speaks Spanish but needs no translation when we catch him for a flash in the bathroom wearing just his little white undies. He then appeared as the sacrificial American soldier in the by-the-numbers Marines vs. Arab terrorists flick *Death Before Dishonor* (1987). During a drunken hazing, he's asked to define "a brother of the golden wing" and answers, "it's a brother with a big thing that makes the girls sing."

In Morrissey's enormously charming comedy about a goombah boxer from Bensinhoist, his neighborhood mob connections, and his career built on fixed fights, Mitchell radiates such lived-in, natural charm and attitude that you're convinced it's not an act. Morrissey hates actors who act. He casts personalities. With the strapping 6'2" Sasha Mitchell, he got a kid with an indigenous sense of character and the looks of a Calvin Klein model.

He really was a Calvin Klein model, too. His gorgeous body and smooth, angular face made for striking compositions in front of Bruce Weber's camera. They were the kind of photos that say less about the product (jeans, whatever) than the form poured into them. Weber had perfected his CK look by 1988, so it's

259

quite possible that you've seen Sasha in an ad and not really seen him. He's been typed into an aesthetic and his minor celebrity is what compels us to take a look back at them.

Spike is a great role. He's an aggressive, vain, and naturally shallow operator. His pop is in jail taking a rap for the local boss and his mom is living with another woman. Spike and his mutha don't exactly get along. "This arrangement here is un-Italian, unreligious, nonsectarian, and definitely anti-nature," he tells her of her lesbian relationship. She and her plump girlfriend return the favor by letting loose a stream of profanities whenever he's near. All the family relationships in the film are hilariously conceived: uncensored, unpredictable, and very unPC. At the time of the film's limited release, some were offended by the barrage of ethnic stereotypes, both Italian and Puerto Rican, but Morrissey has written characters in a social comedy that are completely true to themselves, prejudices and all. This is the "fah-gedda-boutit" movie before *Donnie Brasco* (1997), a cousin to *Saturday Night Fever* (1977) and a stepbrother to *The Wanderers* (1979).

Former-Calvin Klein model Sasha Mitchell as *Spike of Bensonhurst* (1988). EVERETT COLLECTION

260

Spike is a macho, bone-headed, sexist sweetheart. He's a tough guy to pull off, but Mitchell has everything he needs. Watch how he swaggers, how he takes command of every scene, how lost he would be without his eyebrows. His carved and smooth upper body on display in the ring is a sight to behold, but he's got the full-figured physique that makes everything he wears look right. He's got a bod bronzed for clothes—no doubt an important thing for a model—and could sell an all-black muscle T and sweatpants combo to a sponge.

He was lured to serial television first as a regular on *Dallas* (1978-91), playing hunky James Richard Beaumont, J.R. Ewing's illegitimate son and *enfant terrible* during the 1989-91 seasons. An attempt to have him star in the Matt Dillon role for the TV version of *The Flamingo Kid* (1989) didn't last but a few episodes. In 1991, he rejoined *Dallas* co-star Patrick Duffy on the ABC-Television sitcom *Step By Step* (1991-98), where he played the completely airheaded, but lovable Cody Lambert from 1991-96, and then again briefly in 1998.

As for feature films, he lent his considerable athletic skills and extraordinary physical condition to a trilogy of sequels to a middling 1989 Jean-Claude Van Damme opus. In *Kickboxer 2: The Road Back* (1991), he's a nice, handsome, responsible, respectable young man—the last of his dynasty—running his nearly bankrupt gym on a dream and a prayer. He won't go into the corrupt fight business because he's an honest man. He's got integrity. He's also beaten, shot, gets his gym burned, and has a little boy student die in the blaze. Time to bring in the Asian master to help him rehabilitate and get ready to combat the crooks in and out of the ring.

Sasha takes a deep breath every so often while he's on screen, a noticeable behavior that doesn't seem rooted in a character trait, but perhaps conveys his own subconscious boredom with what he's doing. Acting was not his passion, it turns out, though he repeated his role of David Sloan in *Kickboxer 3: The Art of War* (1992) and *Kickboxer 4: The Aggressor* (1994), the latter of which is a leaden rip-off of *Enter the Dragon* (1973), with Sasha at zero energy and the fights moving at the speed of rehearsal. His likability and physical prowess, in numbers 2 and 3 anyway, make the series a lot more enjoyable than I suppose it ought to be. Besides, they could be edited down to a very sexy exercise video.

Though he's supposed to be evil, I admire his single-mindedness to maintain classroom discipline as a vigilante substitute teacher who claims to be the last of a mad scientist's military androids in *Class of 1999 II: The Substitute* (1994). He squeezed in that psycho role just before all hell broke out in his personal life and he made disturbing headlines in 1996 for spousal abuse. He was arrested and convicted for an incident in 1995, sentenced to three years' probation, but then violated that probation. He spent a month in jail in early 1996, then violated his probation again and went to jail for another six months. It was years before a gag order related to his case was lifted and evidence that his wife was a drug addict and allegedly abusive toward their children became known, demonstrating the one-sidedness and inherent sexism of domestic violence arrest records without context. To say the least, this was a troubled family. Shedding further light on the conflict that once caused him to be fired from his TV sitcom and all but ended his professional career at the time, Mitchell is the one who was ultimately awarded custody of his children. He contends he was protecting them from his unstable wife all along and only wishes he had sought custody sooner.

The complex relationship, or lack thereof, between a film star and his audience can be sorely tested when something the actor does off the screen negatively impacts our perception of him, whether we know the full story or not. Should I have been unable to enjoy or recommend *Spike of Bensonhurst* because of the nature of Sasha Mitchell's personal problems? Anyone who sees him in *Spike* will definitely want to find out more about him. For a long time, I was at a bit of a loss. Personally, I loved him in *Spike*, but I couldn't truthfully say I loved the guy who played the part, because I didn't know him. Still don't.

Ignorance of a sort is bliss when it comes to actors. We can't help ourselves, though. When we find somebody we like, somebody who makes our heart beat faster, we're curious to know something about them in real life, running the same risk we'd have asking around about the guy with the nice smile down at the other end of the bar.

People want to know about Rodney Harvey, too. Whatever happened to that guy?

His shot at real stardom finally came when he was cast from a sea of plenty to play Sodapop Curtis (the Rob Lowe role) in the TV series version of *The Outsiders* (1990). The pre-airing publicity was teen star mania, tossing Rodney into a world he could only have imagined in South Philly.

He had arrived...or at least it seemed tangibly close. He was sprawled sexily across two pages of *US*

261

magazine, shirtless and bulging in all the right places in his skintight cyclist's pants. "Who says my body looks so good?" he asks. "I never get any special praise about my body. It must be my brains they go for!"

Time magazine suggested we write the names of the half-dozen new *Outsiders* stars down "and check again in six years," considering that most of the cast of the film version went on to become movie stars in their own rights.

It wasn't going to be that sweet for Rodney. The series was canceled in its first season and the sudden end to the fantasy and the $10,000-a-week paycheck devastated him. A rambunctious, rough and tumble kid who was frightened and freaked by the possibility of success, as well as felt somehow deeply undeserving of it, he was an instantaneous victim of the LA drug scene. He partied, he drank, he smoked pot, he blew his money, he got into fights, and he started slipping.

Gus Van Sant cast him to play the nosey dope fiend from across the street in *Drugstore Cowboy* (1989), but apparently Rodney wasn't together enough to do it. He was also cast to play Scott Favor in Van Sant's *My Own Private Idaho* (1991), but the 2.7 million dollar budget wasn't financed until Keanu Reeves (as Favor) and River Phoenix committed themselves to the project.

Rodney plays Gary in *Idaho*, a far lesser, but still memorable role. He and Scott are already at the older lady's house when Mike is brought in for the warm-up. Gary's also the guy behind the big concert promoters' heist, placing undue emphasis on "*dude*" while he's explaining his gnarly plan.

In *Guncrazy* (1992), he's one of a pair of high school goons who refer to Drew Barrymore as a "sperm bank" and use her in an old drainpipe outside of town. He's still looking pretty good. He's playing a pre-*Boys Don't Cry* hick loser, so we don't really care when it comes time for him to bite it. Drew tells him just before her boyfriend fires the fatal shot: "It'll be okay, Tom. Just think about Jesus."

It's said that Rodney started getting real bad, i.e., started shooting heroin, while he was making *My Own Private Idaho*. Other than an Italian film called *La Bocca* (1990; aka *Silent Love*) and a bit as a "Friend" in the depressing *God's Lonely Man* (1996), there are no more credits for the 1990s. What remains is an immensely tragic, infuriating, and unfortunately unexceptional tale of a young man's violent struggle with a disease. There would follow a cyclical battle with drug addiction, multiple arrests, including for battery, robbery, and possession, stints in halfway houses, prison, and drug rehab, and a life ended on April 10, 1998 in a seedy hotel room from an overdose of junk.

Rodney Harvey's story was powerfully told in "Shooting Star," a first-rate piece of journalism by Holly Millea that appeared in the December, 1998 issue of *Premiere* magazine. Still, no headline or title could be more persuasive than the half-dozen mug shots of Rodney from 1987 to 1996 that header across two pages, from troubled young beauty to burnt-out shell. Dorian Gray's retribution in six panels.

He was supposed to be in Gus Van Sant's *Good Will Hunting* (1997).

Denzel Washington (1954-   ) was cute as George Segal's 17-year old son in *Carbon Copy* (1981) despite the fact that this offensive, dated, and insulting "comedy" about a rich white Jew who discovers he has a black son doesn't merit a single laugh. He was cute, too, during his residency at *St. Elsewhere* (1982-88), NBC's very popular hospital drama that worked well at combining tragedy, comedy, and soap as a primer for *ER*.

He commanded the screen as a militant black soldier demanding equality in *A Soldier's Story* (1984), played South African activist Stephen Biko in *Cry Freedom* (1987), and deservedly won an Oscar for his dynamic role as a soldier in the first all-black unit to fight in the Civil War in *Glory* (1989). You watch that performance and there's no doubt in your mind that you're looking at one of the best actors of his generation...and, well, at one of the best-looking actors of his generation.

Good-looking and sexy aren't necessarily interchangeable. Denzel finally put the two together in *The Mighty Quinn* (1989), in which he plays a Caribbean police chief in all white uniform and black shades. Mimi Rogers thinks he's a "swell dresser," and asks him later if he ever lets down his guard. "A couple of weeks ago I shaved off my mustache," he replies.

Washington is so self-assured and confident playing Xavier Quinn that when he has to take his shirt off several times in the film, he does so without the least bit of self-consciousness. That may sound like an odd compliment given the fact that he has a gorgeous body and taking one's shirt off is not exactly like taking one's pants off. But Washington has a precarious relationship with sexuality on screen. He's famously uncomfortable shooting love scenes (something most actors have in common), but he's also famous for avoiding them. He's had very few in his screen career and is on

Denzel Washington humidifies Easy Rawlins in *Devil in a Blue Dress* (1995).
EVERETT COLLECTION

record as saying that he doesn't do nudity for nudity's sake, preferring a style of movie sexiness from the '30s and '40s to today's bare-all mentality.

Perhaps that's why Denzel Washington is so damned sexy whenever he does something as simple as walk through a scene shirtless. Or when he asks Sarita Choudhury, "Do you mind if I kiss you?" during their stroll along the bayou in *Mississippi Masala* (1991) and the camera actually steps in towards them to capture it. A sexy late night phone call, with both of them in their respective beds barely covered by sheets, is hot and bothersome because of what we don't see, and because his voice is so incredibly seductive, not because we get a quick flash of his bare ass as he gets out of bed.

None of this is to suggest that we don't want to see more of him, only that we're willing to let him decide where and when. In *Ricochet* (1991), of all places, a formulaic good guy cop vs. psycho killer flick, we catch him for a split second in a cup in the police officers' locker room. It may not be a love scene, and the film's audience had to be largely male, but our appreciation knows no bounds.

263

Besides, he's one of those actors who are so attractive that he looks just as lickable completely dressed. You can tell this guy has got a hard body just by the way his clothes mold to him. Catch him in *Much Ado About Nothing* (1993) as Don Pedro, where his dapper uniform and big beautiful smile is all it will take to keep you warm. (If only Shakespeare had saw fit to have Don Pedro turn his brother Don John over his knee for a well-deserved spanking.) Or notice how he spends almost the entirety of the entertaining noir *Devil In A Blue Dress* (1995) in a muscle shirt.

After preparing for an undecided career in either journalism or medicine at Fordham University, Washington discovered his love for acting while doing stage work and joined the American Conservatory Theatre in San Francisco. He's an astonishingly natural actor. There's an incredible ease to his on-screen persona. And he's one of the great listeners, something I've no doubt noticed because it's difficult to keep your eyes off him even when his character isn't the one talking.

His extraordinary powers as a dramatic actor, demonstrated in *Malcolm X* (1992), *Courage Under Fire* (1996), *He Got Game* (1998), *The Hurricane* (1999), and *Training Day* (2001), among others, aren't limited to serious films with serious social issues. He has equal intensity in the submarine flick *Crimson Tide* (1995), and makes stuff like *The Siege* (1998), *The Bone Collector* (1999), and *Remember the Titans* (2000) worth watching.

He infamously advised Will Smith not to kiss another man if he didn't want to in *Six Degrees of Separation* (1993) after the young star called him well into production with serious apprehension. Washington dislikes talking about the incident because it has been politically de-contextualized. It's true, he told Smith not to do it if he didn't feel he could, but personal homophobia wasn't the likely culprit, just good old career planning and image building.

Washington was superb as homophobic attorney Joe Miller in the well-meaning, but eventually pandering *Philadelphia* (1993), and the film's greatest achievements come outside the dramatically rigged courtroom drama as Miller slowly learns to see his feelings towards homosexuality as prejudices, even if that doesn't mean he'll be able to understand or fully accept gays.

So what would a young Denzel Washington have done if he were playing the role Will Smith had in *Six Degrees*? He told Stephen Rebello in *Movieline* magazine: "I'd have chewed it to pieces. And if kissing was part of it, I'd have kissed the hell out of the guy."

Rupert Everett (1959-) looks like a fashion designer's sketch. The relative proportions have been sacrificed for the love of lines. Long limbs, narrow waist, cut pecs, broad shoulders, elongated neck, and large head with rakish angles and great tousled hair.

An imposing 6'4", he should find it easy to play a live-action villain in a Tim Burton animated film without seeming out of place, but he's too soft for that, too sensual. He is, in fact, quite pretty.

He's also clever and sexy and romantic and difficult. And British. Raised in a right-wing, conservative family (his father was a military officer), young Rupert was sent away to boarding school at seven, as custom dictates, and the separation anxiety from his mother was debilitating. He became a moody, almost fatalistic boy. The Catholic school couldn't hold him nor could his first acting school, from which he was expelled for insubordination at age 19.

For about a year and a half, between Paris and London, he supported himself as a rent boy—a male prostitute—and would later allude to it in his semi-autobiographical novel *Hello Darling, Are You Working?* (1992) before deciding not to talk about it anymore. A second novel, *The Hairdressers of St. Tropez*, was published in 1995.

He found himself appropriately cast as the lead in Julian Mitchell's play *Another Country*, whose West End production became a hit. Everett played Guy Bennett, a gay student in 1930s England, whose less than clandestine relationship with another student compromises his standing in the social hierarchy.

He also starred in the 1984 film version of *Another Country* as the almost unbelievably cheeky and openly homosexual Bennett, but his dates with golden boy Cary Elwes (who, perhaps prophetically, dresses to the left) are romantically platonic. They cuddle late at night in a canoe, but there's no kissing or bed-hopping despite Bennett's early admission that "there's a hollow at the base of his throat that makes me want to pour honey all over him and lick it off."

Miranda Richardson asks Rupert if his eyelashes are real in *Dance With A Stranger* (1985), a noirish drama about the fatal relationship between a hard-edged, dyed-blonde café girl and a boorish, alcoholic racecar driver in 1954 London. "Everybody says they'd look better on a girl," he answers.

Rupert Everett pines for his blond boyfriend in *Another Country* (1984). PHOTOFEST

"I think they look nice on you."

Hollywood was brat-packing so Everett didn't have much a chance to break into films here in the States during the '80s, depressing him to no end. He's got the big hair and the androgynous looks to credibly be an '80s rocker singing "Tainted Love" in the awful *Hearts of Fire* (1987), alongside Fiona and Bob Dylan, but there's only a trace of evidence that he's an accomplished pianist and once had a pop band of his own.

His deceptively exquisite physique (later captured full-frontal by photographer Greg Gorman in 1995) is on impressive display in *The Comfort of Strangers* (1991). There's a compressed quality to his leanness and an almost sculptured affect to his nude torso and backside, a far cry from the nearly sunken chest he sports as Ram, the nasty, rapist half-brother in the NBC miniseries *Princess Daisy* (1983). He's gorgeous enough to be stalked by a creepy older couple with an opulent apartment and all of the beauty of Venice at their disposal in *Strangers*. Christopher Walken's character, whose repressed homosexuality has been perverted into sexual fascism in part by his Italian family's Old World masculinity, admits that Rupert looks like an angel. Unfortunately, the horror film finale to the deliberately murky plot seems unearned.

He's a gay activist who falls for a lesbian as one of several subplots in the enjoyable *Inside Monkey Zetterland* (1993), a sexy sexist who sleeps with his wife's sister in Robert Altman's improvised *Ready to Wear* (*Prêt-à-Porter*; 1994), and his thinness cannot be believably disguised in a fat suit as the indolent, bozo-haired Prince of Wales hoping to seize the throne in *The Madness of King George* (1994).

Shockingly, he agreed to star in *Cemetery Man* (1994), an Italian-made horror flick based on a popular comic book, as weary gravekeeper Francesco Dellamorte, whose job it is to blow away the dead after they get up within seven days of first burial. "At a certain point in your life you realize you know more dead people than living," he dryly observes. It's a witty spoof for those familiar with Italian *giallo* films, but you don't have to be a gore or zombie movie aficionado to have one hell of a good time watching it. It's dark, perverse, surreal, blood-drenched, and enormously funny; a slapstick nightmare with garish stylization, clever set pieces, an erotic session of lovemaking on a gravesite, and a fairy tale finale. Everett is perfectly droll and cynical as a man in a dead-end job who turns to serial murder after losing all of his emotional attachments save the one he has with his sweet, blubbering-idiot sidekick Gnaghi (François Hadji-Lazaro).

You'd think that after starring in an Italian zombie epic and co-starring with an orangutan (1996's *Dunston Checks In*, doing his Terry-Thomas), Rupert Everett might have been ready to go back to hustling while he still had what it took to hustle. Instead, he stole *My Best Friend's Wedding* (1997) right from under Julia Roberts and became the gay guy that everybody wanted as his or her best friend. A star was born.

Wedding is an absolute delight of a film, a romantic comedy with enormous charm that channels the Cary Grant/Irene Dunne classics. It's not quite true that Rupert steals the show from Roberts, because she and Dermot Mulroney and Cameron Diaz are all superb, but he's the one who got all the buzz in the press and the boost to his career because audiences fell in love with him big time and felt as though they were discovering an unknown.

His George Downes is not only the most charming boss you could ever want to have, but also a sweet, funny, and outrageously liberating friend. Rupert Everett made us all "fag hags," the indelicate term for insecure single women who find safety and comfort befriending gay men. He was a trendy accessory in the 1990s and every woman should probably have one, or at least get one before everybody else does and they're no longer chic. What makes his homosexuality even more palatable in *Wedding* is that he's as sexless as David Wayne in an old Kate Hepburn flick. He's entirely non-threatening. He has no on-screen sex life. He's fulfilling the age-old next door neighbor or best friend stereotype, but Everett makes the standby refreshing because at least he's a real character. He's got things to do besides being a token.

George's "acceptance" in mainstream cinema is yet another of the leaps and bounds gay men and women made thanks to gay characters or out-and-about and real gay people on TV in the 1990s. Rupert Everett publicly came out of the closet back in 1989, but few were listening or cared. To find out that the gay guy you loved in that Julia Roberts' flick really was gay must have had some sort of impact, and it wasn't necessarily negative.

The studios lined up to star their first openly gay leading man in any number of projects, but he was going to be playing a gay character in all the ones bandied about in the press. A gay James Bond. A gay film star. (Both his own writing projects.) Then he played Madonna's gay best friend who ends up impregnating her in *The Next Best Thing* (2000). And he's an erudite and clever society snob in the screen version of

Oscar Wilde's *An Ideal Husband* (1999), a glittery and armpit-shaven King of the Faeries in the hopelessly earthbound attempt at *William Shakespeare's A Midsummer Night's Dream* (1999), and goes uncredited as gay playwright Christopher Marlowe in the classic *Shakespeare in Love* (1998).

As the aged patriarchal queen in deep trouble with the mob and drinking his life away while plinking at his piano in *B. Monkey* (1999; shot in 1996), Everett has a certain haunted pathos. He dances with Jonathan Rhys Meyers, then gets into a fight with the fiery punk, who threatens him out on the street. The two come face to face.

"So, he doesn't know whether he wants to kill me or kiss me, do you, lover?" asks Everett of the angry youth. I'd like them to kiss, but I'm not sure everyone else feels the same way. Rupert Everett was poised for a moment in time to be the screen's first openly gay leading man film star. If he regains that extraordinary opportunity, despite his temperamental, even rude disdain for the media attendant to such success, it will be fascinating to see how it plays out.

The "other Rupert." Ugh. Everybody uses that one. No matter that both of them don't like the name. No matter that when you were born and raised in Weston-Super-Mare among lower middle class families a snooty name like Rupert was just the excuse needed to tease and torment you...as if anybody needed one.

Rupert Graves (1963-   ) was a precocious, unhappy little boy who didn't get along at school, was sickly, never earned a decent grade, and found himself getting into scraps. He sang in a punk band called The New Lumbago as a teen, washed dishes in a fish and chips shop, and then ran away and joined the circus at age 15. It was the only way out as far as he was concerned. He didn't really have any particular talents, but they were in need of a clown and he was given a day to master a few tricks: spinning plates, a bit of juggling, and a walk along the slack wire. He became Tomato the clown for nine months, never making it across the wire, but trying to turn all failures into comedy. He even stinted as a member of Silly Billy Pickles and The Peanut Street Gang, a children's theatre group.

Without a smidgen of acting school training, but some bit parts here and there, he was cast at age 19 in a London production of *The Killing of Mr. Toad*, where a casting director for Merchant/Ivory spotted his boyish good looks.

"I really think I was cast for my eyebrows," he's since said of the fortuitous choice to have him play Helena Bonham Carter's spunky younger brother in *A Room With A View* (1986). Fourteenth billed, Graves appears as Freddy Honeychurch 43 minutes into the Oscar-winning film and, if you're anything like me, you just might sigh aloud at the sight. The Reverend Mr. Beebe refers to him as "a most unpromising youth," but I can't imagine a more promising example. He's the most beautiful thing in the world lying out there on the cricket lawn in his tennis clothes and suspenders.

"How do you do? Come and have a bathe," are Freddy's first two remarks upon meeting the lovely Julian Sands. He's excited about the prospect, and so are we. But few of us could have been prepared for the bathe itself. Steeped in E.M. Forster's propriety and Victorian propinquity, the film suddenly splashes into a joyous and liberating romp as a trio of men, acting very much like boys, jump into a swimming hole stark naked, frolic, and chase each other around the perimeter.

"There was actually a sequence in it where I've got my back to the camera because I was blushing so much from embarrassment and the shock and the nerves," Graves told *Cinemania*. "I had to be the first one to take my clothes off and take the plunge in the pond."

Humorous, playful, unashamed, and completely natural, as well as *au naturel*, the three-and-a-half-minute bathing sequence assured Merchant/Ivory their biggest crossover hit at the box-office. *A Room With A View* is a gorgeous, properly stuffy, and slowly paced period piece that was suddenly drawing crowds and accolades because, though few would admit it then or now, three men ran around a pond in their altogether.

We can be eternally thankful that one of those men was Rupert Graves, who sheepishly tucks his genitalia between his legs when his mother and sister stumble onto the scene, but doesn't completely cover his pubic hair. Normally, you see a young man that beautiful in a costume drama and you just know you'll have to do all the undressing in your head. How rewarding to be so wrong.

He is, of course, just as gorgeous back in clothes practicing piano with his sister. Freddy wants her to invite Julian for Sunday tennis because he thinks he's "spiffy" and "simply terrific." Graves' hair spikes out over his head in long fronds like a palm tree or a frayed umbrella. Sometimes he pushes it back on his own and sometimes it's obvious that an attentive make-up person does it

Rupert Graves (seated) as the undergamekeeper who falls for a gentleman above his social station, James Wilby's *Maurice* (1987), in the film version of E. M. Forster's suppressed novel of homosexual love. PHOTOFEST

between takes, creating continuity errors.

Even his name sounds delicious. Freddy Honeychurch is as cute as a bug's ear in his striped jacket…or looking very dapper in his cap, vest, cane, and pipe. Moreover, Rupert Graves was a name to watch out for.

He found himself suddenly immersed in stage work, appearing as a gay boyfriend in the London premiere of *Torch Song Trilogy*, and then being directed by his *Room With A View* co-star Simon Callow in the coveted role of *Amadeus* in 1987.

In preparation for going to see Merchant/Ivory's production of E.M. Forster's *Maurice* (1987), I read the novel the day before, fascinated by its having been written by Forster in 1914 and suppressed until after his death by his own wishes (and not published until 1971) because it dealt explicitly with a homosexual love affair.

I had to travel by train into Chicago to see the film at a fine arts theatre, something of a romantic if rather pedestrian venture. It was, nonetheless, a special trip for a special purpose. I was alone and quite anxious to see it, and I still remember the thrill it gave me when I unexpectedly saw the name Rupert Graves come up in the credits. I had no idea he was in it. Some chaps by the names of James Wilby and Hugh Grant were the stars.

Suddenly it occurred to me which role Mr. Graves was undoubtedly to play: Alec Scudder, the undergamekeeper. I had to wait until it was the Autumn of 1913, a full hour and fourteen minutes into the picture, before I caught sight of him. He was still quite lovely to look at, though his role made his speech harsh and unmannered and someone had decided to cut and perm his hair.

I never could quite discern how Scudder knew that Maurice was a homosexual, like himself, but the vagaries didn't matter. Rupert's Alec Scudder is something of an unkempt dream lover, breaking the necks of bunnies, wandering around in the stormy night, standing under windows, climbing up ladders, waiting at the boathouse for you.

"I know, sir," is all he has to say as he climbs into bed with Maurice one night and the right gentleman tormented by his Oscar Wilde affliction gives way to the kisses of a crude servant boy on his chest. Scudder's unpolished, but he's sweet, and only threatens a blackmail he would never carry out because he thinks he's been jilted by class. In truth, he says, "I don't want to hurt your little fing-er."

"Stop the night with me," he asks. Maurice and Alec will spend a night together, waking up the next morning to conversation about why their relationship would never work. Society and class hierarchy would never let them be together. There's truth to what's being said, but there's also something elemental about their nude bodies and embrace.

Rupert Graves once again finds himself naked on-screen, climbing out of bed and dressing himself while we look on, and I'm forced to think about why I find looking at this beautiful young man in the nude so enormously lovely. All he does is get out of bed, glance at himself in the mirror, walk around the other side of the bed, put on his top, get held by his naked lover, then pull on his bottoms and walk out of the room.

I decided I was in love with Rupert Graves, too; not the actor that I didn't know, of course, but his image on the screen. And I couldn't have begun to thank the filmmakers enough for giving me another look at his body, no matter how slightly creepy or pathetic that may sound. Because I don't think there's anything creepy or pathetic about it. Perhaps future writers will find it easier to relate their movie idol crushes, but I came to understand my sexuality in an era and a locale that conspired to make all such pronouncements confessional in nature.

That's probably another reason why I have a complete appreciation for the unlikely but predestined way in which *Maurice* ends. Even critics who otherwise liked the film thought the ending simply far-fetched and fantastic, but that's precisely the point. Film is where fantasies live. So too literature.

"A happy ending was imperative," wrote Forster. "I shouldn't have bothered to write otherwise. I was determined that in fiction, anyway, two men should fall in love and remain in it forever and ever that fiction allows."

For Rupert Graves, who also played a homosexual role in the stageplay *A Madhouse in Goa* (1989), the combination of his sexy roles, nudity, and pretty boy looks had all the hens clucking. "After *Maurice*, a lot of people said I was gay," he told *Genre*, a gay publication, in 1997, "and although I've never had any homophobia directed towards me, I did have some nasty comments made about me in print." He enjoyed playing with the ambiguity, and for awhile simply refused to answer the question if it came up because it was tabloid tease. When his silence on the subject in and of itself became an item, he decided to end the silliness.

"For the record, I'm not gay," he said in the October edition of *Genre*, "but I don't care what anyone thinks about the issue. In fact, I don't give a fuck."

He kept his clothes on in proper, but dry and matter-of-taste literary adaptations of *A Handful of Dust* (1988) and *Where Angels Fear To Tread* (1991). He's also the son of the comically hot-blooded Jeremy Irons in Louis Malle's ludicrously melodramatic *Damage* (1992).

As the handsome equerry of the King, he manages to inject a little spirited romance in between other characters' analyses of the royal chamber pot in *The Madness of King George* (1994), and then, for British television, played out the true story of a drag queen who was a bank robber in *Open Fire* (1994).

He's the hapless drifter whom Julie Walters' Marjorie Beasley falls monstrously for in *Intimate Relations* (1996), a black comedy based on a notorious 1950s British murder trial. Things get intractably complicated when Graves' Harold Guppy finds himself seduced by the household's 14-year old daughter in addition to the smothering old lady with a deadly possessive streak in her.

"Believe it or not, I do get nervous before I strip off my clothes," Rupert admits, though he can't seem to get through a decade without being asked to do it on stage or film. Such are the burdens of being desirable.

In *Different for Girls* (1996), he's making a point to a boyhood best friend who's now an adult post-operative transsexual and he hauls out his dick by the foreskin to prove that this gray piece of flapping flesh is no big deal. Well-taken in terms of the script, but it's nice to see his penis again.

"Are you telling me that Mel Gibson and Harrison Ford are just women with something added on?" he asks on another occasion. His character, Paul Prentice, a crude, feisty leather boy who can't help being sweet, too, is attracted and confused by his attraction to the boy he once knew who's now a woman named Kim. Though Paul says he's straight (so is Kim) and his sexual feelings for her trouble him, he gets a hard-on while she describes her breast development. When we first meet these two characters, Kim is Karl, a beautiful boy lounging in the school showers with his penis and scrotum tucked behind his legs. Fellow students find him there, call him a queer, and threaten to force him to perform sexual services until a young Paul charges into the shower and orders them to leave the boy alone. He comes to Karl's rescue, placing his school jacket over the boy's shoulders, smiling a knowing (loving?) smile after being punched and spat upon by a contingent of other young male students.

It's just a scene in a movie, and another actor plays it, but it may be the reason Rupert Graves resonates so profoundly beyond his own boyish beauty. He seems open to all possibilities, non-judgmental, loving, devoted, protective, and accepting.

That's movie projection for you.

Brad Pitt ushers in the 1990s as one of the era's sexiest stars, seen here in *Seven Years in Tibet* (1997). PHOTOFEST

The 1990s — Take One

"So Use Me Till The Right Guy Comes Along"

Call it congenital panic. In 1986, we had the *Final Report of the Attorney General's Commission on Pornography* thrown at us. In 1987, *Playgirl* magazine, in one of a series of bizarre bad judgments over the next decade, temporarily neutered itself. Heralded as "Entertainment for Women" when it appeared on the scene back in 1973, thereby signifying both political and sexual strides in the movement, the magazine stopped featuring male genitalia because "many attitudes and opinions have evolved or fallen by the wayside, and we wanted as many women as possible to share the enjoyment *Playgirl* provides." Apparently, like the old joke about *Playboy*, they thought their subscribers were buying the damn thing for the articles.

In 1989, thirty-six senators decided that "shocking, abhorrent and completely undeserving art would not get money," and in June of that year the director of the Corcoran Gallery of Art in Cincinnati canceled photographer Robert Mapplethorpe's "The Perfect Moment" exhibition, which included thirteen graphic images of male/male S&M activity, perhaps the least troublesome of which displayed the photographer himself with the end of a bullwhip stuck in his anus. The show eventually opened to record crowds at the Contemporary Arts Center in Cincinnati.

In 1990, somebody else with something up their ass noticed that the videocassette cover art for Walt Disney's *The Little Mermaid* (1989) had a dick on it. It's way back there among the castle spires and there's no denying the resemblance. Phallic would be too ambiguous a description. It's positively penile.

Also in 1990, while reading about *Dirty Dancing* (1987) and *Ghost* (1990) superhunk Patrick Swayze in the August 6 issue of *People* magazine, some shrewd readers with keen eyes and magnifying glasses were sure they had found him frozen in a double-headfirst catapult into his swimming pool. Wearing a tight and skimpy pair of Speedos, Patrick is caught in a mid-air dive and there seems to be something peeking out of the top of his swimsuit. Is it his manhood or is it an optical intrusion involving a looped drawstring? Hard to tell unless you were one of the few who grabbed this issue before it disappeared from store shelves and became an instant collector's item. Using photocopy blow-ups, and turning the photo vertically, I'm inclined to believe that Mr. Swayze is fully accounted for in the bulge to the left inside his trunks. Not that I'd ever take the precious time to look that closely. The article, incidentally, is titled "Ghost with the Most." Closer yet to the real thing, an old photo from Swayze's dancing and modeling days published in an issue of *After Dark* shows him in heavy make-up and sporting a tiny bathing suit that can't quite cover a swatch of man-hairs.

Prudery has a way of making the absence grow fonder. So when America reeled in ludicrous puritanical horror to Madonna's 1992 *Sex* book, it was only sheer coincidence that the repulsion was warranted. At $50 a pop for an obnoxiously designed (spiral notebook binding) and therefore easily damaged collector's curio, *Sex* was allegedly intended to bring the singer's fantasies to fruition in an age of sexual repression and disease.

AIDS had clobbered playful and liberating attitudes about sex with the grim realities—social, political, and medical—of a sexually transmitted disease that demonized gay men and may, in retrospect, metaphorically account for the absence of phallus in *Playgirl*.

Conversely, the sex=death equation of the 1980s and early 1990s unsurprisingly saw the proliferation of provocative sexual fantasy and sexual imagery in the arts. If the safest thing to do was not have it, then the likeliest of places to feed the need was through representation.

Alas, Madonna, the feisty liberator whose self-empowerment and then open embrace of gay culture and homoerotic imagery was enthralling, must not have known what we wanted and needed most from her. Could the cold, unsexy, and often ugly photos by Steven Meisel in *Sex* and the awful *Penthouse*-reject text provided by Madonna herself have been intentional, even subconsciously, as a criticism of the sex-negative world we were living in?

Disappointingly, *Sex* features very little in the way of male nudity. In fact, there's only one full-frontal in the book, though there are some provocative backside shots, including an artful display known to any connoisseur of gay porn as belonging to Joey Stefano.

Otherwise, Madonna shaves a guy's pubes with a straight razor, romps with the boys at The Gaiety strip club, tugs on model/boyfriend Tony Ward's nipple ring with her teeth, and, in my personal favorite, can be seen with her nose in a well-rounded and jockstrapped ass while taking a bite of the lucky boy's cheek.

Somehow we'd adjust. In the mid-1990s, men were able to buy guides and specialized equipment to help them restore foreskins lost to infant circumcision by stretching loose skin from the shaft over the glans and taping it there for months and months and months before employing a series of weights. Viagra®, intracavernosal injection, suspensory ligament snipping, fat injection, knob and frenum piercing were just some of the ways guys thought to augment their penises in the 1990s. By the end of the decade, we'd even been exposed to the leanings of a presidential dick. Less and less seemed to shock us.

"Brad Pitt ruined it for the rest of us," carped actor James Spader in a 1990s interview. "In *Thelma and Louise* we could all see his muscles; now everybody has to do it. I hate Brad Pitt."

Does it help to know that the stomach wasn't intentional? Does it help to know that the guy with that stomach smokes cigarettes, eats junk food, loves Mountain Dew and Twizzlers? Probably not. No, I suppose it makes sense that Brad Pitt is a genetic mutation.

The subject of his looks doesn't just bore him, it turns that stomach. A few interviewers have managed to sneak in there and get a pale response about the pros and cons of image, but most don't get that far. It's not a subject open for discussion and it's one of the surest ways to turn him completely off.

The likelihood that he's just being coy with such denials in order to legitimize himself to the masses, to appear not to be egotistical or narcissistic, is also a dead-end. He would never have lasted in the Golden Age of Hollywood when his golden boy beauty would have been refined and exploited to the hilt by a studio system looking to churn out profitable fantasy figures. He wouldn't have lasted because he wouldn't have put up with it. All I can say is, it's a damned good thing he was born when he was.

William Bradley Pitt (1963-   ) was raised in Springfield, Missouri, the oldest of three children in the family. His father managed a successful trucking company and made sure the entire clan attended the Southern Baptist church every Sunday. In school, young Brad played tennis and found himself in the chorus of his Kickapoo High School musicals. He was even voted "Best Dressed" senior year. He then went off to the University of Missouri in Columbia, pledged Sigma Chi, and majored in advertising through the journalism school there.

Dissatisfied with the field and finding himself two credits short for graduation, he was given the go-ahead to work on an independent study project and laid out plans to produce a "Men of Mizzou" beefcake calendar in answer to the gals' version on campus. The finished product would have even featured his shirtless self, but he gave up on it, told his folks he was heading to California to study at the Art Center College of Design in Pasadena (a lie), and lit out for La La Land in his silver Nissan (Runaround Sue) with $300 in his jeans at age 22.

Among the usual assortment of colorful jobs that actors find themselves doing while waiting to land a gig, Brad dressed in a giant chicken suit and flailed in the sweltering heat outside an El Pollo Loco restaurant and then, out of his chicken suit, chauffeured strip-o-gram dancers.

He landed an agent and, for completists, got his first extra job in *Less Than Zero* (1987), where you can spot him ten and a half minutes in as the second guy to walk across the screen while Andrew McCarthy is staring up at the party TV sets. You won't see much of his face, but he's wearing a light pink and white striped shirt. It's easier to find him in the Charlie Sheen car theft flick *No Man's Land* (1987). Twenty minutes in, he's a waiter in black with a gray vest on as Charlie and D.B. Sweeney attend a social function. We get four good looks at him—one of which has him ordering two drinks in a medium close-up shot just over Charlie's shoulder—but he's done all he's going to do in less than two minutes.

TV work started coming in, with bits on *Head of the Class*, *Growing Pains, 21 Jump Street, Freddy's Nightmares, Another World*, and then a five-episode stint as the boytoy love interest of Shalane McCall's on *Dallas*. He was Randy. And the teen magazines took notice.

Suddenly he found himself in *Teen Beat* holding teddy bears and answering questions about his favorite color and what he likes in a girl. (Feel free to make your own joke.) It wasn't what he was hoping to do,

Brad Pitt, purveyor of the $6600 orgasm, in *Thelma & Louise* (1991). EVERETT COLLECTION

but the work was necessary to build a foundation, get his name out there, and alert industry ephebophiliacs to his availability for film and TV work. The shots from this era are a real hoot, with Brad given all the headband-wearing, bare-chested treatment he could possibly stand.

Somehow fittingly, considering his aversion to being fawned over as a face, his first starring role in a feature film has him wearing a creepy S&M-looking leather mask for a third of its running time. *The Dark Side of the Sun* was shot in Yugoslavia in 1988 on the proverbial shoestring and tells the story of a young man plagued by a skin disease that will kill him if he's exposed to sunlight. Not wishing to live a cloistered life, even at the risk of ending it, he unmasks himself and stares into the mirror for the first time in broad daylight. "I look like mother," he observes. The film suffered financial troubles, as well as from the eruption of regional turmoil, and wasn't cobbled together and put into video release until 1997.

Unofficially then, it was *Cutting Class* (1989), a teen slasher flick, that marked his opening credits debut. He's awfully cute in his gym clothes and you'll quickly notice that he's the only one in the class who wears a muscle T version of the uniform. Though he's pretty, he's also the bad boy with an attitude who rejects a former friend because the kid was sent away to a mental hospital. Try as I might, I can't quite turn Donovan Leitch's unhitched character into a rebuffed gay boy with a thing for Brad's jock. Instead, Leitch wants to know from Brad's girlfriend, Jill Schoelen, "Have you ever felt my tingle?" Brad's just a red-herring, though it's fun to have him back in his gym clothes for the machine shop showdown, a battle of power tools in which he gets his head caught in a big ol' vise and "righty tighty, lefty loosey" is a life lesson well-learned.

Following another *Growing Pains* episode and a spot on television's *thirtysomething*, Brad found himself among the four leads on the Fox television series *Glory Days* (1990), where he played a recently graduated high school football star named Walker Lovejoy who's trying to hash out a living as a newspaper reporter. Nobody watched or cared. The series was dead within three months.

After five minutes playing a pony-tailed, hick cameraman following politician Albert Finney around in HBO's *The Image* (1990), Brad scruffed himself out big time for the first of many such bouts of ugly in the

TV movie *Too Young To Die?* (1990). Bearded and bedraggled, he's a skanky street bum who gets Juliette Lewis drugged up and turning tricks.

The "J.D." he played in his next film has been variously guessed at as standing for "James Dean" or "juvenile delinquent," but I'd throw in "jim dandy." Thirty-nine and a half minutes into *Thelma and Louise* (1991), there he is sitting outside a phone booth foolin' with a water hose between his legs. He's got a southern twang, a white cowboy hat, and dimples. He's polite, too. It's "Miss Thelma" this and "Miss Louise" that. And he comes with a darling philosophy: "When God gives you somethin' special, you should pass it on."

He's hopin' to hitch a ride with the ladies to Oklahoma City, but the surprise arrival of Louise's boyfriend sort of sees to it that he heads out into the rain here and now. "Yep, that's him goin'," says Thelma, as she eyes his perfectly shaped blue-jeaned ass amblin' off. "I love watchin' him go."

He'll be back, though, and I'm sure I wasn't the only one to sigh appreciation when Geena Davis opens her motel room door and sees that handsome boy standing out there dripping wet. He's already shirtless when we cut to the pair playing a game of patty-cake, and then jumps up and down on the bed chanting, "Take me, break me, make me a man."

He's a smooth little hustler, playing coy, but full of ego and completely aware of what he's doin'. He tells Thelma about his bein' a robber and all, even steppin' out of bed and usin' her hairdryer as a gun in playful re-creation of his best liquor store style. "Well now, I always believed that if done properly armed robbery doesn't have to be a totally unpleasant experience." A few heartbeats later he lets loose with the words that will hook, line, and sink her: "I may be an outlaw, but you're the one stealin' my heart."

What follows is that famed camera glide up his rippled torso to his lightly haired nipples, and then...

(Sadly, the original, much longer, and far more Brad-revealing version of the sex scene doesn't turn up on the special edition DVD, though we do learn from Mr. Pitt himself that between takes, while Geena Davis was sitting on his lap, he couldn't help getting a woody.)

"I finally understand what the fuss is about," squeals Thelma the morning after.

Thelma and Louise sparked a fury of debate about its sexual politics and what it may or may not have been saying about feminism and gender relations in the United States at the time. The biggest objections seemed to center on the empowerment of women with the toys and genre conventions usually afforded men: cars, guns, explosions, and even a fatalistic, but transcendental finale (not unlike the one furnished best friend boy outlaws Butch and Sundance). The debate was reactionary, but fascinating, and provided a must-see platform on which, quite happily, an unknown named Brad Pitt caught a lot of people's eyes in a role typically identified as feminine. He became the camera's and the audience's object of beauty; *his* tits were the ones we were looking at, not hers. He was the crafty hooker who used his good looks and bedroom banter to lay one of the leads and walk off with the loot in the morning.

Brad Pitt is in *Thelma and Louise* for just under sixteen minutes, but his impact on the audience and the impact on his career was phenomenal. As the perpetrator of the $6600 orgasm, he wasn't just the hot new actor whom everybody wanted to know by name, he was the hot young actor everybody wanted to get a piece of.

While biding his time for a hit movie that he didn't see coming, because no one knew how big *T&L* would become, Brad played older brother to Ricky Schroder in *Across the Tracks* (1991), an enjoyable, if TV-movieish story about the rocky relationship and eventual rivalry between one "good" brother (Brad) and one "bad" brother (Ricky) who excel as high school track runners. It's probably inappropriate to notice how lovely an angle we're given when a nervous Brad bends over to upchuck before a race and his butt in blue shorts spreads across the screen. (It's the first vomiting scene I've ever had to re-watch because I wondered whether a guy's ass in my face made me miss the cream of mushroom soup.) He and Schroder are both quite good in their roles and it's fun to spend time with them as they talk about women, go on their morning runs together, and get into predictable, but tense and emotional fights. Pitt is a bundle of little quirks, shrugs, half-smiles, fits of frustration and temperament, and shy double-takes. He ends up throwing a lot of stuff away, both lines and looks, but all of it works.

In *The Favor* (1994), also shot in 1991, he's simply too good to be true as the hot, smart, sweet, and unbelievably built artist whom boring Elizabeth McGovern is too dumb to realize is the catch of a lifetime. The first time we see them together they've just finished lovemaking and are all sweaty in bed. Brad climbs out, pulls on a pair of jeans, and when he reaches for a sketchpad, his lean, defined, and comic-book-cut upper half defies sexual orientation. Even straight guys would consider the possibilities.

Brad Pitt plays the catch of a lifetime in *The Favor* (1994), shot in 1991. PHOTOFEST

"Well, if you're going to have a hot fling, you might as well have one with someone who looks like that," says Harley Jane Kozak of McGovern's relationship with Brad. He's so perfect, in fact, that even when things are on the waver, he tells McGovern: "So use me till the right guy comes along." Brad's Elliott Fowler deserves a movie all of his own.

Against his agency's wishes, Pitt took the lead role in the low-budget *Johnny Suede* (1991), playing the dumb bunny title character who idolizes Ricky Nelson, wears funky suede shoes, and sports a monstrous pompadour hair-do that keeps getting in the way of his handsomeness. The film is largely a drag, an oddball experiment that never seems to get underway. The whole thing plays like a set-up for something that doesn't show.

The actor personally ripped and stretched out a pair of dingy jockey shorts for scenes in which he's walking around his apartment with his hand down the baggy front of them, and it's one of the few times you find yourself pleasantly distracted from the hair on his head while checking to see if you can catch a glimpse of hair elsewhere. There's a funny little scene in which he and Catherine Keener are in the bathtub together and she playfully threatens him by grabbing his balls underwater and he counter-threatens to bounce a bar of soap off her head. Another nice moment comes in the bedroom when Keener takes Brad's hand to show him where her love-button is...because he thought it was somewhere else. He tells a friend about his discovery, but gets laughed at for not having known. He did, he insists in sheepish recovery, but now he can find it in the dark.

He's the flesh and blood cut-out amidst a cataclysm of cartoon cut-outs in Ralph Bakshi's *Cool World* (1992), in which almost his entire performance is gamely delivered against blue screens, flattened sets, and opposite animated doodles he can't see. Judged harshly at the time of its release because of comparisons to *Who Framed Roger Rabbit?* (1988), *Cool World* deserves a second look. In typical Bakshi style, sex is largely the pre-occupation of the characters, live or drawn, and Pitt's frustration with having to spend a lifetime dating a doodle he can never diddle is the price he's decided to pay to escape the pain and suffering (a war, his mom's death) in the real world. It's not easy. "I'm like a plug without a socket," he tells his girl.

Pitt's character has assumed the identity of one of those cops he must have seen in the movies of the 1930s and 1940s. He's a cool dick with a hard-ass attitude who's determined to keep law and order in *Cool World*, which means strictly enforcing a no sex with noids regulation. He's got his hands full with the voluptuous and irritating Holly Wood, named for a reason, who graphically represents the desire to fuck with your fantasies. The outcome, however, both in terms of the plot and the quality of the film, is that things start to fall apart as soon as the fantasy has been realized.

Though he eventually gets his doodle balls, Brad seems much more at home back amongst the three-dimensional as a slimy roadrunner with tattoos all over, and a penchant for lasciviously flicking his pointy tongue, in the 1992 "King of the Road" episode of HBO's *Tales From the Crypt*.

Thelma and Louise had by now started a buzz, but his role as Paul Maclean in Robert Redford's film version of *A River Runs Through It* (1992) clinched his stardom. Redford didn't immediately like what he saw at the audition stage, either in person or on tape. But the choice proved to be the right one; so much so, that everybody who saw it figured Redford had perfectly cast Pitt as a younger version of himself. He is very much the golden boy in this poetic memoir of brothers, family values, and the art and philosophy of fly-fishing, but the role's appeal to Pitt had to be Paul's darker side. Seems the only way that Brad Pitt would allow himself to play an attractive man is if he never sees the end credits.

He's got four scenes and less than five minutes screen time as Floyd, the couch-ridden stoner in the hyperviolent *True Romance* (1993), from a Quentin Tarantino screenplay. Christian Slater memorably opens the film by telling a gal he's just met in a bar, "I ain't no fag, but Elvis was prettier than most women. You know, I've always said if I had to fuck a guy, you know, I mean had to, if my life depended on it, I'd fuck Elvis." All Pitt's Floyd wants is someone to watch TV with him or share a bowl.

The pretty boy in *River* became a chain-smoking fuzz-face in *Romance*. In *Kalifornia* (1993), Pitt piled on the ugly. His Early Grayce is the walking definition of white trash, complete with long greasy hair, a bramble bush for a beard, the biggest pit stains imaginable, a hankering for snot-honking, and a drawl that does

Sometimes a loaf of bread is just a loaf of bread.

justice to "put your titty back up, A-dell." So why is he still sexy when he's standing covered in filth in a mud pit, spinning a fantastical tale about California to his pathetically sweet girlfriend (Juliette Lewis), and then climbing out of the pit and standing on top of it butt-naked in the moonlight? I guess it's because we know it's Brad Pitt under there. As fans, we're rooting for him to be taken seriously as an actor by hiding his beauty under all the muck and delving head-on into this creepy performance as a wanton murderer who turns on his car-pooling companions, a liberal writer (David Duchovny) doing a book on serial killers and his chic photographer girlfriend (Michelle Forbes). The scheme works in its own way thanks to the actors, especially Lewis, who wants Early to join her in a sing-along of that timeless classic "Do Your Balls Hang Low?"

He may be the only pretty boy actor never accused of being gay, largely because his relationships with a roster of female co-stars were well documented in the press. (He eventually married television star Jennifer Aniston in 2000.) In a way, that's why his playing the perpetually depressed vampire Louis Pointe du Lac in *Interview with the Vampire* (1994) seemed like inspired casting. If anyone was interested in fucking around with their popular image it was Brad, and so the potential for his biting both ways held quite the allure. Ask just about any gay guy and they'll tell you that, as hackneyed as the premise is, the seduction of a "straight" guy or a guy who's unsure about his sexuality is so much more erotically charged than two raging homos ready for the go.

Sadly, Louis is barely open to the possibility. We can certainly understand why Lestat was initially interested, but sex and sensuality is lost to these damned creatures and Louis is left to feed off rats, poodles, and chickens. The only thing you can say in his favor is that the morose son-of-a-bitch is the sole member of the undead with a conscience. You feel for the guy, and so does Antonio Banderas' bewigged Armand, a nonetheless evil and undeveloped character who comes so close to kissing Louis on the mouth that you know it's the last desperate tease of the de-homofied screen adaptation. And simultaneously, a self-congratulatory moment of "unspeakable daring" served up to scare the considerable heterosexual fan bases of both romantic stars. That's what horror movies are supposed to do. Scare you.

Brad Pitt once said that he didn't fully understand the concept of an entrance until he saw what director Ed Zwick did with him in *Legends of the Fall* (1994). At ten minutes and nineteen seconds into the epic romantic tragedy, absent brother Tristan is seen riding his horse on the horizon and making his way to meet the train. His crotchety pa (Anthony Hopkins) is there, as are his two brothers, elder (Aidan Quinn) and younger (Henry Thomas), and a pale beauty (Julia Ormond) betrothed to the youngest, but destined to ruin them all.

With a mane of long blond hair in a ponytail and a face more beautiful than the countryside, Pitt rides into close-up (though he should have gotten the John Wayne *Stagecoach* treatment), dismounts, and tips his hat to the lady after getting doused with a stream of water by a brother mindful of his cowboy stink. The flick of the hat brim sends a pocket of water droplets aloft and in that single shot, with that simple gesture of cordiality, Brad Pitt immortalizes himself as a movie star. High voltage to the heart. (It's even more mythic played in slow-motion.)

Of course, Brad Pitt doesn't play romance-novel heartthrob for the sake of throbbing hearts. He dismissed the type as a dime a dozen to *Newsweek*, asserting his legitimate and loftier interests at the same time disparaging one of the elemental truths about film as fantasy: we like spending time with pretty people. Tristan could only have appealed to the actor because he's a man ritually immersed in tragedy, haunted by his failures, surrounded by murder, suicide, and devastating loss. Every time he seems to get his act together, his hair grown longer, his face lovelier, he's slapped to the ground. Serves him right for needlessly maiming a grizzly when he was a boy.

Legends was a box-office hit, luring in audiences eager to see the Adonis and unaware of how relentlessly grim the story gets. Walking into *Se7en* (1995), you didn't have that excuse. Serial killers were all the rage at the movies in the 1990s and director David Fincher's literally dark and obsessively grotesque film had the guts to out-wrench the competition. Brad is teamed with retiring veteran Morgan Freeman on a case involving a series of complex murders based on the Seven Deadly Sins. During a chase over car hoods in the pouring rain, Brad slipped and put himself right through a windshield, then gashed a hole through to the bones in his hand while trying to climb out. The injury was incorporated into the script and Brad is bandaged thereafter. Pitt's marquee value and solid performance brought more butts into the theatres than the nervous studio could possibly have imagined, especially considering the filmmakers' insistence on an ending so disturbing and so absolutely right that audiences stumbled out of the theatre in depression and still recommended the movie to friends.

In *Twelve Monkeys* (1995), Pitt plays a twitchy and manic loon in the nuthouse who's really the crazy guy who seems to be making a lot of sense if you listen to what he's saying through all the theatrics. Wearing oversized and slightly askew brown contact lenses, Pitt gets to play the human cartoon he wasn't in *Cool World*; he even gets a sound effect "sproing" as his head comes out of his collar the first time we meet him. He holds the key to understanding why five billion people died in 1997 and why a future underground society is sending Bruce Willis back in time to figure out what happened. His wildly spasmodic monkey boy won him a Golden Globe as Best Supporting Actor and earned him an Academy Award nomination.

He was mortified at being dubbed *People* magazine's "Sexiest Man Alive" in 1995 (they did it to him again in 2000) despite all he had done to put an unattractive face on his career. "When we were kids, my sister had Andy Gibb up on her wall, so that kind of puts it in perspective," he told *Time* magazine in October of 1997.

"It's like he's caught in a body owned by the public," said *Twelve Monkeys'* director Terry Gilliam to the offending *People* in January of 1996. "He's been sold as the new hot bimbo. But he knows there's more to him. He doesn't want to feel trapped by people's expectations."

To his added dismay, Pitt's body was suddenly available for downloading by the public when an asshole paparazzo trespassing on private property and shooting with a telescopic lens captured Pitt and girlfriend Gwyneth Paltrow nude while on holiday in St. Bart's in April of 1995. The photos appeared in the UK and Europe, then on the Internet, and then in a one-shot all-male version of the magazine *Celebrity Sleuth*, one of several publications that subsist on publishing frame enlargements (and the like) of nude scenes from movies, cable television, and paparazzi rolls.

More incensed by the violation of privacy and the exposure of his girlfriend than by his own personal embarrassment, Pitt launched a series of lawsuits to nail the bastards, culminating in the pulling of the August 1997 issue of *Playgirl* magazine off the newsstands. The issue featuring Brad's face on the cover—headlined "Brad Pitt Nude!"—included reprints of eleven of the famous photos. The magazine's subscribers, as well as several big city markets, had already received the issue when the court mandated the recall, so you can imagine how many of those who got it were willing to send it back. Still, the issue was successfully stifled in mass quantities and the message was heard.

Pitt told Diane Sawyer during a rare primetime television interview that he couldn't imagine people were surprised to find out that he has a penis, and was even more dismissive of the whole episode in an October 1995 interview with *US*, though it predates the *Playgirl* profiteering: "But who really cares? I have one of the greatest jobs in the world, we see the country, our families are taken care of, what? I mean, there's a trade-off. [Grins] If it means I do a beaver shot so my kids will go to a good school? So be it."

So what do you do with this irrefutable invasion of privacy when you both respect Mr. Pitt and can't help wanting to see his penis? You look. You tell yourself that he's as blessedly handsome all over as he is from the waist up. Then you stash your magazine or jpeg files and join the chorus against the obscene violation of celebrities' private lives...and mean it.

"The truth is, I don't want people to know me," he told *Rolling Stone* in 1994. "I don't know a thing about my favorite actors. I don't think you should. Then they become personalities."

He's right. We often know too much about celebrities and much of what we know is reported through a notoriously untrustworthy mass media. So while it's not necessary to know what legitimately interests an actor off-screen in order to appreciate his work on-screen, I enjoy the occasional revelation: Brad's frequent championing of *Planet of the Apes* (1968) as religious allegory, his being well-versed in architectural design, his being a devotee of the Arts and Crafts style, his designing his own home, and his shooting the photographs for the book *Greene & Greene: The Blacker House* (Gibbs Smith, 2001).

Back on the big screen, he's the grown up version of Brad Renfro in *Sleepers* (1996), playing an assistant New York district attorney without an accent who walks into the movie after the first hour and cleverly conspires courtroom vigilante justice against the men who sexually abused him and his three buddies while they were serving time at the Wilkinson Home for Boys. In *The Devil's Own* (1997), he's handsome again, so he must come to no good, as an IRA operative failing to remain incognito as a guest of New York cop Harrison Ford's friendly household. The details of the family scenes are handled so well that you selfishly wish the whole political plot could have been dropped and the film turned into a family drama or romantic comedy. It's an insulting suggestion, I know. Sorry, Brad. Believe it or not, there are those of us who would like to see you, as you once joked to *Rolling Stone* after a series of intense roles, "play a guy who just wants to fuck everybody so I can have a good time."

With *Seven Years in Tibet* (1997), the film version of the true story of Austrian mountaineer Heinrich Harrer (Pitt) and his eventual friendship with and tutelage of the Dalai Lama, again we're faced with the dilemma of a first hour of coldhearted autocrat and then bearded sourpuss with a second hour of radiantly beautiful and charming "yellowhead." Can we help it if we wish we had more time with the guy who smirks while a beautiful woman takes measurements of his bare chest or plays passenger to the boy Dalai Lama behind the wheel of a car chassis set up on crates?

Same goes for *Meet Joe Black* (1998), a three-hour variation on a play that made for a 78-minute film in 1934. The young man we meet at the coffee shop is the perfect family man. A real charmer. A dreamer's catch. That's why he gets shockingly bounced off the front of two vehicles passing in opposite directions and is fated to return as soft-spoken and faintly robotic Death in formal wear. I'm not sure why Death is so naive about the world in which we live, though it's fun to watch him discover peanut butter and lovemaking without naturally combining the two. There's a sensual, slow undressing as he stands poolside, then it's into the bedroom for even more longing and lovely close-ups of all the blond hairs he's got on his golden-brown bod. That there's no practicing safe sex with Death is as curious as Brad Pitt's decision (or agreement) to play him without a personality.

He shows up as himself (for a non-speaking second) in *Being John Malkovich* (1999) and then his idealized self in *Fight Club* (1999), a pair of the most inventive, stylish, and heady films at the dawn of the new millennium. *Fight Club* is a dense social satire that examines in metaphorical hyperbole the dilemma of masculine identity in a keystroke society. Edward Norton is a shapeless mess in his cold, materialistic, catalog-order life. Even the material he's surrounding himself with has no intrinsic value. He's a soulless automaton castrated by technology and mired in compartmentalized banality. He starts going to terminal illness support groups just so he can feel something, even if only vicariously.

There are at least four subliminal Brads before we officially meet his Tyler Durden on the airplane and suspect that soap isn't what he's really selling. No, he's offering Edward Norton a way to get back in touch with himself in an absurd escalation from self-abuse and ritualized pummeling of equally lost and emasculated men to a fascist ideology that targets corporate imperialism and promotes terrorism.

The rich and self-aware script based on Chuck Palahniuk's novel crystallizes a potential crisis in gender equilibrium and the loss of our emotional and primal selves in the cyberage. When Ed Norton points out a Gucci men's underwear ad on the street and asks sarcastically if that is what a man looks like, his instigating companion Mr. Durden exclaims that "self-improvement is masturbation." It doesn't occur to Norton that Durden already possesses the body image of the underwear ad. As we're given ample opportunity to see, and as advertising was wise to exploit, Pitt's physique is in exquisite form. He actually uses his body as an accomplice to the plot, a thematic weapon of representation and desire, celebrated as it bloodies and gets bloodied and worshipped as it poses and fucks.

Brad Pitt becomes a perverted ideal in *Fight Club*. "We are the middle children of history, raised by television to believe that someday we'll be millionaires and movie stars and rock stars, but we won't," he says. And yet it's a millionaire movie star who's saying it. The dialogue is fascinatingly self-reflexive. (And a theatre marquee has *Seven Year in Tibet* (sic) on it.)

Considering the amount of resistance to being reduced to a meat puppet during his career, Brad is savvy about the importance of image in his business and has allowed photographers over the years to capture him in some stunning sessions. He also has less an aversion to being photographed with his shirt off than you might have guessed, bless his heart. On the July 1999 cover of *W* magazine, Brad Pitt is actually getting away with showing off some of his pubes, just one striking image of thirty pages worth photographed by Steven Klein that play out the complexity of being desirable and undesirable all at once.

His hard-as-a-nail body does most of the intelligible talking in *Snatch* (2000), too, since his Irish Gypsy boxer Mickey "One Punch" O'Neil's "pikey" accent is nearly impenetrable to others in this comic celebration of anarchic violence and adolescent boys' storytelling. The opposite of a chick flick, it's a dick flick. He steals the show right from under the all-star cast in the unnecessary, but entertaining *Ocean's Eleven* (2001), works better with a dog and a mule than with Julia Roberts in *The Mexican* (2001), and lends his long-haired beauty and beefed physique to Achilles in *Troy* (2004).

No Brad Pitt Experience would be complete without having the unique pleasure of his whispering in your ear as he reads Cormac McCarthy's Border Trilogy (*All the Pretty Horses*, *The Crossing*, and *Cities of the Plain*) as books on tape. There's a terrific intimacy about an audio recording in which every breath of an idol is as clearly and directly received as if he were in the same quiet room with you, as if he were telling you a bedtime story. (The tapes work wonders if you turn out the lights and close your eyes while you listen.)

As an actor who's frequently accused of employing a practical approach to his craft rather than a soul-wringing search for an inner truth, he'd be the first to admit he's a grown man putting on make-up. When he was called upon to pantomime peeing in a bucket for *Johnny Suede* and later it came time to record a suitable sound effect: "There's fifty crew members standing around and a boom girl standing there next to the bucket with a microphone," remembered director Tom DiCillo for *Rolling Stone*. "And Brad just pulled out his pecker and pissed for twenty-five seconds."

When *Time* magazine did their cover story "Leo Up Close" for the February 21, 2000 issue, the subject of the piece instinctively knew it was "going to wind up being about the construction of what to make the article about. That's what it's going to be about: Why the hell is he on the cover of *Time* magazine?"

Leonardo Wilhelm DiCaprio (1974-   ) proved to be, according to the writer, "so self-aware, it's paralyzing." Everything he does, from deciding what to order to eat at a restaurant to happening across *What's Eating Gilbert Grape* while flipping through the channels, is second-guessed and processed for an angle to see how he might be culpable in its calculation. Left without resources, the magazine ended up running a copy of the young actor's grocery bill from Ralph's supermarket, a shopping trip paid for by the journalist—"It seems a little forced," says Leo, "like I'm saying, 'Hey, I'm everyguy, I go to Ralph's too"—and then annotating the actor's dilemmas over waffle and brownie mixes, ginger ale and yogurt, to name just a few.

All I could think of was how many Leo fans were at Ralph's within the week reproducing his $150.87 purchase item per item.

If that seems far-fetched, you may not understand fandom. Lots of people don't. It's a condition associated mostly with women for some reason, particularly young girls, for whom hormone-driven infatuations and crushes are considered part of the embarrassing squeals of adolescence. There comes a time, though, when the notoriously fickle romances with celebrities become by degrees shameful; at best, they're silly remembrances of a time when a boy like Leo did it all for you and there's warm nostalgia in the recollection; at worst, they're mortifying proof of profound immaturity. Arrested development.

It's a sign of intelligence to be a "fan" of an actor, handsome or not, who's also unequivocally an actor of great talent. It takes less bravado to champion Russell Crowe, for instance, despite *Gladiator* (2000) but because of *L.A. Confidential* (1997), than it does to admit that you went to see *Dude, Where's My Car?* (2000) because Ashton Kutcher is cute. The great thing about a Russell Crowe is that you can proudly and simultaneously announce both your admiration of his acting chops and the effect he has on your blood pressure every time he makes an entrance.

Fandom, of course, is not by definition an intellectual pursuit, though make no mistake, it's a serious one. Somebody disses Leo and they're gonna get stomped.

He's not only a quite comely young man, but he's one of our best actors. Those who disagree are entitled to their silly opinions, but they're also most often victims of titanic guilt by association.

He was born and raised in and around Hollywood. Not the picture postcard Hollywood, but the urban decay and tourist trap Hollywood. His father is an Italian-American underground comics illustrator and dealer. His German mother met his dad ten years before Leo was born, and the pair lived a somewhat free-spirited, almost hippie-ish lifestyle. The couple split, though shared parenting duties, less than a year after the arrival of their baby boy—named, so every source is obliged to relate, because of a prenatal kick while the parents stood in front of a DaVinci in Italy.

Little Leo proved a natural entertainer as a child, pre-possessed by the urge to act out (though not fond of doing it in front of a crowd), and predisposed to something along the lines of attention deficit disorder. He was a wild and wily kid, famously (all things being unequal) ejected from the set of television's *Romper Room* at age five because he was uncontrollable.

Motivated by both his need to perform and his awe of how much money could be had doing so, he vigorously pursued commercial and television work as a little kid with the help of his mother and appeared in 20 or 30 commercials, educational and safety short films, and one-shot TV appearances on shows such as *Roseanne* (1988 episode), *The New Lassie* (1989), *The Outsiders* (1990), and *Santa Barbara* (1990 episode).

He then landed a role on NBC-TV's *Parenthood* (1990), the series spin-off from Ron Howard's popular 1989 feature film, in which Leo played Gary Buckman, the chronically depressed and masturbating pre-teen played by Joaquin Phoenix in the movie. The series lasted only thirteen episodes, though it assured his cute little face would be smiling from the covers and pull-out posters of teen magazines.

He's fourth billed in his first feature film, though it ended up going directly to video. *Critters 3: You Are What You Eat* (1991) was the second sequel in the low-budget series about outer space furballs with gnashing teeth. He's a fresh-faced do-gooder trying to warn a kid from falling down into a ravine when the kid's sister runs up and accuses him of being "some kind of pervert." Though he's the first to say, "you can't expect us to believe this horseshit" to a weirdo who warns them about the aliens, he's one of a handful of characters who end up battling the little monsters in a scuzzy L.A. apartment building.

He then landed the role of "new kid on the show" during what turned out to be the final season of the popular sitcom *Growing Pains* (1985-92). His Luke Brower is a homeless teenager sleeping in a broom closet at the school where Kirk Cameron teaches. The Seaver family "adopt" Luke and turn his troubles into their own over a series of episodes that certainly don't prophesy DiCaprio's future stardom in films, but do show a photogenic young actor with remarkable screen presence and natural talent. In particular, episodes devoted to his trucker dad's return and attempt to reach out to his estranged son allow DiCaprio to demonstrate his innate ability to handle emotional scenes and play them far more convincingly than sitcom TV otherwise demanded.

His bit as a "Guy" in the Drew Barrymore potboiler *Poison Ivy* (1992) seems to be an invisible one. In terms of the "Order of Appearance" end credits, he should show up somewhere in the film after we've met both parents, but I've yet to find him, even for a millisecond. The Official Leonardo DiCaprio webpage (www.leonardodicaprio.com) ignores it, too.

For all practical purposes, Leonardo DiCaprio's film debut came in *This Boy's Life* (1993). His performance as young Tobias Wolff opposite the likes of Robert De Niro and Ellen Barkin stands as one of the more astonishing and memorable feats of introduction. Even without knowing that the kid on screen has never had any formal acting training, he's so real, so good, so goddamned honest that acting isn't even in the equation. Based on Wolff's autobiographical book, the film follows a weary and abused woman (Barkin) and her spirited son (DiCaprio) as they settle into yet another abusive relationship, this time with a creepy blue collar factory worker (De Niro) in the remote town of Concrete, Washington in 1958.

Toby is a precocious juvenile delinquent with an awful greased hairdo who engages in macho dirty talk with his friends about Lois Lane before settling into an episode of *Superman*. He's a full-blown kid with awkwardness and insecurities and temperament thanks to DiCaprio and the source material. He seems to genuinely want to be a "better boy," but the hard-knocks tutelage he gets from De Niro's severely stunted and childish brute of a stepfather has him temporarily trapped in a futile cycle of conformity and repression based on the ugly refrain of "kill or cure."

There's a comic edge to De Niro's ignoramus manchild, providing his frequently overexposed talents with one of his best roles of the decade. DiCaprio is right there with him, keeping pace. He got the job by walking into the audition and screaming his lines into De Niro's face to get a reaction. At just 18, though he looks easily three or four years younger, Leonardo hadn't been frightened into submission by De Niro's legendary talent.

The young actor's first on-screen kiss notably comes from another boy, though it's just a sweet peck on the cheek and then disregarded after a silent pause to ponder it and put it away. The kisser is the effeminate Arthur Gayle, who befriends Toby after previously having fought him for calling him a "homo." Boys like Arthur Gayle certainly existed, and I'm sure many of them came complete with their little pups named Pepper, but the character doesn't amount to much more than a useful stereotype and his fate is curiously unrevealed in the end titles.

If *This Boy's Life* proved that there was a great young actor among us, *What's Eating Gilbert Grape* (1993) proved that one of the perks of being a great young actor whom nobody knew yet meant being able to play a part in which everyone was convinced you were not acting it. Arnie Grape is the retarded younger brother of the beleaguered Gilbert (Johnny Depp), and once again DiCaprio's work is so real and so spontaneous that it transcends craft at the very same time it's necessarily full of it. The quirks and spasms and mannerisms with which an actor might self-consciously equip himself playing such a role are simply incorporated into DiCaprio's being. He doesn't so much play Arnie as he becomes Arnie, instinctively, intuitively, though not without having spent time watching tapes of affected people and visiting homes to observe behaviors firsthand.

It may be the first time that an actor has played a handicapped character and it never once crosses your mind that he or she is doing it for some degree of acclaim, even if it's not self-conscious. It's such a beautifully written piece of material, such a masterful film—an American classic, no less—that DiCaprio's Oscar nomination for Best Supporting Actor not only quite rightly acknowledged the presence of a wunderkind, but shocked audiences with the realization that it was an actor playing a part, not a real guy "like that" they found to do the movie.

The universal praise over his performance in *Gilbert Grape* made Leonardo DiCaprio a hot commodity in Hollywood, though with the peculiar caveat of extraordinary talent and not box-office appeal in the buzz. Everybody wanted him for their next film. Sharon Stone, who certainly was an everybody who was somebody in the mid-1990s, wanted him so badly for a supporting role in *The Quick and the Dead* (1995) that she secured his participation by halving her own salary and diverting the balance to pay for his services.

He even gets "And Leonardo DiCaprio" billing in this comic book rip-off of Sergio Leone westerns directed by Sam Raimi, best known for his trio of *Evil Dead* movies and the 2002 blockbuster *Spider-Man*. He's tall and lean and dressed in tans and browns and a big 'ol oversized hat as The Kid, a charming, clear-faced, and cocky gunfighter who assumes every gal in town is interested. He sidles up to Sharon Stone in the saloon, telling her his name is Fee, but everybody calls him The Kid. "I'm so damned fast I can wake up at the crack of dawn, rob two banks, a train, and a stagecoach, shoot the tail feathers off a duck's ass at three hundred feet, and still be back in bed before you wake up next to me."

He's one smooth operator and even manages to win Stone in a drunken poker game, though their coupling is only alluded to because a bed scene they reportedly shot was edited out of the final print. It may not have played out properly in terms of her character, but I can sure as hell see why Sharon wanted the opportunity to do a love scene with The Kid. DiCaprio, then 20, but still looking 17, is finally allowed to shine in all his blond beauty. Skinnier than Jimmy Stewart or Henry Fonda—hell, maybe even skinnier than Anthony Perkins—he conjures early Gary Cooper, except he's got a live wire running through his veins.

The ladies along the sidelines let out a cheer of appreciation each time he's called into the street to gunfight, foreshadowing the actor's adoration as Celebrity Kid within the year. "Whooo-damn am I fast," he tells himself and the crowd after gunning down another opponent. "Is it possible to improve on perfection?" His cockiness is charming, not obnoxious, and I like the beautiful presentation of his gun wares to Russell Crowe and the way he playfully grabs himself after thrilling townsfolk with yet another outrageous tale of gunplay bravado. He's got the cleanest, shiniest hair I've ever seen on a cowboy, and when Sharon Stone suddenly grasps him by the neck and lays one on him—a stark reversal of traditional western roles—he's shocked to play the girl, but more than up to the task of being fancied. He also shocks the gimmicky film out of its artifice by playing a heartbreaking climax using powers far beyond those required by the material.

Literally faced with being the face on teenybopper magazines all over the world, making him feel "like I'm just part of a meat factory," DiCaprio decided to take on the challenge of playing heroin junkie Jim Carroll in the screen version of *The Basketball Diaries* (1995). From a young actor's point of view, I can certainly understand the delicious temptation to play this kind of material, but I can't imagine anyone thinking a good film could have been fashioned from it. Carroll's urban diaries, written between the ages of 12 and 15, are raw glimpses into teenaged addiction and street life in the 1960s. The film takes a period memoir and unproductively and unwisely updates it to the present. The gang of punks is still a gang of punks, but now when they play basketball during a thunderstorm it turns into a music video thanks to a 30-year old director known for such things. Besides, you know it's only going to get worse and worse for the characters. There's no payoff.

If done right, this movie would have been so devastating that it would have been unwatchable. Done wrong, it's an ugly film without poetry, despite a shot of Leo pulling his pud on a darkened rooftop and a voice-over that explains, "time sure flies when you're young and jerkin' off." Honestly, I was hoping for more quiet moments like that before things got too nasty. The film might have even redeemed itself if it had simply re-created the moment in Carroll's recollections when his gym shorts ripped while he was out on the court in the middle of the game. His whole backside was exposed framed only by his jockstrap as he made his way to the hoop.

Carroll's diaries are full of references to "freaks," "fairies," and "fags," and his own street life as a boy who hustled queers, transsexuals, and a woman who had him dress as a woman for drug money is related with a remarkable lack of horror. In the film version, circa 1995, the hustling is represented by a ludicrous and offensive sideshow in a seedy toilet where funhouse mirror shots of the boy's lecherous basketball coach are interspersed with pained, teary-eyed grimaces of personal disgust from Leo while an old guy goes down on him in one of the stalls. Now you tell me, how's a guy supposed to get it up and collect his dough for the blow when he's busy making faces that suggest he's having his privates slowly clamped in the jaws of a vise?

Proof that the material and its adaptation were to blame, the film contains a single scene of blazing honesty and power—a scene in which Leo knocks on his mom's door and makes a devastating plea for money—that was shot the first week of production and was entirely improvised by the actors.

Even more outrageous and attractive material to a young actor could be found in the life of French poet Arthur Rimbaud (1854-1891), whose flash of literary genius lasted from ages 16 to 19. At 20, he renounced his gift. His wild, vulgar, poverty-stricken relationship with the poet Paul Verlaine (1844-1896) is a torrid and picaresque story of love/hate, sexual manipulation, and jealousy, culminating in Verlaine's famously shooting Rimbaud in the hand with a pistol, then being accused of sodomy by the courts and jailed for two years.

The film version, *Total Eclipse* (1995), was originally to have starred John Malkovich as Verlaine and River Phoenix as Rimbaud, but would likely have been just as much a failure. You certainly don't want to blame the actors who eventually played the roles, because David Thewlis, whose performance in *Naked*

Valentino revisited in the feminine beauty and phenomenal popularity of Leonardo DiCaprio, seen here uncharacteristically buoyant for *Marvin's Room* (1996). PHOTOFEST

(1993) is rightly worshipped by a legion of young actors, and Leonardo DiCaprio are two of the best a director could ask for; but Christopher Hampton's screenplay, based on his more literate 1968 stageplay, fails to illuminate the strange and tortured relationship between these two men. The task may have been impossible considering how ugly a man Verlaine was, both in physicality and deed (according to this), and the writer hasn't the kind of rich, juicy material he had when he adapted *Dangerous Liaisons* for the 1988 screen version and won an Oscar for doing so.

Wisely, DiCaprio isn't asked to adopt a French accent, just appear as an unkempt and uncouth little shit who knows he's brilliant and literally pisses on the mundane poets of society circles. "I decided to be a genius," he tells Verlaine. "I decided to originate the future."

Rimbaud's powerful, haunting, dreamlike poems were ahead of their time. He was coarse and wantonly cruel and everything else a young actor would enjoy playing out, except that he also had a homosexual relationship with Verlaine. You can't guess why, but such are the facts. When DiCaprio and Thewlis kiss at 31 minutes into the film, you'll be equally as stumped.

For Leo, the kissing and a later homo-sex scene were difficult hurtles for a young heterosexual actor to jump. He grew up surrounded by icons of the counterculture thanks to his dad's various associations, including R. Crumb, Hubert Selby, Jr., Alan Ginsberg, William Burroughs, and Robert Williams. And his early introduction to the subject of sexuality was illustrated by a plethora of underground sex comics. But just knowing something exists doesn't make it any more appealing to you if you've zero personal interest.

Doing press before the kiss, he seemed uneasy, then playfully fooled with the interviewer, as he often likes to do: "But when I have to do that scene, I'll tell you what I'm gonna do. I'm going to go in there, and I'm going to walk over to him, and I'm going to stick my tongue down his fucking throat and probably swerve it around a bit." (One should take note that the interviewer in this case was female and that Leo casually left the door open while he went into the bathroom to take a pee mid-stream.)

Doing press *after* the kiss, well, he'd rather not talk about it because it makes him sick. Which is something I find both surprising and admirable. Surprising in the sense that he didn't use the "shock" of the homosexual scenes to his tactical advantage as an actor with a reputation for taking risks; admirable in the sense that he was just plain honest about the whole thing. The film seems to concur with his distaste, transitioning directly from the cruel scene in which Rimbaud impales Verlaine's palm with a knife to a tightly framed shot of Rimbaud giving the old boy a painful rear-ending.

Leo still manages to light up the screen with his beauty, but there are other odd indignities to come. For a surprising flash of full-frontal nudity from him, he's afforded the least flattering and foreshortened of angles, shot from street level looking up at him on a ledge. Late in the film, he's plastered with the silliest and phoniest looking mustache this side of high school theatre to effect all of age 37. It's a crêpe caterpillar on a bed of gauze floating on a slick of spirit gum. Leonardo DiCaprio is not the actor you want to play the span of a man's lifetime. He's impossible to age.

He falls out of bed onto the floor naked and they've effectively "removed" half of one amputated leg the same way they took Gary Sinise down to stumps in *Forrest Gump* (1994). Oddly, given the ceiling view angle we're afforded and the time it takes to do that kind of camera set-up, the tip of Leo's penis and both his balls can be glimpsed flattened out on the floor between his skinny legs right before he's lifted back into bed.

Blurry frame enlargements of both his private parts scenes from the film quickly circulated on the Internet after *Titanic* made him a superstar. *Playgirl* magazine notoriously ran a few of them in its October 1998 issue. The magazine had originally announced they were going to run a spread of paparazzo shots of DiCaprio nude that had come from a publicly undisclosed source. *Playgirl*'s editor was fired for refusing to go ahead with the issue. DiCaprio brought legal action against the magazine and a behind-closed-doors settlement was reached in July of 1998. No one seems to know if the magazine had in fact been in possession of candid nudes of the actor—not even the fired editor ever saw them—but the October issue that eventually headlined "Leonardo DiCaprio Nude!" with his face on the cover (an almost identical layout to the infamous Brad Pitt issue) shows only one foggy frame from the floor scene alongside suspiciously awful and ill-chosen additional shots. The clearest frame of Leo's privates in the film is absent, suggesting that was part of the deal.

Total Eclipse is the one pretty awful film in DiCaprio's oeuvre that future fans will always seek out. If for nothing else, to see him crawling on all fours baaing like a sheep or popping a cork out of a wine bottle between his prehensile shoulder blades.

Fans may also be intrigued to hear him talk about masturbation ("I got my girlfriend off on a zucchini, and that got me off") or discuss anatomical pleasure zones ("You have four orgasmic spots in your asshole, that's why gay guys fuck like rabbits") with his friends and acquaintances in *Don's Plum* (1995). Shot in black-and-white over a few days, and largely improvised, the low-budget enterprise from writer-director R.D. Robb plays like a cross between *Diner* (1982) and *Clerks* (1994), throwing a dozen or so actors together for a night of mean-spirited riffing at the title coffee shop. The dramatics veer predictably askew and some of the actors short circuit scenes because they're at a loss where to go and shouting and swearing at each other seems an easy out. The film begins promisingly with a jazzy spontaneity and anything-can-happen vibe, but loses most of that energy as it devolves into undisciplined temper flare-ups. Leo is looking mighty fine and plays the biggest "cock" of the bunch, a jerk among jerks who effortlessly manages to productively upstage Scott Bloom (as a bisexual who probably didn't know it until Leo added the revelation to the improv) and a young Tobey Maguire. Infamously, Maguire and DiCaprio teamed up in a lawsuit against former friend and director Robb when he endeavored to release the film theatrically. The complaint alleged that the two actors understood they were participating in an "acting exercise," not a film intended for the commercial market. The arguments are murky, but the result banned the film from being shown in theatres in North America.

Because he's so well known today, it might be a good idea to interject right here that not a single one of Leonardo DiCaprio's films thus far had been a box-office hit. He was well-respected, highly sought after, but markedly unproven in the purely monetary sense. Until he did *William Shakespeare's Romeo + Juliet* (1996). Tights would have been nice, but he wouldn't have done it if he had to wear them. What director Baz Luhrmann [later of *Moulin Rouge* (2001) fame] had in mind was a garish neon trip into Shakespeare, a popping pop cultural riff that would speak to the teenage audience and bring the Bard to pulsating life. He accomplished that, and more.

Splashed with bright colors and a complex soundtrack, and filmed in hyperstylized, almost operatic fashion, *R+J* (as it most definitely should have been retitled) still manages to wring the essential emotions out of the Shakespearean dialogue in spite of the acid trip. Most all of it works, from the Capulets and Montagues as competing oil companies to the sword fighting relegated to the flash of 9mm Swords and Rapiers. It's disturbing how cool all the gang gunplay appears, but certainly swords and swordplay were just as exciting to young men at one time. Here, the guns are gorgeous, shiny and silver, and wielded with irrevocable grace and style in both slow and fast motion.

Leonardo is quintessentially cast as the sullen Romeo, first seen coolly smoking a cigarette beneath a Gothic seaside arch. He's like James Dean, achingly attractive in his agony. He's also a movie star for teens in this movie, not possessed of a muscular, cut body, but a thin and wispy one, trapped between a boy and a man and yet palpably sexy. And on top of that, as we've already established, he's one helluva an actor, capable of turning the emotional shorthand of in-your-face imagery to powerful, deeply felt drama.

You can feel the love and desire in his Romeo the moment he sees Juliet's face through the neon fish tank. He's nearly iconic. You hang onto every word, note every gesture and facial expression. DiCaprio became a conduit through which a teenaged generation heard, and I mean really heard, Shakespeare's words for the first time. What's more, they may have understood some of them. Sure it's a distillation and it's dressed to the nines in eye candy and violence, but *R+J* flashes like a bolt of lightning to a generation increasingly unexcited unless hit by one.

As Meryl Streep's troubled oldest boy in *Marvin's Room* (1996), he's part of a first-rate ensemble cast that includes Diane Keaton and Robert De Niro. Once again, he seems to live the role, not just play it. Despite the strong source material, in other hands, the character could easily have come across as just the troubled teen in this beautifully written drama; Leo allows us to see many sides of Hank, an angry young man who enjoys hiding behind exaggerated exploits of time spent in a mental home. He's also conducting a fantasy search for his hero-worshipped, but long-absent father.

It's impossible to deny the actor's physical beauty, but I also wonder what impact that beauty has on the way in which he communicates to an audience in purely dramatic terms. Having both great talent and great beauty, he's the unqualified exception to the rule. Are we inclined to feel more for Hank because he's embodied by DiCaprio's natural talent? Natural beauty? Or the conspiracy of both? Probably a dumb question. And yet I find myself investing so much more emotionally in his characters because I'm transfixed by his face. Maybe I'm just in love.

Look at Jack Dawson on paper and try as you might, you'd never find Leonardo DiCaprio there. James Cameron's ingenious decision to cast DiCaprio to play Jack in *Titanic* (1997) was as vital to the success of the 200+ million dollar film as the special effects sinking of the ship itself. Without DiCaprio, *Titanic* is a disaster movie; with him, it's an epic romance.

Jack is the nicest boy a girl could ever meet. He's a common boy. He smokes, he draws, he spits. He's an orphan. He's a free spirit. He's the kind of boy who falls for a one-legged prostitute because she has lovely hands. Oh, and she had a good sense of humor, too. He's a boy who cuts through the pretense, the bullshit. He's devoted, heroic, selfless, and honorable. He also "shines up like a new penny." He dances with a little girl, he's unabashedly romantic, he knows how to have a good time, enjoys life, and rescues a beautiful woman trapped into an awful marriage deal and destined for unhappiness.

He's an idealized lover. And beautiful, too. No wonder it hurts so much.

If he were just a pretty boy, he'd be as dull as the Prince in *Snow White*. So here again we're witnesses to a transcendental conspiracy of beauty and talent. Leo brings Jack Dawson to life, makes him warm-blooded and desirable. Makes us feel the glow of idyll. And then we lose him to the cold water.

Titanic sailed on to become one of the biggest films of all time, grossing a record 1.8 billion dollars worldwide, and creating a phenomenon that rivals only *Gone With the Wind* (1939) in the history of motion pictures. With the monumental success, not unexpectedly, came backlash. Pre-teen and teen girls were lining up to see Leo sail and sink and sail and sink again over and over. Even older women fancied a girlish romance with him. He became an unlikely sex symbol. At last, a skinny sex symbol.

He doesn't have the physique of a Valentino. His body matches the feminine beauty of his face, causing some comedians of the time to joke that the real reason a chick flick like *Titanic* worked for guys was because both leads were so pretty that when they made out it seemed like a lesbian love scene.

DiCaprio's long and lean body and eternally boyish beauty had been captured by photographers years before *Titanic* introduced him to the rest of the world. Bruce Weber, Greg Gorman, Mark Selig, Albert Watson, Bob Frame, and David LaChapelle, to name a few of the best, had been immortalizing those parenthetical eyebrows, sproingy blond locks, penetrating eyes, feminine lips, high cheekbones, and satiny skin as if his eventual stardom was assured.

Titanic premiered in Japan, which seems appropriate given the culture's graphic preoccupation with youth and the fascinating subculture of bishonen (pretty boys) manga (amateur comics) and anime—charged with homoerotic content and same sex love—worshipped by Japanese girls, women, and gay men alike; the art form's leading artists are women, too. DiCaprio was their flesh and blood god.

As with the male response in the West to the sex symbol status of Rudolph Valentino in the 1920s, Leonardo DiCaprio's idolization in the 1990s was scorned by heterosexual men. There quickly came silly rumors about his being gay. And taunts about a so-called sex symbol covered in peach fuzz or equipped with the body of a praying mantis. In short, jealousy erupted, confounded by the fact that the 22-year old object of everyone's affection was almost literally seen as a boy toy.

A timely paper published in August of 1998 in the scientific journal *Nature* reported that cross-cultural studies of sexual dimorphism in faces showed both men and women were actually attracted to and preferred slightly more feminine male faces than slightly more masculine ones. "Feminization of male face shape may increase attractiveness because it 'softens' particular features that are perceived to be associated with negative personality traits," it was reported. Even science acquiesced to male beauty.

I suppose some would argue that negative personality traits might include an inflated ego, a party animal, a media suck-up, and a guy who believes his own press. Leonardo DiCaprio was blamed by a segment of the population for the rabid success of *Titanic* and the tidal wave of DiCaprio photos, posters, fan magazines, books, and nightly news reports devoted to him. In fact, he had zip to do with 99.9% of the multimedia frenzy over the film. He certainly could never have known the impact it was going to have, and he made immediate plans to avoid knowingly repeating the feat. He dodged the press as much as possible, though quite properly refused to become a recluse and was accordingly hunted by paparazzi when he frequented nightspots and went clubbing with friends.

Unlike a Brad Pitt or a Keanu Reeves, or even a Rudolph Valentino, all of whom could have played Jack Dawson and been susceptible to taunts about their skills as an actor in deference to their physical charms as bodies, DiCaprio's work in this gargantuan entertainment is unassailable.

"He is underestimated as an actor because he is a pretty boy," explained *This Boy's Life* director Michael Caton-Jones to *Talk* magazine in February of 2000. "He has a wet panty feel to him. But he's both: pretty and a good actor."

Cast before *Titanic*'s release, he electrifies the screen for just over ten minutes in Woody Allen's otherwise unbearable *Celebrity* (1997). He's an abusive, egotistical, gambling, coke-snorting, pot-smoking, group-sex-indulging movie star snot who beats on his girlfriend-of-the-moment and trashes his hotel room. Unimaginative folks thought he was just playing himself.

He asks a stuttering Kenneth Branagh to join him in bed with two hot young ladies, but Branagh is scared. "You know *we're* not gettin' together," Leo reassures him. "You do like girls?" Sure he does, but he's still nervous about being in the presence of another naked man.

Leo doesn't get it. "Haven't you ever been in a boys' locker room?"

"I don't know really how to put it," says Branagh's Woody alter ego. "It's like, the wave of panic, y'know, in the proximity of unclad male genitalia in conjunction with the specific activity implied..."

I love Woody Allen's work, but it's unfortunate that *Celebrity*, one of his worst ventures, was likely the first of his films ever to be seen by legions of teenagers at the movies. Thank goodness for VHS and DVD. Fast forward to the 54-minute mark and you can watch Leonardo's lively and funny take on celebrity without all the pain and suffering of the other 104 minutes.

Given Leo's extraordinary desire to choose offbeat and challenging material, it's hard to understand what interested him in doing yet another variation on the classic tale of *The Man in the Iron Mask* (1998). It's not a project particularly worth doing, and plays like an old Hollywood studio picture back in the days when stars were assigned films and nobody made an effort to bother with an accent other than their own. As the preening King Louis, with long braided hair and gorgeous clothes, he's only a touch foppish. As Prisoner #64389000, aka identical twin Philippe, he cleans up amazingly well after six years of double imprisonment inside a cell and inside an iron mask. Such lovely skin.

And you'll laugh out loud when Louis orders sweet Philippe back into the mask by screaming with all his might, "Wear it until you love it!"

The Man in the Iron Mask benefited tremendously from Leo's *Titanic* superstardom at the box-office, but evidence that he wanted nothing to do with Leo-frenzy was measured by his absence at the Academy Awards (insultingly, he wasn't nominated) and his retreat from the big screen for two years. To his credit, he did lend that newly supercharged name to several environmental and wild and domestic animal causes close to his heart to rouse public awareness and promote a healthier dialogue about world ecology and conservation. He also made headlines whenever he even considered a movie project, be it *All the Pretty Horses* or *American Psycho*, ultimately choosing the film version of Alex Garland's 1996 novel *The Beach* (2000).

"My name is Richard. So what else do you need to know?" Not much initially. Leonardo DiCaprio brought us here, and the film starts out very strongly. Strictly in physical terms, we can't help noticing that Leo has beefed up his body. He's thicker, but not narcissistically so. He'll be spending a lot of the movie without his shirt on and he obviously wanted to prepare for that. In all other respects as well, he is still quite amazingly beautiful.

The film's overriding theme is Western contamination of paradise, our gross culpability in the destruction, wanton or not, of the world's environment, its natural resources, its diversity and ethnic character. We're turning our planet into a strip mall. Specific to the story, DiCaprio is on vacation in Bangkok and learns the location of a secret beach on a remote island from a suicidal nut staying in the room next to him. The young adventurer then invites a beautiful French couple to join him. Things get less credible and persuasive as soon as they arrive on the island, with complications boiled down to "desire is desire wherever you go."

The actor was paid $20,000,000 to do the film and it largely failed to reach an audience at the box-office, suggesting that his *Titanic* appeal had waned. For true fans, however, the failure came almost as a blessing. DiCaprio was obviously still a talent to be reckoned with; to that end, he provides the best acting I've ever seen of someone getting his balls squeezed.

Seriously, though I meant what I said about the nut-crunch, things can only go back to normal from here; normal being the state of making edgy, off-beat, and even blatantly non-commercial films. Now it's time to get back to work and stagger us with performances in movies that may or may not fill theatres, not *have* to fill them.

Unfortunately, after a long shoot and an additional year's worth of delays before its release, Martin Scorsese's *Gangs of New York* (2002) did not provide DiCaprio with much of a role, despite being the lead. The screenwriters could only cough up one full-fledged character (played by Daniel Day-Lewis) in a 168-minute film that bored with violence and relinquished storytelling for a dry history lesson. Those of us who had been waiting more than two years for DiCaprio's return to the screen were rewarded, however, with Steven Spielberg's *Catch Me If You Can* (2002). Credibly playing a teenager again (at age 28), Leo found plenty of room for nuance as Frank Abagnale, Jr., an enterprising check-forger and con man who had the FBI running in circles in the 1960s. It's an entertaining and necessarily multi-faceted performance, allowing his own celebrity to ingratiate a criminal.

"A long-term career has a lot to do with people not understanding who you are," he told *Time* magazine in February of 2000. That's my boy. And as *Alexander* (2005) the Great, we'll see just how understanding Leo and the filmmakers were of the famed conqueror's pansexuality. Ditto for his turn as Howard Hughes in *The Aviator* (2004).

It's not there. Go and look for yourself if you don't believe me. All those great photos of Marky Mark standing around in his Calvin Klein drawers showing off those pumped arms, that gorgeous six-pack, that million dollar smile (actually he got $100,000), and those perfectly defined pectorals are missing part of the picture: his third nipple, a small, but otherwise quite complete nipple about an inch and a half under his left one. It's not a birthmark. Not a mole. It's a real nipple. And he's awfully proud of it. Its airbrushed absence in the hugely popular CK underwear ad campaign was just one of the subtler signs that the guy they were photographing wasn't really the guy they were photographing.

Mark Robert Michael Wahlberg (1971-) was born and raised the youngest of nine children in the blue collar Dorchester neighborhood of Boston. His father, a truck driver, and his mom, a nurse, were often stretched beyond capability with the children and divorced when Mark was 11. He spent much of his time on the streets, dropped out of school at 14, and got involved with drugs, booze, and a host of criminal activities, from beating up people for cash or liquor to robbing stores and stealing cars.

He says he was on PCP the night he and some buddies attacked a young Vietnamese man because he had a case of beer they wanted. Wahlberg hit the guy with a hooked stick, the kind vendors use to pull down security gates, which reverberated off the victim's arm and took out an eye. The offender was 16. He was jailed for 45 days of a two-year sentence at age 17. Older brother Donnie, meanwhile, was making strides with a little musical group called New Kids on the Block. Mark was part of the group, too, when it first got together, but he didn't care for the bubble gum music and instead occasionally opened for the group by doing some homemade raps as a bro called Marky Mark.

The New Kids might have kept him out of trouble if he'd only swallowed the bubble gum, but maybe they wouldn't have either. The group of working class teens became a teen music phenomenon in 1989 with the release of their *Hangin' Tough* album. The explosion of money and fame helped Donnie and the band's manager to put something together for Mark, who headlined Marky Mark and the Funky Bunch in 1990. Their 1991 album *Music for the People* went platinum, thanks to a throbbing rap song called "Good Vibrations" and the serendipitous discovery of the all-important gimmick.

During a July 1991 concert at the Magic Mountain amusement park in Southern California, Marky Mark pulled his pants down during the last song and the place went up for grabs. This wasn't quite the famed cocks in socks routine that immortalized the Red Hot Chili Peppers in the mid-1980s, but it did the job. No doubt a contributing factor to the success of the impromptu stunt was that young Mr. Wahlberg had a body recently buffed by weight training.

The teenyboppers ate it up and Marky Mark became a street talkin' white rapper with attitude and a trademark of dropping trou and dancing around on stage in his underwear. When he hit the cover of *Rolling Stone* with a boa constrictor around his neck and biceps thicker than the snake, he also had his pants riding low and his Calvin Klein underwear riding high. Record and film mogul David Geffen immediately recognized the advertising angle and called friend Calvin Klein about the kid in the CK shorts.

Klein had been in the clothing business for years and had a penchant for overtly sexy, sometimes controversial, but nearly always lucrative ad campaigns. Hot guys in their undies were nothing new to him. In fact, since 1987, he was finding particular success by taking them out of them. His CK Obsession for Men cologne campaign regularly featured dramatic landscapes of bronzed and carefully posed naked men and women in statuesque display.

Marky Mark was the hot new kid on the modeling block and he signed a contract with Klein to become his Underwear Boy, figuring that the exposure would help sell his music, though far from certain about its impact because he was having serious trouble understanding why people who looked at him found anything remotely sexy.

His idea of masculinity was Steve McQueen. "He was a huge star, too. People went to see a guy, not some doll-looking motherfucker—not some guy who's prettier than the girl he's in the movie with. I like to see a guy I can relate to," he told *Interview* magazine.

The only thing people related to when they saw Marky Mark's sexy and playful underwear ads, including a giant billboard in Times Square, was how incredibly hot and how incredibly built he was in them. Nobody really thought they were going to buy a pair of Calvin Klein undies and stand in the mirror and possibly compete (ok, so a few did), but knew they had to have a pair all the same. Calvin Klein underwear became the fashionable accessory for men who wanted to feel sexy and men who didn't mind the tactical ploy of being perceived as sexy.

The Herb Ritts photos were a hit, stolen from stores and ripped out of display cases and off walls all

Mark Wahlberg, pumped up for his first shot at acting, plays a histrionic hood who knows his teacher is a psychotic killer in the cable-TV thriller *The Substitute* (1993). EVERETT COLLECTION

over the world. Marky Mark was an American male pin-up, sexy all by his lonesome or sharing an embrace with a topless Kate Moss. In a popular and racy black-and-white broadcast commercial, he's even cheeky enough to give himself a tug and admit, "I've had lipstick stains on my underwear a few times."

He memorably lowered his pants and danced around in his white skivvies during the halftime show of MTV's 1991 Rock vs. Jocks basketball tournament in possibly unselfconscious self-promotion of his album via a physical appeal that was so joyful and fun to watch that the music really didn't matter.

The CK ads are classic examples of the successful objectification of the male body as a conveyor of beauty and a conveyance of commerce. What Marky Mark did so incredibly well was bring character, charm, and warm-blooded sex appeal to the unknown male figures of prior campaigns. Marky Mark brought the statue of the beautiful young man selling underwear to life. He somehow made the unreal body he possessed seem real. Not only desirable, but squeezable.

The squeezing quickly became part of the package, too. It wasn't enough to drop your drawers, now you had to grab onto yourself as well. The February 1992 all Bruce Weber edition of *Interview* magazine featured Marky on the cover and ran seven photos of him sans shirt, two of those in full grope. A full-page color shot after a performance has him surrounded by fans. He's got his hand on his crotch, a pucker on his lips, a girl on his bare shoulder, and another gal giving him a kiss on the cheek. That second young lady is wearing a T-shirt that says, "Unbutton Your Fly."

The 1992 HarperPerennial book *Marky Mark* by Marky Mark and Lynn Goldsmith is a glossy color photobook with occasional funky comments from the man himself. It features 41 shots of him without his shirt on, including the front and back covers. Photos of the Markster with his arms behind his head extend his torso exposure, revealing a precipitous amount of skin between that belly button and those low-slung jeans. I'm sure it wasn't the first time such a thing occurred, but even I was somewhat agog when I saw one of the session's photos show up in *SuperTeen* magazine and the light splay of pubic hair was unmistakable.

Marky Mark was a physical phenomenon. Teenagers loved him, older women loved him, and gay men loved him. From the very beginning, Marky's management made no bones about the fact that all three groups were attracted and affectionately welcomed. The white rapper in his undies instantly became the underwear model who sang. And while it lasted, a good time was had by all.

"I'm glad that gay people are so free with their words, and they're not hiding or scared to show their emotions. If I were gay, I wouldn't want to have to hold it in, you know? Just like if I were to meet a girl and I really liked her, you know, I would approach her and at least let her know the way I felt—so it's cool with me when guys do it, you know what I mean? My preference is for females, but I respect anybody for their sexual preference."

Those words were spoken before the gay community turned on him and shamefully called him a homophobe. Those words were spoken when we still liked him. Those words were spoken with sincerity, but some people figured those words were spoken merely to keep the cash flowing.

Concert appearances at gay clubs, AIDS charities, and his pretty pictures on the covers and between the covers of gay magazines meant zip when the three-strikes-you're-out gossip hit the circuit in 1993. 1. His criminal past was revealed and made to appear racially-motivated. 2. His humiliating appearance in December of 1992 on the British tabloid television show *The Word*, where his complexion was ridiculed and they kept trying to get him to take off his shirt, had him on the same guest sheet as openly homophobic rapper Shabba Ranks. Ranks unleashed on gays with his predictable perversion of the Bible and called for their crucifixion. Marky Mark was whipped by association, since people thought he should have said or done something during or immediately after Ranks' asinine on-air diatribe. 3. Minutes after an ugly scuffle at a party attended by Madonna, a publicist contacted the press and claimed that Marky called a member of her entourage, maybe even her brother, a "faggot," and subsequently got his ass kicked off the premises by bodyguards.

Calvin Klein suspiciously decided not to renew Marky's modeling contract, while the gay community leapt to irresponsible and bitchy conclusions. Billboards of him were spattered with red paint and the offices of Calvin Klein received shit-stained returns of their product. Granted, it was a particularly dicey time for gays in this country, what with President Clinton's backing down on the gays in the military issue, the releases of *JFK* (1991), *Silence of the Lambs* (1991), and *Basic Instinct* (1992), all of which were accused of homophobic content, the continuing AIDS health crisis, the appalling practice of outing, and the virulent rise of gay hate crimes, anti-gay legislation, and intolerant religious fanaticism in the face of increased visibility of gay men and women in popular culture and everyday life.

The Marky Mark days.
EVERETT COLLECTION

Marky Mark owed us an allegiance, some claimed, because we were pumping the money into his bank account. When he seemed to turn on us, to reveal himself as something other than what we were buying, we got snotty about it.

The fact is, Marky Mark didn't compromise the product he was selling to us one tit. He was delivering the same goods we craved all along: streetwise street boy wrapped in a skintight, hard, muscled physique with that anomalous third nipple and propensity for dropping his pants and grabbing his package—all to a danceable beat. Did he owe us a mind-set, too? He wouldn't even have garnered the attention of gay boys across the country if it hadn't been for the stunning beauty he cut in his Calvin Kleins and the street-punkish way he flaunted his sex.

The gay community beat up on Marky Mark because it turned out that the guy came in three dimensions and had a life and attitudes and, at worst, an evolving sensibility about homosexuality that wasn't quite up to speed for the liberated queer. Damn, wouldn't you know, the buffed guy in his jockey shorts on that billboard over there is really straight and not so sure what to do with all this attention he's getting from gay guys. Oh, and he's had a criminal past that maybe calls into question some of his feelings about other kinds of people, too. But he says that's all behind him and he doesn't feel that way now.

Could we have been so foolish as to believe that it mattered one iota? It was Marky Mark's body, (for some) maybe his music, that brought about the longings in both gay men and teenaged girls. When the fantasy turned out to have a reality that we didn't like, we dumped on him, as if the context was inseparable from the content. The weirdest part of it all, there was never any evidence he was the least bit homophobic.

Once again, before the tide had turned, in his 1992 book he was asked: "How do you feel about older women and gay men all wanting you?"

"I think it's an honor. You know gay men are not my preference so I'm not as excited as I am about the older women part of it, but people have their likes and dislikes and I respect everybody for that and if I make people happy and entertain them, then cool. But I don't suck dick."

On the printed page, we don't get a sense of how those last five words were said. Did he pause before saying them? Did he smile before or after? Did he say them matter-of-factly or as if he was warning us off? Delivery is where it's at: body language and vocal inflection. All we have is context. I don't think you can read the last five words and ignore the tenor of the first five. After that, it's simply a statement of fact.

291

NBC-TV *Friends'* hunk and former model Matt LeBlanc achieved some level of gay exposure when an early modeling gig unexpectedly turned him into cover boy for the *Spartacus* guide, the international travel book for adventuresome gay men. Assumptions were made, but when asked what, if anything, he had in common with the character he plays on his popular television series, LeBlanc wryly stated, "I, too, am heterosexual."

Is this to be taken as gay-bashing by omission? All you need do is state your true sexual preference these days and it might come off as if you're denigrating the "other" one. Yet you can hardly blame the actors for wanting to set the record straight.

Marky Mark was finally given his chance to address the whole mess in an exclusive interview with *The Advocate*, the national gay and lesbian newsmagazine, in the January 25, 1994 issue. It's an intelligent and articulate response to the too-quick-to-judge community backlash, putting him back in our graces and even posing for a Greg Gorman photo with his shirt wide open and his mouth suspiciously (and certainly unintentionally on his part) poised to suggest receptive fellatio. On the cover, meanwhile, he's pouting like a naughty puppy dog asking for forgiveness. And in the same diplomatic style that got Keanu Reeves gossipers mongering, when asked if he could ever have a sexual relationship with another man, Marky answered, "Uh, not now. But you never know. You never know." (As the October 1997 cover boy on *Out* magazine, he added a bit more emphatically, "I don't want to get up anybody's hopes or anything, but like I said, I wake up every day feeling a little bit different. But I haven't felt *that* different yet.")

He released a second album, *You Gotta Believe*, in 1992, and was ill at ease improvising macho commentary for *The Marky Mark Workout: Form, Focus, Fitness* (1993), a 70-minute workout video that, like all workout videos, was likely bought and rented by lots of folks who had no intention of exercising more than one or the other hand. Catch him in a 1993 *Vanity Fair* two-page spread in which Annie Leibovitz has him recreating the old Coppertone ad, with a German shepherd tugging real hard on the back of his jockey shorts, exposing the top of his heinie and even some up-front hair, and notice the pained expression on his face. It's not one of playful play along. It looks rather like, is this really what it's all come to?

Director Penny Marshall noticed more than just his runway skills when she caught him at a Calvin Klein show pre-hysteria and called him in to audition for a role in *Renaissance Man* (1994). She said he got the part because he was a real guy from a real neighborhood who said "ambalence" instead of ambulance. He plays a hot-tempered Army private from Georgia, though, not one of the script's New Yorkers. The preachy and overlong drama (not comedy, as it was sold) is so good-hearted that you end up liking the delinquent soldiers who unbelievably don't know who Shakespeare is but get into *Hamlet* big time thanks to Danny DeVito. Wahlberg is tapped to play the King, but blanches at the idea of another guy as the Queen: "You know as well as I do a guy playin' a girl is plain filthy, especially if they're gonna be my wife."

He's billed as Mark Wahlberg in *Renaissance Man* and in his film career thereafter, happy to distance himself from the character of Marky Mark, whom he refers to in interviews in the third person. His Marky Mark music video and workout video director Scott Kalvert was still in the picture, though, and cast Mark in the supporting role of Mickey in *The Basketball Diaries* (1995), opposite Leonardo DiCaprio. DiCaprio was openly opposed to Marky Mark's involvement on the project, so was pleased to find out that Mark Wahlberg, on the other hand, was a hard-working and natural acting choice to play a tough kid on the streets of New York.

In *Fear* (1996), he's Reese Witherspoon's new boyfriend, a quietly intense young man who turns out to be dangerously psychotic and possessive. He fingers her to an orgasm while they ride the rollercoaster, but it's at her behest. She's also the dummy who casually gives out the security code to her family's state-of-the-art lockdown house so he can let himself in and visit her bedroom in case she's already fallen asleep. He fashions himself a homemade tattoo across his hard chest and killer abs that says "Nicole 4 Eva" when the pen ink is rubbed into the fresh wounds. By all rights, he should have got to keep her.

He's young Pat O'Hara, whose blood-tie pa was a member of an Irish family of gypsy criminals, in the low-budget film *Traveller* (1997). Partnered with Bill Paxton for a life of scamming on the road, he learns his trade and falls in love with the Boss' daughter on his way to the ugly and bloody finale. Not a whole lot of fun here. Still, considering he was offered the lead in Paul Verhoeven's *Starship Troopers* (1997) and chose this, he's demonstrated intelligent career choices to avoid having his movie career parallel his music and modeling careers.

"I'm definitely not your man," he told director Paul Thomas Anderson, who wanted him to come and read for the role of a porn star in his next feature. "I asked him if he'd seen my underwear ads. If so, he'd have realized I'd never have been able to hide something like that in a pair of Calvin Kleins," he told the *New York Times Syndicate* in November of 1997.

Eddie Adams, all of 17, has a cock four inches shy of his age. He's working as a busboy in *Boogie Nights* (1997) and already charging guys $5 to see it and $10 to have him jack it off. "Everyone's blessed with one special thing," he likes to tell people.

Though I'm sure Leonardo DiCaprio could have pulled it off, and he was the first choice, Mark Wahlberg brings an astonishing charm and sweetness to the boy who will become porn superstar Dirk Diggler during this epic tale of an extended family of pornographers operating out of the San Fernando Valley from 1977-1984. He was reticent about doing it for more than just the numerous sex scenes and attendant nudity. He was worried that his casting was a stunt, that he might end up a goofy piece of meat again.

He didn't end up that way because he gave the kind of performance that no one expected of him. Mark Wahlberg proved himself a real actor with *Boogie Nights*, touchingly playing out the transition from the sweetest boy to ever walk onto a porn set (asking his co-star where she wants him to ejaculate and giving it all he's got to make the scene look sexy) and the pathetic druggie he becomes six years later. Pay close attention to him during his first porn scene, then during the walking tour of his new house, then throughout any of the hilarious action and dialogue scenes from his movies as Brock Landers, and finally as an interviewee in a documentary, and you'll see an actor who knows the guy he's playing very well. *Boogie Nights* is a sharp, funny, and audacious piece of filmmaking—easily one of the year's best movies—and not even the last minute unveiling of the 13" prosthetic penis can upstage the guy attached to it. Sure, we're not likely to be looking anywhere else when it's hauled out, but Mark Wahlberg has made Dirk Diggler a real guy with this "one special thing," not a freak of nature.

He uses his confliction of personality and job description again as the completely whipped, good-hearted, and apologetic hit man in the macho action comedy *The Big Hit* (1998). The actor is something of a study in contrasts himself. With careers in music, modeling, and the movies that owe some degree of success to his sex appeal and body exposure, he's a man, raised Catholic, who often tells interviewers that he thinks sex is a private thing and should be kept private. A weird locker room scene at the beginning of *The Big Hit* has Antonio Sabato, Jr. (who became a Calvin Klein underwear model post-Marky) and Lou Diamond Phillips bare-assed and in a discussion about Bokeem Woodbine's recent discovery of masturbation. Mark's there, too.

"You're gonna stand there and tell me you ain't never jerked your dick in your whole life until last week?" asks Mark. "That's bullshit, man." What's even more unbelievable is how you get away with doing a locker room scene with bare butts left and right and your star keeps his pants on. But that was a conscious decision by the actor and he let the filmmakers know it up front. Compensation can be had in the extraordinary amount of time he spends running around with his shirt completely open and his belly button trail on display. For *The Corruptor* (1999), another boy movie with gunplay and a requisite discussion of dick size, his one nude scene has him face down on a massage table and is completely extraneous, though I enjoyed the view. I also felt sort of embarrassed for him, because I knew it couldn't have been his idea, or something he was eager to do.

The nudity in *Boogie Nights*, minimal as it is, was at least integral to the story, though I'd be the last guy to demand that qualification otherwise. There's no reason to use attractive people in a film if they aren't going to be seen partially or fully naked at some point.

Wahlberg's press comments to horny interviewers about his rarely ever masturbating, disliking giving or receiving oral sex, even being leery of kissing (because he has trouble with all the things that go in that way) have come back to haunt him, especially as a "devout" Roman Catholic. Clark Gable would never have had to worry about being asked such things, let alone ever seeing them in print, but celebrity magazines, especially, have taken a no-holds barred approach to selling themselves.

So what happened to the good old days of verbal discretion and studio-controlled personalities? It used to be that Hollywood brass had a vise grip on their players comings and goings, even if the rest of America figured Tinsel Town was a modern day Sodom and the industry itself gave freakish birth to the infamous scandal sheet rags of the 1950s.

In the 1980s and 1990s, thanks to such publications as *Detour*, *Details*, *Interview*, *Movieline*, and *Spin*, we saw the dawning of a new era marked by shameless celebrity self-exposures. The actors are complicit, too, because the young studs are worshipped by both an industry and a public that revel in their rebellion and willingness to be bold and outrageous. Why else have Stephen Dorff showing off his pubic hair in *Detour*, or caught pissing in the wind (with penis just out of range), or sitting naked on the pot with his hand muffled over his privates in the same magazine?

Brendan Fraser posed nude (again, not full-frontal, but still). Patrick Dempsey is caught filling out his jockey shorts and wearing a ball and chain around one ankle. He's otherwise judiciously nude, but about to chow down on a gorgeous female model's nipple, or with his head between the topless babe's legs. Stephen Baldwin has a secret tattoo next to his genitals and shares that if there's one thing he's learned in this business, "at least have your package looking good." Steve Antin admits he didn't get a boner during either *The Last American Virgin* (1982) or *The Accused* (1988), but only after engaging in a game of Celebrity Pee-Pee with his interviewer in which various celebrities are discussed in terms of genital size and pubic hair density. Antonio Banderas is actually showing some of his pubic hair on the cover of his *Detour* issue; he's posed shirtless and wearing angel wings no less. Jim Carrey went though a phase in which he humped everything in the house, climaxing with a completely nude shag on the fuzzy green rug next to his parents' bed. His father walked in on him.

This is all part of the daily grind in the bitchy old gossip columns, but what's remarkable about the small sample I've provided is that the celebrities were all in on the act. So what does it tell us? That far more revealing than all the garbage people make up about movie stars, when presented with the right opportunity, they're just as sex-crazed, dirty-minded, and reliably human as the rest of us.

Mark Wahlberg once made sick and twisted little movies with his friends and brothers, for instance, in which all sorts of nasty sexual acts are involved, including a desperately horny guy under the influence of a magic sex potion who fails to get any action until he's rear-ended by a pimp. It's titled *Donkey Kong, Gotta Get Off*.

There was a time not so long ago when the idea of Mark Wahlberg directing his own comic perversions, and possibly selling them to eke out a living, seemed a likely scenario for an ex-white rapper and undie boy. But he still has potential as a viable presence on the big screen, despite *The Yards* (2000) and *Planet of the Apes* (2001). He and Said Taghmaoui own the best scenes in the already stylish and very entertaining *Three Kings* (1999), in which Wahlberg is intelligently interrogated and then tortured into the realization that war fought on any ideal means the killing of innocent people. As the devout *Rock Star* (2001) who gets his wish to front for his favorite heavy metal band, he manages to inject some charm and compassion into an obsessive fan before the story flattens into predictable outcomes. The fact that he goes through most of the film with his chest and belly exposed, as well as gets a nipple iced and tweaked in gigantic close-up, helps offset the long-haired disaster above his neckline. His cleaned-up casting as "Cary Grant" in *The Truth About Charlie* (2002), an empty and stillborn re-working of *Charade* (1963), begs us to avoid comparison, however. Even with four character names, he can't find a single one to play. He's a nonentity. As for the equally needless remake of *The Italian Job* (2003), at least he's handsome.

"I wanna dedicate this book to my dick" it says on the third page of Marky Mark's slick, colorful 1992 self-titled tome, accompanied by a playful shot of him grabbing it through the front of his jeans. He had the right idea.

If lots of gay men once felt he made a mistake, it was only in being honest enough to say he wouldn't suck theirs.

Killer bod on that kid, though, huh?

The 1990s — Take Two

"You're Like A Life Support System For A Fucking Cock"

Because it isn't his. It's a fake. And it was a fake at the dawn of fakes, when people were harder to convince. The home computer age moves at such a rapid pace, it might seem unfathomable that less than a decade ago a photo of Marky Mark with a raging hard-on was circulated and most people who saw it believed it was real. Why not? He had an adoring gay fan base and at least half of the men who photographed him were probably gay, so didn't it make sense that he popped a woody during a session and they decided to snap a shot for the hell of it?

No.

What made sense was that some horny guy with a computer and graphics software gave Marky his stiffy. The original photo used for the "nudie" shot of Marky isn't even a rare one. It's one right out of Lynn Goldsmith's book, one of several in which the rapper's pants are riding so low that his hip bones can be seen. It's easier to manipulate a photo in which almost all of your work is done for you. The guy erased the seam of Marky's pants at the bottom of the picture and transplanted a porn model's boner. No balls, because they would hang below the existing frame and the faker would have to use a different photo and be forced to mess with even more denim.

Today, celebrity fakes on the Internet are in known overabundance. Everybody with a home computer can afford the software to do fakes of their own, though there's certainly a skill level required. Some of the Internet fakes look so phony that they're hilarious. Oversized and mismatched heads, discolored neck and hip lines where the meld from star photo to porn body took place, and the age-old movie-making problem of continuity, with as many dicks and dick sizes and body shapes as there are nude models. It's the only way that I found out, for instance, that Freddie Prinze, Jr. is both circumcised and uncircumcised. As if that weren't enough, and it never seems to be when it comes to sexual material, now people are taking photos of already well-endowed porn stars and photographically elongating and fattening their weenies to ridiculous proportions. This may be the only way that the rooftop frontal of Leonardo DiCaprio in *Total Eclipse* can be duly compensated.

In the mid-1990s, celebrity fakes were new enough of a phenomenon to extract elaborate and bizarre justifications to serve the delusion. No one seemed to be asking why a celebrity such as Matt Dillon or Keanu Reeves or Tom Cruise would possibly allow themselves to be photographed with their pricks hanging out, let alone up and ready for action. Each photo came with "secret, underground" knowledge of its veracity: a gay porn shoot early in their careers before they were famous, or snapshots circulated among the rich and famous when the actor was hustling for his first job. We were told they were private photos never intended for release. Well, duh. But gay men should have certainly known better. We'd been looking at naked guys in magazines long enough to recognize the bodies and appendages of some of our favorites transplanted below the necks of stars; or vice versa, since many of us owned or had seen the original photo of the celebrity before it had been altered. So maybe we did know better. Maybe we just didn't care.

After the initial rounds of idiotic debate over whether this preposterous wealth of nude celebrity photos was real, when the fakery was at last acknowledged, you'd think that the interest would have waned. But it didn't. There was such a desire for the material that we simply adapted our expectations to ensure the survival of the species. It's a curious evolution. Something we wanted desperately to be real remained valuable even after it was determined to be fake. Where else in the marketplace can you find such a phenomenon? By altering our mind-set, the celebrity fakes now properly served the fantasy they were catering to in the first place. Okay, so I know that this isn't really Josh Harnett nude, you told yourself, but I've always wanted to see him that way and so I'm able to enjoy looking at what he might look like without

295

his clothes on in this picture. The photo fiddlers are getting better and better at it, too. Seamless creations are out there and they can be a lot of fun to clip and trade amongst friends.

Still, nothing beats the real thing like the real thing being beat. Search the annals of male celebritydom and you'll find a few legitimate treasures along the way. Actors are not always proud of the decisions they made when they were first starting out and trying to get ahead.

At age 19, **Simon Rex** (1974-) answered a modeling ad in a Los Angeles magazine and agreed to be photographed nude, as well as masturbate for the video camera, on three separate occasions in 1993 for photographer Brad Posey and his Club 1821, which catered pictorials of hot young guys to a gay clientele. Billed as "Sebastian," his modeling sessions put him on the covers of the video releases *Young, Hard & Solo #2*, *Young, Hard & Solo #3*, and *Hot Sessions #3* in 1996. (In 2001, some additional footage was parceled and released on both *Hot Sessions #11* and *Hot Sessions #12*.)

Between the time he had shot them and their commercial debut, the strikingly beautiful young man began appearing in mainstream modeling gigs for Calvin Klein and Tommy Hilfiger. He was also "Pretty in Pink" in a five-page spread in *Out* magazine. In 1995, when MTV needed a model for a silly stunt on one of their programs, their original choice was unavailable, so Simon Rex was sent over. While he had to remove an article of clothing each time a caller correctly answered a trivia question, his natural charm and warm personality managed to register through the gag.

He became a bona fide MTV VJ in 1995—one of the few reasons I tuned in anymore—and was looking at a role on a television series produced by Disney when the story broke about his participation in the gay porn videos. Only it wasn't gay porn per se, because all of his scenes were solo acts. But it had the stigma of gay porn, incredibly showed up as a news item in *Newsweek* magazine, and Disney decided not to use him for the show they were developing.

His life at MTV wasn't long-lived, either, though they were supportive of him during his embarrassment, and went on record saying they didn't care one bit. An avowed heterosexual who grew up in San Francisco with a mom and an absent father, Rex has since done quite a bit more modeling and TV work, including a regular stint on the short-lived WB drama *Jack & Jill* (1999), as the young artist who deflowers the title character on the WB's popular *Felicity* (1999-2002), and most recently on *What I Like About You* (2002-).

Watching his nudie video sessions, you might even flatter yourself into guessing that he had the makings of a real career. He's funny, quite natural, good-natured, able to playfully improvise some porn-style dialogue while fooling with a cell phone, and he's non-judgmentally cooperative despite being straight. He even inquires about doing a sex scene with a young lady for the camera sometime and quite properly asks how much more money he can get for ejaculating.

The *Young, Hard & Solo* footage is comprised of stripping off his clothes while watching a porn film on TV and stroking himself. He humps the carpet for a bit and then flips over onto his back for the money shot. The *Hot Sessions* footage is a video record of his nude posing sessions while photographer Brad Posey shoots still photos for sale to gay skin magazines. These documentary looks at several of Posey's models sometimes contain remarkable moments of stripe and candor given the unusual circumstances, such as the one model who refuses to allow Posey to videotape his orgasm because it's something private.

You get a great deal of personality and character coming through while watching Simon Rex in his sessions, but perhaps his most telling moment comes while Posey steps out of the room to get Rex some paper towels for clean up in *Hot Sessions #11*. The naked young man decides to address the lonely camera still recording him. "I hate to do this kind of thing, but I got to pay the rent, and I hope this doesn't come back to haunt me one day when I'm a famous movie star," he says. "But this is what you got to do sometimes to pay the bills, man. I'm in debt. I'll jerk off for, y'know, some money. Fuck it, I don't care. Y'know? So long as nobody touches me, I'm okay."

The hands-off policy was admirable and honest in a hands-on industry. If the 1980s had seen the rise of the male model as blatant sex object, the 1990s saw the legitimate birth of the male supermodel. And everybody wanted a feel.

Marcus Lodewijk Schenkenberg Van Mierop (1968-) was the first male model to achieve the equivalent of female supermodel status in a cutthroat business that has been dominated by women in terms of both exposure and pay. It's a field where women clearly trump men. Like many an AMG model of old, the 18-year-old Schenkenberg was discovered roller-skating along Venice Beach when a photographer stopped him, showed him a series of photos he had already shot of the kid unawares, and told him he had the makings of a model. He signed with an agency and started getting work immediately, which surprised everybody back home in Sweden because he didn't seem to have a plan when he up and left for dreamland USA less than a year before.

The long and lean Schenkenberg's shot to fame was fired with provocative images in a 116-page Calvin Klein advertising supplement sent subscribers of *Vanity Fair* magazine in 1991. It was an instantaneous collector's edition. That's right, a book-length ad was the thing every gay man suddenly had to have. Shot by Bruce Weber, the advert was presented as a travelogue of "candids" while following a young rock and roll band on tour. Though there are both men and women in the group, the photos of Marcus and another beautiful boy band member produced homoerotic heat.

For all the juice those photos generated, and there are plenty more of Marcus without his shirt on (practicing guitar in a towel, for instance), the shots that would be heard around the world have Marcus solo under the pulsating blast of the showerhead. Perhaps to save money on the road, he has taken his pair of CK jeans into the shower with him, but he's not wearing them. He's holding them by the button-fly in front of his privates. The coverage is so miniscule, the skin so exposed, that you know he's been shorn of his pubic hair in order to get away with it. The exposure was seemingly as daring as you could possibly be without "going all the way," though it was the kind of daring that forced you to think about how it was shot. There's no way you could look at that beautiful man in the shower and not contemplate how they'd orchestrated down to the millimeter how to hide his cock.

At nearly 6' 3" and 188 pounds, Schenkenberg's sculpted body is instantly recognizable in a world in which six-pack abs and well-defined pecs became prerequisites for male modeling work. His agency's forceful and savvy decision to bill their model by name after the Calvin Klein ad sensation was met with resistance from an industry that figured nobody cared about such things when it came to the guys. They did, or came to. And Marcus Schenkenberg became the first male model known all over the

Microcosm of the 1990s male sex star: nude model turned professional model turned TV personality turned film and television actor Simon Rex, seen here back in his jack-for-cash video days. PHOTO BY BRAD POSEY, WWW.CLUB1821.COM

globe by name, as well as the first male model to break the six-figure mark for his work. The male model as celebrity.

His phenomenal success reinforced an at first peculiar notion in the mid-1980s that male modeling could be a respectable line of work for anybody who had the right stuff and was willing to work hard in an increasingly competitive industry. In the 1990s, male modeling attracted men of all walks of life and sexual persuasion who were vying for that one lucky break to be shot by the right photographer at the right time or wear the right fashion designer's clothes at the right runway show to propel them into a lifestyle of the rich and famous.

Guys who figured that all male models were homosexual—or more threatening, were perceived as such—suddenly wanted in on the option to exploit their physical beauty for cash and fame. True stories like male supermodel Joel West's, in which he was discovered while on a church outing to the Mall of America in Minneapolis as he was getting some Dairy Queen with his girlfriend, opened up the unreal possibilities of a life in high fashion to a tangible reality. The gyms were filling up with young guys keeping in shape or getting there, part of a cultural response to the "New Man" both in advertising and the movies that brought with it a willingness and readiness to be rewarded for the way they looked. The "new body" was a status symbol as important as the latest sports car. Marky Mark Wahlberg was an inspiration to these model wannabes, whether they would admit it or not, because he was a blue-collar kid whose physique became high fashion. Suddenly, the finest in menswear had become the tailored shape of a body without clothes...or damn few of them. The male body, properly conditioned and formed, was the outerwear of choice. Skin was in. [The workout gym physicality and attendant cult mentality is viciously lampooned by Christian Bale's glorious physique—and his own obsession with viewing it, even during sex—in *American Psycho* (2000).]

The old underwear ads of the *Sears & Roebuck Catalog* days were replaced by full color gigs in *International Male* and *Undergear*, where for several years there was no airbrushing the bulges into a unisex bubble. So now you not only had to have a handsome face, a superbly cut body, and well-shaped buns, but even when you dropped your drawers to model that jock, thong, or brief, you had to properly fill it. Catalog work didn't provide much of a chance to make the big bucks, but it was a start for several who went on to bigger things.

The real money and career potential was as a fashion model for big name designers, thence splashy, attention-grabbing advertising in the slick mainstream magazines. The agency that arguably brought more gorgeous young men into the realm of supermodel possibility than all others was the agency that created the phenomenon. Boss Models was founded in 1988, and in the 1990s became a veritable who's who of the male model as rising star and superstar, handling Marcus Schenkenberg, Simon Rex, and a pair of blonds known as The Brewer Twins, among a stable of classic beauties.

Derek and Keith Brewer (1973-   ), identical twins from Southern California, possess the kind of blonder-than-blond beauty that stereotypes dumb surfer boys even if they're honor students, in better shape than you can ever hope to be, and worship more than the waves. But they are authentic surfer boys, who grew up around Redondo Beach and took to the water like ducks. At 18, they signed with a small modeling agency and were quickly put to work. Their first pro job cover was on *Italian Glamour* in 1992, both seated wearing skintight sheer tops and each with a hand nestled inside their alligator print bikini briefs. Oh, and there's a young lady between them. I think.

They were butt-naked buttresses for Cindy Crawford in a Herb Ritts shoot for *Rolling Stone* and singly and in unison burned holes in the covers and pages of magazines all over the world. But it was a telltale and controversial shoot for Bruce Weber that was to earn them immortality.

Published in 1992 in the first issue of the oversized annual-only magazine *Joe*, which sold for $45 before it even had the chance to become sought as a collector's item, was a series of black-and-white photographs of Derek and Keith that have achieved legendary status among collectors of male homoerotic photography. Progressing like a series of frames from an unreleased film many a gay man would consider selling out to heterosexuality to see just once, the boys are posed playfully undressing one another in the 10-page spread entitled "The Last Days of Summer." Already shirtless, each goes for the other's pants, undoing them and pulling them down. Once butt-naked, one of the twins picks up his brother and puts him over his shoulder. They are thereafter shown holding each other tenderly, intimately, even posed in what looks to be an imminent kiss. In another shot, they are on the ground, one on top of the other, legs intertwined and arms locked in an embrace. A profile full nude shows the brothers again in near embrace while a final indoor shot has them lounging together in bed, both naked, one on top of the other in sweet repose, fingers forked in the other's hair, an arm wrapped around a twin's nude torso, a thumb on the other's nipple, and an elbow resting against a brother's penis.

They are lovely, lovely pictures. Too profoundly beautiful and erotically complex to merit moral debate here, but just the kind of acutely provocative imagery to alarm a pair of admittedly naive, yet presumptively heterosexual and non-incestuous twin brothers. I don't know how Weber got them to pose the way he got them to pose, nor if they had any idea he was going to ask them to do such things when they signed for the shoot. They claimed through their agent that they did not, and Weber was quoted at the time as saying, "in no way did they have a sexual attraction, but they were not afraid to touch each other."

I do know that the twins have been understandably skittish about the session ever since it put them on the map and have not always successfully dealt with the intense affections and expectations of the gay community, igniting just one of many sparks that conjoined for pointless argument among gay periodicals offended by what became called "gay for pay," or the exploitation of gay male currency by straight men willing to cater to gay desires for cash—something we've already hashed out in regard to Keanu Reeves and Marky Mark. If you need a reminder of my take on the subject, I'm thankful for male beauty in whatever guise (or guys) it comes: hetero, homo, or bi. Most often paired with hot young babes, as the industry demands, the Brewers have also not completely lost their cool about appearing nude together or holding hands or staring into each other's eyes whenever the photographer or campaign calls for it.

Full-frontal male nudity in advertising has always been taboo in the West, though in Europe it's rather commonplace comparatively speaking. One way to pin a dick on a model who was wearing more than his undies was to cinch up the trousers again the way they did in the 1970s, only tighter. Designer Donna Karan's 1997 runway show was entitled "The Anatomy of Man," as all the big designers were going for the kind of tight that not only showed which side you dressed, but how you arranged it. "Trousers now have all the mystery of Lycra bike shorts," commented *Newsweek* magazine.

The tighter-than-tight look didn't really stick the way Lycra did, but often the world of fashion is about the fantasy of clothes, usually for certain people, not the strict reality of the times. When Gucci ran an ad in the August, 2000 issue of *Vanity Fair*, among several mags, in which the male model's trouser snake was prominently defined in its khaki nesting place, the image was considered bold in a culture conversely obsessed with sex and hooked on a depressing and dehumanizing trend of so-called "reality" TV shows and shock video programming.

The reality of beautiful male models having something between their legs was never more evident than in the underwear ads of the 1990s. Even Marky Mark wore a pair of support running shorts under his Calvin Kleins to avoid the "offending" delineation of the penile coronal ridge, but the series of starkly beautiful ads featuring model/actor **Michael Bergin** (1969-   ) gave unmistakable weight, girth, and distribution to the front of his white jockeys.

Susan Bordo, writing in *The Male Body: A New Look at Men in Public and in Private* (Farrar, Straus and Giroux; 1999), had the wind knocked out of her when she came across the Bergin CK ad in her 1995 *New York Times Magazine*. Startled by the fact that the model clearly "has a penis," she notes "it seems slightly erect, or perhaps that's his non-erect size; either way, there's a substantial presence there that's palpable (it looks so touchable, you want to cup your hand over it) and very, very male."

She's also taken by the feminization of the image, its docile willingness to invite the erotic gaze. "Feast on me," she writes of the attitude. "I'm here to be looked at, my body is for your eyes."

The progressive and potent sexuality of male underwear, already evident to generations of gay men and rife in their homoerotic photography and periodicals, continued to work its magic on "heterosexual" fronts. A 1990s fashion trend exhibited by teenagers whose bodies were otherwise hopelessly lost inside billowing pants four times larger than they were was to pull the seams of their designer underwear up above the seams of their pants, brandishing their name-brand skivvies and calling attention to their sexuality.

Boy bands caught on to the power of their undies almost as fast as the girls and gay boys who swooned over them. In the 1996 British documentary *A Band is Born*, a quintet of boys chosen specifically for their looks is fashioned into a boy band as one of many such speculative investments from very often gay producers. Though an earlier photo shoot demands only teases from the boys instead of shirtless flaunts, when it comes time to make their first music video, there's a scene in which each must luxuriate in front of a fireplace in their undies.

One of the boys is quite nervous about doing the scene. He tells the interviewer that he feels "vulnerable" and that lying on a rug in just his underpants is "really embarrassing."

 "Why is it so difficult?"

The young man seems momentarily incredulous that the question needs to be asked. Then, "'Cause I'm in my...when you're in your underwear, you know. You don't like people seeing you in your underwear. I mean, it's sexy and all that, but I mean...it will look good in the video I reckon, but, you know, it's just nervous now."

The question is, does he know it's sexy or did someone or some prevailing advertising sensibility tell him it's sexy?

The 1990s were chock-full of openly eroticized men in advertising, film, and television. Beautiful boys were skinny-dipping, getting de-pantsed, slipping back on their undies, horsing around with one another, streaking down Main Street, singing naked on MTV (with blur boxes in place), mooning across magazine pages, enticingly dozing, splayed and unaware, and having their chests felt up by admiring women.

The pretty boys of Bob Mizer's Athletic Model Guild were now the pretty boys of national media. When age-old, but retrofitted Abercrombie & Fitch published its Christmas of 1999 *A&F Quarterly*, a 296-page catalog entitled "Naughty or Nice," it included a wealth of sexualized imagery of young models by (who else?) photographer Bruce Weber. Some people found the photos shockingly inappropriate for the targeted audience. A&F responded by issuing a statement that those who bought the catalog would have to be 18 or older, but most of the 375,000 copies had already been sent out and many were in the hands of teenagers. Future naughty editions, such as their 2001 "Back to School" romp, required a flash of ID and an 18-and-over purchasing policy.

Writing about "Beefcake for the Masses" in the November 14, 1999 edition of *The New York Times Magazine*, Herbert Muchamp discussed the unreality of the "Cult of the Beautiful Boy" and likened them to *kouroi*, the divine sculptures of adolescent boys found in Ancient Greece. "A recent Abercrombie & Fitch catalog carries an editor's note: 'Due to mature content, parental consent suggested for readers under 18.' Actually, it is readers over 18 who should be warned; these pictures could be fatal to your self-esteem."

Straight culture had finally caught up with gay culture of the 1940s.

The male model body archetype directly influenced gay porn as well. Or was it vice versa? There have been beautiful men in gay porn since the industry established itself as an entity in the early 1970s. Casey Donovan, Buster, Leo Ford, Johnny Harden, Todd Baron, Bobby Madison, Billy Gant, Mike Henson, Rob Montessa, Kurt Marshall, Joey Stefano, Ted Cox, Billy Houston, and Kevin Williams, to name a few. Then later, gay porn superstars Jeff Stryker and Ryan Idol. And Billy Brandt.

Since 1993, Slovakian-born filmmaker George Duroy, who studied his craft at UCLA, has almost single-handedly managed to transcend the painful attrition of gay porn in the last decade with a series of gay erotica classics. If he has his detractors, they can only sensibly be found among those gay men for whom Duroy's stable of gorgeous performers are simply not their types. You want beef, you want brawn, you want leather, you want handlebar mustaches, you want vast plains of hairy-chestedness? Look elsewhere.

You want toned young men with gorgeous tanned physiques and pretty faces, boys next door, college guys, and cute farmhands? Look no further than the boys of Bel Ami, a staggering and seemingly endless supply of Eastern and Central European young men eager to have sex with each other in spite of a largely hetero preference in a culture with fewer avowals than our own to a specific identity or orientation.

Though he's been at it long enough now that the product is occasionally susceptible to some annoying habits of American porn (for instance, cutting to sex too quickly), Duroy is responsible for a consistent output of first-class erotica and a roster of multimedia star models unmatched in beauty. Models who also, by the way, have illuminated the cut-crazed American dick culture to the natural beauty and functionality of the foreskin. Bel Ami has brought gay adult films to a golden age. The studio understands the importance of play and fun, passion and sensuality. It has no rivals, only imitators.

Sweet brunette **Johan Paulik** (1975-) and lusty and precocious **Ion Davidov** (1974-) are particular favorites of Bel Ami's first generation of players, but—for my money—there has never been a more beautiful man willing to indulge us in acting out our sexual fantasies on screen than **Lukas Ridgeston** (1974-). He has all the magnetism, warmth, and personality of a beloved movie star, and he radiates heat, playfulness, and desire whether he's doing softcore, picture-postcard posing, or full-fledged hardcore action. I guess it's because he makes hardcore seem the entirely wrong word. Lukas makes love, has sex, seems to be enjoying himself and his partner so much that when he "shoots three feet over my head—the wall is the limit," or unexpectedly all over his partner's hair, or even into his own eye, it's not just another cum shot, it's the well-earned and devoutly-wished orgasm he deserves.

He's also the kind of movie star beauty that we've long-deserved in a porn star; it's as if this young god with his trillion dollar smile, perfect skin, positively hypnotic pale blue eyes, flawlessly formed body, eight beautiful inches of uncircumcised cock, and gloriously well-shaped ass was every underwear model and hot movie star we've ever fantasized about rolled into one. Guys who look this incredible aren't typically the guys you see with their tongue in another stud's butt. Only in our dreams.

300

Slovakian Lukas Ridgeston, arguably the sexiest man to do gay adult films while bringing to them legitimate warmth, playfulness, and charm. BEL AMI PHOTO & VIDEO, INC, WWW.BELAMIONLINE.COM

A porn star who looks like a beautiful movie star gives flesh and blood credence to a beautiful movie star that we always wished would have been a porn star. Rent or purchase *Tender Strangers* (1993), *Lukas' Story* (1994), *Lukas' Story 2* (1994), *Lukas' Story 3* (1995), *Out At Last* (1995), *Frisky Summer 2* (1996), *Lucky Lukas* (1998), *All About Bel Ami* (2001), *Cover Boys* (2001), or the remastered and re-edited (with new Lukas voiceovers) DVD editions of *Lukas' Stories* (2003) and *More Lukas' Stories* (2003) and you'll understand what I'm talking about.

This is why I can never quite believe it when a good-looking guy says he's straight...end of argument. To me, the only reasonable response is James Dean's comment about not going through life with both hands tied behind your back. That many of Duroy's boys identify themselves as "straight" only adds fuel to the fire, tapping into a vast well of fantasy involving the seduction of cute straight men and their initiation into the joys of same-sex sex. Males are intensely sexual creatures by nature, so the notion that hetero-identified men might engage in homo-sex while completely retaining their hetero-identification is an easy leap for me to make. Why limit yourself to just half the population?

If only Nature had seen fit to make the average human male's penis long enough to reach the owner's lips, we'd have an entirely different view on the subject, and a higher incidence of humped backs and broken necks. The distance between sucking your own dick and being receptive to sucking someone else's "under certain conditions" would assuredly be navigated more easily. The sad result is that fewer people would feel the need to go out and try to find someone else to do it with. Besides, then it wouldn't be such an extraordinary thing anymore. Nature played it just right, I suppose. Most guys can't do it on their own and those who can are kept in small enough numbers to make them special attractions.

What makes the Bel Ami boys so consistently enthralling is how natural, affectionate, lusty, passionate, and frolicsome their lovemaking appears on screen.

If part of gauging the complex concept of feeling love for another person means that you despair at their inability to obtain it even without you, then I love **James Duval** (1973-)...deeply. Not James Duval the actor, just the James Duval I know from a cataclysmic trilogy of low-budget films from writer/director Gregg Araki. *(A word of warning: If you haven't seen the Araki trilogy, skip this section until you have. I'll be discussing key plot elements and endings.)*

Duval was hanging out in a Los Angeles café where Araki was working on the script for his next film. The director noticed the dark-haired, dark-eyed beauty and asked him if he was an actor. He wasn't. Not officially anyway, but who wouldn't say "yeah" in L.A. when somebody handed them a script?

James Duval takes a break from his trio of haunted teen roles for director Gregg Araki to play with the big boys in *Independence Day* (1998). PHOTOFEST

    Totally F***ed Up (1993) is Araki's homage to Godard's *Masculin-Feminin* (1966), a docu-interrogatory in which the politics and attitudes of a group of localized teenagers are explored. With Godard, it was "the children of Marx and Coca-Cola." For Araki, it was the queer children of LA ("the alienation capital of the world") and Coca-Cola. One of the group is making a video documentary detailing his friends' thoughts on sex, drugs, shopping, politics, sex, rebellion, relationships, homophobia, sex, ennui, suicide, infidelity, and sex. It's done in 15 chapters, though the problem with using on-screen numbers is that even if you like what you're watching you're still part of a counterproductive countdown.

James Duval plays Andy, a gay teen who's not into anal sex, though the director inserts a graphic video example immediately after Andy voices his disgust. It's a clever way of disenfranchising the stereotype that all gay men have the same attitudes and desires when it comes to sex and particular sexual practices. It's also particularly pointed coming from teenagers growing up during the apocalypse of AIDS.

There are times when the one-liner rips and tears of the often pretentious dialogue have you wondering whether the fault lies with the script or with the characters themselves, but Araki knows what he's doing and some things hit you only after you think about how he's presented them. Andy says, "I think I'm bisexual. I mean, I've never actually dorked a girl or anything, but if it came down to it, I think I could. Like I've gotten a boner before making out with one. And I like them. They're soft and pretty and fun to touch. It's not like I'm afraid of them or anything."

The admission reverberates with connotation. Duval's Andy, with his long black hair and otherwise persistent cynicism, casually addresses the issue of his sexuality from a slyly reversed point of view. Usually a "confession" of bisexuality comes from an otherwise heterosexually-identified character who's fessing up to the possibility of going both ways. Even if he really is gay, the bisexual angle is most often employed to placate the shock associated with an admission that one is homo through and through. Andy is gay, but voices an almost self-reassuring potential for getting it on with a girl while reaffirming his quite natural attraction to boys.

Now if we could only get him to lighten up a bit. Andy is a brooder. He's a sour cynic who believes that love doesn't really exist, it's propaganda. He lays around a lot in his dark sunglasses, dragging on cigarettes. Thematically, he's the hero, the weary spokesperson in this wasteland of pop culture garbage. During a lively exchange between the guys about celebrities they masturbate to, and during which title cards proclaiming "Tom Cruise: Rock Hudson of the 90s" and "Mel Gibson: homophobe a-hole" are flashed, it's Andy who predictably trumps a usual suspect like Matt Dillon with an admission of Michael Stipe, the lead singer of REM.

Totally F***ed Up has a political agenda, but as with most all of Araki's films, it's challenging, conflicting, and hard to discern. A film that opens by showing a newspaper clipping reporting that 30% of teen suicides are committed by gay teens ends with a pointless suicide that has nothing to do with gay self-acceptance. Cynically, if not literally, this is the kind of film that might make kids think life *is* hopeless and they *should* kill themselves. It may not be that blatantly nihilistic, though Araki's work has been accused of worse, but it's self-defeating in a blunt way.

Andy's "poor little fuckin' heart got broken," but it's the filmmaker who killed him.

In a way, *Totally F***ed Up* is the calm before the storm. The storm was *The Doom Generation* (1995), nailed and hailed by one critic as Araki's version of Godard's *Week-end* (1967). Once again, there are anarchic similarities, but you can also throw in *A Clockwork Orange* (1971) and *Natural Born Killers* (1994) if you're determined to find corollaries.

James Duval plays Jordan White, a sweet young man whose loud, caustic girlfriend, Amy Blue (Rose McGowan), is bored in the middle of an intense light show and blaring club music. They could go have sex at the old drive-in, but Jordan is afraid of catching AIDS. Amy points out that they're both virgins. Deciding they might as well, when it comes right down to it, the act isn't quite successful. Jordan is having trouble and the car is cramped. "I feel like a gerbil smothering in Richard Gere's butthole," he says.

Enter Xavier Red (Johnathon Schaech), whom Jordan wants to call "X," but X will only allow it if he can call Jordan "nut licker." Jordan doesn't seem to mind. He's quite taken with this strikingly handsome and violent stranger in the backseat. Amy Blue, on the other hand, can't stand him. In a barrage of traded insults throughout the film, all guys are rectal (or have jism breath) while the gal is all tuna taco and the like.

At least the guys live up to their names. Both Jordan and X show their asses, get a finger pushed up their rectums, and, in the most "shocking" moment in a film filled with cartoonish violence and brutality, X licks up the load of cum he's shot onto his hand after whacking off outside the bathroom where Jordan and Amy are getting it on in the tub.

Araki has created a warped world unto itself where every purchase made comes to $6.66, a severed head talks, a woman slaughters her whole family, a wigged Parker Posey pulls a sword on Jordan in a pool hall to "lop his dick off like a chicken head," characters are routinely steeped in blood, and practically everyone who meets Amy Blue mistakes her for a long-lost and betraying lover in need of payback.

The Doom Generation is a carnival freak show road movie loaded with hit-you-over-the-head symbolism and color schemes. Araki shoots his actors in extreme close-ups, cramming their faces into the frame and forcing them to be in almost constant skin contact. The sexual atmosphere is thick and heavy. Actually, it's pungent.

"Ever feel like reality is more twisted than dreams?" asks Jordan. He's the only one of the trio that seems desperately out of place in this hellhole. He's sweet and honest and forgiving of others, and he has the biggest, brownest eyes this side of a fawn. With only one exception, he's also always on the bottom when he's having sex. He's passive submissive, I guess. In a moment to parallel X's masturbatory peeping session, when Jordan comes back from the store and sees his girlfriend and X going at it through the motel window, he unzips and jacks off from outside, his store-bought yo-yo dangling in front of him so he doesn't lose it.

Jordan White is not ready for the universe of horrors Araki has created for him. Amidst all the gory violence and chaos, Amy believes "life is lonely, boring, and dumb." The first and only emotional breakdown she suffers is when she hits a dog on the highway. X puts it out of its misery.

X is, of course, the unknown quotient, a confessed killer with loads of sex appeal and some kinky ideas about fucking. When he asks quite matter-of-factly whether either of his two road trip partners have had sex with animals, Amy is disgusted. Jordan, always wide-eyed and wanting to participate in the conversation, offers: "I fucked a cantaloupe once."

Jordan is too pure to be long for this world and we somehow instinctively know it, but do everything in our power to deny it. Araki likes to film his actors with their heads upside down on the screen while they're lying down or lounging. It's in this orientation that X first insinuates his skin onto Jordan and Jordan ends up noticing X's elaborate heart tattoo on his upper left chest. The guys share belches in the same air space during the film, a form of odd intimacy, to say the least, but there's a thick sexual tension hanging in there between them. We know that X is interested in getting together with Jordan, but Jordan isn't the kind of guy who takes the initiative.

It's part of Araki's insidious design to have all hell literally break loose at the moment of agonizing expectation—both guys naked together and both aroused—and research reveals that a kiss between the boys was filmed, but cut. Killing Jordan White is Araki's way of killing the puppy. The swastika-wearing freaks who unleash the monstrous violence at the end might be dismissed as part of the director's reputed nihilism, but they finally remind us that people are capable of committing shocking acts of barbarism on one another for little or no reason, let alone homophobia. The climax is a wake-up call in a film and culture otherwise splattered with comic mutilation and an increasingly immune reaction to death and murder.

Poor Jordan. He's the one character in this ugly world who asked, "Do you ever wonder why we exist?" Amy Blue, preoccupied with getting humped and surprising him with a wet finger up his butt, irritably answers, "No. What for?"

"No reason."

Gregg Araki wrote the role of Jordan White expressly for James Duval. He did the same with the role of Dark Smith in *Nowhere* (1997), the third in his teen trilogy. "LA is like nowhere," says Duval's recognizable and airy voice-over. "Everybody who lives here is lost."

The very first shot of Dark has him masturbating in the shower to an assortment of weird and/or threatening mental images. His green-faced mom wants him to stop pulling his pud and open the bathroom door. He drapes himself in the American flag to let her in.

Dark is making a video documentary for school and finds the pretty boy Montgomery (Nathan Bexton) in his viewfinder. He tells Montgomery, the boy with one green eye and one blue, that he has a "prenomination" that he's going to die soon. He means himself.

Drugs, bad TV, doomsday anxiety, bulimia, aliens, spanking and chocolate fetishes, televangelism, suicide, murder, puking, pissing, belching, interracial relationships, Valley mentality, and a *Baywatch* TV actor with the shocking courage to play himself as a celebrity who beats and rapes a teenage fan are just a few of Araki's favorite things. *Nowhere* is a rich concoction of color, fatalism, and the stultifying ennui of plastic people.

Dark has a black girlfriend, but she sleeps with many other boys and girls, and he's having trouble dealing with that. "Sometimes I feel so old-fashioned," he says. At a party, his girl is whisked away by the blinding blond, white, and bronze Brewer Twins, who talk in unison and go by the names Surf and Ski.

"I'm only 18 years old and I'm totally doomed," Dark tells his own video camera. All he wants is one person to love, and to love him back. One person to hold him in his arms and tell him everything is going to be okay. Not being gay ends up not being an obstacle when he thinks he might get his wish at last. But we know better…and I don't think I can stand much more of this kind of abuse. Once again, Duval is cast as the innocent—this time an optimist who wants to fall in love, but will unfailingly be denied as the star player in Araki's relentlessly pessimistic worldview. In its own way, it's an interesting methodology, as the director sets up the same actor time and time and time again and never lets him off the hook. The cumulative effect is an aching sense of sexual frustration. A bad case of blue balls.

James Duval needs to fall in love with a nice guy, or girl. Just once.

Though I wish him every bit of success, somehow he doesn't seem to belong in studio motion pictures, such as *Independence Day* (1998) and *Gone in Sixty Seconds* (2000). The fact that he was waiting tables in a restaurant when *Independence Day* director Roland Emmerich recognized him as the kid from *Totally F***ed Up* and offered him the part of Randy Quaid's oldest boy in the mega-blockbuster is the only reason that I'm okay with it. *Go* (1999) director Doug Liman and *SLC Punk* (1999) director James Merendino barely make use of him, though *Go* is in every other way an extremely fun and wild little movie. As a juvenile delinquent make-up artist terrorized by a killer clown while trapped in an old theatre in *A Clown at Midnight*, he's also an actor trapped in a 1981 teen slasher movie made in 1998. He's a hemophiliac half-Cherokee in *The Doe Boy* (2001), has a key cameo in the coming-of-age head-trip *Donnie Darko* (2001), and manages less than five minutes as a street punk with weird hair who takes a fateful trip to the fridge to get ice for his nipples in the horror flick *May* (2002).

Two gay-themed film appearances sitting on the shelf for years finally showed up thanks to DVD. He's one half of a young couple in crisis in *The Weekend* (1999), with Gena Rowlands and Brooke Shields, and he's a Santa Monica Blvd. hustler sought out by a lawyer dying of AIDS—Richard Chamberlain doing a Peter O'Toole imitation while dressed to evoke Dirk Bogarde's Aschenbach—in *River Made to Drown In* (1999).

Even in the video age, it's fitting that much of Duval's work is incredibly difficult to track down or frustratingly unavailable: *Mod Fuck Explosion* (1994), *How to Make the Cruelest Month* (1998), *Stamp and Deliver* (1998), *Alexandria Hotel* (1998), *The Tag* (2001), and *Amerikana* (2001). You should have to work hard to find him, I think. You should have to belong to a member of a cult to divine him. Bootleg tapes. Unfinished films. Stuff nobody's ever heard of with titles that nobody in their right mind would ever finance. That's Jimmy Duval to me. Not James Duval the actor, of course, just that guy from those three Gregg Araki movies.

It takes a courageous actor to accept a role for which he's asked to lap up his own ejaculate. That, or a gay porn star. The man who put the X in Xavier Red in *The Doom Generation* (1995), and agreed to consume the lifelike concoction off his hand, is **Johnathon Schaech** ("shek;" 1969-   ).

He was studying theatre at the University of Maryland when he met a fella with ties to the famed Chippendales in Los Angeles who suggested he had what it took to be one of their exotic dancers. Chippendales flew him to Hollywood for the butt-shaking audition. He definitely had the face and the body for the gig, but some of the dancers advised him to make a serious effort to act if acting is what he really wanted to do, not dance his way into a career and risk always being labeled the male bimbo and ex-stripper.

He found modeling jobs for which he proved painfully photogenic, but he also had his share of film rejections for being "too pretty." His movie debut came in *The Webbers* (1993), in which Jennifer Tilly thinks he's the perfect man and tries to plaster of paris his face while having sex with him so she can capture his expression at the moment of orgasm.

Next came a lover boy role in Franco Zeffirelli's period piece *Sparrow* (1993), which included a fleeting full-frontal, and then the role of Frank Thompson during the 1994 season of television's *Models, Inc.* American movie audiences were memorably introduced to his amazing physique and too-gorgeous face 24 minutes into *How to Make an American Quilt* (1995). He's a man of amazing parts. We're given his back first, then his front, and finally his face while he waits behind Winona Ryder at the pool concession stand. He's stunning in his bare self from the waist up, shaking his dripping wet hair like a dog, smiling, and habitually running one hand through his coal black locks, allowing for a classic composition of bicep and armpit, like a model posing for a shoot. It's only two minutes of screen time, but it's certainly ample to know we want to see more of this guy. A lot more of this guy.

He returns to woo Winona with a box of freshly picked strawberries, and she awkwardly bites into one as he tries to feed her. Unfortunately, his role amounts to little more than a temptation. There's not really a character there—just a look, even though I'll take all I can get. The problem is he's never around sufficiently during his seven appearances in the film to get enough of him.

When you see a Johnathon Schaech step dripping out of the pool in *Quilt*, if you're like me, you pray to see him take on a queer role. *The Doom Generation* was a gay boy's prayers answered. The fact that he chose to do something like Araki's low-budget road flick while he was still trying to get noticed by the big boys is proof of his willingness to take chances and a conscious decision to demonstrate his versatility and avoid the pitfalls of stereotyping.

Schaech's X is a perfect fit. "Touch it. Go ahead, indulge," he says to his latest sex partner, but the line might as well be spoken to the rest of us. It's a bold, energetic, sexy, and completely realized performance. "You're like a life support system for a fucking cock," Amy Blue tells him. He is.

One of the many reasons I like *The Doom Generation* so much is that the three leads are being played by essentially unknown actors who transcend the idea of performances almost as well as the family in *The Texas Chainsaw Massacre* (1974). They're original, unpredictable, and intriguing. I wanted to know everything I could about them.

The undercurrent of homosexual desire that runs through all of the scenes between Xavier Red and Jordan White makes your palms sweat with antici—pation. X is achingly irresistible, even if he is a killer. His hairy belly button drives me wild. And he's bold, adventurous, and totally uninhibited. He asks Amy to describe Jordan's prick to him in size, shape, cut/uncut, and bend, but she's too self-centered to figure out why he wants to know and so she doesn't answer. Instead, he tells her to "stick your finger up my asshole."

Araki would cast Schaech again in *Splendor* (1999), a nod to the Hollywood screwball comedies the director names as his favorites. Sort of an updated *Design for Living* (1933), it far too conventionally relates the story of a beautiful woman who falls in love with two beautiful men and decides to try keeping them both. This is Araki's true heterosexual film, as opposed to *Doom Generation*'s erroneous "A Heterosexual Movie" subtitle, because it's boring. The boys, Schaech and the lovely blond **Matt Keeslar** (1972-   ), make a gorgeous set of bookends, though.

Outside of a fun shower and clean-up scene late in the film, a game of Truth or Dare provides the sole erotic highlight. Schaech and Keeslar aren't the best of buddies yet, so the game is meant to bring them together. When alternately dared to kiss one another, the second time "full on," it's hot stuff, and only points out the numerous missed opportunities thereafter.

Most audiences probably recognize Johnathon as the temperamental lead singer for the one-hit Oneders in Tom Hanks' charming comedy *that thing you do!* (1996). He was also Jessica Lange's momma's boy in the florid melodrama *Hush* (1998), who brings out the worst in her when he introduces pregnant girlfriend Gwyneth Paltrow.

He spends a fair amount of time shirtless and in his D&G undies as captive in an Outback community of inbred and asbestos-poisoned geeks in *Welcome to Woop Woop* (1997). The follow-up film from the director of *The Adventures of Priscilla, Queen of the Desert* (1994), it's an oddball comic delight with a barely recognizable Rod Taylor as foul-mouthed patriarch, a gigantic legendary (kanga)roo, and scenes scored to songs and melodies from old Hollywood musicals, including *The Sound of Music*, *South Pacific*, and *The King and I*.

He made a serious effort at playing Harry Houdini in the cable-made *Houdini* (1998), which allowed quite a bit of skin exposure, then found himself as a struggling writer who pretends to be gay in order to shack up with a beautiful woman looking for a roommate in *If You Only Knew* (2000). It plays like a pilot for a bad TV show and then gets worse, but it could have worked had it just decided to be sweeter, even mushier. If only the movie captured the spirit of the cute and funny outtakes at the film's very end, it would have been a whole lot of fun.

I confess, though, that I love watching ostensibly straight and inarguably gorgeous men play gay. Josh Brolin was charming as all hell offering the afflicted couple of Ben Stiller and Patricia Arquette advice about oral sex (humming) and circumcision ("Personally, I think a son's dick should look like his father's") in *Flirting with Disaster* (1996), for instance. The only thing that would have improved the famous scene in which Josh licks Patricia's armpit (outside of her returning the favor) is if they had used the earlier take before the actress opted to shave it.

Someone should have licked Johnathon Schaech's armpits. Xavier Red would have done it.

Johnathon Schaech, fresh out of the pool, in *How to Make An American Quilt* (1995). PHOTOFEST

When Dickie Greenleaf catches Tom Ripley looking at his naked bum in *The Talented Mr. Ripley* (1999), he flicks his towel at Tom and Tom gets away with a smile. Dickie certainly has his suspicions about this nerdy young man who has infiltrated his life in Italy at the behest of his father, but he's not yet fully worked out the queer details. The snap of the towel is locker room vernacular to defuse the situation. To Tom, it's a tacit endorsement.

Jude Law (1972-   ), who plays Dickie, has had his ass ogled before. It comes with the territory when you're an actor who looks like a Jude Law, yet it's awfully nice when it comes attached to someone with as much talent as he has looks.

The best piece of ass in Savannah. Jude Law in *Midnight in the Garden of Good and Evil* (1997). PHOTOFEST

Raised in a middle class family in Southeast London by parents who were school teachers, Jude found his own schooling difficult, often getting picked on for his pretty-boy features by boys who called him a poof. Aware that he was in love with the theatre from a very young age, he auditioned for the National Youth Music Theatre at age 13 and was immediately accepted into the girls' dormitory. I guess you could blame it on his face.

Properly gendered, he continued at the school until age 17, playing numerous roles, including the lead in *Joseph and the Amazing Technicolor Dreamcoat*, when he successfully landed a part on the daytime soap opera *Families*. He decided that, in spite of the often lousy material, doing was much more valuable a teacher than classroom instruction, so he dropped out of school to pursue acting full time.

He's a bright-eyed stable boy who wants to be a jockey and gets dramatically unveiled as the plot thickens in the "Shoscombe Old Place" episode of Granada Television's classic *The Casebook of Sherlock Holmes* (1990), starring Jeremy Brett.

His feature film debut was a lead role in *Shopping* (1994), a flashy juvenile delinquent flick about a hot-rodding thief and his slightly more with-it gal pal. It's a movie where the bad boy's cuteness is the reason you're supposed to be on his side even if he's clearly a jerk that ought to be incarcerated and made someone's bitch. Jude's baby face is matched by his baby-smooth (shaved) chest and torso. His Billy is still a 10-year old brat, pulling off MTV-chic crimes by crashing through store windows in stolen cars just to nab a pair of shades, or strolling through a high-end mall with an umbrella because the sprinklers have been set off.

Billy's asexual girlfriend suggests that Billy and his chief rival Tommy (note the little kids' names) just see who has the biggest dick and get over all this childish bullshit. Billy won't give in that easily. He needs his bum paddled good and hard, and I found myself rooting for the cops.

Law says that the film he hoped to make wasn't the film that ended up on the big screen, but at least it provided the time and place for him to meet his future wife and mother of his children, Sadie Frost (her Lucy was one of the few good things about *Bram Stoker's Dracula*), who plays Billy's partner, Jo. (By the way, the tattoo on Jude's right arm is a butterfly fashioned out of his initials. The tattoo on his left arm is a Beatles' lyric—"You came along to turn everyone on, Sexy Sadie"—for his wife, though at the time of this writing divorce was imminent.)

With the disappointment of *Shopping* came the satisfaction of stage work. His role as the incestuous son in the Royal National Theatre's 1994 revival of Jean Cocteau's *Les Parents Terrible* earned him an Olivier Award nomination. The play opened across the pond on Broadway in 1995 as the retitled *Indiscretions*, with Jude in tow and Kathleen Turner as his mum, and his performance here won a Theater World Award and a Tony nomination.

"A lot of people made a big thing about this nude scene that I did," he told *W* magazine in September of 1997 of the famed second act business requiring him to climb out of the bathtub and dry himself on stage.

"He didn't get out of the bath, give you a quick flash, and then turn upstage," recalled director Sean Mathias for *Vanity Fair* in December of 2000. "He did it for real, just dried himself as if he were in his own bathroom at home, so you got to see plenty of him."

On screen, Jude next appeared as an American boy blondie, president of the senior class, captain of the lacrosse team, and the object of Claire Danes' poetic infatuation in *I Love You, I Love You Not* (1996). Fellow schoolmate James Van Der Beek reminds Jude that "every girl on that field wants your jock," but we know that Claire is the only one who could truly appreciate his long lashes and "dreamy accent." The accent is a hybrid; we're told Ethan (Jude's character) is an American boy who was raised in England. Other than a disconcerting spike of melodrama late in the short film, it's an otherwise thoughtful and sweet romance, with a beautiful performance by Jeanne Moreau as Claire's nana.

The movies finally caught up to what Jude Law had to offer when he was brilliantly cast to play Lord Alfred Douglas in *Wilde* (1997), the more or less true story of the love/hate/love/hate relationship between Oscar Wilde and his "Bosie." Stephen Fry, in the role he was born to play, is the famed wit and playwright who replaces the lovely Ioan Gruffud for the bow-tied Jude Law during the reception for *Lady Windermere's Fan*. Bosie, in the guise of Jude, sings the loveliest rendition of "He Loves Me" directly to Oscar during a college sitting room recital. The song alone would be enough to melt a grown man's heart, but Bosie knows precisely how to use the power of a glance. His beautiful, penetrating eyes have an impeccable sense of timing.

Those gorgeous blue-green eyes are also always brimming with the cruelty that lies just behind them. Bosie represents the wickedness of beauty; he's Wilde's flesh-and-blood Dorian Gray, particularly fetching in a straw hat. They engage in interfemoral sex (Bosie fucks Oscar in the crease between his legs, not up the fundament), and afterwards, all Oscar can do is glow at the vision of his spent young lover sleeping entwined in the sheets.

Bosie was a spoiled rotten little lord crybaby, in the event you were unaware, and his cruel and vicious tantrums were acts of selfish determination and ferocious breeding. The young man who penned an ode to "The Love That Dare Not Speak Its Name," and who enjoyed shocking London society as Oscar's boy, was also in open rebellion against his even more cruel and heartless father, the Marquess of Queensbury, and implicated Wilde's allegiance in a court battle to clear the charge of "somdomite" (sic). Unlike in the film version, the real Bosie tried to persuade Oscar to leave the country before the first trial because he feared the worst for him.

Wilde is a beautifully crafted and exceptionally well-acted romantic tragedy. In terms of Jude Law, it was a revelation for those who didn't know what he was capable of doing. There's an intensity and shading of character with which he endows his Bosie, elements that might easily have been lost in the face of an actor who was just another pretty one.

Part of our understanding of Wilde's life-shattering dilemma is our own response to Bosie's undeniable physical attraction and his equally undeniably abusive behavior. It's sad, but not altogether difficult to grasp, that Oscar seems willing to settle for the detached pleasure of watching his young lover have sex in front of him with other young men as opposed to the impossible exclusivity and commitment one idealizes. When Bosie climbs naked out of bed and berates Oscar again upon the imminent arrival of his monstrous father, we're both listening to the now-predictable sass and trying our darndest to catch a glimpse of Bosie's genitalia. (Jude's frontal is itself cruelly shot at the frame line, meaning that most of us only got to see his pubic hair, while others were treated to the full monty in theatres where the projectionist framed the picture too high. Penises at the very bottom of the frame, just like boom microphones at the very top of the frame, are almost always visible at the "fault" of the projectionist, not the filmmaker.)

In "the not-too-distant-future," Jude Law is deemed a genetic superior and Ethan Hawke is prepared to pay extremely well for strands of his hair, clippings of his nails, and bags of his urine and blood in the intriguing sci-fi think piece *Gattaca* (1997). Hawke, whose urinalysis doc tells him he has an "exceptional piece of equipment," was determined at birth to have a life expectancy of 30.2 years due to a congenital heart condition. His dreams of blasting into space on a mission are enhanced by the cooperation of Jude's Jerome, a sullen beauty whose confinement to a wheelchair tramples on the psychology of socially-determined perfection.

When John Cusack walks past Billy Carl Hanson polishing Kevin Spacey's car in *Midnight in the Garden of Good and Evil* (1997), I figured that the reason I didn't get that rush of heady expectation I usually do when a beautiful actor is playing a male hustler was because Jude Law has been given such a bad haircut. It wasn't my only source of trouble as it turned out. Billy, we're told, was a very accomplished hustler of both men and women. He was rumored to be the best piece of ass in Savannah. Then, of course, a rich and powerful bachelor gunned him down on the eve of the socialite's famed Christmas bash. Frankly, I was unconvinced that the guy everybody was talking about was the guy that Jude Law played. There's nothing the least bit sexy, dangerous or otherwise, in his temperamental white trash hick, and the accent is an obvious affectation. In a scenario filled with oddballs, based on John Berendt's best-selling novel, and directed straight-faced by Clint Eastwood, he doesn't even stand out like a sore thumb. You want to suck a sore thumb.

A much more satisfying collage of eccentric characters and situations is Charlie Peters' delightful *Music From Another Room* (1998), in which Jude's hair goes in several directions all at once, and he plays his most completely romantic and endearing role to date. It's impossible not to fall in love with Jude Law in this movie. America shouldn't have had to wait until *Ripley* to discover him. This thoroughly charming and very funny little film is so good that everybody in it—and it has a stellar cast—seems to be making up their lines on the spot. As a boy, Jude's character helped deliver Brenda Blethyn's baby during Thanksgiving, and now, years later, he's returned from England to fall in love with the girl he brought into this world. Like his character's trade, a tiler, the film is a mosaic of quirky characters and lively subplots, one of which has militant Martha Plimpton hiring Jude to play a pig in a production of *Medea or Media* by her feminist theatre company Actors Without Dicks.

He's in search of a woman who will love him "perfectly" in the slow and consistently odd *Wisdom of Crocodiles* (1998; aka *Immortality*), in which he makes a very sexy vampire in a movie that never uses the word. His Grlscz ("grillsh") is a mysterious subspecies with human, mammalian, and reptilian traits, a daylight vamp and medical researcher whose motives are kept unclear for much of the film. The director's motive to employ an overhead shot while Jude scrambles nude out of bed, however, is unquestionable.

Back in 1995, Jude made the papers for having the gall to form a production company with fellow actors and longtime friends Ewan McGregor and Jonny Lee Miller, and actress/wife Sadie Frost. Some perceived the enterprise as a vanity ploy by actors who weren't even on the map yet, but developing projects they were interested in doing was precisely its purpose. The company, Natural Nylon, co-produced David Cronenberg's *eXistenZ* (1999), starring Jude as an unwilling player in the title game. Cronenberg's legendary credentials as writer-director include some of the most fascinating horror films of the 1970s (*They Came From Within, Rabid, The Brood*) and 1980s (*Scanners, Videodrome, Dead Ringers*), as well as director of *The Dead Zone* (1983), *The Fly* (1986), *Naked Lunch* (1991), and *Crash* (1995). Clinical detail, cerebral themes, and a fascination with the viscera and vicissitudes of the flesh characterize his work. There's usually lots of goo in a Cronenberg film, and with *eXistenZ*, he's got Jude playing the "girl's part," he says, though suffering from male penetration anxiety as he's being outfitted with a bioport. The bioport is necessary to upload the game from the nipple/clitoral metaflesh game pods. The port looks like a new asshole, is installed along the spinal column in the lower back, and accepts a wet finger from Jennifer Jason Leigh to help loosen things up.

One wonders if Tom Ripley could ever have been so accommodating. Writer/director Anthony Minghella's 1999 version of the first of Patricia Highsmith's eventual five-book appearances of the multi-faceted Mr. Ripley is a cunning update and throwback. *The Talented Mr. Ripley* is set in 1958, but there's a 1990s' gay sensibility about the way in which we perceive the lead character's troubles. He's been loaded up with the psychological baggage of repressed homosexuality, adding an explicit dimension to his central murder and lending it the sympathetic emotional disposition of a crime of passion. There's still something sticky about the possibility that some dopey viewers might see Ripley as a "gay serial killer," but the homosexual panic is possibly the least of his woes. In fact, from the 1990s vantage point, Ripley's notion of moving in with the man of his dreams seems like a perfectly natural thing to desire.

Matt Damon, who was cast before his celebrity ascended with *Good Will Hunting* (1997), but now had the shine of a full-blown movie star, plays Tom Ripley. The actor lost twenty pounds, donned a pair of Clark Kent glasses, and had the guts to appear in a form-fitting yellow-green swimsuit while white as a ghost at an Italian coast beach resort. His Ripley is geeky, and more than a bit strange, doing voices and making a pathetic attempt to endear himself to his newfound friends, Dickie Greenleaf (Jude Law) and his girlfriend Marge (Gwyneth Paltrow).

It's quite possible for someone to watch *Ripley* and not be immediately aware that he's interested in Dickie in a sexual way, because Dickie represents everything a former washroom attendant traveling to Europe for the first time could want. He's wild, carefree, astonishingly good-looking, comes from money, has a gorgeous girl, plays jazz saxophone, and has a name that will open many doors among the social elite. It's an entire lifestyle that's to be envied—to be *had*—not just a roll in the hay. The idea of personal reinvention, of assuming another identity and remaking your life, even if only in the eyes of others, is common enough in this electronic age not to seem the least bit psychopathic or demented even when viewed backward into the late 1950s. "I've lied about who I am" might be uttered by any of us. Hitchcock would have explored the morality. Today, we empathize all too quickly with the inclination and the motivation: "I always thought it would be better to be a fake somebody than a real nobody."

But Tom Ripley is also a repressed homosexual, thinly veiling a self-loathing that we also want to help him work his way through. Having him sing "My Funny Valentine" to Dickie seems a bit too obvious, but the game of chess in the bathroom is a brilliant device and the only scene that comes close to erotic. The innocent pretense is the discovery that Tom, Dickie, and Marge are all without siblings. Dickie asks what that could mean, and Tom offers, "It means we've never shared a bath together," followed by, "And I'm cold, can I get in?" Dickie sits naked in the bath and Tom sits clothed beside it, fluttering his fingers in the water as if innocently gauging the temperature, and Tom's question comes loaded with an encyclopedia's worth of intent. Damon's delivery of those last four simple words carries suggestion, revelation, fear, and longing. It's a deeply felt moment for both Ripley and for us, and Damon's expression is perfect. He looks at Tom and Tom looks back at him. (As with Jude's Bosie, Damon's Ripley knows how to use his eyes.)

Dickie takes just long enough before saying "no" to suggest he's understood the question, but his answer comes as curiously ambiguous. Tom quickly recovers by adding, "I don't mean with you in it." Perhaps it's this diversion that's to blame for his not looking at Dickie's cock and balls when he stands up naked in the tub and gets out. Instead, he stares at Dickie's butt in the mirror.

Somehow I think that a straight man's mentality got in the way there. Full-frontal male nudity is still said to "shock" audiences, or at least make them uncomfortable, so someone decided to avoid the absolute certainty of Matt Damon sneaking a longing peek at Jude Law's genitalia and go for the butt in the mirror thing to convey the same idea. It works, don't get me wrong. But Tom would have done both. To suggest otherwise is to admit knowing nothing about gay men and dicks. We can never get too much of them.

Blond and bronzed, Jude gives Dickie a vibrant and vain persona. At the advice of the costumer, the actor decided not to wear underwear for the role because Dickie would know that his clothes hung better without them. Dickie's utterly lovely to look at, but we don't like him much. We recognize the type, and we know we wouldn't otherwise care for him unless we happened to *be him*. That's the beauty of the part. We know why Ripley falls in love with the idea of Dickie, why he puts up with his pettiness, unreliability, mood swings, and temper, even though we know it won't last. If the spoiled brat is beautiful, you might forgive all sorts of indignities to remain in his circle of intimates; that is, if you were the kind of person who habitually wished you could take a great big eraser and rub everything out, starting with yourself.

With the help of Matt Damon's star power, and excellent performance, *The Talented Mr. Ripley* was the vehicle that finally introduced the rest of the planet to the enormous physical charms and talent of Jude Law. He was rewarded with a Best Supporting Actor Oscar nomination, and a bevy of lucrative career offers. His beautiful blue eyes starred in the unforgivably boring WWII sniper flick *Enemy at the Gates* (2001). His Gigolo Joe, a mecha built for pleasuring women (though it seems odd he's not also available to men) in Steven Spielberg's realization of Stanley Kubrick's dream project *A.I.—Artificial Intelligence* (2001), curiously spends most of the time looking like a Kewpie doll even though he's able to change his hairstyle at will.

The decision to ugly him up with cruddy teeth, a plucked hairline, and dirty fingernails for his role as a sleazy photographer and hired killer in *The Road to Perdition* (2002) only ends up calling attention to his natural beauty in a fruitless attempt to give him character role credibility where none is required. *Cold Mountain* (2003) was next.

Jonathan Rhys Meyers (1977-   ) needs to play a vampire. His gaunt frame, pale complexion, high cheekbones, black eyes, and succulent lips demand it. It's probably too obvious a move, but he'd go a long way toward putting the dark sex appeal back into the disparaged Goth movement. He could be the first dark angel to properly show a vampire whose lusts aren't limited to quenching his thirst. And he could continue to promote an alluring theme of bisexuality present in much of his work thus far. The man can't make a move without evoking some homoerotic response.

The eldest of four brothers raised by their mother in County Cork, Ireland, he was brought up in poverty and found it difficult to remain in school. He was finally kicked out at age 14. He enjoyed hustling pool at a local pub where—in one of those movie moments—he was approached by a casting agent who wanted him to audition for a role in the 1994 version of *The War of the Buttons*. Surprisingly, since he was god-awfully beautiful, he didn't get the part. Taking a do-or-die approach to this peculiar intrusion of a career into his bleak life, he continued to audition for roles and made his debut in a single scene as—what else?—the "First Young Man" playing pool, alongside Albert Finney and Rufus Sewell, in *A Man of No Importance* (1994).

While auditioning for a role in *Michael Collins* (1996), the true story of the heroic Irish rebel, young Jonathan caused director Neil Jordan to write in his notes: "Comes into the casting session with alarming certainty. Obviously gifted." Jordan thought the lad looked like Tom Cruise. He cast him as Collins' assassin, the pretty boy who's sorted out as a spy while watching Collins in a pub near the end of the film, and then fires the fatal shot during the haunting, lyrical finale.

"It's us...your bitches," the dark-haired young man wearing a red collar says to his mistress. "Remember us? Little fluffy things." Jonathan is one of four queer and color-dyed poodles transformed into human gay boys after slurping up extraterrestrial soup in *Killer Tongue* (1996). With his short hair and American accent, he's Rudolph, the least queeny of the quartet of canines whose human mommy is now possessed by—and in possession of—a ten-foot talking tongue with homicidal tendencies. Sort of a freaked cousin

Jonathan Rhys Meyers, as a troubled boy genius in *The Maker* (1997). PHOTOFEST

to *From Dusk Till Dawn* (1996), this low-budget gore flick would have benefited tremendously from having the four human pups remain naked (except for their doggie collars), or at least from having them occasionally sniffing each other's behinds or trying to lick their own balls.

He went from a mutant poodle to playing a 14-year old Samson in the Italian-British television co-production of *Samson and Delilah* (1996). His first lead, however, came with the title role in *The Disappearance of Finbar* (1996) as an Irish lad afforded the opportunity to play in an international soccer festival. He returns in shame and jumps off a bridge, disappearing for years while his childhood best friend tries to track him down.

A trip to Hollywood to try his game there resulted in Jonathan's surprise casting as an American teenager in two films. He's little more than the school bully and has only a half dozen scenes in *Telling Lies in America* (1997), set in Cleveland, 1961. He breaks Brad Renfro's radio in the boys' bathroom and generally behaves like a little shit. Later, Renfro will hide in the Catholic school confessional as Jonathan's character confesses to obsessive masturbation to the point of making himself raw. He's worried about going blind, too. Then he provides a disturbing glimpse into his tortured home life that immediately changes our attitude towards his own abusive behavior, but there isn't time to develop that angle.

He plays the lead in *The Maker* (1997), a troubled boy genius who discovers on his 18th birthday the truth about his parents' deaths thanks to the return of his smarmy older brother (Matthew Modine). He's quickly initiated into the life of conning and thievery that his brother conveys as a blood tie, upsetting the young man's promising future, college scholarship, and crush on a pretty cop. Rhys Meyers is excellent in the role, but it's curious why he was cast. He is, after all, an Irish boy, and had all of two weeks to master an American accent. The accent is flawless, by the way. You'd never guess he wasn't an American kid, but there must have been any number of young American actors who could have played the role. Leave it to director Tim Hunter. Rhys Meyers is an almost interchangeable double in terms of his long, moppish dark hair and smoldering good looks for two earlier Hunter film luminaries: Matt Dillon in *Over the Edge* (1979) and Keanu Reeves in *River's Edge* (1986).

The Maker did not get theatrical exhibition, however, turning up on cable years later. The brief American film experience ended without a viable career for the Irish actor, much to his chagrin, and he returned to the UK—where he promptly snatched the lead in a British-American co-production set in the surreal world of glam rock in the early 1970s.

Velvet Goldmine (1998) stars Jonathan Rhys Meyers as glam rock singer Brian Slade, an androgynous, gender-bending phenomenon (a la David Bowie), whose career came to a crashing end after he faked his own assassination on stage during his tour as alter ego Maxwell Demon. Ten years after Slade's disappearance in the wake of outrage at the publicity stunt, a Brit reporter played by Christian Bale is asked to do a follow-up piece. Poor Bale. The actor has a considerable cult fan base, and the role is juicy enough to warrant new devotees, but he's habitually victimized by distractingly bad make-up. As our surrogate hero, who's caught masturbating to newspaper photos of Brian kissing American punk Curt Wild, he's also our groupie initiate into the joys of gay sex with our sex god celebrities, so it's a shame he has to look so bad doing it.

Then again, the glam rock movement made all sorts of beautiful people look ugly. A totem to sexy androgyny in all of his other films, Rhys Meyers has the most trouble making Brian Slade, an openly bisexual character, appear physically attractive. It's not just the make-up, it's the wigs. The exaggerated, drag-queenish crossover obliterates the beautiful femininity of the actor's features, leaving him his feline strut and the Oscar-nominated costumes to do the work, though it also helps that Jonathan sings his own songs and ably evokes the vocal quality of the era.

Ewan McGregor is a highlight as the long blond-haired Curt Wild, who lives up to his name and garners Slade's attention during an outdoor concert in which he drops his pants in front of the live audience, bends over to show them his ass, and then turns around and lets it all flop and fly about while giving the crowd the finger. It's an Iggy Pop-ish moment of bestial defiance and musical disinhibition. It's also just one of many welcome full-frontal exhibitions in the film career of Mr. McGregor, notably in *Trainspotting* (1996) and *The Pillow Book* (1996), before being cast as Obi-Wan Kenobi in the long-awaited prequels to *Star Wars* (1977) and romancing Nicole Kidman, along with the rest of us out there in the dark, in the extraordinary postmodern musical *Moulin Rouge* (2001).

Slade and Wild are paired by an enterprising agent and kiss passionately during a press conference. Their stage theatrics include Slade performing mock fellatio on Wild while he's playing guitar. (Bowie did the same to Mick Ronson in real life.) In one of the film's best scenes, we're treated to a scenario played out by two Barbie dolls outfitted with Brian and Curt heads as they admit their mutual attraction and lay down together. The voices and plot are provided by a child who has received the dolls for Christmas and modified them accordingly. It manages to broach a complex response toward celebrity, fantasy, and acceptance before prejudice has been ingrained by the culture. It also brings to mind *Velvet* director Todd Haynes' controversial ultra low-budget film *Superstar: The Karen Carpenter Story* (1987), enacted entirely by Barbie-style dolls.

Haynes was labeled one of the New Queer Cinema's premiere directors with *Poison* (1991), which won the Grand Prize at the Sundance Film Festival. Eschewing political correctness and demonstrating a unique and heady talent for storytelling and filmmaking, Haynes nevertheless indulges in a disturbing tendency toward gay stereotyping that makes several scenes in *Velvet Goldmine* come off like a gay/bi freak show— predatory, unseemly, and in need of psychological treatment. It was, admittedly, a freaky time period, when the sexual revolution in rock triggered a trend of avowed bisexuality or homosexuality among fans. Boys who proclaimed to like boys as much as they liked girls, whether true or not, were the latest practitioners in rock's innate politics of youthful rebellion and shock value.

Doing a television interview on the street in front of a throng of glam devotees, Curt Wild says, "Everyone's into this scene because it's supposedly the thing to do right now. But you can't just fake being gay. You know, if you're gonna claim that you're gay you're going to have to make love in the gay style. And most of these kids just aren't going to make it. That line, everyone's bisexual, it's a very popular thing to say right now. Personally, I think it's meaningless."

Predictably, the three male leads in the film were teasingly grilled, and seriously grilled, about their own sexual predilections. Add Rhys Meyers' inescapably effete beauty into the mix and you have a recipe everyone was eager to make.

In November of 1998, *Jane* magazine asked him, "Exactly what are you sexually?"

"Acceptable. I've never...I can see men as beautiful, and I can see their sexual attractiveness. I don't want to have sex with them, though. I can respect that they're beautiful, but I suppose I find having sex with a woman better for me. But I'm only 21 years old, so things might change. You might meet me in 30 years and I'll be queer as a sixpence. Or I might be married with a drove of fifteen kids, living in a tenement."

The ambiguity of the response, its deliberate lead into a realm of possibility, is just what we wanted to hear from Jonathan. He also told the press diplomatically, and quite purposefully, "I wouldn't say I'm essentially straight, but I have never been to bed with a man." Could he? "Well, I couldn't say, because I haven't made the decision yet. I've never fancied a man, but that's not saying I won't," he told *UK Vogue* in January of 2000.

The victim of some real life and very frightening experiences with violence and threats of violence in his youth, Jonathan also enjoyed fucking with his interviewers in a fashion befitting a Warhol superstar. When asked about an attempt to rape him when he was 14, he relates, "Yeah, I was putting some barrels outside the nightclub and some guy came up to me and wouldn't take no for an answer. I can just picture him now. He was 27, and really, really beautiful."

Velvet Goldmine was publicized up the wazoo, and expectations were high that it would make a career, but it failed to find an audience at the box-office. Jonathan Rhys Meyers was destined to keep showing up in movies that appealed to only a limited audience, a depressing fact that he made plainly clear to subsequent interviewers. Fidgety, full of energy, and eager to work, he was enormously frustrated by his inability to catch on, though there were those among us who enjoyed being able to introduce him on video to friends and lovers. It's bad enough having to share Keanu or Tom or Rob or Johnny with the rest of the world.

Forty minutes into our napping through *The Governess* (1998), a thin, pale, vampirish-looking youth arrives unexpectedly from Oxford and wakes us up to ripe possibilities. He's a moody bad boy ejected from school because, or so he claims, he was discovered in an opium den carousing with a whore. He wants to shock Ms. Blackchurch (Minnie Driver), the new tutor to his little sister and confidant to his studious father, but she's not the least shaken. Naturally, he falls for her like the juvenile romantic he is at heart, and his puppy dog devotion comes with melodramatic pronouncements: "I would walk into the sea if you were not here."

Boyish and fey, he steals into her empty bedroom and lounges in her bed, sniffing and caressing her pillow. On a second occasion, he arrives when she's both still in it and distraught, moving to comfort her.

"Take your clothes off," she quietly orders him. "Let me look at you." She has him lie down naked on his stomach and runs her hands over his smooth little butt and along his back. You can well imagine how such a sensual manipulation by an older woman works on a boy with raging hormones and nothing but an oppressive family and home asphyxiating him.

Unfathomably, as far as I'm concerned, Minnie heads for the hills, leaving poor Jonathan to the devices of gothic romance literature. Like a tragic nymph, he makes good on his threat to walk into the sea, but then at least has the common sense to crawl out of it completely naked and collapse on the beach in anguish. This, of course, is when I enter the picture as the kindly gentleman out for a stroll who offers the shivering, nude young man my overcoat, takes him back to my cozy cottage, and dries him by the fire while he confesses that women no longer hold an interest for him. He wonders if he can be happy with a man.

He seems to be having similar troubles in *B. Monkey* (1998), in which his bisexual street boy Bruno is in love with Asia Argento's title character, but must first shuck off the love/hate relationship he has with Rupert Everett. The two have a scuffle on the street. Bruno is throwing a hissy. He's a foul-mouthed and sexy little fuck. He's the teary-eyed, purple-lipped little boy who parallels the troubled child whom teacher Jared Harris has been trying to reach in his classroom.

Nearly stereotyped playing bad boys, the actor got a welcome break playing two seven-minute sequences as a lovely and quite charming 16-year old who unbelievably grows up to be blond Julian Sands in Mike Figgis' artsy-fartsy *The Loss of Sexual Innocence* (1999). Jonathan doesn't have much to do in the weird film, but the shortness of his hair somehow calls even more attention to the fullness of his lips, and he demonstrates an enormous talent for nuanced and completely natural performing outside the constraints of angry or violent characters. It's also fun to watch him make out with his girlfriend. (During the non-

Jonathan Adam & Eve interchapters, by the way, Adam is inexplicably circumcised. His penis isn't the only thing that should have been cut. I'd have been grateful to lose everything else and just follow Jonathan's story for the full running time. They could even have kept the title.)

Long-haired again in Ang Lee's Civil War-era western *Ride with the Devil* (1999), Jonathan makes a demonic impression as the bloodthirsty Bushwhacker who vows to kill Tobey Maguire.

His mean-streak is extended, his long hair dyed blond, as Chiron, one half of a wicked brotherhood of rabid pups, in director Julie Taymor's grand opera screen version of Shakespeare's *Titus Andronicus*. At first glance, he seems little more than bare-chested and consigned to the sidelines in *Titus* (1999), lurking there like an epicene in an old Cecil B. DeMille biblical epic. Taymor's designer-styled reworking allows him to emerge as a rock and roll punk in sleek silver lamé and pitch black. He bickers and fights with his brother like two petulant brats over their mutual "love" for Titus' daughter, but they are cunningly conspired to commit rape and murder to get what they want. In a pantomimed sex act, just one scene after his brother Demetrius had mock-humped him during their squabble, Chiron assumes the role of the girl, allowing Demetrius to spread his legs and then hurl Chiron's crotch up into his face for cunnilingus. Chiron sits up in midair, his legs around his brother's neck. He moves like a cat.

But he's a dog, toying with his prey before mutilating her. In the boys' dungeon lair, complete with billiards table, Chiron is seen spasming like a punk on acid while listening to his headset. His hair is in pigtails while he plays with the weapons of murder brought to them. He's partial to red leather pants, and shouting his lines, but he's also willing to go in feathery drag, with bra and tight panties, as a bewitching vision of "Rape."

If you don't know what happens to the brothers in Shakespeare's play, then I suggest you read the original and forego seeing the film until afterwards. *Titus Andronicus* is perhaps the Bard's most relentlessly cruel and heartless tragedy. It's an enormously difficult play to mount, and though Taymor is a brilliant stage director and designer, her debut feature film is almost entirely conceptual, not emotional. Potentially powerful imagery is consistently at a loss. There's no poetry, but plenty of artifice.

There is also, I'm obligated to report, yet another fleeting full-frontal from Jonathan as Titus sends arrows into the palace swimming pool. (Be warned, however, that the DVD widescreen version of the film has been improperly masked and Jonathan's goodies are entirely below the frame line. To catch the whole package, you'll need to find the pan-and-scan VHS version or a non-widescreen cable broadcast.)

Thankfully, the actor seems quite willing to accommodate the desire to see him in his altogether. He implicitly understands the concept, perhaps selfishly. Discussing actresses who seek no-nudity clauses in their contracts with an interviewer from the *Daily Mail* in 1999, he admits, "That really pisses me off. Why is your body something that I can't bloody look at?"

I'm sure the remark requires some context, but I'm enormously pleased he's willing to accommodate those of us who might say to him, "Why is your body something that I can't bloody look at?"

In fact, equal opportunists and Freudians alike would have a field day with grammatical constructions like, "I'll always insist on nudity if it's necessary for my character," something which he told *UK Vogue*. It's sensible actors like Jonathan Rhys Meyers who were put on the silver screen to redress the errors of their brethren. Why, for instance, do lovers in the privacy of their own bedroom take their bed sheets with them when they get out of bed in the movies? Jonathan wouldn't do it. He'd walk about stark ballock-naked, like a real guy, wouldn't he then?

Thirty minutes into *Tangled* (2002), he surprises both Rachel Leigh Cook and an indebted audience by pulling down his pants while she's photographing him. His dangerous brunette believes in "the beauty of the impulsive act" and proves it.

The actor continues to carve himself out a name in the UK, with a bona fide hit as a soccer coach who falls for his Indian star player in the comedy *Bend It Like Beckham* (2002), while US audiences don't know what they're missing. I'm guessing that will change.

In the epic BBC production of *Gormenghast* (2000), based on the first two of three cult fantasy novels published in the 1940s and '50s by Mervyn Peake, he's cast in the coveted role of Steerpike, the ruthless and conniving kitchen urchin who plots to overthrow a lord and take possession of his castle. He plays the devious part with relish and perversely stands out as the most palatable amongst an array of annoying fairy tale oddballs. In a similar vein, though from the side of the haves who become the have-nots, he's a spoiled and ornery Georgie Minafer in the cable television retread of *The Magnificent Ambersons* (2002).

Box-office star or quirky, still-not-quite-known entity, Jonathan Rhys Meyers works either way.

He's come some distance from hustling pool in poverty and never having taken an acting lesson in his life. He is, you might say, one of those born to it. It helps that he's also open to all that it entails, including the passionate attentions of both women and men.

"A lot of men are very uptight," he told *Pavement* magazine, "but I don't distinguish between male and female beauty. Beauty is beauty."

I like that sensibility in a man. Especially a beautiful one.

Jared Leto (1971-   ) has a habit of showing up for a scene or two in movies in which you had no idea he was going to make an appearance. His fleeting on-screen life in a half-dozen or so films suggests the enigma of the rest of his off-screen life. Without intending to set himself up as a man of mystery, he's noted for his unwillingness to fill in the blanks on his celebrity bio rap sheet. We know he was born in Bossier City, Louisiana. We know he and his older brother were brought up by their mother in something approaching poverty. We know the family were nomads, living variously in at least eight different cities, as well as Haiti, when Jared was growing up. We know he went to the School of Visual Arts in New York City to study film and painting. We

The poolboy fantasy gets played out with Jared Leto providing the bod in *Highway* (2001). EVERETT COLLECTION Inset: Jared Leto as "Pre," the golden runner from the University of Oregon, in the film bio *Prefontaine* (1997). PHOTOFEST

know he's interested in music, plays the guitar, and sings. (His band is called 30 Seconds to Mars.)

A few bit roles on TV, then a key role in the series *My So-Called Life* (1994) in which he played the brooding, beautiful, and enigmatic Jordan Catalano. At first glance, it might seem just the dumb jock role, but Jared gave Jordan a haunted quality, a soft-spoken uneasiness. There were only 19 episodes shot, but the series found cult status among teens when MTV picked it up for airing. Jared Leto was a teen idol by default. It was a sticky and untenable position to find himself in, but the show proved a great training ground.

His feature film debut comes one hour and twelve minutes into *How to Make an American Quilt* (1995). He's a handsome, slick-haired white boy who falls for a black servant girl in one of the quilter's flashback stories. The young lady is out looking up at the stars and Jared leans in for a tender kiss on her cheek.

"I once took my coat off and put it around this girl," he tells her, "and she told me she could feel the heat from my body still in the lining. You feel that?"

"Yeah, it's there."

But in just over three minutes of screen time, he no longer is.

He went to Ireland to film executive producer Gabriel Byrne's adaptation of the coming-of-age novel *The Last of the High Kings* (1996), which then became known without much purpose as *Summer Fling* when it was released to video in the States in 1998. I'm not sure why young Jared was cast to play an Irish teen in Howth circa 1977, since there must have been plenty other lads to do it, but his accent is good and it's hard to find fault with filmmakers who wanted him on screen in nearly every single scene.

Still, *High Kings* is a curiously dull affair chronicling the six-week wait for our hero Frankie Griffin's exam results to come out. His family is loaded with queer ducks, including a shrill politico mom played by Catherine O'Hara, but for all of their professed oddity, they're not odd enough. Without pandering, the liveliest scene is the one in which Frankie loses his virginity. His immediate and joyous infatuation with the girl he's just done it with is touching and sweet in its naiveté. (By the way, Jared says that a butt-double was used for his character's nude descent from the drainpipe outside the girl's house. If true, at least they made a nice choice.)

With *Prefontaine* (1997), the story of famed University of Oregon runner Steve Prefontaine's short life, Leto was afforded his first real opportunity to show that he was an actor of exceptional talent. Even his amazing good looks work to his advantage. His Pre is a true golden boy, ego and all, and so while you might take a moment or two to note that Leto's eyes look like a pair of prize marbles, or that his body is beautifully shaped and tapered, you also watch an actor who's able to illuminate some of the inner psychology of the man he's playing. The race scenes don't have the nail-biting tension of the Tom Cruise-produced version of the story, *Without Limits* (1998), starring Billy Crudup as Pre, but there's less Hollywood gloss.

He's a bearded hitchhiker who gets picked up by Danny Glover in the serial killer thriller *Switchback* (1997), in which the snowy mountain locales don't prohibit a breathtaking shirtless scene after a shower. Besides that, though, it's a well-made and exciting entry in the subgenre.

Even more curious than his lead as an Irish teen was his playing the title role of the future Lord of Windermere Hall, and son to Derek Jacobi, in *Basil* (1998). In a British period piece, decked out in his stovepipe hat, he's victimized by a perfectly dreary and unconvincing romantic tragedy that threatens to destroy family name and fortune. The object of Basil's affliction is entirely unworthy of it, while the stomping on Christian Slater's face until it's mush could be viewed as a worthwhile attempt to prevent him from using his accent again.

First-billed in *Urban Legend* (1998), Jared plays the Pendleton University journalism student who gets fired from the paper not because he's callous and sensationalistic, which he is, but because he's digging into the mystery of a psychotic Abnormal Psychology professor's murder spree on its 25th anniversary.

"Did it seem like he was giving me the eye?" asks one girl to another after Leto leaves the room.

"It was probably the mirror behind us."

After *Legend*, which is the only one of his films thus far to be considered a hit in spite of him, Jared began his series of surprise visitations in a string of films. Emblematically, he's the first soldier killed in Terrence Malick's *The Thin Red Line* (1998). Sixty-five minutes into *Black and White* (1999), he's a platinum blond party guest who sniffs Robert Downey, Jr.'s cologne and discovers they both wear Aramis. Stay tuned during the film's end credits, but even with that, Jared's on-screen time is just forty seconds.

Still platinum blond, he's Angel Face in *Fight Club* (1999). When Edward Norton decides, "I felt like destroying something beautiful," Jared is the symbol of his rage. After showing up in three brief flashbacks—complete with handlebar mustache—and finding suicide not to be his favorite topic in the bedroom in *Girl, Interrupted* (1999), he's fully-bearded when he comes to visit Winona Ryder in the mental hospital and tries to persuade her to run away with him to Canada. He doesn't think she's crazy and he doesn't plan on getting sent to Vietnam. All in all, less than five minutes. Heavily made up and wearing a sequined head scarf, he's a sexually confused singer who shows up at a party in *Sol Goode* (2001) and tells a psych student about a dream he's had in which he's recruited by a boy band member who sticks a finger up his butt; less than two minutes, though hang around and/or fast-forward to the end credits for more.

He gets third billing for his five minutes in *American Psycho* (2000), playing business snob Paul Allen, who mistakes Christian Bale for another office clone. He meets Bale for dinner, insults the guy he doesn't know Bale really is, and foolishly comes back to the maniac's sterile apartment. He notices that he's sitting in a room in which the *Style* section of the newspaper has been strategically taped to the floor, but can't guess its purpose. In the business world, I think they call it getting axed.

He's a colorful and egocentric singer in the empty throwback to 1972 showbiz fringe dwellers along the *Sunset Strip* (2000), then shed twenty pounds off his already trim physique by starving himself to play Harry Goldfarb, a tragic heroin abuser, in Darren Aronofsky's *Requiem for a Dream* (2000). He's so lean it's like looking at pressed meat. Harry's addiction to heroin is paralleled by his mother's debilitating addiction to diet pills. Ellen Burstyn was Oscar-nominated for her devastating performance. The scene in which Harry brings his mom a birthday present and learns of her fantasy to go on television will break your heart.

In a fashion, Jared Leto himself is supposed to be a heartbreaker. He has the beautiful face and body of an actor from whom little else might be expected, but much more comes. It may or may not be tied to his insistence on privacy, but he's one of those actors who seems to legitimately have his eyes set on something else. It's why the line in *Urban Legends* about the mirror doesn't work. It's up to us to recognize his beauty while he's playing a role. He plainly isn't interested. Good lord, look at the cornrows he wears in *Panic Room* (2002) as one of Jodie Foster's more interesting and manic tormentors.

A rarity, a lead performance in *Highway* (2001), further proves the point. Not even a spiky mullet or pseudo-mohawk can spoil his visceral attraction. Here he once again shows us how resourceful and winning he can be if given the opportunity, clearly capable of holding a film on his own. Yet there's no denying we're consistently drawn to his physical aesthetics as well: his expressive face, his crystal clear eyes, his perfect teeth inside a wicked smile, and the impossible skin-tightness of his bronzed body, which looks as though it was gleaned from a master sculptor's wheel. Jared Leto without his clothes on is a Michelangelo in motion.

"I feel like any scene could be shot without my dick and be just fine," he told *Notorious* magazine when asked about his willingness to do full-frontal nudity. Even earlier, in August of 1998, he told *Interview* magazine point-blank, "I don't want to do full-frontal nudity. I don't think anybody has a right or need to see my penis. No one needs that to continue living their life."

So what about his ass?

"My rationale is that an ass is an ass—and that's one thing everyone has. But it's gotten to the point where I don't want to become known as the guy who shows his ass. I don't want to bend down and do the requisite ass shot in every movie," he told *Premiere* in April of 1999.

Who said anything about bending down? Bending over would be nice.

What **Matthew Ryan Phillippe** ("fill-a-pea;" 1974-   ) will eventually come to terms with is that he was being paid a compliment when people wanted to see him naked. His legitimate fear about the shameless objectification is that he's being reduced to body parts, like one of a million pretty boys and girls served, eaten, and turned into waste products in the meat market of visual consumption. He's fighting a principled battle for longevity and it makes a world of sense. Reduction is not what an actor serious about establishing and maintaining a career is hoping to achieve. But an actor's body is part of the package. To a great extent, it's his physical appearance that got him through the casting office door. After that, it's his talent and intelligence and plain dumb luck that dictates whether he's relegated to that piece of meat or able to carve himself out a diverse career as a prime

Ryan Phillippe on his way from busboy to bartender at Studio *54* (1998). PHOTOFEST

leading man.

What Ryan has going for him that others might not is a sincere disbelief in his own good looks. I've always maintained that pretty people know that they are pretty, but knowing and comprehending are two different things. The guy who knows he's pretty when he looks in the mirror might be a very different animal than the guy who looks in the mirror and sees himself, a somebody who knows he's pretty to other people because they can't help telling him so.

He was born in New Castle, Delaware, but raised just south of Philadelphia, and it couldn't have been the first time he'd been complimented on his angelic face when he was sitting in a barber's chair getting his haircut and a woman in the shop told him he should be a model. But it may have been one of the first times that he figured he should try and do something about it. The woman had a friend who was a talent agent, and with his mom's permission and accompaniment, Ryan pursued the lead and was signed by the agency. He started getting modeling jobs here and there, then made the leap and move to New York City, where seven long months later he was fortuitously cast at age 17 on the daytime soap *One Life to Live* for the 1992-93 season.

His role, Billy Douglas, was the first openly gay teenager on daytime television, an historic fact that didn't go unnoticed by Ryan's parents, a DuPont chemist dad and a mom who ran a daycare center out of their home. They were concerned about the social repercussions the association might have on their heterosexual son, as well as on his future career. He, in turn, was worried about them getting hate mail. And there may have been the little matter of his somewhat conservative religious background. He was part of the Homecoming Court of his class at New Castle Baptist Academy, as well as editor of the 1992 senior year yearbook.

He decided to make his professional acting debut as a gay teenager after learning the staggering statistics involving gay teens and suicide. Not surprisingly, even while wholeheartedly committed to the role, he received a bit of bashing in some of the gay press for being a straight actor playing a gay teen while there were plenty of unemployed gay teen actors to consider. Some people are never happy, let alone gay.

The role lasted only six months. The soap seemed hesitant or unwilling to develop the character once they got him on screen and then decided to ship him off to divinity school, a tie-in to the controversial friendship between Billy and the town minister.

Ryan shipped himself off to Los Angeles to seriously pursue a television and film career, but didn't own a car in a slavishly driven culture. He would often bike or skateboard through the hot and humid LA smog to auditions, making pit stops to mop up all the perspiration. He landed bits on episodes of *Matlock*, a *Perry Mason Mystery* ("The Case of the Grimacing Governor"), and *Due South* in 1994, and then was given almost nothing to do despite third billing in TV's *Deadly Invasion: The Killer Bee Nightmare* (1995). He wears a scruffy little goatee, his hair is tightly curled on top, and he's the dope who brings about the surprisingly undeadly attack on Robert Hays and family.

His big screen debut came as a little seaman in *Crimson Tide* (1995), glimpsed gazing into a fish tank twenty-four and a half minutes into the macho submarine thriller, then occasionally seen in the background before helping to fix the all-important radio. He's Private Ryan, an Army soldier spooged by a Martian maggot, in the idiotic sci-fi flick *Lifeform* (aka *Invader*; 1996). He looks too young to play a serious soldier, though I'm sure it was a good thing to have him use his own name. Coming up with a different one would have taxed the writer's imagination.

With things not quite working out the way he intended, Ryan and fellow actor friends Breckin Meyer and Seth Green battled their anguish and depression by running around Los Angeles committing property damage and engaging in other petty crimes to keep themselves occupied, including breaking into display cases and selling hocked movie posters.

Director Ridley Scott, of *Alien* (1979) and *Gladiator* (2000) fame, cast Ryan as one of a bevy of beautiful young men in the coming-of-age adventure *White Squall* (1996), based on a true story about a group of troubled boys sent out to sea to come back young men. In many ways, it's an old fashioned movie about growing up, facing your fears and insecurities. Male bonding. Ryan plays Gil Martin, a sad young man with an even sadder reason for his nightmares and fear of heights. He plays the role sensitively and memorably, and quite in spite of the obvious distractions provided by all the half-naked and handsome young actors around him, including Scott Wolf, Eric Michael Cole, Peyton Thomas, David Lascher, Balthazar Getty, Jason Marsden, and Ethan Embry. In fact, he's half-naked himself from the get-go, already displaying the hard physique that would figure prominently in films to come.

When Charlotte Rae reads Ryan's palm in Gregg Araki's *Nowhere* (1997), she says, "Death." He says, girlfriend. He tells her, "Your tongue is cool." Earlier that night, he told her a story about a dead guy who got half his face eaten off by his own dog. "Dogs eating people is cool," she replies.

Shad is a reckless party animal and Ryan Phillippe gives himself over completely. We see him with a gag in his mouth and crying out "Mommy!" during sex, then catch him in the midst of the party fucking his girl up against the wall while his own sister reminds him that dad wants the lawn mowed. That's the kind of bump and grind Araki is known for in his wildly colorful and outrageous films.

"Let the love feast begin," announces the death-obsessed Shad after having his girlfriend insert a piece of chocolate in her vagina while they make out in his car. And down he goes for some sugar-fortified cunnilingus. "Mmmmmm. I just love the milk-chocolatey goodness," he gloats, his mouth all smeared in melted brown stuff. "Yum." Now it's her turn to go down on him. He's having such a good time he figures he should just drive off the cliff in front of them with his dick in her mouth. "I want to die. Let's all die!"

Not exactly the kind of role you'd seek to play if you were hoping to capitalize on your teenybopper good looks, which is why I'm glad that he did it. Shows he's got spunk. And that he needed a job.

Even when he agreed to play a spoiled rotten jock in a teen slasher flick, he had no idea that it would be a big hit or lead to other things. Fortunately, it did. He gets third billing in *I Know What You Did Last Summer* (1997), yet another of *Dawson's Creek* creator/writer Kevin Williamson's own knock-offs in the wake of his phenomenally popular *Scream* (1996). Not as skillful or funny as *Scream*, *Last Summer* does share some of its self-awareness about teen horror flick conventions. Ryan looks like a blond popsicle in his white muscle T and Raphaelite curls. For contrast, Freddie Prinze, Jr. wears a black muscle T.

We see Ryan working out with a punching bag, then strolling around the locker room and into the shower all by himself late one night. The generous helpings to his physique are appreciated in not quite the same way as Janet Leigh's nude vulnerability in a motel room shower in *Psycho* (1960). A guy who looks as hot as Ryan deserves to be stalked in a locker room while he's showering or wandering around in a towel. It's the appropriate place to mix suspense with heartthrobbing anticipation. If the filmmakers are only fooling us by having us believe that he's going to be offed here and now, then it may be the first time

321

we can fully appreciate the inevitability of a long fake-out. In the unlikely event of an actual attack, however, we can still hope for a lengthy chase and struggle, with lots of slipping on the wet floor and the necessity of pulling off that towel to fashion protection from sharp, pointy objects.

He's one of three dopes (including Hank Azaria and Billy Bob Thornton) who decide to go into business for themselves with a $5,000,000 crop of marijuana after they see their boss gunned down in *Homegrown* (1998). Azaria and Thornton are frequently hilarious in what seem to be improvised exchanges. Ryan has spiky, butterscotch hair and twitches to a boom box playing a song called "So Fuckin' Dumb." Kelly Lynch tells him to take his shirt off to chop wood for her, and then rubs emollient on his belly in close-up after he's taken a beating. We see him butt-nekkid bunny-humping Lynch, and he spends one whole sequence of the film completely nude with his hands covering his privates while being threatened by a masked gunman. It's a low-budget, unconventional, and strangely likeable little movie with a cast chocked full of recognizable names.

An even more unconventional low-budget appearance was playing the lead in *Little Boy Blue* (1998), a dark and disturbing tale about a young man physically abused by his drunken Nam vet father (John Savage) and forced to have sex with his own mother (Nastassja Kinski). It's a progressively weird story that one can't imagine how someone got financing for, but the cast plays it with a straight face and Phillippe is quite good, balancing the peculiar and perplexing sexual material with a tender and compassionate side.

Frustrated by his inability to latch onto film roles—save a slasher one—that might further his career, Ryan suddenly found himself the "It Boy" when Miramax green-lighted Mark Christopher's *54* (1998), the story of the famous New York City nightclub where hand-picked revelers were allowed to snort and carouse with celebrities at a Dionysian orgy of disco, sex, and drugs.

Into this hedonistic cult is thrown a 19-year old Jersey gas station attendant named Shane (our boy Ryan), with "the body of David and the face of a Botticelli." Before he can even get into the joint, his apparel is called into question by club owner Steve Rubell, played by Mike Meyers, who tries hard but can't overcome the character inventions of his *Saturday Night Live* sketch work. Rubell won't let Shane into 54 the way he's dressed. "Not with that shirt" turns out to mean not with that shirt on, so off it comes—peeled like a second skin—and in he goes.

Intended as a whirling descent into debauchery, with Shane's rise from busboy to coveted bartender detailed in drug addiction and sexual excess, *54* was nearly closed down by test screenings, and writer/director Christopher was plunged into a battle for his movie that resulted in the studio mandating massive cuts, plot and character alterations, and the re-assembly of the shocked cast for what amounted to a re-shoot only two months before the film's scheduled release.

Sadly, the theatrical version of *54* gives decadence a bad name. Without a trace of self-indulgence, the film's saving grace is the decision not to ask Ryan Phillippe to shave his belly button trail. In fact, Ryan is worth the whole movie. He's the only thing that consistently works, wearing tight shirts all the time, including a "Senior Wrestling 76-77" T-shirt, and, once he's made it, tight little shorts to match. (Phillippe told the press that when he saw the shorts he was going to have to wear in the film he thought they might be making *Showguys*.) In the censored and reworked version, Shane is no longer a drug addict, nor necessarily even bisexual. His two on-screen male/male kisses—one with Meyers, the other with real-life best friend Breckin Meyer—were cut, and suddenly this working class kid from Jersey seems like a junior league Tony Manero (Travolta's character in *Saturday Night Fever*). When he comes into Rubell's office wearing fringes and ready to take his pants off for the boss, he's just a young guy willing to do whatever he has to in order to get ahead in the business.

Shane gets a spread in *After Dark* magazine, but no article, a sign that his celebrity is as a piece of boy candy, not a real person. He looks darling in his Christmas garb—blue jeans with white fur cuffs—and he affords us a very lovely glimpse at his bare ass, but none of that helped the actor's career when *54* was roasted over the fire by critics. As if he were to blame.

He's also not to blame for *Cruel Intentions* (1998), a teenaged reworking of the wicked sexual game-playing in *Les Liaisons Dangereuses*. It has its moments, but the cast seems too young for this material, rendering the crude sexual dialogue silly, not sexy. The bet between step-siblings Kathryn (Sarah Michelle Gellar) and Sebastian (Ryan) is predicated on the deflowering of a famous virgin (Reese Witherspoon), with Sebastian's prize: "You can put it anywhere" in his step-sister.

The problem, of course, is that the pretty boy schmuck actually falls in love. Since he does, and even goes so far as to tell her the truth about himself, the script mandates he must pay the ultimate price, which is a pretty bizarre thematic for an R-rated teen sex flick whether it's based on an 18th century novel or not. Joshua Jackson shows up as an equally scheming gay friend and willingly sets up a closeted football jock to advance the plot.

The film was a controversial success at the box-office and a generation of teenagers were exposed to its sexual shenanigans and seemed to take them in stride because they liked the actors playing them out. Ryan gets teased to erection inside his pants by Gellar, Gellar and actress Selma Blair French kiss, and Ryan shows his gorgeous bare backside again before a skinny-dip into the pool. It's safe to say we'd come some distance from *Little Darlings* (1980).

For Phillippe, one of the pleasures of doing the film was enticing his real-life girlfriend (now wife) Reese Witherspoon to play the part of the virgin he's trying to seduce. During a particularly intense scene between the two of their characters, Reese decided to slap Ryan full on, and the actor broke down and got physically ill following the take.

Less than two weeks after the exhausting *Intentions* shoot, Phillippe was scheduled to begin filming *Dancing About Architecture*. He decided to give himself blue hair to help facilitate the transition and showed up Day One of the new film wearing it. He convinced the filmmakers it was right for the role, so he kept it, playing the cool and mysteriously sullen Keenan, who likes to dance alone, in the generically retitled *Playing By Heart* (1998). Angelina Jolie, giving verve and lifeblood to the film's most engaging character, a hot red-headed actress, gets precious little out of the spiky blue-haired boy she exhaustively talks to at the club. He's a hard nut to crack. He doesn't date, he drinks Coke, and he doesn't sit down to pee is about the extent of it until after a late night show of *Texas Chainsaw Massacre* brings them together again. Their story is one of several that will eventually connect in this somber and emotional drama. Phillippe is heartbreakingly good and ably delivers a scene in which everything he says is so perfect that it should make you cry.

"Shut that cunt's mouth or I'll come over there and fuck-start her head," is how the cool, dirty blond, and scruffy Mr. Parker handles a confrontation during the brilliant opening scene of *The Way of the Gun* (2000). The mouthy lady in question is berating Mr. P with a barrage of homosexual accusations and threats to his personal orifices. His reaction when they come face to face, alongside her long-haired boyfriend, is the kind of moment that jumpstarts cult classics. It's followed by another first-rate series of exchanges when Phillippe's Mr. Parker and Benicio Del Toro's Mr. Longbaugh are interviewed in preparation for sperm donation.

If the rest of the film, written by Christopher McQuarrie, who wrote *The Usual Suspects* (1995), doesn't sustain the level of its first two scenes, it is nonetheless brimming with lots of smart dialogue, oddball characters, double-crossings, and overlapping plot lines before it overkills into a nasty bloodbath.

Ryan's three scenes as a Russian ballet star who wants to "defecate" to the US in the amateurish and unfunny *Company Man* (2001) aren't helped by the lack of even a single shot of him in dancer's tights.

In *AntiTrust* (2001), he's a computer geek nabbed by software megalomaniac Tim Robbins and quickly learns the murderous methods behind staying number one in the cutthroat world of high tech. For fun, his character has a deadly allergy to sesame seeds that makes for the film's best scene when his girlfriend decides for the first time in their relationship to prepare a home-cooked meal.

His role as an equal opportunity hustler in Robert Altman's *Gosford Park* (2001) earned him his career-best reviews while dropping him in the midst of a stellar British cast for a 1932 period piece. Eventually we may all be able to pay attention to more than his full red lips, feline brow, and lean physique, but until that time he'll continue to be accused by his critics of doing a pretty boy act.

Ryan Phillippe doesn't have a pretty boy act, though. He just happens to be one.

Casper Van Dien (1969-) has a perfect face. His jaw muscles flex when he's emoting and the only ripple on his otherwise preternaturally smooth visage is the becoming scar slash on his cleft chin that he's lifted from Harrison Ford.

TV bits as a surfer on *Freshman Dorm*, cutie pie Tyler "Ty" Moody on the daytime soap *One Life to Live,* and as Griffin Stone, a *Flintstone* name for a cartoon kind of handsome, on the 1990 season of *Beverly Hills 90210* dot the early years. He's even King Tal in *Beastmaster III* (1995). But he was quintessentially cast in *Starship Troopers* (1997). Given his long family history of distinguished military service, the role must have seemed predestined.

As Johnny Rico, in this vastly entertaining jab at militarism in the consumer age, he looks exactly like

Casper Van Dien demonstrates the pin-up boy look as a member of the *Freshman Dorm* (1992). PHOTOFEST

a toy soldier. Only his perfect set of gleaming white teeth help identify him when the masses of uniforms are in motion.

Out of uniform, he's a doll all right: flawlessly coifed in a "This is Dick…Dick is a boy" sort of way. His head makes an almost perfect tetragon—it's straight out of a beginner's sketchbook (start with your rectangle, then add on ears and you're done), and comes atop a hairless bod of cut masculinity that suggests a rubber mold out of the prop truck. His ass is revealed just as divinely wrought as the rest of him during the famous coed shower sequence in which a very uncomfortable cast was told to strip and mingle. (Dutch director Paul Verhoeven, incensed by his American actors' fuss over nudity, pulled down his own pants on a dare to set the example.)

The film's comic book take on patriotic jingoism comes dangerously close to an evocation of fascism, but it's very self-aware and revels in its proximity to seeing warfare as a pop culture commercial venture, a live-action video game. It makes one yearn for a little joystick action in the shower sequence. Or even during the "administrative punishment" scene in which a bare-torsoed Casper is tied, legs spread and arms splayed, for ten nasty lashes across the back. As we have seen time and time again in the movies, the eroticism of the male body is being psychosexually exploited in torture scenes like this, offering the male physique in erotic spectacle but subjugating the overt eroticism by subjecting it to torment. It's audience S&M. The hero's body ravaged for our enjoyment.

Van Dien, whose Dutch lineage traditionally mandates firstborn males be named Casper, comes complete with a Casper the Friendly Ghost tattoo on the inside of his considerable left bicep. He took on the role no other mainstream actor would dare to play at the time, that of James Dean, in what turned out to be a dreadful junior high school attempt at screen biopic called *James Dean: Race With Destiny* (1997). The lure of the loincloth had his fans drooling when he took a stab at *Tarzan and the Lost City* (1998), but someone forgot to make his Greystoke sexy in this B-movie retread. They also insisted he shave his chest again. Check out Casper in *Shark Attack* (1998) for proof that he's a naturally hairy guy up front.

Short and amazingly beautiful, Casper would make a perfect Joe Dallesandro in a Warhol Factory film bio if he could only do the New York accent. Physically, the only problem he'd have is tiny nipples. Joe has got big ones. He has the right look though, especially when he plays sober.

His career quickly became a guilty pleasure, with lead roles in one horrifically bad film or television show after another. The September 29, 2000 issue of *Entertainment Weekly* pictured him alongside co-stars Yasmine Bleeth and John Barrowman to hype their D.O.A. prime time soap parody *Titans*. Casper and Barrowman are in their boxer shorts on either side of Bleeth, who's groping each of the boy's crotches. Looks like she's got her hand full with Casper, who playacts a wince. It's a frisky and audacious photo shoot gimmick, but it's also something of a career highlight. I wish I had the money spent on trash like *On the Border* (1998), *The Collectors* (1999), *Modern Vampires* (1999), *Python* (2000), *Partners* (2000), and *Sanctimony* (2000) so that I could make my own movie with Casper Van Dien. He's too incredibly gorgeous a man not to take full advantage.

When Dina Meyer dies in his arms in *Starship Troopers*, she looks up at the bereaved Casper and tells him what everyone else in the audience is thinking: "It's all right, because I got to have you." One night with that boy in the sack and you'd be ready to die too.

It's a boy, Mrs. Walker. It's a boy.

Paul William Walker IV (1973-   ) was born and raised in sunny Southern California. His mother was a model. Genetically predisposed for such work, so was he. Baby Paul was modeling diapers, hawking breakfast cereal, and appearing at age 10 as a geeky scientist in the juvenile schlock film *Monster in the Closet* (1986), which was shot in 1983. By the time he was 11, he had done bits on a number of television shows, including *Charles in Charge*, *Who's the Boss*, and three episodes of *Highway to Heaven*.

A healthy interest in a variety of outdoor sports, including surfing, water skiing, and snorkeling, kept him in shape between gigs as he grew into manhood. In addition to modeling jobs, the young man nicknamed "pretty boy" by friends was cast as Brandon Collins in the 1993 season of the hugely popular daytime soap *The Young and the Restless*.

Paul Walker developed the kind of striking good looks that would get him noticed in a catalog surrounded by other male beauties, but seeing him move is an altogether deeper experience. In the unbelievably stupid *Tammy and the T-Rex* (1994), he saunters into the high school gym to watch his new girlfriend (Denise Richards) finish cheerleading practice. He's just come off the field, still dressed in his dirty football pants and wearing that sexy little half-undershirt that leaves his belly button exposed. Denise's gay schoolmate approves. So do we.

During a fight with Richards' gang-banger ex, there's an exquisite moment in which the punk grabs Paul by the nuts and gives him a long and painful squeeze. Paul sure makes it *look* painful, but then he's able to nail the other guy in the nuts in retaliation and suddenly seems personally unfazed. One of the cops who appears on the scene asks: "What's the matter with you, boy? Ain't you got no balls?"

"I've got a cup on," Paul proudly relates with a smile.

Unfortunately, a cup won't help him when he's cruelly nabbed, tossed inside a wildlife park, and left to be mauled by a lion. Even the beast must have recognized the beauty, though, because the young man is looking quite gorgeous, if comatose, in the hospital afterwards. About a half hour into the flick, our lovely jock gets the top of his head sawed off by mad scientists and has his brain put inside a mechanical dinosaur. In one of just many weird moments in this so-awful-you've-got-to-see-it-once teen horror flick, you'll note the substantial woody our boy sports under his hospital gown while he's spasming on the table. (About the woody: The "PG-13" video release of the film cuts the tabletop seizure altogether, as well as some of the language. I caught the pup-tent scene when the film aired on a commercial-laden cable channel. My best guess, given the context, is that the mad docs are testing his limb reflexes by probing the brain and an electrode jab brings on the boner.)

Still not sure it was acting he wanted to do with his life, and *Tammy and the T-Rex* must have made him seriously reconsider, Paul took community college courses in marine biology.

His first big break came with a starring role in Walt Disney's *Meet the Deedles* (1998), playing one half of a pair of lovable Hawaiian twins who wake up to discover it's their 18th birthday. Caught playing hooky while parasailing, thus jeopardizing their future stakes in the Deedle empire, the boys are shipped off to Camp Broken Spirit in Wyoming to make men out of them. They find themselves stranded without a camp, but glide right into Yellowstone Park on their motorized skateboards, where they're mistaken for a pair of experts sent to rid the park of its prairie dog problem.

If the plot sounds an awfully lot like one of those Disney live-action escapades that Kurt Russell used to make, it is. But it's also silly, upbeat, and lots of fun thanks to the guys. Paul plays Phil Deedle, the sweeter and dumber of the pair, with a bronzed bod and frosted highlights in his hair. He's two minutes older than Phil (Steve Van Wormer). He also heats up a pair of sweatpants. At age 24, Paul Walker doesn't look a day over 18. He brings all his Southern California model/athlete physicality to the role, then gives Phil warmth and endless charm as the airheaded Adonis who befriends a P-Dog named Petey and feeds him Twizzlers. I like these guys much better than Bill and Ted. I also can't take my eyes off of Paul no matter what he's doing. "I'm 100% male," he tells his new boss as the twins prepare for ranger training and hope to earn their badges by the end of the week. He is, too. Just look at the 3-D evidence squeezed between his leg harnesses during the parasail behind the truck. Or notice how dark and distinct the trail of hair is that goes from under his belly button and into his pants. Shame on you. This is a Disney film. Okay, so he's also one half of a goofy, but affectionate live-action recreation of the spaghetti noodle scene from *The Lady and the Tramp* (1955), only this time he and the pretty gal are sharing an extra long earthworm.

Twenty minutes into *Pleasantville* (1998), he drives up to say "Hello, Mary Sue" to Reese Witherspoon and suddenly black-and-white television looks a whole lot more inviting. His Skip Martin is captain of the high school basketball team, and he has the most endearing way of delivering the simplest of lines. "Hi ya, Bud." Such a sweetie. So cute.

"I think you're just about the keenest girl in the whole school," he says to Reese, who finds herself trapped along with brother Tobey Maguire in a 1950s TV show. He orders his regular at the café, a cheeseburger and a Cherry Coke, and is working up the nerve to give Reese his school pin. She hauls his innocent self out to Lover's Lane and tells him that she might just pin him. "That's silly, Mary Sue. How can you possibly pin me?" Oh, that smile. That complete innocence.

He thinks he might be ill when he gets his very first hard-on, but the rest of his education is fast and furious...and life-altering. Skip is the first one in Pleasantville to see color—a rose—after the awakening of sex. (In terms of plot consistency, though, he should have also been the first one to flush into full color.) Sex and emotion and the unpredictability of life are what forever change the tiny black-and-white town. It's a thoughtful and entertaining story about self-knowledge and self-expression rendered through the stark conservatism of white bread Middle American values piped into our homes through role-model television.

In *Varsity Blues* (1999), a teen melodrama set in the religion of Texas high school football, Paul is afforded a deity's low-angle shot as he emerges from the house in front of which his parents have erected a billboard with his name and likeness. He is town hero Lance Harbor, #7 of the West Canaan Coyotes, and the angle is one of those where you find yourself staring right into his crotch and heading up from there. The cult of jock celebrity is akin to the cult of movie celebrity. When Lance addresses the school at a pep rally and starts out hesitantly, "Um, I was lyin' in bed last night," all the girls "whoooo" it up at the very thought. In the locker room after a game, fellow player and funnyman Scott Caan mimes giving Lance head in comic worship, but it seems less a joke than a good idea.

For a football movie that includes a sex-ed classroom scene in which the discussion is focused on slang for the male erection, as well as not one but two scenes offering a look at Caan's very nice white butt, it's a rip-off that there are no shots of guys walking around bare-assed or in their jockstraps in the locker

Paul Walker is stalked by a psychotic trucker who thinks the pretty boy is a pretty girl in *Joy Ride* (2001). PHOTOFEST

room. There's some female nudity at a strip club, and one of the pretty lead actresses has the unenviable and embarrassing task of stepping into the room wearing only whipped cream on her breasts and down-below, but that ain't going to cut it for the rest of us.

As consolation for then having the gall to seriously injure Paul Walker's character at the 30-minute mark, leaving him unavailable for play, the movie offers a quick glimpse of his tensing naked butt while he's interrupted boffing a gal on top of a clothes dryer. Sadly, he's wearing a flesh-colored neoprene cup up front.

He's the bad boy who picks the girl Freddie Prinze, Jr. has six weeks to turn into a prom queen in the teen romantic comedy *She's All That* (1999). Other than a nice topless scene during a brief game of beach volleyball, though, he spends most of his time laughing it up and baring his big eyeteeth as the jerk who tries to turn the ugly bet to his advantage and nail the young lady for himself on prom night.

He's not even billed in the end credits for playing Claire Danes' stateside boyfriend in *Brokedown Palace* (1999), where we see him at high school graduation and at a party for less than a minute of screen time. He doesn't have a single line. He's just a kiss and a smile.

He looks great in a tux, and sensational all sweaty and pumped in his boxing shorts, as Caleb Mandrake in *The Skulls* (2000). He's an initiate in a secret fraternal society at an unnamed Ivy League school, but it's impossible to believe such a stupid organization could remain secret for long. Paul is supposed to be grimacing in pain when he's branded by The Skulls on the topside of his wrist, but the eyebrow-raising look he provides can also be read as conveying utter disbelief at the frat's brainless decision where to leave their mark. Plot cover-up: all The Skulls get fancy new watches to conceal the burn.

Paul Walker is one of those young actors (first discovered by teenage girls and gay men) on the verge…of doing what no one knows for sure, though he's gleefully indiscriminate about his projects. Before *2 Fast 2 Furious* (2003), of course, came the surprise box-office hit original, *The Fast and the Furious* (2001), a thoroughly bad hot rod flick in which there are no credible characters, just dopey attitudes. Walker's cute and nicely freckled and gets some great close-ups, but may not be aware he's required to do anything more. There's a carelessness to his body language—the way his shoulders sway and both forearms swing when he walks—that suggests he must saunter in precisely the same fashion when he's not on camera. The only clue that the Southern California surfer boy knows he's in a movie comes with his insistence on giving all his dialogue pretty much the same weight. "Hey bro, you gotta bathroom?" is delivered with the inflection of a line equal to all others, accompanied by a sober face, so that for a moment it seems as if his undercover cop is seriously inquiring whether there's a john on the premises, as opposed to the rhetorical "where's the can?" it's meant to be. (If some have decided that Paul Walker is just a bad actor, I'm satisfied to enjoy him as perpetually green.)

In *Joy Ride* (2001), previously known as *Squelch*, he and his brother (Steve Zahn) find a practical joke backfiring on them big time when a humorless trucker chases them through Nevada because the pretty boy isn't the pretty girl he pretends to be on the CB. Personally, I can't see what the trucker from hell's big problem is; Paul Walker would make an awesome one-night stand. A scene in which our two young leads show up completely naked at a busy roadside diner was nearly snipped out because studio test screenings found it thematically incongruous with the rest of the scary stuff. I'm sure marketing ultimately played a hand in its retention, because the opportunity to see Paul Walker's picture-perfect bare ass was bound to sell tickets, but it's also the scene where the heretofore exciting, funny, and thrilling thriller starts to resemble a typical maniac movie instead of one about these particular characters in trouble, and that's a bit disappointing. There are better excuses to make for keeping in male nudity, but my DVD player's slow-motion, frame-by-frame, and freeze-frame buttons aren't complaining and neither will I.

Asked by an 18-year old male reader of *Teen People* about the "issue of homosexuality," Mr. Walker replied: "Hey, if some dude finds me good-looking, that's a compliment. I say be whatever you want to be."

Scott Diggs is personally responsible for the body **Taye Diggs** (1972-   ) has been known to unveil both on screen and off with regularity and aplomb. "Scottaye," as friends called him, was eventually abbreviated to "Taye" and became his professional name. Raised in poverty by his mother and a difficult stepfather, Taye attended Rochester's School for the Arts when he was 16, at his mother's behest. He graduated from Syracuse University with a degree in musical theatre and began appearing in shows in New York.

Taye Diggs is *How Stella Got Her Groove Back* (1998), with Angela Bassett. YESTERDAY

I suppose you might say he was a quintuple-threat: he could sing, dance, and act, but he also was extraordinarily good-looking and had the body of a male model. A nude male model. He played the role of Benny, the insidious landlord, in the Tony Award-winning Broadway production of *Rent*, and famously streaked through the theatre after learning he had won a key role in his very first motion picture.

Eighteen minutes into *How Stella Got Her Groove Back* (1998), there he is, inviting Angela Basset to join him for breakfast during her holiday in Jamaica. She puts up a half-hearted front to admonish his flirtations and attempts to make a big deal out of the fact that she's 40 and he's 20.

They get it on at the 39-minute mark.

He's really quite the perfect young man, and if the film struggles with finding a dramatic hook outside of one supporting character's sudden hospitalization and terminal illness, it's convincing Bassett what we already know. He's a keeper.

As the young beauty, Diggs is playing a role traditionally assigned to the ingenue, and it comes complete with his washing up in a clear glass shower while the older woman (and the rest of us) take stock of his perfectly toned backside.

He's a non-ejaculating Tantric sex disciple in the frenetic *Go* (1998), whose famed story about a lover's contact lens ending up on the tip of his dick is stolen by another character as his own. Continuing the sexual entendre in many of his movie titles, he's the drunk who's supposed to get married in three hours in *The Wood* (1999), a sweet, well-written, and well-acted story of the friendship of three childhood buddies. After spending nearly half the film with dragon breath and then puking all over himself and his pals, he and the boys are ordered by a friend to clean up in the backyard, where they hose each other down in the nude. Taye Diggs reveals a body so incredibly well-honed and cut that holding his hands over his genitalia seems a smart move. It's not that we're not interested, we are, but the competition with the rest of him would have been stiff.

He had such a great time working on *The Wood* that he immediately signed to do *The Best Man* (1999), another marriage/relationships comedy-drama enriched significantly by the performances. This time Taye is an author on the verge of a best-seller, but an advance review copy has circulated amongst all his friends and they have no trouble recognizing themselves in the fiction. The four guys, superbly played and with great chemistry by Diggs, Morris Chestnut, Harold Perrineau, and Terrence Howard, easily transcend the

329

gimmick of the plot and some otherwise predictable development. Personally, I think some predictable love scenes would have been nice additions. As it is, a close-up that starts panning from between Taye's legs and traverses up his beautiful bod while he sits with his lady in a bathtub strewn with flower petals is an early tease that keeps us hopeful for more.

He's wasted in the pointless remake of *House on Haunted Hill* (1999) and plays a ruthless and taciturn bodyguard in *The Way of the Gun* (2000). Proving himself once again a natural as a romantic lead in *Brown Sugar* (2002), it's a shame the boring film is as victimized by mass-market romance flick formulas as the commercialized hip-hop music is in the film's plot. He's also surprisingly upstaged, though that's the trick of his part, opposite Christian Bale in the entertaining and appreciatively pensive martial arts/sci-fi flick *Equilibrium* (2002). Then he's reduced to little more than a pretty head as the MC pianist in *Chicago* (2002).

Taye Diggs remains one of those pseudo-stars who seems a hit film away from major stardom, though he's not yet revealed self-conscious concern about his being seen as a body first, then an actor. He's known to take his roles quite seriously while preparing for them and working on the set, but he's not unaware of the persistence of vision associated with his smile, pecs, glutes, and everything else a picture postcard man needs. The guy who once told an interviewer that he enjoys answering the door in his boxers when he orders carry-out, and then when he returns with the money likes to have his boxers down around his ankles, is clearly happy just to have someone looking at him at this point. Make no mistake. We're looking.

Taye Diggs made his feature film debut as the perfect boyfriend and lover in *How Stella Got Her Groove Back* (1998).
PHOTOFEST

2000 and Beyond

The Shape Of Things To Come

It's a guessing game, but I'm going to take the guess out of it. Who will be the next hot male sex star? What young actor will rise to the top of his field, if only briefly? One of the magazine industry's perfunctory leads when covering a new "hottie" is to concede that the movies have a voracious appetite for fresh meat, but "this guy stands a damned good chance of making the grade. Why? Because he's not interested in his looks. He's determined to show the rest of us that he's got talent." It's a pseudo-flattering way of hedging the magazine's bet. If the guy really does make it big, then they can say they knew it first and gain extra mileage out of reprinting old photos or convincing the star's agency for a follow-up because they were there to help launch him when he was a nobody. If, as is more often the case, he disappears after a flash, nobody will remember anyway.

So who's next? The next one, that's who. It can be fun to play along, and even more fun to champion a fella you saw in a movie last week who had one scene where he was walking a dog and ran into a lamppost, but the only sure thing is that there will be another…and another…and another one after that.

Josh Hartnett (1978-   ) became the poster boy for Pretty Boys in the New Millennium on a hunch. *Pearl Harbor* (2001) hadn't opened when I decided to add him to this book's first draft. But I had seen the trailer and I was thinking this Hartnett kid could be huge. He already is. At 6' 3", he was a football and soccer jock at his respective high schools in Minneapolis/St. Paul, Minnesota, but tore a ligament in his knee and killed the football career. An aunt encouraged him to audition for a stage production of *Tom Sawyer*, and after getting cast as Huck Finn, he was certain it was what he wanted to do with his life. (For fellow sports injury to theatre junkie Tom Cruise, it was a production of *Guys and Dolls* that did the trick.)

He made the big move to Los Angeles after a quickly derailed attempt at higher theatrical education in New York and within two months was cast as rebel son Michael Fitzgerald on ABC-TV's short-lived series *Cracker* (1997). His small screen debut had him on the toilet, then gagged and cuffed to a bed for a day. Okay, so maybe that's where you saw that guy you thought might just be the next big thing. You saw him sitting on a toilet in this TV show you channel-surfed by last week. Wonder whatever happened to that guy?

Well, you might say he's following in the footsteps of Jamie Lee Curtis…literally. He plays Curtis' strapping son in *Halloween H2O: Twenty Years Later* (1998). Even gets "Introducing Josh Hartnett" billing. Seventeen-year-old John wants to join his friends on a trip to Yosemite, but mom is finding it very hard to let him out of her sight. After all, she has this psycho killer brother she's been haunted by for the last two decades and today is Halloween. One of John's friends teases him that with a mother like that he'll probably end up running a weird motel with her 20 years from now.

I give him more credit. This promising sequel after so many unpromising ones has some clever scenes in it, and though Josh isn't given much to do, it's kind of an honor, or at least a distinction, to find himself alongside Curtis in her return to the series that launched her career. The plotting requires Jamie Lee to face up to her own monster, and that works, but Josh does such a good job filling the screen top to bottom that I figured he could kick Michael Myers' ass no problem.

The Faculty (1998) was next on the teen horror film circuit, with Josh playing Zeke, the senior-year repeat with the coolest car, the latest in feel-good drugs, and "full-frontal" videotapes of Neve Campbell and Jennifer Love Hewitt. He's also the closet genius with a full-size lab in his garage who needs to figure out how to dry up the waterlogged aliens taking over the bodies of the students and school faculty. "I'm a contradiction," he says.

With a screenplay by *Scream* (1996) teen horror-maven Kevin Williamson and direction by Robert Rodriguez [of *From Dusk Till Dawn* (1996) fame], *The Faculty* is a fast-paced, inventive, and very entertaining sci-fi/horror flick. Josh puts a trademark stamp on his curiously unkempt (only in back)

331

Josh Hartnett in need of a nut in *Here on Earth* (2000). PHOTOFEST

bedhead hair-do (meaning the look in *H2O* wasn't a fluke of styling) and gives us plenty of opportunities to try and count the number of parentheses in the dimples of his smile.

Even with his imposing on-screen size, he's still too good to be the simple bad guy brunette in the somber teen romance *Here on Earth* (2000), thankfully thwarting our expectations when he's been cast opposite a sublime looker like Chris Klein. The slow-paced film begs for both of these guys to strip off their shirts while they're hard at work rebuilding the diner they caused to burn down, but only Klein does the honors, which should have been a clue to where our sympathies were supposed to lie. Still, Josh is clearly the better boy and Leelee Sobieski's senseless choice is dictated entirely by the script.

This taking-off-the-shirt business makes Josh kind of queasy. "I'm not good at that whole shirt-off thing," he told *Detour* magazine in 2000. "I'm just a scrawny little thing, and there are lots of people who are in good shape. Girls would rather see their bodies than mine."

Interview magazine predictably asked him about doing nude scenes in its February, 2000 issue: "I'm not comfortable with it yet, but we'll see. Some people have this meat-market mentality, so you've got to take your shirt off because it will bring girls into the theater...I don't have a very good body. Some of these guys work out every day. I work out maybe once a year, so they've got me beat."

When he answers the door wearing just a towel to accept a plate of frosted brownies from a cute girl in *The Virgin Suicides* (2000), the thought that Josh Hartnett needs a tone or a tuck here and there never crosses your mind. He's lean and beautiful, with a generous splay of dark black hair overrunning his belly button. The fact that he's not sporting a six-pack or otherwise endowed with the severe ridges of male model-dom may be to blame for an actor in great shape and with a gorgeous physique somehow thinking he's not up to snuff. We should all be so disappointed.

He's on screen for just under 30 minutes in *The Virgin Suicides*, writer-director Sofia Coppola's dreamy and poetic evocation of Jeffrey Eugenides' novel about the deaths of five beautiful teenagers in Michigan during the mid-1970s, easily one of the best films of the year. Josh plays Trip Fontaine (a great name for a teen idol), a charming, egocentric pothead who wears tinted shades and can't get his mind off of Lux Lisbon (Kirsten Dunst). He's obsessed with her, mostly because she seems completely indifferent to him. Trip's gay dad isn't much help in the advice department, but Trip works up the courage to ask Lux to the prom after attempting to ingratiate himself with her oddball and strictly religious parents (Kathleen Turner and James Woods) by coming over to watch TV.

The prom date turns out to be life-altering for Trip, who's played in flash-forwards by Michael Paré, the young actor who came out of "nowhere" for his shot at being the next big thing with *Eddie and the Cruisers* (1983).

His first time on screen with a mop of hair, Josh makes all the right moves as Trip. He has the body language down pat. Even the small space between his front teeth seems right. And the darkness around his eyes.

He's billed as Joshua Hartnett for his inconsequential role as Warren Beatty's and Diane Keaton's teenaged son in the notoriously long-delayed, reworked, and still messed-up *Town & Country*, shot in 1998, but not released until 2001. Likewise held-up, though this time because the studio was nervous about the violent content post-Columbine, *O* (2001) appeared on screens three years after it was shot. Josh plays a sulking beauty named Hugo, a steroid-shooting basketball player who mercilessly plots the downfall of the team's African-American star player (and several others) in this teenaged variation on Shakespeare's *Othello*. He's surprisingly cast in *Blow Dry* (2000) as Alan Rickman's son in the small British comedy about a dysfunctional family of hairdressers, but handles the chore nicely and the accent quite well.

Then there's the matter of that obscure little movie about *Pearl Harbor* that launched Josh Hartnett into worldwide heartthrob status, something he has dramatically shied away from while making use of the attention to try and fashion himself a career that's here today and here tomorrow.

"Everybody is objectified in it because it's a heroic, epic love story," Josh told *Elle* magazine in September of 2000. "So I do take my shirt off, which is kind of a cheesy way to get people into the theater."

I would have preferred much more of that kind of cheese than the stuff they fashioned the script out of; *Pearl Harbor* is recycled tripe. It's so pathetically a retread of B-movie romances and dumb dialogue that you wouldn't miss an emotional nuance or plot contrivance if the movie were played with the sound turned off. Why spend 135 million dollars on a film that features one of the most devastating events in American military history as its centerpiece and then decide not to tell a story worth telling? For Josh Hartnett, the opportunity to be swallowed up by a shameful summer blockbuster and spat out a pretty boy symbol of why we fought a war was a decision that made perfect sense. It wasn't calculation on his part, only an opportunity, and I'm sure he hoped he was making a good film.

Something tells me he'll have plenty more opportunities. Even before the year was out, his role in *Black Hawk Down* (2001) served up a powerful repudiation of *Pearl Harbor*'s schmaltz despite having the same producer. A proven dramatic actor, he's also eminently deserving of a romantic comedy on a grander scale than *40 Days and 40 Nights* (2002), in which he's saddled with unfunny and awkward situations, such as the one that has him walking around the office unaware that he's

British *Queer As Folk* star Charlie Hunnam (left), the very essence of goodness, as Dickens' *Nicholas Nickleby* (2002), with Jamie Bell as Smike. PHOTOFEST

got a hard-on. Wisely, he subsequently turned down a three-picture deal to become the new millennia's *Superman*. His buddy cop romp with Harrison Ford in *Hollywood Homicide* (2003) was sadly undone by a substandard script that failed its two stars, who were left with clumsy scenes that wouldn't have played at all with less familiar faces. Meanwhile, Josh continues to look for a hairstyle that works and I'm enjoying the pursuit. Another film: *Wicker Park* (2004).

The parade of male beauty at the movies continues its inevitable march forward into the new millennium. Discovered while joking around at a shoe store in front of a television producer, who promptly put him in the BBC-teen series *Byker Grove* (1998-), Newcastle-born **Charlie Hunnam** (1980-　) didn't take long to make his mark. His breakout performance came playing 15-year-old Nathan in the original British series *Queer As Folk* (1999-2000), endearing himself to gay men, young and old alike, as the selfish, but lovable teenager making his first foray into the gay scene in Manchester. He was a welcome guest star on the short-lived American television series *Young Americans* (2000) and a lovely and very cocky co-star during the equally short run of *Undeclared* (2001). Disgracefully under-employed as a malevolent boyfriend who's gone missing in *Abandon* (2002), a runner-up for the worst film of the year, he then received his glorious due as the heavenly lead in *Nicholas Nickleby* (2002). Lean and tall in his striking funereal garb, the white blond of his shiny clean hair ornamenting his angelic features, Nicholas is "the very definition of goodness." His innate kindness, profound sense of honor, and deep love of family are manifest throughout, but especially touching in his loving commitment to Smike (*Billy Elliot*'s Jamie Bell). Other films: *Whatever Happened to Harold Smith?* (1999), *Cold Mountain* (2003).

Male model, then actor Ian Somerhalder desires another young man to share his bed in *The Rules of Attraction* (2002). PHOTOFEST

Ian Somerhalder (1978-   ) was also on *Young Americans* (2000), playing a schoolboy who questions his sexuality after falling for a butch young lady posing as a guy. He pimps out troubled Hayden Christensen after taking a glance at him in the shower in *Life As A House* (2001), then enjoys a brief but sweaty love affair with lucky Mary Steenburgen, his girlfriend's mom. He's also counterproductively good-looking as one of the boys who torments Matthew Shepard in the TV-made *Anatomy of a Hate Crime* (2001), and plays a depressed orderly who learns about love from a breast cancer patient in the sappy, but well-intentioned *Changing Hearts* (2002). His turn as a gay college student with a crush on James Van Der Beek and a penchant for dancing in his undies in *The Rules of Attraction* (2002) is a revelation, however. A former male model with hypnotic blue eyes and the thickest, sexiest belly button trail you've ever seen, Ian steals this vastly-underrated social satire, and companion piece to *American Psycho* (2000), as the sole character worth caring about. Another film: *In Enemy Hands* (2004).

Colin Farrell (1976-   ) is the bad boy flavor of the moment. His media-magnified proclivity for talking a blue streak and championing a lifestyle of booze, chain-smoking, and inveterate rutting (he's a fuckaholic) makes him, in some ways, the ideal young male actor of the here and now. Unapologetic about who he is and what he likes to do, he's toying with the threatening potential of the in-your-face hedonist as sex star. The son of famed Irish footballer Eamon Farrell, the Dublin-born Colin studied acting at the Gaiety Drama School, then dropped out for two seasons' work riding horses and looking very much the romantic lead on the BBC sitcom *Ballykissangel* (1996-97). He made his feature film debut 26 minutes into Tim Roth's disturbing incest drama *The War Zone* (1999), showing up for two scenes, then was spotted by Kevin Spacey, who saw to his casting as a member of a Dublin heist team in *Ordinary Decent Criminal* (2000). The kid arrived, as the saying goes, with his lead performance as a charismatic Texan rebel caught up in the macho-shaping, psychologically-shattering, and brutal physicality of young soldiers training for war in Vietnam in Joel Schumacher's low-budget *Tigerland* (2000). Despite, or perhaps because of, the subject matter, we can be grateful for Colin's fleeting full-frontal eleven minutes in, thanks to frame-by-frame advance.

Fifteen minutes into the wasteful *American Outlaws* (2001), his Jesse James has got his shirt off for one scene, helping distract us for two minutes from an uninspired treatment that manages to be even less entertaining than *Young Guns* (1988). Here are good actors playing Old West without any of the fun of playing. *Hart's War* (2002), also a genre throwback, at least gave Colin a well-written role in this WWII prison camp film that segues into a courtroom thriller with nebulous definitions of heroism provided by Bruce Willis. Set up as a dark-haired villain, Danny "the Fed," in Steven Spielberg's *Minority Report* (2002), he's also the one quite sensibly questioning a system of justice based on arresting people for premeditating homicide. His shitheel in *Phone Booth* (2002), a gimmicky drama shot in 12 days that has a morally corrupt man facing his personal demons while being held hostage in a phone booth by an unseen sniper, allows him to play the hell out of the climax, while *The Recruit* (2003) offers him as a CIA trainee embroiled in a profoundly underwhelming game of charades. Other films: *Daredevil* (2003), *Intermission* (2003), *S.W.A.T.* (2003), *A Home at the End of the World* (2003), *Alexander* (2004).

The biggest male star in all of Mexico also happens to be one of the most beautiful men to occupy an entire country's devotion since Alain Delon's heyday in France. **Gael Garcìa Bernal** (1978-   ), whose parents are both performers, became an actor at age six. At 18, he starred in the 16-minute Oscar-nominated live-action short film *De tripas, corazón* (1996), playing a virginal milkboy hauled to a brothel by friends. With *Amores Perros* (2000), an Oscar nominee for Best Foreign-Language Film, he burnt up the screen as the tragically romantic young man hoping to run off with his elder brother's abused wife on winnings from illegal dogfights. He's easily the most tempting, as well as most passionate, of Monica Potter's five potential boyfriends in the otherwise dull English-language romance drama *I'm With Lucy* (2002). Back to Mexico for *El Crimen del Padre Amaro* (2002), also an Oscar nominee, he's the title young priest who falls in love with a parishioner and then must face the spiritual, moral, and physical consequences of that relationship. A soap opera loaded with religious political corruption, and based on a 19th Century Portuguese novel, the film proved a cultural flash point for Catholics in Mexico and became the highest-grossing film in the country's history.

Box-office history had also been made the year before. *Y Tu Mamá También* (2001), released in the US in 2002, and my candidate for the best film of the year, is a potent sexual and sociopolitical fable undressed as a low-budget teen-sex flick. Pants-down the hottest, sexiest, most erotic film I've seen in ages, it takes us on a journey with two perpetually-horny teenaged boys (real-life best friends Bernal and Diego Luna)

336

Colin Farrell as Jesse James in *American Outlaws* (2001). EVERETT COLLECTION

as they escort an unhappy older woman on a weekend trip to a fictional beach. Along the way, while the boys are thoroughly self-obsessed with all things sexual, the countryside outside their car windows reveals itself alternately desolate, impoverished, violent, political, militaristic, quaint, and classist—a remarkable snapshot of Mexico. The hierarchical distinctions of class are also made evident amongst the friends: one rich, one poor; one circumcised, one uncircumcised.

Both boys are beauties and their macho competitiveness, juvenile sex talk, and delicate egos are given full work-outs, but Bernal is exceptionally pretty and brings an infectiously joyful and uninhibited life to his character. He smiles ear-to-ear at the least provocation, has a big, hearty laugh, and big green eyes that invite the whole world to step in closer. Beyond his good looks, and they are hard to get beyond, is a performance that doesn't seem like a performance. He and Luna are absolute naturals.

The film also delivers the sensual goods. Balking at having to cut the film for an R-rating (though such a version exists, so be careful), director Alfonso Cuaron released the film unrated. We're treated to sexy nude swims, shower room towel-snapping, comic and mighty-quick couplings, an intensely erotic commingling late in the film, and both boys masturbating simultaneously while laid out on diving boards over the pool. Other films: *Dreaming of Julia* (2001), *Don't Tempt Me* (2001)*, Lily and the Secret Planting* (2002), *Fidel* (2002, as Che Guevara), *Dot the I* (2003), *The Motorcycle Diaries* (2003), and Pedro Almodovar's *La Mala educación* (*Bad Education*; 2004).

As we look ahead and wonder who, we might also look back at the wealth of who. Lists are horrible things, because there's either too much to include or too much to leave off, and in this case you're bound to omit somebody's favorite, as well as several hundred foreign film heartthrobs yet to be appreciated in the west. And though I'm quite sure that Jack Elam was beautiful to someone, he didn't make the cut. Given the fact that most leading men, by definition, have to be pleasing to look at if they're going to play in the movies, one could argue that you might as well include everybody at one time or another in their career. I've been slightly pickier, though this list should still be viewed as a starter. As to who's handsome, who's

Gael García Bernal is Mexico's hottest male film star, shown here in tight close-up from *Amores Perros* (2000). PHOTOFEST

pretty, and where's so and so, I leave that up to you. The single movie listed after each name is a recommendation of where to catch the actor in a state approaching bliss, whether the movie sucks or not. Yes, there's a tendency toward early roles for most, but I'm only listing one title and when you're faced with guys like Connery and Newman it's possible to find stunning examples at different periods of their maturity.

If this seems like a hell of a lot of people, it is. If it's any consolation, there's another beauty born every minute.

I'm a sucker for all of them.

A: Willie Aames (*Paradise*); Leonardo Abaraglia (*Burnt Money*); Rodolpho Acosta (*Bullfighter and the Lady*); Ben Affleck (*Chasing Amy*); Edward Albert (*Butterflies Are Free*); Ross Alexander (*I Married A Doctor*); Bill Allen (*Rad*); Ray Allen (*He Got Game*); Björn Andresen (*Death in Venice*); Jean-Hugues Anglade (*L'Homme Blesse*); Steve Antin (*The Last American Virgin*); Thomas Arklie (*Heaven's A Drag*); Alessandro Ascoli (*The Son's Room*); Dana Ashbrook (*Twin Peaks: Fire Walk With Me*); Armand Assante (*Private Benjamin*); Nils Asther (*The Blue Danube*); Mackenzie Astin (*In Love and War*); Christopher Atkins (*The Blue Lagoon*); Edward Atterton (*Far Harbor*); Jean-Pierre Aumont (*Dark Eyes*); Frankie Avalon (*Muscle Beach Party*); Lew Ayres (*Iron Man*); Eloy Azarin (*All About My Mother*); Charles Aznavour (*Paris in the Month of August*)

B: Kevin Bacon (*Footloose*); Chet Baker (*Hell's Horizon*); Alec Baldwin (*Prelude To A Kiss*); Stephen Baldwin (*Threesome*); William Baldwin (*Backdraft*); Christian Bale (*American Psycho*); Anderson Ballesteros (*Our Lady of the Assassins*); Cameron Bancroft (*Love and Human Remains*); Antonio Banderas (*Evita*); Lex Barker (*Tarzan's Magic Fountain*); Jean-Marc Barr (*The Big Blue*); Matthew Barry (*Luna*); Neill Barry (*O.C. & Stiggs*); John Barrymore, Jr. (*Quebec*); Richard Barthelmess (*Tol'able David*); Peter Barton (*Friday the 13th: The Final Chapter*); Mikhail Baryshnikov (*White Nights*); Danté Basco (*The Debut*); Randall Batinkoff (*For Keeps*); Steven Bauer (*Scarface*); Adam Beach (*Squanto: A Warrior's Tale*); Randy Becker (*Love! Valour! Compassion!*); John Beal (*The Little Minister*); Sean Bean (*Stormy Monday*); Warren Beatty (*Splendor in the Grass*); Kuno Becker (*Lucia, Lucia*); Jason Beghe (*Monkey Shines*); Jason Behr (*Rites of Passage*); Harry Belafonte (*Carmen Jones*); Rex Bell (*Wild West Romance*); Bill Bellamy (*How To Be A Player*); Michael Bendetti (*Netherworld*); Dirk Benedict (*Georgia, Georgia*); Angus Benfield (*Lex and Rory*); Jonathan Bennett (*Mean Girls*); Robby Benson (*Ode to Billy Joe*); Tom Berenger (*In Praise of Older Women*); Peter Berg (*Shocker*); Helmut Berger (*Dorian Gray*); Michael Bergin (*The Broken Hearts Club*); Tim Bergmann (*Regular Guys*); Gael García Bernal (*Y Tu Mamá También*); Jack Beutel (*The Outlaw*); Nathan Bexton (*Nowhere*); Turhan Bey (*Sudan*); Richard Beymer (*West Side Story*); Michael Biehn (*Coach*); Won Bin (*Guns & Talks*); William Bishop (*Girl Crazy*); Gerard Blain (*Deadlier Than the Male*); Pierre Blaise (*Lacombe Lucien*); Jon Blake (*Freedom*); Michael Blodgett (*Beyond the Valley of the Dolls*); Brian Bloom (*Deuce Coupe*); Orlando Bloom (*The Lord of the Rings*); Hart Bochner (*Islands in the Stream*); Dirk Bogarde (*The Blue Lamp*); Volker Bohnet (*The Bridge*); Pat Boone (*April Love*); Charley Boorman (*The Emerald Forest*); Simon Bossell (*Spider & Rose*); Barry Bostwick (*Movie Movie*); Joseph Bottoms (*The Dive*); Timothy Bottoms (The *Last Picture Show*); John Bowers (*Day Dreams*); David Bowie (*The Man Who Fell To Earth*); Bruce Boxleitner (*The Baltimore Bullet*); Alan Boyce (*Permanent Record*); Stephen Boyd (*Ben Hur*); Greg Bradford (*Lovelines*); Jesse Bradford (*Swimfan*); Lillo Brancato (*A Bronx Tale*); Marlon Brando (*A Streetcar Named Desire*); Steve Braun (*The Trip*); Rossano Brazzi (*Brute Force*); Derek Brewer (*Nowhere*); Keith Brewer (*Nowhere*); Jeff Bridges (*Thunderbolt and Lightfoot*); Pat Briggs (*All Over Me*); Herman Brix/Bruce Bennett (*Tarzan & Green Goddess*); Matthew Broderick (*Torch Song Trilogy*); James Brolin (*Westworld*); Josh Brolin (*Flirting with Disaster*); John Bromfield (*Hold That Line*); Pierce Brosnan (*The Fourth Protocol*); Jordan Brower (*Speedway Junky*); Jimmy Brown (*The Road Warrior*); Peter Brown (*Kitten With A Whip*); Johnny Mack Brown (*The Fair Co-Ed*); Georges Bruggeman (*The Sign of the Cross*); Jack Buchanan (*Confetti*); Horst Buchholz (*One, Two, Three*); Rick Burks (*Blood Diner*); Tom Burlinson (*The Man from Snowy River*); Niall Byrne (*The Miracle*); Walter Byron (*Queen Kelly*)

C: Jason Cadieux (*Lilies*); Eddie Cahill (*Miracle*); Dean Cain (*The Broken Hearts Club*); Rory Calhoun (*Something For the Boys*); Michael Callan (*Because They're Young*); Kevin Callisher (*Voodoo Academy*); Kirk Cameron (*Like Father, Like Son*); Bruce Campbell (*Evil Dead II: Dead By Dawn*); Webster Campbell (*Oh, Daddy*); Chris Campion (*Field of Honor*); Bruno Campos (*O Quatrilho*); Keith Carradine (*The Duellists*); Matthieu Carriere (*Young Torless*); Nino Castelnuovo (*The Umbrellas of Cherbourg*); Maxwell Caulfield (*Grease 2*); Jim Caviezel (*The Thin Red Line*); Henry Cavill (*The Count of Monte Cristo*);

George Chakiris (*West Side Story*); Richard Chamberlain (*Petulia*); Justin Chambers (*The Musketeer*); Damian Chapa (*Bound by Honor*); Ben Chaplin (*The Truth About Cats & Dogs*); Chayanne (*Dance With Me*); Christopher Scott Cherot (*Hav Plenty*); Craig Chester (*Swoon*); Chad Christ (*Gattaca*); Hayden Christensen (*Life As A House*); David Christopher (*The M.O. of M.I.*); Eddie Cibrian (*Living Out Loud*); Pierre Clementi (*Belle de Jour*); Nicolai Cleve (*Sebastian*); Montgomery Clift (*The Heiress*); Elmer Clifton (*Intolerance*); George Clooney (*Out of Sight*); Steve Cochran (*Shark River*); Ronald Colman (*The Dark Angel*); Scott Colomby (*Caddyshack*); Vince Colosimo (*Moving Out*); Trax Colton (*It Happened in Athens*); Sean Connery (*Dr. No*); Robert Conrad (*Palm Springs Weekend*); Gary Cooper (*A Farewell to Arms*); Anthony Corlan (*Something for Everyone*); Nick Cornish (*Psycho Beach Party*); Nick Corri (*Tropical Snow*); Joaquin Cortes (*The Flower of My Secret*); Ricardo Cortez (*The Cat's Pajamas*); Daniel Cosgrove (*Valentine*); Maurice Costello *(A Tale of Two Cities)*; Nicolaj Coster-Waldau (*Misery Harbour*); Kevin Costner (*No Way Out*); Christian Coulson (*The Hours*); Jerome Courtland (*Together Again*); Larry "Buster" Crabbe (*Tarzan the Fearless*); James Craig (*Thunder Trail*); Grant Cramer (*Hardbodies*); Mathieu Crepeau (*Terminale*); Stanislas Crevillén (*The Closet*); Richard Cromwell (*The Age of Consent*); Harry Crosby (*Friday the 13th*); Russell Crowe (*Proof*); Billy Crudup (*The Hi-Lo Country*); Tom Cruise (*All the Right Moves*); Vladimir Cruz (*Strawberry and Chocolate*); Macaulay Culkin (*Party Monster*); Tony Curtis (*Houdini*); Zbigniew Cybulski (*Ashes and Diamonds*)

D: Mark Dacascos (*Only the Strong*); Joe Dallesandro (*Flesh*); Timothy Dalton (*The Lion in Winter*); Timothy Daly (*Diner*); Mark Damon (*The Rebel Breed*); Matt Damon (*Good Will Hunting*); Hugh Dancy (*The Sleeping Dictionary*); Helmut Dantine *(Hotel Berlin)*; Ray Danton (*The Night Runner*); James D'Arcy (*Dot the I*); James Darren (*Gidget*); John Darrow (*High School Hero*); Richard Davalos (*East of Eden*); John Davidson (*The Happiest Millionaire*); Brad Davis (*Midnight Express*); Clifton Davis (*Lost in the Stars*); Bruce Davison (*Last Summer*); Daniel Day Lewis (*Last of the Mohicans*); James Dean (*East of Eden*); Simon de la Brosse (*Pauline At the Beach*); Cristian de la Fuente (*Driven*); Alain Delon (*Purple Noon*); Xavier Deluc (*La Triche*); Guillaume Depardieu (*All/Mornings of the World*); Johnny Depp (*Cry-Baby*); John Derek (*Knock On Any Door*); Patrick Dewaere (*Going Places*); Brandon de Wilde (*Hud*); Leonardo DiCaprio (*Titanic*); Taye Diggs (*The Best Man*); Matt Dillon (*The Flamingo Kid*); Alex Dimitriades (*Head On*); Jerry Dinome (*Tomboy*); Stéfano Dionisi (*Farinelli*); Troy Donahue (*Parrish*); Robert Donat (*The Private Life of Henry VIII*); Stephen Dorff (*Blade*); Christoph Dostal (*For God and Country*); Kenny Doughty (*Crush*); Tom Douglas (*The Country Flapper*); Robert Downey, Jr. (*Chances Are*); Charles Drake (*Now, Voyager*); David Duchovny (*The Rapture*); Michael Dudikoff (*American Ninja*); Josh Duhamel (*Win a Date with Tad Hamilton*); Keir Dullea (*The Hoodlum Priest*); James Duval (*The Doom Generation*); Cameron Dye (*Body Rock*)

E: Michael Ealy (*Barbershop*); Edward Earle (*Through Turbulent Waters*); Jeff East (*The Hazing*); Clint Eastwood (*Lafayette Escadrille*); Pablo Echarri (*Burnt Money*); Nelson Eddy (*Naughty Marietta*); Vince Edwards (*Mr. Universe*); Jérémie Elkaïm (*Come Undone*); Cary Elwes (*The Princess Bride*); Omar Epps (*The Wood*); John Ericson (*Teresa*); Rob Estes (*Halfway House*); Will Estes (*New Port South*); Chris Evans (*Not Another Teen Movie*); Robert Evans (*The Sun Also Rises*); Chad Everett (*Johnny Tiger*); Rupert Everett (*Another Country*)

F: Peter Facinelli (*Dancer, Texas Pop. 81*); Jeff Fahey (*Psycho III*); Douglas Fairbanks, Jr. *(A Woman of Affairs)*; Sean Faris (*The Brotherhood II: Young Warlocks*); Charles Farrell (*Lucky Star*); Colin Farrell (*Tigerland*); Nicola Farron (*Body Count*); Oded Fehr (*The Mummy*); Alex Feldman (*Mr. Smith Gets A Hustler*); Joseph Fiennes (*Shakespeare in Love*); Ralph Fiennes (*The English Patient*); Fabrizio Filippo (*Waydowntown*); Peter Firth (*Equus*); Sean Patrick Flanery (*A Tiger's Tale*); Errol Flynn (*Adventures of Robin Hood*); Sean Flynn (*The Son of Captain Blood*); Scott Foley (*Below*); Ralph Forbes (*The Trail of '98*); Harrison Ford (*Star Wars*); Trent Ford (*Deeply*); Mark Forest (*Son of Samson*); Philippe Forquet (*Take Her, She's Mine*); Fabian Forte (*Hound-Dog Man*); Earle Foxe (*The Love Mask*); Jamie Foxx (*Any Given Sunday*); Robert Francis (*The Long Gray Line*); James Franciscus (*Youngblood Hawke*); James Franco (*Whatever It Takes*); Noah Frank (*The Brotherhood II: Young Warlocks*); Brendan Fraser (*George of the Jungle*); John Fraser (*The Trials of Oscar Wilde*); Mark Frechette (*Zabriskie Point*); Drew Fuller (*Voodoo Academy*)

G: Clark Gable (*It Happened One Night*); Peter Gallagher (*The Idolmaker*); Adam Garcia (*Bootmen*); Andy Garcia (*Internal Affairs*); Leif Garrett (*Peter Lundy and the Medicine Hat Stallion*); Alessandro Gassman (*Devils of Monza*); Dan Gauthier (*Teen Witch*); John Gavin (*A Time To Live and A Time To Die*); Mitch Gaylord (*American Anthem*); Jason Gedrick (*Promised Land*); Giuliano Gemma (*Day of Anger*); Race Gentry (*The Lawless Breed*); Jason George (*Clockstoppers*); Richard Gere (*Days of Heaven*); Zen

Gesner (*Wish Me Luck*); Giancarlo Giannini (*Love & Anarchy*); Reynaldo Gianecchini (*Overwhelming Women*); Mel Gibson (*The Bounty*); Thomas Gibson (*Sleep With Me*); John Gilbert (*The Big Parade*); Luigi Gillianni (*Boccaccio '70*); Massimo Girotti (*Ossessione*); Gaston Glass (*Humoresque*); Iain Glen (*Mountains of the Moon*); Ricky Paull Goldin (*Hyper Sapien*); Nicholas Gonzalez (*The Princess and the Barrio Boy*); Cuba Gooding, Jr. (*Jerry Maguire*); Joseph Gordon-Levitt (*Manic*); Todd Graff (*Not Quite Paradise*); Farley Granger (*Strangers on a Train*); Cary Grant (*Holiday*); Hugh Grant (*Maurice*); Rupert Graves (*Maurice*); Brian Austin Green (*Laws of Deception*); Richard Greene (*Kentucky*); Adrian Grenier (*Drive Me Crazy*); Richard Grieco (*If Looks Could Kill*); Gary Grimes (*Cahill—United States Marshall*); Ioan Gruffud (*Wilde*); Lance Guest (*The Last Starfighter*); Giovanni Guidelli (*Where Angels Fear to Tread*); Mehmet Gunsun (*Steam: The Turkish Bath*); Jake Gyllenhaal (*Bubble Boy*)

H: Lukas Haas (*johns*); Raymond Hackett (*The Trial of Mary Dugan*); Reed Hadley (*Zorro's Fighting Legion*); William Haines (*The Midnight Express*); James Hall (*Hell's Angels*); Jon Hall (*The Hurricane*); Brett Halsey (*Return to Peyton Place*); Ashley Hamilton (*Beethoven's 2nd*); George Hamilton (*Where the Boys Are*); Neil Hamilton (*Beau Geste* - 1926); Harry Hamlin (*Clash of the Titans*); John Hansen (*The Christine Jorgensen Story*); Lars Hanson (*The Saga of Gosta Berling*); Ty Hardin (*PT 109*); Marek Harloff (*The Deathmaker*); Tom Harper (*What A Girl Wants*); Josh Hartnett (*The Faculty*); Laurence Harvey (*Room at the Top*); Rodney Harvey (*Mixed Blood*); Hurd Hatfield (*Picture of Dorian Gray*); Ethan Hawke (*Before Sunrise*); Sessue Hayakawa (*The Cheat*); Karl Held (*Ready for the People*); David Hemmings (*Blow-Up*); Josh Henderson (*Leeches*); Martin Henderson (*Windtalkers*); William Henry (*China Seas*); Andreas Herder (*The Blue Hour*); Jay Hernandez (*crazy/beautiful*); David Hewlett (*Where the Heart Is*); Martin Hewitt (*Endless Love*); Jon-Erik Hexum (*The Bear*); Darryl Hickman (*Fighting Father Dunne*); Ken Higelin (*A' La Mode*); Terence Hill (*God Forgives...I Don't!*); Peter Hinwood (*The Rocky Horror Picture Show*); Emile Hirsch (*The Dangerous Lives of Altar Boys*); Robert Hoffman (*Grand Slam*); Thom Hoffman (*The 4th Man*); Marco Hofschneider (*Europa, Europa*); William Holden (*Golden Boy*); Phillips Holmes (*An American Tragedy*); Charles Homet (*Beginner's Luck*); Tom Hompertz (*Lonesome Cowboys*); Adam Horovitz (*Lost Angels*); Djimon Hounsou (*Gladiator*); Adam Coleman Howard (*Quiet Cool*); C. Thomas Howell (*To Protect and Serve*); Reed Howes (*Lightning Romance*); Rock Hudson (*Taza, Son of Cochise*); Charlie Hunnam (*Nicholas Nickleby*); Jeffrey Hunter (*Red Skies of Montana*); Tab Hunter (*Island of Desire*)

I: Sacha Iakovlev (*Ivan and Abraham*); Ben Indra (*Voodoo Academy*); Tom Irish (*Hondo*)

J: Jonathan Jackson (*Tuck Everlasting*); Richard Jaeckl (*Come Back, Little Sheba*); Dalton James (*My Father, the Hero*); Oliver James (*What A Girl Wants*); Thomas Jane (*The Velocity of Gary*); Cas Jansen (*Leak*); Daniel C. Jenkins (*O.C. & Stiggs*); Brad Johnson (Always); Don Johnson (*Zachariah*); Andras Jones (*Far From Home*); Christopher Jones (*Three in the Attic*); Richard T. Jones (*The Wood*); Sam Jones (*Flash Gordon*); Jeremy Jordan (*Leaving Las Vegas*); Rhett Jordan (*Voodoo Academy*); Ben Jorgenson (*The Break*); Louis Jourdan (*Bird of Paradise*)

K: Antonie Kamerling (*Suite 16*); Dayton Ka'Ne (*Hurricane*); Takeshi Kaneshiro (*Fallen Angels*); Lee Kang-Sheng (*Vive L'Amour*); Vincent Kartheiser (*Another Day in Paradise*); William Katt (*Carrie*); Yasuke Kawazu (*Cruel Story of Youth*); Billy Kay (*L.I.E.*); Raymond Keane (*April Fool*); Andrew Keegan (*The Broken Hearts Club*); Matt Keeslar (*Urbania*); Donald Keith (*Secrets*); Hiram Keller (*Fellini Satyricon*); Gene Kelly (*For Me and My Gal*); Jim Kelly (*Enter the Dragon*); Paul Kelly (*Fit to Fight*); Matty Kemp (*The Magnificent Flirt*); Bobby Kendall (*Pink Narcissus*); Udo Kier (*Mark of the Devil*); Val Kilmer (*Real Genius*); Perry King (*Andy Warhol's Bad*); Luke Kirby (*Mambo Italiano*); Justin Kirk (*Love! Valour! Compassion!*); Alf Kjellen (*Torment*); Chris Klein (*Election*); Christopher Knight (*Studs Lonigan*); Esmond Knight (*77 Park Lane*); Michael Knight (*Date With an Angel*); Boris Kodjoe (*Brown Sugar*); Shin Koyamada (*The Last Samurai*); Brian Krause (*Sleepwalkers*); Kurt Kreuger (*The Strange Death of Adolf Hitler*); Ashton Kutcher (*Dude, Where's My Car?*); Aaron Kwok (*Saviour of the Soul*)

L: Lorenzo Lamas (*Body Rock*); Christopher Lambert (*Greystoke, Legend of Tarzan*); Burt Lancaster (*The Crimson Pirate*); Michael Landes (*An American Summer*); Michael Landon (*I Was A Teenage Werewolf*); Jonny Lang (*Blues Brothers 2000*); Frank Langella (*Dracula*); Mario Lanza (*That Midnight Kiss*); Rod La Rocque (*Filling His Own Shoes*); Robert La Tourneaux (*The Boys in the Band*); Matt Lattanzi (*My Tutor*); John Laughlin (*Crimes of Passion*); Adam LaVorgna (*I'll Be Home for Christmas*); John Phillip Law (*The Russians Are Coming...*); Jude Law (*Wilde*); Peter Lawford (*The White Cliffs of Dover*); James Layton (*The Wolves of Kromer*); Justin Lazard (*Spike of Bensonhurst*); Vincent Lecoeur (*Deep in the Woods*); Francis Lederer (*Pandora's Box*); Heath Ledger (*A Knight's Tale*); Brandon Lee (*The Crow*); Bruce Lee (*The Chinese Connection*); Mark Lee (*Gallipoli*); Jason Scott Lee (*The Jungle Book*);

Michael Legge (*Angela's Ashes*); Leon (*Cool Runnings*); Robert Sean Leonard (*Dead Poets Society*); Marco Leonardi (*Cinema Paradiso*); Djellil Lespert (*Human Resources*); Jared Leto (*Prefontaine*); Yehuda Levi (*Yossi & Jagger*); Andrew Levitas (*Psycho Beach Party*); George Lewis (*His People*); Jason Lewis (*Next Stop Wonderland*); Thierry Lhermitte (*Going Places*); Mitchell Lichtenstein (*Streamers*); Ye Liu (*Lan Yu*); Robert Locke (*'68*); Calvin Lockhart (*Salt and Pepper*); Harold Lockwood (*The Lost Address*); Jason London (*Man in the Moon*); Jeremy London (*Dazed & Confused*); John Lone (*The Last Emperor*); Richard Long (*Kansas Raiders*); Carlos Lopez (*Savage Nights*); Mario Lopez (*Outta Time*); Alexis Loret (*Alice and Martin*); Daniel Lortie (*Danny in the Sky*); Rob Lowe (*The Hotel New Hampshire*); Derek Luke (*Antwone Fisher*); Diego Luna (*Y Tu Mamá También*); Michael Lutz (*Leeches*); Michael Lyndon (*The Lightship*); Jeffery Lynn (*Four Daughters*); Steve Lyon (*Campus Man*); Greg Lyczkowski (*Brotherhood II: Young Warlocks*)

M: James MacArthur (*Swiss Family Robinson*); Angus MacFadyen (*The Lost Language of Cranes*); Malcolm MacGregor (*Smouldering Fires*); Kyle MacLachlan (*Blue Velvet*); Guy Madison (*Till the End of Time*); Benoit Magimel (*Les Voleurs*); George Maharis (*Sylvia*); Costas Mandylor (*Mobsters*); Frederic Mangenot (*A Summer Dress*); Byron Mann (*Street Fighter*); Kris Mann (*Slugs*); Ettore Manni (*She Wolf*); Valerio Foglia Manzillo (*The Embalmer*); Jean Marais (*Orpheus*); Frederic March (*The Royal Family of Broadway*); Georges Marchal (*Vautrin the Thief*); Saverio Marconi (*Padre Padrone*); James Marsden (*Disturbing Behavior*); Alan Marshal (*The Garden of Allah*); James Marshall (*Gladiator*); Dewey Martin (*The Big Sky*); A Martinez (*The Cowboys*); Olivier Martinez (*The Horseman on the Roof*); Vincent Martinez (*The School of Flesh*); Vladimir Mashkov (*The Thief*); Marcello Mastroianni (*The Accusation*); Kerwin Mathews (*7th Voyage of Sinbad*); Maximillian (*Vatos*); Lon McCallister (*Stage Door Canteen*); David McCallum (*The Great Escape*); Malcolm McClintock (*On Your Own*); Doug McClure (*Because They're Young*); Matthew McConaughey (*A Time To Kill*); Joel McCrea (*The Sport Parade*); Shane McDermott (*Airborne*); Francis McDonald (*Mr. Dolan of New York*); Peter McEnery (*Entertaining Mr. Sloane*); Ewan McGregor (*The Pillow Book*); Malcolm McGregor (*All the Brothers Were Valiant*); Scott McGinnis (*Sky Bandits*); Stephen McHattie (*James Dean* -TV); Gardner McKay (*The Pleasure Seekers*); William McNamara (*Texasville*); Ricardo Meneses (*O Fantasma*); Paul Mercurio (*Strictly Ballroom*); Marco Mestriner (*The Flavor of Corn*); Gerald Meynier (*Romeo and Juliet*); Arturo Meza (*Doña Herlinda and Her Son*); Ray Milland (*Easy Living*); Jonny Lee Miller (*Trainspotting*); Ty Miller (*Slaughterhouse Rock*); Eddie Mills (*Dancer, Texas Pop. 81*); Sal Mineo (*Rebel Without A Cause*); Sasha Mitchell (*Spike of Bensonhurst*); James Monks (*How Green Was My Valley*); Paolo Montalban (*American Adobo*); George Montgomery (*The Lone Ranger*); Robert Montgomery (*Hell Below*); Geoffrey Moody (*Leather Jacket Love Story*); Roger Moore (*The Last Time I Saw Paris*); Shemar Moore (*The Brothers*); Esai Morales (*My Family*); Nick Moran (*Lock, Stock & Two Smoking Barrels*); Antonio Moreno (*The Exciters*); Chester Morris (*Second Choice*); Viggo Mortenson (*The Lord of the Rings*); Anson Mount (*Tully*); Danny Mousetis (*Reversal*); Patrick Muldoon (*Starship Troopers*); Dermot Mulroney (*My Best Friend's Wedding*); Cillian Murphy (*28 Days Later*); Chad Murray (*Freaky Friday*)

N: Mike Nadler (*Beach Blanket Bingo*); Conrad Nagel (*Little Women* – 1918); Johnny Nash (*Take A Giant Step*); Adam Nathan (*Parting Glances*); Francois Negret (*Night and Day*); Rick Negron (*The Next Step*); Sam Neill (*My Brilliant Career*); Rick Nelson (*Rio Bravo*); Franco Nero (*Camelot*); George Newbern (*It Takes Two*); David Newell (*Murder on the Roof*); Paul Newman (*The Long Hot Summer*); M.A. Nickles (*Hamburger Hill*); Allan Nixon (*Pickup*); Eduardo Noriega (*Burnt Money*); Jeremy Northam (*Emma*); Ryan Northcott (*Ripper*); Ramon Novarro (*Scaramouche*); Ivor Novello (*The White Rose*); Danny Nucci (*Crimson Tide*); Edward Nugent (*Our Dancing Daughters*)

O: George O'Brien (*The Iron Horse*); Diether Ocampo (*Soltera*); Andrea Occipiniti (*Bolero*); Mauricio Ochmann (*Message in a Bottle*); Chris O'Donnell (*The Three Musketeers*); Michael O'Keefe (*Caddyshack*); Miles O'Keeffe (*Tarzan, the Ape Man*); Ryan O'Neal (*The Big Bounce*); Peter O'Toole (*Lawrence of Arabia*); Ken Olandt (*April Fool's Day*); Christian Oliver (*Eat Your Heart Out*); Laurence Olivier (*Friends and Lovers*); Michael Ontkean (*Slap Shot*)

P: Russell Page (*Kick*); Richard Panebianco (*China Girl*); Kip Pardue (*Remember the Titans*); Michael Paré (*Eddie and the Cruisers*); Michael Parks (*Bus Riley's Back in Town*); Steve Parlevecchio (*Amongst Friends*); Michael Pas (*Love is A Dog from Hell*); Adrian Pasdar (*Streets of Gold*); Jason Patric (*The Lost Boys*); Allen Payne (*Jason's Lyric*); John Payne (*Kid Nightingale*); Guy Pearce (*Memento*); Gregory Peck (*Spellbound*); J. Eddie Peck (*Lambada*); Thierry Pepin (*Danny in the Sky*); George Perez (*Toy Soldiers*); Vincent Perez (*Indochine*); Anthony Perkins (*The Matchmaker*); Jens Peter (*Wild Orchid*); Paul Petersen (*In the Year 2889*); William L. Petersen (*Amazing Grace and Chuck*); Mekhi Phifer (*Soul*

Food); Gerard Philipe (*Devil in the Flesh*); Ryan Phillippe (*54*); Lou Diamond Phillips (*Young Guns*); Joaquin Phoenix (*To Die For*); River Phoenix (*Running on Empty*); Jean-Francois Pichette (*Being at Home with Claude*); Jack Pickford (*The Gangsters of New York*); Andreas Pietschmann (*Regular Guys*); Brad Pitt (*A River Runs Through It*); Michael Pitt (*The Dreamers*); Federico Pitzalis (*Devil in the Flesh*); Sidney Poitier (*No Way Out*); Carlos Ponce (*My Gardener*); Stathis Popadopoulos (*From the Edge of the City*); Marc Porel (*Secret World*); Martin Potter (*Fellini Satyricon*); Georges Poujouly (*And God Created Woman*); Tyrone Power (*Jesse James*); Tyrone Power, Jr. (*Cocoon*); Elvis Presley (*Jailhouse Rock*); Jason Priestley (*Love and Death on Long Island*); Freddie Prinze, Jr. (*She's All That*)

Q: Dennis Quaid (*Breaking Away*); Tim Quill (*Hamburger Hill*); Aidan Quinn (*Reckless*)

R: Howard Ralston (*A Daughter of Luxury*); Wes Ramsey (*Latter Days*); Julien Rassam (*The Accompanist*); Robert Redford (*Butch Cassidy and Sundance Kid*); Mathew Reed (*Perfect*); Philip Reed (*College Coach*); Christopher Reeve (*Somewhere in Time*); Keanu Reeves (*My Own Private Idaho*); Steve Reeves (*The Giant of Marathon*); Wallace Reid (*The Roaring Road*); Duncan Renaldo (*Trader Horn*); Brad Renfro (*Apt Pupil*); Jeremie Renier (*La Promesse*); Simon Rex (*Shriek If You Know What I Did Last Friday the 13th*); Ryan Reynolds (*Buying the Cow*); William Reynolds (*Has Anybody Seen My Gal?*); Jonathan Rhys Meyers (*The Maker*); Cliff Richard (*Expresso Bongo*); Jeff Richards (*Seven Brides for Seven Brothers*); Kane Richmond (*Spy Smasher*); Paul Richter (*Siegfried*); Stephane Rideau (*Wild Reeds*); Vince Rimoldi (*Camp*); Huntley Ritter (*Bring It On*); Linus Roache (*No Surrender*); Eric Roberts (*Raggedy Man*); Leonard Roberts (*Joe and Max*); Andrew Robertson (*The Cement Garden*); John Robinson (*Elephant*); Sam Rockwell (*Box of Moonlight*); Charles "Buddy" Rogers (*Wings*); Clayton Rohner (*April Fool's Day*); Gilbert Roland (*Men of the North*); Peter Ronson (*Journey to the Center of the Earth*); Robbie Rosa (*Salsa*); Gerry Ross (*The Kid and the Killers*); Brad Rowe (*Billy's Hollywood Screen Kiss*); Paul Rudd (*The Object of My Affection*); Robert Rusler (*Vamp*); John Russell (*The Man Who Dared*); William Russell (*Robin Hood* – 1913)

S: Antonio Sabato, Jr. (*The Big Hit*); Sabu (*The Thief of Bagdad*); Bill Sage (*Flirt*); Russell Sams (*The Rules of Attraction*); Julian Sands (*A Room With A View*); Tommy Sands (*Sing, Boy, Sing!*); Stark Sands (*Die Mommie Die!*); Giuseppe Sanfelice (*The Son's Room*); Rodrigo Santoro (*Behind the Sun*); Al Santos (*Santa Monica Boulevard*); Jorge Sanz (*Lovers*); Adé Sapara (*Crusoe*); Chris Sarandon (*Lipstick*); Michael Sarrazin (*They Shoot Horses, Don't They?*); Alejo Sauros (*La Mujer de mi vida*); John Saxon (*The Unguarded Moment*); Johnathon Schaech (*The Doom Generation*); Joseph Schildkraut (T*he King of Kings*); Charlie Schlatter (*18 Again!*); Michael Schoeffling (*16 Candles*); Werner Schreyer (*Bandits*); Travis Schuldt (*Candy*); Til Schweiger (*Maybe...Maybe Not*); Coltin Scott (*Kraa! The Sea Monster*); Gordon Scott (*Tarzan's Greatest Adventure*); Randolph Scott (*Man of the Forest*); Tom Everett Scott (*The Love Letter*); William Lee Scott (*The Opposite of Sex*); Nick Scotti (*Kiss Me, Guido*); Joey Sculthorpe (*The Longshot*); Ivan Sergei (*The Opposite of Sex*); Jacques Sernas (*Helen of Troy*); Diego Serrano (*The 24 Hour Woman*); Matthew Settle (*I Still Know What U Did Last Summer*); Corey Sevier (*The Edge of Madness*); Rufus Sewell (*Cold Comfort Farm*); Dirk Shafer (*Man of the Year*); Charlie Sheen (*Lucas*); Martin Sheen (*Badlands*); Craig Sheffer (*That Was Then, This Is Now*); Travis Sher (*Voodoo Academy*); Johnny Sheffield (*Bomba on Panther Island*); Stephen Shellen (*Gimme an 'F'*); Jean Shepard (*Scarlet Diva*); Antrim Short (*Please Get Married*); Marc Singer (*If You Could See What I Hear*); Christian Slater (*Pump Up the Volume*); Kerr Smith (*Possession*); Rex Smith (*The Pirates of Penzance*); Riley Smith (*Voodoo Academy*); William Smith (*Run, Angel, Run*); Wesley Snipes (*Streets of Gold*); Andrei Sokolov (*Little Vera*); Ian Somerhalder (*The Rules of Attraction*); Kevin Sorbo (*Slaughter of the Innocents*); Jean Sorel (*From A Roman Balcony*); Sandor Soth (*Time Stands Still*); Vincent Spano (*Good Morning, Babylon*); Eddie Spears (*The Slaughter Rule*); Jesse Spencer (*Uptown Girls*); Klinton Spilsbury (*The Legend of the Lone Ranger*); Robert Stadlober (*Crazy*); Terence Stamp (*Billy Budd*); Charles Starrett (*Fast and Loose*); Alexandre Sterling (*French Lesson*); Robert Sterling (*Two-Faced Woman*); Andrew Stevens (*Massacre at Central High*); Parker Stevenson (*A Separate Peace*); Michael St. Gerard (*Hairspray*); Dean Stockwell (*Sons and Lovers*); John Stockwell (*Christine*); Eric Stoltz (*Some Kind of Wonderful*); Adam Storke (*Mystic Pizza*); Scott Strader (*Jocks*); Rider Strong (*Cabin Fever*); Nick Stuart (*High School Hero*); Stephen Swan (*Leeches*); Patrick Swayze (*Roadhouse*)

T: Sean Tataryn (*Leather Jacket Love Story*); Larenz Tate (*Love Jones*); Robert Taylor (*Camille*); Rod Taylor (*Raintree County*); John Terlesky (*Chopping Mall*); Fabio Testi (*China 9, Liberty 37*); Thierry Tevini (*Tendres Cousines*); Sean Patrick Thomas (*Save the Last Dance*); Jonathan Taylor Thomas (*Speedway Junky*); C.J. Thomason (*Brotherhood II: Young Warlocks*); Cyrille Thouvenin (*Confusion of Genders*); Andrew Tiernan (*Edward II*); Jason J. Tobin (*Yellow*); Richard Todd (*The Hasty Heart*); Russell

Todd (*Friday the 13th Part 2*); Saguan Tofi (*The Wind in My Pocket*); Adam Tonsberg (*Twist and Shout*); Stuart Townsend (*Queen of the Damned*); John Travolta (*Grease*); Armando Trovajoli (*Yesterday, Today & Tomorrow*); Glenn Tryon (*The White Sheep*); Tom Tryon (*Three Violent People*); Barry Tubb (*Warm Summer Rain*); Kristopher Turner (*The Brotherhood III*); Matt Twining *(The Frightening)*; Tom Tyler (*Red Hot Hoofs*); Tyrese (*2 Fast 2 Furious*)

U: Gaspard Ulliel (*Summer Things*); Skeet Ulrich (*Touch*); Blair Underwood (*Set It Off*)

V: Maris Valainis (*Hoosiers*); Rudolph Valentino (*The Son of the Sheik*); Raf Vallone (*Bitter Rice*); Nicolas Van Burek (*On Your Own*); Jean Claude Van Damme (*No Retreat, No Surrender*); Casper Van Dien (*Starship Troopers*); Vincent Van Patten (*Rock n Roll High School*); Mario Van Peebles (*Last Resort*); Michael Vartan (*Fiorile*); Robert Vaughn (*The Young Philadelphians*); Vince Vaughn (*The Locusts*); Lino Ventura (*Crime and Punishment*); Eduardo Verastegui (*Chasing Papi*); Jordi Vilasuso (*The Last Home Run*); Jan-Michael Vincent (*The World's Greatest Athlete*); Mike Vogel (*Grind*)

W: Robert Wagner (*Stars and Stripes Forever*); Ken Wahl *(The Wanderers)*; Mark Wahlberg (*Boogie Nights*); Liam Waite (*Simpatico*); Tyler Waldrop (*The M.O. of M.I.*); Justin Walker (*Clueless*); Paul Walker (*Meet the Deedles*); George Walsh (*The Fencing Master*); James Walters (*Shout*); Simon Ward (*Quest for Love*); Tony Ward (*Hustler White*); Denzel Washington (*The Mighty Quinn*); Ken Watanabe (*The Last Samurai*); Nathan Watkins (*The Brotherhood*); John Wayne (*The Big Trail*); Patrick Wayne (*The Young Land*); Dewey Weber (*Chain of Desire*); Victor Webster (*Bringing Down the House*); Nick Wechsler (*Chicks, Man*); Johnny Weissmuller (*Tarzan and His Mate*); Niles Welch (*Emmy of Stork's Nest*); Peter Weller (*Butch and Sundance: The Early Years*); Tom Welling (*Cheaper By the Dozen*); Oskar Werner (*Jules and Jim*); Samuel West (*Reunion*); Leonard Whiting (*Romeo and Juliet*); Johnny Whitworth (*Somebody is Waiting*); Johan Widerberg (*All Things Fair*); Crane Wilbur (*The Perils of Pauline*); John Wildman (*My American Cousin*); Jason Wiles (*Kicking and Screaming*); Earle Williams (*Masters of Men*); Grant Williams (*The Incredible Shrinking Man*); Lee Williams (*The Wolves of Kromer*); Treat Williams (*The Ritz)*; Billy Wirth (*War Party*); Greg Wise (*Feast of July*); Scott Wolf (*Go*); Russell Wong (*Eat A Bowl of Tea*); Montgomery Wood (*Adios Gringo*)

Y: Michael York (*Cabaret*); Aden Young (*Hotel de Love*); Chris Young (*Book of Love*); Jim Youngs (*The Wanderers*); Jeremie Yuen (*Hey, Happy!*); Rick Yune (*Die Another Day*)

Z: Billy Zane (*Dead Calm*); Kevin Zegers (*The Hollow*); Roberto Zibetti (*Radiofreccia*)

Guy Madison on the beach, circa 1945, getting felt up by admirers. PHOTOFEST

The Author

A life-long film aficionado, Michael Ferguson has published articles, interviews, reviews, and short stories in *City NY*, *Cult Movies*, *Outré*, *Bikini*, *Spacemen*, and *It's Only A Movie*. His previous book, *Little Joe, Superstar: The Films of Joe Dallesandro* (Companion Press, 1998), was the authorized account of the life and career of Warhol "Superstar" Joe Dallesandro, a cult film icon and male beauty of the 1960s and 1970s – Visit www.joedallesandro.com. The author lives in Chicago.

Cover Photos

Cover/Spine/Back Cover Photo Credits:
All photos courtesy of Photofest except Valentino

Cover (from bottom left clockwise)
James Dean
Rob Lowe in *Youngblood*
Elvis Presley
Errol Flynn
Taye Diggs in *How Stella Got Her Groove Back*
Rudolph Valentino in *Monsieur Beaucaire*
Johnathon Schaech in *The Doom Generation*
Jan-Michael Vincent in *The World's Greatest Athlete*
Paul Walker in *Joy Ride*

Spine: Alain Delon

Back cover (from top)
Rock Hudson
Marlon Brando
Keanu Reeves in *Point Break*
Richard Gere in *American Gigolo*